HISTORICAL DICTIONARIES OF LITERATURE AND THE ARTS

Jon Woronoff, Series Editor

Historical Dictionary of French Cinema

Dayna Oscherwitz
MaryEllen Higgins

Historical Dictionaries of
Literature and the Arts, No. 15

The Scarecrow Press, Inc.
Lanham, Maryland • Toronto • Plymouth, UK
2007

SCARECROW PRESS, INC.

Published in the United States of America
by Scarecrow Press, Inc.
A wholly owned subsidiary of
The Rowman & Littlefield Publishing Group, Inc.
4501 Forbes Boulevard, Suite 200, Lanham, Maryland 20706
www.scarecrowpress.com

Estover Road
Plymouth PL6 7PY
United Kingdom

British Library Cataloguing in Publication Information Available

Library of Congress Cataloging-in-Publication Data

Oscherwitz, Dayna, 1970–
    Historical dictionary of French cinema / Dayna Oscherwitz, MaryEllen
  Higgins.
      p. cm. — (Historical dictionaries of literature and the arts ; no. 15)
    Includes bibliographical references.
    ISBN-13: 978-0-8108-5491-8 (hardcover : alk. paper)
    ISBN-10: 0-8108-5491-0 (hardcover : alk. paper)
      1. Motion pictures—France—History. 2. Motion pictures—France—
  Dictionaries. I. Higgins, MaryEllen, 1967– II. Title.
  PN1993.5.F7O83 2007
  791.430944'03—dc22
                                                                    2006033688

737 42358

For Brian Oscherwitz, Evan Oscherwitz, and Amine Yahya

In memory of William J. Higgins

Contents

Editor's Foreword

Cinema has always held a very special place in French culture. France is where some of the first cameras were invented, it was among the first to make films, both silent and sound, and for well over a century French directors, producers, and actors have enjoyed exceptional prestige at home and abroad while some of the best and most innovative films appeared. Although repeatedly overshadowed by Hollywood, especially in this age of globalization, the "seventh art" is still flourishing, to judge by the results of major film festivals if not always the box office. This is a long and prodigious story, and one that deserves to be retold, since French cinema has so many fans around the world. But it is exceedingly complex, and not always glorious, and it is hard to keep track of the broader current and the many details.

That is the purpose of this *Historical Dictionary of French Cinema*, which first traces over a century of history in the chronology. The broader currents are summarized in the introduction. Then a very substantial dictionary section provides numerous details in entries on inventors and commercial entrepreneurs, cinema companies and journals, major trends and forms, and especially a broad circle of directors, producers, and actors. In addition, there are over two dozen memorable films, films that have contributed both to French cinema and world cinema. Most of these will be familiar names; others have been forgotten but brought back to mind thanks to careful investigation. Yes, even this will obviously not be enough for many readers, who can find useful suggestions for further reading in the bibliography.

This book was written by two American scholars who have long admired and studied French cinema, Dayna Oscherwitz and MaryEllen Higgins. Fortunately, one is a specialist on the early period while the other deals more with recent and contemporary cinema. Dr. Oscherwitz is an assistant professor of French and Francophone studies at Southern

Methodist University in Dallas, Texas. She has published widely in specialized journals and edited works and is currently writing a book on film and identity politics in France. Dr. Higgins is an assistant professor of comparative literature at the Greater Allegheny campus of the Pennsylvania State University. She, too, has published in specialized journals, and is presently writing a book on Senegalese cinema. As will be obvious from reading it, this reference work is more than just a compilation of facts, but a tribute to one of the world's great cinemas.

Jon Woronoff
Series Editor

Preface

Preparing a single-volume reference work on the history of the cinema in France is an impossible task. Let us admit this from the beginning. Cinema emerged in France in 1895, and since the year following its emergence, the French have, for the most part, produced hundreds of films a year. Many of world cinema's major avant-garde movements came from France, or were influenced by it. Many of cinema's great directors, great screenwriters, great actors, and great films are French. A work of this nature can only scratch the surface. It can present the broad outline of a subject, but not the shades of gray.

And yet, it seemed to us that this was a necessary project. It appeals to a diverse audience, from well-informed academics looking for a concise reference, to students of the cinema seeking to broaden their knowledge, to the individual who is passionate about the cinema, but still has a good deal to learn. We have tried to bear these diverse types of readers in mind in conceiving and constructing this book. We have tried to create a sense of the movement and development of the cinema in France, a sense of film's social role in France, a sense of French cinema's place in the larger world, and a sense of who and what has been involved in making French cinema what it is.

Some important people, events, ideas, films, and movements have been left out. They had to be. The scope of this project is to present a broad overview of French cinema and its development; it is not to present an exhaustive analysis of how French cinema became what it is. However, we have tried to choose carefully and to include those individuals who have had a significant impact on French cinema, and we have tried to be mindful that impact can be measured a number of ways. We have, as the film industry does, privileged directors over producers, cinematographers, screenwriters, and the myriad other artists involved in film production. We have privileged lead actors over supporting actors. This is not because we regard individuals other than lead actors and directors as unimportant. It is because we had limited space, and we chose, therefore, to mirror the perceptions that exist in the wider world.

We have also included a sampling of producers, cinematographers, and screenwriters whose work simply could not be overlooked. We have tried to include and recognize the theoretical contributions of scholars and critics as well as the contribution of actors and filmmakers, but there again, we had to limit ourselves to those who have earned a sacred space in French film history. We have also attempted to convey a sense of the organization and development of the film industry in France, and to that end we have looked at certain technological developments and the roles of several of the major studios. We have included among the entries several particularly memorable films, but this does not in any way imply that there are not other films worthy of entries.

With respect to the people included, the task was made a little bit more complicated by our having to ask the question, "Who is French?" This is no small question, as anyone familiar with debates in contemporary France no doubt knows. We have not tried to answer that question definitively here. It is far too complex. However, for the purposes of cinema, we have included only those whose major works were made in France, those who spent the majority of their careers in France, or those who are closely associated with French cinema. We did not necessarily consider country of birth, as French cinema has been, from the beginning, greatly enriched by the contributions of many who were born outside of France, just as Hollywood has been greatly enriched by many who were born in France.

The work is introduced by a chronology, which lays out some of the major events and developments in the history of French cinema, and includes a listing of the French films that won major awards. This is followed by an introduction, which traces the broad trajectory of French film both as an industry and an art form. The entries that follow are intended to serve as elaborations of the development of French cinema through a presentation of the work of various individuals, studios, and movements. And the bibliography, which completes the work, is intended to provide guidance on where to look for more in-depth studies of the numerous subjects, questions, and issues this work introduces.

We would like to thank our families for their support of us as we worked on this, and for being willing to share us so that we could share what we knew. We would also like to thank Jon Woronoff at Scarecrow Press for his guidance, his patience, and for setting limits.

Dayna Oscherwitz
MaryEllen Higgins

Reader's Note

For various reasons, including considerations of space and of the fact that the same film may be released under several translated titles, we have used only the French titles of films in the work. Likewise, movements or terms that are French in origin and the major French prizes are listed under their French names, although they are cross-referenced in English.

Terms found in bold are cross-referenced within the body of the dictionary.

Acronyms and Abbreviations

AATC	L'Académie des Arts et Techniques du Cinéma
ACAD	Association des Compositeurs et des Auteurs Dramatiques
AEAR	Association des Écrivains et des Artistes Révolutionnaires
AFHRC	Association Française de Recherche sur l'Histoire du Cinéma
BAFTA	British Academy of Film and Television Arts
BFI	British Film Institute
CNC	Centre National de la Cinématographie
COIC	Comité d'Organisation de l'Industrie Cinématographique
FEMIS	École Nationale Supérieure des Métiers de l'Image et du Son
FIPRESCI	Fédération Internationale de la Presse Cinématographique
FSA	Film Service Association
GATT	General Agreement on Tariffs and Trade
IDHEC	Institut des Hautes Études Cinématographiques
INA	Institut National de l'Audiovisuel
MPCC	Motion Picture Patents Company
ORTF	Office Radio Télévision Française
SCAGL	Société Cinématographique des Auteurs et des Gens de Lettres
SEC	La Société d'Éditions Cinématographiques
SNEG	Société Nouvelle des Établissments Gaumont
UFI	Unifrance Film International
UNESCO	United Nations Educational, Scientific, and Cultural Organization

Chronology

1888 Étienne Jules Marey develops the *Chronophotographe*, a precursor to the film camera.

1892 Emile Reynaud projects early, hand-painted animated films at the Musée Grévin in Paris.

1895 Auguste and Louis Lumière develop the *Cinématographe*, the first fully functional motion picture camera. Henry Joly collaborates with Charles Pathé to market his film camera. Pathé Frères is founded to sell cameras and make films. Ambroise Parnaland founds Parnaland Frères using a camera Parnaland invented himself. **22 March:** The Lumière Brothers give a demonstration of the film *La Sortie de l'usine* to a group of scientists. **28 December:** The Lumière Brothers hold a projection of twenty of their films. Léon Gaumont, Alice Guy, and Georges Méliès are in attendance. Films screened included *L'Arrivée d'un train en gare de La Ciotat*. This is generally regarded as the birth of cinema.

1896 Léon Gaumont has a film camera constructed for his company. Ambroise Parnaland patents his *Cinépar* film camera and goes on to found Parnaland Frères. Pathé constructs its first studio at Vincennes. Alice Guy makes *La Fée aux choux*, the first narrative film. Several months later, George Méliès releases his first film.

1897 Alice Guy becomes head of production at Gaumont. Gaumont perfects its *Chronographe* camera. Charles Pathé transforms Pathé Frères, once a company that sold phonographs, into the Compagnie générale des cinématographes, phonographes, et péllicules. Lumière by this time has two permanent projection cinemas. Georges Méliès constructs the first glass-house studio in Montreuil-sous-bois and goes on to found Star Film. **May:** A fire breaks out in a temporary film-screening pavilion at the Bazar de la Charité and 121 people are killed.

1898 Georges Méliès releases *Salle à manger fantastique*, which uses reverse motion photography. Léon Gaumont negotiates with A. C. Bromhead, a British firm, to market and sell his film cameras and projectors in Great Britain and the United States.

1900 Gaumont markets a new version of its film projector at the Paris Exposition. The device wins an award and later becomes the dominant projector used in France. At the same exposition, Paul Decauville has an exhibit with an early version of synchronized sound projection.

1901 Pathé releases Ferdinand Zecca's *Histoire d'un crime*, one of the first realist dramas.

1902 Georges Méliès releases the early science fiction film *Le Voyage dans la lune*. **November:** Léon Gaumont demonstrates his synchronized sound film and projection equipment, the *Chronophone*, to the Société française de photographie.

1903 Pathé releases *La Vie et la passion de Jésus Christ*. The film uses interchangeable tableaux allowing it to be screened at any length ranging from one to thirty-two tableaux, offering flexible pricing and view time. **March:** Gaston Méliès opens a U.S. distribution office for Star Film.

1904 **February:** Pathé opens a distribution office in Moscow. **March:** Pathé moves into its new studio at Montreuil. **August:** Pathé opens a distribution office in New York.

1905 Gaumont constructs the largest glass-house studio yet built in Paris. Pathé has so invested in the American film market that it is, by this time, the dominant film distributor in the United States. **February:** Ambroise Parnaland loses a suit by Paris surgeon Dr. Doyen to distribute films he made of surgeries performed by the doctor. As a result Parnaland Studios ultimately goes bankrupt.

1906 Gaumont releases Alice Guy's *Madame a des envies*. The film utilizes a dramatic close-up well before D. W. Griffith utilizes such a thing in film. **May:** Pathé opens a distribution office in Milan. **July:** Pathé opens a distribution office in London. **November:** Pathé begins its project to construct cinemas throughout France.

1907 Pathé begins progressive mechanization of the film production process by mechanizing its coloration process, again reducing costs. It also moves to the "director-unit" method of film creation. Pathé also creates Société Cinématographique des Auteurs et des Gens de Lettres (SCAGL). Louis Feuillade replaces Alice Guy as head of production at Gaumont and begins streamlining the Gaumont film production process. Gaumont releases Émile Cohl's *Un drame chez les fantôches*, the first film to feature live animation. **May:** Marcel Vandal and Charles Jourjon found Éclair Studios and build a studio at Épinay. **July:** Pathé begins renting prints of its films, rather than selling them, undercutting competitors. **November:** Pathé begins printing a weekly summary of its new releases in the United States in an effort to maintain dominance in the American market.

1908 SCAGL releases *L'Arlésienne*, which is probably the first true film d'art. Gaumont opens the Cinéma-Palace, later known as the Gaumont Palace, its first permanent cinema. The studio also releases Émile Cohl's *Fantasmagorie*, the first fully animated feature film. Pathé begins a restructuring of its global film distribution, in part triggered by its loss of dominance in the American market. **February:** Paul Lafitte founds Studio Film d'art. **November:** Studio Film d'art premières Charles Le Bargy's *L'Assassinat du Duc de Guise*.

1910 Gaumont sends Jean Durand and Joë Hamman south to the Camargue, where they make a series of Westerns, including *Calino veut être Cowboy* and *Pendaison à Jefferson City*. This marks the first indication that France feels the need to compete with Hollywood in a genre that is uniquely American.

1911 Pathé releases *Le Siège de Calais*, one of the first historical films to use a crowd scene.

1913 Gaumont releases Louis Feuillade's *Fantômas*.

1915 Gaumont releases Louis Feuillade's *Les Vampires*. The series is banned for promoting disorder, but ultimately goes on to become a classic of the cinema.

1919 Films Albatros is founded by the expatriate Russians Alexandre Kamenka, Alexandre Volkoff, and Victor Tourjanksy, among others. The studio will produce films by Jean Renoir and Jean Epstein, among others. Serge Sandburg founds Studios de la Victorine in Nice. The studio will produce films by such directors as Jean Durand, Émile Cohl,

René Le Somptier, and Marcel Carné. Louis Delluc releases his first film, *Le Chemin d'Ernoa*.

1920   Popular director André Hugon leaves Pathé to found Films André Hugon. The production company remains in existence until 1952 and will produce all of Hugon's films after 1920. Hugon will become the most successful self-produced director in France.

1921   Louis Delluc launches the film journal *Cinéa*, which quickly becomes the premier film journal of the day. **June:** Jacques Feyder releases *L'Atlantide*, widely regarded as one of the greatest silent films ever made.

1922   Pathé founds its Société d'Éditions Cinématographiques (SEC) division to replace SCAGL. Henri Diamant-Berger leaves Pathé to found Le Studio de Billancourt. He goes on to produce a number of films, including Abel Gance's classic *Napoléon* (1927), which nearly bankrupts the studio.

1923   Marcel L'Herbier leaves Gaumont and founds Cinégraphic, which will produce his later films, as well as several films by Jacque Catelain. **28 September:** Jean Epstein releases *L'Auberge rouge*, inaugurating impressionist cinema.

1925   20 March: Jean Renoir releases his first film, *La Fille de l'eau*.

1926   Bernard Natan founds Productions Natan along with director Henri Diamant-Berger. The company will produce such films as Diamant-Berger's *Rue de la Paix* (1926) and Gaston Ravel's *L'Affaire du collier de la reine* (1928).

1928   Charles Pathé begins liquidating Pathé Frères, which is having financial difficulty. **August:** Éclair releases the first sound film in French. It is *L'Eau du Nil*, a silent film to which sound had been added. Pathé-Natan produces the first film to be shot with sound that same year, André Hugon's *Les Trois masques*.

1929   1 March: Bernard Natan takes over control of Pathé studios from Charles Pathé. The studio becomes Pathé-Natan. Natan proceeds to modernize the firm, adapting it for sound production, streamlining distribution, bringing back the *actualités* newsreel series, and improving the quality of film productions.

1930 Charles Pathé begins a whisper campaign against Bernard Natan, accusing him of embezzling as an effort to discredit Natan, and deflect attention away from his own mismanagement.

1931 Marcel Pagnol founds Films Marcel Pagnol. The company produces *Marius* (1932) the following year, and will go on to produce all of Pagnol's subsequent films.

1933 Max Glass founds Flora film. The company goes on to produce films by Marco de Gastyne, Jean de Limur, and others. **7 April:** Jean Vigo releases *Zéro de conduite*. The film is immediately censored.

1934 **12 November:** Jean Vigo releases his landmark film *L'Atalante*. The film is cut and edited before release, and it is detested by critics and audiences alike, but goes on to be considered one of the greatest films ever made.

1935 **3 December:** Jacques Feyder releases *La Kermesse héroïque*, inaugurating what would later be called Le Réalisme poétique or Poetic Realism. Marcel Carné assists Feyder on the film.

1936 Henri Langlois founds the Cinémathèque Française, along with Jean Mitry and Georges Franju, among others. Jean Zay, the minister for education and fine arts, proposes the establishment of an international film event in Cannes. **January:** The French government, under the Tribunal de Commerce, seizes Pathé-Natan and places it under receivership. It will be reorganized and become La Société Nouvelle Pathé Cinéma. The company is healthy, and it is Bernard Natan's modernization that ensures its continuity.

1937 Max Glass founds Arcadia Film, which produces several films by Marcel L'Herbier, among others. **8 June:** Jean Renoir releases *La Grande illusion*. The film seems to announce the coming war and the fall of the Front Populaire. It goes on to become a classic. **1 September:** The first Cannes International Film Festival is scheduled to begin, with Louis Lumière as president. Germany invades Poland. **3 September:** France and others declare war on Germany. The Cannes Film Festival is postponed and will not be held until 1946. **December:** The Prix Louis-Delluc is established. Jean Renoir's *Les Bas-Fonds* wins the first year.

1938 **18 May:** Carné releases *Quai des brumes*, continuing the trend of Poetic Realism. The film causes a scandal because of scenes hinting at sexual relations between Jean Gabin and Michèle Morgan. **December:** Jeff Musso's *Le Puritain* wins the Prix Louis-Delluc. Bernard Natan is arrested by the French authorities.

1939 December: Marcel Carné's *Quai de brumes* wins the Prix Louis-Delluc.

1940 22 June: France surrenders to Germany. Many in the French film industry leave France for Britain or the United States. The Prix Louis-Delluc is suspended and is not given again until 1945. **3 October:** Subsequent to the French surrender to Nazi Germany, the Nazis create Continental Films, the only official production company during the German Occupation.

1941 André Paulvé founds Films André Paulvé to produce his avant-garde scientific documentary films.

1943 Marcel Carné, Jean Grémillon, Jacques Becker, and others found *Écran Français*, a precursor to *Cahiers du cinéma*. La Comité de Libération du Cinéma Français is secretly formed by Jacques Becker, Louis Daquin, Jean Painlevé, Jean-Paul Le Chanois, André Zwaboda, and Pierre Blanchar, among others, to make films to prepare for liberation. **January:** Director Marcel L'Herbier founds Institut des Hautes Études Cinématographiques (IDHEC) to train future professionals in the film industry.

1944 6 June: The D-Day invasion ultimately liberates France from Germany. Many collaborators are tried and condemned, including many from the film industry. **August:** La Comité de Libération du Cinéma Français secretly films the battle for Paris during liberation. The film will later be released as *La Libération de Paris*.

1945 2 March: Marcel Carné releases *Les Enfants du paradis*, marking the end of Poetic Realism. **December:** André Malraux's *L'Espoir* wins the Prix Louis-Delluc.

1946 Léon Moussinac publishes *L'Âge ingrat du cinéma*. The Prix Méliès is established. René Clément's *La Bataille du rail* wins the first award. Marcel Pagnol is elected to the Académie Française. **20 September–5 October:** The first Cannes Film Festival takes place, after its delayed inauguration in 1939. René Clément's *La Bataille du rail* wins the Grand Prix that year. **December:** Jean Cocteau's *La Belle et la bête* wins the Prix Louis-Delluc.

1947 September: Jacques Becker's *Antoine et Antoinette* and René Clément's *Les maudits* win the Grand Prix at the Cannes Film Festival. **December:** Nicole Védrès's *Paris 1900* wins the Prix Louis-Delluc.

1948 March: Maurice Cloche's *Monsieur Vincent* wins an Oscar for Best Foreign Film. Jean Dréville's *Les Casse-pieds* wins the Prix Louis-Delluc.

1949 Georges Sadoul publishes *L'Histoire du cinéma*. **December:** Jacques Becker's *Le Rendez-vous de juillet* wins the Prix Louis-Delluc.

1950 The Fédération française des ciné-clubs de jeunes is created. **March:** René Clément's *Au-delà des grilles* wins an Oscar for Best Foreign Film. **December:** Robert Bresson's *Le Journal d'un curé de campagne* wins the Prix Louis-Delluc.

1951 April: Jacques-Doniol-Valcroze, André Bazin, and others found the journal *Cahiers du cinéma*. The first issue is published. *Cahiers* will go on to become one of the most respected film journals in the world. The Cannes Film Festival is moved to the spring. **December:** The Prix Jean-Vigo, which awards filmmakers for their originality and independence, is established. Jean Lehérissy's *La montagne est verte* wins that year.

1952 Henri Schneider's *La Grande Vie* receives the Prix Jean-Vigo. **March:** René Clément's *Jeux-interdits* wins an Oscar for Best Foreign Film. **May:** The film journal *Positif* is founded. It goes on to become the principal rival to *Les Cahiers du cinéma*. **December:** Alexandre Astruc's *Le Rideau cramoisi* wins the Prix Louis-Delluc.

1953 Albert Lamourisse's *Crin-Blanc* receives the Prix Jean-Vigo. **May:** Henri-George Clouzot's *La Salaire de la peur* wins the Grand Prix at Cannes. The number of internationally co-produced films rises from three in 1949 to twenty-five in 1953. **December:** Jacques Tati's *Les Vacances de Monsieur Hulot* wins the Prix Louis-Delluc.

1954 François Truffaut publishes "Une certaine tendence du cinéma français" in *Cahiers du cinéma*. Alain Resnais and Chris Marker's *Les statues meurent aussi* receives the Prix Jean-Vigo. **November:** The first edition of the journal *Cinéma* is published under the editorship of Pierre Billard. **December:** Henri-Georges Clouzot's *Les Diaboliques* wins the Prix Louis-Delluc.

1955   Alice Guy receives the Légion d'honneur for her contributions to French culture. Jean Cocteau is elected to the Académie française. Jean Vidal's *Zola* receives the Prix Jean-Vigo. The prestigious Palme d'Or is added at the Cannes Film Festival. **December:** René Clair's *Les Grandes manoeuvres* wins the Prix Louis-Delluc.

1956   Agnès Varda's *La pointe courte* is released. It is considered an important precursor to the New Wave. Alain Resnais and Jean Cayrol's *Nuit et brouillard* receives the Prix Jean-Vigo. **March:** Jacques-Yves Cousteau and Louis Malle's *Monde du silence* wins the Oscar for Best Documentary and the Palme d'Or. **December:** Albert Lamorisse's *Le Ballon rouge* wins the Prix Louis-Delluc.

1957   André Bazin publishes his "Politique des Auteurs" in *Cahiers du cinéma*. **December:** Louis Malle's *Ascenseur pour l'échafaud* wins the Prix Louis-Delluc.

1958   The first volume of André Bazin's collected writings on the cinema, *Qu'est-ce que le cinéma?* is published. Françoise Giroud publishes *La Nouvelle Vague: portraits de la jeunesse*. Louis Grospierre's *Les femmes de Stermetz* receives the Prix Jean-Vigo. **March:** Jacques Tati's *Mon Oncle* wins the Oscar for Best Foreign Film. **December:** Jean Rouch's *Moi, Un Noir* wins the Prix Louis-Delluc.

1959   Claude Chabrol's *Le beau Serge* and *Les cousins* are released. They are considered the first New Wave films. François Truffaut releases another benchmark of the New Wave, *Les quatre-cent coups*. Jean-Luc Godard directs the landmark New Wave film, *À bout de souffle*, which is released in 1960. Chabrol's *Le beau Serge* receives the Prix Jean-Vigo. **May:** Marcel Camus's *Orfeu Negro* wins the Palme d'Or. François Truffaut wins the prize for Best Director. **December:** Michel Drach's *On n'enterre pas le dimanche* wins the Prix Louis-Delluc.

1960   René Clair is elected to the Académie française. Jean-Luc Godard's *Le Petit soldat,* a film that refers to torture in Algeria, is censored. Jean-Luc Godard's *À bout de souffle* receives the Prix Jean-

Vigo. **December:** Henri Colpi's *Une aussi longue absence* wins the Prix Louis-Delluc.

1961 Jean-Paul Sassy's *La Peau et les os* receives the Prix Jean-Vigo. **May:** Henri Colpi's *Une aussi longue absence* wins the Palme d'Or. **December:** François Reichenbach's *Un Coeur gros comme ça* wins the Prix Louis-Delluc.

1962 Yves Robert's *La Guerre des boutons* receives the Prix Jean-Vigo. **December:** Alain Robbe-Grillet's *L'Immortelle* and Pierre Étaix's *Le Soupirant* share the Prix Louis-Delluc.

1963 Jean Mitry publishes the first volume of *Esthétique et psychologie du cinéma*. Frédéric Rossif's *Mourir à Madrid* receives the Prix Jean-Vigo. **December:** Jacques Demy's *Les parapluies de Cherbourg* wins the Prix Louis-Delluc.

1964 Robert Enrico's *La Belle Vie* receives the Prix Jean-Vigo. **May:** Jacques Demy's *Les parapluies de Cherbourg* wins the Palme d'Or. The journal *Jeune Cinéma* is established. **December:** Agnès Varda's *Le Bonheur* wins the Prix Louis-Delluc.

1965 The second volume of Jean Mitry's *Esthétique et psychologie du ciné is published*. **March:** Claude Berri's *Le Poulet* wins the Oscar for Best Short. **December:** Jean-Paul Rappeneau's *La Vie de château* wins the Prix Louis-Delluc.

1966 Jacques Rivette's *Suzanne Simonin, la religieuse de Diderot* is banned. France's best-selling film of the twentieth century, Gérard Oury's *La Grande vadrouille*, is released. **March:** Claude Leouch's *Un homme et une femme* wins the Oscar for Best Foreign Film. It also wins the Palme d'Or at Cannes in May. **December:** Alain Resnais's *La Guerre est finie* wins the Prix Louis-Delluc.

1967 Noel Burch publishes *Une praxis du cinéma*. William Klein's *Qui êtes-vous, Polly Magoo?* receives the Prix Jean-Vigo. **December:** Michel Deville's *Benjamin ou les mémoires d'un puceau* wins the Prix Louis-Delluc.

1968 Christian Metz publishes *Essais sur la signification au cinéma*. Christian de Chalonge's *O Salto* receives the Prix Jean-Vigo. **February:** Minister of Culture André Malraux intends to replace Cinémathèque president Henri Langlois with Pierre Barbin. Over three hundred directors protest, and thousands of others follow suit. The Comité de défense de la Cinémathèque is formed by Marcel Carné, Jean Renoir, François Truffaut, Jean-Luc Godard, and Claude Chabrol, among others. **April:** Langlois is reinstated. **May:** In the spirit of the rebellion of May 1968, Godard, Truffaut, Louis Malle, Claude Berri, Jean-Gabriel Albicocco, Claude Lelouch, and Roman Polanski interrupt the Cannes Film Festival and call for its suspension. **December:** François Truffaut's *Baisers volés* wins the Prix Louis-Delluc.

1969 Maurice Pialat's *L'Enfance nue* receives the Prix Jean-Vigo. **March:** Constantin Costa-Gavras's Z wins the Oscar for Best Foreign Film. Z will become a seminal film of the militant cinema of the 1970s. **December:** Claude Sautet's *Les choses de la vie* wins the Prix Louis-Delluc.

1970 Raoul Coutard's *Hoa Binh* receives the Prix Jean-Vigo. **December:** Eric Rohmer's *Le genou de Claire* wins the Prix Louis-Delluc.

1971 Christian Metz publishes *Language et cinéma*. Jean-Louis Bertucelli's *Les Remparts d'argile* receives the Prix Jean-Vigo. **December:** André Delvaux's *Rendez-vous à Bray* wins the Prix Louis-Delluc.

1972 Jérôme Laperrousaz's *Continental Circus* receives the Prix Jean-Vigo. **March:** Luis Buñuel's *Le Charme discret de la bourgeoisie* wins the Oscar for Best Foreign Film. **December:** Constantin Costa-Gavras's *État de siège* wins the Prix Louis-Delluc.

1973 Guy Gilles's *Absences répétées* receives the Prix Jean-Vigo. **March:** François Truffaut's *La Nuit américaine* wins the Oscar for Best Foreign Film. **December:** Bertrand Tavernier's *L'Horloger de Saint Paul* wins the Prix Louis-Delluc.

1974 Bernard Queysanne and Georges Pérec's *Un homme qui dort* receives the Prix Jean-Vigo. **March:** Jean Renoir receives an Oscar for his life's work. **December:** Claude Pinoteau's *La Gifle* wins the Prix Louis-Delluc.

1975 René Féret's *Histoire de Paul* receives the Prix Jean-Vigo. **December:** Jean-Charles Tachella's *Cousin, cousine* wins the Prix Louis-Delluc.

1976   **March:** Jean-Jacques Annaud's *La Victoire en chantant* wins the Oscar for Best Foreign Film. **3 April:** The first cérémonie des Césars du cinéma, established by Georges Cravenne, takes place. Jean Gabin presides. Robert Enrico's *Le Vieux Fusil* wins the César for Best Film that year. **December:** Yves Boisset's *Le Juge Fayard dit 'Le Shériff'* wins the Prix Louis-Delluc.

1977   Joseph Losey's *Mr. Klein* wins the César for Best Film. Christian Bricourt's *Paradiso* receives the Prix Jean-Vigo. **March:** Moshe Mizrahi's *La Vie devant soi* wins the Oscar for Best Foreign Film. **December:** Diane Kurys's *Diabolo Menthe* wins the Prix Louis-Delluc.

1978   Alain Resnais's *Providence* wins the César for Best Film. Jacques Champreux's *Bako, l'autre rive* receives the Prix Jean-Vigo. **March:** Bertrand Blier's *Préparez vos mouchoirs* wins the Oscar for Best Foreign Film. **December:** Christian de Chalonge's *L'Argent des autres* wins the Prix Louis-Delluc.

1979   Christian de Chalonge's *L'Argent des autres* wins the César for Best Film. Jacques Davila's *Certaines nouvelles* receives the Prix Jean-Vigo. **December:** Paul Grimault's *Le Roi et l'oiseau* wins the Prix Louis-Delluc.

1980   Roman Polanski's *Tess* wins the César for Best Film. René Gilson's *Ma blonde, entends-tu dans la ville* receives the Prix Jean-Vigo. **December:** Alain Cavalier's *Un étrange voyage* wins the Prix Louis-Delluc.

1981   Jack Lang becomes minister of culture. He criticizes American dominance in the film industry. François Truffaut's *Le Dernier Métro* wins the César for Best Film. Jean-Pierre Sentier's *Le Jardinier* receives the Prix Jean-Vigo. **December:** Pierre Granier-Deferre's *Une étrange affaire* wins the Prix Louis-Delluc.

1982   Michel Chion publishes *La Voix au cinéma*. Constantin Costa-Gavras becomes the president of the Cinémathèque. He also wins the Palme d'Or for *Missing*. Jean-Jacques Annaud's *La Guerre de feu* wins the César for Best Film. Philippe Garrel's *L'Enfant secret* receives the Prix Jean-Vigo. **December:** Andrzej Wajda's *Danton* wins the Prix Louis-Delluc.

1983   Bob Swaim's *La Balance* wins the César for Best Film. Gérard Mordillat's *Vive la Sociale* receives the Prix Jean-Vigo. **December:** Maurice Pialat's *À nos amours* wins the Prix Louis-Delluc.

1984   Mehdi Charef releases *Le Thé au harem d'Archimède*, one of the first *beur* films, or films directed by second- and third-generation immigrants of Arab descent. It wins the Prix Jean-Vigo. Maurice Pialat's *À nos amours* wins the César for Best Film. **December:** Richard Dembo's *Le Diagonale du fou* wins the Prix Louis-Delluc.

1985   Michel Chion publishes *Le Son au cinéma*. Claude Zidi's *Les Ripoux* wins the César for Best Film. Jacques Rozier's *Maine Océan* receives the Prix Jean-Vigo. **December:** Claude Miller's *L'Effronté* wins the Prix Louis-Delluc.

1986   Coline Serreau's *Trois hommes et un couffin* wins the César for Best Film. Laurent Perrin's *Buisson ardent* receives the Prix Jean-Vigo. **December:** Leos Carax's "look" film *Mauvais Sang* wins the Prix Louis-Delluc.

1987   Jean Rouch becomes president of the Cinémathèque. Alain Cavalier's *Thérèse* wins the César for Best Film. Louis Malle's *Au revoir les enfants* receives the Prix Jean-Vigo. **May:** Maurice Pialat's *Sous le soleil de Satan* wins the Palme d'Or. Alain Cavalier's *Thérèse* wins the César for Best Film. **December:** Malle's *Au revoir les enfants* and Jean-Luc Godard's *Soigne ta droite* share the Prix Louis-Delluc.

1988   Luc Moullet's *La Comédie du travail* receives the Prix Jean-Vigo. Louis Malle's *Au revoir les enfants* wins the César for Best Film. **December:** Michel Deville's *La Lectrice* wins the Prix Louis-Delluc.

1989   The top best-selling films in France are American. More than half of French films are co-productions, sparking fears that the French film industry is in serious trouble. Bruno Nuytten's *Camille Claudel* wins the César for Best Film. Dai Sijie's *Chine, ma douleur* receives the Prix Jean-Vigo. **December:** Eric Rochant's *Un monde sans pitié* wins the Prix Louis-Delluc.

1990   Bertrand Blier's *Trop belle pour toi* wins the César for Best Film. Patrick Grandperret's *Mona et moi* receives the Prix Jean-Vigo. **December:** Patrice Leconte's *Le Mari de la coiffeuse* and Jacques Doillon's *Le Petit criminel* share the Prix Louis-Delluc.

1991 Jean-Paul Rappeneau's *Cyrano de Bergerac* wins the César for Best Film. Eric Barbier's *Le Brasier* receives the Prix Jean-Vigo. **December:** Alain Corneau's *Tous les matins du monde* wins the Prix Louis-Delluc.

1992 Alain Corneau's *Tous les matins du monde* wins the César for Best Film. Olivier Assayas's *Paris s'éveille* receives the Prix Jean-Vigo. **December:** Christine Pascale's *Le Petit Prince a dit* wins the Prix Louis-Delluc.

1993 Pathé opens its first méga-complexe in Toulon. Cyril Collard's *Les nuits fauves* wins the César for Best Film. Anne Fontaine's *Les histoires d'amour finissent mal en général* receives the Prix Jean-Vigo. France succeeds in obtaining special status for its cinema industry under the General Agreement on Tariffs and Trade (GATT) agreements by arguing for film as an integral part of the French cultural exception. These agreements restrict foreign access to French markets, while guaranteeing French access to foreign markets. **March:** Régis Wargnier's *Indochine* wins the Oscar for Best Foreign Film. **December:** Alain Resnais's *Smoking/No Smoking* wins the Prix Louis-Delluc.

1994 Alain Resnais's *Smoking/No Smoking* wins the César for Best Film. Cédric Kahn's *Trop de bonheur* receives the Prix Jean-Vigo. **December:** André Téchiné's *Les Roseaux sauvages* wins the Prix Louis-Delluc.

1995 André Téchiné's *Les Roseaux sauvages* wins the César for Best Film. Xavier Beauvois's *N'oublie pas que tu vas mourir* receives the Prix Jean-Vigo. **December:** Claude Sautet's *Nelly et M. Arnaud* wins the Prix Louis-Delluc.

1996 Film directors and actors participate in the *mouvment des sans-papiers*, in which they express their solidarity with illegal immigrants in France who face deportation. They also oppose pending legislation that would compel French citizens to report the *sans-papiers*. Bertrand Tavernier and Emmanuel Béart were among those leading the protests. Mathieu Kassovitz's *La Haine* wins the César for Best Film. Pascale Bonitzer's *Encore* receives the Prix Jean-Vigo. **March:** Juliette Binoche wins the Oscar for Best Supporting Actress for *The English Patient*. **December:** Sandrine Veysset's *Y aura-t-il de la neige à Noël?* wins the Prix Louis-Delluc.

1997 Patrice Leconte's *Ridicule* wins the César for Best Film. Bruno Dumont's *La Vie de Jésus* receives the Prix Jean-Vigo. **December:** Robert Guédiguian's *Marius et Jeanette* and Alain Resnais's *On connaît la chanson* share the Prix Louis-Delluc.

1998 Alain Resnais's *On connaît la chanson* wins the César for Best Film. Claude Mourieras's *Dis-moi que je rêve* receives the Prix Jean-Vigo. **December:** Cédric Kahn's *L'Ennui* wins the Prix Louis-Delluc.

1999 Eric Zonca's *La Vie rêvée des anges* wins the César for Best Film. Noémie Lvovsky's *La vie ne me fait pas peur* receives the Prix Jean-Vigo. **May:** Bruno Dumont's *L'humanité* wins the Grand Prix at Cannes. **December:** Otar Iosselani's *Adieu plancher des vaches* wins the Prix Louis-Delluc.

2000 French films account this year for only about 30 percent of all film viewers in France. Tonie Marshall's *Vénus beauté (institut)* wins the César for Best Film. Patricia Mazuy's *Saint-Cyr* receives the Prix Jean-Vigo. **December:** Claude Chabrol's *Merci pour le chocolat* wins the Prix Louis-Delluc.

2001 France more than doubles the number of foreign-film viewers who see its films, attracting 37.4 million foreign viewers. Agnès Jaoui's *Le goût des autres* wins the César for Best Film. Emmanuel Bourdieu's *Candidature* receives the Prix Jean-Vigo. **May:** Michael Haneke's *La pianiste* wins the Grand Prix at Cannes. **December:** Patrice Chéreau's *Intimité* wins the Prix Louis-Delluc.

2002 Jean-Pierre Jeunet's *Le fabuleux destin d'Amélie Putain* wins the César for Best Film. Charles Najman's *Royal Bonbon* receives the Prix Jean-Vigo. **May:** Roman Polanski wins the Palme d'Or for *Le pianiste*. **December:** Nicolas Philibert's *Être et avoir* wins the Prix Louis-Delluc.

2003 Roman Polanski's *Le pianiste* wins the César for Best Film. Jean-Paul Civeyrac's *Toutes ces belles promesses* receives the Prix Jean-Vigo. **December:** Lucas Belvaux's triology *Un couple épatant, Cavale*, and *Après la vie* and Noémie Lvovsky's *Les sentiments* share the Prix Louis-Delluc.

2004 Patrick Mimouni's *Quand je serai star* receives the Prix Jean-Vigo. **December:** Arnaud Desplechin's *Rois et Reine* wins the Prix Louis-Delluc.

2005 Abdellatif Kechiche's *L'Esquive* wins the César for Best Film. Jérôme Bonnell's *Les Yeux clairs* receives the Prix Jean-Vigo. **December:** Philippe Garrel's *Les Amants réguliers* wins the Prix Louis-Delluc.

2006 Jacques Audiard's *De battre mon coeur s'est arrêté* wins the César for Best Film. Laurent Achard's *Le Dernier des fous* wins the Prix Jean-Vigo.

Introduction

Although everywhere the cinema is associated with Hollywood, there is near universal agreement that moving pictures as we know them were a French invention. That is to say, as with all technological innovations, cinema belongs to everyone and to no one. It was the product of several decades, if not centuries, of thought. That being the case, it was, perhaps by accident, in France in 1895 that it reached the form in which we recognize it as cinema. Thomas Edison, an American, brought technology developed in France, Great Britain, and elsewhere very close to the point of being cinema and yet he could not quite resolve the issue of continuity of the image, and he did not bring the form to external projection. That would be achieved, as many already know, by Auguste and Louis Lumière in France near the end of the nineteenth century.

So it was, in a way, perhaps, by accident, and yet, not quite by accident, that the cinema was a French invention. In many ways, the cinema is emblematic of France of the late nineteenth century. It reflected a belief in progress, a spirit of innovation that characterized France at that time. It was in France in that same century that the camera and photography were perfected, that Louis Pasteur made the world aware that our eye was an imperfect organ, that there were realities it could not perceive, therefore challenging the accuracy of what it did perceive. It was in France, in the nineteenth century that revolution after revolution sought to establish democracy and equality, albeit not altogether successfully. It was in France in the nineteenth century that the Industrial Revolution brought people from all spheres of life together in the same space, that Paris, the modern city as we know it, was conceived and constructed. The cinema reflects all of this. As the Lumière brothers presented it to the world, the cinema represented the scientific capacity to create an alternative reality, placing humankind in the position of creator in a way they had not previously been. It was a collective experience, reflecting both the mixing of classes

1

and types suggested by democracy and the experience of the crowd (hailed by the poet Charles Baudelaire in the same place and time) that characterized the modern city. It offered the potential for individuals, whatever their status in the world, to have their existence reflected back to them in reality or in kind.

THE SILENT CINEMA: 1895–1930

It is a commonplace that the early films were documentary, that the next wave of filmmaking involved spectacle, and that narrative did not evolve until the 1920s in Hollywood. However, a closer look shows that cinema was already interested, on some level, in fiction and narrative from the beginning. Louis Lumière's *La Sortie de l'usine* (1895), a film of workers leaving the Lumière factory, is, for example, less documentary than it might appear. It seems that Louis Lumière invited, or required, that the workers leave the factory at a time and in a way prescribed by him for the precise purpose that he might film them. That is to say, the scene was staged. The workers were not leaving the factory at all, but acting as though they were, acting before the camera, presenting an image in the way Louis Lumière wished it to be seen. Nor was this a unique example. Although one of the dominant early forms produced by Lumière et Cie, and the major studios that followed them, were *actualités*, documentary or newsreel films, many of these were not actual footage, but studio re-creations of events that could not be witnessed firsthand. Among these so-called re-created actualités are such films as the famous *Éruption du Mont Pelé* (1902), which reconstructed the explosion of the volcano on the island of Martinique. Sisters of these reconstructed actualités were the historical reconstruction films, such as Georges Méliès's *The Coronation of Edward VII* (1902), which also ostensibly depicted significant events, but were, in fact, reenactments. Taken together, these two types of film indicate early tension and play with the boundaries between documentary and fiction, a tension that recurs in later movements in French cinema.

Moreover, from 1896 onward, when Alice Guy and Georges Méliès both began creating fiction films, cinema was, in a very real sense, narrative cinema. That is to say, most films created from that point on sought to tell a story, even if they did not yet use the narrative conventions, and particularly the continuity editing and the condensing of time and action associated with later Hollywood film. And even if film genre was not fully developed for several decades, by 1915, French studios were producing films that could easily be classified as comedy, farce, melodrama, costume drama, science fiction, fantasy, horror, literary adaptation, detective film, the religious film, the animated film, and even the Western.

Georges Méliès was experimenting in science fiction and horror nearly from the beginning, producing films such as *Le Voyage dans la lune* (1902) and *Barbe-bleue* (1901). He was also involved in the creation of historical drama, most notably *L'Affaire Dreyfus* (1899), a film that early on positioned film as a vehicle for social and political criticism. Méliès can also be seen as a pioneer of special effects as well as a pioneer of sequencing and of *mise-en-scène*. He used elaborate sets and costumes in his films, creating a fictional world in which narratives unfolded. In addition, he was unsatisfied with the black and white images the film cameras of the day offered, and began using a colorizing process to bring color to his films. Méliès, who was also a meticulous filmmaker, more interested in the quality and artistic elements of his films than their commercial potential, was the absolute master of every element of his filmmaking, from scriptwriting to cinematography to costume design, and was the first independent filmmaker and very probably the first *auteur*, although no such concept existed at the time.

Alice Guy at Gaumont, the director of the first narrative film, *La Fée aux choux* (1895), was also a pioneer of the medium. Although she is not credited, she is believed to have directed or to have overseen the direction of most of the films produced at Gaumont during her tenure as head of production, from 1896 to 1907. She was particularly a pioneer of the melodrama, but under her direction the comedy, the farce, and numerous other genres were developed. Guy was also a pioneer of the shot. She experimented with the use of the camera, and was, for example, already using a dramatic close-up in her 1906 film, *Madame a des envies*. She was also a pioneer in the use of synchronized sound, utilizing Gaumont's *phonoscènes* to produce early sound films. If Méliès was the first independent director, Guy made of Gaumont perhaps the first art-house studio, as quality was also a foremost consideration at the studio, which strove for original creation and innovation in its films.

And then there was Pathé, the first large, corporate studio. Charles Pathé, the founder of the studio, was, as heads of studios are today, more concerned about market share, profits, and global dominance than he was about what kinds of films the studio produced. He hired Ferdinand Zecca, a like-minded director of production, who streamlined the filmmaking process, putting the director at the center. Zecca oversaw the creation of formulaic film production, finding out what worked and repeating that formula. If something was successful, Pathé repeated it, even when it was a question of a film made by another studio. Pathé streamlined production in every way it could. It utilized teams of writers to churn out scripts, mechanized coloration of films to reduce the cost, recycled film stock to make films cheaper, began renting films instead of selling them to cut cost, and aggressively marketed and established distribution networks to insure it remained dominant. In fact, Pathé studios, dominant in France, was also dominant worldwide. As Georges Sadoul once noted, during its period of dominance, Pathé released approximately twice as many films in the United States as all American studios combined.

Apart from its interest in mass, formulaic production, Pathé was also instrumental in evolving another current in film that remains today, that of *film d'art*. Film d'art was a conception of the cinema as a high art form, setting it above the fairground attraction it had been early on, separating it from the characterization of the medium as a "low," popular form rooted in burlesque and physical comedy. Film d'art sought to use established theatrical actors and, for the time, high production values, to produce adaptations of great literary works or great historical events. In particular, film d'art sought to rival the theater, and establish film as the "seventh art," a status it now holds in French culture. Although the term comes from the Studio Film d'Art, established in 1908, film d'art was also developed by a division of Pathé devoted to the development of art film, the Société Cinématographique des Auteurs et des Gens de Lettres (SCAGL). SCAGL, in fact, released the first art film, *L'Arlésienne*, in 1908, closely followed by Film d'Art's *L'Assassinat du Duc de Guise* the same year. Éclair Studio's division Association des Compositeurs et des Auteurs Dramatiques (ACAD) also developed art films, and both Éclair and Pathé distributed for Studio Film d'art, at least until it went bankrupt in 1911.

The development and failure of Studio Film d'Art represents one of the central tensions that has existed in cinema since that time, the tension between cinema as a form of popular entertainment and the cinema as an art, as represented by film d'art. And if that tension has always existed internally in French cinema, just as it existed internally within Pathé itself, it has certainly described the tension between the French cinema and Hollywood cinema. In fact, Studio Film d'Art is emblematic of the struggle of substantive, artistically oriented films in the cinema marketplace. These films may please critics, they may be the films historians remember, they may be what gives cinema legitimacy, but they are very rarely blockbusters, and they have trouble competing with the formulaic productions put out by large studios. Not much, it seems, has changed.

GLOBAL DOMINANCE AND DECLINE

France was the dominant producer of films in the world until just before World War I, and in 1910, at the peak of production, nearly all films distributed in the world were French. Moreover, the French were key in establishing the film industries in such European countries as Belgium, Italy, and Portugal. France was the force to be reckoned with in film production. It was a global industry that accounted for a significant amount of revenue to France, and studios such as Pathé were dependent on foreign revenue to maintain their profits. It is in this context that Hollywood began moving to limit access to the American market, at the same time engaging in a campaign to specifically discredit Pathé. These two coordinated thrusts might not have been lethal to the French film industry, had they not been accompanied by the double blow of an increase in production values in Hollywood film, which forced a struggling French film industry to keep up, and the advent of the First World War. By 1914, France had lost its position of dominance, and Hollywood had taken that position, a position it holds to this day.

French cinema continued on throughout the war years, despite the fact that numerous film personnel were mobilized and that a good deal of industry and capital had to be diverted to the war. By this time, many of the smaller studios had been pushed out of business, and there remained Pathé, Gaumont, and Éclair, as well as a handful of established directors who managed to produce independently. If the industry suffered in terms of financing and market share, it did not necessarily suffer in terms of quality of production. The period produced such remarkable works as

Feuillade's *Les Vampires* (1915), Jacques Feyder's *L'Atlantide* (1920), and Marcel L'Herbier's *L'Argent* (1928), as well as the films of Louis Delluc and Jean Epstein. It was the decade that produced impressionist cinema and surrealist cinema, and that established consciously artistic, often avant-garde filmmaking as a staple of the French cinema.

And yet, financially, the industry was in crisis, seemingly overcome by the American film industry at home as well as abroad. When, in 1927, Hollywood released *The Jazz Singer*, and pushed the cinema firmly into the sound era, it seemed a devastating blow from which the French film industry might not recover. Enormous costs were associated with updating cinemas and equipment to accommodate sound, and there were many who feared that the 1930s might see the end of film in France. A great deal of restructuring went on to ensure viability. A case in point was Pathé Frères, where Charles Pathé sold a controlling interest in the company to Bernard Natan, who completely rebuilt the company, ensuring its longevity for years to come.

THE ARRIVAL OF SOUND AND THE "GOLDEN AGE"

If French film was no longer globally dominant in the 1930s, neither had it lost all of its force. The cinema was the fastest growing industry in the country that decade, and French films had regained their footing, at least in France, accounting for approximately half of all viewers during the decade. This rebirth was in part due to the innovations, both artistic and technical, that sound film required, as well as the fact that sound had made domestically produced films more marketable. The resurgence was also due in part to the fact that France instituted protectionist measures to keep Hollywood from taking over completely. Hollywood also had a bit of bad luck in that the economic downturn in the United States at the end of the 1920s gave France the opportunity to resurrect its film industry. Whatever the particulars, many film historians now look back on the 1930s as the Golden Age of French cinema.

The cinema in France moved firmly along trajectories it would follow for several decades. There were several types of film produced, popular films, such as comedies, romantic comedies and melodramas made by such directors as René Clair, who became an international star. The avant-garde struggled on, heralded by filmmakers such as

Louis Buñuel, Marcel Pagnol, and to a lesser extent André Hugon, who created regional cinema, heralding France's disappearing rural heritage. The directors associated with *Le Réalisme poétique* or Poetic Realism fused art, the avant-garde, and the popular to produce a cinema that was decidedly urban and decidedly popular, reflecting the political currents of the day, but also reflecting the filmmaking of French silent film pioneer Louis Feuillade, who had also been interested in a stylized representation of urban France. The 1930s was the decade of Jean Renoir and Marcel Carné, the decade of Jean Vigo and Jean Gabin. The cinema produced in France was decidedly French, but marketable internationally, if not all that profitable in the United States. Still the decade was not without its anxieties. The economic problems of the United States had, by that time, reached Europe, and the film industry had some tense periods during the decade. Gaumont Studios was even forced into bankruptcy and liquidation at the end of the decade, but was bought out and reorganized into the Société Nouvelle des Établissements Gaumont (SNEG). The studio still exists in that reorganized form today.

By the 1940s, government assistance and protection of the film industry had turned to government oversight and regulation of production. This, and various other factors, including the film d'art legacy itself, had pushed French cinema to become one of the preeminent cinemas in the world, widely regarded in that decade and after as one of the most artistic cinema industries to exist. French cinema became associated with talented actors and talented directors, substantive films with complex thematic resonance. If that did not entirely account for all film production in the 1930s and 1940s, it did at least accurately describe the vision of French cinema that existed in France and internationally, and that continues to exist, cinema, not as popular entertainment, but as a superior expression of a valuable culture.

OCCUPATION, LIBERATION, AND THE TRADITION DE QUALITÉ

When Germany took control of France after the French capitulation in 1940, much changed. The Germans allowed the cinema to continue in France, and permitted it to operate, albeit under the control of the

German government. Many experienced film industry professionals left France during the Occupation. Others, particularly those whose origins or political orientation were objectionable to the occupying power, were not allowed to work. The Germans also seized all films made in France prior to their arrival, and melted many existing prints down to reuse film stock, which was expensive and in short supply. However, not all interventions by the Germans negatively affected the industry as a whole. The Germans continued the process of standardization that the French government had begun. The Nazis set up the Comité d'Organisation de l'Industrie Cinématographique (COIC) to oversee and manage film production [the center still exists today, although in its postliberation iteration the Centre National de la Cinématographie (CNC)]. They also standardized ratings and ticket prices, and even created production companies, such as the infamous Continental Films, which allowed sanctioned individuals to continue to work. They also established the Institut des Hautes Études Cinématographiques (IDHEC) to train professionals in the film industry. That institution also survived several decades past the occupation that created it. The Germans also created the system of *avances sur recettes*, or government advances on films in production, that also still exists today. In fact, some scholars have argued that without German intervention, the French film industry might not be what it is today.

The Germans also oversaw all film production, and set up their own production company, Continental Films, as the dominant, official studio. Perhaps surprisingly, most of the films produced under the Occupation were not propagandistic drivel, but rather, some of the better and better-known films of French cinema. This is certainly due to a will on the part of directors to make films that did not alarm the censor, but which did not conform to their vision of cinema either. Among the films produced by Continental Films, for example, were Christian-Jacques's *L'Assassinat du Père-Noël* (1941), Georges Lacombe's *Le Dernier des six* (1941), Henri-Georges Clouzot's *Le Corbeau* (1943), and André Cayatte's *Au bonheur des dames* (1943). Marcel Carné also independently directed his *Les Visiteurs du soir* (1942) and his legendary *Les Enfants du paradis* (1945) during the Occupation at Les Studios de la Victorine in Nice. The role of Continental Films and of the Nazis in general in French film development and production was a virtual nontopic for many decades after the war, but has recently been explored. Of course, the film industry has offered its own meditation on the subject, in the form of Bertrand Tavernier's film *Laissez-passer* (2002).

After Liberation, the French film industry emerged intact, and in some ways strengthened, but the French economy was in a shambles. The United States, eager to reconstruct Europe in order to create markets for U.S. products, saw its chance to once again dominate the French film market that had managed to elude it after the arrival of sound. The series of trade agreements that would ultimately become the General Agreement on Tariffs and Trade (GATT) was engineered in large measure to give the United States unrestricted access to European markets. In France and elsewhere this meant the film market as well. At first, the Americans succeeded in getting what they wanted, when, in May 1946, France signed the Blum-Byrnes agreement. However, only a short time later, under pressure from the French film industry itself, the French government backed down on the agreement, restricting the number of Hollywood films that could be imported into France. Thus began the cinema wars between France and Hollywood.

In terms of production, the late 1940s and 1950s were characterized by the same sorts of trends that had existed previously in French film history, and in some ways, there was a return to the kinds of divisions seen in the silent era. The sort of film most closely associated with this period is the type of film belonging to what is called "*la qualité française*" or "*la tradition de qualité*." In many ways, this is a return to the film d'art tradition, in that these films were largely costume dramas or literary adaptations with high production values, featuring recognizable stars. Examples of this type of film include Claude Autant-Lara's *L'Auberge rouge* (1951) and *Le Rouge et le noir* (1954) and Christian-Jacque's *Lucrèce Borgia* (1953) and *Madame du Barry* (1954). This particular type of film would attract the scorn of later filmmakers, most notably the filmmakers of the Nouvelle Vague or New Wave, who saw it as stale and formulaic. It was not always so, but, in a sort of reversal of roles the tradition de qualité did, over time, come to occupy the same studio-controlled, formula-based position that the burlesque had in the silent era.

There were other types of films made during the decade. There were crime and detective films, such as Gilles Grangier's *Le Rouge est mis* (1957) and Jean Delannoy's *Maigret tend un piège* (1958). There was also a play with this form in films such as Henri-Georges Clouzot's *Les*

Diaboliques (1955) and of course Jean-Pierre Melville's *Bob le flambeur* (1955). If many of these films were popular, they were not entirely without a basis in earlier French "high" cinema. The fascination with crime and noir stretched back to Louis Feuillade through to *Le Réalisme poétique*, and it was perhaps not entirely by accident that Jean Gabin reinvented his career through such films. French cinema had likewise reinvented itself, but it did so by following well-established patterns. And there were still filmmakers who were decidedly avant-garde. These filmmakers, most notably Max Ophüls, Jacques Becker, and Robert Bresson, were truly experimenting. Becker's experimentations were influenced by the past, as he in some ways carried Le Réalisme poétique forward into the next generation, but his use of the form was innovative, and his style more forward looking. Bresson and Ophüls were breaking new ground entirely, breaking such new ground that they often left audiences baffled, if they had audiences at all. This vein of the 1950s was not grounded in the past, but would become the prehistory of the later resurgence of the avant-garde movements that followed.

NEW WAVES, NEW REVOLUTIONS, MILITANT CINEMA

The year 1951 saw the inauguration of the highly influential journal *Cahiers du cinéma,* which would play a crucial role in defining the direction of French cinema for the next several decades. Its cofounder and patron, André Bazin, was in many ways the father of the Nouvelle Vague, giving New Wave film directors their theoretical vision of cinema and laying the groundwork for their assertion of director as auteur. Armed with a background in film theory and a desire for directorial innovation, New Wave directors François Truffaut, Claude Chabrol, Jean-Luc Godard, Jacques Rivette, and Eric Rohmer scorned script-driven directors like Claude Autant-Lara and René Clément, who were representatives of the French tradition of quality. Truffaut coined the term *cinéma du papa*, a derogatory expression meant to dismiss such filmmakers and the style they represented.

But the "papa" against which the New Wave raised its fist was not, perhaps, only the cinematic father. There is a good deal of evidence that it was an entire social and political order that was being questioned. The period that preceded the New Wave was one of great instability, marked by efforts to move the nation beyond the specter of Nazi collaboration, by an ongoing, brutal, colonial war in Algeria, and by visions of the end of the empire, on which, for so long, France had built its identity. It was a period of censorship, in which these very pressing issues could not be represented or questioned in film, although some recent scholars have asserted that, in very coded ways, the films of the New Wave did just that. It was also a period of rapid industrialization and economic growth. In some ways, this was a moment very similar to the one in which cinema was born. This moment did not erase the tradition de qualité, but it was certainly the type of moment in which revolutions are born.

The New Wave auteurs asserted their independence from the demands of the industry and the constraints of the studio, and from the control of government by avoiding and subverting all of these structures. They made unscripted or minimally scripted, low budget films, using handheld cameras, filming out in the streets. They looked away from the past and squarely at the present. Their films were dark, often pessimistic, always philosophical. A spirit of revolt characterizes many of the New Wave films, such as Truffaut's *Les quatre-cents coups* (1959) and Godard's *À bout de souffle* (1960). If they broke with tradition, these directors did not break completely with the establishment, since they relied on the newly instituted system of *avances sur recettes*, which funded films against their eventual box-office income. In some ways, this system of government patronage allowed the movement to occur. The figurative march of the New Wave directors out of the film studios and into "real" locations anticipated in some ways the subsequent massive marches of students, workers, and others out onto the streets of Paris in May 1968, the point at which most critics believe the New Wave ended. Godard once asserted that the New Wave altered cinema to such a degree that, after a certain point, all films were New Wave. While this is not entirely true, there was a fairly significant transformation in audience expectations and in filmmaking possibility that has survived to the present day.

Although France returned to what is considered a commercially oriented cinema by the end of the 1960s (even the New Wave directors moved in this direction), some have pointed to the influence of the movement in the militant cinema that emerged in the 1970s. Its directors would be Godard, whose films became intensely politicized, and Constantin Costa-Gavras, who was a master of the political thriller. Additionally,

Chabrol mocked the bourgeoisie in films like *Le Boucher* (1970), as would Luis Buñuel in his remarkable *Le Charme discret de la bourgeoisie* (1972). Other trends of the 1970s have been described using the word "new"—new quality, new naturalism—although their corresponding films are, obviously, extensions of earlier styles. Feminist waves of the time were also continuations of earlier movements, and gender remained an important issue, as it was with Alice Guy. In the 1970s, women directors became more visible, a trend that continued in subsequent decades. Duras released her most innovative films in the 1970s, a decade that also hosted the directing debuts of Diane Kurys, Colline Serreau, and Nina Companeez. All of this seems to reflect the spirit of innovation embodied in the New Wave.

The film industry was also busy reorganizing. The increasing popularity of television caused people to go to the movies less frequently, and there were dramatic changes in the types of cinemas that existed in France and in the channels of distribution that got the films to the theaters. The government at the same time broke up the Office Radio Télévision Française (ORTF), which had previously controlled television production, creating separate companies, all of which also began producing films. This in turn created a trend toward collaboration between film and television in France that endures to the present day. Television companies like Canal + or TF1 routinely produced or coproduced cinematic films. Television also became an important market for filmmakers, with many films being made directly for television.

HERITAGE, PLURALITY, AND THE LOOK

By the 1980s, film audiences were again increasing, and the cinema in France seemed to undergo yet another transformation. Film has almost always been viewed as a representation of culture, yet the definitions of culture are often sources of conflict. The surge of international coproductions, the cosmopolitan migrations of prominent film figures from early on until the present, and the diversity of France itself made identity, particularly French identity, a central issue in contemporary film. The question of French identity, and especially of French national identity, has a very long history, yet it has received particularly intense critical attention—and especially interrogation—from the 1980s to the present.

Issues of class, gender, ethnicity, belonging, and discrimination have long been present in French cinema, yet they have received concentrated scrutiny in cinema and cinema studies recently. The heritage film figures quite pointedly into such identity politics. In the 1980s, Minister of Culture Jack Lang invited filmmakers to make heritage films (with state funding), and it produced some interesting results. Like the films in the tradition de qualité, heritage films often carry high production costs. They often linger on French landscapes, revisit idealized periods in French history, or highlight French works of art. One of the first examples of the genre is Daniel Vigne's *Le Retour de Martin Guerre* (1982). Claude Berri's and Yves Robert's respective adaptations of the work of Marcel Pagnol are also examples. This type of film has been a dominant force in French cinema since the 1980s.

At the same time, French cinema produced the *cinéma du look*, a cinema focused on youth and slick visual spectacle. The cinéma du look seemed less interested in history or ethnicity, and more concerned with location, age, and technology. *Look* films like Jean-Jacque's Beneix's *Diva* (1981) or Luc Besson's *Subway* (1985) flirt with questions of identity, but refuse to take them very seriously. One might read this as an alternate articulation of identity, an assertion that none of it matters.

There also emerged the *cinéma de banlieue*, which seemed to revalorize the filmmaking aesthetics of the New Wave as well as to foreground the experience of those in France of immigrant descent. Examples of the cinéma de banlieue include Malik Chibane's *Hexagone* (1994) and Mathieu Kassovitz's *La Haine* (1995). Thus it seems that identity politics, perhaps the defining feature in French politics since the 1980s, was also the defining feature of the cinema of the same period.

The battles about identity between pluralists and purists are not only about national identity itself, but about having the privilege and power to define national identity—or any identity—in the first place. It should come as no surprise that this thematic focus on identity in cinema would coincide with the heating up of the film wars between France and Hollywood. The battlefield was, again, the GATT negotiations, this time in the early 1990s. Central to the turf wars between France and Hollywood was France's assertion that its cinema was exceptional, not mere spectacle, but art, and an art form intricately bound to the identity of the nation itself. If these assertions were tied to debates about immigration, integration, and globalization, they also reflect ideas about French cinema that stretch back to the silent era.

The contemporary period is, thus, one where seemingly incongruous filmmaking styles co-exist, where support for pluralist cinemas by international festival juries, scholars, and fans has been in conflict with a conservative nostalgia for a "purer" past identity associated with a more narrowly constructed heritage. Paradoxically, the French film industry seems to fare better under such conflicts. It has been gaining, although not always steadily, in global market share, and it entered the twenty-first century stronger than it had been almost since the silent beginnings. And even in the filmmaking climate, there is something of the silent era. The cinéma du look in some ways recalls the so-called *cinéma d'attraction*s of filmmakers like Méliès, where image and visual spectacle count as much as narrative. The heritage film harkens back to the tradition of film d'art, and the cinéma de banlieue recalls Feuillade, out documenting the turbulent city life of his day. Much has changed, but not much has changed. And if French cinema has not managed to find a way to best Hollywood in terms of ticket sales, it has found a way to gain some access to the American market as "art film" becomes increasingly interesting to American audiences. What is more, the Hollywood remake of French films has become an increasing staple in large studio production. Perhaps even Hollywood recognizes the "exception" of French cinema.

The Dictionary

– A –

***À BOUT DE SOUFFLE* (1960).** Film. *À bout de souffle* was the first feature-length film of *La Nouvelle Vague*, or New Wave director **Jean-Luc Godard**. Based on a story by **François Truffaut**, *À bout de souffle* narrates the flight of its romantic antihero, Michel Poiccard (**Jean-Paul Belmondo**), from the French police. At the beginning of the film, Michel steals a car and shoots an officer. He plans to escape to Italy with his American girlfriend, Patricia Franchini (Jean Seberg), after collecting money owed to him. He takes risks and delays his flight in part because he is intent upon sleeping with Patricia and convincing her to accompany him. In the end, Patricia reveals his location to the authorities. She says it is an attempt to prove that she does not love him, to avoid being looked after, and to force him to leave. Stating that he is tired, Michel lingers and is later shot to death by police as he flees crookedly down a Paris street.

Godard dedicated *À bout de souffle* to Monogram Pictures, a low-budget American company that produced B movies. As several critics have remarked, Godard's film is a tribute to cinema, and especially to American film noir, as reflected in Michel's expressed admiration for Humphrey Bogart. Godard clearly treats cinema as an art with its own set of conventions. His own unique style of filmmaking reflects such a conception of cinema, and also led to the development of the **auteur** theory, often closely associated with the New Wave.

There are several allusions to the cinema in *À bout de souffle*. Patricia was modeled after a character Seberg played in Otto Preminger's *Bonjour tristesse* (1958). Director **Jean-Pierre Melville** makes an appearance in the film as a celebrity author, a reference to

Melville's own filmmaking, and presumably, Godard's admiration for him. Michel and Patricia kiss in a theater during the screening of Budd Boetticher's *Westbound* (1959), another reference to Hollywood cinema. Finally, the ending of *À bout de souffle* recalls that of Raoul Walsh's *High Sierra* (1941), a film that stars Bogart, whom Poiccard references during the course of the film.

Melville's presence in the film is especially interesting, given that he had contributed to the film noir genre in France in the 1950s. Film noir, with its chiaroscuro lighting, crime-centered narratives, criminal antiheroes and femmes fatales, was viewed by some as an assault on the high production values, moral codes, and perceived good taste of the French *tradition de qualité* or tradition of quality. This type of cinema was disdained by the critics of **Cahiers du cinéma**, many of whom went on to become New Wave directors. Given that, it is not surprising to find so many references to film noir and other popular Hollywood genres in *À bout de souffle*.

Because Godard's first feature film radically challenged the conventions of the film industry, *À bout de souffle* has sometimes been regarded as the first New Wave film. However, some critics instead cite either **Claude Chabrol**'s *Le beau Serge* (1958) or **François Truffaut**'s *Les Quatre cents coups* (1959) as the first. Whatever the case, Godard was clearly working in the same vein as Chabrol and Truffaut, and he obviously vowed to start his art from the ground up, ignoring standard film practices. Godard used natural lighting, a handheld camera, unorthodox film stock usually reserved for photography, and on-site locations. He saw film as a medium that could mix "high" art and popular culture. He rejected the communication of clear points of view, fragmented dialogues, and used jump cuts that interrupt the flow of the narrative. All of this was enhanced by masterful cinematography by Raoul Coutard. The result is a classic of French cinema, and probably one of the most recognized and recognizable films ever made.

ADJANI, ISABELLE (1955–). Actress and producer. Isabelle Yasmine Adjani was born in Gennevilliers, France, the daughter of a German mother and an Algerian-Turkish father. In the 1970s she entered the Comédie Française and later landed her first cinematic role in Bernard Toublanc-Michel's *Le petit bougnat* (1970), followed by supporting roles in Nina Companéez's *Faustine et le bel été* (1972) and **Claude Pinoteau**'s *La gifle* (1974). **François Truffaut** cast her in her breakthrough role in *L'Histoire de Adèle H.* (1975), in which she plays Victor Hugo's daughter. She has since won four **César** Awards for Best Actress—the most of any French actress to date— for her performances in Andrzej Zulawski's cult film *Possession* (1981), Jean Becker's *L'Été Meurtrier* (1983), Bruno Nuytten's *Camille Claudel* (1988), and **Patrice Chéreau**'s *La Reine Margot* (1994). She also received Best Actress awards at the **Cannes Film Festival** for *Possession* and American director James Ivory's *Quartet* (1981). At the American Academy Awards, she received Oscar nominations for *L'Histoire de Adèle H.* (1975) and *Camille Claudel,* a film she coproduced. Although she often plays the role of the emotionally fragile lover, Adjani is known for her versatility and the complexity that she brings to her characters. She is simultaneously famous for her political activism in campaigns against racism, genocide, torture, the deportation of immigrants, and imperialism. In the 1980s, her public arguments in favor of research on HIV/AIDS caused a stir in the popular media.

Other notable acting performances include her work in **André Téchiné**'s *Barocco* (1976) and **Luc Besson**'s *Subway* (1985), both of which won her nominations for the César for Best Actress. She also had leading roles in Roman Polanski's *Le Locataire* (1976), Jacques Rouffio's *Violette et François* (1977), Téchiné's *Les soeurs Brontë* (1979), Werner Herzog's *Nosfertu the Vampyre* (1979), Jacques Monnet's *Clara et les chics types* (1980), Jean-Loup-Hubert's *L'Année prochaine . . . si tout va bien* (1981), **Jean-Paul Rappeneau**'s *Tout feu tout flamme* (1982), Carlos Saura's *Antonieta* (1982), **Claude Miller**'s *Mortelle randonée* (1983), **Agnès Varda**'s short *T'as de beaux escaliers tu sais* (1986), Merzak Allouache's *L'Après Octobre* (1989), and Philomène Esposito's *Toxic affair* (1993). In the twenty-first century, she starred in Laetitia Masson's *La Repentie* (2002), **Benoît Jacquot**'s *Adolphe* (2002), and Rappeneau's *Bon Voyage* (2003). She plays the role of a **Brigitte Bardot** in François Dupeyron's *Monsieur Ibrahim et le fleurs du Coran* (2003). Adjani also acted in American films such as Walter Hill's *The Driver* (1978) and Elaine May's *Ishtar* (1987). She worked for Canadian director Jeremiah Chechik in his remake of **Henri-Georges Clouzot**'s *Diabolique* (1996). She acted as jury president for the fiftieth **Cannes Film Festival**.

AIMÉE, ANOUK (1932–). Actress. Anouk Aimée was born Nicole Françoise Dreyfus in Paris. The daughter of actors, she studied theater and dance in France and England. She made her film debut at the age of thirteen in Henri Calef's *La Maison sous la mer* (1947), and adopted the name Anouk after the character she played in that film. The surname Aimée was suggested by the writer Jacques Prévert, who wrote the screenplay for her second film, André Cayatte's *Les amants du Vérone* (1949). She later starred in **Alexandre Astruc**'s sketch *Le rideau cramoisi*, (1953) and his first feature-length film, *Les mauvaises rencontres* (1955). She played a supporting role in **Georges Franju**'s debut feature *La Tête contre les murs* (1958), where she worked alongside **Jean-Pierre Mocky**. Mocky would later cast her in his first feature, *Les Drageurs* (1959). Two of her most prominent performances were in Italian director Federico Fellini's pivotal films *La Dolce Vita* (1960) and *8½* (1963). She is equally renowned for her work in **Jacques Demy**'s *Lola* (1961), and **Claude Lelouch**'s *Un homme et une femme* (1966), for which she won a Golden Globe and a British Film Academy Award. She starred in Lelouch's sequel, *Un homme et une femme: vingt ans déjà* (1986).

Aimée has received international accolades for her work in art films, and speaks French, Italian, and English fluently. She received the Best Actress Award at the **Cannes Film Festival** for her role in Marco Bellocchio's *Le saut dans le vide* in 1980. In the 1980s and 1990s, she gave cosmopolitan performances in films by Bernardo Bertolucci, Jerzy Skolimowski, and Robert Altman. Throughout her career, Aimée has continued to work with Lelouch in *Si c'était à refaire* (1976), *Viva la vie!* (1983), *Hommes, femmes: mode d'emploi* (1996), and *Une pour toutes* (1999), in addition to Demy in *The Model Shop* (1968) and *La table tournante* (1988). She has also worked extensively with her husband, Elie Chouraqui. She acted in his *Mon premier amour* (1978), *Qu'est-ce qui fait courir David?* (1981), and *Les Marmottes* (1993). Her celebrity was mirrored somewhat in fiction as she portrayed a famous actress in Henri Jaglom's *Festival in Cannes* (2001). She received an honorary **César Award** in 2002 and an honorary Golden Berlin Bear in 2003.

ALLÉGRET, MARC (1900–1973). Director. Born in Switzerland, the son of Protestant minister Elie Allégret, Marc Allégret would become one of the first great directors of sound cinema in France. From a very young age, Allégret became a protégé of André Gide, who was a friend of his father's. Gide served as mentor and guide to Allégret, and in fact, it has often been said (although this is not true) that Allégret was Gide's nephew. Marc often traveled with Gide, including on his famous trip to Africa in the late 1920s (the trip is inscribed into Gide's writing, most notably in *Les Faux monnayeurs*). It was these travels that would inspire Allégret's first films, a series of travel documentaries, the most famous of which is titled *Voyage au Congo* (1927). Presumably, these documentaries gave Allégret a taste of what was to come, and he began his career in cinema.

Allégret initially spent time codirecting and working with other directors, most notably silent-film director Robert Florey. The two made several films together, most notably *Le Blanc et le noir*, a film adaptation of a play by **Sacha Guitry** about a black baby born of adultery who is switched with a white baby. The film was a success, and it set the tone for Allégret's career. Moreover, many of the themes in *Le Blanc et le noir*—race relations, love, and betrayal—would recur in Allégret's later films, such as *Zou-zou* (1934), starring Josephine Baker.

La Meilleure bobonne (1930), codirected with Claude Heymann, inaugurated another career of sorts for Allégret, for it featured a young actor named **Fernandel**, whose long career in film Allégret would launch. Besides Fernandel, Allégret would go on to discover **Raïmu**, **Brigitte Bardot**, **Roger Vadim**, **Jean-Pierre Aumont**, **Jean-Louis Barrault**, **Odette Joyeux**, Danièle Delorme, **Alain Delon**, and **Jean-Paul Belmondo**, among others. In fact, he is considered one of the foremost talent scouts of his time.

In 1931, with the help of film producer Pierre Braunberger, Allégret made his first solo feature films, *Mam'zelle Nitouche* and *La Petite Chocolatière*. Both were commercially and critically successful melodramas that cemented Allegret's reputation as a filmmaker. *Mam'zelle Nitouche* also marked the beginning of a series of directorial collaborations between Allégret and his brother, Yves.

Following *Mam'zelle Nitouche*, Allégret made *Fanny* (1932), an adaptation of **Marcel Pagnol**'s play of the same title, which introduced another star to the screen, the Marseillais actor Raïmu. Raïmu was cast because he had played in Pagnol's original theatrical production, but it was Allégret's film that made him a star. Allégret made numerous films in the 1930s, and these are considered some of his best. Among Allégret's other noteworthy films from the 1930s are *Lac aux dames* (1934), *L'Hôtel du libre échange* (1934), *Les Beaux jours* (1935), *Les Amants terribles* (1936), *La Dame de Malacca* (1938), and *Entrée des artistes* (1939), which is often considered his best film. Allégret's work during the 1930s ranged from literary adaptation to exotic travel film, and it is his breadth as much as anything else that made him a landmark director.

The year 1942 was another great one for Allégret. The two films made in that year, *L'Arlésienne* and *La Belle aventure*, are both French film classics. That decade saw the occupation of France by Germany. Allégret remained in France and continued to make films. Most of his films from the period, like *Les Petites du quai aux fleurs* (1946), were lighthearted and lacked much substance, no doubt in part due to Nazi censorship.

Allégret's films of the 1950s are largely unremarkable. In fact, they are probably responsible for a sort of fall from grace in the eyes of the film public and of film historians. There are one or two exceptions to this, including *En effeuillant la marguerite* (1956), the film that really launched Bardot's career, and *Un Drôle de dimanche* (1958), starring Belmondo and **Arletty**. Allégret continued to make films until just before his death. His last film was *Le Bal du comte d'Orgel* (1970). Allégret's brother, Yves, is also a director of some note.

ANDRÉANI, HENRI (1877–1936). Director and film pioneer. Henri Andréani got his start in film in much the same way as his contemporary, **Alice Guy**, by being the right-hand man to the boss. He was, in fact, **Charles Pathé**'s secretary at the time when Pathé was just breaking into film. Andréani found himself lured by the cinema, and began acting in small roles in **Gaston Velle**'s films. He went on to become a film producer and director himself, making some twenty films over the course of his career.

Historical films were Andréani's forte, and he made many of them. The most celebrated of these are his *Napoléon* (1909), *Cléopatre*

(1910), *Siège de Calais* (1911), and his multipart serial adaptation of *Les Trois Mousquetaires* (1921). *Cléopatre* is an exotic orientalist rendering of the story of the mythical Egyptian queen. It uses elaborate décor and costumes, and was shot entirely in-studio, which emphasizes the "otherworldliness" of its subject matter. The *Siège de Calais*, by contrast, is a nationalist historical film on the Hundred Years War, and it was one of the grandest and most widely publicized historical films of the time. It was filmed on location, rather than entirely in a studio, and featured rather elaborate battle scenes and some of the first true crowd scenes in cinema.

Apart from historical films, Andréani made biblical histories, although he tended to avoid the more widely celebrated stories from the Bible. His biblical films include *Le Sacrifice d'Ismaël* (1912) and *Rebecca* (1913). Andréani was also an early experimenter with the spy film. It is perhaps fitting, given the grandeur of his own historical films, and his production of a film on Napoleon, that, near the end of his career, Andréani formed part of the production crew of **Abel Gance**'s legendary *Napoléon Bonaparte*.

ANTOINE, ANDRÉ (1858–1943). Director and film pioneer. André Antoine came to the cinema late in life, at the age of fifty-two. By that time, he was already a celebrated stage director and producer. He was also the founder of the Théâtre-Libre, a realist, naturalist theater in early twentieth-century Paris that circumvented censorship by selling tickets through subscriptions only. The cinema, for Antoine, brought together two great passions, the theater and photography (a passion inspired by his friend Émile Zola). Moreover, Antoine had many connections in the cinema, having trained a number of leading actors who had, themselves, gone on to become filmmakers, including **Albert Capellani** and **Léonce Perret**.

Antoine made nine films in France, all between 1915 and 1922, most of them for either the **Société Cinématographique des Auteurs et des Gens de Lettres** (SCAGL), which was **Pathé**'s *film d'art* division, or for la Société d'Éditions Cinématographiques (SEC), which succeeded it. His films were for the most part literary adaptations: *Les Frères corses* (1916) adapted from the novel by Alexandre Dumas, *Quatre-Vingt-Treize* (made in 1915 but not released until 1920) adapted from Victor Hugo, *La Terre* (1921) adapted from Émile Zola, and *L'Arlésienne* (1922) adapted from the novel by Alphonse Daudet, for example.

This tendency toward literary adaptation, however, was the only aspect of Antoine's filmmaking that could be considered consistent with the film d'art vision. In place of formal, theatrical style, Antoine often sought out unprofessional actors, average people on the street, to include in his films. In place of the studio and costumes of film d'art, Antoine took his actors and film crew outside into nature or onto the streets. Antoine's filmmaking was influenced far more by his experiences working in avant-garde naturalist theater than they were of any film d'art credo. In the end, this is what did him in. He was, probably, too visionary for his time, and certainly for his studio. His final film, *L'Hirondelle et la Mésange* (1920), was not released because Pathé so disapproved of it (the print was later found and distributed by Henri Colpi in 1938).

For Antoine, this rejection was a last straw. He could not and would not work in film under censorship when he had refused to work in the theater under such terms. He gave up filmmaking and became a film critic.

ARDANT, FANNY (1949–). Actress. Fanny Ardant's career in French cinema began in 1979 when she caught the eye of **François Truffaut** while acting in a television soap opera. Trained in classical theater, Ardant had been unable to do better than bit parts on television and in film until that point. Truffaut's decision to cast her opposite **Gérard Depardieu** in *La Femme d'à côté* (1981) changed the course of Ardant's career. Her performance drew wide critical acclaim and won her a nomination for the **César**.

Since her film debut, Ardant has been a consistent presence on the screen in France. She is known for her capacity to bring to life independent, intelligent, but very sensual older women, quite often in historical periods during which women were allowed to be none of these things. Some of her best-known performances can be found in **Alain Resnais**'s *La Vie est un roman* (1983) and *L'Amour à Mort* (1984), Truffaut's *Vivement dimanche* (1983), **Costa-Gavras**'s *Conseil de famille* (1985), **Michel Deville**'s *Le Paltoquet* (1986), Pierre Beuchot's *Aventure de Catherine C.* (1990), **Yves Angelo**'s *Le Colonel Chabert* (1994), **Patrice Leconte**'s *Ridicule* (1996), Gabriel

Aghion's *Le libertin* (2000), François Ozon's *Huit Femmes* (2001), and **Anne Fontaine**'s *Nathalie* (2003). She again received a César nomination for her performance in *Vivement dimanche*, but did not win the award until 1997, when she received the César for her performance in Aghion's *La Pédale douce*.

Probably because of the success of *Le Colonel Chabert* and *Ridicule* in the English-speaking world, Ardent has also been cast in several English-language films. In 1995, she was cast in Sydney Pollack's *Sabrina*, and in 1998 Shekkar Kapur cast her as Marie de Guise in his biopic, *Elizabeth*, based on the life of Elizabeth I of England. Other international films in which Ardant has appeared include Michaelangelo Antonioni's *Al di là delle nuvole* (1995), Franco Zeffirelli's *Callas Forever* (2001), Ettore Scola's *La cena* (1998), and Mario Martone's *L'Odore del sangue* (2004). Ardant married Truffaut in 1981.

ARLETTY (1898–1992). Actress. Born Léonie Bathiat to a miner and his wife in the Auvergne region of France, Arletty, as she came to be known onstage and onscreen, is one of the best-known actresses in French film history. Arletty made her debut onstage acting opposite actors such as **Jean Gabin**. She did not act in films during the silent era, but seemed to be awaiting the arrival of sound, and made her onscreen debut in 1930 in Rene Hervil's *La Douceur d'aimer*. Her performance in that film was unremarkable, some might even say bad, but despite this less than promising start, she went on to make several other films immediately after, including Jean Choux's *Un Chien qui rapporte* (1931), Roger Le Bon's *La Belle aventure* (1932), and Karl Anton's *Un soir de réveillon* (1933). In each of these films, she gave much better performances, and it is these films that cemented her popularity as a screen actress.

Throughout the early 1930s, Arletty's screen roles were primarily light comic parts. They ensured her status as a popular actress, if not an acclaimed one. That began to change in 1935 with her role in **Jacques Feyder**'s *Pension Mimosas*, in which she played a childless woman who adopts a young boy later sought by his biological father. The role was one of Arletty's first dramatic performances, and it gave her credibility as an actress of some range. It was, however, her collaborations with two important screen icons, **Sacha Guitry** and **Marcel Carné**, that ultimately made Arletty a star.

Guitry cast Arletty in three different films: *Faisons un rêve* (1936), *Les Perles de la couronne* (1937), and *Désiré* (1937). The first film cast her opposite **Raïmu**, himself a screen icon, which considerably enhanced her reputation as an actress. The film also presented Arletty as a woman of the working classes, the type of role that she would later play for Carné. The second film, radical in its difference from the first, cast Arletty as the queen of Sheba. The stark contrast between the two roles again pointed to a dramatic range that previous films had not permitted. In her third Guitry film, she would again play a tough, streetwise, working-class woman, and it is this type of role with which she would become associated.

Carné met Arletty during the filming of *Pension Mimosas*, where he had served as Feyder's assistant. The two became friends. Carné would go on to become a director and in 1938, he decided to cast Arletty opposite **Louis Jouvet** in *Hôtel du nord*. Arletty played the role beautifully, giving depth and dimension to the character of Renée. It was not an easy role in 1938, since it was fairly clear that Renée was a sexually available woman. Nonetheless, Arletty managed to give the character a dignity others might not have found. The film became a classic.

Renée, however, was not the only role Carné would create for Arletty. He cast her again in 1939 in *Le Jour se lève*, opposite her former stage partner Gabin. In this film, Arletty played Clara, the amoral assistant to a completely malevolent dog trainer named Valentin. Arletty's greatest role under Carné's direction, however, undoubtedly came in his 1945 class film, ***Les Enfants du paradis***, in which she plays Garance, a working-class actress in early nineteenth-century France. It is probably the role for which Arletty is best known and best remembered. Arletty made two other films with Carné, *Les Visiteurs du soir* (1942), in which she played an envoy of the devil, and *L'Air de Paris* (1954), in which she again played opposite Gabin.

During the late 1930s and 1940s, Arletty, by then a superstar, tried her hand at lighter roles onscreen as well. She had a number of noteworthy comic roles, including those in Jean Boyer's *Circonstances attentuantes* (1939) and **Claude Autant-Lara** and Maurice Lehmann's *Fric-Frac* (1939). She also did several other films, besides those with Carné, during the 1940s, the period of the Nazi Occupation of France. Those include Bernard-Deschamps's *Tempêtes*

(1940), **Roger Richebé**'s *Madame Sans-Gêne* (1941), and Boyer's *Boléro* (1942).

Arletty's very open cooperation with the Nazi occupiers during the war, and particularly her open liaisons with various Germans more or less put an end to her film career after the war. She was even placed under surveillance for a number of years following the war as a result of her Occupation-era activities. She managed a handful of films in the 1950s and early 1960s, including Carné's *Air de Paris*, and **Marc Allégret**'s *Un drôle de Dimanche* (1962), in which she starred opposite **Jean-Paul Belmondo**. However, Arletty had so permanently damaged her reputation that the public found it difficult to embrace her as it once had. She made her final film in French in 1962.

ARNAUD, ÉTIENNE (1880–1955). Director and film pioneer. Étienne Arnaud was born Chiaffredo Arnaud. He became a silent film–era director during the pioneer days of cinema. He was hired on at **Gaumont** in about 1905, along with numerous other writer-directors, including **Louis Feuillade**. At first, Arnaud specialized in chase films, such as *Un Coup de vent* (1906) and *La Brouette* (1908), but over time, he began to cross genres and ultimately made films ranging from *féeries*, to social dramas such as *Le Crime du braconnier* (1908), to historical films such as *Le Dernier requiem de Mozart* (1909) and *André Chenier* (1912). His best-known film is undoubtedly *La Course aux potirons* (1908) made with **Emile Cohl**.

Aranud remained at Gaumont until 1914, when he was hired away by **Éclair** to head up production at its U.S. studios. He streamlined Éclair's production and developed films more in keeping with American tastes, but much of his work was for nothing, as the Fort Lee studios at which Éclair was based burned down in 1914. Arnaud was replaced as head of production the same year. He remained in the United States, but appears to have given up filmmaking after that point.

ARNOUL, FRANÇOISE (1931–). Actress. Françoise Arnoul was born Françoise Gautsch in Algeria (at that time a French colony). Her father was an officer in the French army and her mother was an actress. In 1945, she went to Paris to study theater and dance, and she made her film debut in 1949 in *l'Épave*. The same year she also appeared in

Charles Boyer's comic film *Nous irons à Paris*. In 1951, Arnoul got her first starring role in *La Plus belle fille du monde*, in which she played a beauty pageant contestant willing to do anything to win. This role led to several others in which she played ruthless or unscrupulous women or temptresses of various kinds. Films that cast Arnoul in this type of role include *Le Fruit défendu* (1952), in which she starred opposite **Fernandel**, *Dortoir des grandes* (1953), in which she starred with **Jean Marais**, *La Rage au corps* (1953), *Les Amants du tage* (1955), and *La Chatte* (1958).

Arnoul's first great role came in 1955 in **Jean Renoir**'s *French Cancan*, in which she played opposite **Jean Gabin** as an ordinary girl transformed into a cancan dancer. She would star opposite Gabin again the following year in **Henri Verneuil**'s *Des Gens sans importance*. In 1956, Arnoul had a starring role in a film directed by another icon of French cinema, **Marcel Carné**'s *Le Pays d'où je viens*. 1962 would see her directed by two other greats, **Marc Allégret** in *Les Parisiennes* and **Julien Duvivier** in *Le Diable et les dix commandements*, in which she starred opposite **Charles Aznavour**.

In 1963, Arnoul starred in **Pierre Kast**'s *Vacances portugaises*, and then left acting to work for the actors union. She has since made only a handful of films: Jacques Rouffio's *Violette & François* (1977), Jean-Claude Missiaen's *Ronde de nuit* (1984), Jean Marboeuf's *Voir l'éléphant* (1990) and *Temps de chien* (1996), Philippe Leriche's *Les Années campagne* (1992), Brigitte Roüan's *Post coitum* (1997), and Claude Faraldo's *Merci pour le geste* (2000).

ASSAYAS, OLIVIER (1955–). Actor, critic, director, and screenwriter. Olivier Assayas is the son of director Jacques Rémy, so Assayas was born into film, in a manner of speaking. He began his career making short films, such as *Copyright* (1979), *Rectangle* (1979), and *Laissé inachevé à Tokyo* (1982). Assayas then went on to work on film from the critical and theoretical side. He was an editor for **Cahiers du cinéma** from 1980 to 1986, and he gained particular recognition for the journal's special issue on Hong Kong cinema, a foreign cinema that would later influence his own filmmaking.

From the mid-1980s, Assayas moved to screenwriting. He worked on the scripts of **André Téchiné**'s *Rendez-vous* (1985), *Le lieu du crime* (1986), and *Alice et Martin* (1998), before trying his hand at directing feature-length films. His debut feature was *Désordre* (1986), followed by *L'enfant de l'hiver* (1989). His third feature, *Paris s'éveille* (1991), won the **Prix Jean-Vigo** in 1992.

His film *Irma Vep* (1995), based on the character from the **Louis Feuillade** silent film serial *Les Vampires* (1915), was also widely acclaimed. This film stars Hong Kong action heroine Maggie Cheung, whom Assayas married. To date, he has been nominated for the Palme d'or at the **Cannes Film Festival** for three films: the period piece *Les destinées sentimentales* (2000), the cyber thriller *Demonlover* (2002), and the drama *Clean* (2004), which casts Cheung as the lead. His other feature films include *Une nouvelle vie* (1993), *L'eau froide* (1994), and *Fin d'août, début septembre* (1999). He also directed a documentary on the prominent Taiwanese director Hou Hsiao-Hsien, titled *HHH, un portrait de Hou Hsiao-Hsien* (1997).

ASTRUC, ALEXANDRE (1923–). Film theorist and director. Alexandre Astruc began his film career as an assistant to **Marc Allégret** in *Blanche Fury* (1947). He is famous for his concept of the "**caméra-stylo**," which he articulated in "Naissance d'une nouvelle avant-garde: La caméra-stylo" (The Birth of a New Avant-Garde: The Caméra-Stylo), an essay that appeared in 1948 in *L'Ecran français*. He was also a screenwriter for Marcello Pagliero, Fernando Cerchio, and Jean-Daniel Pollet. His first independent work as director was the sketch *Le rideau cramoisi* (1953), which won the **Prix Louis-Delluc**. He is known for his adaptations of literary works, especially *Une Vie* (1958), a feature based on the story by Guy de Maupassant, and *L'éducation sentimentale* (1962), based on Gustave Flaubert's classic novel. He also directed *Les mauvaises rencontres* (1955), *La proie pour l'ombre* (1961), *La longue marche* (1966), *Flammes sur l'Adriatique* (1968), and, with Michel Contat, the documentary *Sartre par lui-même* (1976). He plays himself in Michel Pascal and Serge Toubiana's *François Truffaut: portrait volés* (1993). Critics often place him as a precursor to the *Nouvelle Vague* or New Wave.

AUDIARD, MICHEL (1920–1985). Director and screenwriter. Michel Audiard was one of France's most popular and prolific crafters of film dialogue. He began his film career in the late 1940s, writing screenplays. His first major work as screenwriter was for André

Hunébelle's *Mission à Tangier* (1949). He won the **César,** with **Claude Miller** and Jean Herman, for the screenplay of Miller's *Garde à vue* in 1982. The screenplay was later used in American director Stephen Hopkins's *Under Suspicion* (2000). He was also nominated for César awards for best film script for **Georges Lautner**'s *Mort d'un pourri* in 1978 and **Jacques Deray**'s *On ne meurt que deux fois* in 1986. He worked frequently for Lautner, and wrote several dialogues acted by **Jean Gabin**, **Lino Ventura**, and **Jean-Paul Belmondo**. He directed *Faut pas prendre les enfants du bon Dieu pour des canards sauvages* (1968), *Une veuve en or* (1969), *Elle bois pas, elle fume pas, elle drague pas, mais . . . elle cause!* (1970), *Le cri du cormoran le soir au-dessus des jonques* (1971), *Le drapeau noir flotte sur la marmite* (1971), *Elle cause plus . . . elle flingue!* (1972), *Comment réussir quand on est con et pleurnichard* (1974), and *Bon baisers, à lundi* (1974). His son is director Jacques Audiard.

AUDRY, JACQUELINE (1908–1977). Director and screenwriter. One of the early female directors, Jacqueline Audry got her start writing screenplays and assisting for the likes of **Jean Delannoy** and **Max Ophüls**. Her sister Colette was a playwright who also occasionally wrote screenplays (most notably for **René Clément**'s 1943 *La Bataille du rail*), and her husband, Pierre Laroche, was a screenwriter. Audry made her directorial debut in 1943 and directed her first feature film, *Les Malheurs de Sophie*, in 1945. She made eighteen films between 1945 and 1972, the most notable of which were either literary adaptations or had literary connections. These films included *Gigi* (1948), *Minne, l'Ingénue libertine* (1950), and *Mitsou* (1956), all adaptations of novels by Colette, *Huis Clos* (1954), an adaptation of the play by Sartre, and *La Garçonne* (1957), based on a controversial novel. *Olivia* (1951), starring **Edwige Feuillère** and Simone Simon, *Le Secret du Chevalier d'Éon* (1959), starring **Bernard Blier**, and *Les Fruits amers* (1967), starring Emmanuelle Riva and based on her sister's play *Soledad*, are also noteworthy. For the most part, Audry's films reflect the classic French cinema *tradition de qualité*, with fairly classic narration, editing, and mise-en-scène. Her films often centered around strong female characters or female leads that challenged conventional ideas of women's roles or social rules in general.

AUMONT, JEAN-PIERRE (1911–2001). Actor. Born Jean-Pierre Salomons into a wealthy French family, Jean-Pierre Aumont had acting in the blood. His mother was an actress, as were other family members. He was discovered by **Louis Jouvet** after studying at the Paris Conservatoire d'art dramatique, and began his acting career on the stage. He made his film debut in 1931 in *Jean de la lune*, a film in which he had a small role. He soon had much larger roles in several other films, including *Le Voleur* (1933), *Dans les rues* (1934), and then two fairly important roles, one in **Marc Allégret's** *Lac aux dames* (1934) and the second in Julien Duvivier's *Maria Chapdelaine* (1934).

Following his work with Allégret and Duvivier, Aumont became established as a major film actor. He made films with many of the major directors of the day, including *La Porte du large* (1936) with **Marcel L'Herbier**, *Les Beaux jours* (1935) with Allégret, *La Femme du bout du monde* (1937) with **Jean Epstein**, and *Drôle de drame* (1937) and *Hôtel du nord* (1938) with **Marcel Carné**. He tended to play suave, handsome, charming leading men, mostly in comedies. His attractive appearance and natural charm lent themselves naturally to lighter, happier films.

Aumont's real life, however, was anything but light and happy. He fled France in 1942 during the Nazi Occupation, in part because of his Jewish background and in part because of political conviction. He went first to the United States, where he succeeded in obtaining a contract with MGM, with whom he made the wartime (propaganda) film *The Cross of Lorraine* (1943), but then went to Tunisia to fight for the Free French. He was wounded twice and once nearly killed during his service and would later receive the *Croix de guerre* and the *Légion d'honneur* for his service.

After the war, Aumont returned to the United States, with trips back and forth to Europe. He made several films in English, including *Shéherazade* (1946), *Lili* (1953), *The Devil at 4 O'Clock* (1961) with Frank Sinatra and Spencer Tracy, and *Castle Keep* (1969) with Sidney Pollack. In French he also made several films, including *Si Versailles m'était conté* (1954) with **Sacha Guitry**, *Vacances portugaises* (1963) with **Pierre Kast**, and *La Nuit américaine* (1974) with **François Truffaut**. Shortly before his death, he appeared in two Merchant and Ivory costume dramas, *Jefferson in Paris* (1995) and *The Proprietor* (1996), which starred **Jeanne Moreau**.

AU REVOIR, LES ENFANTS **(1987).** Film. Director **Louis Malle** completed *Au revoir, les enfants* in the latter part of his career, yet it is based on a story that haunted him well before he started to make films. Set in a Catholic boarding school in 1944, this autobiographical feature recounts a pivotal episode from Malle's childhood. Set during the Nazi Occupation of France during World War II, the film focuses on two schoolboys, Julien Quentin (Gaspard Manesse) and his Jewish classmate, Jean Bonnet (Raphaël Fejtö). Quentin is modeled on the young Malle and Bonnet on his childhood friend, Hans-Helmut Michel.

The film portrays the growing friendship between the two boys, and particularly Quentin's discovery that Bonnet's last name is really Kippelstein, and that he is, in reality, a Jew who has been hidden at the school to protect him. The climax of the film occurs near the end of the film, when the Gestapo, apparently alerted to the presence of hidden Jewish children, searches the school, discovers Bonnet, and takes him away to the concentration camps. Arrested along with Bonnet are a number of other Jewish students and the school priest, Père Jean (Philippe Morier-Genoud), who hid them. It is revealed at the end of the film that a recently fired school caretaker named Joseph (François Négret), had alerted the Gestapo either for revenge or in return for compensation. In voiceover at the end of the film, Malle himself tells the audience that Bonnet died in Auschwitz and that Père Jean died in Mauthausen-Gusen.

Au revoir, les enfants is an ambiguous rendering of French guilt during the Occupation. It recalls Malle's exploration of the subject of French collaboration in his earlier film, *Lacombe Lucien* (1974). Using a director's poetic license, Malle added various fictional details to his story, for example, changing the events such that Quentin inadvertently gives his friend away. Malle also added the detail of Joseph as the informer. While the actions of the Gestapo are clearly horrendous, Malle's Joseph, like the character Lucien Lacombe in *Lacombe Lucien*, is not an evil character. Rather, he is a human character who acts selfishly, without, perhaps, fully considering the consequences of his actions.

The film also acknowledges that there were heroes even in such a dark period. Le Père Jean is a case in point. Nonetheless, it also suggests that many French nationals were more focused on self-preservation or self-interest than in resisting the Occupation. In some way, the film reflects the interrogation of the Occupation associated with the *Mode Rétro*, with which *Lacombe Lucien* is often associated. Although produced a decade later than most works linked to the *Mode Rétro*, the film shares with them the less than idealistic image of France's collective wartime response to the Occupation, images that many in France clung to in the postwar years.

AUTANT-LARA, CLAUDE (1901–2000). Director. Born in 1901, the son of Édouard Autant, an architect, and Louise Lara, an actress, Claude Autant-Lara left France with his mother and spent his early childhood abroad in Great Britain. Autant-Lara returned to France at the age of eighteen to study art and soon after began working for director **Marcel L'Herbier** as a set and costume designer, a job that put him in contact with Fernand Léger and Alberto Cavalcanti, among others. This prompted an interest in cinema, and more specifically in directing films, and as a result, Autant-Lara made two shorts, *Fait divers* (1923) and *Construire un feu* (1923), both influenced by the surrealists with whom he had ties.

Autant-Lara subsequently went to work as an assistant to **René Clair** for a time, and then to Hollywood where he made French versions or remakes of American hit films, largely films by Buster Keaton. In 1930, he returned to France and made his first solo feature film, *Ciboulette*, based on the story by Francis Croissent and made in collaboration with Jacques Prévert. The author, however, unhappy with Autant-Lara's vision of his text, initiated a smear campaign that resulted in excessive cutting during the editing process, and the results were that the film was a failure and Autant-Lara's reputation was tainted.

Following the *Ciboulette* debacle, Autant-Lara returned to England, where he assisted Maurice Lehmann on *L'Affaire du courrier de Lyon* (1937), *Le Ruisseau* (1938), and *Fric-Frac* (1939). He then returned to France, which was shortly afterward occupied by Germany, and it was the Occupation that breathed new life into Autant-Lara's career. His first Occupation films were *Le Mariage de Chiffon* (1942) and *Lettres d'amour* (1942), both starring **Odette Joyeux**. These were quickly followed by *Douce* (1943) and then by an adaptation of Raymond Radiguet's novel, *Le Diable au corps* (1946), which was Autant-Lara's first great success. The true nature of these Occupation films is disputed. Some see them as nostalgic but light period pieces that conformed to the censorship of the day. Others see in them hidden critiques of the hypocrisy and treachery of the time.

After the war, Autant-Lara was one of the most popular directors making films in France. He was, in fact, one of the practitioners of the *tradition de qualité*, one of the "papas" who would be criticized by the members of the French *Nouvelle Vague* or New Wave. Films such as *L'Auberge rouge* (1951), *Le Blé en herbe* (1954), *Le Rouge et le noir* (1954), *La Traversée de Paris* (1956), and *En cas de malheur* (1958) were traditional, sometimes entertaining, sometimes patriotic, but, as the New Wave would point out, did little to move cinema forward and did not in any way reflect the tremendous changes France had undergone.

The critiques of the New Wave notwithstanding, Autant-Lara made films all through the 1960s, although few, if any of them, were remarkable. Autant-Lara's last film was *Gloria*, made in 1977. In the 1980s, he gave up filmmaking and began to dabble in politics, particularly in the politics of the extreme right, which was on the rise in France. He was elected to the European parliament, but resigned in scandal after denying the Holocaust and making other, similarly objectionable claims.

AUTEUIL, DANIEL (1950–). Actor. Daniel Auteuil was born in Algeria to a father who was an opera singer. Auteuil started his career as a stage actor at the Théâtre National Populaire in Paris and a performer in musicals, forming part of the chorus in the Paris production of *Godspell* in 1972. A few years later, he debuted onscreen in Girard Pires's *L'Agression* (1974). Early in his film career Auteuil played one of the "under-gifted"—a title that would carry quite a bit of irony later on—in **Claude Zidi**'s comedies *Les sous-doués* (1978), *Bête mais discipliné* (1979), and *Les sous-doués en vacances* (1981). He also played in **Edouard Molinaro**'s *Pour cent briques, t'as plus rien* (1982), *L'Amour en douce* (1984), and *Palace* (1985), where he first worked alongside his former wife, **Emmanuel Béart**.

Although Auteuil is talented in comedy, his very best performances would be in drama. He won a **César Award** for Best Supporting Actor in **Claude Berri**'s *Jean de Florette* (1986), the **heritage**

film that launched his stardom. He went on to win a number of prestigious awards, including two Césars for Best Actor in Berri's ***Manon des sources*** (1986) and **Patrice Leconte**'s *La fille sur le pont* (1999), and Best Actor at the **Cannes Film Festival** in Jaco van Dormael's *Le huitième jour* (1996). He also won two European Film Academy Best Actor Awards, one for **Claude Sautet**'s *Un coeur en hiver* (1992) and one for Michael Haneke's *Caché* (2005), as well as a Lumière Award for his title role in **Benoît Jacquot**'s *Sade* (2000), and the Golden Goblet at the Shanghai International Film Festival in Francis Veber's *Le Placard* (2001). Auteuil is often a presence at the César awards. He received nominations for Best Actor in Sautet's *Quelques jours avec moi* (1988), Girod's *Lacenaire* (1990), **André Téchiné**'s *Ma saison préférée* (1993), Christian Vincent's *La séparation* (1994), **Philippe de Broca**'s *Le Bossu* (1997), Pierre Salvadori's *Après vous* (2003), and Olivier Marchal's *36 Quai des Orfèvres* (2004). He has worked with a number of female directors, including **Coline Serreau** on *Romuald et Juliette* (1989), **Josiane Balasko** on *Ma vie est un enfer* (1991), **Nicole Garcia** on *L'Adversaire* (2002), Hélène Angel on *Recontre avec le dragon* (2003), and Laetitia Masson on *Pourquoi (pas) le Brésil* (2004).

Auteuil is one of France's most respected contemporary actors, well known for his ability to master diverse genres. He has delivered leading roles in numerous comedies, dramas, period pieces, heritage films, romances, and thrillers. His additional noteworthy performances are in **Patrice Chéreau**'s *La Reine Margot* (1994), **Régis Wargnier**'s *Une femme française* (1995), Téchiné's *Les Voleurs* (1996), Girod's *Passage à l'acte* (1996), Berri's *Lucie Aubrac* (1997), Michel Blanc's *Mauvaise passe* (1999), Leconte's *La Veuve de Saint-Pierre* (2000), Roberto Andò's *Sotto falso nome* (2004), Bob Swaim's *Nos amis les flics* (2004), Arnaud and Jean-Marie Larrieu's *Peindre ou faire l'amour* (2005), and Veber's *La Doublure* (2006).

AUTEUR/CINÉMA D'AUTEUR. Coined by the critics of the *Cahiers du cinéma*, the auteur or *cinéma d'auteur* concept refers to a type of filmmaking defined as a body of work by a single director that exhibits certain identifiable and stable characteristics across the body of work, among which is a tendency away from seamless narration and the classical Hollywood style and more toward avant-garde or experimental tendencies.

The notion of auteur is rooted in the structuralist writings of Roland Barthes, wherein texts are authored to be either "readable" (that is, easily understood by a reader) or "writable," where the reader is required to do a certain amount of analytical work in order to derive meaning from the texts. Auteurism posits that films, like texts, are "authored" by their directors, and in auteurist films, the film is more "writable" than "readable," which is to say, it requires a certain amount of work on the part of the spectator.

The term was first widely applied to the cinema of the directors of the *Nouvelle Vague* or New Wave, most notably **Jean-Luc Godard** for films such as *À bout de souffle* (1960) and *Éloge d'amour* (2004), and to **Eric Rohmer** for films such as *Ma Nuit chez Maude* (1969) and *Conte d'automne* (1998). The term has been applied also to directors such as **Robert Bresson**, particularly for films such as *Journal d'un curé de campagne* (1951) and *Lancelot du lac* (1974). **Agnès Varda**, known for films such as *Jacquot de Nantes* (1991) and *Les Glaneurs et la glaneuse* (2000), is also frequently cited as an auteur. Younger auteur directors include **Jean-Jaques Beineix**, best-known for *Diva* (1981), **Mathieu Kassovitz**, best-known for *La Haine* (1995), and **Claire Denis**, known for films such as *Chocolat* (1988) and *Beau Travail* (1999). The concept of auteur may be tied to the constant anxiety of placing cinema in the realm of art, rather than of popular culture, an anxiety that stretches back to the *film d'art* tradition. **Alexandre Astruc**'s notion of the *caméra-stylo* is also closely related to the concept of auteur.

AZNAVOUR, CHARLES (1924–). Actor, composer, and singer. Charles Aznavour was born in Paris to Armenian parents. During his youth he acted in the Théâtre du Petit Monde. His first appearance onscreen was in a very small role in Eugene Deslaw's *La Guerre des gosses* (1938). In 1958 he acted in **Georges Franju**'s *La Tête contre les murs*, which starred **Jean-Pierre Mocky**. He would later act in Mocky's *Les Dragueurs* (1959) and *Les Vièrges* (1964). One of his first major roles was as the pianist in **François Truffaut**'s famous *Tirez sur le pianiste* (1960).

In addition to being a celebrity actor, Aznavour is a renowned music hall singer and composer, writing songs for films and for his mentor, the late Edith Piaf. In the 1960s, he became an international film star, appearing alongside Marlon Brando, Ringo Starr, and Richard Burton in his first English-language film, Christian Marquand's *Candy* (1968). He also appeared in Michael Winner's *The Games* (1970), Lewis Gilbert's *The Adventurers* (1970), Clive Rees's *The Blockhouse* (1973), Peter Collinson's *And Then There Were None* (1974), and Douglas Hickox's *Sky Riders* (1976). He acted in German films as well, such as Volker Schlöndorff's *Die Blechtrommel* (1979) and Hans Geissendörfer's *Der Zauberberg* (1982). In 1982, he costarred with the beloved actor **Michel Serrault** in **Claude Chabrol**'s *Les Fantômes du chapelier*. In 1986, he worked as the scenarist and lead actor for Paul Boujenah's *Yiddish Connection*.

Aznavour has also had leading roles in several French films, among them Denys de La Patellière's *Un Taxi pour Tobrouk* (1961), Michel Boisrond's *Cherchez l'idole* (1963), Pierre Granier-Deferre's *Paris au mois d'août* (1965), Jean Larriaga's *La part des lions* (1971), Phillipe Leriche's *Les Années campagne* (1991), Bernard Favre's *Pondichery, dernier comptoir des Indes* (1996), and Christian de Chalonge's *Le Comédien* (1996). He received an honorary **César** in 1997. In 2001, he sang alongside **Anna Karina** in Jonathan Demme's *The Truth About Charlie*. In 2002, he starred in Atom Egoyan's *Ararat*, a film about coping with the genocide against Armenians in Turkey. He also appeared in Denis Berry's *Laguna* (2002) and Edmond Bensimon's *Emmenez-moi* (2004).

– B –

BALASKO, JOSIANE (1950–). Actress and director. Josiane Balasko started her career in café-théâtres with the Troupe du Splendid alongside Michel Blanc, **Thierry Lhermitte**, **Gérard Jugnot**, and **Christian Clavier**. She would collaborate with this team of well-known comedians in several films. Her feature films as director are generally comedies, including *Sac de noeuds* (1985), *Les keufs* (1987), *Ma vie est un enfer* (1991), the popular *Gazon Maudit* (1995), and *Un grand cri d'amour* (1998). *Gazon Maudit,* a social comedy that portrays the lesbian affair of a married woman, was nominated for an Oscar for Best Foreign Film.

Balasko has acted in several films by **Jean-Marie Poiré**, including *Les petits calins* (1978), *Retour en force* (1980), *Les hommes préfèrent les grosses* (1981), and *Le père Noël est une ordure* (1982). She challenged more typical depictions of sexual attraction in **Bertrand Blier**'s *Trop Belle pour toi* (1988), where **Gérard Depardieu**'s character leaves the lovely Carole Bouquet in favor of the plainer, yet more interesting Balasko. Balasko also acted in **Patrice Leconte**'s *Les bronzés* (1978) and *Les bronzés font du ski* (1979), **Claude Berri**'s *Le Maître d'école* (1981), Jean-Loup Hubert's *La Smala* (1984) and *Les Acteurs* (2000), Jean-Jacques Zilberman's *Tout le monde n'a pas eu la chance d'avoir des parents communistes* (1993), **Claude Zidi**'s *Arlette* (1997), Gérard Lauzier's *Le Fils du français* (1999), Jean Becker's *Un crime au paradis* (2000), Gabriel Aghion's *Le libertin* (2000) and *Absolument fabuleux* (2001), Djamel Bensalah's *Le raid* (2002), and Guillaume Nicloux's *Cette femme-là* (2003).

BARDOT, BRIGITTE (1934–). Actress. Probably the most famous starlet French cinema or world cinema has ever produced, Brigitte Bardot came to the screen at the age of sixteen, after having modeled for several French women's magazines, most notably *Elle*. Bardot's first film role was in Jean Boyer's *Le Trou normand* (1952). While it did not make her a star, it was a successful enough performance to start her career. Bardot attracted the attention of **Marc Allégret**, who cast her in his 1955 film *Futures vedettes* and in his 1956 film *En effeuillant la marguerite*. Her roles in both films gave Bardot considerable visibility and launched her on the road to stardom. The film, of course, that made Bardot a household name, was husband **Roger Vadim**'s (the two had married in 1952) *Et Dieu créa la femme* (1956). In it, Bardot played the voluptuous, yet naïve Juliette, the woman who unwittingly comes between two brothers. The film made Bardot an international sex symbol and French cinema icon. It did not, however, do much for her marriage to Vadim, and the two divorced in 1957.

Following *Et Dieu créa la femme*, Bardot would go on to work with many of France's leading directors. In 1958, **Julien Duvivier** cast her in *La Femme et le pantin*, **Claude-Autant Lara** directed her in *En cas de malheur* (1958), **Jean-Luc Godard** directed her in *Le*

Mépris (1963) and *Masculin, feminine* (1966), **Louis Malle** directed her in *Vie privée* (1962) and *Viva Maria!* (1965), and **Michel Deville** directed her in *L'Ours et la poupée* (1969). She made two other films with Vadim, *Les Bijoutiers du clair de lune* (1958) and *Don Juan* (1973).

Bardot's films tend to reflect the role she came to play in the public eye at the height of her career. As her untamed, wild blond hair always suggested, Bardot the icon came to stand for the ability of **women** to refuse to conform to those roles thrust upon them, be they by society or by men. Bardot also represented an overt, if not fully conscious sexuality. She stood for an uninhibited demand for women to be who they were and to go where they wanted. It is small wonder her popularity coincided with an era that saw the rise of the women's movement and the general throwing over of traditional values. It is also no surprise that she was as popular in the United States as she was in France.

Bardot gave up her film career in 1974, in part because she really did not like fame and in part because she no doubt realized that her physical appearance was a great deal of her appeal, and that as she aged and her appearance changed audience interest in her would likely diminish. Since that time, she devoted her life to the cause of animal rights, and, for the most part, stayed out of the public eye. However, Bardot, who is married to a senior member of France's extreme right-wing party, the Front National, has attracted a fair degree of controversy since 1997. She has made numerous racist and anti-homosexual remarks and has been fined several times, since such remarks are illegal under France's hate crimes laws. In 2003, she published a book, *A Cry in the Silence*, which was filled with many of the same kinds of racist and extremist rhetoric, and for which she was also fined.

BARONCELLI, JACQUES DE (1881–1951). Director and screenwriter. Born Jacques de Baroncelli-Javon in Bouillarges in Languedoc-Roussillon, Jacques de Baroncelli went on to become one of the best-known silent-film directors and a modestly well-known sound film director as well. Baroncelli at first aspired to journalism, but around 1909 turned to cinema. His first known film is *L'Arlésienne* (1909), an adaptation of the novel by Alphonse Daudet that was made for the **Société Cinématographique des Auteurs et des Gens de Lettres** (SCAGL), the *film d'art* division of **Pathé**. The film stars **Stacia Napierkowska,** one of the great silent film actresses. In some ways, this film established the tone for much of Baroncelli's career, as literary adaptations are seen as one of his strengths.

Although he is today better remembered for his sound films, Baroncelli was, in his day, considered a master of the silent film. He made more than forty silent films, many of them with the great silent-film actors, most of them for Pathé, although he did make an occasional film for **Éclair** and **Gaumont**. His better films include *La Nouvelle Antigone* (1916), *Soupçon tragique* (1916) with Georges Wague, *Le Jugement de Salomon* (1916) with Léontine Massart, *Le Revenant* (1917), *Le Delai* (1918), *Le Scandale* (1918), the classic silent film, *La Légende de la Soeur Béatrix* (1923), based on the play by Maurice Maeterlinck, *Ramuntcho* (1919), based on the novel by Pierre Loti, *La Rafale* (1920), *Père Goriot* (1921), based on the novel by Honoré de Balzac, *Champi-Tortu* (1921), based on the novel by Gaston Chérau, *Le Rêve* (1921), based on the novel by Émile Zola, *Roger la honte* (1922), based on the novel by Jules Mary, *Pêcheur d'Islande* (1924), also based on a novel by Loti, *Nitchevo* (1926), *Le Duel* (1927), starring **Jean Murat**, and *La Femme et le pantin* (1928), based on the novel by Pierre Loüys.

Baroncelli's early sound films include several remakes of his silent films. These include *L'Arlésienne* (1930), *Le Rêve* (1930), and *Nitchevo* (1936). He also made a number of melodramas, another genre he had developed during his silent film years. His early sound melodramas include *Le Dernier choc* (1932), *Gitanes* (1933), and *Le Calvaire de Cimiez* (1934). His aristocratic origins show through in *Soyez les bienvenus* (1940), a satire on the nouveau riche. After this he seems to have gone in several directions, making costume dramas such as *Michel Strogoff* (1935) and gritty dramas like *Le Pavillion brûle* (1941), starring **Jean Marais**.

Perhaps his best-remembered film is his so-called ethnographic drama, *L'Homme du Niger* (1939), an epic ode to French colonialism. Some have seen this film as an anomaly in Baroncelli's work. However, there are, to those who look closely, a number of similarities between this film and his larger body of work. Baroncelli had a long-standing interest in the exotic travel writer Pierre Loti, also known for his glorification of colonialism, and he had adapted a number of Loti's novels. It is also worth noting that there is a distinctly exotic colonial backdrop to his film *SOS Sahara* (1938). What is more, even when he was filming in or about France, there is a certain exotic tone to some of Baroncelli's films, particularly those that deal with those who lie outside the mainstream of French culture. *Le Roi de camargue* (1934) is a case in point.

Near the end of his career, Baroncelli seems to have returned to what he knew best, literary adaptation. He made *La Duchesse de Langeais* (1942), adapted from the novel by Balzac and starring **Edwige Feuillère**, as well as *Rocambole* (1948) and *La Revanche de Baccarat* (1948), both based on novels by Pierre-Alexis Ponson du Terrail and both starring **Pierre Brasseur**.

BARRAULT, JEAN-LOUIS (1910–1994). Actor. Jean-Louis Barrault got his start on the Paris stage at the Atélier in 1931. He became acquainted with **Antonin Artaud** and the surrealists in 1935, and then went on to debut in film while continuing his stage career, acting alongside his wife, **Madeleine Renaud**. The two formed a renowned theatrical company, the Compagnie Renaud-Barrault in 1946.

Barrault's first film role was in **Marc Allégret**'s *Les Beaux jours* (1935). The following year, he was cast in **Abel Gance**'s *Le Grand amour de Beethoven* (1936) and Allégret's *Sous les yeux d'occident* (1936), as well as two **Marcel Carné** films, *Drôle de Drame* (1936) and *Jenny* (1936). Barrault worked again with Allégret in 1938 in the film *Orage* and in 1941 in *Parade en sept nuits*. He worked with Gance again in 1938 on the film *J'Accuse!* One of Barrault's most memorable roles came in 1945, in Carné's classic film ***Les Enfants du paradis***.

Barrault tended to be cast as powerful, almost mythical men, but men who were sometimes physically challenged or physically unimpressive. He played Louis XI in **Christian-Jacques** and **Sacha Guitry**'s *Les Perles de la couronne* (1937) and Napoleon in Ettore Scola's *La Nuit de Varennes* (1982), for example. The mythical quality extended even to his completely fictional roles, such as Baptiste in ***Les Enfants du paradis***, probably one of the most memorable characters in French film history. Other films in which Barrault appears include Anatole Litvak's *Mayerling* (1936), **Max Ophüls**'s classic film *La Ronde* (1950), Guitry's *Si Versailles m'était conté* (1954), and Philippe Agostini's *Le Dialogue des Carmélites* (1960). Barrault also had a significant, but unusual, English-language role in the classic war film *The Longest Day* (1962).

BAUR, HARRY (1880–1943). Actor. Born Henri-Marie Baur in Paris, Harry Baur was the son of a watchmaker. Sent to Catholic school, Baur rebelled and ran away to Marseille, having been refused entry to the Paris Conservatoire d'art dramatique. In Marseille he studied acting and made his debut onstage shortly thereafter. He went on to become probably one of the greatest character actors of French cinema.

Baur got his start in silent film at **Pathé** in 1909 under the direction of **Victorin-Hippolyte Jasset** in *La Légende du bon chevalier*. He went on in silent film to play in Michel Carré's films *Arsène Lupin* (1909), *La Miniature* (1910), and *Le Noce à Canuche* (1910). He also starred in **Albert Capellani**'s *film d'art* adaptation of Émile Zola's *L'Assomoir* (1909), and he starred as Shylock in **Henri Desfontaines**'s *Shylock* (1910), based on Shakespeare's *Merchant of Venice*. This role made Baur quite famous, and in 1911, **Sacha Guitry** invited him to join stars like **Sarah Bernhardt** and **Mistinguett** in Guitry's theater troupe. Baur accepted the invitation but did not let his film career languish, making such films as Maurice Tourneur's *Monsieur Lecoq* (1914), **André Hugon**'s *Le Chignon d'or* (1916), Henry Roussel's *L'Âme du bronze* (1918), and Léon Abram's *La Voyante* (1923). In several of these films, Baur appeared with his theatrical counterparts such as Sarah Bernhardt and Mistinguett.

In the early days of sound cinema, Baur seems not to have acted in film. That changed in 1930 when he met **Julien Duvivier**. Duvivier cast Baur in the title role of *David Golder* (1930), a film about the transformation of an avaricious banker. One of the classic French films of all time, *David Golder* made Baur an instant star. The film allowed him to reveal his dramatic range as well as his unique ability to fully realize the characters he played. From 1930 until his death, Baur was one of the most recognized stars of French cinema, playing a diverse range of characters and giving a stunning range of performances.

Between 1930 and 1934, Baur made a number of films including *Les Cinq gentlemen maudits* (1931) and *La Tête d'un homme* (1931), both with Duvivier, and *Les Trois Mousquetaires* (1932) with **Henri Diamant-Berger**. Probably his best performance of this period, however, was in Duvivier's remake of *Poil de carotte* (1932).

In 1934, Baur played Jean Valjean in Raymond Bernard's *Les Misérables*, the adaptation of Victor Hugo's classic novel. The same year he also gave strong performances in Alexis Granowsky's *Les Nuits moscovites* (1934) and Victor Tourjansky's *Les Yeux noirs* (1934), both melodramas set in Russia. These films were followed by two classic Duvivier films, *Golgotha* (1935), a film about the life of Jesus Christ, and *Golem* (1935), the story of seventeenth-century Jews who fight back against persecution. Baur also played in **Pierre Chenal**'s *Crime et châtîment* (1935), adapted from the Fyodor Dostoyevsky novel, in **Jacques de Baroncelli**'s *Nitchevo* (1936), and in **Abel Gance**'s *Le Grand amour de Beethoven* (1936). He also played Rasputin in **Marcel L'Herbier**'s *La Tragédie impériale* (1937), and gave a masterful performance as Czar Paul I in Tourneur's *Le Patriote* (1937).

As the Nazi Occupation began, Baur became increasingly afraid of being denounced as a Jew. There is some evidence he attempted collaboration with the Nazi occupiers. This seems to have worked for a time. Under the Occupation, he made *Volpone* (1941) with Tourneur, and *L'Assassinat du Père Noël* (1941) with **Christian-Jacque**. The film is a satire about the disappearance of Santa Claus, sometimes seen as a political critique of the Occupation. Baur would manage only one more film in France, *Les Pechés de Jeunesse* (1941), again with Tourneur. In 1942, he left for Berlin to film *Symphonie eines Lebens* (1942). While in Berlin, his second wife, the actress Rike Radifé, who was Jewish, was arrested (his first wife, the actress Rose Grane, had died in 1930). Shortly thereafter, Baur was also arrested and tortured. He was released in April 1943, but was in very poor health. He died shortly after his release, whether from the aftereffects of his detainment or from other mysterious happenings is unclear. His wife also died in 1943. Baur died at the height of a brilliant career. It is not certain that his career would have lasted beyond the war if he had lived, but that is perhaps beside the point.

Baur was very closely associated with the cinema of the 1930s and 1940s, and was, along with **Jean Gabin** and **Pierre Brasseur**, one of the most recognizable faces of *Le Réalisme poétique*, or poetic realism.

His very somber appearance and his powerful dramatic force as an actor, in combination with his use of gesture and expression (as cultivated in silent film), made him a natural fit with the somber, almost noir yet highly emotionally charged style of directors like Duvivier. His death is a stain on one of the darkest periods of French history.

BAYE, NATHALIE (1951–). Actress. Nathalie Baye first appeared in cinema in Robert Wise's American film *Two People* (1972). She made her debut in French film in Nina Companeez's *Faustine et le bel été* (1973), and later played a small part in **François Truffaut**'s *La Nuit américaine.* Baye would rejoin Truffaut for *L'homme qui aimait les femmes* (1977) and *La Chambre Verte* (1978). She partook in Michel Pascal's homage, *François Truffaut: portraits volés* (1992).

Some of Baye's first major roles were in Maurice Pialat's *La geule ouverte* (1974), Alain Cavalier's *Le plein de super* (1976), Philippe Monnier's *Monsieur Papa*, and Daniel Vigne's *Le retour de Martin Guerre* (1981). She received her first **César** nomination for Best Actress in **Bertrand Tavernier**'s *Une semaine de vacances* (1980). In the early 1980s, she won three consecutive Césars: Best Supporting Actress in **Jean-Luc Godard**'s *Sauve qui peut (la vie)* in 1981, Best Supporting Actress in Pierre Granier-Deferre's *Une étrange affaire* in 1982, and Best Actress in Bob Swaim's *La balance* in 1983. She gained another César nomination for her performance in Robin Davis's *J'ai épousé une ombre* (1983).

Baye would team with several prominent directors more than once. She acted in **Bertrand Blier**'s *Beau-père* (1981) and *Notre Histoire* (1984), and would find Godard again in *Detective* (1984). She starred in Bruno Chiche's *Le pinceau à lèvres* (1990) and *Barnie et ses petites contrariétés* (2000). To date she has worked with **Tonie Marshall** three times: in *Enfants de salaud* (1996), *Vénus beauté (institut)* (1999), which earned her another César nomination, and *France boutique* (2002). She has also starred in Jeanne Labrune's films *Si je t'aime, prends garde à toi* (1998) and *Ca ira mieux demain* (2000), and in Xavier Beauvois's *Selon Matthieu* (2000) and *Le petit lieutenant* (2004). Baye played leading roles in Philippe Labro's *Rive droit, rive gauche* (1984), Patrick Jamain's *Lune de miel* (1985), Alain Jessua's *En toute innocence* (1987), Robert Enrico's *De guerre lasse* (1987), Diane Kurys's *La Baule-les-Pins* (1990), **Nicole Garcia**'s *Un* *week-end sur deux* (1990)—which earned her yet another César nomination—François Margolin's *Mensonge* (1992), Catherine Bottaro's *La mère* (1995), and Alain Berberian's *Paparazzi* (1999).

Baye won the Volpi Cup for Best Actress at Venice for her interpretation in Frédéric Fonteyne's *Une liaison pornographique* in 1999. She is still prolific in the twenty-first century. She plays key roles in Gabriel Aghion's *Absolument fabuleux* (2001), **Claude Chabrol**'s *La Fleur du mal* (2002), and Noémie Lvovsky's *Les sentiments* (2002). She has worked in anglophone films as well, including Stephen Poliakoff's *Food of Love* (1998) and Steven Spielberg's *Catch Me If You Can* (2002). She continues to be regarded as a major actress in France, playing significant roles in films such as Thierry Klifa's *Une vie à t'attendre* (2003), **Claude Berri**'s *Un reste, l'autre part* (2005), and Martial Fougeron's *Je t'aime tant* (2005).

BAZIN, ANDRÉ (1918–1958). Film critic and theorist. Best known as the cofounder of the film journal *Les Cahiers du cinéma* and as one of the motivating forces behind the *Nouvelle Vague* or New Wave, André Bazin was a film scholar in every sense of the word, and one who worked at every level to bring intelligent analysis and understanding of film to the average viewer. Bazin was, from an early age, a very gifted student with an analytical mind. Intending to become a teacher, he studied at the École Normale Supérieure. Bazin completed his studies in 1941 but was denied a teaching post, ostensibly because he stuttered. However, he was able to find an informal teaching position of sorts in a *Maison de lettres*, a facility set up during World War II to help educate those children who had been displaced or whose education had been otherwise disrupted.

In 1942, during the Occupation, Bazin became interested in the cinema. He organized lectures and debates on film, and also founded the first of his famous ciné-clubs or film clubs, which would expose people like **François Truffaut** to cinema. It is clear from these efforts that one of Bazin's interests was the popularization of the study of film, not only through formal intellectual channels, but also through less formal, more open channels. So intent was Bazin on realizing this goal that he was willing to risk the ire of the Nazi occupying forces. His ciné-clubs, in particular, were organized in direct defiance of the Nazi régime.

Bazin also began writing about film. His first forum was as film critic for the newspaper *Le Parisien Libéré*. Prior to founding *Les Cahiers du cinéma* in 1951, along with Jacques Doniel-Valcroze, Bazin wrote for numerous film journals, including *L'Écran français* and *La Revue du cinema*. One of his main contributions to film scholarship and criticism was his attention to what most scholars would now consider the fundamental elements of film composition, mise-en-scène, cinematography, and editing. He was one of the first scholars to move from simple narrative analysis to an analysis of the visual field, shot composition, camera angle, camera movement, staging, costume, lighting, etc. In fact, there are many in film studies today who would say, not without grounds, that Bazin founded film studies as we know it.

Perhaps as a result of his very focused attempt to understand and explain *how* films meant not simply *what* they meant, Bazin was much more open than many of his contemporaries to the experimentation of avant-garde filmmakers. For Bazin, cinema was essentially an active engagement between spectator and film, and the degree to which a film called upon a spectator to engage with the work, that is to have to interpret the images on the screen, was in many ways the degree to which the film was a success. If he is remembered as an avid fan of realism, this in no way diminishes his openness to film's numerous other possibilities. Bazin died of leukemia at the very young age of forty. By that time, he had published something like two thousand writings on film. A collection of what was considered his most important work was published in a volume titled *Qu'est-ce le cinema?/What is Cinema?* It was first published in 1967, but has been reedited several times. The book remains a canonical text in film scholarship.

BÉART, EMMANUELLE (1963–). Actress. Emmanuelle Béart was born in Saint Tropez, the daughter of the composer and singer Guy Béart. She rose to stardom with her role in **Claude Berri**'s 1986 film *Manon des sources*, for which she won a **César** for Best Supporting Actress. It starred her former husband **Daniel Auteuil**. She has since become one of France's major actresses, working with both **auteur** and popular directors. Béart received international attention for her work in **Jacques Rivette**'s *La Belle noiseuse* (1991), **Claude**

Sautet's *Un coeur en hiver* (1992), **Claude Chabrol**'s *L'enfer* (1994), and Sautet's *Nelly et Monsieur Arnaud* (1995). She also played significant roles in **Edouard Molinaro**'s *L'amour en douce* (1985), **André Téchiné**'s *J'embrasse pas* (1991), **Régis Wargnier**'s *Une femme française* (1995), Raoul Ruiz's *Le Temps retrouvé* (1999), Danièle Thompson's *La Bûche* (1999), **Olivier Assayas**'s *Les destinées sentimentales* (2000), Francis Ozon's *8 femmes* (2002), Rivette's *Histoire de Marie et Julien* (2003), and Anne Fontaine's *Nathalie* (2003). Béart has appeared in a few Anglophone films, including Tom McLoughlin's *Date with an Angel* (1987), Brian de Palma's *Mission: Impossible* (1996), and Sam Miller's *Elephant Juice* (1999). In addition to her work in cinema, Béart works as an ambassador for the United Nations Children's Fund (UNICEF).

BECKER, JACQUES (1906–1960). Director and screenwriter. Jacques Becker was born into the world of the Parisian intellectual and artistic elite. His father was a Scotsman and his mother, a member of the French haute bourgeoisie. Becker was brought up in Paris, where he became friends with Paul Cézanne. However, it seems that it was an American director, King Vidor, who attracted Becker to cinema. Vidor even invited Becker to work with him as an assistant. Becker declined the offer and instead began a long collaboration with **Jean Renoir**, whom he knew through family connections. The two worked closely on a number of Renoir's great works, including *Boudu sauvé des eaux* (1932), *Chotard et cie* (1932), *Madame Bovary* (1933), *Les Bas-fonds* (1936), *Une partie de campagne* (1936), *La Vie est à nous* (1936), **La Grande illusion** (1937), and *La Marseillaise* (1938). The two were at one time very close, even living together during the filming of *La Grande illusion*. In fact, Renoir once compared their friendship to that between Boieldieu and Von Rauffenstein, two of the primary characters in Renoir's film.

Becker made a brief attempt at directing on his own from 1934 to 1935, but the few films produced during this period were either incomplete or not significant. He was mobilized during the war and spent time in a German prisoner of war camp, an experience that would mark his future films. He went on to make what is considered his directorial debut, properly speaking, on the eve of the German Occupation. His first film as director, *Le Dernier atout* (1942), reflects the social and political climate, while at the same time problematizing both. The story of two apprentice police officers who challenge the authorities by investigating a murder that those in power want forgotten, *Le Dernier atout* is set in a "safe" and distant Latin American city, and in that regard, it shares characteristics with other Occupation-era films, which were often set in distant places or ages. This film was followed by *Goupi mains rouges* (1943), the story of a young village man who is framed for murder. The film continues the theme of abuse of power present in *Le Dernier atout*, and has the same noiresque plot elements. These would later come to be seen as characteristics of Becker's work.

Becker's third film, *Falbalas* (1945), seems to be a complete anomaly, breaking from the first two films and having no obvious connection with Becker's later works. Set in a Parisian fashion house, *Falbalas* is essentially a melodrama, and it is, on the surface, atypical of his work. However, the careful cinematography and realist mode (reminiscent of Renoir) do tie it in, in some ways, to Becker's other works. Moreover, the film gives a very detailed portrait of the fashion industry, and in that regard, it shares characteristics with Becker's subsequent films, which would also feature meticulous depictions of different facets of French society.

The immediate postwar films are, in many ways, chronicles of the lives of average people. However, in every film, there is also the near constant interrogation of power and oppression. *Antoine et Antoinette* (1947) is the story of a working-class couple who lose a winning lottery ticket and the tensions this loss provokes. *Rendez-vous de juilliet* (1949), which won the **Prix Louis-Delluc**, is the story of an aspiring jazz musician and his struggles with his disapproving father. *Edouard et Caroline* (1951) is the story of a young couple torn apart by class differences.

Similarly, *Casque d'or* (1952), which is often considered Becker's masterpiece, is also a highly realist period film chronicling life in the lower classes in turn of the century Paris. Some see in the film a late return to *Le Réalisme poétique* or poetic realism. The film returns to the subject of romantic love and also explores the effects of outside interferences on the romantic couple, in keeping with Becker's previous late films. This film, more than any other, affirms the degree to which human beings are subject to the outside power structures in the world, and the degree to which love cannot simply conquer all.

Following *Casque d'or*, Becker's films moved more toward something quite close to film noir, a direction that may be seen in the progressive pessimism of his worldview, at least as expressed through his films, and that was heralded by the return to *Le Réalisme poétique*, which was, itself, quite pessimistic. This move to noir is best embodied by *Touchez pas au grisbi* (1953), also considered one of Becker's greatest films. In *Grisbi*, the noir elements are fairly evident—the film is about questionable people and the influence of money, and the tangled structure of plots and subplots is highly reminiscent of film noir. There is also a level of tense discomfort to this film that was not evident in Becker's previous works, an element also linked to film noir. Some critics consider *Grisbi* the greatest French crime film ever made.

Becker's final film, *Le Trou* (1960), is also considered one of his masterpieces. It retains the tone of imminent danger and unease found in *Touchez pas au grisbi*, but the context has changed. This is a prison/escape film, but, as is typical with Becker's films, the focus is on issues of power and exploitation and not really on the escape itself.

Between *Grisbi* and *Le Trou*, Becker made *Ali Baba et les quarante voleurs* (1954), a classically orientalist, popular film; *Arsène Lupin* (1957), a period piece recounting the adventures of the gentleman burglar; and *Modigliani-Montparnasse 19* (1957), a biopic about Amadeo Modigliani that Becker took over after the death of **Max Ophüls**. The latter film was something of a disappointment, as might be expected when a noir director like Becker takes over a spectacular costume drama from someone like Ophüls.

Apart from the interest in Becker as a filmmaker, several critics have been interested in the connection between Becker and Le Réalisme poétique, and particularly in the issue of Renoir's influence on Becker's work. Traces of Renoir may be seen in the interest in the lower classes and most obviously in the camera's realist gaze. After all it was from Renoir that Becker learned how to make films. However, certain of Becker's films are also reminiscent of **Marcel Carné**. *Casque d'or* evokes *Les Enfants du paradis* (1945) at certain points (as is obvious by its setting and story), and films like *Touchez pas au Grisbi* bring Carné's *Quai de brumes* (1938) to mind.

There are certain connections between Becker and some of his contemporaries as well. There is often a psychological and moral component communicated through silence and minimalism that is reminiscent of **Robert Bresson**. **Jean-Pierre Melville** was another kindred spirit and a great admirer of Becker's work. Although Melville's films are less psychological than Becker's, a connection between the two filmmakers' work certainly exists, especially a shared interest in film noir. Like both Bresson and Melville, Becker would become an influence on the filmmakers of the *Nouvelle Vague* or New Wave. It was they, in particular, who would regard him as a bridge between the realist impetus of poetic realism and the experimental mode of their own sociological realism.

BEINEIX,' JEAN-JACQUES (1946–). Director, screenwriter, and producer. Jean-Jacques Beineix initially planned to become a doctor, and in fact, began studying medicine in 1966 before the events of May 1968 inspired him to turn to a career in film. He first studied under Jean Becker as he directed the television series *Les Saintes Chéries*. He later became an assistant to **Claude Berri**, **René Clément**, and **Claude Zidi**. Their influence, however, is difficult to detect in Beineix's work, as he has been something of an avant-garde filmmaker. Beineix's films are emblematic of the *cinéma du look*, a movement or style that was, at first, criticized for its alleged adaptation of superficial advertising styles and abandonment of narrative development. More recently, critics have praised Beineix's innovative use of color, his artistic blending of genres, and his mélange of "high" art with popular culture, all of which reflects a reconsideration of the cinéma du look.

Beineix's first film, the short *Le chien de monsieur Michel,* was nominated for a **César Award** for Best Short Fiction Film in 1979. His debut feature film, *Diva* (1981), is considered the first "look" film, the first of France's postmodern films, an **auteur** film, and a prototype of *jeune cinéma* (young cinema). The film won Césars for Best First Film, Best Photography, Best Musical Score, and Best Sound in 1982. *Diva*'s reception was mixed. Some considered it an uncritical display of meaningless images, while others pointed to its clever engagement with youth culture and psychoanalytic theories.

Beineix subsequently directed the "look" film *La lune dans le caniveau* (1983), a less commercially successful feature starring **Gérard Depardieu**, Nastassja Kinski, and Victoria Abril. It was nominated for a Golden Palm at **Cannes**, yet was also booed by some spectators at its festival screening. This second film received several negative reviews—including scorn from Depardieu. Those who disliked the film denounced Beineix's emphasis on an often seductive look over narrative substance. Beineix's third feature, *37° 2 le matin* (1986), like *Diva,* continued in the vein of *cinéma du look* and became a cult classic. It won the Grand Prix des Amériques and Most Popular Film at the Montreal World Film Festival in 1986. It stars Béatrice Dalle and Jean-Hughes Anglade, two emerging young actors of the 1990s. It was followed by the romantic drama *Roselyne et les lions* (1989). The much beloved actor **Yves Montand** starred in Beineix's *IP5, l'île aux pachydermes* (1992). The film was Montand's last, as he died before Beineix finished shooting, leaving the director in some turmoil. Montand's death occurred very close to that of Beineix's mother, and the two deaths in combination seem to have constituted a devastating blow.

After the deaths of Montand and his mother, Beineix departed from feature filmmaking to make documentaries, including *Otaku: fils de l'empire du virtuel* (1994) codirected with Jackie Bastide. In 1994, he began his presidency of the Association des Auteurs, Réalisateurs, et Producteurs, a post he resigned from in 1995. He returned to fictional films with *Mortel transfert* (2001), which depicts more mature characters. It is based on a novel by Jean-Pierre Gattegno and casts Anglade as the lead protagonist.

Debates over Beineix's films reflect the larger debates about the value of postmodern filmmaking and the increased role of technology in contemporary cinema. Beineix's films, especially *Diva* and *37° 2 le matin*, were very popular among young audiences. While the criticisms of these films were scathing, they were largely confined to the more established commentators for **Cahiers du Cinéma**. This is, as some scholars have noted, ironic inasmuch as Beineix's challenges to French filmmaking recall **Nouvelle Vague** or New Wave's challenge to the *tradition de qualité*, a challenge that was intimately bound to the *Cahiers*. For his part, Beineix has contended that the New Wave is, at this point, outdated, and that cinema must move on. Despite Beineix's critiques of the New Wave, his work shows signs of the **auteur** cinema often associated with figures like **Jean-Luc Godard**, **François Truffaut**, and **Eric Rohmer**.

BELLE DE JOUR (1966). Film. Based on the 1928 novel by Joseph Kessel, Louis Buñuel's *Belle de Jour* is a psychological portrait of the character Séverine (**Catherine Deneuve**), a bourgeois housewife, who is unfulfilled by her relationship with her husband Pierre (Jean Sorel). Sexual relationships and desires form the core of the film, as is evident from the opening sequence, in which Pierre and Séverine ride together in a horse-drawn carriage. At first, the two proclaim their love for each other. However, in an abrupt change that reflects the logic of dreams, Pierre pulls Séverine out of the carriage, ties her to a tree, and offers to let the driver of the carriage have sex with her. At this point, it seems that the film has replayed for the viewer one of Séverine's sexual fantasies, an impression reinforced by the subsequent cut to a shot of Séverine in her bed.

The division between fantasy and reality evident in the opening sequence is one of the more stunning and complex aspects of Buñuel's film. This division is manifested most clearly by Séverine's double life as a housewife and prostitute. Séverine becomes a prostitute after learning about an underground brothel from a friend. She seeks out the location of the brothel, which is ultimately revealed to her by a friend of her husband's named Husson (**Michel Piccoli**). The title of the film comes from the name Séverine takes for her prostitute persona, that name being Belle de Jour. It is apparently only by prostituting herself that Séverine can be sexually satisfied, although the line between fantasy and reality in the film is always vague. During the course of the film, the viewer discovers that Séverine was molested as a child, and this provides some clues as to her masochistic tendencies.

Buñuel's film has been read on a number of levels. On one level, *Belle de Jour* can be interpreted as the psychological portrait of a guilt-ridden, bourgeois woman, whose sexual fantasies are inextricably tied to the humiliation she experienced during her childhood. There are, in fact, a number of masochists in the film, male as well as female. The influence of psychoanalytic theory is clear in the repressed desires of the film's characters and in the dreamlike structure of the film itself. Some critics have read the film through such theories, attributing Séverine's behavior to her childhood trauma, coupled with the guilt instilled in her by her Catholic, upper-middle-class background. Other critics have objected to the film's depiction of

Séverine, reading the film as suggesting that all women have a repressed desire to be humiliated and that they therefore secretly crave abuse. Read this way, the film seems to justify gender-based violence.

Yet other critics have read *Belle de jour* through the director's connections to the European surrealists. Like **René Clair**, **Claude Autant-Lara**, and **Jean Painlevé**, Buñuel was embraced by the surrealists, particularly Salvador Dalí. And there is clearly a surrealist influence on Buñuel's filmmaking. His first film, *Un Chien andalou* (1929), is often cited as a surrealist masterpiece that participated in artistic attacks against the perceived constraints of religious and bourgeois values. Similar themes are apparent in Buñuel's 1972 film, *Le charme discret de la bourgeoisie*, and in his last film, *Cet obscur objet du désir* (1977). They are also evident in *Belle de Jour*. The character Husson, for example, acts as a commentator on the dullness of the bourgeois marriage, and Séverine's association of sex with punishment draws from the church's linkage of sex with sin.

Buñuel is also known for his creative manipulation of sound and image, for example the merging of the bells on the horses in Séverine's dreams with ice tapping against glass, or the image of the wilderness superimposed onto modern buildings. The boundary between reality and dreams becomes more blurred as Séverine gives way to her libido, and the spectator is left to wonder how much of the film is a representation of fantasy, and whether all of the fantasies are indeed Séverine's. However it is read, *Belle de Jour* remains an enigmatic and highly original film, and it provided its star with probably one of the best-known roles she has had.

BELMONDO, JEAN-PAUL (1933–). Actor and producer. Jean-Paul Belmondo is an internationally recognized film celebrity and an icon of the French *Nouvelle Vague* or New Wave. He once aspired to a career in boxing before turning to acting at the Conservatoire d'art dramatique in Paris from 1952 to 1956. He debuted in film in the 1956 short *Molière*, by Norbert Tildian. In 1957, he began his career in feature-length films such as Henri Aisner's *Les copains du dimanche* and Maurice Belbez's *À pied, à cheval, et en voiture*. He later played memorable roles for **Marc Allégret** in *Sois belle et tais-toi* (1958), where he worked alongside fellow icon **Alain Delon** for the first time. He also appeared in Allégret's *Un drôle de dimanche* (1958).

Belmondo subsequently landed a supporting role in **Marcel Carné**'s drama *Les Tricheurs* (1958). He went on to work with **Jean-Luc Godard** in the short *Charlotte et son Jules* (1958), then launched into stardom through his portrayal of the internationally famous character Michel Poiccard in Godard's benchmark New Wave film, *À bout de souffle* (1960). He worked with New Wave directors on several important films: **Claude Chabrol**'s *A double tour* (1959) and *Docteur Popaul* (1972), Godard's *Une femme est une femme* (1961) and *Pierrot le fou* (1965), and **François Truffaut**'s *La Sirène du Mississipi* (1969). He also costarred with one of the New Wave's most prominent actresses, **Jeanne Moreau**, in **Marcel Ophüls**'s *Peau de banane* (1963). Belmondo developed a film persona that seemed to embody the insouciant, rebellious, cinematic antihero of the 1960s. The term "Belmondo style" immediately recalls this image. Indeed, Belmondo's face is displayed on the cover of several books about film.

Belmondo's celebrity stretches beyond his status as a New Wave icon. He played eclectic roles in both art and commercial cinema. In the 1960s and up until the mid-1980s, he was one of France's biggest box-office attractions, often starring in thrillers like **Claude Sautet**'s *Classe tous riques* (1960), **Jean-Pierre Melville**'s *Le Doulos* (1962), **Jacques Deray**'s *Borsalino* (alongside Alain Delon), and **Georges Lautner**'s *Le Professionel* (1981). He frequently led in comedy-adventure films such as **Phillipe de Broca**'s *Cartouche* (1962) and *L'Homme de Rio* (1964), Gérard Oury's *Le cerveau* (1968) and *L'As des as* (1982), **Jean-Paul Rappeneau'**s *Les Mariés de l'an II* (1971), and Deray's *Le solitaire* (1987). He was also featured in parodies of spy films, including the cosmopolitan James Bond spoof *Casino Royale* (1967) and de Broca's *Le Magnifique* (1973). His range was further demonstrated in his roles as a priest in Melville's *Léon Morin: Prêtre* (1961), a Resistance fighter in **René Clément**'s war drama *Paris Brûle-t-il?* (1966), and as Henri Fortin in **Claude Lelouch**'s *Les Miserables* (1995), a loose adaptation of Victor Hugo's classic novel. He paired up with Delon again in **Patrice Leconte**'s *Une chance sur deux* (1998), then starred in **Cédric Klapisch's** science-fiction film *Peut-être* (1999). He won a **César** in 1989 for Best Actor for his role in **Claude Lelouch**'s *Itinéraire d'un enfant gâté*. In 2000, he played himself in **Bertrand Blier**'s *Les Acteurs,* and starred again for de Broca in 2000 in the science-fiction film *Amazone.*

BENOÎT-LÉVY, JEAN (1888–1959). Director. Jean Benoît-Lévy was a film director during the classical era of French film. Although directing popular cinema was not his primary profession, Benoît-Lévy directed a number of fairly popular and critically well-received films during the 1930s and 1940s. His best-known films are *La Cygne* (1937) and *Altitude 3200* (1938), a *Lord of the Flies*–type story of several friends who withdraw to the Alps and found their own republic. The film stars **Odette Joyeux** and **Jean-Louis Barrault**. He also codirected several films with **Marie Epstein**, the sister of renowned impressionist director **Jean Epstein**. Their collaborative films include *Âmes d'enfants* (1928), a history of decline and redemption between two families, and *La Maternelle* (1933). Outside of narrative films, Benoît-Lévy also made a number of documentary films for various social and humanitarian agencies. He also taught film studies for a time in New York, and eventually went on to work for UNESCO.

BERLING, CHARLES (1958–). Actor, director, and producer. Charles Berling acted in the theater before appearing in his first film, Marc Lobet's 1982 *Meurtres à domicile.* He appeared on television and played minor roles in the early 1990s before being nominated for a **César** for Most Promising Actor in Pascale Ferran's *Petits arrangements avec les morts* in 1994. He played prominent roles in **Claude Sautet**'s *Nelly et Monsieur Arnaud* in 1995 and Marion Vernoux's *Love, etc.* in 1996. In 1997 he received a César nomination for Best Actor for his work in **Patrice Leconte**'s *Ridicule*. He was again nominated for Césars for Best Actor for his performances in Anne Fontaine's *Nettoyage à sec* in 1998, Cédric Kahn's *L'Ennui* in 1999, and **Olivier Assayas**'s *Les Destinées sentimentales* in 2001.

Since 1995, he has been very prolific, playing leading roles in **Claude Pinoteau's** *Les Palmes de M. Schutz* (1997), **Patrice Chéreau**'s *Ceux qui m'aiment prendront le train* (1998), Raoul Ruiz's *La Comédie de l'innocence* (2000), Bernard Rapp's *Une affaire de goût* (2000), Frédéric Schoendoerrfer's *Scènes de crimes* (2000), Fontaine's *Comment j'ai tué mon père* (2001), Laurent Tuel's

Le Jeu d'enfants (2001), Patrick Alessandrin's *15 août* (2001), Assayas's *Demonlover* (2002), Frédéric Jardin's *Cravate Club* (2002), Abdelkrim Bahloul's *Le soleil assassiné* (2002), **Diane Kurys**'s *Je reste!* (2003), Michel Boujenah's *Père et fils* (2003), Schoendoerrfer's *Agents secrets* (2004), **Michel Deville**'s *Un fil à la patte* (2005), Luc Jacquet's *La Marche de l'empereur* (2005), and Cyril Gelblat's *Les Murs porteurs* (2005). He has also tried directing, with one film to his credit to date, *La cloche* (1998).

BERNHARDT, SARAH (1844–1923). Actress. Born Henriette-Rosine Bernard, Sarah Bernhardt was probably the greatest stage actress of the late nineteenth and early twentieth century. Born of French and Dutch Jewish parents, she was sent to a convent school and converted to Christianity. She studied acting at the Paris Conservatoire d'art dramatique, where she excelled and won prizes for both tragedy and comedy. Bernhardt went on to debut at the Comédie Française at the age of seventeen. Despite her success at the Conservatoire, success on the stage did not come immediately. However, by 1880 or so, after very hard work and several great performances, most notably in Racine's *Phèdre* (1874) and in Victor Hugo's *Hernani* (1877), she had become recognized as the greatest actress of her time, so great that her reputation as a temperamental, hypochondriac diva did little to diminish her standing as an actress.

Given Bernhardt's standing, she did not seek out the cinema. Rather, the cinema came to her in order to advance its own prestige. Bernhardt's first appearance on film came in 1900, when Clément Maurice filmed part of her performance in Shakespeare's *Hamlet*. She starred in 1908 in **Charles Le Bargy**'s ill-fated *La Tosca*, which was never formally released. She went on to star in **André Calmettes** and **Henri Pouctal**'s *La Dame aux camélias* (1912), **Henri Desfontaines** and **Louis Mercanton**'s *Les Amours de la reine Elizabeth* (1912) and *Adrienne Lecouvreur* (1913), and Mercanton and René Hervil's *Jeanne Doré* (1915) and *Mères voyantes* (1917). She died during the filming of Mercanton and Léon Abrams's *La Voyante* (1923), although her role was included in the final film.

BERRI, CLAUDE (1934–). Actor, director, producer, and screenwriter. Born Claude Langmann, Claude Berri, as he would come to be known, was one of the most successful directors of the 1980s and 1990s. He started in film as an actor, appearing in **Jacques Becker**'s *Rue de l'Estrapade* (1953), **Claude Chabrol**'s *Les Bonnes Femmes* (1960), and **Henri-Georges Clouzot**'s *La Verité* (1960). He soon turned his hand to other aspects of film, writing the screenplay for **Maurice Pialat**'s *Janine* (1961), a film in which he also appeared. He won an Oscar for the short *Le poulet* (1963), a film he wrote, directed, and produced.

By the late 1960s, Berri had turned his full attention to activities behind the camera. In 1967 he directed his first feature film, *Le vieil homme et l'enfant*, which starred **Michel Simon**. It was followed by *Mazel Tov ou le mariage* (1968), *Le pistonné* (1970), *Le cinéma de papa* (1970), *Sex shop* (1972), *Le mâle du siècle* (1975), *La première fois* (1976), *Un moment d'égarement* (1977), *Je vous aime* (1980), and *Le maître d'école* (1981). His features *Tchao pantin!* (1983), *Jean de Florette* (1985), *Uranus* (1990), and *Germinal* (1993) were all nominated for **César Awards** for Best Film and Best Director.

In addition to the awards he won for directing, Berri's films have launched or established the careers of several major actors in France. **Coluche** won Best Actor at the **César** Awards for his work in *Tchao pantin!* and **Gérard Depardieu** gained considerable acclaim for his performances in *Jean de Florette*, *Uranus*, and *Germinal*. The career of actor **Daniel Auteuil** was made famous by the film *Jean de Florette*, and particularly its sequel, ***Manon des sources***.

Berri is often associated with high-budget **heritage** or nostalgia films. Though Berri has written many of the scripts for his films, he has also made several cinematic adaptations of French literary oeuvres: *Tchao Pantin!* was derived from a novel by Alain Page, and both *Jean de Florette* and *Manon des sources* (1985) were adapted from **Marcel Pagnol**'s two-part novel, *L'Eau des collines*. *Uranus* is an adaptation of a Marcel Ayme novel, and *Germinal* was adapted from the epic novel by Émile Zola. *Lucie Aubrac* (1997) was inspired by Aubrac's own memoir, *Ils partiront dans l'ivresse*. Berri's *Une femme de ménage* (2002) was based on a novel by Christian Oster. Berri also directed *La débandade* (1999) and *L'Un reste, l'autre part* (2004). He has also produced a number of films inspired by literary works, for example, Roman Polanski's *Tess* (1979), **Patrice Chéreau**'s *La reine Margot* (1994), and Jean-Jacques Annaud's

L'amant (1992). Berri was elected president of the **Cinématheque Française** in 2003.

BESSON, LUC (1959–). Director, producer, and screenwriter. Luc Besson is best known for his contribution to the *cinéma du look*. His first feature, *Le Dernier Combat* (1983), is a science-fiction film. His three films that are often associated with the *cinéma du look—Subway* (1985), *Le Grand Bleu* (1988), and *Nikita* (1990)—were nominated for **César Awards** for Best Film and Best Director. He later directed films in English using international actors. *The Fifth Element* (1997) won him a César for Best Director. His other English-language films include *Léon* (1994) and *The Messenger: The Story of Joan of Arc* (1999), which won the Lumière Award in 2000. His documentary, *Atlantis*, was released in 1991. He generally works with actor **Jean Reno**. He cofounded Les Films du Loup with Pierre Jolivert.

BINOCHE, JULIETTE (1964–). Actress. Juliette Binoche was born in Paris. Her father, Jean-Pierre Binoche, is a sculptor and her mother, Monique Stalens, a professor and actress. Initially trained in the theater, Binoche is both a highly professional actress and a model (for Lancôme's perfume, Poême). She landed her first film role in Pascal Kané's 1982 film, *Liberty Belle*. In 1984, Binoche received a minor part in **Jean-Luc Godard**'s *Je vous salue, Marie* and played a supporting role in the all-female cast of Annick Lanoë's *Les Nanas*. Her first major role was in **André Téchiné**'s *Rendez-vous* (1985), for which she won the Prix Romy Schneider. In the same decade, she also appeared in Jacques Doillon's *La Vie de famille* (1985) and **Jacques Ruffio**'s *Mon beau-frère a tué ma soeur* (1986). She reached the status of art-house icon with starring roles in two films by the demanding *cinéma du look* director **Leos Carax**, *Mauvais sang* (1986) and *Les Amants du Pont Neuf* (1988).

In addition to being a *vedette*, or star, of French **auteur** films, Binoche has become one of France's most internationally recognized contemporary actresses. She first appeared in international film productions in Philip Kaufman's *The Unbearable Lightness of Being* (1988), followed by Peter Kosminski's *Wuthering Heights* (1991), Chantal Ackerman's *Un divan à New York* (1995), and Krzysztof Kieslowski's *Trois couleurs: bleu* (1993), for which she won prizes for Best Actress at the **César Awards** and the Volpi Cup at the Venice Film Festival. In 1997, she won an Oscar and a British Film Academy Award for Best Supporting Actress in Anthony Minghella's *The English Patient*. She was later nominated for an Oscar for Best Actress in Lasse Hallström's *Chocolat* (2000). In 2004, she costarred with Samuel Jackson in John Boorman's *In My Country*, a film about an interracial romance during the Truth and Reconciliation hearings in post-Apartheid South Africa. In the 1990s and beyond, she also delivered key performances in several notable French films, including **Louis Malle**'s *Damage* (1992), **Jean-Paul Rappeneau**'s **heritage film** *Le Hussard sur le toit* (1995), Diane Kurys's *Les Enfants du siècle* (1999), Téchiné's *Alice et Martin* (1998), **Patrice Leconte**'s *La Veuve de Saint-Pierre* (2000), and Danièle Thompson's *Décalage horaire* (2002). She played leading roles in Michael Haneke's *Code inconnu* (2000) and *Caché* (2005). In 2005, she led opposite Richard Gere in Scott McGehee and David Seigel's *Bee Season*, a film based on the novel by Myla Goldberg. Also in 2005, she played Mary Magdalene in Abel Ferrara's *Mary*.

BLIER, BERNARD (1916–1989). Actor. There are few actors in France or in the world whose careers lasted as long as that of Bernard Blier. There is some poetic justice in that, no doubt, given that he nearly missed his childhood dream of becoming an actor, barely gaining admission to the Paris Conservatoire d'art dramatique. He only succeeded at being admitted on the fourth attempt. Blier would have given up after the third refusal, so the story goes, only he had a chance encounter with **Louis Jouvet**, at the time an instructor at the Conservatoire, and the great Jouvet apparently encouraged Blier not to quit. As fate would have it, Jouvet became Blier's teacher and had a profound influence on him.

Blier began his long film career in 1937, appearing with **Edwige Feuillère** and René Bergeron in **Marc Allégret**'s *La Dame de Malacca*. The same year he also made *Trois, six, neuf . . .* (1937) with **Raymond Rouleau**. In addition to Allégret (with whom Blier worked again in *Entrée des artistes* in 1938, alongside Jouvet), Blier worked with other major directors of the day. He was directed by **Marcel Carné** in *L'Hôtel du nord* (1938) and *Le Jour se lève* (1939) and by **Claude Autant-Lara** in *Le Ruisseau* (1938). Blier was mobilized and sent off to war in 1939. He was ultimately captured and made a prisoner of war, but managed to escape and returned to France, where he met director **Christian-Jacque**, with whom he made a number of films, including *L'Enfer des anges* (1941), *La Symphonie fantastique* (1942), and *Carmen* (1943).

After the war, Blier's career lost none of its momentum, as he had a number of key roles in important films. He starred in **Henri-Georges Clouzot**'s *Quai des Orfèvres* (1947), Henri Calef's *La Sorcière* (1949), Yves Allégret's *Manèges* (1949), **Jean-Paul Le Chanois**'s *Les Misérables* (1958), and **Julien Duvivier**'s *L'Homme à l'imperméable* (1957) and *Marie-Octobre* (1959), among other films. He also reforged ties with directors he had worked with before, most notably Yves Allégret and Autant-Lara.

In the later stages of his career, Blier divided his time between France and Italy. The Italians had developed a great appreciation for him, and he was able to do a number of films there. In France, Blier seemed to narrow the scope of his work to the films of a few, preferred directors, although this did little to limit the number of films in which he appeared. He had a long collaboration with **Georges Lautner**, starring in a number of his films, including *Marche ou crève* (1958) and *Les Barbouzes* (1964). Blier's relationship with Lautner led to new collaborative efforts with **Michel Audiard**, who had been the screenwriter for Lautner before becoming a director himself. Blier starred in Audiard's films, starting with *Faut pas prendre les enfants du Bon Dieu pour des canards sauvages* (1968) to *Elle cause plus . . . elle flingue* (1972) and often appeared in small roles in later films. Similarly, he was a favorite of Lautner and starred in such films as *La Grande sauterelle* (1967) and *Mort d'un pourri* (1977). He was also a regular in the films of **Philippe de Broca**, **Claude Miller**, **Jean Yanne**, and **Edouard Molinaro.**

Blier was a large, round man. As such, he had a formidable dramatic presence that made a great impression when he played somber, serious characters. It was this persona that often dominated in his roles. However, he could play much more inscrutable, psychologically subtle, even bizarre characters. He did comedy as well as he did drama, as proven by his performance in **Yves Robert**'s *Le Grand blond avec une chaussure noire* (1972). He did romantic comedy as well as he did farce. His forte in comedy was to play a parody of his dramatic roles. It is, perhaps, noteworthy that he gave one of his most memorable performances in *Buffet froid* (1979), directed by his son, **Bertrand Blier**.

BLIER, BERTRAND (1939–). Actor, director, and screenwriter. In the late 1950s, Bertrand Blier assisted directors such as John Berry and **Jean Delannoy**. In the early 1960s he worked as a second assistant to **George Lautner** before directing his first two films, the shorts *Hitler, connais pas* (1963) and *La Grimace* (1966). His first feature film was the thriller *Si j'étais un espion* (1967), starring his father, the great actor **Bernard Blier**. Bertrand Blier emerged as a significant filmmaker in the 1970s after the release of *Les Valseuses* (1974), which was based on his own novel. It was followed by *Calmos* (1976) and *Préparez vos mouchoirs* (1977), which won the Oscar for Best Foreign Film in 1978. Both *Les Valseuses* and *Préparez vos mouchoirs* helped to launch **Gérard Depardieu**'s career and both costarred **Patrick Dewaere**.

Depardieu played leading roles in several of Blier's films, including *Buffet Froid* (1979)—which also featured Bernard Blier—*Tenue de soirée* (1986), *Trop belle pour toi* (1989), *Merci la vie* (1991), and *Les Acteurs* (2000). *Trop belle pour toi* won **César**s for Best Film, Best Director, and Best Scenario, in addition to the Grand Prize of the Jury at **Cannes**. Blier is also an accomplished screenwriter, having won Césars for Best Scenario for *Buffet Froid* and *Notre Histoire* (1984). In the 1990s films, Blier worked with actress Anouk Grinberg, who played leading roles in *Merci La Vie*, *Un, deux, trois soleil* (1993) and *Mon homme* (1996). His other films include *Beau-père* (1981), starring Dewaere; *La femme de mon pote* (1983), featuring **Coluche** and **Isabelle Huppert**; *Les côtelettes* (2003), with Philippe Noiret and **Michel Bouquet**; and *Combien tu m'aimes?* (2005), with Monica Bellucci and Bernard Campan.

Critics have observed that Blier's films are grounded in theater. His work has been compared especially to the theater of the absurd. Scholars have noted several characteristics of the absurd in Blier's work, such as the use of incongruous plots and audience alienation, or the abandonment of traditional conflict resolutions and character development. He also worked with actors whose careers were fostered in

France's *café-théâtres*, such as Michel Blanc and **Josiane Balasko**. Blier has often been accused of misogyny because of the recurrent scenes of violence against women and the negative portrayals of female characters. Other critics have recognized his reversal of conventional gender roles that complicate established notions of femininity and masculinity.

BOHRINGER, RICHARD (1941–). Actor, director, and screenwriter. Richard Bohringer made his start in film as an actor. He first role was in Gérard Brach's comedy *La Maison* in 1970. In 1972, he landed his first starring role in Charles Matton's *L'Italien des roses*. His popularity rose in the 1980s with his roles in *cinéma du look* director **Jean-Jacques Beineix**'s *Diva* (1981) and Robin Davis's *J'ai épousé une ombre* (1981). He won a **César** for Best Supporting Actor in Denis Amar's *L'Addition* in 1985. He also played memorable roles in **Luc Besson**'s *Subway* and **Jean-Pierre Mocky's** *Agent trouble* (1987) and *Les Saisons du plaisir* (1988). Bohringer won a **César** for Best Actor in Jean-Loup Hubert's *Le Grand chemin* in 1988. He then appeared in his first English-language film, Peter Greenaway's *The Cook, the Thief, His Wife, and Her Lover* (1989). Bohringer played subsequent leading roles in Hubert's *Après la guerre* (1989), **Edouard Molinero**'s *A Gauche en sortant de l'ascenseur* (1989), Jean-Charles Tacchella's *Dames Galantes* (1990), and **Gérard Jugnot**'s *Une époque formidable* (1991).

In 1992, Bohringer acted alongside his daughter, Romane Bohringer, in **Claude Miller**'s *L'Accompagnatrice*. He later played significant parts in Jérôme Boivin's *Confessions d'un barjo* (1992), **Patrice Leconte**'s *Tango* (1993), Matton's *La lumière des étoiles mortes* (1993), Burkinabé director Idrissa Ouedraogo's *Le cri du coeur* (1994), Miller's *Le sourire* (1994), Aline Issermann's *Dieu, l'amant de ma mère et le fils du charcutier* (1995), Bernard Giraudeau's *Les Caprices d'un fleuve* (1996), Amar's *Saraka Bo* (1996), Enki Bilal's *Tyko Moon* (1996), Thomas Gilou's *La Vérité si je mens !* (1997), Pierre François Limbosch's *Requiem pour un décor* (1998), Francis Girod's *Mauvais genres* (2001), and Alain Bévérini's *Total khéops* (2002). He has also acted extensively in television. He directed one feature film, *C'est beau une ville la nuit* (2003).

BONNAIRE, SANDRINE (1967–). Actress. Sandrine Bonnaire first appeared in minor roles in **Claude Zidi**'s *Les Sous-doués en vacances* (1982) and **Claude Pinoteau**'s *La Boum 2* (1982). She rose to acclaim with her leading performance at age sixteen in Maurice Pialat's *À Nos amours* (1983), for which she won a **César** for Most Promising Actress in 1984. In 1986, she won the César for Best Actress for her performance in **Agnès Varda**'s *Sans toit ni loi* (1985). She played key roles in Pialat's *Sous le soleil de Satan* (1987), **Claude Sautet**'s *Quelque jours avec moi* (1988), **Patrice Leconte**'s *Monsieur Hire* (1989), and Raymond Depardon's *La Captive du désert* (1989). She played Joan of Arc in **Jacques Rivette**'s *Jeanne la Pucelle: les prisons* (1994) and *Jeanne la Pucelle: la bataille* (1994), and later acted in Rivette's *Secret Défense* (1998). In Venice, Bonnaire won the Volpi Cup for Best Actress in **Claude Chabrol**'s *La cérémonie* (1995). She later played leading roles in Yves Angelo's *Voleur de vie* (1998), Chabrol's *Au coeur du mensonge* (1999), **Régis Wargnier**'s *Est-Ouest* (1999), Philippe Lioret's *Mademoiselle* (2001), Leconte's *Confidences trop intimes* (2003) and *L'Equipier* (2004), Jean-Pierre Améris's *C'est la vie* (2001) and *Maman est folle* (2005), and Safy Nebbou's *Le Cou de la giraffe* (2004). As her performances in Varda's *Sans toit ni loi* (1985) and Rivette's *Jeanne la Pucelle* (1994) attest, Bonnaire is an actress known for her ability to play strong **women** who challenge the rules of society, and for that reason, she is a favorite of several **auteurs**.

BOSETTI, ROMÉO (1879–1948). Actor, director, and screenwriter. The precise trajectory of Roméo Bosetti's career is not entirely clear, largely because he was ignored by the first several generations of film scholars and has only recently become a subject of interest. It is clear he was an entertainer from the age of ten, first in the circus, then in theaters and dance halls of Paris. P. T. Barnum seems to have hired him into his very well-known circus in 1905, and in 1906, he may have gone to work at **Pathé**, along with a number of other well-known Parisian entertainers.

If indeed Bosetti was at Pathé at this time, he did not remain there for very long, for it seems he went that same year to **Gaumont,** where he worked as a director first under **Alice Guy** then under

Louis Feuillade. In fact, he is wrongly credited with having directed several of Guy's films. At first, Bosetti specialized in the chase film, but it was at Gaumont that he developed his talent for burlesque or farce, directing and also acting in a number of films in which the characters were either unwitting victims of ridiculous circumstances, or were possessed of ridiculous characteristics that created such circumstances.

The most successful of Bosetti's burlesques were those that featured the eponymous character Roméo, who appeared in films such as *Roméo pris au piège* (1906), *Roméo et le cheval de fiacre* (1907), and *Roméo a mangé du lion* (1907). The comic figure Calino (played by Clément Migé), who was featured in films such as *Calino au théâtre* (1909), *Calino se bat en duel* (1910), and *Calino a mangé du cheval* (1910), was also one of Bosetti's creations. Both Calino and Roméo were, in great measure, inspired by the outlandish, grotesque, and wildly popular character Boireau, developed by **André Deed** for Pathé.

In addition to these two series, Bosetti also wrote and directed two classics of early film comedy while at Gaumont: *Le Tic* (1907), which features a beautiful young woman who has a tic that makes her wink at men as she passes by, and *Une dame vraiment bien* (1908), which features another beautiful woman who attracts a good deal of attention as she walks down the street.

Bosetti left Gaumont in 1910, when Pathé lured him away by giving him the directorship of a special comic division in Nice, the Pathé Comica. At Pathé, he developed two other well-known comedic characters, Rosalie, played by Sarah Duhamel, and Bigorneau, played by René Lantini. The films featuring Rosalie ran in 1912 and featured titles such as *Rosalie veut engraisser* (1912) and *C'est la faute à Rosalie* (1912). The films featuring Bigorneau also began in 1912 and featured titles such as *Bigorneau fait son café* (1912) and *Bigorneau surveille Madame* (1912). This series ran until 1915. His later series include the Casmir series, which ran from 1913 until 1916, and the Gavroche series, which ran from 1912 until 1914. His career was briefly interrupted by service in World War I, but he quickly returned to filmmaking after being discharged due to injury. Bosetti made more than one hundred films between 1912 and 1916 alone.

Bossetti seems also to have been allowed to develop his own production unit, Nizza, which remained attached to Pathé but which operated semi-independently. His films are seen to have been important in the early development of the comedy, focusing it in a working-class milieu (one might note the influence of Feuillade, perhaps, in this regard), and moving the genre toward narrative and away from pure gags.

BOUQUET, MICHEL (1925–). Actor. Michel Bouquet was born in Paris. His career as an actor began with a meeting with Maurice Escande, who would later become one of his professors at the Conservatoire National d'Art Dramatique in Paris. He became a respected theater actor who worked closely with the acclaimed French playwright Jean Anouilh. His first appearances onscreen were in 1947 in Gilbert Gil's *Brigade criminelle* and Maurice Cloche's *Monsier Vincent*. He subsequently worked under several notable French directors, including **Henri-Georges Clouzot** (in *Manon*, 1949), **Jean Grémillon** (in his 1949 *Pattes blanches*, which was cowritten by Anouilh), and **Abel Gance** (in *La Tour de Nesle* in 1955). He also acted in Anouilh's film *Deux sous de violettes* in 1951. Bouquet is well known for his work with *Nouvelle Vague* or New Wave director **Claude Chabrol**, which started in 1965 with *Le tigre se parfume à la dynamite*, followed by *La Route de Corinthe* in 1967. Bouquet's most prominent role with Chabrol was alongside Stéphane Audran in *La Femme infidèle* (1968). He paired again with Chabrol in *La Rupture* (1970), *Juste avant la nuit* (1971), and *Poulet au vinaigre* (1985). Bouquet was chosen by New Wave director **François Truffaut** for a leading role next to **Jeanne Moreau** in *La Mariée était en noir* (1967) and a supporting role in his *La Sirène du Mississippi*.

In the 1970s, Bouquet veered away from New Wave directors and toward other then-emerging cinéastes. He starred in Yves Boisset's *Un Condé* (1970), Édouard Luntz's *Le dernier saut* (1970) and *L'Humeur vagabonde* (1972), Nelly Kaplan's *Papa, les petits bateaux* (1971), Roger Pigaut's *Comptes à rebours* (1971) and *Trois millards sans ascenseur* (1972), René Gainville's *Le Complot* (1973), Nadine Trintignant's *Défense de savoir* (1973), and Alain Corneau's *France société anonyme* (1974). He also played supporting roles in **Jacques Deray**'s *Borsalino* (1970), Harry Kümel's *Malpertuis* (1971), Jean-Louis Bertucelli's *Paulina 1880* (1972), and Francis Veber's *Le Jouet* (1976).

Bouquet acted largely in television films in the 1980s, with a few exceptions such as his work in *Poulet au vinaigre,* his role as Javert in **Robert Hossein**'s 1982 *Les Misérables,* and his leading performance alongside **Bernard Blier** in Christian Zerbib's *Fuite en avant.* In 1990, he starred in Belgian director Jaco van Dormael's *Toto le héros*, for which he won Best Actor at the European Film Awards.

In the 1990s, Bouquet played supporting roles in Corneau's *Tous les matins du monde* (1991) and Jean Becker's *Élisa* (1995) and a leading role in Roger Guillot's *Joie de vivre* (1993). In 1997, he became a professor at the Conservatoire. He appeared again with Moreau to play the writer Guisseppe Tomasi di Lampedusa in the Italian film *Manoscritto del principe* (2000), by Roberto Andò. He won his next major awards—a **César** Award and a Lumiere Award for Best Actor—for his work in Anne Fontaine's *Comment j'ai tué mon père* (2002). He then costarred with Philippe Noiret in **Bertrand Blier**'s *Les Côtelettes*, and with **Miou-Miou** in Michelle Porte's *L'Après-midi de Monsieur Andesmas* (2004). In 2005, Bouquet gave a memorable interpretation of President François Mitterrand in **Robert Guédiguian**'s *Le Promeneur du Champ de Mars*.

BOURVIL (1917–1970). Actor and singer. Born André Raimbourg in 1917, Bourvil, as he was known professionally, would go on to become a beloved actor, singer, and comedian in France. He never knew his father, who was killed in World War I. He spent his childhood in northwestern France, where he lived with his mother and brother.

In 1945, Bourvil made his film debut, appearing very briefly in the film *La Ferme du pendu* by Jean Dréville. At the time Bourvil was already a known singer and radio personality, and the entire role consisted of him singing a song. As a result in 1946, Pathé offered him an exclusive contract to record his routines and songs. The same year Jean-Jacques Vitray gave him a role in the film *La Bonne hôtesse*, also a singing role. As his career in cinema began to pick up, the roles became larger, the range required became broader, and fewer and fewer of the parts required him to sing. Bourvil would star in such films as Jean Boyer's *Le Trou normand* (1952), **Claude Autant-Lara**'s *La Traversée de Paris* (1956), Michel Boisrond's *Le Chemin des écoliers* (1958), Jean-Paul Le Chanois's *Les Misérables* (1958), in **Marc Allégret**'s *Un drôle de dimanche* (1958), André Hunébelle's *Le Bossu*

(1960), in René Clair's *Tout l'or du monde* (1961), **Alex Joffe**'s *Le Tracassin ou les plaisirs de la ville* (1961), **Jean-Pierre Mocky**'s *L'Étalon* (1970), and **Jean-Pierre Melville**'s *Le Cercle rouge* (1970). Bourvil must have considered 1963 as the pinnacle of his career, however, since it was in that year that he starred opposite his long-time hero, Fernandel, in Gilles Grangier's *La Cuisine au beurre*. From 1964 on, Bourvil worked predominantly with Gérard Oury and Jean-Pierre Mocky. Perhaps he preferred to work with familiar faces at that point, since in 1968, he was diagnosed with Kahler's disease, a fatal form of bone cancer. He well exceeded the few weeks the doctors gave him to live, going on to appear in Melville's *Le Cercle rouge* (1970), among other films. Like some of the other great icons of his day, he has remained popular long after his departure. He seems to be fixed eternally into a privileged space of French cinema. Some thirty years after his death, people who were not even born when he died recognize him and know his films.

BOYER, CHARLES (1899–1978). Actor. Charles Boyer was born in Figeac, in Southern France. From an early age, Boyer was interested in acting, theater, and the newly invented cinema. When he finished his studies at the lycée, he went to Paris, where he studied at both the Sorbonne and the Paris Conservatoire d'art dramatique.

After an earlier debut on the Paris stage, Boyer appeared onscreen for the first time in 1920, in **Marcel L'Herbier**'s *L'Homme du large*. He had a starring role, fairly significant for a new actor, and the film served to launch his screen career. During the silent-film era, Boyer made a number of successful films that established him as an international star. These included *Esclave* (1922), directed by **Georges Monca**, and *Le Capitaine Fracasse* (1929), directed by Alberto Cavalcanti. As sound gradually came to dominate the film industry, Boyer, for a time, lost his international appeal, since English was not among the four languages he spoke. During the first half of the 1930s, Boyer made films predominantly in France, most notably *La Bataille* (1933) and *L'Épervier* (1933), both directed by L'Herbier. Boyer also worked with Hollywood studios doing dubbing work for French versions of Hollywood films.

In 1934, Boyer, who had been learning English, gave a boost to his language skills as well as his personal life when he married British actress Pat Peterson (the two would remain married until Peterson's death in 1978). Boyer's new fluency gave him new access to Hollywood, and he played opposite Claudette Cobert in Gregory LaCava's *Private Worlds* (1935). The film and Boyer's successful onscreen pairing with Colbert inaugurated a new Hollywood phase to Boyer's film career, and for many years he would work in both France and Hollywood. In France Boyer starred in such films as L'Herbier's *Le Bonheur* (1935), Anatole Litvak's *Mayerling* (1936), **Marc Allégret**'s *Orage* (1938) and *Le Corsaire* (1939), **Max Ophüls**'s *Madame de . . .* (1953), **Christian-Jacque**'s *Nana* (1954), **Henri Verneuil**'s *Maxime* (1958) and *Les Démons de minuit* (1962), again with Allegret, **René Clement**'s *Paris brûle-t-il* (1966), and **Alain Resnais**'s *Stavisky* (1974).

In Hollywood, Boyer became the quintessential Frenchman, refined and elegantly romantic, making such films as *I Loved a Soldier* (1936) and *The Garden of Allah* (1936), both with Marlene Dietrich; *Algiers* (1938), an English-language remake of **Julien Duvivier**'s *Pépé le Moko* (1937); *Love Affair* (1939); *Gaslight* (1944), in which he played a villain; *Arch of Triumph* (1948), with Ingrid Bergman; *The Thirteenth Letter* (1951), a remake of **Henri-Georges Clouzot**'s *Le Corbeau* (1943); *The Bucanneer* (1958); the English-language version of **Marcel Pagnol**'s *Fanny* (1961); *Barefoot in the Park* (1967); and his final film, *A Matter of Time* (1976), in which he again starred opposite Ingrid Bergman as well as Liza Minelli.

Although Boyer worked on both continents, he became an American citizen in 1942, and resided in the United States for most of the rest of his life. He took his own life shortly after the death of Peterson, his wife of fifty-four years, from cancer. The great onscreen gigolo and playboy was, in real life, a devoted and loyal husband.

BRASSEUR, CLAUDE (1936–). Actor. The son of the actors **Odette Joyeux** and **Pierre Brasseur**, Claude Brasseur studied at the Conservatoire National d'Art Dramatique in Paris and became a reputable theater actor in the 1950s, working in plays such as **Marcel Pagnol**'s *Judas*. His first film appearance was in Georges Lampin's 1956 comedy *Rencontre à Paris* (1956), followed by a role in **Marcel Carné**'s *Le Pays d'où je viens* (1956). In 1959, he appeared with his father in **Georges Franju**'s *Les Yeux sans visage*. In addition to acting, Brasseur had a reputation as a daredevil. His pastimes included racing in the Paris-Dakar rally and parachuting.

In the 1960s, Brasseur worked for some of France's most significant directors, including **Jean Renoir** in *Le Caporal épinglé* (1961) and Yves Allégret in *Germinal* (1962). He was also cast in several films associated with the *Nouvelle Vague* or New Wave, including **Claude Chabrol**'s *Les Sept Péchés capitaux* (1962), **Jean-Luc Godard**'s *Bande à part* (1964), and **François Truffaut**'s *Une belle fille comme moi* (1972). Brasseur appeared in a number of thrillers, among them **Costa-Gavras**'s *Un homme de trop* (1967) and **Georges Lautner**'s *Les Seins de glace* (1974). He also flourished in comedies. In 1976, he won a **César Award** for Best Supporting Actor in *Un éléphant, ça trompe énormément* (1976). The following year, he appeared in **Yves Robert**'s *Nous irons tous au paradis*.

Brasseur worked in a variety of genres alongside other well-known French actors. For example, he acted in Christian de Chalonge's thriller *L'argent des autres* (1978) with **Jean-Louis Trintignant**, **Michel Serrault**, and **Catherine Deneuve**, in **Claude Sautet**'s *Une histore simple* (1978) with **Romy Schneider**, and in Joël Santoni's *Ils sont grands, ces petits* (1979), again with Deneuve. He remained active in the 1980s, playing Guy de Maupassant in Michel Drach's 1982 film of the same name, and starring in Serge Leroy's *Légitime violence* (1982); Philippe Labro's *La Crime* (1983); **Edouard Molinaro**'s *Palace* (1985); Francis Girod's *Descente aux enfers* (1986); Godard's *Détective* (1985); Roger Planchon's *Dandin* (1987), based on the play by Molière; Alain Page's *Taxi boy* (1986); Yves Boisset's *Radio corbeau* (1988); and Jacques Rouffio's *L'Orchestre rouge* (1989), among other films.

In the 1990s, Brasseur was less engaged in cinema acting, but still landed major roles in Catherine Breillat's *Sale comme un ange* (1990), Gilles Béhat's *Dancing Machine* (1990), Molinaro's *Le Souper* (1992)—for which he received a César nomination for best actor—Francis De Gueltz's *Les Ténors* (1993), Dominque Cabrera's *L'Autre côté de la mer* (1996), and Robert Enrico's *Fait d'hiver* (1998). Brasseur also acts in television. In the 1970s, he played the lead in the French TV series *Vidocq*; more recently, he led the cast of the television detective series *Franck Keller*, and acted in the television film *Edda*, in which he plays Benito Mussolini.

BRASSEUR, PIERRE (1905–1972). Actor. Born Pierre-Albert Espinasse in Paris, Pierre Brasseur studied drama at the Paris Conservatoire d'art dramatique and then went on to make his debut in the theater at the age of eighteen. His early years in theater were with an itinerant troupe, but he went on to join the Compagnie Renaud-Barrault, a more accomplished theatrical company.

Brasseur made his screen debut in 1924 in **Leonce Perret**'s *Madame Sans-Gêne*. It was a fairly respectable although not a starring role, reflective of a certain reputation in the theater. This debut gave Brasseur a footing in cinema, and he went on from there to make nearly one hundred films, working with directors as diverse as **Jean Renoir**, **Marc Allégret**, **René Clair**, **Marcel Carné**, **Claude Autant-Lara**, **Christian-Jacque**, and **Philippe de Broca**.

In the early part of his career, Brasseur is probably best remembered for his work with Carné in two of his legendary films, *Quai de brumes* (1938) and *Les Enfants du paradis* (1945). Other noteworthy performances of the period were in **Georges Lacombe**'s *Café de Paris* (1938) and André Cayatte's *Les Amants de Vérone* (1949).

Among the films in which he appeared during this period are Yves Mirande's *Papa sans le savoir* (1931), Robert Siodmak's *Le Sexe faible* (1933), Maurice Cammage's *Prête-moi ta femme* (1936), **Serge de Poligny**'s *Claudine à l'école* (1936), Carné's *Les Portes de la nuit* (1946), **Marcel Pagnol**'s *Le Schpountz* (1938), Marcel Achard and Allégret's *Les Deux timides* (1938), **Jean Grémillon**'s *Lumière d'été* (1938), and Pierre Montazel's *Croisière pour l'inconnu* (1947).

In his later career, Brasseur found himself cast in various thrillers and crime films. Among these, probably the most interesting are **Georges Franju**'s *Les Yeux sans visage* (1960) and Pierre Granier-Deferre's *La Métamorphose des cloportes* (1964). Other films in which he had roles include **Christian-Jacque**'s *Barbe-bleue* (1951), **Max Ophüls**'s *Le Plaisir* (1952), **Sacha Guitry**'s *Napoléon* (1955), **René Clair**'s *La Porte des lilas* (1957), Clément Duhour's *La Vie à deux* (1958), Henri Diamant-Berger's *Messieurs les Ronds de cuir* (1959), Philippe Agostini's *Dialogues des Carmélites* (1960), **Claude Autant-Lara**'s *Vive Henri IV vive l'amour* (1961), de Broca's *Le Roi de coeur* (1966), and **Jean-Paul Rappeneau**'s *La Vie de château* (1966).

Brasseur acted all the way, more or less, up to his death. He made his last film, *La Plus belle soirée de ma vie*, with Ettore Scola in

1972. In fact, Brasseur died in Italy during the making of the film. He left to the world of cinema his son, **Claude Brasseur**, who is an accomplished actor in his own right, and his grandson, Alexandre Brasseur, who has also decided to continue the family business.

BRESSON, ROBERT (1901–1999). Director and screenwriter. Robert Bresson was born in Bromont-Lamothe in central France. His original interest was painting, and it was this path that he had intended to pursue until he wandered into cinema in 1934. His first film was a short-to-medium-length film (once believed lost, but since rediscovered) called *Affaires publiques*, a satire starring **Marcel Dalio** and that recounted, in Bresson's words, "three days in the life of an imaginary dictator." The shift from painting to cinema was made. Painting, however, would influence Bresson's filmmaking to the end, in the visual composition and in the legendary minimalism of his work.

Bresson did not make another film of his own until 1943. However, in the interim, he is known to have worked on the screenplay for Pierre Billon's *Courrier Sud* (1936) and on Claude Heymann's *Jumeaux de Brighton* (1936). He was the assistant director on **Henri Diamant-Berger's** production of *La Vièrge folle* (1938) and he also worked with **René Clair** in 1939 on his film *Air pur*. Bresson may have collaborated, uncredited, on other films as well, as he was apparently gaining more experience in filmmaking before again venturing out on his own.

Then World War II intervened. Bresson, who was called up for service, was taken prisoner, and spent time as a German prisoner of war, an experience that had a profound effect on his life and his filmmaking. Upon his release, Bresson returned to France, definitively abandoned painting, and resumed filmmaking. His second film was *Les Anges du péché* (1943), the story of an order of nuns, and was based on a play by Jean Giradoux. This film was reportedly made at the request of a Catholic priest. The film is the first that shows evident signs of what would become the hallmarks of Bresson's style, the very restrained, almost emotionless surface that masks the turmoil of human existence, the minimalism of presentation, the nonpsychological or anti-psychological presentation of characters, and most of all the very stark and stoic worldview that many have read as the fusion of Bresson's Jansenist religious upbringing and the existential atheism brought on by his experiences during the war. The convent is perhaps a natural setting in which to bring these aspects to the fore, and the Occupation, with its own very limiting constraints on film production, perhaps a natural context.

Les Anges du péché (1943) marked the beginning of a unique, creative filmmaking style that would evolve over several films. This film, although marked by the beginnings of what was to come, is still fairly traditional in its conception and orientation. It is a straightforward literary adaptation that, in spite of the Bressonian elements, adheres fairly closely to the filmic conventions of the day. As time went on, Bresson would move further and further away from these conventions and into the aesthetic universe that was uniquely his own.

Bresson's next feature film, *Les Dames du Bois de Boulogne* (1945), was also a literary adaptation (from a Diderot story, with dialogue written by **Jean Cocteau**), and was the story of a love triangle characterized by manipulation and distortion. Bresson's third film, *Journal d'un curé de campagne* (1951), is the story of a young, idealistic, religious priest, whose faith is challenged and ultimately denounced by the inhabitants of a small French village. This film marks an important turning point in Bresson's filmmaking and differs from the first two films in significant ways. First of all, although the film is adapted from Georges Bernanos's novel of the same name, Bresson clearly took the liberty of creating a film inspired by the novel and not simply filming the novel. Secondly, it was in this film that Bresson moved away from the use of professional actors and began using only nonprofessionals, a practice he would continue throughout his career. Finally, a significant move toward the silent opacity that would characterize the later films is evident between the first two feature films and the third. The film was critically acclaimed from the time of its release and won the prestigious **Prix Louis-Delluc**.

The other films of the 1950s, *Un condamné à mort s'est échappé* (1956) and *Pickpocket* (1959), are both considered excellent examples of Bresson's work. The first is the story of French prisoners in a German prison camp during World War II, who retain religious faith even when faced with abuse and cruelty. The film focuses on acts of resistance and attempts at escape. Unlike Bresson's earlier films, the source was not literary. Rather, the film was inspired by true events. It was and remains Bresson's most commercially successful film.

The second film is the story of an intelligent, quiet, polite man, who is driven by a compulsion to steal, despite his efforts to resist. Although it is not certain, many have seen similarities between this story and Fyodor Dostoyovsky's *Crime and Punishment*. It is possible that Bresson had the novel in mind, particularly given the literary connections in so many of his films. Both films mark the peak of the development of Bresson's spare, bleak filmmaking style, and of the Christian existentialist worldview that dominates in his films. Both are also considered classics of French cinema.

Bresson would make only eight more films during the course of his life: *Le Procès de Jeanne d'Arc* (1962), believed to have been inspired by Theodore Dreyer's classic silent film *La Passion de Jeanne d'Arc* (1928), which was also noted for its stark cinematography; *Au hazard Balthazar* (1966), the story of the parallel lives of Balthazar the donkey and the young woman Marie, both of whom are often harshly treated and unloved; *Mouchette* (1967), the story of a troubled and abused young girl, also based on a novel by Bernanos; *Une Femme douce* (1969), the story of young husband's reaction to his wife's suicide; *Quatre nuits d'un rêveur* (1971), the story of an aborted suicide attempt and an encounter that results from it; *Lancelot du lac* (1976), a very mythlike, Bressonian retelling of classic Arthurian legend; *Le Diable probablement* (1977), the story of the mysterious death of young, depressed, suicidal man; and *L'Argent* (1983), the story of a young man whose life is ruined for unwittingly passing a counterfeit five hundred franc bill.

Like his films, Bresson's canon is relatively minimal given the fifty-year span of his career. Moreover, of the thirteen films he did make, very few were commercially successful. Audiences tended not to like Bresson's films for precisely the reasons that make them so clearly his own—they make the viewer work rather hard to gain an understanding of life and of humankind that is often not reassuring. Limited audience appeal notwithstanding, Bresson is regarded by scholars and filmmakers alike as one of the master **auteurs** of French cinema. His films cannot really be tied to any movement or wave in French cinema during any period during which he was making films. He embodies, in many ways, a train of existentialist thought that is uniquely French as well as a Jansenist tradition that is also uniquely French, but his view of humankind has an element of the universal about it. His filmmaking style, muted, yet bold, spare, yet emphatic has inspired filmmakers from France to Hollywood to Japan.

BRIALY, JEAN-CLAUDE (1933–). Actor, director, and screenwriter. Jean-Claude Brialy was born in Aumale, Algeria, the son of a French colonel. He later entered military service himself, where he worked for the Service cinématographique des Armées. While performing his service he met the cinematographer and director Pierre Lhomme, who subsequently introduced him to the writers at *Cahiers du cinéma*, many of whom went on to become directors of the *Nouvelle Vague* or New Wave. Brialy's primary introduction to cinema came, however, when he appeared in Lhomme's short, *Paris mon copain* (1954). He became a star of early New Wave shorts, the first among them being **Eric Rohmer**'s *La sonate à Kreutzer* (1956). He also acted in **Jacques Rivette**'s *Le coup du berger* (1956), **Jean-Luc Godard** and **François Truffaut**'s *Une histoire d'eau* (1957), and Godard's *Tous les garçons s'appellent Patrick* (1959). At about the same time, he appeared in Jacques Pinoteau's feature-length film, *L'Ami de la famille* (1957).

Brialy's career gained momentum when he was cast in **Claude Chabrol**'s landmark films *Le Beau Serge* (1958) and *Les Cousins* (1959). He went on to deliver acclaimed performances in Godard's *Une femme est une femme* (1961) and Truffaut's *La Mariée était en noir* (1967). Rohmer's *Le Genou de Claire* (1970) made Brialy, like **Jean-Paul Belmondo,** a masculine icon of the New Wave.

Brialy later managed to build a solid cinema career outside of the New Wave. He has appeared in nearly two hundred films, including **Pierre Kast**'s *Le Bel Age* (1959), Roberto Rossellini's *Vanina Vanini* (1961), **Roger Vadim**'s *Un château en Suède* (1963), **Edouard Molinaro**'s *Arsène Lupin contre Arsène Lupin* (1962) and *La Chasse à l'homme* (1964), **Marc Allégret**'s *Le Bal du compte d'Orgel* (1970), **Philippe de Broca**'s *Un monsieur de compagnie* (1964) and *Julie pot de colle* (1977), and **Claude Miller**'s *Mortelle randonnée* (1982) and *L'Effrontée* (1986). In 1988, he won a **César** for Best Supporting Actor in **André Téchiné**'s *Les Innocents*.

Brialy also began directing in the 1970s and 1980s. His first film, *Églantine* (1971), was a semi-autobiographical film based on the relationship with his grandmother. He also directed *Les volets clos* (1973), *L'oiseau rare* (1973), *Un amour de pluie* (1974), *Les malheurs de Sophie* (1981), and *Un bon petit diable* (1983).

Brialy developed an energetic television and stage presence as well. He has been director of the Théâtre des Bouffes Parisiens. He appeared in the television film *Anna* (1967) alongside Anna Karina. He acted in several French television series in the 1990s and beyond, including *Les Rois Maudits* (2005). In 1995, he was a member of the jury at the **Cannes Film Festival**.

BROCA, PHILIPPE DE (1933–2004). Actor, director, producer, and screenwriter. Philippe de Broca is well known for his comedies and adventure films. He started as an assistant to director **Henri Decoin**, and then worked as a documentary filmmaker in Africa, before becoming an assistant director to **Claude Chabrol** and **François Truffaut**. De Broca's first feature was *Les jeux de l'amour* (1960), which won a Silver Berlin Bear for best comedy. This established a fairly long series of critically acclaimed films. His film *L'amant de cinq jours* (1961) received a nomination for a Golden Berlin Bear. His *L'homme de Rio* (1964), which starred **Jean-Paul Belmondo**, received an Oscar nomination for Best Screenplay. *Chère Louise* (1972) was nominated for a Golden Palm at the **Cannes Film Festival**. His more recent film, *Le Bossu* (1997), was nominated for a **César** for Best Film and a British Film Award for Best Foreign Language Film.

De Broca also had a fair degree of commercial success. His film *Cartouche* (1962), starring Belmondo, was a big hit, and most of his films have been quite popular. Other major films by de Broca include *Les tribulations d'un Chinois en Chine* (1965), *Le roi de coeur* (1966), *Le diable par le queue* (1969), *Les caprices de Marie* (1970), *Le poudre d'escampette* (1971), *Le magnifique* (1973), *L'incorrigible* (1975), *Julie pot-de-colle* (1977), *Tendre poulet* (1978), *Le cavaleur* (1979), *On a volé la cuisse de Jupiter* (1980), *Psy* (1981), *L'Africain* (1983), *La gitane* (1986), *Chouans!* (1988), *Les 1001 Nuits* (1990), *Les clés du paradis* (1991), *Amazone* (2000), and *Vipère au poing* (2004).

– C –

CAHIERS DU CINÉMA. A film journal founded in 1951 by Jacques Doniol-Valcroze and **André Bazin**, *Les Cahiers du cinéma* is today one of the leading, authoritative French film journals, and it was the first to offer film analysis beyond the level of diegesis or plot analysis. Bazin's essays in the journal were highly influential, as were his efforts in bringing stylistic, structural, and formal analysis of film into the mainstream. Although Bazin and the journal were known for the championing of realism, Bazin's openness to innovations of technique and form made the journal one of the *Nouvelle Vague* or New Wave's most prominent advocates. The New Wave directors **Claude Chabrol**, **Jean-Luc Godard**, **Jacques Rivette**, **Eric Rohmer**, and **François Truffaut** contributed regularly to the journal. One of the most strongly associated critical veins of the journal is its championing of the concept of the **auteur**, or the director who is total creator of cinema. Much of what is and has been written by the critics of the journal is informed by this idea, which can be traced back to Bazin. *Positif*, the principal competitor to *Les Cahiers du cinéma*, rejects the auteur concept altogether.

CALMETTES, ANDRÉ (1861–1942). Actor, director, and producer. André Calmettes was born in France. He began his career, as so many of the film pioneers did, in the theater, where he was an actor. In 1908, the newly formed **Studio Film d'Art** hired Calmettes on as head of production. While at Film d'Art Calmettes directed several films, including *Un Duel sous Richelieu* (1908); *L'Assassinat du Duc de Guise* (1908), made in collaboration with **Charles LeBargy**; *MacBeth* (1909); *La Dame aux camélias* (1912); *Madame sans gêne* (1911); and *Les Trois mousquetaires* (1912).

Calmettes's directorial style was heavily influenced by classical French theater and might be considered overly theatrical by some. This, however, is not surprising given his background in theater and the artistic pretensions of Film d'Art. He is credited with having elevated film by raising the expectations of both content and performance. He is also known for having brought famed stage actress **Sarah Bernhardt** to the screen. When Film d'Art folded in 1913, Calmettes returned to the stage. He did not work in film again except occasionally as an actor, notably in *Le Petit chose* (1923).

CAMARGUE WESTERN. Camargue Westerns were a series of Western films shot in the silent era in France's southern Camargue region, which bears certain similarities to the American West, with respect to terrain and to the culture of cattle rearing and horseback riding. Some films were also shot elsewhere in Provence. The principal director of Camargue Westerns was **Jean Durand**, and all films of this type starred **Joë Hamman**, an actor who had gone to the American West and had performed with the Buffalo Bill traveling show. Of Durand's Westerns, examples include *Calino veut être Cowboy* (1911), *Onésime sur le sentier de guerre* (1913), *Une pendaison à Jefferson City* (1912), and *Le Railway de la mort* (1912). Another important group of Westerns made in the Camargue were the *Arizona Bill* series, which ran from 1910 to 1912. It is believed that Hamman himself directed five of these films, and that the remainder were directed by **Gaston Roudès**. This, at least, is what Hamman reported in his autobiography.

These early Westerns imitated the American Western, but substituted France's Camargue region for the American West. A forerunner of the Spaghetti Western, the Camargue Western reflected the popularity of the Western in France as well as France's anxiety about losing its dominance in the period leading up to World War I. Other examples of the Camarge Western include *Un drame sur une locomotive* (1910), *Le Fer à cheval* (1910), *Reconaissance d'un Indien* (1910), *L'Attaque d'un train* (1910), *Le Feu à la Prairie* (1911), *Le Mariage au revolver* (1911), and *Cent dollars vif ou mort* (1911). Most of these were made for either **Gaumont** or Éclipse studios. Many have been lost, although copies of *Le Mariage au revolver* and *Une pendaison à Jefferson City* are known to exist.

CAMÉRA-STYLO. Caméro-stylo is the name given to a theory of filmmaking articulated by **Alexandre Astruc** in an article titled, "Naissance d'une nouvelle avant-garde: la caméra stylo," which appeared in *L'Écran français* in 1948. Essentially the theory consisted of the idea that a truly artistic filmmaker used the camera in the same way a writer uses a pen in order to author his or her film, and that there were, therefore, certain stylistic particularities that could be identified in the work of every truly gifted filmmaker. The theory implicitly and explicitly invited experimentation and a break with classical narrative form. This is one of the theories that contributed to the development of the notion of the *cinéma d'auteur* or **auteur** cinema.

CANNES FILM FESTIVAL. *See* FESTIVAL INTERNATIONALE DU FILM DE CANNES.

CAPELLANI, ALBERT (1870–1931). Actor, director, and screenwriter. Albert Capellani was one of the few pioneers of cinema to have any formal training in the dramatic arts. He studied drama at the Paris Conservatoire d'art dramatique (where **Charles LeBargy** was also a student) and went on to become a dramatic actor in the Parisian theater, and then later a stage manager and theater manager, lastly at the Alhambra Music Hall. In 1905, Capellani abandoned the stage for the cinema on the conviction that the cinema would become the dominant art.

He went directly to **Pathé**, where he worked and trained under **Ferdinand Zecca**. Capellani also distinguished himself early as a talented director of the melodrama, which was emerging as a genre. His 1906 film *La Loi du pardon* was hailed by his contemporary Victorin Jasset as one of the first great films and one of the first commercial successes in the genre, and his *Pauvre mère*, from the same year, did nearly as well.

In 1907, Capellani directed *La Légende de Polichinelle*, the story of a robot who falls in love with a doll. The film, which starred film icon **Max Linder**, was an enormous success. And as a result, **Charles Pathé** moved Capellani over to the newly created **Société Cinématographique des Auteurs et Gens de Lettres** (SCAGL), which Pathé had created to make *films d'art*. As a director for this series, Capellani brought to the screen a number of French classics, ranging from fairy tales to histories. These included *Le Chat botté* (1908); *La Belle au bois dormant* (1908), codirected with **Lucien Nonguet**; *L'Assommoir* (1909), codirected with Michel Carré; *Germinal* (1912), an adaptation of the novel by Émile Zola; and a sweeping, four-part adaptation of Victor Hugo's *Les Misérables* (1912), which is still regarded as a masterpiece of cinema. Capellani's films elevated the cinema from a popular distraction toward an art form, and his longer-than-average films are seen to have established the trend toward feature-length films.

Capellani is also credited with bringing a number of talented actors and directors to the filmmaking industry. He cast the great stage performer **Mistinguett** in *Les Misérables*, her first film, and established her as a silent-film star. He also brought theater actors such as Paul

Capellani (his brother) and Berthe Bovy to film. The directors he helped to train include **Georges Monca** and Michel Carré.

In 1914, when the war began to interfere with French film production, Capellani left France for the United States. He remained in the United States for several years, making films there for various studios, including Pathé Exchange, Metro Film, and World Film. Capellani fell ill in 1923 and returned to France with the intention of going back to the United States when he recovered. His health deteriorated, however, and he became paralyzed and was forced to give up filmmaking altogether.

CARAX, LÉOS (1960–). Actor, director, and screenwriter. Léos Carax was born Alexandre Oscar Dupont. He was a film student at Université de Paris III, when he began working as a reviewer for *Les Cahiers du cinéma* under the editorship of Serge Daney. His experience writing for *Les Cahiers* may have influenced his filmmaking, and it has certainly affected the reception of his films. His first films were shorts, including the unfinished *La fille rêvée* and *Strangulation Blues* (1979). He subsequently made three feature-length films, *Boy Meets Girl* (1984), *Mauvais sang* (1986), and *Les amants du Pont Neuf* (1991). These three films form a trilogy, the latter two featuring **Juliette Binoche**. Carax later directed the short *Sans titre* (1997) and the feature film *Pola X* (1999). **Catherine Deneuve** appears in both.

Carax is often characterized, along with **Jean-Jacques Beineix** and **Luc Besson**, as a director of the *cinéma du look*. Carax's reception among the critical elite in France was more positive that that of Beineix's and Besson's, however, perhaps because of his connection to *Les Cahiers*. Carax's "look" films have been seen as more intellectual, more visually stunning, and more contemplative than those of Beineix or Besson. However, it is not entirely clear that this is accurate, and in fact, recent criticism has challenged that assertion, giving more credit to the other two directors.

Carax's emphasis on décor and lighting has also led critics to describe his films (and those of other *cinéma du look* directors) as baroque or neobaroque. Further comparisons have been made between the styles of Carax and **Jean-Luc Godard**. Just as Jean-Pierre Léaud appears to be an autobiographical figure or "fetish" actor for Godard, the actor Denis Lavant, who plays protagonists named Alex in the first three features, seems to be Carax's stand-in. Carax acted in Godard's *King Lear* (1987).

CARL, RENÉE (1875–1954). Actress and director. Renée Carl was one of the first major leading ladies of the cinema. She began her career, like most silent-film stars, in the theater. Carl was one of those stars of the stage lured to the screen in order to elevate the status of cinema from spectacle to art. She went to **Gaumont** in 1907, where she acted in **Roméo Bosetti**'s celebrated silent film, *Une dame vraiment bien* (1908). She also appeared in a number of the films in the *Bébé* series, which was directed by **Louis Feuillade** and which ran from 1911 to 1913. She was also the heroine of Feuillade's *Fantômas* films. She starred in many other of Feuillade's films as well, including *Le Roman de soeur Louise* (1908), *Le Collier de la reine* (1909), *La Cigale et la fourmi* (1909), *Judith et Holopherne* (1909), *La Fille de Jephté* (1910), *Esther* (1910), *Mater Dolorosa* (1910), *André Chénier* (1911), *Aux lions les chrétiens* (1911), *Les Vipères* (1911), *Androclès* (1912), *La Maison des lions* (1912), *Le Proscrit* (1912), *Le Revenant* (1913), *Severo Torelli* (1914), the *Heures* series, which ran in 1909, and Feuillade's celebrated series *Les Vampires* (1915).

During her career Carl also worked with **Léonce Perret** and **Marcel L'Herbier** and was the leading lady in Robert Peguy's *L'Aviateur* series (1921–1922). She also appeared as Madame Thenardier in **Henri Fescourt**'s *Les Misérables* (1925). Carl managed, briefly, to transition into talking films. She had a role in **Julien Duvivier**'s film noir classic, *Pépé le Moko* (1937). That role would be her last.

In addition to acting, Carl tried her hand at directing. She directed herself in *Un cri dans l'abîme* (1923), at a period when female directors were still a rarity. What stands out about her work onscreen, apart from her sheer longevity during a time when the names of film actors, much less actresses, were rarely known, and when actresses disappeared forever after only a few roles, is her breadth. She performed in burlesque just as well as she did in biblical histories, and was as compelling in *Fantômas* as she was in *Androclès* (1912). All in all, Carl appeared in more than 160 films. *See also* WOMEN.

CARNÉ, MARCEL (1909–1996). Director and film critic. Marcel Carné was born in Paris, the son of a carpenter. His mother died when he was only five years old, after which time he was mostly left in the care of his grandmother and aunt. It was his father's wish that Carné follow in the family trade, but he had little interest in going that route, as he was much more interested in the cinema, theater, and café-concerts even at a young age. He began work in an insurance office while studying photography, becoming certified by the *Arts et Métiers*. Through personal connections, Carné was able to obtain work in the film industry. The first major influence on the aspiring director would be the great **Jacques Feyder**, with whom Carné worked on the film *Les Nouveaux messieurs* (1929). The same year Carné made his first film, a poetic documentary short titled *Eldorado du dimanche*. The film caught the attention of **René Clair**, who invited Carné to come and work with him.

Clair would be the other great influence on Carné's filmmaking, and Carné's celebrated ***Réalisme poétique*** or poetic realism owes a great deal to Clair's own filmmaking style and worldview. Carné worked as Clair's assistant on the classic film *Sous les toits de Paris* (1930), and the vivid depiction of the Parisian working class found in Clair's film is echoed in many of Carné's own works.

During the period of his early formation, Carné had also taken up film criticism. He worked as a journalist and critic for *Cinémagazine* as well as *Hebdo Film*. He continued this throughout the early part of his career. In 1934, Carné again began working with Feyder and was his assistant on several films, most notably *Pension Mimosas* (1935) and *La Kermesse heroïque* (1935).

Carné's first credited film as director is *Jenny* (1936). The film, which stars Feyder's wife, **Françoise Rozay**, is a period melodrama centered on the lives of the working classes and those even lower on the social scale. It has many of the characteristics of what would become Carné's trademark, the focus on the lower classes, the nineteenth-century backdrop, the varied cast of characters, all either pure good or pure evil, caught in a world that is less good than evil. This was also the beginning of Carné's long and successful collaboration with poet and screenwriter Jacques Prévert. The film was a commercial success and established Carné as a reputable director who could attract an audience and the Carné/Prévert team as a recipe for popular success and film magic.

Jenny was followed by *Drôle de drame* (1936), starring **Jean-Pierre Aumont**, a bourgeois drama about a family with domestic help issues. This was followed in 1938 by *Quai des brumes*, the first in a fairly noir trio of films made fairly close together by Carné. It would be followed by *Hôtel du nord* (1938) and *Le Jour se lève* (1939). All three are considered Carné classics and classics of French cinema as a whole.

Quai des brumes, which starred **Jean Gabin**, **Michèle Morgan**, **Pierre Brasseur**, and **Michel Simon**, is a twisted story of the return of Jean, a soldier/deserter, to France (specifically Le Havre) and his love affair with Nelly, a less-than-innocent seventeen-year-old. The film won the **Prix Louis-Delluc**. *Hôtel du nord*, which is the first Carné film to star **Arletty**, is the story of a failed suicide pact between Renée and Pierre. Pierre shoots Renée, then loses his nerve and runs away. The rest of the film centers on the different characters that intersect Renée's life via the hotel. *Le Jour se lève*, starring Gabin and Arletty, is again a twisted story of love gone wrong. François, a young factory worker, falls in love with Françoise, not realizing she is the protégé of the evil dog trainer, Valentin. The film begins with François murdering Valentin, then flashes back to the events that lead up to it. It is for that reason, perhaps, the bleakest of the three films, since it is clear from the beginning that all ends in tragedy.

While these films are clearly part of the tradition of poetic realism associated with Carné, a tradition that he did not create so much as refine, they are, as noted, marked by particularly noir characteristics as well. The chiaroscuro lighting is quite evident in all three, as is the presence of what might be seen as a femme fatale. Carné himself intended these noir elements to be clear in these films, seeing part of his own contribution to poetic realism as a sort of fusion between poetry on film and the noir tradition. The films are less tense than a typical noir, and the characters are less clearly types, but the milieu, lighting, and certain elements of the plot clearly reflect that particular influence.

After *Le Jour se lève*, Carné was operating fully under the constraints of Nazi Occupation. His next film, *Les Visiteurs du soir* (1942), would be very different from the three that preceded it. Again starring Arletty opposite Jules Berry, *Les Visiteurs du soir* is the story of two emissaries sent by the devil to tempt the inhabitants of a medieval baron's court. The film lacks much of what classically defines Carné's early cinema; it is, for example, much less fatalistic in certain respects, and the settings are quite different. Some have explained these differences as the result of the censor, and some as the result of a veiled commentary on the political circumstances in which it was made. Whatever the case, it remains a masterful piece of cinema, although quite different from anything else Carné ever made.

Following *Les Visiteurs du soir*, Carné made what is widely regarded as his masterpiece, **Les Enfants du paradis** (1945). Again starring Arletty, this time with **Jean-Louis Barrault** and Brasseur, *Les Enfants du paradis* is the sprawling tale of a group of artists in 1827 Paris. Baptiste, a mime, is in love with Garance, an actress, but the two are kept apart by fate and outside intervention. Apart from setting, this film has a great deal in common with Carné's earlier films. It is much more in keeping in subject, tone, and theme, and it is seen as having brought to perfection the vision of cinema that was developed in those films.

It would have been difficult under any circumstances for Carné to match the success of *Les Enfants du paradis*. It was an enormous success and hailed as a classic even when it was released, although some critics would argue that time has not been so kind to it. Nonetheless, nothing could have prepared Carné for the precipitous decline in his career that would come after the war. It is often the case that people today forget Carné made films after the war, and that is as much a statement on the reception of those films as anything else. In fact, he made fourteen, and left one unfinished, but not a single of these would come close to the success of any of his early films.

In part, Carné had difficulty finding his voice after the war. Poetic realism seemed to have had no place at that point in time. Carné tried to update his vision to fit the times. His 1946 film, *Les Portes de la nuit*, contains many of the elements of his early films, but was updated to fit the contemporary historical context—it was a failure. He tried his hand at creating a "youth cinema" with films like *Les Tricheurs* (1958) and *Terrain vague* (1960) but audiences and critics found something a bit artificial in these films. He tried religious films, such as *La Merveilleuse visite* (1974) and *La Bible* (1977), but in 1970s France, in the wake of May 1968, there was not much interest in religion.

Outside of these failures there was one modest success. Carné's 1953 adaptation of Émile Zola's *Thérèse Racquin*, which starred

Simone Signoret, was not doomed to the utter failure of many of his later films. But for the most part, the postwar era was a footnote to a brilliant filmmaking career that, for all serious film scholars and for audiences alike, more or less ended with *Les Enfants du paradis*.

CAROL, MARTINE (1920–1967). Actress. Born Marie-Louise Mourer in the Val-de-Marne region of France, Martine Carol had no ambitions of becoming an actress until, in her late teens, she met the actor André Luguet, who is reported to have encouraged her. Following Luguet's advice, Carol enrolled in dramatic courses and then sought a career onstage. Her first role was in Racine's *Phèdre* under the stage name Maryse Arley.

While performing onstage, Carol caught the attention of director **Henri-Georges Clouzot**. Clouzot intended to cast Carol in a film he was making, but the film was never done. He did, however, succeed in getting her a bit part in **Georges Lacombe**'s *Le Dernier des six* (1941). This bit part introduced Carol to the world of cinema and led to a role in Richard Pottier's *La Ferme aux loups* (1943). It was at the encouragement of François Perier, her costar in *La Ferme aux loups*, that Carol adopted the stage name of Martine Carol.

From 1943 until 1955, Carol enjoyed increasing success in her film career. Her presence onscreen was, from the beginning, driven in large measure by her physical beauty and by her willingness to put her body visibly in the frame, so there should be little wonder that she became a first-rate femme fatale. She would incarnate onscreen many legendary historical and literary bad girls in films such as *Lucrèce Borgia* (1953), *Madame du Barry* (1953), and *Nana* (1954), all directed by **Christian-Jacque**, whom she would later marry. She also did a series of films made especially for her, starting with *Caroline Chérie* (1950), a period drama in which she again played an aristocratic heroine and in which she was again directed by Pottier. The sequels included *Caprice de Caroline Chérie* (1953). Other noteworthy films include *Lysistrata* (1953), also directed by Christian-Jacque, and *Secrets d'alcôve* (1953), directed by **Jean Delannoy**.

Ironically, Carol's career was all but undone by another historical femme fatale, as her role in **Max Ophüls**'s *Lola Montès* (1955), itself an enormous failure, put a taint on Carol that she was hard pressed to shake. The film was unusually long, shot in vivid color in a style that was very postmodern and completely at odds with the filmmaking of the time. The avant-garde nature of the film and the overtly sexual and very powerful nature of the character proved too much for audiences of the day. The film anticipates in some ways the characteristics both of the post–1968 sexual liberation that would infuse cinema and the filmmaking style of the *cinéma du look*. Ironically, with time it has come to be regarded as something of a masterpiece, and Carol's performance in it is widely regarded as one of her best. Nonetheless, it nearly ended her career.

Following *Lola Montès*, Carol made a handful of other films, including Christian-Jacque's *Nathalie* (1957), *Austerlitz* (1960), directed by **Abel Gance**, and Michel Boisrond's *Un Soir sur la plage* (1960). She gave a very compelling performance in Roberto Rossellini's *Vanina Vanini* (1961), and also appeared in Gilles Grangier's *La Cave se rebiffe* (1961). Her last film in French was **George Lautner**'s *En plein cirage* (1961).

CASSEL, JEAN-PIERRE (1932–). Actor. Jean-Pierre Cassel was born Jean-Pierre Crochon in Paris, the son of a doctor and an opera singer. His first appearance in film was in Maurice Labro and Giorgio Simonelli's *Saluti e baci* (1953). He then played small parts in Anatole Litvak's French- and English-language *Un acte d'amour* (1953) and Gene Kelly's *The Happy Road* (1958). He later landed a leading role in Claude Boissol's *La Peau de l'ours* (1957).

It was Cassel's work with **Philippe de Broca** that really launched his career. He appeared in such films as *Les jeux de l'amour* (1960), *Le Farceur* (1960), *L'Amant de cinq jours* (1961), and *Un Monsieur de compagnie* (1965). In the 1960s, Cassel also played the title role in Norbert Carbonneaux's *Candide, ou l'optimisme au XXe siècle* (1960). He starred in **Jean Renoir**'s *Le Caporal épinglé* (1962), **Abel Gance**'s *Cyrano et d'Artagnan* (1963), **René Clair**'s *Les Fêtes galantes* (1965), Alain Jessua's *Jeu de massacre* (1967), and **Michel Deville**'s *L'ours et la poupée* (1969).

In the 1970s, Cassel continued to work with celebrated directors from Europe and the United States. He starred in **Claude Chabrol**'s *La Rupture* (1970), Harry Kümel's *Malpertuis* (1971), Deville's *Le Mouton enragé* (1974), and Jean-Louis Bertucelli's *Docteur Françoise Gailland* (1975). He also appeared in Luis Buñuel's *Le*

Charme discret de la bourgeoisie (1972), Richard Lester's *The Three Musketeers* (1973) and *The Four Musketeers* (1974), Sidney Lumet's *Murder on the Orient Express* (1974), Christopher Miles's *That Lucky Touch* (1975), and Chantal Akerman's *Les Rendez-vous d'Anna* (1978).

In the early 1980s, Cassel maintained an international presence while landing significant roles in French films. He starred in **Pierre Kast**'s *Le Soleil en face* (1980), Moshé Mizrahi's *La Vie continue* (1981), Emidio Greco's *Ehrengard* (1982), Kast's *La Guérilléra* (1982), and Joseph Losey's *La Truite* (1982). He appeared in Lester's *Superman II* (1980) and Nino Manfredi's *Nudo di donna* (1981). He also acted in several television productions.

In the 1990s, Cassel acted in a variety of international films. He played starring roles in Marion Hänsel's *Sur la terre comme au ciel* (1992) and Jean Marboeuf's *Pétain* (1993). He also appeared in Philippe Setbon's *Mister Frost* (1990), Ian Toynton's *The Maid* (1991), Ben Lewin's *The Favour, the Watch, and the Very Big Fish* (1991), António de Macedo's *Chá Forte com Limão* (1993), Luís Filipe Rocha's *Amor e Dedinhos de Pé* (1993), Chabrol's *L'Enfer* (1994), **Gérard Jugnot**'s *Casque blue* (1994), and Juan Manuel Chumilla's *Amores que matan* (1996). Cassel played in two Robert Altman films, *Vincent and Theo* (1990) and *Pret à porter* (1994). In 1993 he appeared with his son, **Vincent Cassel**, in **Mathieu Kassovitz**'s *Métisse*, and in 1996, he was nominated for a **César** for Best Supporting Actor for his role in Chabrol's *La Cérémonie* (1996).

In the twenty-first century, Cassel still impresses his cinema and television audiences while working on decidedly more international projects. He has played supporting roles in **Benoît Jacquot**'s *Sade* (2000), Kassovitz's *Les Rivières pourpres* (2000), South African director Ntshaveni Wa Luruli's *The Wooden Camera* (2003), Louis-Pascal Couvelaire's *Michel Vaillant* (2003), Tristan Aurouet and Gilles Lellouche's *Narco* (2004), Denis Thybaud's *Dans tes rêves* (2005), Mabrouk El Mechri's *Virgil* (2005), and Stefan Liberski's *Bunker Paradise* (2005).

CASSEL, VINCENT (1966–). Actor, director, producer, and screenwriter. Vincent Cassel first appeared in cinema in Didier Kaminka's *Les cigognes n'en font qu'à leur tête* (1989), followed by a role in

Philippe de Broca's *Les Clés du paradis* (1991). Vincent's father, **Jean-Pierre Cassel**, had also worked with de Broca early in his career. His pairing with director **Mathieu Kassovitz** in *Métisse* (1993), and especially in *La Haine* (1995), was pivotal to his career. His performance in *La Haine* earned him nominations for **César**s for Most Promising Actor and Best Actor. He also starred in Kassovitz's *Les rivières pourpres* (2000), and acted alongside Kassovitz in Nicolas Boukhrief's *Le plaisir et ses petits tracas* (1997) and Jez Butterwirth's English-language *Birthday Girl* (2001).

Cassel was again nominated for a César for Best Actor in **Jacques Audiard**'s *Sur mes lèvres* (2001). He has acted in films by Jan Kounen, including *Dobermann* (1997) and *Blueberry* (2004). Cassel landed other significant acting roles in Christine Pascal's *Adultère, mode d'emploi* (1995), Gilles Mimouni's *L'appartement* (1996), Olivier Schatzky's *L'Èleve* (1996), Adrian Edmonson's English comedy, *Guest House Paradiso* (1999), **Luc Besson**'s *The Messenger: The Story of Joan of Arc* (1999), Christophe Gans's *Le pacte des loups* (2001), Gaspard Noé's *Irréversible* (2002), and Frédéric Schoendoerffer's *Agents secrets* (2003). He also directed and wrote the script for the short *Shabbat Night Fever* (1997).

CATELAIN, JACQUE (1897–1965). Actor and director. Born Jacques Guerin-Castelain, Jacque Catelain got his start in the silent cinema as an actor for **Gaumont**. His first film role was in René Hervil and **Louis Mercanton**'s *Le Torrent* (1917). Catelain went on to be the dashing star of many of **Marcel L'Herbier**'s films of the day, including *Rose-France* (1918), *Le Bercail* (1919), *Le Carnaval des vérités* (1920), *L'Homme du large* (1920), *Eldoradao* (1921), *Don Juan et Faust* (1922), *L'Inhumaine* (1924), *Le Vertige* (1927), *Le Diable au corps* (1928), and *Nuits de princes* (1929). He also appeared in **Léonce Perret**'s *Koenigsmark* (1923), Viktor Tourjansky's *Le Prince charmant* (1925), and **Henri Fescourt**'s *L'Occident* (1927), among other films.

In 1923, Catelain tried his hand at directing, directing himself in *Le Marchand de plaisirs*. He directed himself again the following year in the film *La Galérie des monstres* (1924). He did not direct again for most of his career, with the exception of two turns at assistant director, one on L'Herbier's *La Porte du large* (1936), and one on the

French version of Giorgi Ferroni and L'Herbier's film *Terra di fuoco* (1939).

Catelain managed the transition to sound with little difficulty. His first speaking role was in **Jacques de Baroncelli**'s *Le Rêve* (1930). He also continued to work with L'Herbier, appearing in films such as *L'Enfant de l'amour* (1930), *Le Bonheur* (1934), *La Route impériale* (1935), *Adrienne Lecouvreur* (1939), *Entente cordiale* (1939), and *La Comédie du bonheur* (1942). He also appeared in **Gaston Ravel**'s *Monsieur de Porceaugnac* (1932), **Abel Gance**'s *Le Voleur de femmes* (1936), Jean de Limur's *La Garçonne* (1936), and **Jean Renoir**'s *La Marseilleise* (1938). Catelain's talent was attested to not only by L'Herbier's strong preference for the actor (he was more than a pretty face), but also by the number of other directors he worked with. It is also attested to by the fact that he maintained a successful stage career as well.

Catelain fled to the United States during the Nazi Occupation of France. There, he had a handful of uncredited roles in Hollywood films but did not have much other luck. The time away from France also took its toll on his French career. After the war, Catelain appeared in such L'Herbier films as *La Révoltée* (1948) and *Les Derniers jours de Pompei* (1950), but apart from that, he managed only small roles in Gilles Grangier's *Amour et compagnie* (1950), Renoir's *French Can Can* (1955), *Élena et les hommes* (1959), and *Le Testament du Docteur Cordelier* (1959), which was his last film.

CÉSAR (1933). *See MARIUS* (1931), *FANNY* (1932), AND *CÉSAR* (1933).

CÉSAR AWARDS. The French awards given for accomplishments in cinema by the l'Académie des Arts et Techniques du Cinéma (AATC), established by **Georges Cravenne** in 1975, after he lamented that France did not have an equivalent to the Oscars. The first César Awards ceremony took place on 3 April 1976, and they recognize Best Film, Best Director, Best Actor and Actress, and a host of similar facets of the filmmaking process.

CHABROL, CLAUDE (1930–). Actor, director, film critic, producer, and screenwriter. Claude Chabrol spent much of his youth during

World War II in Sardent, a village that provided the setting of some of his films. He later met fellow New Wave directors in *ciné-clubs* and wrote for *Cahiers du cinéma*. His film *Le beau Serge* (1958) was the first feature of the Cahiers Group and won the **Prix Jean-Vigo**. It was followed by *Les Cousins* (1959), which was awarded the Golden Berlin Bear. Chabrol's first two features are frequently considered to be the very first films of the *Nouvelle Vague* or New Wave, although some critics cite **François Truffaut**'s *Les 400 coups* (1959) as the first, with **Agnès Varda**'s *La Pointe Courte* being a pivotal precursor.

Chabrol's subsequent films, *A Double Tour* (1959), *Les bonnes femmes* (1959), *Les Godelureaux* (1960), *L'Oeil du malin* (1960), and *Ophélia* (1962), did not achieve the same level of acclaim. *Landru* (1962), which is regarded as his last New Wave film, was a success, and has curiously also been viewed by some critics as Chabrol's entrance into commercial cinema. Others point to his 1964 *Le Tigre aime la chair fraîche* as his debut into profit-oriented mainstream films.

Chabrol went on to make several commercial films, though his direction of art films did not cease. Indeed, critics have observed that Chabrol managed to blur the boundaries between artistic and popular cinema. After a period of salaried directing, which elite critics viewed negatively, Chabrol released his 1968 film *Les biches*, which focuses on a sensual relationship between two **women** and stars his former wife, Stéphane Audran. It received wide critical acclaim. Increasingly, Chabrol became known as an incisive critic of the French bourgeoisie and a master of the thriller, especially in *Le Boucher* (1970).

Chabrol tends to collaborate with a particular group of people when making films, among them cinematographer Jean Rabier, scenarist Paul Gégauff, composers Pierre Jansen and Matthieu Chabrol, producers André Génovès and Marin Karmitz, and actors Audran, **Isabelle Huppert**, **Jean-Claude Brialy**, Bernadette Lafont, **Michel Bouquet**, and **Jean Yanne**. Audran was the key figure in what has been called Chabrol's Hélène cycle, a series of films that include *La femme infidèle* (1968), *Que la bête meure* (1969), *Le Boucher* (1970), *La Rupture* (1970), and *Juste avant la nuit* (1971). The film *Violete Nozière* (1978) marked the transition from Audran to Huppert as Chabrol's leading actress, though Audran is featured in his latter films. *Violette Nozière*, which is based on a nonfictional case of a woman who poisoned her parents, is a prominent example of Chabrol's interest in the stories of female criminals.

In the 1980s and beyond, Chabrol received a fair degree of critical acclaim. His *Une affaire des femmes* (1988), based on the story of the last woman to receive the guillotine in France, was unconventional in its representation of women during the German occupation. It starred Huppert and was nominated for a **César** for Best Director in 1989. Chabrol contributed to the **heritage** genre with *Madame Bovary* (1991), a film based on Gustave Flaubert's classic novel. *La Cérémonie*—arguably Chabrol's most critically acclaimed film—was nominated for a **César** for Best Film, Best Director, and Best Screenplay in 1996, and Huppert won Best Actress for her performance. In 1997, Chabrol made his fiftieth film, *Rien ne va plus*. Afterwards, a special edition of *Cahiers du cinéma* was dedicated to Chabrol, an act that his fans considered long overdue.

Although Chabrol's work was initially considered uneven by several French critics, he has emerged as one of France's most prolific and respected directors. He continues to direct highly regarded films: *Merci pour le chocolat* won the **Prix Louis-Delluc** in 2000 and *La fleur du mal* (2003) was nominated for a Golden Berlin Bear. He received a Lifetime Achievement Award at the European Film Awards in 2003.

In addition to directing, Chabrol has produced films through his production company, AJYM, which was financed with an inheritance from his wife's grandmother. With AJYM he produced his own early films, as well as those of other New Wave directors. For example, he produced **Éric Rohmer**'s *Le signe du lion* (1959) as well as **Jacques Rivette**'s *Le Coup du berger* (1956) and *Paris nous appartient* (1961).

CHENAL, PIERRE (1904–1990). Director. Born Pierre Cohen in Brussels, Belgium, Pierre Chenal, as he would be known in the world of film, showed an early interest in cinema. He made his first film, a documentary titled *Petits métiers de Paris* (1930), at the age of only twenty-six. He would quickly turn his attention to narrative cinema, making some thirty films over the course of his career.

Chenal had a penchant and a gift for literary adaptation. Among the literary masterpieces he brought to the screen were *La Rue sans nom* (1933), based on the novel by Marcel Aymé; *Crime et chatîment*

(1935), based on the novel by Fyodor Dostoyevsky; and the superb *La Maison du Maltais* (1938), from the novel by Jean Vignaud. In 1936, he adapted Luigi Pirandello's *L'Homme de nulle part* for the screen, trumping the earlier silent-film version by the legendary **Marcel L'Herbier**.

Chenal was also able to spot a literary and film masterpiece in the making. He was the first director to bring James M. Cain's novel, *The Postman Always Rings Twice,* to the screen in his 1939 film, *Le Dernier tournant*. In 1950, Chenal also collaborated with American author Richard Wright to bring Wright's highly controversial but acclaimed novel of racial prejudice in America, *Native Son*, to the screen in an Argentine version titled *Sangre negra*, the work being still too controversial to be made in an English-language version.

Chenal made a number of other films in Latin America as well as in France, having spent the war years there. He returned to Latin America from time to time to work, most particularly in Argentina. His Spanish-language films include *Confesiones al almancer* (1954) and *Las Bellas* (1969). Of his films in French, apart from those mentioned, he is best known for *Clochmerle* (1948), *Rafles sur la ville* (1958), and *La Bête à l'affût* (1959). He is considered by some critics to have been an overlooked contributor to *Le Réalisme poétique* or poetic realism.

CHÉREAU, PATRICE (1944–). Actor, director, and screenwriter. Patrice Chéreau started his career in theater, serving as the director of the Théâtre des Amandiers in Nanterre. He made the transition to cinema in the 1970s, and although he continued to work in the theater, the cinema became his primary focus. His early films include *La chair de l'orchidée* (1975), *Judith Therpauve* (1978), and *Hôtel de France* (1987). He first came to prominence with his adaptation of Alexandre Dumas's historical novel *La Reine Margot* (1994), which starred **Isabelle Adjani** and **Daneil Auteuil**. The film won the Jury Prize at **Cannes** and established Chéreau as a powerful director. His later films include *Ceux qui m'aiment prendront le train* (1999), which also received critical acclaim and won a **César** for Best Director, *Son frère* (2003), which won the Silver Berlin Bear in 2003, and *Gabrielle* (2005). He directed *Intimacy* (2001), based on stories by Hanif Kureishi, in English. This won the Golden Berlin Bear.

Quite apart from his directing, Chéreau has proven himself an accomplished film actor. He had roles in Andrzej Wajda's *Danton* (1982), Youssef Chahine's *Adieu Bonaparte* (1985), Michael Mann's *The Last of the Mohicans* (1992), **Claude Berri**'s *Lucie Aubrac* (1997), Tonie Marshall's *Au plus près du paradis* (2002), and Michael Haneke's *Le temps du loup* (2003). He was also the narrator of Raoul Ruiz's *Le temps retrouvé* (1999). His screenwriting has also been acclaimed. He won the César for his writing of *L'homme blessé* in 1984.

CHOMON, SEGUNDO DE (1871–1929). Cinematographer, director, and screenwriter. Segundo de Chomon was a Spanish-born nobleman (of French origin) who was an early pioneer of film. He was a cameraman and cinematographer, as well as a screenwriter and director. Because of his familiarity with the camera and his comfort in front of and behind the camera, Chomon, like other early film pioneers such as **Georges Méliès**, became interested in the possibility of making the camera record things that did not happen, rather than record things that did (the focus of many early filmmakers from **Louis Lumière** on). He developed an early reputation as a creator of *truc* films and special effects.

It was this reputation that attracted the attention of **Charles Pathé**, who, in 1903, recruited Chomon to work for **Pathé** studios as part of Pathé's attempt to rival Méliès. Pathé's efforts proved worthwhile. Chomon was a master of both the truc film, which had been Méliès's dominant genre, and other genres. His tricks and special effects were more elaborate than Méliès's and his films often more visually spectacular. It is widely believed that over the course of his work at Pathé Chomon was able to surpass Méliès in the genre that Méliès had created. It is no mystery why Pathé named Chomon head of production for truc films in 1907, after **Gaston Velle** left Pathé to go work for an Italian studio.

Of Chomon's truc films, the best known are *Le Sorcier arabe* (1906), *Les Roses magiques* (1906), *Le Charmeur* (1907), and *La Scarabée d'or* (1907), all of which involve men and women making each other appear or vanish, and *Les Invisibles* (1906), which was the first film to represent invisibility onscreen. Other films he made include *Le Roi de dollars* (1905), *La Poule aux oeufs d'or* (1905), *La*

Canne récalcitrante (1906), *Le Courant él7lectrique* (1906), *La Maison hantée* (1906), *Ali Baba* (1907), *Armures mystérieuses* (1907), *Les Chrysanthèmes* (1907), *Le Pêcheur de perles* (1907), *Le Spectre rouge* (1907), *Les Affiches animées* (1908), *La Belle au bois dormant* (1908), *Chevalier mystérieux* (1908), *Sculpteur moderne* (1908), *Au fond de la terre/Voyage au centre de la terre* (1909), *La Forge du diable* (1909), and *La Maison des revenants* (1912).

Beyond his directorial talent, Chomon was, as noted, an important innovator in the domain of special effects. He is often credited with the first traveling shot, for example, for his film *Hôtel électrique* (1908). The camera in this film leaves its fixed axis on the floor and shoots from a specially constructed frame that allowed filming while the camera was moved backward or forward. Chomon was also in charge of special effects for **Abel Gance**'s legendary biopic *Napoléon*. Chomon's collaboration with Gance took film's technical capacity to an entirely new level.

Chomon's collaboration with Gance was far from his only collaborative effort. During his time at Pathé, he worked with **Ferdinand Zecca, Albert Capellani**, and **Gaston Velle**, among others. His collaborations with Zecca include *Le Roi des dollars* (1905) and Zecca's remake of *La Vie et la passion de notre seigneur Jésus Christ* (1905). Chomon's collaborations with Velle include the legendary *La Poule aux oeufs d'or* (1906), for which Chomon wrote the screenplay, and the equally legendary *Les Invisibles* (1906). Chomon also worked on occasion with **Émile Cohl**, the father of the modern animation film.

Chomon left Pathé in 1912, lured, like Velle before him, to Italy to work for the Italian cinema. However, he returned to France in 1925, near the end of his life, to work with Abel Gance on *Napoléon*. By the time of his early death, he had worked on more than one hundred films.

CHRISTIAN-JACQUE (1904–1994). Director and screenwriter. Christian-Jacque was born Christian Maudet in Paris. He apparently had no intention of becoming a filmmaker, but instead studied architecture after finishing his studies at the lycée. His introduction to cinema came quite by accident while designing posters for a film-production company as a way to make money to help pay for his studies. So the story goes, his cocreator was someone named Jacques, and the two signed their posters, Christian-Jacque. Christian-Jacque would later use the same name to sign his films. His architectural background may, in part, explain some of Christian-Jacque's reputation as a masterful technician—his studies may well have shaped his sense of form and structure.

From poster design, Christian-Jacque was introduced to directing by the film director Henry Roussell, whose assistant he became. Following Roussell, he would work with **Julien Duvivier**, and these two are the principal influences on Christian-Jaccque's own filmmaking style. Around 1926, he also began writing film criticism, so the early period of assisting Roussell and Duvivier and working as a film journalist may be seen as the formative years.

Christian-Jacque made his first film in 1932, *Le Bidon d'or*. It was rather unremarkable except that it was sufficient to permit him to establish his career. Although his first films are rather diverse, as was his entire corpus, the two dominant trends of his career are apparent from these early films, namely, an interest in historical romance and literary adaptation and an interest in comedy or farce. And in fact, when Christian-Jacque's name is mentioned it is invariably one of these types of film that comes to mind.

His first historically oriented film would be *François Ier* (1937), which is sort of a historical farce, shortly followed by *Les Perles de la Couronne* (1937), made with **Sacha Guitry**. His first literary adaptation would be *Les Disparus de Saint-Agil* (1938), based on the novel by Pierre Very. The majority of his other 1930s films, including *La Famille Pont-Biquet* (1935), would be comedies or farces.

During World War II, Christian-Jacque remained in France and continued to make films. His wartime production, like that of many other filmmakers, was influenced by the Occupation and the censorship that accompanied it. He worked with the Nazi-owned production company **Continental Films**, and several of his wartime films were produced by Continental.

Some of Christian-Jacques's prewar tendencies manifested in the film *L'Assassinat du Père Noël* (1941), often considered one of his masterpieces. Like *Les Disparus de Saint-Agil*, the film is based on a novel by Pierre Very. However, like much of the wartime production, it stands apart. In *L'Assassinat du Père Noël*, some have seen a discourse of resistance. It is particularly difficult to overlook the fact that the Père Noël of the title is played by the actor **Harry Baur**, and one cannot help but remember that this was one of the last films that Baur would make. This theme of resistance is repeated in the 1945 film *Boule-de-suif*, an adaptation based on the short story by Maupassant. And one must imagine that there was something subversive in his *Carmen* (1945), since it was made during the Occupation, although not released until after it. The other major wartime production, *La Symphonie fantastique* (1942), starring **Bertrand Blier** and **Jean-Louis Barrault**, was a historical melodrama based on the life of Hector Berlioz.

In the immediate postwar years, it was literary adaptation and historical melodrama that would dominate. Christian-Jacque made *La Chartreuse de Parme* (1948), based on the novel by Stendhal, *Barbe-bleue* (1951), *Fanfan le tulipe* (1952), *Lucrèce Borgia* (1953), *Madame du Barry* (1954), and *Nana* (1955), based on the novel by Émile Zola. Some of these adaptations remain to date the definitive versions in French cinema. The immediate postwar period is considered the peak of Christian-Jacque's career, and it is widely accepted that by the 1960s, his films had become largely unremarkable, with the exception perhaps of *Madame Sans-Gêne* (1961), *La Tulipe noire* (1964), and the World War II drama *Le Repas des fauves* (1964). In addition to filming in France, he also made several films in Italy. Many of his best films starred the actress **Martine Carol**, who was his wife for a brief time. Many believe it was he who best captured her on film.

CINÉMA D'AUTEUR. *See* AUTEUR/CINÉMA D'AUTEUR.

CINÉMA DE BANLIEUE. *Cinéma de banlieue* is a term used to describe films that take place in the margins of the city, especially those that focus on working-class neighborhoods. The genre has its roots in the early silent films of **Louis Feuillade**, who was one of the first to go out and shoot the city, at that time in a state of rapid transformation. Feuillade made the city and the working classes a central focus his films, particularly his series, *Les Vampires* (1915).

Following Feuillade, the interest in filming the urban and particularly the working-class areas of the city was developed by the directors in the 1930s, particularly those associated with *Le Réalisme poétique* or poetic realism. These include such directors as **René Clair** in such films as *Sous les toits de Paris* (1930) and **Marcel Carné** in his *Hôtel du nord* (1938). Unlike Feuillade, however, these directors often worked on soundstage re-creations of these milieux and did not actually film in the city.

A further development came with the advent of the *Nouvelle Vague* or New Wave. Directors such **Jean-Luc Godard** took handheld cameras out to film in the city, in a move reminiscent of Feuillade. Godard, like Feuillade, was also particularly interested in the *quartiers populaires*, or the working-class areas. Classic examples are Godard's *À bout de souffle* (1960), and *Deux ou trois choses que je sais d'elle* (1967).

As it is currently used, the term refers mostly to films set in largely immigrant neighborhoods around Paris or Marseille. Films included in this category often focus on issues of racism, exclusion, and unemployment. The term is sometimes used interchangeably with the term *cinéma beur* (*beur* is a term for the children of North African immigrants in France) because many, although not all, of the directors who have made such films have come from this background. It must be noted there are other differences with what is typically termed *beur cinema*. Examples of banlieue cinema include **Malik Chibane**'s *Hexagone* (1994), **Mathieu Kassovitz**'s *La Haine* (1995), **Karim Dridi**'s *Bye Bye* (1996), and Paul Vecchiali's *Zone franche* (1996).

CINÉMA DE PATRIMOINE. *See* HERITAGE FILM.

CINÉMA DU LOOK. The *cinéma du look* is a term used to describe films that emphasize visual style—or *le look*, as well as image, color, and youth. Critics trace the beginnings of the *cinéma du look* to **Jean-Jacques Beineix**'s 1981 film, *Diva*. Additional examples of films that fall into this category include Beineix's *La lune dans le caniveau* (1983) and *37°2 le matin* (1986), **Luc Besson**'s *Subway* (1981) and *Le Grand Bleu* (1988), and **Leos Carax**'s *Mauvais sang* (1986) and *Les Amants du Pont-Neuf* (1991). One might also consider **Jean-Pierre Jeunet**'s *Le fabuleux destin d'Amélie Poulain* (2001) as part of this trend.

The *look* films of Beineix and Besson were at first derided by intellectual French film critics, especially those at *Cahiers du cinéma*, for their alleged fetishism of the image at the expense of artistic, political, or psychological substance. Beineix and Besson both worked in advertising prior to their directing debuts, and *le look* was mocked as the embracement of consumer culture and advertising over intellectual depth and art. Critics argued that the characters in these films—especially those of Besson's *Subway*—were depicted as objects rather than complex individuals. They also objected to what they perceived as meaningless borrowings from, or recycling of, previous film images. The *look*'s perceived reliance on spectacle, surface, the sensual, and the romantic initially repelled critics who valued character development and social commitment. Carax, who had written for *Cahiers*, escaped the critical establishment's denunciations. He was instead regarded as a director who worked artfully with the cinematic image, and as a cinéaste who used the visual in order to convey social meaning.

Beineix countered that his films, in contrast with what he characterized as outdated, albeit beloved **Nouvelle Vague** or New Wave films so closely associated with *Cahiers*, connected with contemporary film audiences. Indeed, the majority of spectators in the early 1980s were under twenty-five, and both *Diva* and *37°2 le matin* became cult films. Critics point out that Beineix's charge mirrors accusations by former *Cahiers* critics that the *cinéma du papa* was irrelevant for young audiences in the 1950s. The *cinéma du look* does have its champions. Respected scholars maintain that *look* directors engaged in the creation of an innovative cinematic language derived from popular culture and influenced by technological advancements. The *look*'s play of images, seemingly detached from any clear significance, in addition to its mélange of high art with popular culture, has led to associations between the *cinéma du look* and the postmodern. Indeed, one of the foremost theorists of the postmodern, Frederic Jameson, selected *Diva* as France's first postmodern film. Regardless of one's position on the value of the *cinéma du look*—and the earlier critical responses have been challenged and reevaluated—it is difficult to deny that Beineix, Besson, and Carax created landmark films.

CINÉMATHÈQUE FRANÇAISE. This important film archive, located in Paris, was cofounded by **Henri Langlois**, **Georges Franju**, and **Jean Mitry** in the 1930s. The Cinémathèque Française preserved and screened historic French silent films, in addition to more contemporary and international works. It is France's—and one of the world's—most important cinema archives.

CINÉMATOGRAPHE. The *Cinématographe* was the film camera and projector developed by **Louis and Auguste Lumière** in 1895. It is, properly speaking, the first true motion-picture camera and projector, and it is from the name of this device, which literally means "moving writing" that the term *cinema* is derived.

Lumière was not the first to conceive of the projection of moving pictures. In fact, all of the four pioneers of the cinema in France, which included **Charles Pathé**, **Léon Gaumont**, and **Georges Méliès**, were all working on similar technologies at approximately the same time, as were other inventors. Their work, in turn, was based on the work of predecessors who stretch back to the invention of the Magic Lantern, the first widely used projector for moving images, which was developed in the seventeenth century. The Magic Lantern projected still images that were painted onto glass slides. These images were "moved" via mechanisms in the projection apparatus. Such devices were extremely popular and widely available during the course of the nineteenth century.

Toward the end of that century, a number of important predecessors to the *Cinématographe* were produced, such as Edweard Muybridge's Zoopraxiscope, developed in 1879, and **Étienne-Jules Marey**'s *Chronophotographe*, developed in 1888. The Zoopraxiscope, like the Magic Lantern, projected images reproduced onto glass. Instead of slides, however, Muybridge's machine used a series of glass disks that held sequences of individual photographs. These disks were rotated by the Zoopraxiscope during projection, in order to produce the effect of motion. The *Chronophotographe* exploited the use of roll film, developed by George Eastman in 1888. Marey's device was a camera that recorded images on a continuous roll of film and then projected them in an intermittent motion. Practically speaking, the *Chronophotographe* had all the necessary characteristics of a motion picture camera, but the images taken by the camera were spaced at intermittent intervals, which disrupted the effect of continuous motion. This was a problem that Marey was not able to resolve.

Thomas Edison saw Marey's device in 1889, and inspired by it, he went on (with the members of his lab) to develop the Kinetoscope in 1891. The Kinetoscope was also a machine capable of recording and projecting images in such a way as to suggest motion. The Kinetoscope photographed images while a shutter in the camera opened and closed rapidly. The same shutter moved when these images were reprojected and viewed via a peephole viewer in the device. The effect of the shuttered photography and shuttered viewing also created the effect of motion.

The *Cinématographe* was really the first apparatus capable of recording and externally projecting images in such a way as to convey motion. The other important innovation in the Lumière brothers' machine was that it allowed for the recording of an image on a roll of 35mm film, and also resolved the problems of intermittent motion that existed with earlier devices. The other key distinction with the Lumière machine was that it was quickly reproduced and marketed as a result of the family's rather large photography business. This more or less guaranteed its status as the dominant film camera and projector at the time of the development of commercial cinema.

CLAIR, RENÉ (1898–1981). Actor, director, and screenwriter. René Clair was born René-Lucien Chomette in the Halles quartier of Paris. A lively, vibrant neighborhood of the city that housed the main market, this area was also a center of the modern renovation of the city and was decidedly working class in its flavor. Many of these influences from childhood would shape Clair's filmmaking later in life.

Clair was a very bright, studious, scholarly child with a passion for literature. He attended the prestigious lycée Louis-le-Grand, and the school gave him genuine literary ambitions. Clair might have gone on to pursue those ambitions, but World War I intervened. Clair served in an ambulance brigade during the war and saw firsthand many of its horrors, and this too had a profound effect on him.

After the war, Clair went to work as a journalist, but also began dabbling in cinema, initially as an actor. He would later state that cinema recalled to him the puppet shows he loved as a child. It was as an actor that he first used the name René Clair. He worked in films principally for **Gaumont**, mostly those directed by **Louis Feuillade**. Feuillade's filmmaking style, which was highly individualized and recognizable, may have had some influence on Clair, whose own films share some of Feuillade's filmmaking characteristics.

In fact, it was while he was working with Feuillade that Clair decided that acting was not really his forte, and that perhaps his interest in cinema might lie behind the camera. Clair got his start directing films as assistant to director **Jacques de Baroncelli** through a connection made by his brother, director Henri Chomette. At the same time, he began writing film criticism for *Paris-Journal* and other publications.

In 1924, Clair started two projects that launched his solo directing career. Francis Picabia, the famed dadaiste, contacted Clair and asked him to film the dadaiste ballet *Relâche*, which would become the film *Entre'acte* (1924), and at about the same time, Clair was named as director of **Henri Diamant-Berger**'s production of *Paris qui dort* (1924). *Entre'acte* established Clair as a member of the avant-garde, a reputation consolidated with his 1926 film *Le Voyage imaginaire*. These two early films were clearly influenced by avant-garde movements such as Dada and surrealism, and Clair's film criticism also shows (in fact before such movements existed) an interest in the same ideas and theories as these two avant-garde movements. Even Clair's later, neorealist films have a surrealist touch to them. Elements like asynchronous sound, fantastic happenings, and distortions of reality all occur in order to present through this seemingly "unreal" an often bitingly critical, but undeniably accurate vision of the real world. Films such as *Sous les toits de Paris* (1930), *À nous la liberté* (1931), and *Le Million* (1931), for which Clair was awarded the **Prix Louis-Delluc,** are examples.

From 1925 on, Clair made films at a regular pace, working exclusively for Albatros films, and writing the screenplays for every film he directed. His films were enormously popular, and he had a tremendous influence on other filmmakers of the time, including Charlie Chaplin, whose classic *Modern Times* (1936) was said to have been inspired by Clair's *À nous la liberté*. Clair was able to make the transition from silent to sound film without much difficulty, and in fact, his early sound films are considered some of his best. Clair was also a popular filmmaker in a second sense. His films were focused on common people (the influence of the milieu of his childhood, no doubt). This continued the tradition of filmmakers like Feuillade, with whom he had worked, and prepared the way for those like **Marcel Carné** and **Jean Renoir** who would follow. Clair is seen as a central filmmaker in this respect. He carried forward certain trends in early film and served as the bridge that established these trends as cinema evolved. Among these trends are not only a populist focus, a critical dynamic, an avant-garde aesthetics (all of which are present to some measure in Feuillade, although Feuillade's films are much more colored by the spirit of their age than Clair's), but also the strongly individual style and vision in his filmmaking that would come to be the signature of an **auteur** (also evident in Feuillade, if less developed).

After ten years of success, Clair encountered the first real setback in his career. His 1934 film, *Le Dernier milliardaire*, was an absolute failure. Clair, quite taken aback by the film's bad reception, left France for England, where he made two films, *The Ghost Goes West* (1934) and *Break the News* (1938). He then went to Hollywood. By this time, France was under occupation, and Clair would remain in Hollywood until the end of the war. While in Hollywood, Clair made a number of films, most of them rather conventional Hollywood films, with actors like Veronica Lake and Charles Laughton. The best known of these Hollywood films are *Forever and a Day* (1943), an epic historical drama of war and peace, and *And Then There Were None* (1945), a rather faithful adaptation of the eponymous Agatha Christie novel.

After the war, Clair returned to France and resumed making films in French. His first film, *Le Silence est d'or* (1947), was a success, and Clair would see it crowned with his nomination to the *Académie française*. But this would be the only great success of Clair's late career. His style seemed to change upon his elevation to classical status, and his films became too intellectual, too stuffy, or simply unappealing to the popular audiences who had once flocked to see them. Clair would have two other major critical successes. The first was the film *Les Grandes manoeuvres* (1955), which won the Prix Louis-Delluc, and the second was his 1957 film *Porte des Lilas,* which was nominated for an Oscar for Best Foreign Film. His other films were unremarkable. He made his last film, *Fêtes galantes*, in 1965.

CLAVIER, CHRISTIAN (1952–). Actor, producer, and screenwriter. Christian Clavier attended the lycée Pasteur de Neuilly with colleagues who would form the *café-théâtre* group, the Troupe du Splendid, including Michel Blanc, **Gérard Jugnot**, and **Thierry Lhermitte**. They were later joined by **Josiane Balasko**, Dominique Lavanant, Bruno Moynot, and Marie-Anne Chazel, whom Clavier eventually married. The group performed in the comedy and standup on the Parisian theater circuit, and many of them eventually went into film. Clavier made his film debut in Jacques Doillon, **Alain Resnais**, and **Jean Rouche**'s *L'An '01* (1973). He went on to appear in **Bertrand Tavernier**'s *Que la fête commence* (1974), Jacques Besnard's *C'est parce qu'on n'a rien à dire qu'il faut fermer sa guele* (1974), Gérard Pirès's *Attention les yeux* (1975), and Maurice Dugowson's *F. comme Fairbanks* (1976).

Clavier landed his first major role alongside Lhermitte in Pierre Lary's *Le Diable dans la boîte* (1977). He also acted in *Vous n'aurez pas L'Alsace et Lorraine* (1977), a film directed by one of France's best-known comedians, **Coluche**. He played significant roles in **Patrice Leconte**'s popular comedies *Les Bronzés* (1978) and *Les Bronzés font du ski* (1979). Leconte, Clavier, and members of the Splendid Troupe cowrote the scripts for these films. He followed these performances with leading roles in François Leterrier's *Je vais craquer* (1980) and *Les Babas cool* (1981). He also cowrote and starred in the play and film adaptation of Jean-Marie Poiré's *Le Père Noël est une ordure* (1982). Clavier would work with Poiré as a writer and actor on several films, among them *Papy fait de la résistance* (1983), *Twist again à Moscou* (1986), *Mes meilleurs copains* (1988), and *Opération corned-beef* (1991), where he starred with Jean Reno, an actor with whom he worked frequently. He was also paired with **Gérard Depardieu** in Poiré's *Les Anges gardiens* (1995).

With Poiré, Clavier cowrote the hugely popular film *Les Visiteurs* (1993), for which he received **César** nominations for Best Screenplay and Best Actor. He also cowrote and starred in its sequel, *Les Couloirs du temps, les visiteurs 2* (1998). He subsequently starred in the less successful American version of *Les Visiteurs*, Jean-Marie Gaubert's *Just Visiting* (2000). He also worked with director Gérard Oury in *La Soif de l'or* (1993) and played Astérix, the most famous and beloved of all French cartoon characters, in **Claude Zidi**'s *Astérix et Obélix contre César* (1999), and in Alain Chabat's *Astérix et Obélix: mission Cléopâtre* (2002). He played leading roles in his brother Stéphane Clavier's *Lovely Rita Sainte Patronne des cas désespérés* (2003), as well as in Hervé Palud's *Albert est méchant* (2004), Alain Berberien's *L'Enquête corse* (2004), Vincent de Brus's *L'Antidote* (2005), and Leconte's *Les Bronzés 3: amis pour la vie* (2005). An actor best known for his comic performances, Clavier has, at times, been compared to the late **Louis de Funès**.

CLÉMENT, RENÉ (1913–1996). Director and screenwriter. René Clément did not initially plan to pursue film as a career, and instead, began studies in architecture when he finished lycée. Clément began experimenting with film while he was a student. He is known to have made one animated film on his own, although this film is lost. Just before World War II, he began making short films, most of them documentary. Some of these films survive in the form of the documentary *L'Arabie interdite* (1938), made in collaboration with ethnographer Jules Barthou. These documentaries are about life and water in what is now Yemen. Another surviving documentary short is *La Bièvre, fille perdue* (1939). He also made one known propaganda film for the Vichy government titled *Les Chefs de demain* (1943).

In 1944, Clément received his first major film project. In a reversal of his wartime filmmaking project, he was charged by the French Film Cooperative with directing a film about the participation of French rail workers in the wartime Resistance against the Nazis. That film project, which would become *La Bataille du rail* (1946), won Clément international acclaim and established him as a talented director of great renown. The film also won the Grand-Prix at the **Festival International de Cannes**.

The early part of Clément's career followed down the path of success established by *La Bataille du rail*. His next film, *Le Père tranquil* (1946), was also a Resistance-focused piece, although not of the depth of its precursor. In 1947, Clément was invited by **Jean Cocteau** to work on his film *La Belle et la bête* (1947), largely because Cocteau had been impressed by Clément's directorial work on *La Bataille du rail*. Clément's next two films, *Au-délà des grilles* (1949) and *Le Château de verre* (1950), were both reasonably successful, both love stories, in a sense, very different from Clément's previous work and different from one another. In *Au-délà des grilles*, Clément began a relationship with screenwriters Pierre Bost and Jean

Aurenche that would serve all three well. The film also won the Oscar for Best Foreign Film.

In 1952, Clément returned to the issue of war in a film that many consider his masterpiece, *Jeux interdits*, a film about two children whose innocence cultivated in a pastoral paradise is completely shattered by war. *Jeux interdits* is regarded as a classic film, a visual poem on the horrors of war that never for a moment valorizes war by giving it space on the screen. The film makes the spectator feel the war only through the shadow of its presence and through its aftermath. *Jeux interdits* was an enormous international and critical success, and it won Clément the Palme d'Or at Cannes, a prize at the Venice Film Festival, and the Oscar for Best Foreign Film.

Jeux interdits was followed by two literary adaptations, *Gervaise* (1956), adapted from Émile Zola's classic novel *L'Assomoir*, and *Barrage contre le pacifique* (1958), from the novel by **Marguerite Duras**. Both were also stylistically, thematically, and technically brilliant films, but both are quite different from one another, the first an exploration of social decay in the fin-de-siècle, the second an exploration of women's subjectivity in the colonies.

Clément's next film would be more different still. Adapted from a Patricia Highsmith novel, *Plein soleil* (1960) is a psychological thriller that explores the eerie depths of sociopathic behavior. Brilliantly detached in its realization, the film places the mesmerizingly chilling Ripley (played by **Alain Delon**) at its center, and leaves the spectator without any moral framework through which to interpret either his character or the substance of the narrative itself. It is, like the four preceding films, a brilliant piece of cinema, but it is, as with the others, absolutely unique. And therein lay the problem for Clément.

In an industry shaped to expect **auteurs** at precisely the moment when the ***Nouvelle Vague*** or New Wave intensified the expectation that filmmakers should have strongly recognizable characteristics to their films, Clément insisted, over and over, on making films that were not only different from everyone else's, but different even from his own. The result was that Clément was never an auteur in the classic sense of the word—he had no predictable or recognizable style or technique that anyone could associate with him. As a result, neither critics nor audiences knew quite what to make of him, and as in all such cases, this began to invite suspicion and, ultimately, scorn. Because his style could not be defined, many, including the New Wave filmmakers, questioned his talent. This may have affected the reception of his later films.

Clément would go on to make seven films after *Plein soleil*: *Quelle joie de vivre* (1961), *Les Félins* (1964), *Paris brûle-t-il?* (1966), *Le Passager de la pluie* (1969), *The Deadly Trap* (1971), *La Course du lièvre à travers le champ* (1972), and *Jeune fille libre le soir* (1976). Of these, the most spectacular in terms of budget and scope was *Paris brûle-t-il?*, another occupation-era film commissioned and funded by the French government with a script written by Gore Vidal and Francis Ford Coppola and an all-star cast. However, this film, like the six others, was widely criticized, and it, perhaps more than the others, left a permanent mark on Clément's reputation just as he neared the end of his career. It is this taint that has remained, and he and his earlier acclaimed films have been all but forgotten.

CLOUZOT, HENRI-GEORGES (1907–1977). Director and screenwriter. Henri-Georges Léon Clouzot got his first taste of film, no doubt, from his father's passion for photography. Clouzot's father, who owned a bookshop, also introduced him to literature and, most important, the theater by sending him to Paris at the age of fifteen specifically to see plays. Clouzot got his start in cinema assisting first the German producer Adolphe Osso. He also began writing screenplays, and so, during the early 1930s, his connections to Osso and his screenwriting talents enabled him to work with directors such as **Jacques de Baroncelli** on *Le Dernier choc* (1932) and **Georges Lacombe** on *Le Dernier des six* (1941). Clouzot also did a number of French adaptations of German works with directors such as Pierre Billon on *Faut-il les marier?* (1931) and Anatole Litvak on *La Chanson d'une nuit* (1932).

Clouzot's first directorial project came in 1933 when he assisted Joe May on *Tout pour l'amour*. His first feature-length film as a solo director came quite late in his career, when he directed *L'Assassin habite au 21* (1942) for the Nazi-owned production company, **Continental Films**. There would be only ten more films that followed. And yet, for a director with a relatively short body of work, Clouzot remains one of the most influential directors in French film history, a director, somewhat like **Robert Bresson**, whose impact and significance cannot be measured in a mere number of films.

Clouzot's second film, *Le Corbeau* (1943), is perhaps his masterpiece. An Occupation-era film made during censorship, the film explores a climate of suspicion and denunciation in a small village, and reflects quite accurately although obliquely on the political climate during which it was made. The film was regarded as scandalous at the time it was made. The source of scandal was as much political allegory as it was the film's subject matter of abortion and the underlying issue of female sexuality. The film more or less assured that Clouzot did direct again until after the Liberation.

Clouzot's third film, *Quai des orfèvres* (1947), shares with *Le Corbeau* a critical gaze at the hypocrisy of society, particularly bourgeois society, and the thriller-type plot. The film is the story of music-hall singer Jenny Lamour (played by **Suzy Delair**) and her jealous husband. The film is also widely considered a classic and rivals *Le Corbeau* in critical appraisals of Clouzot's work.

Manon (1949), Clouzot's third film, cemented his reputation as a formidable filmmaker and established definitively the style that would come to be seen as his. *Manon* is an adaptation of the classic Abbé Prévost novel *Manon Lescaut*, but which adapts the story to a post-Occupation setting, and which, like *Le Corbeau*, visits the thorny issue of collaboration and resistance during the occupation. The decision to adapt *Manon* to the screen says a good deal, in fact, about Clouzot's filmmaking in general. Manon is, like Denise in *Le Corbeau*, an extremely problematic heroine whose own moral and ethical status is extremely questionable. And yet in Clouzot's films, we are asked to consider less how we should judge such characters than how we should judge them with respect to the society in which they live, a society that is always more deeply flawed than the very flawed characters through whom we see it.

Moreover, what has elevated Clouzot's films to classic status, apart from the technical superiority of his films and the smooth, even flow of the narrative, is the pointed neutrality of the camera. His very neutral and distant filmic gaze shares much with **Robert Bresson**, though it is less stoic, and with **René Clément** when he was at his best. It is not a moralizing gaze, but one which looks very clearly and very coldly on the world as it finds it and asks the spectator to draw his or her own conclusions.

Clouzot's fourth film, *Miquette et sa mère* (1950), starring Danièle Délorme, returned to the world of the theater. Unusual for

Clouzot, the film is a comedy, and not typically considered the best example of his work, although it is a particularly beloved film in France. Following the experimentation in *Miquette et sa mère*, Clouzot returned to form with *Le Salaire de la peur* (1953) starring **Yves Montand**. The film is the story of four mercenary-type adventurers on a dangerous mission in Latin America and marks a return to the suspenseful realism verging on naturalism that characterizes much of Clouzot's work. One unusual aspect of this film, however, is its focus on male characters, and one might say on certain characteristics of masculinity. Many of Clouzot's films, particularly those considered his best, focused on female characters.

A case in point was Clouzot's next film, the legendary *Les Diaboliques* (1955), which has been remade by Hollywood in recent years. Starring the legendary **Simone Signoret**, *Les Diaboliques* is the story of a wife and mistress who together plot the murder of their tyrannical lover and husband. The husband, however, manages to disappear after being killed, and to reappear at hauntingly inopportune moments, raising the question of whether the tyrant is really dead. Like all of Clouzot's best films, the substance of this one is in the exploration of the moral universe of the society in which the entire story unfolds.

Following *Les Diaboliques*, Clouzot made four more feature films, *Les Espions* (1957), *La Vérité* (1960), *L'Enfer* (1964), and *La Prisonnière* (1968). *Les Espions* is the story of a director of a psychiatric clinic who agrees to give cover to a spy. *La Vérité*, which stars **Brigitte Bardot**, is the story of a **woman** with a questionable history who is on trial for the murder of a famous musician. *L'Enfer*, starring **Serge Reggiani**, is the story of a man who is obsessed with the fear of his wife's infidelity. *La Prisonnière* is the story of an attraction between a gallery owner's wife and a troubled and troubling artist. *L'Enfer* was remade by **Claude Chabrol** in 1998. All four films are solid Clouzot films, suspense-filled, deeply psychological, and socially critical. None, however, reaches the level of his earlier works.

Like Bresson, Clouzot did not leave a vast catalog of films behind, and probably for the same reasons. He was known, like Bresson, to be a perfectionist, and he was known for wanting total control over his films. Unlike Bresson, Clouzot achieved a measure of commercial success during his lifetime, and this afforded him many opportunities to make films, most notably in Hollywood, which he declined.

His desire to make films that were true to his own vision superseded the desire to make a large number of films, and that is the way he will be remembered.

COCTEAU, JEAN (1889–1963). Director and screenwriter. Jean Cocteau was born in Paris to a family from the wealthy Parisian bourgeoisie. Cocteau's father, a lawyer, was an important force in the young Cocteau's life, and he was deeply affected when his father committed suicide. Cocteau was only nine at the time. Cocteau undertook secondary studies, but abandoned them when he left home at the age of fifteen. He quickly took to literature, publishing his first volume of poetry at the age of only nineteen. His early success, and perhaps his family background, gave Cocteau access to the world of the Parisian literati, and Cocteau, even in his early twenties, found himself in the company of such literary greats as Marcel Proust and André Gide. He kept company with Picasso, with Apollinaire, with the Russian dancer Sergei Diaghilev, who inducted Cocteau formally into the avant-garde, by challenging him to write a ballet. Cocteau did so, and *Parade*, a thoroughly modern ballet, was produced, with the aid of Pablo Picasso, in 1917.

Cocteau was mobilized by the military to serve in World War I. He drove an ambulance during his military service, and in that context, he met the novelist Raymond Radiguet. The two shared an intense personal connection, and Cocteau helped launch Radiguet in his literary career. Possibly as a result of his connection to Radiguet, who died from typhoid in 1923, Cocteau began to experiment with the novel, and he would go on to publish a number of them, most notably *Les Enfants terribles* (1929). In the 1930s, Cocteau also began dabbling in the theater and the cinema. He made his first film, *Le Sang d'un poète*, in 1931, and also collaborated with **Marcel Carné** and **Robert Bresson**.

It was the 1940s, however, before Cocteau undertook filmmaking in earnest. He wrote the screenplay for **Marcel L'Herbier**'s *La Comédie du bonheur* (1942) as well as for **Jean Delannoy**'s classic film *L'Eternel retour* (1943). He then thrust himself into making a series of his own films. *La Belle et la bête* (1947), Cocteau's avant-garde vision of the Madame Le Prince de Beaumont fairytale, is considered a classic film and is perhaps the best film he made. It remains

a stunning cinematic work to this day, and was, for its day, a technically advanced piece of filmmaking, particularly with respect to special effects. This film was followed by *Les Parents terribles* (1948),
starring **Jean Marais** as a twenty-something who is tied to his parents. This in turn was followed by *L'Aigle a deux têtes* (1948), the
story of an impossible love between an anarchist and a queen, played
by Marais and **Edwige Feuillière**, respectively. Cocteau's next film,
Orphée (1949), also starred Marais, and is a retelling of the classic
Greek legend of Orpheus and Eurydice. The film is widely considered one of Cocteau's best works in any genre, and it is a masterpiece
of cinema. Cocteau's last film was *Le Testament d'Orphée* (1960), a
proto-mythical meditation on the role of the poet.

In general, Cocteau's films are meticulously crafted, stunningly
beautiful (even in black and white), lyrical modernizations of classic
stories. There is a timelessness that is conveyed both internally to the
narratives and in the films themselves. Cocteau experimented with
form, with special effects, with film technique, and in this respect
was avant-garde in his filmmaking, but there is, as noted, an underlying classicism of theme and of form that is almost heightened by
such experimentation.

In addition to the films he directed, Cocteau's contribution to cinema includes those films made from his screenplays or based on his
literary works. These include Pierre Billon's *Ruy Blas* (1948), for
which Cocteau wrote a screenplay adapted from the Victor Hugo
novel; **Jean-Pierre Melville**'s adaptation of Cocteau's *Les Enfants
terribles* (1950), for which Cocteau wrote the screenplay; Delannoy's
La Princesse de Clèves (1960), for which Cocteau wrote the screenplay, based on the novel by Madame de Lafayette; and **Georges
Franju**'s adaptation of Cocteau's *Thomas l'imposteur* (1964).

Quite apart from his films, Cocteau remains a literary and avant-
garde figure of some importance. Picasso, not known for his mod-
esty, once referred to Cocteau as "the tail of my comet." Considering
the comet to be esteemed worthy of consideration as part of the same
artistic universe is already an accomplishment. Cocteau, apparently,
was an integral part of that universe.

COHL, ÉMILE (1857–1938). Animator, director, and screenwriter.
Émile Cohl was born Émile Courtet in Paris to an old, well-estab-

lished, but not wealthy Parisian family. Unlike many of the pioneers of the cinema, Cohl did not have much interest in either film or photography. He was far more interested in drawing, and sought to make a career of that. In 1878, he obtained an apprenticeship with André Gill, a leading political cartoonist of the day. Under Gill's guidance, Cohl himself became an established cartoonist, and he developed ties to Parisian intellectual groups, notably "*les incohérents*."

In 1907, Cohl turned his attention to the cinema. Legend has it that it was rather by accident that he found the film industry, although the truth of the matter remains unclear. The story is that Cohl went to **Gaumont** in 1907 not to ask for a job, but to threaten to file suit against the company for allegedly stealing one of his cartoon images and using it in a poster. **Léon Gaumont** supposedly diffused the situation by offering Cohl work at the studio, namely writing screenplays. Whether or not this is how things occurred, Cohl did go to work for Gaumont, at first writing for the studio, and eventually experimenting with film animation. In 1907, he produced his first film, *Un drame chez les fantôches*. The film was not fully animated, but its central character, Fantôche, was completely animated. Fantôche was quite a success with audiences, and he appeared in sequels as late as 1921.

As a result of the success of his first experiment in animation, Cohl was permitted the following year to make *La Vie à rebours* (1908) and *Le Journal animé* (1908), both of which he codirected with **Louis Feuillade**. 1908 was also the year in which Cohl produced *Fantasmagorie*, the first fully animated feature film, considered one of the masterpieces of animated cinema and of early cinema as a whole. *Fantasmagorie*, similar to Cohl's earlier films, did not use color animation (although this was a possibility, since all color in film at the time was hand drawn). Rather, the animation was done in a white-on-black style, reminiscent of a film negative. Cohl's films also broke with the realist vein emerging in live action at the time, as his films were much more stylized and fantastic, in some ways anticipating the surrealist movement of later decades.

Cohl went on to make several other films with Feuillade, including *Le Docteur Carnaval* (1909) and *Les Couronnes* (1910). Additionally, Cohl had some other noteworthy collaborations with other Gaumont directors. These included *La Course aux potirons* (1908), codirected with **Etienne Arnaud**, and *Le Rêve du cheval de fiacre* (1909), codirected with **Roméo Bosetti**. He also continued to write screenplays during his time at Gaumont, as well as to direct animated sequences in live-action films. Some notable examples include *Joyeux microbes* (1909) and *Le Peintre néo impressioniste* (1910), both also directed by Cohl. He also pioneered, during his time at Gaumont, puppetry on film. Notable use of puppets as "actors" may be found in *Les Allumettes animées* (1908) and *Le Tout petit Faust* (1910).

Cohl left Gaumont in 1910. He went, for a very brief time, to **Pathé**, where he made only two animated films. After being forced to make live-action films for the studio, Cohl again left and went to work for Éclipse Studios. While at Pathé, however, he made some important technical advances in animation. The films Cohl made at Éclipse have been lost, so it is not known exactly how long he was there or how many films he may have made. However, it is known that during the time he was working for Éclipse, he also began working for **Éclair**, and ultimately Éclair sent him to New Jersey to work.

While at Éclair, Cohl worked most notably on an animated series titled the *Newlyweds*, which began running in 1913. He also made *Les Allumettes ensorcelées*. His other films have been lost. It is believed that while he was in France, others may have learned of Cohl's animating techniques and patented them, thereby wrongly taking credit for the development of film animation.

Cohl remained in the United States and directed films there until 1914, at which point he returned to France. From about 1916 to 1918, he worked independently with another illustrator, Benjamin Rabier, to produce an animated series titled *Les Dessins animés de Benjamin Rabier*. He also produced independently an animated series titled *Les Aventures des Pieds Nickelés*. There were four series of these produced, all released between 1917 and 1918. He also managed to produce one more *Fantôche* film independently in 1921, but the film was largely ignored.

Cohl was financially devastated and alone (his wife, Suzanne, had died in 1930), when, in 1937, he was severely burned by a gas lamp while drawing in his home. He was using a gas lamp because he could not afford to pay the electric bill. He died penniless in a charity hospital, all but forgotten. Before Cohl's death, Georges Dureau, the editor of the *Ciné-Journal*, had attempted to draw attention to Cohl's rightful place in film history, citing him as the father of modern animation. Since then, several of Cohl's films have been rediscovered, and today, Dureau's claim is difficult to challenge.

COLUCHE (1944–1986). Actor, director, and screenwriter. Born Michel Colucci, Coluche was an acclaimed stand-up comedian and beloved actor. He performed live in the nightclub Café de la Gare with Romain Bouteille, **Miou Miou**, and **Patrick Dewaere**, and created his own theater troupe, *Au vrai chic parisien*. He also worked alongside celebrities such as **Josiane Balasko** and **Thierry Lhermitte** in the Splendid Troupe.

In the 1970s, his stand-up performances drew large crowds. His film acting career began with **Claude Berri**'s *Le pistonné* (1970). He often collaborated with the famous comedy director **Claude Zidi**, playing leading roles in the popular *L'Aile ou la cuisse* (1976), *Inspecteur la bavure* (1980), and *Banzai* (1983). He played smaller roles in Zidi's *Le Grand Bazar* (1973) and *Les Rois du gag* (1985). Coluche's fame only increased when he ran for president of France in 1980.

Though he is popularly remembered for his comic roles, Coluche was a talented actor in more serious films. He won a **César** for Best Actor for his performance in Berri's drama *Tchao Pantin* in 1984. He also starred in Berri's comedies *Le Maître d'école* (1981) and *La femme de mon pote* (1983). Throughout the 1970s and 1980s, he acted in many of France's most commercially successful films. He also directed one film in which he starred, *Vous n'aurez pas l'Alsace et la Lorraine*, in 1977. He played notable roles in **Patrice Leconte**'s *Les vécés étaient fermés de l'intérieur* (1975), **Jean Yanne**'s *Deux heures moins le quart avant Jésus Christ* (1982), Italian director Dino Risi's *Le Bon roi Dagobert* (1984) and *Scemo di guerra* (1985), and Gérard Oury's *La Vengeance du serpent à plumes* (1984).

Coluche was the longtime companion of the actress **Miou-Miou**. He is almost as beloved in France for his charity work as for his comedy and film work, particularly on behalf of the homeless and hungry. He founded the charity Les Restos du Coeur. He died unexpectedly in a motorcycle accident, but has remained a cultural icon since his death.

CONTINENTAL FILMS. Continental Films was a German, Nazi-owned film production company founded in 1940. Its specific mission was to produce films for French audiences. Theoretically, the company was supposed to produce films friendly to the occupying power, and it operated under the censorship of the occupying forces, although many critics argue that at least some of the filmmakers whose films were produced by Contintental found ways to thwart that censorship. Disbanded in 1944 at the end of the Occupation, the company produced thirty films during the four years it was in existence. Many of these films are today regarded as classics, and the philosophical position they occupy with respect to the German Occupation is, in many cases, quite ambiguous and interesting. Films such as **Christian-Jacque**'s *L'Assassinat du père Noël* (1941), **Henri Decoin**'s *Premier rendez-vous* (1941), **Georges Lacombe**'s *Le Dernier des six* (1941), and **Henri-Georges Clouzot**'s *Le Corbeau* (1943) were produced by Continental.

COSTA-GAVRAS, CONSTANTIN (1933–). Actor, director, producer, and screenwriter. Born in Greece as Konstantinos Gavra, Constantin Costa-Gavras, who is also known simply as Costa-Gavras, studied at the Sorbonne and then at the **Institut des Hautes Études Cinématographiques** (IDHEC) in the 1950s. He became a French citizen in 1968. He assisted **René Clair**, **René Clément**, **Jacques Demy**, and **Henri Verneuil** before venturing out on his own. His first film was a short, *Les rates* (1958), and it was followed by two thrillers, *Compartiment tueurs* (1965) and *Un homme de trop* (1967). One of his most notable works is *Z* (1969), an adaptation of the novel by Vassilis Vassilikos based on the assassination of the Greek politician Gregorios Lambrakis in 1963. *Z* won the Jury Prize at **Cannes** and an Oscar for Best Foreign Film in 1969. It has been considered one of the classics of the political thriller genre. Costa-Gavras's frequent casting of actor **Yves Montand** in starring roles rendered Montand an emblem of the political thriller.

Z was followed by several other political thrillers, including *L'aveu* (1970), *État de siège* (1972), which won the **Prix Louis-Delluc**, and *Section spéciale* (1975). Costa-Gavras's 1970s films are important contributions to what critics call "militant cinema." Indeed, several of his films can be viewed as attempts to inspire political action. He was awarded a Golden Palm at Cannes for *Missing* (1982), an Anglophone feature that called attention to human rights abuses in Argentina. He won the Golden Berlin Bear for *Music Box* in 1990, and a César for Best Adapted Screenplay for *Amen* (2003), a film that critiques the negligence of the Vatican during the Nazi Occupation. This film starred actor and director **Mathieu Kassovitz**.

CRESTÉ, RENÉ (1881–1922). Actor. René Cresté was a silent-film actor best known for his portrayal of Judex, the crime fighting hero of **Louis Feuillade**'s eponymous series. Cresté got his acting start in 1908 but did not appear in anything significant until 1912, when **Léonce Perret** cast him in three of his films, *L'Amour et la lumière*, *La Bonne hôtesse*, and *Le Mariage de Suzie*. Perret went on to cast Cresté in numerous other films, including *Le Roi de la montagne* (1915), *Les Mystères de l'ombre* (1915), *Le Retour du passé* (1916), and *Dernier amour* (1916).

In 1916, Cresté was cast by Feuillade as the title character in *Judex*. The series made him a film legend. Feuillade cast Cresté again in 1918, in his *Tih-Minh* series, but his performance here could never rival his incarnation of Feuillade's legendary crime fighter. Cresté would forever remain Judex to the film public, a reality cemented by his reprisal of the role in the second series made by Feuillade in 1918. Cresté played in other Feuillade films, including *Vendémiare* (1918). But his untimely death from tuberculosis never afforded him the opportunity to create another legend onscreen.

– D –

DALIO, MARCEL (1900–1983). Actor. Marcel Dalio was born Israël Blauschild in Paris. He aspired to be an actor from early on, and began training at the Paris Conservatoire d'art dramatique before being mobilized for military service in 1916. Dalio returned from the war in 1919 but did not resume his studies, preferring instead to try his hand at acting. He got his start in theater and in live revues, working full-time by the 1920s. It was in the theater that he met screenwriters Marcel Achard and Henri Jeanson, and it was perhaps the influence of one, the other, or both that got Dalio his start in cinema.

Dalio's first film role was in *Une nuit à l'hôtel* (1931). He later appeared in **Marc Allégret**'s *Les Quatre jambes* (1932), **Robert Bresson**'s *Les Affaires publiques* (1934), and **Serge de Poligny**'s *Retour au paradis* (1935). From the early 1930s on, he was a fairly constant presence in films made by the leading directors of the day, particularly historical dramas. He appeared in **Julien Duvivier**'s *Le Golem* (1935), **Abel Gance**'s *Le Grand Amour de Beethoven* (1936), and **Christian-Jacque**'s *Les Perles de la couronne* (1937). He went on to appear in Duvivier's *Pépé le Moko* (1937) and was in **Jean Renoir**'s *La Grande Illusion* (1937). In both films, Dalio worked alongside **Jean Gabin**. These are two of Dalio's best-remembered roles.

Dalio went on to work with another director associated with *Le Réalisme poétique* or poetic realism, appearing in **Pierre Chenal**'s 1938 film *La Maison du maltais*. He also worked again with Renoir in *La Règle du jeu* (1939), again costarring with Gabin. He also gave memorable performances in films such as **Roger Richebé**'s *La Tradition de minuit* (1939), Robert Bibal and **Léon Mathot**'s *Le Bois sacré* (1939), and Dominique Bernard-Deschamps's *Tempête* (1939). The fact that Dalio was never a star on the order of someone like Gabin says far more about France in the 1920s and 1930s than it does about Dalio as an actor. As he himself once remarked, with his olive skin and dark curly hair, in the society in which he worked, he found himself limited to certain types of roles, those of the Arab or the Jew. Only Renoir, in *La Règle du jeu*, would break from the stereotype, casting Dalio as an aristocrat. There is near universal agreement that it was an inspired decision, and the performance is one of Dalio's best.

Dalio spent the war in Hollywood. He managed to find roles in films like *Casablanca* (1942) and *To Have and Have Not* (1944). He also gave a memorable performance as Georges Clemenceau in Henry King's lauded but disastrous biopic, *Wilson* (1944). Dalio also worked with King on films such as *The Snows of Kilimanjaro* (1952) and *The Sun Also Rises* (1957). Upon returning to France after the war, he found that his entire family had been deported to concentration camps and killed. Not a single member survived. He continued to work in American films in the 1950s and 1960s, appearing in *Gentlemen Prefer Blondes* (1953), *Sabrina* (1954), *The Man who Understood Women* (1959), *Pillow Talk* (1959), *Can-Can* (1960), and *How to Steal a Million* (1966), among others.

In France, he appeared in films such as **Marc Allégret**'s *Petrus* (1946), opposite **Fernandel** and Simone Simon; in André Cayatte's *Les Amants de Vérone* (1946), with **Pierre Brasseur**; in **René Clément**'s *Les Maudits* (1947); and in Bernard-Roland's *Portrait d'un assassin* (1949), opposite Erich Von Stroheim, Maria Montez, and **Arletty**. In the 1950s and 1960s, he appeared in **Henri Decoin**'s *Razzia sur la Chnouf* (1955), **Claude Sautet**'s *Classe tous risques* (1960), **Philippe de Broca**'s *Cartouche* (1962), and **Henri Verneuil**'s *La Vingt-cinquième heure* (1967).

The 1970s saw something of a renaissance in Dalio's career. He appeared in Joël Santoni's *Les Yeux fermés* (1973) as well as in Gérard Oury's *Les Aventures de Rabbi Jacob* (1973). He also appeared in Walerian Borowcyzk's controversial film, *La Bête* (1975) and in René Féret's *La Communion solonelle* (1977). The 1970s also saw him in a number of made-for-television pieces, including the acclaimed and very popular miniseries, *La Famille Cigale* (1977). It also marked his return to the stage. Dalio continued working in all three mediums, television, cinema, and theater, almost right up to his death.

DAQUIN, LOUIS (1908–1980). Director. A director of instruction at the **Institut des Hautes Études Cinématographiques** (IDHEC) near the end of his career, Louis Daquin began as a filmmaker. He worked with **Pierre Chenal** on *La Rue sans nom* (1933), *Les Mutinés de l'Elseneur* (1936), and *L'Homme de nulle part* (1937) and with **Jean Grémillon** on *Guele d'amour* (1936) and *Remorques* (1940) before venturing out on his own as a director on the eve of the Occupation. His first films, *Le Joueur* (1938), in collaboration with Gerhard Lamprecht, and *Nous les gosses* (1941), were made before the Occupation. His subsequent films, such as *Le Voyageur de la Toussaint* (1943), *Madame et le mort* (1943), and *Premier de cordée* (1944), would be made under the Occupation and are interesting as a result of their own internal tensions. Daquin was a member of the Communist Party and was influenced by leftist filmmaking tendencies. He was, however, forced to make films under the strict control of a fascist regime, and these conflicting ideologies find interesting mixes in his films.

Daquin's gradual transition to public service and away from filmmaking began after the war as he was elected as head of the Liberation committee on film. Nonetheless, he continued to make films into the 1960s, predominantly literary adaptations, including *Patrie* (1946), based on a play by Victorien Sardou, *Bel Ami* (1955), based on the novel by Maupassant, and *Les Arrivistes* (1959), based on Honoré de Balzac's *La Rabouilleuse*. Daquin ceased making films in the 1960s, focusing on his duties at IDHEC. He also authored several books on the cinema.

DARRIEUX, DANIELLE (1917–). Actress. One of the major actresses of French cinema, Danielle Darrieux was born in Bordeaux but was raised in Paris. She had not intended, it seems, to become an actress, but was instead studying the cello at the Conservatoire de musique, when in 1931 she was cast as Antoinette in Willhelm Thiel's French remake of his German film *Le Bal* (1931). There are different versions of how this came about. Some sources say Darrieux's mother arranged the audition, others that Theil discovered Darrieux at the conservatoire. However it happened, the film launched Darrieux's career, and she would go on to work in both cinema and theater.

Darrieux has had a very long and fairly continuous career in cinema lasting from *Le Bal* up to the present. Immediately following *Le Bal*, she found herself cast in similar juvenile roles in fairly sentimental films, such André Berthomieu's *Coquecigrole* (1931) and Michel Bernheim's *Panurge* (1932), but by 1936 that would change. Her role in Anatole Litvak's *Mayerling* would make her a genuine star.

After *Mayerling*, Darrieux was offered a wider variety of roles. The same year she appeared in **Marcel Carné**'s *Jenny* (1936) and Alexis Granowsky's *Tarass Boulba* (1936). There followed a number of other excellent films including **Henri Decoin**'s *Mademoiselle ma mere* (1937) and Maurice Tourneur's historical film *Katia* (1938). Darrieux's work with Decoin launched not only several years of collaboration between the two, but also a romance, and Darrieux and Decoin married the same year. During their marriage, Decoin typically cast Darrieux in melodramas, and these are regarded as some of her best performances. Decoin/Darrieux collaborations include *Abus de confiance* (1938) and *Retour à l'aube* (1938).

In 1938, Darrieux also crossed the Atlantic to film in Hollywood, where *Mayerling* had also made her a star. She made one film in Hollywood, *Rage of Paris* (1938), and then quickly returned to France and remained there during the war and occupation, continuing to make films. She, like **Arletty** and other actors and filmmakers who remained, would later suffer criticism for what was seen as their collaboration with the Nazi authorities. In Darrieux's case, the criticism stemmed not from her personal relationships, as with Arletty, but from her willingness to work for the Nazi-owned production company, **Continental Films**. During this period, Darrieux appeared in such films as Decoin's *Premier rendez-vous* (1941), a comedy, **Léo Joannen**'s *Caprices* (1942), André Cayatte's *La Fausse maîtresse* (1942), and **Marcel L'Herbier**'s *Au petit bonheur* (1945). Darrieux and Decoin parted ways during the Occupation, divorcing. They would not work together again for a number of years.

After Liberation, Darrieux did not have the difficulty some of her contemporaries faced in resuming her career. She would also periodically return to Hollywood to film. Some of her best and best-known roles, in fact, are from the postwar period. In 1948, she appeared as the queen opposite **Jean Marais** in Pierre Billon's adaptation of Victor Hugo's *Ruy Blas*. The film remains a classic and the performance is regarded as one of Darrieux's best. She also appeared in two landmark **Max Ophüls** films, *La Ronde* (1950) and *Madame de . . .* (1953).

This period would find Darrieux doing more comedy in films. Noteworthy examples are **Claude Autant-Lara**'s *Occupe-toi d'Amélie* (1949) and Carlo Rim's *Escalier de service* (1954). She did mystery films, such as Joseph L. Mankiewicz's *5 Fingers* (1952) and **Julien Duvivier**'s *Marie-Octobre* (1959), and also literary adaptations, such as Autant-Lara's *Le Rouge et le noir* (1954) and Duvivier's *Pot-Bouille* (1957). She also worked again with Decoin on two fairly dark films, *La Vérité sur Bébé Dongé* (1952) and the historical film *L'Affaire des poisons* (1955). Darrieux, who has a very good singing voice, also produced a number of records during this period, and even made one musical, *Rich, Young, and Pretty* (1951).

Just as she had little difficulty in continuing her career after the war, the transformations in film caused by the filmmakers of the **Nouvelle Vague** or New Wave did little to put an end to Darrieux's filmmaking career. Although she concentrated her efforts more on her stage career in the 1960s and 1970s, even replacing Katharine Hepburn on Broadway in the stage production *Coco*, Darrieux acted

in film. She appeared in such films as Autant-Lara's *Vive Henri IV
. . . vive l'amour* (1961), Duvivier's *Le Diable et les dix commandements* (1962), **Claude Chabrol**'s *Landru* (1962), and **Jacques Demy**
and **Agnès Varda**'s *Les Desmoiselles de Rochefort* (1967).

Although she has slowed to one film every year or so since the
1970s, Darrieux has produced a fairly constant body of work even
over the past thirty years. Dominique Delouche featured her in *Divine* (1975). She also appeared in **Philipe de Broca**'s *Le Cavaleur*
(1979), **André Téchiné**'s *Le Lieu du crime* (1986), and **Benoît
Jacquot**'s *Corps et biens* (1986). She has quite recently appeared in
several films, including Jeanne Labrune's *Ça ira mieux demain*
(2000) and Thierry Klifa's *Une vie à t'attendre* (2004), and she gave
a fabulous performance in François Ozon's acclaimed *8 femmes*
(2002). After more than seventy yearson screen and onstage, Danielle
Darrieux has demonstrated a talent and a star power that few actors
or actresses have ever had.

DARY, RENÉ (1905–1974). Actor. Born Anatole Mary Dary, René
Dary was probably the first child star of the cinema. He made his film
debut in 1908 at the age of three as Bébé Abelard in **Gaumont**'s *Bébé*
silent films series. Directed in many of the films by the legendary
Louis Feuillade and starring with **Renée Carl**, herself a veritable
star at the time, Dary's early beginnings were illustrious. Dary would
appear in more than fifty films from 1910 to 1914, including *Bébé
fume* (1910), *Bébé marie son oncle* (1910), *Bébé Hercule* (1911),
Bébé et son âne (1911), *Bébé est socialiste* (1911), *Bébé devient
féministe* (1911), *C'est Bébé qui boit le muscat* (1912), *Napoléon,
Bébé et les cosaques* (1912), *Bébé se venge* (1912), *Bébé et la lettre
anonyme* (1912), *Bébé en vacances* (1913), and *Bébé à la ferme*
(1914).

Dary abandoned the cinema in 1914. He did not leave the public
eye, however, turning to boxing, and then to singing and performing
in musicals. Gradually, cinema lured him back, and he attempted to
resume his film career as an adult. He started appearing in films again
in 1934, and made appearances in such films as **Yves Mirande**'s *A
Nous deux, madame la vie* (1936), **Jacques de Baroncelli**'s *SOS Sahara* (1938), and Robert Bibal's *Le Révolté* (1938). Perhaps because
of his days as a boxer, Dary developed a reputation for playing a

tough guy, and he would play such characters in Jean Choux's *Café du port* (1939) and *Port d'attache* (1943), in Maurice Cloche's *Nord Atlantique* (1939), in **André Hugon**'s *Moulin Rouge* (1941), and above all in **Jacques Becker**'s *Touchez pas au Grisbi* (1953), which is probably Dary's best-known role as an adult actor.

Dary continued to act until 1968, and although he never became an adult star, he made a career of playing supporting roles. Near the end of his career, he appeared in such films as André Cayatte's *Piège pour Cendrillon* (1965) and *Les Risques du métier* (1967) with Jacques Brel.

DAUPHIN, CLAUDE (1903–1978). Actor. Born Claude Legrand, Claude Dauphin wanted, from a very early age, to become an actor. Discouraged by his father, the poet Franc-Nohain, he was instead trained as a set decorator, and entered the world of theater by the back door, as it were. His brother, Jean Nohain, would also become an actor. After ten years, Dauphin sought out the stage, and ultimately, in the 1930s, he appeared onscreen. He would go on to make some eighty films in France and in Hollywood during a career that spanned fifty years.

Dauphin made his screen debut in Solange Bussi's adaptation of Colette's *La Vagabonde* (1930). This was quickly followed by roles in **Henri Diamant-Berger**'s *Tout s'arrange* (1931) and *Clair de Lune* (1932) and Jean Hémard's *La Fortune* (1931), *Paris-Soleil* (1932), and *Aux urnes, citoyens!* (1932), among other films. As the decade considered the golden age of French cinema unfolded, Dauphin would be right in its midst, appearing in films such as Jean de Limur's *Le Voyage imprévu* (1934), **Georges Lacombe**'s *La Route heureuse* (1935), and **Henri Decoin**'s *Battement de coeur* (1940).

Dauphin also worked often with directors associated with *Le Réalisme poétique* or poetic realism, most notably **Marc Allégret**. He appeared in Allégret's *Entrée des artistes* (1938), *La Belle aventure* (1942), *Les Deux timides* (1943), and *Félicie Nanteuil* (1943). He also worked with **Jacques Feyder** in *Une Femme disparaît* (1944).

During the occupation, Dauphin fled France for Great Britain, where he joined the Free French Forces under the command of Charles de Gaulle. While in Britain, he worked with **Jean Renoir** on the film *Salute to France* (1946). Dauphin returned to France after Liberation and resumed his film career, appearing in such films as Pierre Mon-tazel's *Croisière pour l'inconnu* (1947), Marcel Achard's *Jean de la lune* (1948), **Max Ophüls**'s *Le Plaisir* (1952), and **Jacques Becker**'s *Casque d'or* (1952). He also spent time in Hollywood, appearing in such films as *April in Paris* (1952), *Little Boy Lost* (1953), *Phantom of the Rue Morgue* (1954), and *The Quiet American* (1958).

The 1960s brought different types of roles to Dauphin, who went from playing suave, seductive young men in his early career to play older, sometimes hard-boiled men in his later career. He appeared in such films as **Jacques Deray**'s *Symphonie pour une massacre* (1963), **Roger Vadim**'s *Barbarella* (1968), Ettore Scola's *La Plus belle soirée de ma vie* (1972), and Otto Preminger's *Rosebud* (1975).

DECOIN, HENRI (1896–1969). Director and screenwriter. Henri De-coin came to the cinema somewhat late in life. In his youth, he was very athletic, an avid sportsman and an Olympic athlete, participat-ing on the French swimming team in the 1912 Olympic games. He spent his early adult years fighting in World War I first as an in-fantryman, then as an airman, and after the war, became a sports-writer and author, writing one boxing novel titled *Quinze combats* as well as a play.

Decoin began his career in cinema in the mid-1920s. He started out as a screenwriter. Among the silent films made from his screenplays are Maurice Champreux's *Le Roi de la pédale* (1925) and Luitz-Morat's *La Ronde infernale* (1928). Decoin also wrote a number of screenplays during the early years of sound cinema, including several literary adaptations. Sound films made from his screenplays include Carmine Gallone's *Un soir de rafle* (1931), **Jacques de Baroncelli**'s *Roi de Camargue* (1934), and **Abel Gance**'s *Poliche* (1934).

It was in the 1930s that Decoin turned to directing, taking on proj-ects he had written himself. He made his first films in 1933, *Les Bleues du ciel* and *Les Réquins du pétrole*, with a fair degree of suc-cess. The following year, 1934, while working with the German di-rector Kurt Bernhardt on the French version of *L'Or dans la rue* (1934), Decoin met the seventeen-year-old actress **Danielle Dar-rieux**. The two married shortly thereafter and began an onscreen col-laboration that lasted several years and marked one of the high points of both their careers.

Decoin and Darrieux made five films together before parting company in 1941. Those five films, *Mademoiselle ma mère* (1937), *Retour à l'aube* (1938), *Abus de confiance* (1938), *Battement de coeur* (1939), and *Premier rendez-vous* (1941), were primarily well-written melodramas (the last being the exception) that cast Darrieux in lead roles. They were a great success during the late 1930s and early 1940s, and Decoin-Darrieux became a power couple in cinema.

During the Occupation, Decoin remained in France, working with **Continental Films**, the German, Nazi-owned production company. He would ultimately make three films for Continental, *Premier rendez-vous* (1941), *Les Inconnus dans la maison* (1942), starring **Raïmu**, and *Mariage d'amour* (1942). Decoin parted ways with Continental in 1942, about the time he parted ways with Darrieux. He went on to make films independently. His other films from the Occupation era include *Le Bienfaiteur* (1942), also starring Raïmu, *Je suis avec toi* (1943), and *L'Homme de Londres* (1943), an adaptation of a Georges Simenon novel.

After the war, Decoin's films took on a more sober edge, and he broadened his range (perhaps after the taste of Simenon) to include a touch of noir. His later films include *La Fille du diable* (1946), *Les Amoureux sont seuls au monde* (1947), *Les Amants du Pont St. Jean* (1947), *Non coupable* (1947), *Entre onze heures et minuit* (1949), and *Au grand balcon* (1949). He continued directing into the 1950s, working again with Darrieux on *La Vérité sur Bébé Dongé* (1952) and *L'Affaire des poisons* (1955). Other films from the decade include *Dortoir des grandes* (1953), starring **Jean Marais**, *Razzia sur la Chnouf* (1955), starring **Jean Gabin**, and *La Chatte* (1958), starring **Françoise Arnoul**, with whom he made a number of films during the decade. These, like many of Decoin's later films, were primarily film noir or experiments with noir. There were, however, also some Hollywood-style musicals thrown into the mix in the form of *Charmants garçons* (1957) and *Folies Bergère* (1957).

Decoin's production slowed noticeably in the 1960s, although he did some television productions and a handful of films. Among these were *Le Masque de fer* (1962), an adaptation of the Alexandre Dumas novel, and *Nick Carter va tout casser* (1964), a reprisal of the silent-film classic detective. Overall he left a body of some forty-five films comprising an interesting range of styles and stories, and a fair number of other films for which he had written screenplays. Although he may always be best known for having boosted the career of Danielle Darrieux, Decoin made a significant contribution to film history himself.

DEED, ANDRÉ (1879–1938). Actor. André Deed was born André de Chapais, the son of a customs inspector. He seemed, early on, to follow the appointed bourgeois path that had been set out for him, studying at lycée, then at various postsecondary institutions, finally becoming a clerk in a bank. Deed, however, was restless, and gave up the quiet life, at first for the sea, then for the theater, or more particularly the café-concerts. He performed as both a singer and an acrobat before being hired on at the Folies-Bergères, and then the Châtelet. He appeared in several early **Georges Méliès** films, including *Dislocation mystérieuse* (1901), *Les Aventures de Robinson Crusoé* (1902), *Le Royaume des fées* (1903), and *Le Barbier de Seville* (1904).

Around 1905, Deed was hired on at **Pathé** by **Charles Pathé**, who was scouring the café-concerts at the time looking for potential talent for his films. Deed was at Pathé from 1905 to 1908. At the beginning of his time at Pathé, he made several films with **Georges Hatot**, including *Les Débuts d'un chauffeur* (1906) and *La Course à la perruque* (1906), a classic early chase film. However, Deed's most important contribution to cinema at Pathé came in his development of the "Boireau" character. Appearing for the first time in the film *La Course à la perruque*, Boireau was a fool or idiot character at the center of burlesque silent-film comedies and was one of the first regular and reappearing characters in cinema. The character and the comedies in which he appeared were also some of the first film comedies and are seen as central to the development of the genre in film.

Boireau would reappear in series of films, many of them bearing the character's name, which was also quite unusual at the time. The first of these sequels was *Boireau démenage* (1906). Major titles in the first series (during Deed's initial term at Pathé from 1905 to 1908) include *Les Apprentissages de Boireau* (1907), *Les Débuts d'un canotier* (1907), both directed by **Albert Capellani**, and *Boireau fait la noce* (1908). Deed also starred in a number of non-Boireau films during his time at

Pathé, including *Le Chevalier mystère* (1908) and *Les Tribulations du roi Têtaclaque* (1908), both directed by **Segundo de Chomon**, and *Apaches mal avisés* (1908), among others.

In 1909, Deed left Pathé for Italy, hired away by Itala Film due to the success of Boireau (in Italy called "Beoncelli"). His departure was a blow to Pathé, since Boireau was, at the time, a bigger draw even than **Max Linder**. In Italy, Deed created the character of "Cretinetti" (called "Gribouille" in French), and made some seventy films with that character for Itala Film. He also directed films while in Italy. Pathé meanwhile tried, in vain, to continue the *Boireau* series without Deed, hiring another actor, Paul Bertho, to play Boireau. They made four films with Bertho and then gave up. The type, however, remained in film. **Roméo Bosetti**, among others, created Boireau-inspired characters, most notably "Calino" and "Romeo." Boireau's influence on film comedy lasted well beyond 1909.

Deed remained in Italy until 1912, at which time he returned to France, lured back by Pathé. He again reincarnated the Boireau character for Pathé, who cleverly debuted him in a film titled *Gribouille redevient Boireau* (1912). To add a bit of farce to the mix, Pathé paired Deed with the Italian actress Valentina Frascaroli. The pair was a hit and would appear together in many of the twenty or so films Deed would make for Pathé between 1912 and 1915. Of these, the best known include *Boireau se venge* (1912), *La Fête de Boireau* (1912), *Boireau et Gribouillette s'amusent* (1912), *Boireau magistrat* (1912), and *Boireau empoisonneur malgré lui* (1913).

Deed seems to have left Pathé again for Itala, around 1915. He made five films with Valentina Frascaroli in 1915 and 1916 and may afterwards have been mobilized for war, and possibly injured. In any case, he seems to have returned to France and continued his career, which, at that point, had gone into decline. He made a handful of films in the 1920s and early 1930s, appearing in **Gaston Ravel**'s *Tâo* (1923) and *Monsieur de Pourceaugnac* (1932), Georges Pallu's *Phi-Phi* (1926) and *La Rose effeuillée* (1936), **Georges Monca**'s *Miss Helyett* (1927), and Bernard-Deschamps' *Le Rosier de Madame Husson* (1931), among others. He also wrote, directed, and starred, alongside Frasacaroli, in an early science-fiction film titled *L'Uomo Meccanico* (1921), which exists in a fragment. He seems to have disappeared after 1936 and died more or less forgotten.

DELAIR, SUZY (1917–). Actress. Born Suzanne Delaire, Suzy Delair apparently wanted to pursue acting from a very young age, although her parents attempted to discourage her. Delair persisted, nonetheless, and began her career as a costume designer for the theater and the cinema. She went on to become a stage actress and music-hall performer, singing and dancing as well as acting, before making her debut in film.

Delair's first screen appearances were in 1930, when she had a small role in Willy Wolff's *Le Caprice de la Pompadour* (1930). This role was followed by roles in Henry Roussel's *Les Violettes impériales* (1932) and Alexander Korda's *La Dame de chez Maxim's* (1932). The following year, Delair had a supporting role in Maurice Champreux's *Touchons du bois* (1933) and in Robert Siodomak's *Le Sexe faible* (1933). Slowly, the roles increased in number and in importance, as Delair appeared in Curtis Bernhardt's *L'Or dans la rue* (1934), Siodomak's *La Crise est finie* (1934), **René Guissart**'s *Dédé* (1934) and *Les Soeurs Hortensias* (1935), and Jean Boyer's *Prends la route* (1936).

The 1940s, and particularly the cinema of the Occupation, were what really made Delair a star. Much credit for her early celebrity goes to **Henri-Georges Clouzot**, who created the character of Mila Malou for Delair, in **George Lacombe**'s *Le Dernier des six* (1941). Clouzot had written the original screenplay for *Le Dernier des six* by adapting a work by Stanislas-André Steeman, but the character of Mila, the somewhat annoying singer/girlfriend of Inspector Wenceslas Wens, was the original creation of Clouzot. Delair as Mila was a hit, and Clouzot reprised the character for her in his own film *L'Assassin habite au 21* (1942). Delair would also star in Clouzot's *Quai des Orfèvres* (1947).

Apart from her work with Clouzot, Delair starred in a number of other significant films during the decade, including Richard Pottier's *Défense d'aimer* (1942), **Marcel L'Herbier**'s *La Vie de bohème* (1942), Jean Dréville's *Copie conforme* (1947), Gilles Grangier's *Par la fenêtre* (1948), Henri Jeanson's *Lady Paname* (1949), and **Jean Grémillon**'s *Pattes blanches* (1949).

Delair managed to maintain her star power during the 1950s, appearing in films such as **Christian-Jacque**'s *Souvenirs perdus* (1950), **Léo Joannen**'s *Atoll K* (1951), Guy Lefranc's *Le Fil à la* *patte* (1955), **René Clément**'s *Gervaise* (1956), and Boyer's *Le Couturier de ces dames* (1956). After the mid-1950s, however, she was offered only very occasional roles, such as in **Claude Autant-Lara**'s *Les Regates de San Francisco* (1960), **Marcel Carné**'s (1962), and Gérard Oury's *Les Aventures de Rabbi Jacob* (1973).

Over the course of her career, Delair has showed an impressive range as an actress, appearing in everything from comedies to detective films to literary adaptations. A number of films also showcased her lovely singing voice. Despite that, however, Delair abandoned cinema in the late 1970s, because, in her words, people were simply not asking her to work.

DELANNOY, JEAN (1908–). Actor, director, film editor, and screenwriter. Jean Delannoy at first pursued a fairly traditional path and studied the classics at university. However, he took up acting while he was a student in Paris in the 1920s. He was one of the few who entered cinema in the early part of the century who has a university degree.

His career as an actor was fairly short-lived. He appeared in a handful of films, such as Alexandre Volkoff's *Casanova* (1927) and **André Hugon**'s *La Grande passion* (1928), before taking up film editing for Paramout Studios Paris. He quickly developed a reputation as a master film editor and did the editing for such films as Max Nosseck and Robert Siodomak's *Le Roi des Champs-Elysées* (1934), **Jacques de Baroncelli**'s *Michel Strogoff* (1934) and *Nitchevo* (1936), and Jacques Deval's *Club de femmes* (1936).

Delannoy began directing himself in the early 1930s. He assisted Deval on *Club de femmes*, and also assisted Felix Gandara on *Tamara la complaisante* (1937) as well as *Le Paradis de Satan* (1938). At about the same time, he began directing feature-length films on his own. Delannoy's early films include *Macao, l'enfer du jeu* (1939), *Le Diamant noir* (1940), *Pontcarral, colonel d'empire* (1942), and *L'Assassin a peur la nuit* (1942). These films are all fairly conventional, solid, but unremarkable.

Delannoy's work came into its own when he directed *L'Eternel retour* (1943). A classic of French cinema, the film, which stars **Jean Marais**, is the story of a tragic love affair. With a powerful screenplay written by **Jean Cocteau** that replayed the Tristan and Isolde story, the film, in Delannoy's hands, became a modern myth onscreen. It launched Delannoy into the ranks of power directors. Delannoy went on to make *Le Bossu* (1944) and *La Symphonie pastorale* (1946), which won the Palme d'Or at the **Cannes Film Festival**. Other films from the 1940s include *Les Jeux sont faits* (1947), *Le Secret de Mayerling* (1948), and *Aux yeux du souvenir* (1949).

While the 1940s probably mark the high point of Delannoy's career, his reputation as a first-rate director held into the 1950s. His most acclaimed film of that decade is undoubtedly *Maigret tend une piège* (1958), starring **Jean Gabin**. Probably the only other truly noteworthy film is Delannoy's adaptation of *La Princesse de Clèves* (1960). His other films from the 1950s and 1960s are more similar to his first films, fairly conventional and fairly unremarkable. These include *La Route Napoléon* (1953), *Notre Dame de Paris* (1956), *Vénus impériale* (1963), *Les Amitiés particulières* (1964), *Le Majordome* (1965), *Le Soleil des voyous* (1967), *Bernadette* (1988), *La Passion de Bernadette* (1989), and *Marie de Nazareth* (1995). Delannoy wrote the screenplays for a number of his films.

On the whole, there are varying interpretations of Delannoy as a director. Some regard him as a once talented, artistic director who, in the latter half of his career, declined into producing second-rate films. Others who are more critical say that the vast majority of his films are unremarkable, and that only one, *L'Eternel retour*, really amounts to a great film. And even though there is general agreement on that point, there is disagreement as to whether the greatness of the film lies in the work of Cocteau, the work of Delannoy, or the work of the two together. In any case, Delannoy's peers and colleagues in the film industry considered that he had made a sufficiently significant contribution to French cinema to grant him an honorary **César** for Lifetime Achievement in film in 1986.

DELLUC, LOUIS (1890–1924). Director, film critic, and screenwriter. Louis Delluc suffered his entire life from ill health. He was a bookish boy and pursued his studies with the intention of attending the prestigious École Normale Supérieure in Paris. He was also an avid writer and seemed to have literary ambitions from quite a young age. At the age of fifteen, he published a volume of poetry titled *Les Chansons du jeune temps*, and he would ultimately write a number of novels, some of which were published during his lifetime and some posthumously. Interestingly, at least as a young man, he disliked the cinema, although he was an avid follower of the theater.

All that changed in 1915, it seems, when he met the actress Eve Francis, whom Delluc would marry in 1918. She reportedly took him to see Cecil B. DeMille's *The Cheat* (1916), which apparently changed Delluc's entire vision of cinema. Suddenly taken with the power of cinema, he became a convert and began writing film criticism in publications like *Le Film* and *Paris-Midi*. He also launched film journals of his own, including *Cinéa* in 1921. The journal is regarded as one of the first to engage in an intellectual criticism of the cinema, and the critics who wrote for the journal, including **Jean Epstein**, are considered the first generation of film scholars.

For his own part, Delluc was an advocate of an impressionist cinema, a cinema less preoccupied with constructing a story than with transmitting its message through more subtle sensory and psychological means. When he began to make films in 1919, after he demobilized from military service, he put his theories into practice onscreen. He made eight films before his death, *Le Chemin d'Ernoa* (1919), *Le Silence* (1920), *Fumée noire* (1920), *Fièvre* (1921), *Le Chemin d'Ernoa* (1921), *Le Tonnere* (1921), *La Femme de nulle part* (1922), and *L'Inondation* (1924). Francis is the lead actress in all of Delluc's films. Of these, without a doubt, *Fièvre* (1921) and *La Femme de nulle part* (1922) are considered the greatest, but all of the films have retained classic standing in the French film cannon.

In addition to his own films, other filmmakers adapted some of Delluc's writings for the cinema. **Germaine Dulac**, whose filmmaking style is often said to have influenced Delluc's own, made *La Fête espagnole* (1920) from a Delluc screenplay. And Alberto Cavalcanti adapted *Le Train sans yeux* (1927) for the screen. Delluc is probably better known for the prize that bears his name, the **Prix Louis-Delluc**, than for his writings or his films.

DELON, ALAIN (1935–). Actor, director, producer, and screenwriter. A former member of the French army's parachutists, the French version of commandos, Alain Delon began acting with no formal training. His military background immediately established him as a masculine onscreen tough guy, and that reputation held throughout most of his career. Delon made his film debut in a small part in Yves Allé-gret's *Quand la femme s'en mêle* (1957). He later appeared in **Marc Allégret**'s *Sois belle et tais-toi* (1958) with **Jean-Paul Belmondo**, the fellow icon with whom he later costarred in **Jacques Deray**'s *Borsalino* (1970). Belmondo and Delon would participate in the creation of French tropes of masculinity in the French cinema of the 1970s that favored tough, virile, and rebellious playboys. Delon subsequently acted in Pierre Gaspard-Huit's *Christine* (1958) and Michel Boisrond's *Le Chemin des écoliers* (1959) and *Faibles femmes* (1959). He received international attention for his role in **René Clement**'s *Plein soleil* (1960), adapted from a Patricia High-smith thriller. He starred in prominent Italian films, including Luchino Visconti's *Rocci e i suoi fratelli* (1960) and *Il gattopardo* (1963) and Michelangelo Antonini's *L'Eclisse* (1962), and won the Étoile de Cristal de l'Académie du Cinéma for Best Actor for his role in Clement's *Quelle joie de vivre* in 1962.

Delon's fame soared with his leading roles in **Jean-Pierre Melville**'s gangster film trilogy *Le Samouraï* (1967), *Le Cercle Rouge* (1970), and *Un flic* (1972), which made excellent use of his tough-guy aura. He was cast in other police thrillers, including De-ray's *Flic Story* (1975) and José Pinheiro's *Parole de flic* (1985), and he also appeared in adventure films such as **Christian-Jacque**'s *La Tulipe noire* (1963) and Duccio Tessari's *Zorro* (1974). His portrayal of fictional criminals onscreen was mirrored by his own alleged connection to the mafia.

Delon also appeared in artistic films, including Joseph Losey's *Mr Klein* (1976), for which he was nominated for a **César Award**, and **Bertrand Blier**'s *Notre Histoire* (1984), for which he won a César for Best Actor. He played in a few American films, for example, in *Scorpio* (1973) and *The Concorde: Airport '79* (1979). He has directed two films to date: *Pour la peau d'un flic* (1981), in which he stars beside one of French cinema's tough and sexy women, Anne Parillaud, and *Le Battant* (1983), which features Delon and François Périer. Alain Delon's star status, however, is primarily due to his career as an actor. He has produced a number of films, among them Deray's *Doucement les basses* (1970), *Borsalino, Borsalino & co* (1974), *Le gang* (1977), *Trois hommes à abattre* (1980), and *Un crime* (1992). In 1990, Delon was awarded the Legion of Honor. After costarring in **Patrice**

Leconte's *Une chance sur deux* (1997) with Belmondo, he announced his retirement from film acting. Since then, he has appeared on French television and in Blier's *Les Acteurs* (1999). Delon made a guest appearance as the mentor of the infamous bank robber, kidnapper, and arms smuggler, Jacques Mesrine (played by **Vicent Cassel**), in Barbet Schroeder's *The Death Instinct* (2006).

DELPY, JULIE (1969–). Actress, director, producer, and screenwriter. Julie Delpy was born in Paris to actors Albert Delpy and Marie Pillet. She first appeared onscreen when she was seven in Joël Farges's *Guerres civiles en France* (1978). In the 1980s, she appeared in films by some of France's major directors, such as **Jean-Luc Godard**'s *Détective* (1985) and **Leos Carax**'s *Mauvais sang* (1986). Her first major role was in **Bertrand Tavernier**'s *La Passion Béatrice* (1987), for which she received a **César** nomination for Most Promising Actress. She later landed a leading role in Jean-Pierre Limosin's *L'Autre nuit* (1988).

In the late 1980s and especially in the 1990s, Delpy developed a solid cosmopolitan presence. International coproductions are prevalent in modern cinema, and sophisticated actors like Delpy travel well. In 1989 she played in Spanish director Carlos Saura's *La Noche oscura*. In the 1990s, she played significant roles in coproductions such as Agnieszka Holland's *Europa, Europa* (1991), Volker Schlöndorff's *Homo Faber* (1991), and Krzysztof Kieslowski's *Trois couleurs, blanc* (1993). She appeared in German director Percy Adlon's Anglophone *Younger and Younger* and starred in Roger Avary's French and American production, *Killing Zoe* (1994).

In 1995, Delpy directed her first film, a short titled *Blah Blah Blah*. She cowrote the script with American actress and screenwriter Emily Wagner, who also acts in the film. Also in the mid-1990s, she starred in and composed songs for American director Richard Linklater's *Before Sunrise* (1995) and later starred in his sequel *Before Sunset* (2004). Delpy continued to work in international films, among them Enki Bilal's science-fiction film *Tykho Moon* (1996), Anthony Waller's *American Werewolf in Paris* (1997), and Mika Kaurismäki's *L.A. Without a Map* (1998).

Delpy directed and produced the English-language film *Looking for Jimmy* (2001), a film cowritten again with Wagner. In 2003,

Delpy released a music CD. She later directed a short in French, *J'ai peur, j'ai mal, je meurs* (2004). In 2005, she appeared with Bill Murray in Jim Jarmusch's *Broken Flowers*. That same year, she played the lead in John Stimpson's *The Legend of Lucy Keyes* (2005).

DEMAZIS, ORANE (1904–1991). Actress. Orane Demazis was born Burgard Demazis in Oran, Algeria, to a family of Alsacian immigrants. The name Orane Demazis is a stage name, after Oran, where she was born. Demazis studied at the Paris Conservatoire d'art dramatique before starting her career on the stage. She made her debut at the Théâtre de l'Atélier, where she was discovered by **Marcel Pagnol** in 1928.

Demazis left the Théâtre de l'Atélier to join Pagnol at the Théâtre des Arts, where he worked with actors such as **Harry Baur** and Pierre Blanchar. Demazis got her start in cinema in 1931, when Pagnol decided to bring his play *Marius*, in which she had starred, to the screen. Demazis starred in the film, opposite **Pierre Fresnay**. She would go on to make several other films with Pagnol, most notably *Fanny* (1932), *Angèle* (1934), *César* (1936), and *Regain* (1937). The two also had a son together. However, they never married, and in 1939, they parted ways.

Demazis went on to make films with other directors. She worked with Raymond Bernard in *Les Misérables* (1934), Marc Didier on *Le Moulin dans le soleil* (1938), with Jean Benoît-Lévy in *Le Feu de paille* (1940), with Jacques Houssin in *Le Mistral* (1943), with Henri Calef in *Bagarres* (1948), and with Jacqueline Audry in *La Caraque blonde* (1954), among others. Her film career seemed more or less over in the 1960s, although it had a short renaissance in the 1970s, when Demazis appeared in Rene Allio's *Rude Journée pour la reine* (1973), Luis Buñuel's *Le Fantôme de la liberté* (1974), **André Téchiné**'s *Souvenirs d'en France* (1975), and Michel Andrieu's *Bastien, Bastienne* (1979). Demazis remains for many in France forever Fanny, the star of Pagnol's *Fanny* (1932) and *Marius* (1931), and she once said that for many years after the films were released, people would stop her in the streets and ask her what news she had of Marius.

DEMONGEOT, MYLÈNE (1936–). Actress and producer. Mylène Demongeot was born Marie-Hélène Demongeot in Nice. She studied acting under René Simon and Marie Ventura, and later became a model. She made her screen debut at the age of sixteen in Léonide Moguy's *Les Enfants de l'amour* (1953), and subsequently appeared in **Marc Allégret**'s *Futures vedettes* (1955). She was initially viewed as a sex symbol, and her role in Allégret's *Sois belle et tais-toi* (1958) was therefore rather interesting from a feminist standpoint.

Demongeot's breakthrough performance was in **Raymond Rouleau**'s 1957 film *Les Sorcières de Salem*, in which she played Abigail Williams. Some of her other memorable early roles were in Otto Preminger's *Bonjour, tristesse* (1958), Michel Boisrond's *Faibles femmes* (1959), Bernard Borderie's *Les Trois mousquetaires: La vengeance de Milady* (1961) and *Les Trois mousquetaires: Les ferrets de la reine* (1961), **Michel Deville**'s *L'Appartement des filles* (1963) and *À cause, à cause d'une femme* (1963), and Jean Becker's *Tendre Voyou* (1966). She played alongside **Jean Marais** in **André Hunébelle**'s remake of **Louis Feuillade**'s *Fantômas* (1964), and in the sequels *Fantômas se déchaine* (1965) and *Fantômas contre Scotland Yard* (1966).

Demongeot also ventured into British cinema with parts in Val Guest's *It's a Wonderful World* (1956), Ralph Thomas's *Upstairs and Downstairs* (1959), and Roy Ward Baker's *The Singer Not the Song* (1961), and into Italian cinema with roles in Mauro Bolognini's *La Notte brava* (1959) and Dino Risi's *Un Amore a Roma* (1960). In 1974 Demongeot acted in her husband Marc Simenon's film *Par le sang des autres*. She later appeared in his *Signé Furax* (1981). With Simenon, she leads the production company Kangourou Films. She has continued her film career into the twenty-first century and was nominated for a **César** for Best Supporting Actress for her performance in Olivier Marchal's *36 Quai des orfèvres* in 2005. She also played in **Bertrand Blier**'s *Tenue de soirée* (1986), Liliane de Kermadec's *La Piste du télégraphe* (1994), Stéphanie Murat's *Victoire* (2000), and Fabien Onteniente's *Camping* (2006).

DEMY, JACQUES (1931–1990). Actor, director, producer, and screenwriter. Jacques Demy got his start in film assisting director Georges Rouquier. He went on to direct his first short, *Les sabotiers du Val de Loire* (1955), shortly thereafter. He gained acclaim with his first feature film, *Lola* (1961), which was followed by the classic *La*

Baie des anges (1963), a rather dark film about compulsive gambling on the sunny French Riviera. Demy is most famous for his musicals, most notably *Les parapluies de Cherbourg* (1964) and *Les Demoiselles de Rochefort* (1967), both of which helped to launch the career of megastar **Catherine Deneueve**. *Les parapluies de Cherbourg* won the Golden Palm at **Cannes** and the **Prix Louis-Delluc**. It was restored by his wife, the ground-breaking director **Agnès Varda**. Demy's musical *Une chambre en ville* (1982) also received **César** nominations for Best Director and Best Film.

Demy's other films include *The Model Shop* (1969), *Peau d'ane* (1970), *The Pied Piper* (1972), *L'événement le plus important depuis que l'homme a marché sur la lune* (1973), *Lady Oscar* (1979), *Parking* (1985), and the animated film *La table tournante* (1987), codirected with Paul Grimault. His last musical was *Trois places sur le 26* (1988). Varda's films *Jacquot de Nantes* (1991) and *L'Univers de Jacques Demy* (1995) are both about Demy.

DENEUVE, CATHERINE (1943–). Actress. Catherine Deneuve is one of France's most celebrated film actresses. The actor Maurice Dorléac is her father, and the actress Françoise Dorléac was her sister. Deneuve went into the family business, but took her mother's name as a stage name, not her father's.

Deneuve made her film debut in **André Hunébelle's** *Les Collégiennes* in 1957. She went on to do a number of other films with remarkable directors, including **Marc Allégret's** *Les Parisiennes* (1962), **Roger Vadim's** *Le Vice et la vertu* (1963), **Pierre Kast's** *Les Vacances portugaises* (1963), and **Jacques Demy's** popular and critically acclaimed *Les Parapluies de Cherbourg* (1964). Deneuve won the Etoile de Cristal de l'Académie du Cinéma for Best Actress for her performance in the film. Other films made during this early, "starlet" part of her career include **Edouard Molinero's** *Chasse à l'hommes* (1964), **Claude Chabrol** and **Jean-Luc Godard's** *Les Plus belles escroqueries du monde* (1964), Roman Polanski's *Repulsion* (1965), **Jean-Paul Rappeneau's** *La Vie de Château* (1966), and Demy's *Les Demoiselles de Rochefort* (1967).

There was a turning point of sorts in her career in 1967, when she starred in Luis Buñuel's ***Belle de jour*** (1967). The film, which scandalized some in France, established Deneuve as a serious actress, allowing her to shed her starlet aura. The range of roles she was able to play increased from that point forward. She appeared in such films as **François Truffaut**'s *La Sirène du Mississipi* (1969), Demy's *Peau d'âne* (1970), Buñuel's *Tristana* (1970), **Jean-Pierre Melville**'s *Un flic* (1972), Rappeneau's *Le Sauvage* (1975), **Claude Lelouch**'s *Si c'était à refaire* (1976) and *À nous deux* (1979), **Yves Robert**'s *Courage fuyons* (1979), and Truffaut's *Le Dernier métro* (1980), a film for which she won the **César** for Best Actress.

In 1985, Deneuve's cultural standing was demonstrated by the fact that her face was used as the model for the statue of Marianne, the symbol of the French Republic. Another indication of this cultural prestige is her appearance in a number of **heritage films**, including Alain Corneau's *Fort Saganne* (1984), **Régis Wargnier**'s *Indochine* (1992), and Raoul Ruiz's *Le temps retrouvés* (1999), an adaptation of the novel by Marcel Proust. She won a César for Best Actress and was nominated for an Academy Award for her performance in *Indochine*.

Other films in which Deneuve has appeared include **André Téchiné**'s *Le Lieu du crime* (1986), *Ma saison preférée* (1993), *Les voleurs* (1996), and *Les temps qui changent* (2004), **Philippe de Broca**'s *L'Africain* (1983), **Jean-Pierre Mocky**'s *Agent Trouble* (1987), **Alain Resnais**'s *Contre l'oubli* (1991), Ruiz's *Généaologies d'un crime* (1997), **Léos Carax**'s *Pola X* (1999), Wargnier's *Est-Ouest* (1999), and François Ozon's *8 femmes* (2002).

In 1998, Deneuve won the award for Best Actress at the Venice Film Festival for her performance in **Nicole Garcia**'s *Place Vendôme*, and the Silver Bear for life achievement at Berlin in 1999. She has acted in several international productions, including Sergio Citti's *Casotto* (1977), Dick Richards's *March or Die* (1977), Lars von Trier's *Dancer in the Dark* (2000), Peter Hyams's *The Musketeer* (2001), Tonie Marshall's *Au plus près du paradis* (2002), and Manoel de Oliveira's *O Convento* (1995) and *Un Filme Falado* (2003).

DENIS, CLAIRE (1948–). Director. Claire Denis grew up in West Africa where her father was a French colonial administrator. She interned at Télé Niger in educational filmmaking, then studied at the **Institut des Hautes Études Cinématographiques** (IDHEC). She trained under **Jacques Rivette**—the influential *Nouvelle Vague* or

New Wave director, who has, by Denis's own admission, had a profound influence on her own filmmaking style. She once made a documentary about Rivette, *Jacques Rivette, le veilleur* (1990), which was something of an homage to his work. In addition to her work with Rivette, Denis also assisted **Robert Enrico** and **Constantin Costa-Gavras**, with whom she collaborated in Israel. She was later invited to work for Wim Wenders in the United States. During the time she worked with Wenders, she also met with Jim Jarmusch.

Denis's formative experiences in Africa would frequently influence the settings, themes, and focus of her films. Her exposure to expatriate colonialists fueled her interest in the French Empire, migration, and race relations and her films have drawn rather extensive interest from postcolonial French film scholars, with one of them sometimes even being counted as an African film. Her first feature film, the autobiographical *Chocolat* (1988), is set in colonial Cameroon. The screenplay was cowritten by Jean-Pol Fargeau, who would help to pen the scripts of almost all of Denis's feature films. As it narrates the journey of an adult French **woman** who revisits the place of her childhood, *Chocolat* also explores relationships between the colonizer and colonized. The film pays particular attention to gender and race as it experiments with the cinematic gaze, shifting it away from the standard white male gaze, and placing the gaze instead with a woman or girl-child. Denis's interest in African and Caribbean migrations from former French colonies is also demonstrated in *S'en fout la mort* (1990) and in her documentary *Man no run* (1989), about the European tour of the Cameroonian band, Les Têtes Brûlées.

Denis's emphasis on the visual and the silent is especially evident in *Beau travail* (2000), a film set in Djibouti and based on Herman Melville's *Billy Budd, Sailor*. The film has received critical attention for its representation of the male body, specifically for the way in which the cinematic gaze lingers on members of the French Foreign Legion. The film, which features stunning cinematography, was shot by Agnès Godard, with whom Denis worked on Wenders's *Wings of Desire* (1987). Denis's later film, *Vendredi soir* (2002), is based on a literary work by Emmanuèle Berheim and, like *Beau travail*, it uses only sparse dialogue.

Denis's avoidance of dialogue or explanations of her characters' motives is also seen in *J'ai pas sommeil* (1993), which is based on a serial-killer case featured in the French press. *Trouble Every Day* (2001), an experiment in vampire films and the horror genre, is a further representation of her propensity to highlight silence and visual depth over dialogue. Although Denis tends to underemphasize dialogue, her soundtracks are often a strong presence in her films, and her films often underscore her passion for music: her feature *Nénette et Boni* (1995) takes some of its inspiration from a song by the Tindersticks, a British band whose music is also featured in *Trouble Every Day*.

Apart from the privileging of silence and music and the use of Africa, family dynamics are sometimes a connecting feature that unites some of Denis's films. Both *Nenette et Boni* and the episode she directed for the television series *US Go Home* (1994) explore the relationship between a sister and brother. Both also star the actors Grégoire Colin and Alice Houri. Denis often works with the same actors, especially Colin, Houri, Isaach de Bankolé, Béatrice Dalle, Alex Descas, and Vincent Gallo. Denis later directed *l'Intrus* (2004), which features Michel Subor alongside Colin and Dalle. Because of the recognizable filmmaking style and the commonalities of theme, Denis is one of the few female filmmakers to have been deemed an **auteur**. In addition to her activities as a film director, Denis is currently an instructor at the Fondation Européenne des Métiers de l'Image et du Son (FEMIS).

DEPARDIEU, GÉRARD (1948–). Actor and director. Gérard Depardieu is France's—and perhaps Europe's—most internationally recognized actor of the 1970s and beyond. Depardieu dropped out of school at an early age and started in the theater in the 1960s, then moved to a film acting career with Roger Leenhardt's short *Le beatnik et le minet* (1965). In 1971, he acted in **Michel Audiard**'s *Le Cri du cormoran le soir au-dessus des jonques* and **Jacques Deray**'s *Un peu de soleil dans l'eau froide*. He worked in **Marguerite Duras**'s *Nathalie Granger* (1973) and *Le Camion* (1977) and rose to stardom with **Bertrand Blier**'s *Les Valseuses* (1973). He acted again for Blier in *Préparez vos mouchoirs* (1978), *Buffet Froid* (1979), *Tenue de soirée* (1986), *Trop belle pour toi* (1989), *Merci la vie* (1991), and *Les Acteurs* (2000).

Depardieu has starred in international blockbusters such as **Claude Berri**'s ***Jean de Florette*** (1986) and is likewise recognized for his work with **auteur** directors such as **Alain Resnais** in *L'an 01* (1973), *Mon Oncle d'Amérique* (1980), and *I Want to Go Home* (1989) and **François Truffaut** in *La femme d'à côté* (1981) and *Le Dernier Métro* (1980), for which he was awarded a **César** for Best Actor. His performance in **Maurice Pialat**'s *Police* (1985) won him a Best Actor Award at Venice. Pialat also chose him for leading roles in *Loulou* (1980), *Sous le soleil de Satan* (1987), and *Le garçu (*1995).

Depardieu is adept in multiple genres. Several of his successful comic roles were in films by Francis Veber: *La Chèvre* (1981), *Les Compères* (1983), *Les Fugitifs* (1986), and *Le Placard* (2000). He also played Obélix in **Claude Zidi**'s *Astérix et Obélix contre César* (1999), animating one of the most beloved of France's comic-book heroes.

Depardieu has done a number of what could be considered **heritage films**, including Daniel Vigne's *Le retour de Martin Guerre* (1982), Alain Corneau's *Fort Saganne* (1984) and *Tous les matins du monde* (1991), Depardieu's own *Le Tartuffe* (1984), Bruno Nyutten's *Camille Claudel* (1988), Berri's *Uranus* (1990) and *Germinal* (1993), Yves Angelo's *Le Colonel Chabert* (1994), and Josée Dayan's television series *Balzac* (1999). One of his most acclaimed heritage roles was in **Jean-Paul Rappeneau**'s *Cyrano de Bergerac* (1990), for which he won Best Actor at both the César Awards and **Cannes**. Another acclaimed heritage performance was in Andrzej Wajda's *Danton* (1982), for which he won the National Society of Film Critics Award and the Best Actor Award at the Montreal World Film Festival.

Depardieu appeared in other notable French films, including **André Téchiné**'s *Barocco* (1976) and *Les temps qui changent* (2004), **Claude Miller**'s *Dites-lui que je l'aime* (1977), Jean-Marie Poiré's *Les anges gardiens* (1995), Jean Becker's *Élisa* (1995), and Anne Fontaine's *Nathalie* (2004). He has also acted in several Anglophone features, including Peter Weir's *Green Card* (1990), for which he received an Oscar nomination, Ridley Scott's *1492: Conquest of Paradise* (1992), Randall Wallace's *The Man in the Iron Mask* (1998), Roland Joffé's *Vatel* (2000), Matt Dillon's *City of Ghosts* (2002), Wayne Wang's *Last Holiday* (2006), and Sam Weisman's *Knights of Manhattan* (2006).

Other international films in which Depardieu has appeared include Bernardo Bertolucci's *1900* (1976), Luigi Comencini's *L'Ingorgo:*

una storia impossibile (1979), Guiseppi Tornatore's *A Pure Formality* (1994), and Brad Mirman's *Wanted* (2003). Depardieu directed *Un pont entre deux rives* (1999) with Frédéric Auburtin. An actor who has excelled at embodying an impressive range of characters—literary heroes, historical legends, canonical writers, macho criminals, romantic sensitive leads, and closet homosexuals, among many others—Depardieu was awarded a Career Golden Lion at the Venice Film Festival in 1997.

DERAY, JACQUES (1929–2003). Actor, director, and screenwriter. Jacques Deray was born Jacques Deray-Desrayaud. While in his early teens, Deray studied drama under René Simon in Paris. He acted in the theater and played a small part in Jean Boyer's *Le Trou normand* (1952). In the 1950s, he was an assistant director to filmmakers such as Luis Buñuel, Jules Dassin, and Gilles Grangier. He assisted in a number of crime dramas featuring **Lino Ventura**, who would later become one of Deray's preferred leads, next to **Alain Delon**.

In 1960, Deray directed his first film, *Le Gigolo*, an interesting title given the playboy image of the stars he would employ most frequently. He ultimately became known for his slick gangster films, detective films, and crime dramas, which were often based on novels by Robin Cook, Jean-Patrick Manchette, or Georges Simenon. His 1960s films, *Du rififi à Tokyo* (1962), *Symphonie pour un massacre* (1963), *Par un beau matin d'été* (1965), and *L'Homme de Marrakesh* (1966), all reflect this interest in crime. The popularity of Deray's films was enhanced by his collaboration with some of France's biggest actors, most notably **Jean-Claude Brialy**, **Jean-Paul Belmondo**, Delon, and Ventura.

In the 1960s, Deray directed *Avec la peau des autres* (1966), *La piscine* (1969), and *Borsalino* (1970), the last pairing masculine icons Belmondo and Delon. Many of Deray's 1970s films featured the superstar Delon. Examples include *Doucement les basses* (1971), *Borsalino & Co.* (1974), *Flic story* (1975), and *Le gang* (1977). Delon was not the only actor Deray worked with during the decade. **Jean-Louis Trintignant** starred in Deray's 1972 film, *Un homme est mort*, and Ventura starred in his 1978 *Un papillon sur l'épaule*. Throughout his career, however, Deray continued to favor Delon, who starred in *Trois hommes à abbatre* (1980), *Un crime* (1993), and Deray's last big-screen film, the thriller *L'ours en pelouche* (1994). Deray collaborated again with Belmondo in *Le marginal* (1983) and *Le solitaire* (1987).

In 1981, Deray served as president of the jury at the **Cannes Film Festival**. His *On ne meure que deux fois,* starring **Michel Serrault**, won the Jury Prize at the Montreal World Film Festival in 1985. He directed romances, too, such as the 1987 *Maladie d'amour*, featuring Nastassja Kinski and a more fragile leading man, Jean-Hughes Anglade. In the 1990s, he worked with the French thriller icon, actor **Yves Montand**, on the spy film *Netchaïev est de retour* (1991). After *L'ours en pelouche*, Deray turned to directing for television.

DESFONTAINES, HENRI (1876–1931). Actor, director, and screenwriter. Henri Desfontaines began his career in the theater. He was a noted stage actor who worked with **Sarah Bernhardt** and the great **André Antoine** at the Théâtre de l'Odéon. It may have been Antoine who introduced Desfontaines to the screen, and he was one of those actors whose presence in a film served as a draw for film audiences. He appeared in various *film d'art* productions for both **Pathé** and **Studio Film d'art** at the beginning of his career, and he was strongly associated with the more artistic vein of filmmaking, particularly literary adaptation, throughout his life.

Desfontaines's acting career extended from the early silent era into the 1930s. Films in which Desfontaines starred included **Albert Capellani**'s *Don Juan* (1908), *L'Arlésienne* (1908), and *La Peau de chagrin* (1909), **Abel Gance**'s *Roman d'une jeune fille pauvre* (1909), **André Calmettes** and **Henri Pouctal**'s *Camille Desmoulins* (1911) and *La Dame aux camélias* (1912), **Jacques de Baroncelli**'s *Soupçon tragique* (1916), **Jean Kemm**'s *L'Obstacle* (1918), **Henri Fescourt**'s *La Maison de la flèche* (1930), and Viktor Tourjansky's *L'Aiglon* (1931).

Desfontaines also directed films. His first film may have been *La Résurrection* (1909), which he codirected with Calmettes. His directing activities gained momentum in 1910 or so, when he took over the direction of the *film d'art* division of Éclipse Studios. Over the course of his career, Desfontaines directed a number of important films, most of them literary adaptations in the film d'art tradition. These include *Les Puits et le pendule* (1909), an early adaptation of the Edgar

Allen Poe story; *Shylock* (1910), an adaptation of Shakespeare that starred **Harry Baur**; *Cromwell* (1911), *L'Assassinat d'Henri III* (1911), *Les Amours de la reine Elisabeth* (1912), *Anne de Boleyn* (1913), and *Adrienne Lecouvreur* (1913), all of which he codirected with **Louis Mercanton**; *Jésus de Nazareth* (1911) and *Madame Sans-Gêne* (1911), both codirected with Calmettes; *Le Secret de Polichinelle* (1913); *La Reine Margot* (1914); *Les Bleus de l'amour* (1918); *La Marseillaise* (1920); *Les Trois lys* (1921); *La Fille des chiffonniers* (1922); and *Le Capitaine Rascasse* (1926).

Desfontaines also directed two series, *L'Espionne aux yeux noirs* (1925) and *Belphégor* (1927), the infamous series of a mysterious phantom who haunts the Louvre, and which starred **René Navarre.** *Belphégor*, like Desfontaines's early film, *Les Puits et la pendule*, was also an experiment in the horror genre. In many of his films, Desfontaines also starred and, therefore, directed himself.

DEVILLE, MICHEL (1931–). Director, producer, and screenwriter. Michel Deville was born in Boulogne-sur-Seine. He got his start in cinema as an assistant to director **Henri Decoin** in the early 1950s before codirecting his first film, the crime drama *Une balle dans le canon* (1958) with Charles Gérard. His first independently directed feature was *Ce soir ou jamais* (1961), starring **Anna Karina** and co-written with Nina Companeez. Deville would collaborate with Companeez on the scripts of several comedies, including *Adorable menteuse* (1962), *L'Appartement des filles* (1963), *À cause, à cause d'une femme* (1963), *Lucky Jo* (1964), *On a volé la Jaconde* (1965), *Martin Soldat* (1966), *Benjamin ou Les Mémoires d'un puceau* (1967), and *Bye bye, Barbara* (1969). Karina starred again in *Tendres Requins* (1967), another film he cowrote with Companeez. Many of Deville's films were commercially successful. His *Benjamin* was also critically successful, winning the prestigious **Prix Louis-Delluc.**

Deville has some connection to French *Nouvelle Vague* or New Wave directors, of whom he is a contemporary. He often worked, for example, with prominent New Wave actresses such as Karina and **Brigitte Bardot**. The latter starred in his comedy *L'Ours et la poupée* (1970), a film emblematic of Deville's interest in sexual politics. However, Deville departed from the New Wave in his use of more tra-ditional photography and his emphasis on creating entertaining films.

While directors such as **Jacques Deray** profited from the use of male superstars, Deville is noted for his work with several major actresses. In the 1970s he cast **Françoise Fabian** and Brigitte Fossey in *Raphaël ou le débaché* (1971) and the legendary **Romy Schneider** in *Le mouton enragé* (1974) alongside British star Jane Birkin. He also collaborated with important French actors such as **Michel Piccoli** and **Jean-Louis Trintignant**. Aside from his selection of fine actresses, Deville is known as a talented scenarist. In 1979 he won a **César** for Best Writing with Gilles Perrault for *Le Dossier 51*. The film also received the French Syndicate of Cinema Critics Award for Best Film. Perrault later scripted Deville's *La petite bande* (1983).

In the 1980s, Deville's work continued to be critically lauded as well as popular. Much of what is appreciated in his films is his tendency to utilize postmodern techniques, particularly with respect to the blending of different art forms into his films, and for his play with genre. He won a César for Best Director and a second French Syndicate of Cinema Critics Award for Best Film for *Péril en la demeure* (1985), another detective thriller with decidedly postmodern traits. His *La Lectrice* (1988), which stars **Miou-Miou**, also plays with genre and blurs the boundaries between fiction and reality. It won the Prix Louis-Delluc and the Grand Prix des Amériques at the Montreal World Film Festival. Rosalinde Deville collaborated on the scripts for both films and continued this collaboration with Deville into the 1990s and beyond. Both *Le Voyage en douce* (1980) and *Péril en la demeure* were also nominated for the Golden Berlin Bear.

No doubt because of his popular and critical standing, Deville has still been able to work with some of the best actors and directors in France. He cast Trintignant and **Isabelle Huppert** in *Eaux profondes* (1981), and his film *Le Paltoquet* (1986) features **Fanny Ardant**, **Daniel Auteuil**, **Richard Bohringer**, and **Jeanne Moreau**. His recent collaborations with French directors include *Contre l'oubli* (1991), a film about political prisoners initiated by Amnesty International. He has also cooperated with emerging French actors such as Jean-Hughes Anglade in *Nuit d'été en ville* (1990) and Élodie Bouchez in *La Divine poursuite* (1997). His *Toutes peines confondues* (1992) features celebrity singers Patrick Bruel and Jacques Dutronc. In the 1990s, Deville received further acclaim. His film *La Maladie de Sachs* (1999) received yet another French Syndicate of

Cinema Critics Award for Best Film. It was also nominated for a César for Best Director. Deville subsequently directed *Un monde presque paisible* (2002) and *Un fil à la patte* (2005), a film starring Emmanuel Béart and Charles Berling.

DEWAERE, PATRICK (1947–1982). Actor. Patrick Dewaere was born Jean-Marie Patrick Bourdeau in Saint-Brieuc. He made his first screen appearance at the age of four in **Henri Diamant-Berger**'s *Monsieur Fabre* (1951) and later appeared in Jean Boyer's *La Madelon* (1955) and Victor Vicas's *Je reviendrai à Kandara* (1956) under the name Patrick Maurin. He used the name Maurin for several years in films such as **Henri-Georges Clouzot**'s *Les Espions* (1957) and Robert Darène's *Mimi Pinson* (1958). He also appeared in the television series *Jean de la tour miracle* (1967). In the late 1960s, Dewaere established himself as an actor at the Café de la Gare, where he worked with figures like **Gérard Depardieu** and his future costar and wife, **Miou-Miou**. His adult screen-acting career included small roles in **Jean-Paul Rappeneau**'s *Les mariés de l'an II* (1971) and Claude Faraldo's *Themroc* (1973).

Dewaere's breakthrough role came in 1974 in **Bertrand Blier**'s *Les Valseuses* (1974). It costarred Depardieu, with whom he would also pair in Blier's Oscar-winning *Préparez vos mouchoirs* (1978). After *Les Valseuses*, Dewaere landed significant roles in two Maurice Dugowson films: *Lily, aime-moi* (1975) and *F. comme Fairbanks* (1976), both featuring Miou-Miou. He later starred in **Claude Miller**'s *La Meilleure façon de marcher* (1976), Yves Boisset's *Juge Fayard dit Le Shériff* (1977) and *La Clé sur la porte* (1978), Jean-Jacques Annaud's *Coup de tête* (1979), Didier Haudepin's *Paco l'infaillible* (1979), and Alain Corneau's *Série noire* (1979). He also acted in films by Italian directors: Marco Bellocchio's *Marcia trionfale* (1976), Dino Risi's *La Stanza del vescovo* (1977), and Luigi Comencini's international production, *L'Ingorgo, Una storia impossible* (1979). His ability to portray gentle and emotional, yet decidedly masculine characters earned him a vast array of roles in comedies, dramas, and crime films. Dewaere, with his colleague Depardieu, was one of the most popular French actors in the 1970s.

In the 1980s, Dewaere remained active. He starred in **Claude Sautet**'s *Un mauvais fils* in 1980 and led the cast of **Philippe de**

Broca's *Psy* in 1981. He collaborated again with Blier in *Beau-père* (1981) and shortly thereafter starred in Luc Béraud's *Plein sud* (1981), **André Téchiné**'s *Hôtel des Amériques* (1981), and **Henri Verneuil**'s *Mille milliards de dollars* (1982). His last completed role was in Alain Jessua's *Paradis pour tous* (1982). It is perhaps ironic that Dewaere's character in *Paradis pour tous* commits suicide, because shortly after the film's release, Deware took his own life. He was, at the time, working in **Claude Lelouch**'s *Edith and Marcel*.

No doubt because of his standing in French cinema, Dewaere has continued to be something of an icon long after his death. In 1992, director Marc Esposito made a documentary about Dewaere's life, *Patrick Dewaere*. The film aptly features Blier and Miou-Miou. A second documentary, this time for television, was made in 2003 by director Alexandre Moix. This documentary was titled *Patrick Dewaere, l'enfant du siècle* and featured Blier, Jean-Jacques Annaud, Yves Boisset, Dewaere's daughter Lola Dewaere, and **Vincent Cassel**, among others.

DHÉLIA, FRANCE (1894–1964). Actress. Born Franceline Benoît, France Dhélia was one of the great stars of the silent screen. She started her film career under the stage name Mado Floréal, but later changed to France Dhélia. She made her screen debut in **Camille de Morlhon**'s *L'Ambitieuse* (1912) under the name Floréal, and went on to make several other silent film appearances in films such as Georges Denola's *Joséphine vendue par ses soeurs* (1913), de Morlhon's *Coeur de Gavroche* (1916), and René Le Somptier's *Épave de l'amour* (1916). Dhélia appeared for the first time as Dhélia in Charles Burget and Le Somptier's *Sultane de l'amour* (1918). She went on to do several other Le Somptier films including *La Croisade* (1920), *La Montée vers l'acropole* (1920), and *La Bête traquée* (1922), which Le Somptier codirected with Michel Carré. Other silent films in which Dhélia played include **Germaine Dulac**'s *Malencontre* (1920), **Jacques de Baroncelli**'s *Nène* (1923), Pierre Colombier's *Petit hôtel à louer* (1923), and **Jean Epstein**'s *Sa tête* (1929).

Dhélia made a number of films, both silent and sound, with director **Gaston Roudès**, including *Les Rantzau* (1923), *L'Ombre du bonheur* (1924), *L'Éveil* (1924), *La Douleur* (1925), *Le Prince Zilah*

(1926), *Le Chemin de la gloire* (1926), *La Maison au soleil* (1928), *L'Ami de Pierre* (1928), *Un coup de mistral* (1933), *Roger la Honte* (1933), *L'Assomoir* (1935), and *Une main a frappé* (1939). Apart from her roles in Roudès's films, she had one other speaking role, in Marc Didier's *Le Billet de mille* (1935). She disappeared from the screen after 1935.

DIAMANT-BERGER, HENRI (1895–1972). Director, producer, and screenwriter. Henri Diamant-Berger began his career as a journalist and film critic, ultimately becoming the editor of the journal *Le Film*. He began dabbling in screenwriting just prior to the war, and several of his film adaptations were made into **Pathé** silent films, no doubt in part because of Diamant-Berger's connections to André Heuzé, who had founded *Le Film*. Silent films based on Diamant-Berger's adaptations include Heuzé and **Léonce Perret**'s *Debout les morts* (1916) and Raymond Bernard's *Le Petit café* (1919), starring **Max Linder**.

Diamant-Berger soon added directing to his repertoire. He directed for Pathé a twelve-episode serial adaptation of Alexandre Dumas's *Les Trois mousquetaires* (1921). The film was exceptionally well done, enormously popular, and is still regarded as one of the classics of silent film.

In 1922, Diamant-Berger left Pathé to found his own production company, Le Studio de Billancourt, buying an old aviation works that had been converted into a film studio. The studio was one of the first independent studios, outside of Pathé and Gaumont, and it was the first studio that was not made of open-glass. He began producing his own films there in the same year, continuing the Musketeers saga with a sequel series, *Les Trois mousquetaires: vingt ans après* (1922–1923). The series was an enormous success, which was a great triumph for Diamant-Berger. He went on to make yet another sequel, *Milady* (1923), and in the same year produced and directed *Gonzague* (1923), *L'Affaire de la rue Lourcine* (1923), *Le Mauvais garçon* (1923), and *Par habitude* (1923), all of which featured Maurice Chevalier.

Diamant-Berger continued directing films in the sound era. He made some twenty or so sound films including *Les Trois mousquetaires: Milady* (1932), *Les Trois mousquetaires: les ferrets de la reine* (1932), *Miquette et sa mère* (1933), *Arsène Lupin détective* (1937),

Arsène Lupin contre Arsène Lupin (1937), *La Maternelle* (1948), *Monsieur Fabre* (1951), *Mon curé chez les riches* (1952), and *Messieurs les ronds de cuir* (1959). Diamant-Berger was largely a popular director. Outside of *Les Trois mousquetaires* (1921), and possibly *Arsène Lupin detective* (1937), none of his films was particularly critically acclaimed. However, many of his films, particularly *Miquette et sa mère* (1933), have achieved a particular status in French-film history, and certainly memory.

In addition to producing his own films, Diamant-Berger also produced the films of a number of other directors. He produced **René Clair**'s *Paris qui dort* (1925) at Billancourt, as well as **Abel Gance**'s spectacular *Napoléon* (1927). The film had to be cut from ten episodes to only one because of the enormous costs involved. He also produced Karl Théodor Dreyer's *La Passion de Jeanne d'arc* (1929), although he sold Billancourt shortly thereafter to Pierre Braunberger and **Roger Richebé**.

In later years, Diamant-Berger produced several of Robert Dhéry's films, including *Branquignol* (1949) and *La Belle Américaine* (1961). He also produced Robert Lamoureux's *Ravissante* (1960) and **Jean-Pierre Mocky**'s *Un drôle de paroissien* (1963) and *Les Compagnons de la marguerite* (1967).

DIEUDONNÉ, ALBERT (1889–1976). Actor, director, and screenwriter. Albert Dieudonné began his career on the stage, following in the footsteps of his uncle, who was also an actor. He ventured into cinema fairly early in his career. His first roles were in productions done by **Studio Film d'art**, and he appeared in Henri Burguet's *L'Empreinte ou la main rouge* (1908) as well as **Charles le Bargy**'s *L'Assassinat du Duc de Guise* (1909). He also appeared in several **Pathé** films including Michel Carré's *Le Roi s'amuse* (1909), as well as **Georges Monca**'s *Jim Blackwood Jockey* (1909) and **André Hugon**'s *Angoisse* (1917) and *Jacques Landauze* (1920).

Without a doubt, the role for which Dieudonné is best known is that of Napoléon Bonaparte. He played Napoléon several times in his career, three of them in films directed by **Abel Gance**. It is the first film, *Napoléon vu par Abel Gance* (1927), that tied Dieudonné to the emperor, and his face, for many filmgoers, became the face of the emperor with Gance's film.

Dieudonné reincarnated the emperor again in Gance's *Napoléon Bonaparte* (1935) and again in *Bonaparte et la révolution* (1971). So intertwined were Dieudonné and that role that near the end of his life, he gave lectures on the life of Napoléon. Other films in which Dieudonné appeared include **Alfred Machin**'s *Le Diamant noir* (1913), Gance's *L'Héroïsme de Paddy* (1915), *La Folie du Docteur Tube* (1915), and *Le Périscope* (1916), **Jean Renoir**'s *Catherine/Une vie sans joie* (1927), and **Roger Richebé**'s *Madame Sans-Gêne* (1941), a film in which Dieudonné also played Napoleon.

In addition to his acting, Dieudonné also tried his hand at writing and directing. He assisted Jean Renoir on the film *Catherine/ Une vie sans joie* and wrote the scenario for Hugon's *Les Chacals* (1917), **Jacques de Baroncelli**'s *L'Homme du Niger* (1940), and René Hervil's *La Douceur d'aimer* (1930). He also directed three films of his own, *Sous la griffe* (1921), *Son crime* (1921), *Gloire rouge* (1923), films in which he also starred.

DIVA (1981). Film. Based on novel of the same name by Delacorta (the pseudonym of Swiss writer Daniel Odier), **Jean-Jacques Beineix**'s debut feature film, *Diva,* at first appears to be a crime drama. The protagonist, Jules (Frédéric Andréi), clandestinely records the concert of the diva Cynthia Hawkins (the American opera singer Wilhelmenia Fernandez), who has refused all reproductions of her voice. Jules becomes the target of a corrupt police chief, Jean Saporta (Jacques Fabbri), whose mistress makes a tape exposing his connections to a prostitution and drug ring and then places this tape in Jules's carrying case. Jules is then chased by Saporta and by Taiwanese bootleggers, who want his opera recording in order to force Hawkins into a contract. Jules is aided by Serge Gorodish (Richard Bohringer) and a young shoplifter named Alba (An Lu Thuuy).

At once a parody of the popular French *policier* and a playful mixture of images and sounds from "high" art and popular culture, *Diva* has been regarded as the first film from the ***cinéma du look***. Beineix's emphasis on visual beauty prompted some critics to compare his films to commercial advertising and even to the experience of window shopping, comparisons that point to the elements of postmodernism in the film. However, *Diva* has since been viewed as a clever artistic engagement with the reproduction of images and sounds.

The film is structured around the idea of theft, and multiple thefts punctuate the narrative: the pirating of music for pleasure and profit, the theft of the diva's dress, and the shoplifting of records. These thefts contrast, for example, with the idea of the legitimate recording of music and with Hawkins's own reproductions of older musical works. As a backdrop to the narrative, there is Beineix's filmmaking, which relies heavily on borrowings (or reproductions) from other films. These numerous examples of borrowing and reproduction point to the fact that all of art is rooted in such borrowing and that sometimes it is legitimate, sometimes illegitimate. Since it is specifically the marketing of art, and not its reproduction for enjoyment, that Hawkins resists, the film seems to suggest that borrowing and reproduction for "art's sake" is sanctioned, while borrowing or reproduction for purely commercial purposes is problematic.

Diva also abounds in visual and auditory manipulation. Saporta manipulates his mistress's recording to efface blame. Gorodish uses optical illusion to lure Saporta into an elevator shaft, and the film itself records the sound and image of the opera singer Fernandez, despite the fact that it encodes this recording as taboo. There is also Beineix's own manipulation, whereby he borrows images from **Louis Feuillade**'s *Fantômas* (1913), **Marcel Carné**'s *Les Enfants du Paradis* (1945), and various other films. Film is also referenced in the stereotyped images of thugs in dark sunglasses, characters who mirror those often found in film noir or crime films. Through his own borrowings, Beineix draws attention to filmic images that are reproduced over and over again in popular cinema, and he blurs the lines between cinematic reproduction and invention, between marketing and art.

Diva has been said to have heralded a number of film movements, some of which overlap. These include the *cinéma du look*, postmodern French cinema, the new baroque, *le visuel*, and the "new New Wave." Some superficial comparisons can also be made between *Diva* and **Jean-Luc Godard**'s landmark *Nouvelle Vague* or New Wave film, *À bout de souffle* (1960). Similarities between the two films include the protagonist's obsession with an American woman, the presence of slick cars, the dominance of music, and the preoccupation with youth. Additionally, both works make overt references to other films. Yet one might also see a stark divergence from the New

Wave with *Diva*'s return to the vivid color and gorgeous imagery of the *tradition de qualité*, yet without any pretensions toward stable meaning. It is interesting that the film that marks this "new" cinema is a clever play of reproduced images and sounds. Its foregrounding of the visual suggests a rejection of the search for narrative truths and a concentration on the cinema as a purely visual form, a move similar to postmodernism's renunciation of grand narratives and its constant play with signs.

DONIOL-VALCROZE, JACQUES (1920–1989). Actor, director, and film critic. Jacques Doniol-Valcroze was the cofounder, with **André Bazin**, of the *Cahiers du Cinéma*, a journal for which he also wrote criticism. He also worked as editor for *Cinémonde* and *La Revue du Cinéma*. Apart from his role as critic, he also acted and directed. Films in which he appeared include Alain Robbe-Grillet's *L'immortelle* (1963) and *Le jeu avec le feu* (1975), **Alain Resnais's** *Je t'aime, je t'aime* (1968), **Claude Lelouch's** *Le voyou* (1970), Jean-Daniel Pollet's *L'amour c'est gai, l'amour c'est triste* (1971), and **Michel Deville's** *L'apprenti salaud* (1977). He directed *L'eau à la bouche* (1960), *Le coeur battant* (1962), *La dénonciation* (1962), *Le viol* (1967), *La maison des Boiries* (1970), *L'homme au cerveau greffé* (1972), and *Une femme fatale* (1977).

DULAC, GERMAINE (1882–1942). Director. Born Charlotte Elisabeth Germaine Saisset-Schneider in Amiens, Germaine Dulac, whose father was a cavalry officer, was raised primarily by her grandmother. Dulac had an early interest in literature and the arts and was, unusually, encouraged to pursue those. She was an early and outspoken feminist and suffragette. Her marriage, contrary to what might be expected, only encouraged these tendencies, as her husband, Marie-Louis Albert Dulac, shared similar interests and ideas.

Dulac began her professional life in journalism, becoming editor of the feminist journal *La Française*. In her capacity as editor, Dulac was obliged to function as a film and theater critic. It was in this way that she met the silent film actress **Stacia Napierkowska**, who is reported to have encouraged Dulac's interest in cinema. Dulac turned her hand to directing in 1915 and was only the second French **woman** to take up directing, after **Alice Guy**, although the actress **Musidora** would not be far behind.

Dulac would ultimately direct more than thirty narrative or fiction films and a handful of documentaries, although her reputation in the present day stems from only three films, *La Fête espagnole* (1920), a film about a love triangle involving a Spanish dancer that is based on a scenario by **Louis Delluc,** and which is widely considered the first impressionist film, *La Souriante Madame Beudet* (1923), about an abused bourgeois wife and widely considered the first feminist film, and *La Coquille et le clergyman* (1927), a truly surrealist film that is often considered the first.

Many of Dulac's other films are more conventional and less experimental than the three for which she is best known. Many are romantic stories involving love triangles in particular. These include *Âme d'artiste* (1925), a forbidden love story about a married playwright, *Antoinette Sabrier* (1928), the story of a wife tempted by adultery, and *Le Picador* (1932), the story of forbidden love of a man for an orphan he has raised and the love triangle involving her and another. Some of her films, such as *La Belle dame sans merci* (1920), *Mort du soleil* (1921), and *La Folie des valiants* (1925) deal with explicitly feminist themes, while others such as *Malencontre* (1920), *Gosette* (1923), and *Le Diable dans la ville* (1924) deal with oppression more generally than in a specifically gender-based sense. In any case, nearly all of her films, both the more popular and the more experimental, often reflected the social concerns that drove her life.

In addition to their thematic similarities, Dulac's films tend to be visually compelling, organized in a way that is more visual than traditionally narrative. They are often psychologically motivated, focusing on the psychology and the mental state of the characters involved, and distinctly nonlinear in their narrative composition, tending to insert scenes and images that convey other meanings than merely the advancement of plot. This also is consistent with Dulac's philosophical position outside of her filmmaking, since she held, in opposition to the dominant trends of her day, that film should not seek to imitate literature or theater, but rather to evolve into its own form.

Dulac made films independently from 1915 until the early 1930s, when the arrival of talking films rendered her theories and filmmaking style permanently obsolete. After that she became the head of newsreel production for **Pathé** and then **Gaumont**, responsibilities she exercised until her death.

DURAND, JEAN (1882–1946). Actor and director. Jean Durand got his start, as did many of the film pioneers, in the café-concerts or music halls of Paris. In 1908, Georges Fagot introduced Durand to **Charles Pathé**, who was constantly recruiting talent from the Parisian stage for his studio, and Durand went to work very briefly at Pathé. He left Pathé for Société Lux, where he made more than forty films, most of which have been lost.

In 1910, **Gaumont** hired Durand as a replacement for **Roméo Bossetti**, who had gone to Italy, and he was charged with directing the burlesque *Calino* series. Durand, it turns out, was a master of burlesque. He directed *Calino* from 1910 until 1913, turning out such titles as *Calino cocher* (1911), *Calino médecin par amour* (1911), *Calino chef de gare* (1912), and *Calino et les deux candidats* (1913).

Durand went on to create two other very successful burlesque series for Gaumont, the *Zigoto* series, which ran in 1912, and the *Onésime* series, which ran from 1912 until 1915, including such titles as *Onésime a un duel à l'américaine* (1912), *Onésime contre Onésime* (1912), *Onésime et la panthère de Calino* (1913), *Onésime se marie, Calino aussi* (1913), and *Onésime et le drame de famille* (1914). Durand's burlesque was extremely physical, even more so than Bosetti's, and to that end he pioneered the use of stunt people (as things were always getting broken and people hit). His influence was far-reaching in later burlesque and slapstick performances like the Keystone Cops or the Marx Brothers.

In about 1910, Durand began working with the Wild West actor/director **Joë Hamman**. Some of these Westerns were episodes of his burlesque series. Examples are *Calino veut être cowboy* (1911) and *Onésime sur le sentier de la guerre* (1913). Others, such as *Pendaison à Jefferson city* (1911) and *Le Railway de mort* (1912), are newly created Westerns. These films, at Hamman's suggestion, were shot in France's Camargue region of France, which is somewhat reminiscent of some Wild West landscapes. The **Camargue Western** was one of the casualties of the war, but Durand's influence may have ultimately led to the Spaghetti Westerns of later days. The famous and enormously popular *Arizona Bill* series, which ran from 1911 to 1913, and in which Hamman starred, is sometimes attributed to Durand. However, there is evidence that five of the episodes were directed by

Hamman himself when he left to work for Éclipse Studios in about 1910 and that others were directed by **Gaston Roudès**.

Most of the Camargue Westerns have been lost, although *Un mariage au revolver* (1911), *Une pendaison à Jefferson City* (1911), and *Le Railway de la mort* (1912) are known to have survived. Interestingly, Durand's comic touch is something he does not seem to have been able to turn on and off, and many of his Westerns have elements of burlesque and therefore come off as parodies of the more classic vein of the genre.

On the whole, Durand made a number of films of a wide variety. There are more than one hundred titles that he is known to have made. He was the third-most-important director during his time at Gaumont, after **Louis Feuillade**, of course, and **Léonce Perret.** Outside of the burlesque series and the Westerns, his other films include *Belle-maman bat les records* (1908), *Mignonne* (1911), *Sous le griffe* (1912), *Le Collier vivant* (1913), *Le Chasseur de lions* (1913), *La Pipe de master Pouitte* (1913), *Les Enfants de France* (1918), *Palaces* (1927), *L'Île d'amour* (1928), and *La Femme rêvée* (1928). Despite his enormous contribution to early film, Durand was ignored by the first generation of film historians and was thus more or less forgotten by film scholars until quite recently. His work has lately been reevaluated.

DURAS, MARGUERITE (1914–1996). Director and screenwriter. Marguerite Duras was born Marguerite Donnadieu in Gia Dinh, Vietnam, during the period of French colonization of what was then Indochina. Her parents were teachers. Her father fell ill and returned to France in 1918 and died in 1921. Duras lived in France with her family for a few years and then relocated to Indochina with her mother and brothers in 1924. Her mother struggled to support them on a teacher's salary. Duras left for France again in 1932, and earned a degree in law and political science at the Sorbonne. She later worked for the French Colonial Office. In 1942, during the German Occupation, Duras joined the French Resistance. Her husband, Robert Antelme, was taken to the Dachau concentration camp and was rescued by François Mitterand. The Holocaust would become one of the central themes of her work. Her first novel, *Les Impudents*, was published in 1943. Her later novel, *Un barrage,* was the basis for **René**

Clement's 1958 film, *This Angry Age*. In 1960, *Moderato Cantabile* was adapted for Peter Brook's film of the same name.

Duras entered the cinema more directly when **Alain Resnais** invited her to write the script of his film, *Hiroshima mon amour* (1959), and in fact, both she and Resnais would often be grouped under the same critical rubrics by scholars, including *le nouveau cinéma*, or new cinema, and *cinéastes rive gauche*, or Left Bank directors. She has also been linked with **Agnès Varda**, both through her feminist approaches and her categorization as an avant-garde artist. Duras also scripted Henri Colpi's *Une aussi longue absence* (1961) and codirected *La Musica* (1967) with Paul Seban. Duras was a widely respected novelist, screenwriter, and left-wing intellectual before her independent directorial debut, *Détruire dit-elle* (1969). She also published a text of the same name with Les Editions de Minuit in 1969. Both works were shaped in part by the events of May 1968.

Duras's films were frequently interwoven with her novels and plays—she referred to films as "un livre sur la pelicule" (a book on film), though she resisted conventional cinematic adaptations of her texts. While her films, like her novels, are clearly autobiographical, intentional contradictions in her interviews and writing suggest both a resistance to readings of her work as strictly autobiographical and also recognition of the fragility of powerful, yet unreliable and chaotic memories. Her preoccupation with the voice (and also the sound of silence) in her writing was reflected in her foregrounding of sound in her films.

In the 1970s, Duras directed some of her most well-known works, among them *Nathalie Granger* (1972) and *India Song* (1975). *India Song*, starring **Delphine Seyrig**, is Duras's most prominent film. In *India Song*, off-screen voices are dislocated from the image track and seem to function independently. Duras reemployed the soundtrack of *India Song* for her next film, *Son Nom Venise dans Calcutta désert* (1976), yet created a new set of images.

Duras's next major film was *Le Camion* (1977), in which she appeared with **Gérard Depardieu**. Filmed in Duras's home, *Le Camion* features Depardieu reading from an unrehearsed script. The film's unusual approach to acting, her real recording of an imagined film, and her complex presentation of narrative has received energetic critical attention. Duras continued to foreground actors' reading of scripts in *Le Navire Night* (1979), where she reads alongside director **Benoît Jacquot**. The soundtrack of the film recounts a romance conducted via telephone, while the visual track conjures images of Paris. The disjuncture between sound and image is a hallmark of Duras's films. Duras directed lesser-known works in the 1970s, some of which have limited distribution: *Jaune le soleil* (1971), *La Femme du Gange* (1973)—both starring Catherine Sellers—*Des journées entières dans les arbres* (1976), with **Madeleine Renaud** and **Bulle Ogier**, and *Baxter, Vera Baxter* (1976), with Seyrig and Claudine Gabay. In 1979, four short films by Duras were released: *Césarée, Les Mains négatives*, *Aurélia Steiner (Melbourne)*, and *Aurélia Steiner (Vancouver)*. The last and longest of the four was inspired by Elie Wiesel's memories of the Holocaust recorded in his autobiographical novel, *Night* (1958).

In the early 1980s, Duras directed *Agatha et les lectures illimités* (1981), a film about forbidden love featuring the images of actors Ogier and Yann Andréa and the voices of Andréa and Duras. In *L'Homme atlantique*, Duras projected a black screen through much of the film as she reads from her novel of the same name. After *L'Homme atlantique*, she made *Il Dialogo di Roma* (1982) and her final film, *Les Enfants* (1985), codirected with her son, Jean Mascolo, and Jean-Marc Turine. In the mid-1980s, Duras departed from the cinema and focused on her writing. Her novel *L'Amant* won the prestigious Goncourt Prize in 1984. Jean-Jacques Annaud adapted the novel for his film, *The Lover*. Duras disagreed with his representation of her work. *See also* WOMEN.

DUVIVIER, JULIEN (1896–1967). Director. Julien Duvivier was born in Lille, in northern France. He had a great love of the theater and had ambitions of becoming an actor. Indeed, he began his career as an actor at the Odéon in Paris under the direction of the great **André Antoine**. It would later be said that this early period influenced him greatly and that he learned from Antoine to strive for perfection and to aspire to an art that mirrored reality. It was Antoine himself who encouraged Duvivier to leave the theater to go into cinema. Remembered as one of the master technicians among the practitioners of *Le Réalisme poétique* or poetic realism, it would seem that although Duvivier left the theater, he kept some of what he learned there.

Duvivier began his career in cinema during the silent-film era. Antoine had been hired by **Pathé** to direct films for the **Société Cinématographique des Auteurs et des Gens de Lettres** (SCAGL), Pathé's *film d'art* division, and Duvivier came along to work as his assistant. His first experience in film was on *Les Travailleurs de la mer* (1918), an adaptation of a work by Victor Hugo. Duvivier also assisted Antoine on *La Terre* (1921), adapted from the Émile Zola novel. Duvivier would work also with **Albert Capellani** at Pathé, and he assisted on such films as *Quatre-vingt-treize* (1921), the classic silent-film adaptation of the Hugo novel. He also worked for **Louis Feuillade**, at the time the head of production at **Gaumont**, with Henri Étiévant, with Dominique Bernard-Deschamps, and with **Marcel L'Herbier**.

This early period in the cinema must have been as important in forming Duvivier as his time in the theater. Capellani, Etiévant, and L'Herbier were masterful directors. Feuillade was himself a master technician and a hyperperfectionist. Most important, his films are seen as important forerunners of poetic realism. It would be naïve to overlook the influence the great director must have had on the young director, just starting out.

Duvivier, for his part, tried his hand at solo filmmaking quite early. His first film, *Haceldama ou le prix du sang,* was made in 1919. From 1922 on, Duvivier was working almost exclusively alone, often writing the screenplays for his films as well, something he would do throughout his career. His early films include *Les Roquevillard* (1922), based on the novel by Henry Bordeaux, and the sequel, *L'Ouragon sur la montagne* (1923), *Credo ou la tragédie à Lourdes* (1924), *La Machine à refaire la vie* (1924), and the melodramatic religious films, *L'Agonie de Jerusalem* (1927) and *La Divine Croisière* (1929).

The coming of sound to cinema moved Duvivier into another dimension of filmmaking, and some would say that the early decades of sound cinema, particularly the 1930s, were the best years of Duvivier's career. At that time, he was counted among the best directors making films and was often identified with other major realist and poetic realist filmmakers of the day, including **Jean Renoir**, **Marcel Carné**, **René Clair**, and **Jacques Feyder** (together considered the great five directors of the golden age of French cinema).

Duvivier set the pace for his filmmaking in the 1930s with *David Golder* (1931), the film in which he introduced **Harry Baur** to sound cinema. The film restarted Baur's film career, making of him a major film star of the day, and was the first in a fairly long series of solidly realist, somber, almost noir films that would dominate Duvivier's career for more than a decade. Shortly after *David Golder*, Duvivier made *Allô Berlin, Ici Paris* (1931), a film that captures quite clearly much of the spirit of the prewar era. This film, the story of two telephone operators, one in Berlin, one in Paris, who can speak to and understand one another but who are prevented by circumstances from meeting, seems, in retrospect, a proleptic comment on the failure of those who might have prevented war to come to power.

In 1932, Duvivier made *La Tête d'un homme*, again starring Harry Baur, a very dark Maigret mystery about a man who frames a mentally challenged man for a crime he, himself, committed. In this film, there was a glimpse into the darker side of Duvivier's realism, a side that would show itself more and more frequently over time. This film was followed by *Poil de Carotte* (1932), a sound remake of a 1925 Duvivier silent film about reconciliation between an emotionally abusive father and his son. *Poil de Carotte* is considered among the best films Duvivier ever made.

Duvivier's 1934 historical film *Maria Chapdelaine* marked the first time the director worked with legendary actor **Jean Gabin**. The collaboration was a fruitful one, and the two would go on to do a number of films together. Gabin would star in the passion film *Golgotha* (1935), the war film *La Bandera* (1935), the classic film *La Belle équipe* (1936)—often read as a commentary on the Front populaire, with which Gabin was identified through his work with **Jean Renoir**—the classic noir film *Pépé le Moko* (1937), and the darkly realist *Voici le temps des assassins* (1956).

Apart from his work with Gabin, Duvivier directed a number of other classic films, particularly in the 1930s. The costume drama *Golem* (1935), starring Harry Baur, remains a solid, well-crafted example of Duvivier's work. The sentimental drama *Un Carnet de bal* (1937) is also among the best films Duvivier ever made, and it inspired many similar films. *La Fin du jour* (1939), starring Pierre Jouvet and **Michel Simon**, about retired actors in a nursing home, is also one of Duvivier's better films. His talent for casting great actors to perfection clearly shows in this particular film.

Following the success of his films in France, particularly *Pépé le Moko*, Duvivier was called to work in Hollywood. He did several films in English, particularly during the 1940s, but also continued to work in France. His English-language films include *Lydia* (1941), starring Merle Oberon; *Tales of Manhattan* (1942), with an all-star cast including **Charles Boyer**, Rita Hayworth, Henry Fonda, and Edward G. Robinson; *The Imposter* (1944), starring Gabin in an English-speaking role; and *Anna Karenina* (1948), starring Vivien Leigh. Duvivier's French films from the same period include *Untel père et fils* (1943), starring **Raïmu** and **Michèle Morgan**, and *Panique* (1946), starring Simon and Viviane Romance.

After the war, Duvivier concentrated the majority of his efforts on filmmaking in France. He had a hit with *Le Petit monde de Don Camillo* (1951), starring **Fernandel**, and more particularly with the sequel, *Le Retour de Don Camillo* (1953). In that respect, Duvivier was able to restart his career after the war, whereas many filmmakers seemed at a loss to do so. Other important films from this later period include *Voici le temps des assassins* (1956), starring Gabin and Danièle Delorme, and *Le Diable et le dix commandements* (1962), starring Fernandel. Duvivier might have gone right on making films, but he was killed in a car crash in 1967.

Often criticized during his lifetime for making "popular" films, Duvivier has proven to be one of the more enduring of the so-called great five filmmakers of the 1930s and 1940s. The standing of his work has not been diminished by the critiques of the filmmakers of the ***Nouvelle Vague*** or New Wave, nor has the appreciation of them been changed by the innovations those filmmakers introduced. The great Renoir once said that if he built a monument to cinema, he would place Duvivier's statue above the front door. Perhaps Duvivier's films have taken just such a place in the monument that is film history.

– E –

ÉCLAIR STUDIOS. Éclair film studios were founded in May 1907 by two Parisian lawyers, Marcel Vandal and Charles Jourjon, who bought out the operations of Parnaland studios, at the time involved in legal action. Shortly after the company was founded, however, **Ambroise Parnaland** was ejected as a partner and Vandal and Jourjon managed the studio on their own. In order to jump-start film production, Vandal and Jourjon had a glass-house studio, which was a type of early film studio constructed of steel and glass in order to allow for maximum exposure to natural light, built at Épinay-sur-Seine in 1908, and this became the company's principal studio.

Vandal and Jourjon then hired the directors **Georges Hatot** and **Victorin Jasset**, who immediately began making films for the studio. The most famous and successful of these were serials, including the *Nick Winter* (1908–1909) detective films, the *Riffle Bill* (1908–1909) films, and the *Morgan le pirate* (1909) series.

In 1910, Hatot left Éclair to found his own studio, and Jasset continued on alone. During the same period, the studio began production operations, which constituted an important expansion of its influence in the French cinema market. The studio opened operations in the United States (in Fort Lee, New Jersey, site of **Alice Guy**'s Solax studios) in 1911, and films were made here until 1920. In France, 1920 marked the entry of Éclair into the equipment market, and in the late 1920s, Éclair ventured into the production of sound or talking pictures.

Éclair ultimately became the third largest studio in France, after **Pathé** and **Gaumont**. It is still located at Épinay-sur-seine. During the golden age of French cinema, its studios produced films by **Jacques Feyder** and **René Clair**. Today it has diversified its film operations and is a pioneer of digital video.

EPSTEIN, JEAN (1897–1953). Director, film theorist, and screenwriter. Jean Epstein was born in Warsaw, Poland. He later immigrated to France with his family. Epstein, like his contemporary **Louis Delluc**, was extremely literate and had an intellectual and philosophical as well as aesthetic engagement with film. Like Delluc, Epstein began by writing criticism and then went on to make films on his own. Epstein's theories, which have been ignored for long periods, were at odds with the strongly realist and mimetic trends that dominated cinema from the beginning. He wrote about film's ability to comment on, interpret, and distort reality, through the manipulation of the image and through editing techniques and special effects and later through sound, but he was not a proponent of film's ability to capture or reflect the real. His theories have influenced filmmakers as diverse as **Jean Vigo**, **Marcel L'Herbier**, **Jean-Luc Godard**, **Alain Resnais**, and the filmmakers of the *Cinéma du look*, such as **Léos Carax**.

Epstein's own films were, obviously, avant-garde. In his early films made during the silent-film era, the image dominates. These films are deeply psychological and visual and often border on expressionism. They typically use effects such as montage, rapid cuts, or multiple exposure to convey emotional or psychological states of characters or to create such emotional or psychological states in the spectator. Films from this early period include *Les Vendanges* (1922) and *Pasteur* (1922), both of which are documentaries, and *Coeur fidèle* (1923), *La Belle Nivernaise* (1923), *L'Auberge rouge* (1923), and *La Chute de la maison D'Usher* (1928), an adaptation of the Edgar Allen Poe story. He was assisted in some of these first filmmaking efforts by his sister, **Marie Epstein**.

Epstein's attempts to render the psychological visual in film are evident from his first narrative film, *Coeur fidèle*, in which the use of the close-up, in particular, becomes a device for conveying the psychological and emotional rather than the seen world. These techniques are developed in *L'Auberge rouge*. Without doubt, however, it is *La Chute de la maison d'Usher*, considered one of Epstein's greatest films, in which Epstein's techniques reach a level of mastery. The film conveys not only character emotions and psychology, but also captures the eerie and tense atmosphere of the original Poe story through Epstein's visual presentation and through the film's unusual use of time. Luis Buñuel, who worked as Epstein's assistant director on the film, was profoundly influenced by his experience.

Shortly after making *La Chute de la maison d'Usher*, Epstein spent a significant amount of time in Brittany, particularly on coastal islands and in rural areas. *Finis terrae* (1929) was the first of several documentaries in which Epstein tried to capture life as he found it in that very undisturbed region of France. Breton documentaries include *Mor Vran* (1931), *L'Or des mers* (1932), and *La Bretagne* (1936).

With the arrival of sound, Epstein sought new ways to experiment with film. His later films include *L'Homme à l'Hispano* (1933), *La Châtelaine du Liban* (1934), *Coeur de gueux* (1936), and *La Femme du bout du monde* (1937), all of them crime or espionage films. The most notable of Epstein's later films is the experimental Breton documentary *Le Tempestaire* (1947), in which Epstein attempts to use sound to re-create the natural environment of the Breton landscape, particularly the sea and the wind.

World War II, and specifically the Nazi Occupation, more or less put an end to Epstein's film career. He was prevented from working, suffered constant persecution, and only narrowly escaped deportation (due to the influence of friends in high places). After Liberation, Epstein became a professor at the **Institut des Hautes Études Cinématographiques** (IDHEC), where his students included Resnais, a filmmaker on whom Epstein had a profound influence.

EPSTEIN, MARIE (1899–1995). Director and screenwriter. Marie-Antoinette Epstein was born in Warsaw, and later immigrated to France with her family. She got her start in film writing screenplays for her brother, **Jean Epstein**. She wrote the screenplays for the films *Coeur fidèle* (1923), *Le Double amour* (1926), and *Six et demi onze* (1927). She also acted in *Coeur fidèle* (1923).

Epstein then went to work for director **Jean Benoît-Lévy**, for whom she also wrote screenplays and codirected. Films on which she collaborated with Benoît-Lévy include *Il était une fois trios amis* (1928), *Peau de pêche* (1929), *Âmes d'enfants* (1929), *Coeur de Paris* (1931), *La Maternelle* (1933), *Itto* (1934), *Hélène* (1936), *La Mort du cygne* (1937), *Le Feu de paille* (1940), *Le Poignard* (1952), and *Agence matrimoniale* (1952). She was one of the founders, along with **Henri Langlois**, of the **Cinémathèque française**, and in 1953, she gave up filmmaking in order to devote her energies to film preservation and archiving at the Cinémathèque.

– F –

FABIAN, FRANÇOISE (1933–). Actress. Françoise Fabian was born Michèle Cortès de Leone y Fabianera in Touggourt, Algeria, to a Polish-Jewish mother and Spanish father. She studied piano at the Conservatoire de musique of Algiers and later moved to Paris, where she entered the Conservatoire d'art dramatique. She debuted in cinema in

Pierre Foucaud and **André Hunébelle**'s 1955 *Mémoires d'un flic*. She subsequently acted in Michel Boisrond's *Cette sacré gamine* (1956), Jean Boyer's *Le Couturier de ces dames* (1956), Alex Joffé's *Les Fanatiques* (1957), **Henri Decoin**'s *Le Feu aux poudres* (1957), Clause Boissol's *Chaque jour a son secret* (1958), and Henri Calef's *Les Violents* (1958). In 1957, she married director **Jacques Becker**.

In the 1960s, she played in **Alexandre Astruc**'s *L'Éducation sentimentale* (1962), Gilles Grangier's *Maigret voit rouge* (1963), and **Louis Malle**'s *Le voleur* (1967). Her international fame soared with her performance in Luis Buñuel's *Belle de jour* (1967), and especially with her starring role in **Éric Rohmer**'s *Ma nuit chez Maud* (1969). She was highly active in the early 1970s, with leading roles in Yves Boisset's *Un condé* (1970), **Michel Deville**'s *Raphaël ou le débauché* (1971), Juan Luis Buñuel's *Au rendez-vous de la mort joyeuse* (1973), **Claude Lelouch**'s *La Bonne année* (1973), François Leterrier's *Projection privée* (1973), and **Yves Robert**'s *Salut l'artiste* (1973). She also appeared in Czech director Zbynek Brynych's German-language feature *Die Weibchen* (1970) and **Jacques Rivette**'s *Out 1: Spectre* (1972).

Fabian has also worked with several Italian directors, among them Sergio Corbucci in *Gli Specialisti* (1971), Carlo Lizzani in *Torino nera* (1972), Romolo Guerrieri in *Un Uomo, una città* (1974), Damiano Damiani in *Perché si uccide un magistrato* (1974), Mauro Bolognini in *Per le antiche scale* (1975), and Marco Leto in *Al piacere di rivederla* (1976). Later in the 1970s, she starred in Françoise Sagan's *Les Fougères bleues* (1977) and Just Jaeckin's *Madame Claude* (1977). She also played in a number of television productions directed by Nina Companeez.

In the 1980s and 1990s, Fabian acted again for Lelouch in *Partir, revenir* (1985) and for Rivette in *Secret défense* (1998). In the 1980s, she also appeared in André Delvaux's *Benvenuta* (1983), Pierre Granier-Deferre's *L'Ami de Vincent* (1983), Jean-Claude Guiguet's *Faubourg Saint Martin* (1986), **Jacques Demy**'s *Trois places pour le 26* (1988), for which she received a **César** nomination for Best Supporting Actress, and American director Jerry Schatzberg's *Reunion* (1989). In the 1990s, she acted in the films of prominent **women** directors: Nelly Kaplan's *Plaisir d'amour* (1991) and Danièle Thompson's *La Bûche* (1999). More recently, she had a supporting role in François Ozon's *5x2* (2004).

FABRE, SATURNIN (1884–1961). Actor. Saturnin Fabre began his career as a comic stage actor. He made a name for himself in the theater before turning to cinema. Although he had tried his hand at cinema during the silent-film era in films like **André Antoine**'s *Mademoiselle de la Seglière* (1919) and **Jacques de Baroncelli**'s *La Rafale* (1920), Fabre awaited the coming of sound before transitioning into film.

His first sound film was Robert Florey's *La Route est belle* (1930). Thereafter, Fabre appeared in more than seventy films, establishing himself as a comic actor on a par with **Fernandel**, who was his contemporary. He could, however, play other types of parts as well. The 1930s and 1940s marked the height of Fabre's career. During the 1930s, he appeared in such films as Henry Roussel's *Atout coeur* (1931); **René Guissart**'s *Le Fils improvisé* (1932), *Le Père prématuré* (1933), and *Toi, c'est moi* (1936); **Léo Joannen**'s *On a trouvé une femme nue* (1934), *Train de plaisir* (1935), and *Vous n'avez rien à déclarer* (1937); **Abel Gance**'s *Roman d'un jeune homme pauvre* (1935) and *Le Voleur de femmes* (1937); Yves Mirande's *Sept hommes et une femme* (1936) and *Messieurs les ronds de cuire* (1937); **Julien Duvivier**'s *Pépé le Moko* (1937); and **Sacha Guitry**'s *Ils étaient neuf célibataires* (1939).

In the 1940s, Fabre's career remained strong. During the Occupation, he remained in France, continuing to make films and working for the Nazi-owned production company, **Continental Films**. Fabre's films from the decade include **Henri Decoin**'s *Battement de coeur* (1940), **Marcel L'Herbier**'s *La Nuit fantastique* (1942), **Jacques de Baroncelli**'s *Fausse alerte* (1945), **Marc Allégret**'s *Lunegarde* (1946), **Roger Richebé**'s *Les J3* (1946), **Marcel Carné**'s *Les Portes de la nuit* (1946), **Pierre Chenal**'s *Clochmerle* (1948), and Maurice Cloche's *Docteur Laënnec* (1949).

Fabre made only a handful of films in the 1950s, and the decade was the last in which he made films. His film roles from that period include parts in **Henri-Georges Clouzot**'s *Miquette et sa mère* (1950), Marcel Aboulker's *La Dame de chez Maxim's* (1950), Duvivier's *La Fête à Henriette* (1952), and Carlo Rim's *Escalier de service* (1954), which was his final film.

FANNY (1932). *See MARIUS* (1931), *FANNY* (1932), AND *CÉSAR* (1933).

FANTÔMAS (1913–1914) AND *LES VAMPIRES* (1915). Films. Written and directed for **Gaumont Studios** by **Louis Feuillade**, the *Fantômas* series and the *Vampires* series were two of Feuillade's most significant contributions to the cinema and two of the most important works in French silent cinema. *Fantômas* was not a film, but a series of five films: *Fantômas* (1913), *Juve contre Fantômas* (1913), *Le Mort qui tue* (1913), *Fantômas contre Fantômas* (1914), and *Le Faux magistrat* (1914). The series was based on the best-selling serial novels by Pierre Sylvestre and Marcel Allain. The films chronicle the activities of the criminal mastermind Fantômas, who is played by **René Navarre**. Fantômas is a master manipulator and a master of disguise. He transforms identities and personalities, and among his various incarnations are a doctor, a bellhop, a gentleman, and a detective.

The series centers on Fantômas's crime sprees and the efforts of his enemy, Inspector Juve (Edmond Bréon), to put an end to them. The world of *Fantômas* is one in which anyone is capable of anything, and in which the veneer of normal daily life disguises a frighteningly unstable, often brutal, reality. Feuillade's interpretation of *Fantômas* is noteworthy both in its use of narrative technique (Feuillade experiments with different shots and continuity editing in a way that prefigures much later French filmmaking) and in its mise-en-scène, which is also characterized by the use of social or fantastic realism (he was one of the first directors to film outside, using the real backdrop of the city).

Les Vampires (1915) is also a series of films including the titles *La Tête coupée*, *La Bague qui tue*, *Le Cryptogramme rouge*, *Le Spectre*, *L'Évasion du mort*, *Les Yeux qui fascinent*, *Satanas*, *Le Maître de la foudre*, *L'Homme des poisons*, and *Les Noces sanglantes*. The series repeats the preoccupation with crime and instability, replacing the criminal mastermind with a gang of criminal masterminds, equally capable of morphing into everyday identities and disappearing into the urban space. The series also repeats and develops Feuillade's earlier progress in narrative, editing, and mise-en-scène.

Perhaps the most interesting addition to story in *Les Vampires* is the character of Irma Vep (**Musidora**), a female criminal mastermind, who is sexually liberated, and who uses her status as a working woman to gain access to her victims. A precursor to the femme fatale, Irma Vep is something like the missing link between nineteenth-century literary **women** such as Nana and Emma Bovary and the very twentieth-century film figure, Cat Woman. Irma Vep is often figured onscreen in a black cat suit that emphasizes her female form, and her use of her body to get what she wants is a theme in the series. She has sometimes been read as a prefeminist figure, but it is likely that this is an anachronistic rereading. Given her function within the films, it is more likely that she functions as a strategic warning against the dangers of granting women economic and sexual freedom.

Similarly, some have seen Feuillade's crime series as an avant-garde renunciation of his conservative upbringing. This is also a likely misreading of his films. Feuillade's techniques and his poetics were avant-garde, however, which is why he was beloved by the surrealists a generation after his films were first released. However, in terms of thematics, his films remain quite conservative. Order is always restored, and the criminals ultimately die or are brought to justice. Those who have argued that Feuillade's films revel in chaos are probably overstating matters. It is true that there is a good deal of chaos, but it is a source of disquiet in the films and the spectators who watch them.

It is first and foremost difficult to believe that an avowed monarchist who had previously published a defense of Catholicism would suddenly and inexplicably become an anarchist and a feminist, and there remains the fact that Feuillade made more biblical dramas than any other director of his day. More important, if *Fantômas* and *Les Vampires* revel in chaos, they do so only for a short space, within the relatively safe confines of the cinema and, not insignificantly, they do so only until they again restore order, which occurs at the end of each series.

FERNANDEL (1903–1971). Actor and director. Fernandel was born Fernand Joseph Contandin in Marseille. His father was a performer (the stage name was Sined) in the café-concerts, and Fernandel and his younger brother frequently joined him onstage as children. The father's mobilization for war in 1915 put an end to this, but the desire to become an entertainer was instilled early in Fernandel. Obliged to work to help support his mother, Fernandel found jobs at a bank and soap factory and elsewhere. He continued to pursue the stage in his spare time. During this period, Fernandel met Jean

Manse. The two became close friends. Manse would go on to work on nearly all the screenplays for Fernandel's films, and Fernandel married Jean's sister, Henriette, in 1925. The stage name, Fernandel, is reputed to have come from Jean's mother, Mme. Manse, who referred to Fernand as "Henriette's Fernand" or "her Fernand," that is, "le Fernand d'elle."

Fernandel's first big career break came in 1926, when he was hired on as a feature act at the Odéon theater in Marseille. From there, Fernandel traveled from theater to theater. At about the same time, the cinema began to take note. In 1929, Paramount Europe hired Fernandel to do minifilms of his act as entertainment between films in their movie theaters. And in 1930, **Marc Allégret**, who had seen Fernandel onstage, cast him in *Le Blanc et le noir*, an adaptation of a play by **Sacha Guitry**. Fernandel was an enormous success, and he went on to make 150 or so films.

There is no mistaking the fact that Fernandel was a popular actor and primarily a comic actor. He is probably the best-known comic actor in French film history. Most of his films are not critical masterpieces, but they were nearly all popular successes. That he is an icon of French cinema is attested to by the fact that more than thirty years after his death, you could stop any one of nearly any age in France and ask who Fernandel was and they could tell you.

Some of his best-known films from the first half of his career include Dominique Bernard-Deschamps's *Le Rosier de Madame Husson* (1931); **Marcel Pagnol**'s *Angèle* (1934), *Regain* (1937), *Le Schpountz* (1938), and *La Fille du puisatier* (1941); **Christian-Jacque**'s *Josette* (1936), *François Ier* (1937), *Raphaël le tatoué* (1939); and **Claude Autant-Lara** and Maurice Lehmann's *Fric-Frac* (1939). In these, as in most of his films, and certainly most of those made up to World War II, Fernandel is cast in predictably warm and amusing roles, as the type of characters that cannot help but inspire warm-hearted laughter.

During the war, Fernandel remained in France. He worked for the Nazi-owned production company **Continental Films**, and not only acted, but also tried his hand at directing, perhaps at the request of the management of Continental, who may have sought to exploit his popularity and his good-natured image. He directed two films with Continental, *Simplet* (1942) and *Adrien* (1943). He would make only one other attempt at directing and that much later, in 1951, with *Adhemar ou le jouet de la fatalité*.

After the war, Fernandel continued to make films at a steady pace. Although comedy remained his mainstay, there is a bit more diversity to the films' roles in the postwar period, as Fernandel also began to perform in melodrama and crime films. The best-known films from the latter half of his career include Richard Pottier's *Meurtres* (1950); Autant-Lara's *L'Auberge rouge* (1951); **Julien Duvivier**'s *Le Petit monde de Don Camillo* (1951), *Le Retour de Don Camillo* (1953), *L'Homme à l'imperméable* (1956), and *Le Diable et le dix commandements* (1962); Jean Boyer's *Coiffeur pour dames* (1952), *Le Couturier de ces dames* (1956), and *Sénéchal le magnifique* (1958); **Henri Verneuil**'s *Le Fruit défendu* (1952); Yves Allégret's *Mam'zelle Nitouche* (1954); Clément Duhour's *La Vie à deux* (1957); Christian-Jacque's *La Loi c'est la loi* (1958); and Gilles Grangier's *La Cuisine au beurre* (1963), *L'Âge ingrat* (1964), and *L'Homme à la Buick* (1966).

Without a doubt, the Don Camillo films, particularly the two directed by Duvivier, *Le Petit monde de Don Camillo* and *Le Retour de Don Camillo*, are Fernandel's best-known films. In them, he plays a country priest in a village in postwar Italy. The film gives Fernandel a format for his comedy, but also for the warmth with which he is often associated. Duvivier's realist eye also explores, in a warm and funny way, the tensions in Italian life between Communism and Catholicism, between the forces of tradition and those of change, forces that France also had to grapple with. The films, which were French-Italian coproductions, remain classics in both countries. Fernandel, a devout Catholic, once said of the films that they were the proof he was, despite what anyone might say, a great actor, since his costar in the films was God himself (Don Camillo dialogues with God in the films, and God sometimes answers). Though he made many other films, it is these that have left the most vivid imprint in the cultural memory.

FESCOURT, HENRI (1880–1966). Director and screenwriter. Henri Fescourt began his career as a journalist. He was recruited to **Gaumont** by **Louis Feuillade** in 1908 or so, initially as a screenwriter, although he shortly thereafter turned his hand to directing. Since film credits were rarely used during the silent-film era, it is not known precisely which films he worked on at Gaumont. However, it is known that he began directing in about 1912.

Fescourt directed an impressive number of films during the silent-film era, including early films such as *Le Mensonge* (1912), *Le Bonheur perdu* (1912), *Un grand seigneur* (1912), *La Bienfaitrice* (1912), *La Lumière qui tue* (1913), *La Mort sur Paris* (1913), *Son passé* (1913), *Les Trois ombres* (1914), *Petit coeur d'enfant* (1914), *Fille de prince* (1914), *Maman* (1914), and *L'Affaire du collier noir* (1914).

His career was interrupted by World War I, but he resumed it without much difficulty afterwards, specializing in film serials, notably *Rouletabille*, which ran from 1922 to 1923. Other postwar films include *Les Grands* (1924), *Mandrin* (1924), *Un fils d'Amérique* (1925), *Les Misérables* (1925), *La Maison du Maltais* (1927), *L'Occident* (1927), and *Monte-Cristo* (1929). Of these, his best film is no doubt *Les Misérables*, which stars Gabriel Gabrio as Jean Valjean.

Fescourt made a handful of films in the sound era, including *La Maison de la flèche* (1930), *Service de nuit* (1931), *Serments* (1931), a sound remake of *L'Occident* (1937), *Bar du sud* (1938), and *Retour de flamme* (1943). However, he never seemed to quite find his footing in sound film. He finished his career teaching at **Institut des Hautes Études Cinématographiques** (IDHEC) and writing on the cinema.

FESTIVAL INTERNATIONALE DU FILM DE CANNES/CANNES FILM FESTIVAL. Arguably the most prestigious of international film festivals, the Cannes Film Festival was scheduled to begin in September 1939, but because of World War II, was not fully realized until September 1946. Its first jury president (in 1939) was **Louis Lumière**. The highest award granted is the Palme d'Or (Golden Palm), which was called the "Grand Prix du Festival International du Film" (Grand Prize of the International Film Festival) until 1955. At present, the festival is generally held in May.

FEUILLADE, LOUIS (1873–1925). Director, film pioneer, producer, and screenwriter. Louis Feuillade was born in Hérault in southern France to a bourgeois family of wine merchants. The young Feuillade received a traditional, Catholic education and had a strong interest in literature. He wrote poems and short articles for the local press and dreamed of becoming a writer. Upon leaving school, he went briefly into the family business. In 1898, however, after the death of his father and the failure of the family business, he went to Paris to become a journalist.

In Paris, Feuillade struggled at first, but ultimately found work writing for the *Revue mondiale*. He also began writing screenplays, perhaps to earn extra money to support his wife and daughter, and he began to sell to film studios, including **Gaumont**, in about 1905. **Alice Guy** hired Feuillade on as a screenwriter at Gaumont in 1906, and he replaced her as head of production when she left that post in 1907.

During his time at Gaumont, Feuillade made or participated in the making of some seven hundred films. His enormous catalog includes an impressive array of titles including *films à truc* or trick films (many of them copies of the films of **Georges Méliès**), mystery films, farces, dramas, historical dramas, and biblical dramas. Among the films he directed at Gaumont are *L'Amour et Psyché* (1908), *Le Journal animé* (1908), *La Légende de Daphné* (1908), *La Vie à Rebours* (1908), *Aveugle de Jérusalem* (1909), *La Cigale et la fourmi* (1909), *Le Collier de la reine* (1909), *Benvenuto Cellini* (1910), *Esther* (1910), *Le Festin de Baltazar* (1910), *Aux lions, les chrétiens!* (1911), *Le Fils du locuste* (1911), *Quand les feuilles tombent* (1911), *Le Trust ou les batailles de l'argent* (1911), *André Chenier* (1912), *Androclès* (1912), *Le Bracelet de la marquise* (1912), *L'Homme de proie* (1912), *La Maison des lions* (1912), *L'Agonie de Byzance* (1913), *Erreur tragique* (1913), *La Mort de Lucrèce* (1913), *Le Revenant* (1913), *Le Calvaire* (1914), *Manon de Montmartre* (1914), *Le Fer à cheval* (1914), *Le Sosie* (1914), *Les Fiançailles d'Agénor* (1916), *Les Fourberies de pinguoin* (1916), *Notre pauvre coeur* (1917), *La Femme Fatale* (1917), *Aide-toi* (1918), *Vendemiaire* (1918), *Barrabas* (1919), *Le Nocturne* (1919), *Les Deux gamines* (1920), *La Fille bien gardée* (1921), *L'Orpheline* (1921), *Parisette* (1921), *Le Fils du filibustier* (1922), *Vindicta* (1923), *Lucette* (1924), *Le Stigmate* (1924), and *Pierrot-Pierrette* (1924).

Feuillade is best known, however, for his serials, which he began developing shortly after he took over production at Gaumont. His first serials were rather mundane and included comedy serials, such as the *Bébé* series, which ran from 1912 to 1914, and the *Bout de Zan* series that also ran from 1912 to 1914. He also did a realistic series titled *La Vie telle qu'elle est,* which ran in 1913, and in which his technique of social realism or "fantastic realism" is often seen as a precursor to **Le Réalisme poétique** or poetic realism. The best known of all of Feuillade's serials, however, and probably the best known of his films are his crime serials, particularly the **Fantômas** series, which ran in 1913 and 1914, and the **Vampires** serial, which ran in 1915.

The *Fantômas* series, which consists of five stories totaling twenty-one episodes, was based on the best-selling serial novels by Pierre Sylvestre and Marcel Allain. The films chronicle the activities of the criminal mastermind Fantômas (**René Navarre**), master manipulator and a master of disguise. They center on Fantômas's crime sprees and the efforts of his enemy, Inspector Juve (Edmond Bréon), to put an end to them. *Les Vampires* is similar to *Fantômas* in its subject matter and poetics. In place of a criminal mastermind, Feuillade offers a criminal gang. In place of Inspector Juve, Feuillade offers the journalist Philippe Guerande, but the violence and instability that underlie the everyday world remain.

Feuillade made several other series subsequent to *Fantômas* and *Les Vampires*, the most notable being *Judex*, which ran in 1916 and 1917, *Tih-Minh*, which ran in 1918, and *Barrabas*, which ran in 1918. He remained as head of production at the Gaumont Studios in Paris until his death (from exhaustion, it seems) in 1925. He continued to direct films, as his contract stipulated, right up to the end. Feuillade's films, particularly his crime serials, have been experiencing something of a revival in recent years. They have been released on DVD and are screened at film festivals throughout the world. This should be of little surprise, the world we find ourselves in today being as chaotic and unstable as the world in which Feuillade lived, the spirit of which he so adeptly captured.

FEUILLÈRE, EDWIGE (1907–1998). Actress. Born Edwige Cunati, Edwige Feuillère intended to pursue an acting career from an early age. She attended the Conservatoire d'art dramatique in Dijon, and then began her career in theater. She was in residence at the Comédie Française from 1931 until 1933.

Feuillère made her film debut in 1931 (using the name Cora Lynn) in Karl Anton's *Le Cordon bleu*. The same year she appeared in **Marc Allégret**'s *Mam'zelle Nitouche* (1931) and Jean Dermont's *La Fine combine* (1931). Between 1932 and 1935, Feuillère worked steadily in films such as **René Guissart**'s *La Perle* (1932), Anton's *Monsieur Albert* (1932) and *Une petite femme dans le train* (1933), Pierre Colombier's *Les Messieurs de la santé* (1933), and Alexis Granowsky's *Les Aventures du roi Pausole* (1933). The roles steadily increased in prominence and Feuillère became a darling of the screen.

In 1935, she was cast in the title role in **Abel Gance**'s *Lucrèce Borgia*. The role added momentum to Feuillère's career, proving she was not merely a screen darling, but a serious actress as well. Her performance was widely acclaimed and the role earned her professional respect that would carry forward. Feuillère went on to star in Louis J. Gasnier's *Topaze* (1935), **Julien Duvivier**'s *Golgotha* (1935), Allégret's *La Dame de Malacca* (1937), **Max Ophüls**'s *Sans lendemain* (1939), **Léo Joannen**'s *L'Émigrante* (1940) and *Lucrèce* (1943), Maurice Tourneur's *Mam'zelle Bonaparte* (1942), and **Jacques de Baroncelli**'s *La Duchesse de Langeais* (1942). From the period of 1935 to the Occupation, in fact, Feuillère was one of the most popular leading ladies on the French screen.

Feuillère's career was interrupted during the Occupation, but she resumed it without much difficulty after Liberation, regaining her status as one of the foremost actresses of the day. She appeared in such films as **Jean Delannoy**'s *La Part de l'ombre* (1945); de Baroncelli's *Tant que je vivrai* (1946); Georges Lampin's *L'Idiot* (1946); **Jean Cocteau**'s *L'Aigle a deux têtes* (1948), in which she starred opposite **Jean Marais**; Jacques Manuel's *Julie de Carneilhan* (1949), adapted from Colette; **Christian-Jacque**'s *Souvenirs perdus* (1950) and *Adorables créatures* (1952); **Jacqueline Audry**'s *Olivia* (1951); **Claude Autant-Lara**'s *Le Blé en herbe* (1954) and *En cas de malheur* (1958); and Clément Duhour's *La Vie à deux* (1958).

Feuillère continued acting until the 1990s, although in the 1980s and 1990s, her screen roles were primarily on the small screen. Her later performances include roles in Gérard Oury's *Le Crime ne paie pas* (1962), **Patrice Chéreau**'s *La Chair de l'orchidée* (1975), and Nina Companéez's *Les Dames de la côte* (1979), which was her last film role.

FEYDER, JACQUES (1885–1948). Actor and director. Born Jacques Frédérix in Bruxelles, Jacques Feyder decided to become an actor. While this seems unremarkable, it required him to go against the wishes of his family. The Frédérix family was quite prestigious, had military and literary ties, and had planned a military career for Jacques. Feyder went to Paris to pursue his career as a stage actor, but without the blessing of the family. During his time in the theater, he met the actress Françoise Rosay, and the two married in 1917.

Not long after beginning his stage career, Feyder turned to the cinema, initially as an actor. He had a role in **Georges Méliès's** *Cendrillon ou La pantoufle mystérieuse* (1912) and in one or two other films before signing at **Gaumont** in 1912, on the eve of World War I. At Gaumont, Feyder appeared in such films as **Henri Pouctal's** *Le Trait d'union* (1913), **Gaston Ravel's** *Autour d'une bague* (1915), **Louis Feuillade's** *Les Vampires* (1915), and Charles Burguet's *Quand minuit sonna* (1916).

Feyder began directing in 1915. His first effort was *Les pieds et les mains* (1915), which he codirected with Ravel. From there, Feyder went on to direct a number of silent films on his own, including *Le Pied qui étreint* (1916), *Têtes de femmes, femmes de tête* (1916), *L'instinct est maître* (1917), *Le Ravin sans fond* (1917), and *Le Frère de lait* (1917). These early films are generally light, comic films and really gave no hint of what was to come later in Feyder's career.

In 1917, Feyder's career was interrupted, as he was mobilized for war. The experience marked him, as it did so many of that time. His filmmaking, when he returned, showed evidence of this mark and began to move in a different direction. His first postwar film, *La Faute orthographe* (1919), was another comedy, but it had a depth and an attention to technical artistry that his early films had not.

His next film, *L'Atlantide* (1921), was markedly different from his earlier works. Based on the novel by Pierre Benoît, the film was the story of two soldiers lost in a mythical, African kingdom. Feyder used the story to explore a completely fantastic world in a highly realistic mode. The film is highly exotic in the most orientalist way, presenting the non-Western world as foreign, strange, alluring, and dangerous. The mise-en-scène is probably the primary element of the film, in which image dominates over narrative. With *L'Atlantide*, Feyder established himself as a master of the visual image. The film was an enormous success, in France and internationally, and it has gone down as not merely one of the great silent films, but one of the great films of all time.

Following *L'Atlantide*, Feyder made *Crainquebille* (1923), which developed his realist style, and then another masterpiece, *Visages d'enfants* (1925), the story of a young boy who must deal with the death of his father. Regarded as a piece of visual, psychological poetry on film, *Visages d'enfants* is also widely regarded as one of the greatest silent films ever made.

All of Feyder's last silent films are solid works and all of them follow his realist trajectory, based on a desire to reveal the more invisible, intangible elements of life, such as individual psychology or the human spirit, through extremely concrete, clear images. *Gribiche* (1915), starring his wife, **Françoise Rosay**, is an exploration of class mobility and class identity; *L'Image* (1925) explores the effects a single photograph has on several different people; *Carmen* (1926) is a brilliantly realized adaptation of the Prosper Mérimée novel; and *Les Nouveaux messieurs* (1926) is a satire on the bourgeoisie. Feyder is also known to have made a silent-film version of Honoré de Balzac's *Thérèse Raquin* (1928); however, that film has been lost.

In 1929, Feyder, whose international reputation was well established, went to Hollywood to work for MGM. He found Hollywood a disappointment and remained there only two years. Notable films from this period are *The Kiss* (1929) and *Anna Christie* (1930), both starring Greta Garbo.

The return after Hollywood was slow, and it was not until 1934 that Feyder again released a truly substantive film. It came in the form of *Le Grand jeu* (1934), the story of a lawyer who joins the foreign legion and falls in love with a prostitute. The film was followed by *Pension Mimosas* (1935), the story of a woman who adopts a child abandoned by his father. This was in turn followed by *La Kermesse héroïque* (1935), which stars Rosay, and which is considered yet another of Feyder's masterpieces. The film, which is a meditation on a Flemish painting, explores what happened in the eighteenth century when the marauding Spanish army sought shelter in a small Flanders town. It seeks to explore the period and the subject of the painting in much the same way as the painting it imitates, and in so doing, seeks to place film on an artistic level equal to painting. Its own artistic and thematic brilliance aside, *La Kermesse héroïque* is significant in that it is widely regarded as the film that heralded the arrival of *Le Réalisme poétique* or poetic realism.

La Kermesse héroïque is also considered to be the last of Feyder's great films. He made several more following that film, including *A Knight without Armour* (1937), starring Robert Donat and Marlene Dietrich, *Les Gens du voyage* (1938) and *Une femme disparaît* (1944), both starring Rosay, *La Loi du nord* (1939), starring **Michèle Morgan** and **Pierre Richard-Willm**, and *Macadam* (1946), which he codirected with Marcel Blistène and was his last film. None of these, however, had the depth or the poetry of his earlier works. It is perhaps an irony that the movement Feyder announced would be developed by other filmmakers, but it is also true that he was a generation earlier than directors such as **Marcel Carné** and **Jean Renoir**, and Carné, at least, acknowledged the importance of Feyder's influence on his own work.

FILM D'ART/ART FILM. *Film d'art* or art film is a theory or category of film that considers film as very closely tied to and perhaps an extension of the literary arts, specifically, theater and the novel. Prior to the development of *film d'art*, the cinema was a largely popular, almost purely diversionary medium, driven by spectacle, and while there was a move toward narrative from the very beginning, and even an effort to link cinema to art, it was film d'art that represented the most serious effort to tie cinema to high culture forms like literature and the theater. The term comes from the name of a short-lived studio and production company, **Studio Film d'art**, which specialized in the genre. Film d'art was not the only studio, however, to develop the film d'art. **Pathé**, which had been one of the investors in Studio film d'art, also started up a film d'art division, called **Société Cinématographique des Auteurs et des Gens de Lettres** (SCAGL).

The investment in film d'art helped elevate the status of cinema, especially in France, where the form is considered "the seventh art." It pushed early cinema firmly in the direction of narrative cinema (as opposed to the *cinéma d'attractions*) and created a demand for more developed storylines and certainly for better costumes and scenery, which lead to escalating production costs. It also had one other, probably unintended, consequence. Since films based on theatrical productions created an appetite for well-known theater actors, Pathé and the other studios which were engaged in the production of films d'art began to advertise the presence of well-known stage actors in their films, and it was this practice that led to the much more widespread practice of listing credits for performances and technical contributions in film production. Prior to the development of film d'art, nearly all performances and technical contributions were anonymous.

Early examples of films d'art include **André Calmettes** and Charles Le Bargy's *L'Assassinat du Duc de Guise* (1907), Calmettes's *La Duchesse de Langeais* (1910) and *La Dame aux Camélias* (1912), and **Albert Capellani**'s *Notre-Dame de Paris* (1911) and *Les Misérables* (1913). Several of **Abel Gance**'s films, including *Napoléon* (1927) and *Lucrèce Borgia* (1935), are also in the film d'art tradition. The influence of film d'art may be seen in later directors including **Christian-Jacque** in films such as *Nana* (1955) and *Madame Sans-Gêne* (1962) and **Claude Autant-Lara** in films such as *Le Rouge et le noir* (1954) and *Le Comte de Monte Cristo* (1961). Heritage films such as **Claude Chabrol**'s *Madame Bovary* (1991) and **Claude Berri**'s *Germinal* (1993) also follow in the tradition of film d'art.

In contemporary film terminology, film d'art signifies something quite different from high-production costume dramas, which is essentially what the term signified in the beginning. It is now more closely associated with independent, experimental film than with high-profile stars and large studios. French films such as the more recent films of directors **Jean-Luc Godard** and **Eric Rohmer** are examples, and films by directors such as **Marguerite Duras** and **Agnès Varda** also represent this type of cinema. For many around the world, French cinema in any form is associated with film d'art, since the films that France exports tend to reflect either the **heritage** or experimental tendencies.

FRANCEN, VICTOR (1888–1977). Actor. Born in Belgium, Victor Francen began his acting career in the theater. He made his screen debut during the silent-film era, appearing in such films as Henri Étiévant's *Crépuscule d'épouvante* (1921) and *La Neige sur les pas* (1923). It was the sound era, however, that made Francen a veritable star. He appeared in 1931 in **Léonce Perret**'s *Après l'amour*, and that same year in **Abel Gance**'s *La Fin du monde* and Viktor Tourjanksy's *L'Aiglon*. After 1931, Francen's reputation as a first-rate actor was solidified and he appeared in film after film until the German Occupation. He starred in such films as Paul Czinner's *Mélo* (1932), André Berthomieu's *Les Ailes brisées* (1933), Maurice Tourneur's *Le Voleur* (1933), Pierre Colombier's *Le Roi* (1936), Gance's *J'Accuse* (1937), **Henri Diamant-Berger**'s *La Vieille folle* (1938), **Julien Duvivier**'s *La Fin du jour* (1939), and **Jacques de Baroncelli**'s *L'Homme du Niger* (1940). Francen was also a favorite of **Marcel L'Herbier**, starring in a number of his films during the 1930s, including *L'Aventurier* (1934), *Veilles d'armes* (1935), *La Porte du large* (1936), *Forfaiture* (1937), *Nuits de feu* (1937), and *Entente cordiale* (1939).

Francen fled France with the advance of the Nazis and went to Hollywood. Although Hollywood gave him plenty of work, Francen had to abandon the status of leading man he had held for a decade in France and accept lesser roles, usually that of the villain. Nonetheless, he chose to spend the better part of the remainder of his career in Hollywood, appearing in such films as *Hold Back the Dawn* (1941), Duvivier's *Tales of Manhattan* (1942), *Madame Curie* (1943), *San Antonio* (1945), *Devotion* (1946), *The Adventures of Captain Fabian* (1951), *A Farewell to Arms* (1957), and Joshua Logan's English-language remake of **Marcel Pagnol**'s *Fanny* (1961). Francen returned to France to film only occasionally, appearing in L'Herbier's *La Révoltée* (1948), Pierre Méré's *La Nuit s'achève* (1950), and **Jean-Pierre Mocky**'s *La Grande frousse* (1964). Francen did, however, spend his final days in France and died in Aix-en-Provence.

FRANJU, GEORGES (1912–1987). Director and screenwriter. Georges Franju was born in Fougères. He began his career in cinema working as a set director, and then in 1934 codirected the short film *Le Métro* with **Henri Langlois**. In 1936, Franju cofounded, with Langlois, the **Cinémathèque Française**, the most important film archive in France, and, for two years, Franju worked as an archivist at the cinémathèque. In 1938, Franju expanded his role in the archiving of film and became executive secretary of the International Federation of Film Archives and later the general secretary of the Institut de cinématographie scientifique.

In 1949, Franju returned to active filmmaking with the documentary *Le Sang des bêtes*, an exploration of Parisian abattoirs or slaughterhouses. He went on to make several more shorts immediately following, including *Hôtel des Invalides* (1952), the short biopic *Le Grand Méliès* (1952) about the filmmaker **Georges Méliès**, *Sur le pont d'Avignon* (1956), and *Monsieur et Madame Curie* (1956). In 1959, Franju made his first feature-length film, *La Tête contre les murs*. This film was followed by *Les Yeux sans visage* (1959), a horror film about a mad doctor who attempts to reconstruct his daughter's disfigured face with the faces of murdered women. Franju went on to make only a handful of other films, including *Pleins feux sur l'assassin* (1961), *Thérèse Desqueyroux* (1962), *Judex* (1963), a remake of the classic **Louis Feuillade** silent film series, and *Thomas l'imposteur* (1964), based on the novel by **Jean Cocteau**.

Franju's influence on French cinema was enormous, despite the small body of work he produced. His involvement in the creation of the Cinémathèque already ensured him a role in French film history. However, his films themselves, although forgotten for some time, also merit him a place. The influences on his filmmaking are evident in the subjects of the films he undertook. His homages to Méliès and Feuillade reveal that he was interested in those early pioneers who attempted to capture the sublime on film, both the horror and the beauty of human existence. His interest in Cocteau reveals a belief in film as a transcendent art form, as a form of visual poetry. In fact, a study of Franju's own filmmaking style bears these influences out. He is a late link to these early figures, who sought to push film to the limits of art.

FRESNAY, PIERRE (1897–1975). Actor. Born Pierre Laudenbach in Paris, Pierre Fresnay studied drama at the Paris Conservatoire d'art dramatique and then went on to begin his acting career on the stage. He established himself as a talented stage actor and was in residence at the Comédie Française from 1915 until 1929. Fresnay made his film debut during the silent-film era, appearing in such films as **Henri Pouctal**'s *France d'abord* (1915), Charles Burguet's *L'Essor* (1920), *Les Mystères de Paris* (1922) and his series *La Bâillonnée* (1922), **André Hugon**'s series *Le Diamant noir* (1922), Charles Maudru's series *Rocambole* (1924), and Luitz-Moratz's *La Vièrge* *folle* (1929). Fresnay married the actress Berthe Bovy in 1923, but the two divorced in 1929.

The breakthrough role in Fresnay's career came early in the sound era, however, when **Marcel Pagnol** cast him as the lead in *Marius* (1931). Fresnay, not at all from the south, had to learn the Marseille accent for the role. However, his efforts were worth it, and the film made him an instant star. He reprised the role in two subsequent Pagnol films, *Fanny* (1932) and *César* (1936).

After *Marius*, Fresnay worked steadily in cinema, with one major role after another throughout the 1930s and 1940s. He had starring roles in **Abel Gance**'s *La Dame aux camélias* (1934) and *Roman d'un jeune homme pauvre* (1935), Maurice Tourneur's *Königsmark* (1935) and *La Main du diable* (1943), **Marc Allégret**'s *Sous les yeux d'occident* (1935), **Léon Mathot**'s *Chéri-Bibi* (1937), Pierre Billon's *La Bataille silencieuse* (1937), **Jean Renoir**'s *La Grande illusion* (1937), **Marcel L'Herbier**'s *Adrienne Lecouvreur* (1938), **Julien Duvivier**'s *La Charette fantôme* (1939), **George Lacombe**'s *Le Dernier des six* (1941), *Le Journal tombe à cinq heures* (1942), and *L'Escalier sans fin* (1943), **Henri-Georges Clouzot**'s *L'Assassin habite au 21* (1943) and *Le Corbeau* (1943), Jean Anouilh's *Le Voyageur sans bagages* (1944), **Henri Decoin**'s *La Fille du diable* (1946) and *Au grand balcon* (1949), Jean Dréville's *Le Visiteur* (1946), Maurice Cloche's *Monsieur Vincent* (1947), and Richard Pottier's *Barry* (1949). Fresnay's costar in many of these films was the actress Yvonne Printemps, whom he married in 1934.

As evidenced by the sheer number of films in which he starred during the 1930s and 1940s, Fresnay was a major star on a par with **Jean Gabin**. The two were very different actors, however, fulfilling different roles in cinema. This is, perhaps, best illustrated by the characters the two played in Renoir's classic film, *La Grande illusion* (1937). Fresnay's De Boeldieu is clearly an aristocrat, the last of a disappearing class, whereas Renoir's Maréchal is clearly a man of the people.

Fresnay, despite the broad range of characters he brought to the screen (including the very "man of the people" Marius), always had a classical air to his performances, a bit of a sophisticated edge, whereas Renoir, however refined his characters, was always of the people. Beyond *La Grande illusion* and the Pagnol trilogy, Fresnay's best-known, and probably greatest, film is Clouzot's *Le Corbeau* (1943), in which Fresnay played the very complex Dr. Rémy Germain. It is also worth noting that he had a very brief, but central, role as Louis Bernard in Hitchcock's *The Man Who Knew Too Much* (1934).

In the 1950s, Fresnay continued to act in films, but the roles became either less prominent or more difficult to find. He, like Gabin and **Arletty**, was an icon of a previous age, of the classic era of French film, and cinema was trying to move in different directions. He appeared in such films as **Jean Delannoy**'s *Dieu a besoin des hommes* (1950) and *La Route Napoléon* (1953), **Henri Diamant-Berger**'s *Monsieur Fabre* (1951), **Jean-Paul Le Chanois**'s *Les Évadés* (1955), **Léo Joannen**'s *L'Homme aux clefs d'or* (1956) and *Tant d'amour perdu* (1958), Alex Joffé's *Les Fanatiques* (1957), Allégret's *Les Affreux* (1959), and Gilles Grangier's *Les Vieux de la vieille* (1960), among other films. For the most part, however, Fresnay returned to working on the stage. He did not act in films after 1960, his only screen roles being on the small screen after that.

FUNÈS, LOUIS DE (1914–1983). Actor. Louis de Funès was one of France's best-known comic actors, alongside **Bourvil** and **Coluche**. His parents were Spanish immigrants, and Funès also became a celebrity in Spain. He played the piano in clubs and acted in the theater before first appearing in cinema in Jean Stelli's *Tentation de Barbizon* (1945). He played minor roles in films such as **Henri Verneuil**'s *Le Mouton à cinq pattes* (1954), **Jean-Paul Le Chanois**'s *Papa, maman, la bonne, et moi* (1954) and *Papa, Maman, ma femme et moi* (1955), and **Claude Autant-Lara**'s *La Traversée de Paris* (1956), where he became known for his comic acting ability. Funès later found leading roles in Yves Robert's *Ni vu ni connu* (1958) and **Jean Girault**'s *Pouic-pouic* (1963). His performance in Girault's mainstream commercial comedy *Le Gendarme de Saint-Tropez* (1964) and in André Hunnebell's 1964 remake of **Louis Feuillade**'s *Fantômas* won Funès acclaim.

Funès worked with Girault again in his popular *Gendarme* series: *Le Gendarme à New York* (1965), *Le Gendarme se marie* (1968), *Le Gendarme en balade* (1970), *Le Gendarme et les extra-terrestres* (1978), and *Le Gendarme et les gendarmettes* (1982). Known as

"Fufu," Funès starred in some of the most popular French films of the 1960s and 1970s. These films owe much of their success to his popularity. In addition to his work with Girault, Funès worked frequently with **Gérard Oury**. He played leading roles in *Le Corniaud* (1965), *La Grande vadrouille* (1966), and *Les aventures de Rabbi Jacob* (1973). He appeared alongside the comic actor **Bourvil** in several of his films. Jerry Lewis presented Funès with an honorary **César** in 1980.

– G –

GABIN, JEAN (1904–1976). Actor. Born Jean Gabin Alexis Moncorgé into a family of entertainers, Jean Gabin first tried to avoid becoming one himself. Both of his parents were performers in the café-concerts, and Jean, in his early life, tried other careers, including construction, before coming back to the theater to join his parents. He got his start at the Folies-Bergères in 1922 and remained in live entertainment until 1930, when he debuted in René Pujol's *Chacun sa chance*. Film work came steadily after that, but it was not until Gabin's role in **Julien Duvivier**'s *Maria Chapdelaine* in 1933 that he really became a force on the screen.

From 1933 until the war, Gabin was probably the biggest male star on the screen in France. He was, in many ways, the face of the *Le Réalisme poétique* or poetic realism, playing real-world tragic characters and conveying as much through facial expression as through dialogue. He worked with Duvivier in *La Bandera* (1935), *Golgotha* (1935), *La Belle équipe* (1936), and *Pépé le Moko* (1937), with **Jean Renoir** in *Les Bas-fonds* (1936), *La Grande illusion* (1937), and *La Bête humaine* (1938), with **Marc Allégret** in *Zouzou* (1934), and with **Marcel Carné** in *Le Quai des brumes* (1938) and *Le Jour se lève* (1939).

The types of characters Gabin played in these films, particularly the Carné films, typify his work from the 1930s and 1940s. He was very often an everyman type of character, strong, silent, often brooding, more often than not caught in circumstances well beyond his control. His best-known roles from the period are probably that of Jean, the silent former soldier in Carné's *Le Quai des brumes* (1938),

François, the factory worker caught in a tragic love relationship that leads to murder in *Le Jour se lève* (1939), Pépé, the gangster trapped in the medina of Algiers in Duvivier's *Pépé le Moko* (1937), and Lieutenant Maréchal, the prisoner of war in Renoir's classic, *La Grande illusion* (1937). Gabin's other noteworthy roles from this period include **Jean Grémillion**'s *Guele d'amour* (1937) and *Remorques* (1941). Other films in which he appeared include Hans Behrendt and Yvan Noé's *Gloria* (1931), Jean Godard's *Pour un soir* (1931), Jacques Tourneur's *Tout ça ne vaut pas l'amour* (1931), Harry Lachman's *La Belle marinière* (1932), Anatole Litvak's *Cœur de lilas* (1932), John Daumery and Howard Hawks's *La Foule hurle* (1932), **Serge de Poligny**'s *L'Étoile de Valencia* (1933), and Maurice Gleize's *Le Récif de corail* (1939).

Gabin left France at the time of the German Occupation during World War II to fight with the Free French. He also tried his hand at acting in Hollywood, but his two English-language films, *Moontide* (1942) and *The Imposter* (1944), were unremarkable. Gabin returned to France after the war but had some difficulty restarting his career. He starred in **Georges Lacombe**'s *Martin Roumignac* (1946), Raymond Lamy's *Miroir* (1947), and **René Clément**'s *Au-delà des grilles* (1949). Gabin's film career did not begin to pick up momentum until 1952, when he was again offered memorable roles in memorable films. His films that year included **Max Ophüls**'s *Le Plaisir* and **Henri Decoin**'s *La Vérité sur Bébé Dongé*. The following year, Gabin starred in **Jacques Becker**'s classic noir film *Touchez pas au grisbi* (1953), and his second star turn was cemented.

In its second phase, his career was characterized by three types of roles. He frequently played detectives (most notably Maigret) in *polars* or crime films. Examples include Gilles Grangier's *Le Sang à la tête* (1956), *Le Rouge est mis* (1957), and *Maigret voit rouge* (1963), **Jean Delannoy**'s *Maigret tend un piège* (1958) and *Maigret et l'affaire Saint-Fiacre* (1959). Alternatively, he played tough guys in crime films or occasionally parodied them in comedies. Examples include, of course, Becker's *Touchez pas au grisbi* (1953), Decoin's *Razzia sur le Chnouf* (1955), Duvivier's *Voici le temps des assassins* (1956), Grangier's *Le Cave se rebiffe* (1961), Denys de la Patellière's *Du rififi à Paname* (1966), and **Henri Verneuil**'s *Le Clan des Siciliens* (1969).

The other type of role that dominated was that of the distinguished gentleman, in which Gabin would play a mature and grounded older man of means. Films that feature him in this capacity include Decoin's *La Vérité sur Bébé Dongé* (1952), **Claude Autant-Lara**'s *En cas de Malheur* (1958), Delannoy's *Le Baron de l'écluse* (1960), **Jean-Paul Le Chanois**'s *Monsieur* (1964), Pierre Granier-Deferre's *La Horse* (1970), and Verneuil's *Le Président* (1973). There were also occasional roles as the everyman, as in Le Chanois's *Les Misérables*, in which Gabin gave the screen one of its most memorable incarnations of Jean Valjean.

The tone for the second career was, no doubt, set by the success of the 1952 Decoin and Becker films, which broke with Gabin's earlier association with the tragic everyman figure and greatly broadened his range. It is also no doubt the result of the fact that such roles better suited the older Gabin. Gabin also continued to act in theater throughout his career. His last film was *L'Année sainte* (1976), released the year of his death.

It is difficult to summarize Gabin's career except to say that he was and is probably the most beloved actor to have graced the screen in France, that he had and has a very intimate connection to several generations of moviegoers, and that the face and the persona that each generation associates with him is different. One element that holds true for all generations, inside and outside of France, however, is that he is one of the most recognizable and one of the most legendary actors to have worked in cinema. It is also true that whether he is remembered for *La Grande illusion* (1937) or for *Mélodie en sous-sol* (1963), or for any of his other films, what made Gabin so memorable was his quiet, yet forceful way of capturing the human experience.

GANCE, ABEL (1889–1981). Actor, director, and screenwriter. Born the illegitimate son of a Jewish doctor and a working-class girl, Abel Gance rose to prominence as one of the most visionary directors of the silent-film era. Until the age of eight, Gance lived with his grandparents in rural France. At the age of eight, he moved to Paris to live with his mother, who had married Adolphe Gance, the man whose name Gance ultimately took. Although officially the son of Adolphe Gance, Gance's natural father, Abel Flamant, continued to support him. This support allowed the young Gance an education well beyond the reach of his working-class family (Adolphe Gance was a mechanic).

It was clear from an early age that Gance was attracted to literature and theater. He read voraciously and, in 1908, went to Brussels to become an actor, defying his father's wish that he become a lawyer. In 1910, he was hired on as an actor by **Gaumont** and was cast by **Léonce Perret** in his 1910 film *Molière*. He also wrote several screenplays for films directed by Perret, including *Le Portrait de Mireille* (1910) and *Le Crime du grand-père* (1910).

In 1911, Gance left Gaumont to form his own production company, *Le Film français*, which produced many of Gance's first films, including *La Digue* (1911), a costume drama set in Holland, which Gance both wrote and directed. This was shortly followed by several other films, both written and directed by Gance, including *Le Nègre blanc* (1912), an antiracist drama, and *Le Masque d'horreur* (1912), a short narrative film. He continued also to write scripts for other studios, and some of these were turned into successful films, one example being *Un tragique amour du Mona Lisa* (1912) directed by **Albert Capellani**.

Gance's vision of cinema, however, stretched beyond that medium's developed capacity, and his experimentation, particularly with light, can be seen even in his early films. As his career developed, this ambition to push the cinema beyond its limits began to find greater form in his work. Experimentation with special effects, for example, characterizes his 1915 film *La Folie du docteur Tube*. His film *Barberousse* (1917), a serial made for **Studio Film d'art**, brought Gance much audience acclaim, if not critical acclaim, and also demonstrates experimentation with camera angles, shot distance, editing, and narrative style. He is often called one of the fathers of the close-up.

Gance's experimental style matured in 1917 in what is considered his first great work, *Mater Dolorosa*, a psychologically and socially oriented film about an unhappily married bourgeois **woman**. The subject matter and Gance's stylized cinematography, particularly his use of lighting, garnered the film much attention, and it was a huge success both in France and internationally.

In 1919, Gance went to work for **Pathé**, where he made another of his great works, the serial film *J'Accuse*, a war epic that prominently features the carnage of the so-called Great War and which literally calls upon the living to answer for the deaths of those killed. The film's deeply traumatic subject is beautifully rendered in Gance's experimental cinematography, which includes tracking shots, rapid cuts, close-ups, and his typical play with lighting. The film was an enormous success, both domestically and internationally, and it cemented Gance's reputation as one of the great directors of his day.

Gance's second great epic work, *La Roue* (1923), was begun shortly after the release of *J'Accuse*. The story of railroad workers in France, *La Roue* has elements of the poetic realism that would follow a generation later, but it retains the element of artistic self-consciousness that Gance's earlier films demonstrated. *La Roue*, which Gance once called "a white symphony fading to black," was filmed on location in Provence. Gance makes of the natural landscapes of the Southern Alps living symbols, and of the steam engines around which the narrative centers, contrasting symbols. To his growing repertoire of cinematographic and editing tricks, Gance, in this film, adds montage, which functions to highlight the already symbolic stature of the images on the screen. A long poem on film, *La Roue* remains one of the great films of all time.

It is perhaps because of the success of films like *La Roue* and *J'Accuse* that Gance was given the freedom that he was in making his next film, the famed (infamous) **Napoléon vu par Abel Gance** (1927), a historical epic that sought to re-create the early political career of Napoléon Bonaparte and that took three years to make. The film was produced by **Henri Diamant-Berger**, through the director's own, small production company. The cost of the film nearly bankrupted the studio.

The technical innovation that Gance brought to *Napoléon*, perhaps the greatest technical innovation of his career, was a superexpanded screen that he called polyvision. Polyvision allowed for the projection of enormous panoramic shots and series of tryptich images, in which three screens were visible at once. Both techniques were created by filming simultaneously with multiple cameras, and both pushed filmmaking well beyond anything that had been seen up to that time. *Napoléon* also draws on the earlier innovations in Gance's films, including montage, rapid cutting, tracking, and experimental lighting.

Although the original, which premiered in Paris in 1927, did not do well at the box office, it remains one of the masterworks of cinema, albeit a controversial one. This may, in part, be due to the fact that few audiences of the day ever saw the full, six-hour version, as the film was often shown in pieces because of its length. Gance made several attempts to redeem the film, which he considered a masterpiece. He added sound to the film in 1934, and he reedited and rereleased it in 1971 under the title *Bonaparte et la révolution*. However, it is widely believed that it is only the most recent rendering of the film by film historian Kevin Brownlow (done in 1981) that truly brings Gance's vision to the screen.

The enormous production costs of *Napoléon* (the most expensive film made at the time), coupled with its commercial failure, undermined what had previously been Gance's reputation as a cinematic great. Gance received backing for one more epic film, *La Fin du monde* (1931), his first sound film, but producers intervened during production and editing, fearing another *Napoléon*. The version that was released was a mere shadow of Gance's vision for the film, and it, like its predecessor, did not do well. As a result, Gance earned a reputation as an eccentric with overambitious ideas, and he had trouble finding the financial backing to make films for a period of twenty or so years.

Gance continued to make films, including *La Dame aux Camélias* (1934) starring **Pierre Fresnay**, *Lucréce Borgia* (1935), *Le Roman d'un jeune homme pauvre* (1935), *Le Grand amour de Beethoven* (1936), *Paradis Perdu* (1939), *Le Capitaine Fracasse* (1942), *Quatorze juillet* (1953), *Austerlitz* (1960), and *Cyrano et d'Artagnan* (1963), his final film. However, none of these ever achieved the acclaim won by his silent-film era epics. His fame during this period came more from previous achievements than contemporary ones, as he was awarded an international prize for invention for his technical contributions to cinema in 1954, and was named first laureate of the French national cinema in 1974. He was also given an honorary **César** in 1980.

GARCIA, NICOLE (1946–). Actress, director, and screenwriter. Nicole Garcia was born in Oran, Algeria. She debuted as an actress in 1968 in Etienne Périer's *Des Garçons et des filles* and Jean Girault's

Le Gendarme se marie. She later played supporting roles in **Jacques Rivette**'s *Duelle* (1976), Laurent Heynemann's *La Question* (1977) and *Le Mors aux dents* (1979), and **Jacques Deray**'s *Un papillon sur l'épaule* (1978). In 1980, she received a **César** for Best Supporting Actress in **Philippe de Broca**'s *Le Cavaleur* (1979). In the 1980s, Garcia was nominated for Césars for Best Actress three times for her performances in **Alain Resnais**'s *Mon Oncle d'Amérique* (1980), José Pinhiero's *Les Mots pour le dire* (1983), and **Michel Deville**'s *Péril en la demeure* (1985). She starred in **Claude Lelouch**'s *Les uns les autres* (1981), Heynemann's *Stella* (1983), Joël Santoni's *Mort un dimanche de pluie* (1986), Jacques Ruoffio's *L'État de grâce* (1986), and Francesca Comencini's *La Lumière du lac* (1988). Garcia directed a short, *15 août* (1986), which was nominated for a Golden Palm for Best Short at **Cannes**. In addition to *La Question*, she played in a number of films that reflected upon France's relationship with Algeria: Pierre Schoendoerffer's *L'Honneur d'un capitaine* (1982) and Brigitte Roüan's *Outremer* (1990).

Garcia's first feature film as director was *Un week-end sur deux* (1990). It received a César nomination for Best First Work. It was followed by *Le fils préféré* (1994) and *Place Vendôme* (1998). Garcia was nominated for Césars for Best Director for both films, and **Catherine Deneuve** won the Volpi Cup for Best Actress at Venice for her performance in the latter. In addition to directing, Garcia maintained her acting career. She shared an award for Best Actress with costar **Sandrine Kiberlain** at the Montreal World Film Festival for her work in **Claude Miller**'s *Betty Fisher et autres histoires* (2001). She later played a leading role in Miller's *La petite Lili* (2003). She also starred in Sam Karmann's *Kennedy et moi* (1999), Rodolphe Marconi's *Le Dernier jour* (2004), and Luc Bondy's *Ne fais pas ça* (2004). Her film *L'adversaire* (2002) was nominated for a Golden Palm. It was followed by *Selon Charlie* (2006).

GARREL, PHILIPPE (1948–). Director and screenwriter. Philippe Garrel was born in Paris, the son of stage and television actor Maurice Garrel, who would later appear in his son's films. Garrel directed his first film, the short *Les Enfants désaccordés* (1964), at the age of sixteen. He released a second short, *Droit de visite*, in 1965. His first feature-length film was the 1967 *Marie pour mémoire*. Also in the

1960s, he directed *Anémone* (1968), a made-for-television film that was subsequently released in theaters. Then-emerging actress Anémone apparently derived her stage name from this film. Garrel's next film was *Le lit de la vièrge* (1969).

In the 1970s, several of Garrel's films centered on his relationship with the Velvet Underground singer Nico. She costarred with Garrel in *La cicatrice interieure* (1972) and collaborated with him on the dialogue. She also contributed to the soundtrack. She also appears in Garrel's *Athanor* (1972), *Les Hautes solitudes* (1974), *Un ange passe* (1975), *Berceau de cristal* (1976), *Voyage au jardin des morts* (1975), and *Le Bleu des origines* (1979).

In addition to writing and directing autobiographical pieces, Garrel created portraits of Jean Seberg, Nico, and actress Tina Aumont in his biopic *Les Hautes solitudes* (1974). The film focuses especially on Seberg, the costar of **Jean-Luc Godard**'s *Breathless*. Garrel would later employ another *Nouvelle Vague* or New Wave star, this time a favorite of **François Truffaut**'s, as Jean-Pierre Léaud appeared in his *Naissance de l'amour* (1993). Maurice Garrel also became one of his son's preferred actors, appearing in films such as *Le Coeur fantôme* (1996).

Garrel received a number of prizes in the 1980s, though his fans argue that he is still highly underappreciated. In 1982, Garrel won the **Prix Jean-Vigo** for *L'Enfant secret* (1982). In 1984, he won the Perspectives du Cinéma Award at **Cannes** for *Liberté, la nuit* (1983), a film about revolutionaries in the Algerian War starring his father and actress Emmanuel Riva. Also in the 1980s, Garrel directed *Elle a passé tant d'heures sous les sunlights* (1985) and *Les Baisers de secours* (1989), in which he appears with Anémone and his wife, Brigitte Sy. *Les Baisers de secours* marks his first collaboration on a feature film with writer Marc Cholodenko, who would script later films.

In the 1990s and beyond, Garrel received several awards at the Venice Film Festival. He won the Silver Lion for *J'entends plus la guitarre* (1991), in part a tribute to Nico, who died in 1988. The film is also a moving contemplation of drug addition and the disillusionment following May 1968. His *Le Vent de la nuit* (1999), with **Catherine Deneuve**, was nominated for a Golden Lion. In 2001, he won the Fédération Internationale de la Presse Cinématographique

(FIPRESCI) Prize for *Sauvage innocence*. In 2005, he won the Silver Lion a second time for *Les Amants réguliers* (2005).

Described as a poet-filmmaker, Garrel has developed a relatively small but dedicated following of cinéphiles, intellectuals, and fellow directors. Garrel was not a contemporary of New Wave directors, nor is he viewed as a New Wave director. However, he has incorporated ideals of New Wave filmmaking into his work, including the focus on the autobiographical and the experimental, and the conception of cinema as an art with its own unique aesthetics.

GATLIF, TONY (1948–). Actor, composer, director, producer, and screenwriter. Tony Gatlif was born Michel Dahamani in Algeria. He is of gypsy origin. He moved to France in 1960, where he studied drama and, like many directors of the period, attended ciné-clubs. He debuted in cinema in the mid-1970s, and his first feature was *La tête en ruines* (1975). He also worked as an actor and screenwriter for Eric Le Hung's 1975 *La rage au poing* (1975). In 1979, he released *La Terre au ventre,* a feature film set during the Algerian War. His gypsy heritage and his transnationality have influenced several of his films, including the short *Corre gitano* (1982), the documentary *Latcho drom* (1993), and the features *Mondo* (1996), *Gadjo Dilo* (1997), and *Exils* (2004). While he often works with nonprofessional actors, Gatlif has directed several French stars. He directed **Gérard Depardieu** in *Rue du départ* (1986), **Fanny Ardant** in *Pleure pas, my love* (1987), and Vincent Lindon in *Gaspard et Robinson* (1990).

As noted, many of Gatlif's films have centered on gypsy music, gypsy culture, and the social position of gypsies as outside of every culture in which they find themselves. Through these films, Gatlif illuminates historic and contemporary struggles with discrimination and persecution. *Les Princes* (1983), the first in Gatlif's "gypsy trilogy," exposes the hardships faced by gypsy communities in Parisian suburbs. *Latcho Drom*, the second work in the trilogy, portrays diasporic gypsies in India, Egypt, and Europe. The documentary is unique in its foregrounding of music and its absence of voice-over narration. It won the Un Certain Regard Award at the **Cannes International Film Festival**. The third part of the trilogy, *Gadjo Dilo*, a feature that offers a critical look at European commodification of Roma culture and the violent treatment of gypsies in Romania, won a Silver Leopard at the Locarno International Film Festival. It stars Romain Duris, who also appeared in Gatlif's *Je suis né d'une cigogne* (1999) and *Exils*. Although not considered part of his trilogy, *Mondo* focuses on a homeless gypsy child in Southern France. Gatlif's *Swing* (2002) revisits *Gadjo Dilo*'s story of a French protagonist who is fascinated with gypsy music; however, in this film, the focus is the Manouche in France.

Gatlif has won prestigious awards for his music: both *Gadjo Dilo* and *Vengo* (2000), a drama about flamenco, won **César Awards** for Best Musical Composition. In 2004, Gatlif won Best Director at the Cannes Film Festival for *Exils*. Like his previous films, *Exils* contemplates experiences of exile and nomadism as it narrates the journey of protagonists who travel from France to Algeria to discover part of their heritage. Gatlif has been praised by critics across cultures for his sensitive and affectionate portrayals of gypsies and his moving celebrations of cosmopolitan gypsy music.

GAUMONT, LÉON ERNEST (1864–1946). Film pioneer, producer, and studio head. Léon Gaumont came from a modest family, and he started his professional life in 1881, working at the atelier of Jules Carpentier, who would later build the *cinématographe* for **Louis Lumière**. Quite apart from his experience with optical equipment, Gaumont had an avid interest in cameras and photography. This led Gaumont, in 1893, to leave Carpentier to work for Félix Richard, a manufacturer of optical and photographic equipment. When Richard became entangled in a nasty lawsuit with his brother in 1895, he offered to sell his shop to the ambitious Gaumont, who convinced Richard's clients Gustave Eiffel and Joseph Vallot, the director of the Mont Blanc Observatory, to back him. The company L. Gaumont et Cie. was founded.

At first, Gaumont, like Lumière, was interested primarily in marketing photographic and film equipment. He obtained the rights to manufacture and distribute the *Chronophonographe*, an early film camera invented by Georges Demenÿ that was capable of synchronized sound recording, and the accompanying projection device, the Phonoscope. That same year, Gaumont's secretary, **Alice Guy**, had the idea of using the camera to film several short story films to use to market the equipment, and the idea of the **Gaumont Studios** was born.

While acting as head of Gaumont, Léon Gaumont was able to ride out a number of financial crises and even the emerging American monopoly on the film industry. The firm remained largely intact until Gaumont's retirement in 1930, although it was heavily subsidized by foreign investors at that point.

GAUMONT STUDIOS. Gaumont Studios began in 1895 as a camera manufacturing company founded by **Léon Gaumont**. That same year, as a result of Gaumont secretary **Alice Guy**, the company was also turned into a film production company and ultimately a movie studio and production and distribution company. Guy was the first studio head, and she was later replaced by **Louis Feuillade**.

For a number of years, Gaumont et Cie. engaged in both the manufacture and sale of camera equipment and the making and distribution of films. In addition to Guy and Feuillade, Gaumont brought in a number of other directors, including **Romeo Bosetti**, **Camille de Morhon**, and **Victorin Jasset**. However, in 1906, shortly after the construction of the Gaumont Studios at Les Buttes Chaumont, the filmmaking and distribution was split off into a subsidiary called Les Établissements Gaumont, and Gaumont et Cie. focused on camera equipment manufacture and sales.

The performance of the equipment side of the firm was uneven. The first attempts to market the chronophone failed. This was, at first, due to the nonstandard nature of the equipment (the camera used unperforated film, unlike the **Lumière** camera). Gaumont, along with help, made some modifications and was able to develop a camera that used more standard 35mm perforated film, and this model fared somewhat better. However, problems with the image quality persisted. In fact, Guy herself had to reshoot entire scenes on occasion due to poor image quality. Nonetheless, the chronophone and the *phonoscènes* shot with it remain part of one of the first attempts to produce synchronous sound and image in cinema, and they preceeded the "talkies" by several decades.

In the domain of film production and distribution, Gaumont Studios was also a pioneer. It was the first studio to utilize the system of distribution rentals rather than direct film sales. This system still governs film distribution today. Prior to Gaumont, films were purchased by those who wished to show them, and this made it much more expensive. Gaumont was also one of the studios to construct its own movie theaters in which to show his films, the first and most magnificent of which was the famed Gaumont Palace, built by Gaumont in 1900 by converting the Hippodrome at the Place Clichy into a cinema.

In 1938, under the direction of Gaumont's replacement, Louis Aubert, Gaumont was declared insolvent. The company was seized and reorganized under the name Société des Nouveaux Établissements Gaumont. It underwent several subsequent reorganizations. However, it has managed to remain one of the three largest film production and distribution studios in France, as well as one of the most important in the world.

GIRARDOT, ANNIE (1931–). Actress. Annie Girardot was born in Paris and graduated from the Paris Conservatoire d'art dramatique with honors. She began her career on the stage, appearing at the Comédie Française from 1954 to 1957 and in cabarets before making her debut in **André Hunébelle**'s *Treize à table* (1956). Her early major roles were in **Jean Delannoy**'s *Maigret tend un piège* (1957) alongside **Jean Gabin**, **Marc Allégret**'s *L'amour est en jeu* (1957), and Jean-Charles Dudrumet's *La corde raide* (1960). She debuted in Italian cinema under the direction of Luchino Visconti, who had directed Girardot in the play *Deux sur la balançoire*. She also appeared in Visconti's *Rocco e i suoi fratelli* (1960) with her husband Renato Salvatori.

In the 1960s, Girardot established a career in both French and Italian cinema. She starred in Franco Rossi's *Smog* (1962), Denys de La Patellière's *Le Bateau d'Émile* (1962), Marco Ferreri's *La Donna scimmia* (1963), Robert Thomas's *La Bonne soupe* (1963), François Villiers's *L'Autre femme* (1963), **Roger Vadim**'s *Le Vice et la vertu* (1963), Ugo Gregoretti's *Le Belle famiglie* (1964), and Philippe Clair's *Déclic et des claques* (1965). She also appeared with a multinational cast in *La Guerre secrete*, directed by **Christian-Jacque** and others, in 1965. She won a Volpi Cup for Best Actress at the Venice Film Festival for her performance in **Marcel Carné**'s *Trois chambres à Manhattan* (1965). Later in the 1960s, she acted with **Yves Montand** in **Claude Lelouch**'s *Vivre pour vivre* (1967) and starred with **Jean-Paul Belmondo** in Lelouch's *Un Homme qui me plaît* (1969).

In the 1970s, Girardot was one of France's most beloved and versatile actresses. She starred in André Cayatte's *Mourir d'aimer* (1970), Michel Audiard's *Elle boit pas, elle fume pas, elle drague pas, mais . . . elle cause!* (1970), and *Elle cause plus, elle flingue* (1972), Guy Casaril's *Les Novices* (1970), **Edouard Molinaro**'s *La Mandarine* (1972), Jean-Pierre Blanc's *La vieille fille* (1972), Alain Jessua's *Traitement de choc* (1973), Cayatte's *Il n'y a pas de fumée sans feu* (1973), Rémo Forlani's *Juliette et Juliette* (1974), and **Claude Pinoteau**'s *La Gifle* (1974). Girardot won a **César** for Best Actress in Jean-Louis Bertucelli's 1975 film, *Docteur Françoise Gailland*. She landed further leading roles in Cayatte's *À chacun son enfer* (1977) and *L'Amour en question* (1978), **Philippe de Broca**'s *Tendre poulet* (1977), **Claude Zidi**'s *La Zizanie* (1978), Nicole de Buron's *Vas-y maman* (1978), Yves Boisset's *La Clé sur la porte* (1978), Molinaro's *Cause toujours . . . tu m'intéresses* (1979), and Walter Bal's *Bobo Jacco* (1979).

In the early 1980s, Girardot added to her repetoire with leading roles in films such as de Broca's *On a volé la cuisse de Jupiter* (1980), Franck Apprenderis's *Le Coeur à l'envers* (1980), José Giovanni's *Une robe noire pour un tueur* (1981), Moshé Mizrahi's *La Vie continue* (1981), Pierre Lary's *La Revanche* (1981), Alain Bonnot's *Liste noire* (1984), and Lelouch's *Partir, Revenir* (1984). She also appeared in Jean-Claude Tramont's *All Night Long* (1981) with Gene Hackman and Barbara Streisand. Later in the 1980s she was less active in cinema, but appeared on television. She also starred in Bob Decout's *Adieu blaireau* (1985), Charlotte Silvera's *Prisonnières* (1988), and Michel Legrand's *Cinq jours en juin* (1989).

Later in her career, Girardot was awarded two Césars for Best Supporting Actress in Lelouch's *Les Misérables* (1995) and Michael Haneke's *La Pianiste* (2000). She also appeared in Lelouch's *Il y a des jours . . . et des lunes* (1990), **Bertrand Blier**'s *Merci la vie* (1991), Gérard Mordillat's *Toujours seuls* (1991), Italian director Aldo Lado's *Alibi perfetto* (1992), Jean-Paul Salomé's *Les Braqueuses* (1994), Leduc's *L'Âge de braise* (1998), Grégoire Delacourt's *Préférence* (1998), Haneke's *Caché* (2003), and Eric Toledano and Olivier Nakache's *Je préfère qu'on reste amis* (2005).

GIROUD, FRANÇOISE (1916–2003). Director and screenwriter. Born Françoise Gourdji in Switzerland, Françoise Giroud got her start in cinema at the age of only fifteen. She worked as the script girl on **Marc Allégret**'s *Fanny* (1932) and went on to work as assistant director, often under the name "Gourdji" on a number of films, including **Jacques de Baroncelli**'s *Roi de Camargue* (1934), Edmont T. Gréville's *Remous* (1934), René Sti's *Le Bébé de l'escadron* (1935), **Yves Mirande** and Léonid Moguy's *Baccara* (1935), Pierre Billon's *Courrier Sud* (1936), Allegret's *Aventure à Paris* (1936) and *Les Amants terribles* (1936), Alexander Esway's *Hercule* (1937) and *Barnabé* (1938), and Pierre Colombier's *Rois du Sport* (1938).

Giroud also worked as a screenwriter, writing or cowriting the screenplays for André Berthomieu's *Promesse à l'inconnue* (1942), Baroncelli's *Marie la misère* (1945), **Marcel L'Herbier**'s *Au petit bonheur* (1946), **Jacques Becker**'s *Antoine et Antoinette* (1947), Jean Stelli's *Dernier Amour* (1949), Allégret's *Julietta* (1953), and Francis Girod's *Le Bon plaisir* (1984), which was adapted from her own novel.

Ultimately, Giroud left cinema for a career in journalism. She wrote for *L'Express* and *Elle*, and while at *L'Express*, she coined the term *Nouvelle Vague* or New Wave to describe the innovations in cinema brought about by directors such as **François Truffaut, Jean-Luc Godard, Alain Resnais, Claude Chabrol, Agnès Varda, Louis Malle**, and others associated with the *Cahiers du cinéma*. Giroud would also go on to hold several cabinet-level positions in the French government.

GODARD, JEAN-LUC (1930–). Director and screenwriter. Jean-Luc Godard was born in Paris and spent his childhood in Switzerland before returning to Paris to attend lycée. In 1940, when Germany initially defeated France, he obtained Swiss citizenship and returned to Switzerland. He went back to Paris after World War II and studied ethnology at the Sorbonne. He frequented the **Cinémathèque française** and ciné-clubs in the late 1940s along with colleagues who would also later become part of the *Nouvelle Vague* or New Wave.

In the early 1950s, Godard wrote regularly for *La Gazette du cinéma* with **Éric Rohmer, Jacques Rivette**, and **François Truffaut**. Godard began acting in Rivette's short, *Quadrille* (1950). In 1952 he published influential essays in the *Cahiers du cinéma*, often under the pen name Hans Lucas. He directed his first film, the short documentary *Opération Béton,* in 1954, and followed with the short films *Une femme coquette* (1956), *Tous les garçons s'appellent Patrick* (1957), *Une histoire d'eau* (1958) with Truffaut, and *Charlotte et son Jules* (1959).

Godard's first feature film was the loosely scripted *À **bout de souffle*** (1960). Based on a story idea by Truffaut, the film was a landmark for the Nouvelle Vague, and some historians see this film, along with Truffaut's own *Les 400 coups* (1959), as the starting point of the movement. The star of *À bout de souffle,* **Jean-Paul Belmondo**, became a film icon. The film won the **Prix Jean-Vigo** for its cinematography and its use of jump cuts, unusual camera mounts, fragmented narratives, and incongruities between sound and image. Because of these elements, *À bout de souffle* had a dramatic influence on later films.

In 1960, Godard made *Le Petit soldat,* a film that presented a less than flattering picture of French colonial practices in Algeria. The representation of torture alarmed French censors, who blocked its release until 1963. *Le Petit soldat* is also noteworthy in that it was the first of several films to feature Godard's former wife **Anna Karina**. Other Godard films starring Karina include *Une femme est une femme* (1961), *Vivre sa vie* (1962), which won the Special Jury Prize at Venice, *Les Carabiniers* (1963), *Le mépris* (1963), *Bande à part* (1964), *Une femme mariée* (1964), *Alphaville* (1965), which won a Golden Berlin Bear, *Pierrot le fou* (1965), *Masculin, féminin* (1966), and *Made in U.S.A.* (1967).

Apart from criticism of the Algerian War, there is also a clear undercurrent of anticonsumerism and a critique of the establishment in many of Godard's films, including *Deux ou trois choses que je sais d'elle* (1967), *La Chinoise* (1967)—which won the Special Jury Prize at Venice—and *Week-end* (1967). Commentators have noted that all three films seem to foreshadow the political upheavals of May 1968, which followed shortly thereafter.

Other political films of Godard's include his 1968 documentary, *One Plus One,* which investigates American and European countercultures, including the Black Panthers and the Rolling Stones. The producers revised the film so that the concluding song is played in its entirety and retitled it *Sympathy for the Devil.* Godard, interestingly, disassociated himself from the revised version.

After May 1968, Godard departed from what he called "bourgeois" films and teamed up with Maoist Jean-Pierre Gorin to form the leftist Dziga Vertov Group, named after the filmmaker Denis Arkadievitch Kaufman. Godard and Gorin codirected *Pravda* (1969), *Un film comme les autres* (1968), *Le Vent de l'est* (1969), *Vladmir et Rosa* (1971), and *Tout va bien* (1972), a feature starring Jane Fonda and **Yves Montand**.

In the 1970s, Godard directed experimental videos. He collaborated with Anne Marie Miéville on *Numéro deux* (1975) and *Comment ça va?* (1978). In 1979, *Sauve qui peut (la vie)* marked Godard's return to cinema proper, and it inaugurated a fairly long run of critically acclaimed films. *Sauve qui peut (la vie)* and Godard's next film, *Passion* (1982), were both nominated for Golden Palms at the **Cannes Film Festival** and the **César** Awards for Best Director and Best Film. His film *Prénom Carmen* (1983) won the Golden Lion at Venice and the controversial *Je vous salue, Marie* (1985) was nominated for a Golden Berlin Bear.

Godard also directed *Détective* (1984), *Soigne ta droite* (1986), *King Lear* (1988), *Nouvelle Vague* (1990), *Allemagne année 90 neuf zéro* (1991), *Hélas pour moi* (1993), *JLG/JLG—Autoportrait de décembre* (1994), *Forever Mozart* (1996), *Éloge de l'amour* (2001), and the multilingual *Notre Musique* (2004), among other films. He was given an honorary César award in 1987 and another in 1998 for his acclaimed series on the histories of film, *Histoire(s) du cinéma*.

Godard's filmmaking has evolved in a number of ways over the course of his career. During the Nouvelle Vague, he was known for his innovative, on-the-street shooting style, his use of the handheld camera, and the rough, unpolished feel to his films. In this respect, he embodied the movement's reaction against the overly polished, almost stilted filmmaking of the previous decade and heralded the move toward a new, more experimental cinema. On the surface these films often seem to be experimental imitations of American B movies, but closer analyses reveal a high degree of complexity, including complex discourses on time, history, social class, and, it has been argued, the Algerian War, at the time a censored topic.

The events of May 1968 and the experimentation that followed created a definitive break with the Nouvelle Vague. The narrative films that emerge after this period are much more classically realist, although they lose nothing of the harshness of the scrutiny of his gaze. These in turn have been followed by more and more experimental explorations in film, from experiments in form, as with *Je vous salue, Marie* (1990), to experiments in genre, such as *JLG/GLJ* (1994).

Godard remains one of France's most enigmatic and revered filmmakers. Through all of its transformations, his cinema has never lost the thing that makes it distinctly his, his ethnographic gaze. His films, from *Vivre sa vie* (1962) to *Éloge de l'amour* (2001), are all pointed explorations of individuals in society, and somehow, the question of social class is always just under the surface. Godard's 2004 film, *Notre Musique*, marked a return to the exploration and condemnation of war, although, as might be expected, it is an antiwar film in radically altered form.

GRÉMILLON, JEAN (1901–1959). Director. Jean Grémillon began his career as a musician. He went to Paris in 1920 to study music at the Schola cantorum, where he met the actor Charles Dullin. At the same time Grémillon began performing in film orchestras to make money. This initial contact with the cinema cultivated an interest in filmmaking, which in turn ultimately led him to a career in the cinema.

Grémillon began his filmmaking career as a documentary filmmaker, with films such as *Étirage des ampoules éléctrique* (1923), *Chartres* (1923), *La Bière* (1924), *Les Parfums* (1924), *Photogénie mécanique* (1924), *L'Auvergne* (1925), *La Vie des travailleurs italiens en France* (1926), and *Un tour au large* (1926), which has been lost. All sixteen of his documentaries are centered on issues of work and particularly workers, and the two that are considered his best, *Photogénie mécanique* (1924) and *Un tour au large* (1926), are both also situated in the domain of the avant-garde for their use of montage, their fragmented structure, and their impressionistic visual techniques.

In 1928, Grémillon made his first narrative film, *Maldone*, a film for which he also composed the music. The film, which starred Charles Dullin, was made partly with the help of Dullin's cinema connections. The film was fairly well received, both critically and commercially, and again revealed an avant-garde sensibility, with expressionist underpinnings. Grémillon followed the next year with *Gardiens de phare* (1929), a film that had been a project of **Jacques**

Feyder, another friend of Grémillon's. Grémillon made some modifications to the project when he received it, and the final film, therefore, reprised certain elements of Grémillon's filmmaking technique, including a cinematic gaze that is very reminiscent of documentary filmmaking.

If Grémillon's narrative film debut went rather well, Grémillon's sound film debut did not repeat the pattern. *La Petite Lise*, made for **Pathé-Natan** in 1930, was an enormous failure. And while Grémillon would go on to make other films immediately after *La Petite Lise*, they would not be worthy of him. His films from the period include the colonial melodrama *Dainah la métisse* (1931) and the relatively conventional melodramas *Pour un sou d'amour* (1931), *Gonzague* (1933), and *Pattes de mouche* (1936), and the historical melodrama *Valse royale* (1935).

In 1937, Grémillon redeemed his reputation as a filmmaker with excellent films produced back-to-back. The first of these, *Guele d'amour* (1937), starred **Jean Gabin** and Mireille Balin, and is one of the classic Gabin films of all time. The second film, *L'Étrange Monsieur Victor* (1937), starred screen legend **Raïmu** as a criminal and murderer, a role that was highly uncharacteristic of the beloved star. These two were followed by another acclaimed film, *Remorques* (1941), a sea adventure, again starring Gabin. It is a testament to Grémillon that the film was made at all, as the outbreak of the war prevented access to the sea, which is nearly a character in itself in the film, and Grémillon had to be quite inventive in finding ways to finish it. Some critics consider these films, as well as those made in the 1940s, under the rubric of *Le Réalisme poétique* or poetic realism.

In 1943, Grémillon made *Lumière d'été*. The film, which stars **Pierre Brasseur** and **Madeleine Renaud**, is the story of a young, working-class girl, exploited by a rich lover, and is overt in its critique of the exploitation of the lower classes by the upper classes. Made from a screenplay written by Jacques Prévert, the film carried forward the message of the defeated Front populaire, even into the era of Nazi Occupation. This trend was continued with Grémillon's next film, *Le Ciel est à vous* (1943), which is often seen as an example of French neorealism.

After the Liberation, Grémillon made *Le 6 juin à l'aube* (1946), a film about the Liberation itself, and *Pattes blanches* (1949), the story of a family brought to its knees by a love rivalry between half brothers. The film, which starred **Suzy Delair**, also has very overt class messages and may be read as a comment on the perceived self-destruction of elites, such as the aristocracy. Apart from these two films, Grémillon did not have much luck getting his films produced and devoted his energies to the **Cinémathèque française**, of which he had become president, and film union work. He also returned to documentary filmmaking, with such films as *Les Désastres de la guerre* (1949), *Les Charmes de la vie* (1949), about the Art Salons of the nineteenth century, *Astrologie ou le miroir de la vie* (1952), and *La Maison aux images* (1955).

Grémillon made only two other narrative films before his death, *L'Étrange Madame X* (1951), starring **Michèle Morgan**, and *L'Amour d'une femme* (1953), starring **Gaby Morlay** and France Asselin. Both are essentially romantic melodramas. However, *L'Amour d'une femme* is quite progressive in its representation of **women**'s roles and might be read, without much of a stretch, as a feminist film. In that respect, Grémillon ended his career as he started it—ahead of his time.

GROUPE OCTOBRE. An amateur theater troupe started in 1932 by Maurice Baquet, the Groupe Octobre had strong ties to the socialist Front Populaire. Formed from the Prémices group of the *Fédération du théâtre ouvrier*, the group sought to advance socialist and revolutionary ideas through theater and was particularly influenced by the avant-garde and revolutionary works of Revolutionary Russian writers (the group's name was a reference to the Russian Revolution). Perhaps the most famous member of the group was the poet Jacques Prévert. A number of the members also appear in **Jean Renoir**'s *Le Crime de Monsieur Lange* (1936). In cinema, the group's most evident influence comes through Prévert and his influence, particularly on the films of **Marcel Carné** and, therefore, on the larger movement of *Le Réalisme poétique* or poetic realism, which is grounded in the proletarian ideals of the group.

GUÉDIGUIAN, ROBERT (1953–). Director, producer, and screenwriter. Robert Guédiguian was born and raised in L'Estaque, Marseille, of Armenian and German parents. He studied sociology in Aix-en-Provence and later received a master's degree in sociology in Paris. In 1979, he met René Féret, who invited him to coscript his film, *Fernand* (1980). In 1980, he began shooting his first film, *Dernier été*, with codirector Frank Le Wita. It stars his wife, Ariane Ascaride, and Gérard Meylan, who appear in the majority of Guédiguian's films. Guédiguian's second feature was *Ki lo sa?* (1985), which features Jean-Pierre Daroussin, another of his favorite performers. His next features were *Rouge midi* (1985) and *Dieu vomit les tièdes* (1991).

Guédiguian's *À la vie, à la mort* (1995) really established his career as a filmmaker, a career which continued into the 1990s and beyond. The film was cowritten with Jean-Louis Milesi, who would collaborate on the scripts of his future films. Guédiguian has become known as a socially engaged filmmaker who gives intimate, multilayered portraits of the struggles of the working class. He has also been an incisive critic of conservative calls for French "purity," using drama and comedy to illuminate discriminatory French policies against immigrants. He has also been described as a regional filmmaker. Marseille, and particularly its working-class neighborhoods, provides the setting for most of his films.

Guédiguian won the **Prix Louis-Delluc** and a Lumière Award for his fourth feature, the box-office success *Marius et Jeanette* (1997). The film also received three **César Award** nominations for Best Director, Best Film, and Best Screenplay. Ascaride won the César for Best Actress for her performance. In 1998, Guédiguian released *À la place du coeur,* which won a Silver Seashell at the San Sebastián International Film Festival. It was followed by *À l'attaque!* (2000) and *La vie est tranquille* (2000), which won the Fédération Internationale de la Presse Cinématographique (FIPRESCI) Prize at the European Film Awards. His next feature, *Marie-Jo et ses deux amours* (2002), was nominated for a Golden Palm at **Cannes**. In 2004, he released *Mon père est ingénieur*. His 2005 film, *Promeneur du champ de Mars*, departs from his previous films in the selection of setting, actors, and writers. It offers a provocative depiction of former president François Mitterand, who is played by the talented **Michel Bouquet**. The film is based on a book by Georges-Marc Benamou, who collaborated on the script. It received a nomination for a Golden Berlin Bear.

GUISSART, RENÉ (1888–1960). Cinematographer and director. René Guissart was born in Paris but began his career in film in the United States. Guissart started out in cinema as a cinematographer during the silent-film era, working with companies such as Fox, Paramount, MGM, and Pathé's American division. While in the United States, Guissart worked with a number of silent-film directors. He was the cinematographer for director James Vincent on films such as *Sins of Men* (1916), *Ambition* (1916), *Love and Hate* (1916), and *Sister against Sister* (1917). He worked with Harley Knoles on *Stolen Orders* (1918), *The Cabaret* (1918), *Little Women* (1918), and *Land of Hope and Glory* (1927). He also worked on other well-known silent films, such as Fred Niblo's *Ben Hur* (1925). Guissart also worked with both Maurice Tourneur and **Léonce Perret** on their American films. He worked with Tourneur on films such as *Women* (1918), *Treasure Island* (1920), and *While Paris Sleeps* (1923), and with Perret on *Empire of Diamonds* (1920), *The Money Maniac* (1921), and *Madame Sans-Gêne* (1924).

In the late 1920s, Guissart returned to Europe. He worked as a cinematographer in Great Britain, Germany, and France. He worked most notably with **Louis Mercanton** on *Chérie* (1930), Charles de Rochefort on *Le Secret du docteur* (1930), and Alberto Cavalcanti on *Dans une île perdue* (1930).

At about the same time, Guissart also began directing films himself. He made a number of films during the 1930s, including *Rien que la vérité* (1931), *Tu seras duchesse* (1931), *Coiffeur pour dames* (1932), *La Poule* (1932), *Ah! Quelle gare!* (1932), *Le Père prématuré* (1933), *Primerose* (1934), *Dédé* (1934), *Prince de minuit* (1934), *Bourrachon* (1935), *Parlez-moi d'amour* (1935), *Ménilmontant* (1936), and *Visages de femmes* (1938). He also codirected a number of films with various other directors, most notably *Passionnément* (1932), codirected with Mercanton, *On a volé un homme* (1933), codirected with **Max Ophüls**, and *La Chance* (1931) and *Sept homes . . . une femme* (1936), and *A nous deux, madame, la vie* (1936), all codirected with **Yves Mirande**.

For the most part, although there were some exceptions, Guissart's films were largely light, romantic, or sentimental comedies. *Coiffeur pour dames* (1932), *Primerose* (1934), and the films he codirected with Mirande are typically considered his best films. Guissart gave up the cinema after the 1930s.

GUITRY, SACHA (1885–1957). Actor, director, producer, and screen-writer. Born Alexandre Guitry in Moscow in 1885, Sacha Guitry was the son of the renowned French stage actor Lucien Guitry and Renée de Pontry, an actress. Like his parents, Guitry had a passion for the theater. He acted from childhood, began writing plays in his teens, and produced and staged plays starting in 1918. Over the course of his life, he wrote 124 plays, along with a number of other works, including newspaper articles, poems, essays, and of course, screen-plays. Guitry's first love was the theater, and it was as a writer of the-ater that he was introduced to the screen, when, in 1917, he was asked to write the screenplay for René Hervil and **Louis Mercanton**'s silent film, *Un roman d'amour et d'aventures* (1918). The film starred Yvonne Printemps, who would become Guitry's second wife.

Guitry ultimately wrote more than fifty screenplays. In addition to writing the screenplays for all of his own thirty-four films, he wrote the screenplays for such films as **Léonce Perret**'s *Les Deux couverts* (1935), Pierre Caron's *L'Accroche coeur* (1938), and **Fernandel**'s *Adhémar ou le jouet de la fatalité* (1951).

Guitry began directing films in 1935, when he codirected *Pasteur* with Fernand Rivers. The film, a biopic, was an adaptation of a play that Guitry's father had made famous. In many ways, this film was a harbinger of the type of film Guitry went on to make. An intellectual in every sense of the word, Guitry was fascinated with history, and many of his films are biopics, historical films, or historically inspired dramas of one sort or another. These include films such as *Les Perles de la couronne* (1937), codirected with **Christian-Jacque**, *Remontons les Champs-Elysées* (1938), *Le Destin fabuleux de Désirée Clary* (1942), *Le Diable boiteux* (1948), *Si Versailles m'était conté* (1954), *Si Paris nous était conté* (1955), *Napoléon* (1955), and *Assassins et voleurs* (1957).

The other dominant type in Guitry's filmmaking is a type of light, pure entertainment film. One of the first examples of this is another film that was codirected with Rivers, *Bonne Chance* (1935). Other well-known examples of this type of film include *Le Nouveau testament* (1936), *Mon père avait raison* (1936), *Le Roman d'un tricheur* (1936), *Faisons un rêve* (1937), *Quadrille* (1938), and *Ils étaient neuf célibataires* (1939). Guitry played leading roles in all of his films, as did his various wives, ranging from Printemps to Jacqueline Delubac, to Geneviève de Sérérville to Lana Marconi. Guitry was famous for his wit, which, at times, could be quite biting. In his filmmaking, a bit of this shows through, such that even films that seem, on the surface, to be fairly light and entertaining, often have a sharper edge to them, unmasking aspects of society that people generally prefer to keep hidden and forcing the audience to confront what might be some uncomfortable truths. Some examples of films that can be viewed in this light are *Ils étaient neuf célibataires* (1939), *La Poison* (1951), and *La Vie d'un honnête homme* (1958).

During his lifetime, Guitry's work was often ridiculed. He was reproached for his interest in history, his satiric realism, and his eclectic style, which incorporated everything from standard historical epic to the skit film. In fact, **François Truffaut** once famously quipped that Guitry's most egregious fault, in the eyes of his critics, was that he lived. Truffaut's defense of Guitry should make it clear why Guitry's work has lately been reevaluated. Truffaut and other members of the *Nouvelle Vague* or New Wave, seem to have been interested in Guitry's filmmaking, and as an independent, he clearly stood apart from the filmmaking tradition that they, themselves, sought to break with. As film has evolved since the New Wave, scholars, filmmakers, and filmophiles have also had a chance to revisit Guitry's work and to rethink it. Like **Max Ophüls**, who was his contemporary, Guitry may have been a bit ahead of his time, and it may be that an audience familiar with the films of the New Wave, postmodernism, and the *Cinéma du look* can better appreciate Guitry's films than those contemporary critics who so disdained them.

GUY, ALICE (1873–1968). Director and screenwriter. Alice Guy was born to Émile and Mariette Guy, the youngest of four daughters. Although the family lived in Chile, Guy was raised by her maternal grandmother in Switzerland and then sent to a Paris boarding school. She did not even meet her father until the age of four. In 1893, after a series of misfortunes following the death of her father, Guy was forced to leave school to train as a typist and stenographer so as to be able to support herself. She began a career as a secretary, first at a varnish company, and then, in 1894, with **Léon Gaumont**, who was, at the time, working for Felix Richard at his photography works.

When Richard abandoned the business later that year, Gaumont bought the company out, and Guy remained as his secretary. She was, therefore, present when Georges Demenÿ demonstrated his *phono-scope* to Gaumont, and more important, in the following year, when **Louis Lumière** demonstrated his *cinématographe*. It was as a result of the Lumière demonstration that Guy entered the world of cinema. Moved by what she had seen, she persuaded **Gaumont** to loan her their newly patented *biographe* motion picture camera (which Gaumont purchased from Demenÿ) so that she could make one or two "story" films.

La Fée aux choux, a short film that tells the story of a woman who makes babies in a cabbage patch, was written and directed by Guy and produced in 1896, several months before **Georges Méliès**'s first film. The date is significant, since Méliès is often cited as having made the first narrative film when the credit rightly belongs to Guy. While it is true that Guy made this film as a sort of advertisement for Gaumont's cameras (at that time Gaumont was still in the equipment business), her film is nonetheless a narrative film, and her title of "first **woman** director" notwithstanding, Guy's true place in film history has often been overlooked. In fact, even Gaumont, who made Guy the head of film production at Gaumont Studios in 1897 (a post she held until 1906), failed to mention her in his 1930 history of the studio.

As head of film production from 1897 to 1906, Guy trained most or all of the future directors of Gaumont silent film, including **Louis Feuillade**, **Victorin-Hippolyte Jasset**, and **Roméo Bossetti**. Alison McMahan, Guy's biographer, has concluded that Guy was responsible for most if not all narrative films made at Gaumont during that period, although very few are attributed to her. McMahan notes that in 1927, when Guy went looking for examples of her films, she could not find a single one. If indeed Guy did make or collaborate on all narrative films made by Gaumont between 1897 and 1906, then her work consists of a catalog of several hundred films. Of those several hundred, there are a number of films that are universally attributed to Guy. Among the most important are *Madame a des envies* (1906), which features what is probably the first dramatic close-up (typically attributed to the American director D. W. Griffith), *La Guérite/Douaniers et contrebandiers* (1905), *La Fée printemps* (1906), and the tableau film, *La Vie du Christ* (1906).

In 1907, Guy married Herbert Blaché, a Belgian cameraman who worked for Gaumont. Shortly after their marriage, the Blachés moved to the United States, where Herbert was to manage the New York offices of Gaumont. Alice gave up film for a time. She had two children, Simone in 1908, and Reginald in 1911. However, in 1912, she went back to work, founding the Solax Film Company (with her own money) in rented Gaumont studio space. Solax became a success, producing largely Westerns and melodramas, and the company moved to new studios in Fort Lee, New Jersey, in 1912. In 1913, Herbert joined Guy at Solax, and the studio prospered. The company enjoyed great popular and commercial success until 1917, when Herbert moved to Hollywood, both of Guy's children became seriously ill, and Solax began to feel the pressure from the increased centralization of the American film industry.

Solax was forced into bankruptcy in 1920, and the Blachés divorced in 1922. Guy returned to France in the hope of rebuilding her career in the French film industry, but since she was unable to find a single copy of her films to serve as proof of her expertise, she was unable to find work. She became financially dependent on her children, who were by that time old enough to support her. In 1940, Guy's daughter, Simone, began a career with the U.S. embassy service, and she and Guy moved to Washington, D.C., in 1947, where they began work on her memoirs. Guy moved again with Simone to New Jersey in 1967, near to the site where Solax Studios had been located. She died there in 1968.

In 1954, shortly before Guy's death, attention was refocused on her place in film history. Louis Gaumont gave a speech on her, "the first woman director," whom, he said "had been unjustly forgotten" and in 1955, Guy was honored with the *Légion d'Honneur* for her contributions to film. This contribution cannot be overstated. She rooted cinema firmly in a narrative tradition, seeing from the very beginning the possibility for telling stories through the use of the film camera. Taking into account the broad range of films she produced during her early career, it is also clear that she helped conceive or establish many of the existing film genres, including fantasy films, such as *La Fée aux choux* (1897), comedies such as her remake of *Les Apaches pas veinards* (1903) and the original *Le Matelas alcoolique* (1906), historical dramas, such as *L'Assasinat du courier de Lyon* (1903), melodramas such as *Le Fils du garde-chasse* (1906) and *La Marâtre* (1906), and literary adaptations, such as *Faust et Mephistopholes* (1903) and *La Esmerelda* (1905). She was, as McMahan has noted, an early pioneer of sound film, working with Gaumont's *chronographe*, and filming many early synchronized sound films both for Gaumont and subsequently for Solax.

In recent years, attention has been refocused on Alice Guy's work. In 1963, just prior to her death, Guy met with Belgian film scholar Victor Bachy, who spent several years researching Guy and her work. Bachy's book on Guy, which was published in 1994, did much to shed light on her role as a filmmaker. Guy's memoirs, along with a filmography, were published in French in 1976 and in English in 1986. In addition, a number of television documentaries have been done on her life and work. She is progressively becoming recognized as a woman who was well ahead of her time and who was one of the most influential and unsung pioneers of silent film.

– H –

HAMMAN, JOË (1885–1974). Actor and director. Joë Hamman was born Jean Hamman in Paris. His father was a painter and his mother a lady in waiting to the Empress Eugénie, so Hamman was surrounded by the world of arts and letters and Parisian high society. He studied art and was presumed to follow in his father's footsteps. However, the Wild West called Hamman, and when he was seventeen, he went to the United States, specifically to Montana and Nebraska. There, Hamman apparently spent time on an Indian reservation, learned to ride horses, and met Buffalo Bill, his childhood idol. He later joined Buffalo Bill's Wild West Show, and it was when traveling with the show that he returned to France in 1905.

Upon his return, Hamman, who had adopted the name Joë, was recruited by **Jean Durand** to star in Western films for **Gaumont**. He appeared in *Pendaison à Jefferson City* (1910) and *Le Railway de la mort* (1911). He also appeared in the burlesque Western *Calino veut être cow-boy* (1911). Apart from starring in the films, it was apparently Hamman who had the idea to shoot the films in France's southern Camargue region, finding the terrain and the horseriding tradition similar to what he had seen in the United States. This **Camargue**

Western, as Hamman would develop it, was an important precursor to the Spaghetti Westerns of later decades.

Hamman remained at Gaumont until 1910 or 1911, appearing in other films, including **Louis Feuillade**'s *La Fin d'une révolution américaine* (1912), *Dans la brousse* (1912), and *Au pays des lions* (1912). However, at that time, he was lured away by Éclipse Studios exclusively to develop the Camargue Western, and he was given full creative control. It is not entirely clear whether or not the famous and enormously popular *Arizona Bill* series in which Hamman starred was done at Gaumont, or whether it was done for Éclipse. The series, which ran from 1911 to 1913, is typically credited to Durand, but it seems more likely that Hamman directed several of the episodes and that the rest were directed by **Gaston Roudès**. World War I interrupted Hamman's activities, and he seems not to have made another film until it was over.

After the war, Hamman again directed films, beginning with *Le Gardien* (1920) and including *Un caprice de la Pompadour* (1930), *Les Monts en flammes* (1931), and *Grock* (1931). However, he spent most of the rest of his career acting, appearing in such films as **Gaston Ravel**'s *Tao* (1923), **Jean Kemm**'s *L'Enfant roi* (1923), **René Leprince**'s *Le Vert galant* (1924), Feullade and Maurice Champreux's *Le Stigmate* (1924), and **Henri Desfontaines**'s *Le Capitaine Rascasse* (1926).

Hamman's career extended past the silent-film era into the 1930s. He starred in the films he himself directed in the 1930s, and also in **Léo Joannen**'s *Adieu les copains* (1934) and Marie-Louise Iribe's *Le Roi des Aulnes* (1930). He also had supporting roles in Pierre Caron's *Notre Dame d'amour* (1936), **Henri Fescourt**'s *L'Occident* (1937), *Bar du sud* (1938), and *Vous seule que j'aime* (1939), as well as in Félix Gandara's *Tamara la complaisante* (1937). His last role was an uncredited one in **Sacha Guitry**'s *Napoléon* (1955). Although Hamman did not make Westerns after World War I, his place in film history was defined by his role in those early Westerns he did make. He is remembered to this day as "the French John Wayne."

HATOT, GEORGES (1876–1959). Director and film pioneer. Georges Hatot, like so many early film pioneers, began his career in the Parisian theatrical world. He had worked in Parisian theater, most notably as a crowd scene manager at the Hippodrome Theater, when, in 1896, he was hired on by the **Lumière** brothers as one of their team of film directors. He became the principal "story" film director for Lumière, making principally historical reconstruction films, most notably *L'Assasinat du Duc de Guise* (1897), *L'Exécution de Jeanne d'Arc* (1897), *Mort de Marat* (1901), and *La Vie et la Passion de Jésus-Christ* (1897). Hatot remained with the Lumières until they shut their studio and ceased film production in 1901. At that time, Hatot did a brief stint at **Gaumont** and then moved to **Pathé** studios, where he directed a number of mostly comic films, many written by André Heuzé. These included films such as *Dix Femmes pour un mari* (1905), *La Course à la perruque* (1906), *Boireau déménage* (1906), and *Les Débuts d'un chauffeur* (1906), the last three all starring comic actor **André Deed**.

Hatot remained at Pathé until 1908, at which time he moved to **Éclair** studios, where he teamed up with director **Victorin Jasset**. The two collaborated on nearly all films produced at Éclair in 1908 and 1909, although Hatot is often omitted on the credits. Hatot and Jasset produced predominantly film series such as the *Riffle Bill* series, which ran from 1908 to 1909, *Morgan le pirate* (1909), and *La Vautour de la Sierre* (1909). The most famous of their collaborations is the *Nick Carter* detective series, which ran in 1908 and 1909 and which was adapted from popular serial detective stories printed in contemporary newspapers. The *Nick Carter* series was an enormous success and spawned numerous detective series at other studios. Hatot and Jasset also collaborated on many other films, including *Dans les ruines de Carthage* (1910), *La Résurrection de Lazare* (1910), and *La Reconaissance de l'arabe* (1910), all of which were filmed on location in North Africa in 1909 and early 1910. Hatot stopped making films in 1910. At that time he started his own production company, Société du film négatif. Jasset directed the enormously popular series *Docteur Phantom* (1910) for Hatot's company, but the company was forced to close when its studio, located in Montreuil, burned down shortly after the company was founded. Hatot gave up cinema after that.

HERITAGE FILM. The Heritage film is the name given to a type of film encouraged by Minister of Culture Jack Lang that began in the

1980s and stretched into following decades. In some measure a return to the *tradition de qualité*, heritage films are characterized by high production values, by their foregrounding of French heritage properties and landscapes, and by their focus on privileged periods of French history. Many heritage films also feature great works of art or classical music or are adaptations of France's literary classics. Some critics consider the heritage film to be an extension or revision of earlier genres such as the period genre or *film historique*. What distinguishes heritage films from the other similar types of films, however, is that they are often inherently nostalgic. The past they create is often simultaneously glorified and mourned. Even in those cases where the presentation of the past is less straightforwardly nostalgic, there tends to be a glorification of the history of France, and the complications in presentation typically serve less to interrogate the past than to critique the present.

The term was first used in English to describe a similar type of British film from approximately the same period. However, it was quickly applied to French film, where the terms *cinéma de patrimoine* or sometimes *cinéma de terroirs* is used. In both cases the source of anxiety about the past seen to provoke the heritage wave is the loss of empire and with it the sense of national glory that empire once conveyed.

While opinions differ, Daniel Vigne's *Le Retour de Martin Guerre* (1982) is sometimes cited as the first French heritage film. The choice is apt, since the film is based on a historical event that has passed into folklore, and the narrative deals with the return of the past into the narrative present. The heritage director par excellence is probably **Claude Berri**. His *Jean de Florette* (1986) and *Manon des sources* (1986), both remakes of works by **Marcel Pagnol**, are doubly nostalgic in their references to the classical era of French film and in their representation of France's rural past. His *Gérminal* (1993) is also an oft-cited example. Other heritage films include **Patrice Chéreau's** *La Reine Margot* (1994), **Jean-Paul Rappeneau's** *Cyrano de Bergerac* and *Le Husard sur le toit* (1995), and **Edouard Molinaro's** *Beaumarchais, l'insolent* (1996). All of these are literary adaptations or are based on the biographies of literary figures. Alain Corneau's *Tous les matins du monde* (1991) has been cited as the quintessential heritage film for its ability to combine costume drama, literary adaptation, and classical music into an inherently nostalgic piece.

HISTOIRE D'UN CRIME **(1901).** Film. Directed by **Ferdinand Zecca** for **Pathé**, *Histoire d'un crime* is an early narrative film, probably the first crime film ever made, and one of the early realist films. The film, which runs approximately eight minutes, was a commercial success. It is a moralizing story about a carpenter who develops a gambling problem and who ultimately commits murder. The story, which seems as though it might have been adapted from something in period newspapers, was, according to film scholar Richard Abel, actually inspired by waxwork displays at the Musée Grevin just prior to its production.

The film is noteworthy not only for its narrative content and its use of realism, but also through its use of flashback sequences, which occur as dreams the carpenter has while in prison. The flashback is achieved by juxtaposing two sets in the same scene, one above the other. In the frame, the sleeping prisoner and the sleeping guard, who is supposed to be watching him, are in the lower set, while the action of the flashback or dream sequence occurs in the upper set. Although this is a technique that had previously been used in the theater, it pushes the boundaries of early cinema, pointing to the possibility of representing more abstract realities than simply the filmic present of narrative action.

HOSSEIN, ROBERT (1927–). Actor, director, and screenwriter. Robert Hossein was born Robert Hosseinoff in Paris, the son of Iranian composer André Hossein. He studied drama at the René Simon School and later acted in the theater. He first appeared as a cinema actor in **Sacha Guitry**'s *Le Diable boiteux* in 1948. He also appeared in Jules Dassin's *Du rififi chez les hommes* (1955). In the mid-1950s, Hossein acted, wrote, and directed his first film, *Les Salauds vont en enfer* (1956), a film noir starring his first wife, Marina Vlady. Hossein's next feature was *Pardonnez nos offenses* (1956). In addition to performing in his own films, Hossein maintained an energetic acting career. In the 1950s, he began working for **Roger Vadim** in *Sait-on jamais?* (1957), and Vadim would later cast him as a leading man in *Le repos du guerrier* (1962) opposite **Brigitte Bardot**. He also appeared in Vadim's *Le Vice et la Vertu* (1963), with **Annie Girardot** and **Catherine Deneuve**, and in *Don Juan* (1973), again with Bardot. In the late 1950s, Hossein directed *Toi le venin* (1958) and *La Nuit des espions* (1959), featuring Vlady, and *Les Scélérats* (1959), where he costars with **Michèle Morgan**.

In the 1960s, Hossein directed *Le goût de la violence* (1961), *Le jeu de la vérité* (1961), *La Mort d'un tueur* (1964), *Les yeux cernés* (1964), *Le Vampire de Düsseldorf* (1965), and *J'ai tué Raspoutine* (1967). In 1962, Hossein costarred with Sophia Loren in **Christian-Jacque**'s *Madame Sans Gêne* (1962). Hossein was the lead actor, alongside actress Michèle Mercier, in Bernard Borderie's *Angélique marquise des anges* (1964). He later paired with Mercier in Borderie's "Angélique" sequels: *Angélique et le roy* (1956), *Indomptable Angélique* (1967), and *Angélique et le sultan* (1967). Hossein cast Mercier in his French Western *Une corde, un colt*. Also in 1967, he starred with **Delphine Seyrig** in **Marguerite Duras**'s *La musica*. He costarred with **Charles Aznavour** in Sergio Gobbi's *Le Temps des loups* (1969).

After directing *Point de chute* (1970), Hossein temporarily halted his career in the cinema to take over direction of the Théâtre Populaire de Reims. He acted in a few films in the 1970s, among them Jean Larriaga's *La Part des lions* (1971), where he costarred again with Aznavour, and **Henri Verneuil**'s *Le Casse* (1971). In 1981, he returned to cinema with *Les Misérables*, which was nominated for a **César** for Best Adaptation. His last film as director, to date, is *Le caviar rouge* (1986). However, he has also acted in **Claude Lelouch**'s *Les Uns et les Autres* (1981), Vadim's *Surprise Party* (1983), Yannick Bellon's *Les enfants du désordre* (1989), Gobbi's *L'Affaire* (1994), and **Tonie Marshall**'s *Vénus beauté (institut)* (1998). He replaced the late **Jean Yanne** in Frédéric Auburtin's *San Antonio* (2003) after Yanne's death.

HUBERT, ROGER (1903–1964). Cinematographer. Roger Hubert began his career during the silent-film era. His first film experience was as the cameraman and cinematographer for **Jean Epstein** on his legendary film, *L'Auberge rouge* (1923). During the 1930s and 1940s, no doubt because of his talent and his early formation with a technical master, Hubert was invited to work with some of the greatest directors in France, particularly the directors associated with *Le Réalisme poétique* or poetic realism.

Hubert worked with **Marc Allégret** on *Mam'zelle Nitouche* (1931), *La Petite chocolatière* (1932), *Fanny* (1932), and *L'Hôtel du libre échange* (1934), with **Marcel Carné** on *Jenny* (1936), *Les Visiteurs du soir* (1942), **Les Enfants du paradis** (1945), and *La Fleur de l'âge* (1947), with **Julien Duvivier** on *Pension Mimosas* (1935), and *L'Homme du jour* (1937), and with **Jacques Feyder** on *La Piste du nord* (1939).

Hubert was also in demand with other, mostly artistically inclined directors. He was the preferred cinematographer of the director **Abel Gance**, and worked with Gance on *La Fin du monde* (1931), *Mater Dolorosa* (1932), *Napoléon Bonaparte* (1934), *La Dame aux camélias* (1934), *Le Roman d'un jeune homme pauvre* (1935), *Lucrèce Borgia* (1935), *Le Voleur de femmes* (1936), and *J'Accuse* (1938). He also worked with **Jean Delannoy** on *L'Éternel retour* (1943), with **Marcel L'Herbier** on *L'Affaire du collier de la reine* (1946), and with **Georges Lacombe** on *Martin Roumagnac* (1946).

In the 1950s and 1960s, as French filmmaking changed directions, Hubert found himself working on different kinds of films for different kinds of directors. He worked with **Henri Verneuil** on crime films and Gilles Grangier on comedies, but he also found occasion to work with some familiar directors. He worked with Duvivier again on *La Fête à Henriette* (1952) and *L'Homme à l'imperméable* (1957) and with Carné on *Thérèse Raquin* (1953). He also worked with Jean Dréville on his films *La Reine Margot* (1954) and *La Fayette* (1961).

HUGON, ANDRÉ (1886–1960). Director, producer, and screenwriter. André Hugon was born in Algiers, at the time a French territory. He began his career in the silent-film era as a screenwriter for **Pathé**, where he worked on **Georges Monca**'s *Rigadin* series (1912), among other projects. Hugon also directed films for Pathé or one of its subsidiaries for a number of years. These included *Beauté fatale* (1916), *L'Empreinte* (1916), *Le Bonheur qui revient* (1917), *Mariage d'amour* (1917), *Requins* (1917), *Un crime a été commis* (1919), and *Les Chères images* (1920). He did a number of films featuring the stage and screen star **Mistinguett**, such as *Chignon d'or* (1916), *Fleur de Paris* (1916), and *Mistinguette Détective* (1917), as well as several films with the actress **Musidora**, including *Mam'zelle Chiffon* (1917), *Les Chacals* (1917), and *Johannès fils de Johannès* (1918).

In 1920, Hugon left Pathé and established his own production company, Films André Hugon. The company produced all of Hugon's films for the rest of his career, lasting from 1920 to 1952. In fact, it is as an independent director that Hugon is best remembered. Working independently gave Hugon the freedom to make the type of films he was most interested in, and it is the films from this independent period that best define his work. There is a clear affinity between many of Hugon's films and those of another important independent filmmaker of the time, **Marcel Pagnol**, of whom Hugon was a close friend. Both made films with a strong southern French influence and both often worked with the actor **Raïmu**. Both also made films that were extremely popular in their time. However, whereas Pagnol has become something of an icon of French cinema, Hugon's works have been all but forgotten, for reasons that are not entirely clear.

Of the films that Hugon made between 1920 and 1952, a number have close Provence connections. These include *Roi de camargue* (1922), *Le Diamont noir* series (1922), *Notre dame d'amour* (1924), all based on novels by the Provençal writer Jean Aicard, *Le Petit chose* (1923), based on the novel by Alphonse Daudet, and *Les Trois masques* (1929), *Maurin des Maures* (1932), *L'Illustre Maurin* (1933), *Gaspard de Besse* (1935), *Romarin* (1936), *La Rue sans joie* (1938), *Chambre 13* (1940), and *L'Affaire du Grand Hôtel* (1946), all of which are set in Provence. In addition to the Provence connection, a number of Hugon's films also feature the Maghreb, or North Africa, where Hugon himself was born. These include *La Croix du sud* (1931), *Le Marchand de sable* (1931), and *Sarati, le terrible* (1937).

Other films made by Hugon include *Jacques Landauze* (1920), *La Preuve* (1921), *Rue du pavé d'amour* (1923), *L'Arriviste* (1924), *La Grande passion* (1928), *La Femme et le rossignol* (1930), *Les Vingt-huit jours de Clairette* (1933), *Chourinette* (1933), *Gangster malgré lui* (1935), *Le Héros de la Marne* (1939), and *Moulin Rouge* (1940).

Hugon's career made the transition to sound cinema, and in fact, his film, *Les Trois masques* (1929), was the first sound film made in French. His filmmaking seemed to lose no momentum with the coming of sound. In fact, he seemed to embrace sound, even making musicals during his career. Hugon actually had quite a broad range as a filmmaker, making everything from comedy to drama to mystery.

One testament to Hugon's stature as a filmmaker was the fact that his production company was able to survive at a time when most other independent studios failed in a period of a year or two. Another indicator of his stature was the type of actor he was able to attract to his films. At various points, Hugon worked with Lucien Baroux, **Harry Baur**, Jules Berry, Pierre Blanchar, **Pierre Brasseur**, Julien Carette, **René Dary**, Josette Day, Jean Debucourt, Hugette Duflos, Duvallès, **Ginette Leclerc**, **Françoise Rosay**, Dita Parlo, **Albert Préjean**, and of course Raïmu. The comic actress Mireille also frequently appeared in his films.

As noted, Hugon fell from grace in the 1950s. His films were no longer appreciated, and they ceased to be distributed. This may, in part, explain why so little attention has been paid to him since. One may imagine that if almost no one has seen his films for more than fifty years, there is no reason for anyone to have any interest in them. However, it is difficult to imagine that someone who once had the degree of popular appeal that Hugon had, someone who was once able to draw the best actors and supporting actors in French cinema, someone who was once regarded as on a par with one of the icons of French cinema, has nothing in his work that is worth remembering.

HUNÉBELLE, ANDRÉ (1896–1985). Director, producer, and screenwriter. André Hunébelle began his career as a director in the postwar era in France, the period that the filmmakers of the *Nouvelle Vague* or New Wave would refer to as the era of the "cinema du papa" and Hunébelle, no doubt, was one of the filmmakers those directors had in mind when coining the term. He was a popular director in the most often used sense of the word and was often accused by critics of producing an overly commercial, insufficiently aesthetic cinema. Today he might be regarded as a master of the B movie.

Hunébelle's first film was *Métier de fous* (1948), based on a screenplay written by the equally popular Gilles Grangier. He went on to make more than thirty other films, most of them in the 1950s and 1960s, before the New Wave permanently altered the composition of cinema. There was a certain diversity to Hunébelle's filmmaking, commercialism aside, although some trends are evident. He made adventure films, mostly literary adaptations or remakes of classic films. These included *Les Trois mousquetaires* (1953), *Le Bossu*

(1960), *Le Capitain* (1960), and *Le Miracle des loups* (1961). He also did other literary adaptations, producing mostly melodramas. These included *Les Mystères de Paris* (1962), based on the novel by Eugène Sue, and an interpretation of Alexandre Dumas in *Sous le signe de Monte Cristo* (1968).

Hunébelle was also inspired by the cinema, remaking again (it had already been remade) and adapting **Louis Feuillade**'s *Fantômas* films, in *Fantômas* (1964) and *Fantômas contre Scotland Yard* (1967). Other types of films that were his forte included thriller or spy films. These included *OSS 117 se déchaîne* (1963), *Banco à Bangkok pour OSS 117* (1964), and *Furia à Bahia pour OSS 117* (1965). Hunébelle also had some favorites with whom he liked to work. **Jean Marais** starred in many of his films, and many of his screenplays were written by **Michel Audiard**.

Apart from directing, Hunébelle also produced films and wrote screenplays. He worked on the screenplays for several of his films and produced many of his own films, as well as films for Gilles Grangier and **Claude Berri**, among others. His last film was *Ça fait tilt*, which was made in 1978.

HUPPERT, ISABELLE (1953–). Actress. Isabelle Huppert is one of France's major film actresses of the 1970s and beyond. She was born in Paris and grew up in Ville d'Avray. She studied at the Versailles Conservatory and the Conservatoire National d'Art Dramatique in Paris. Huppert debuted in film during her teens in Nina Companéez's *Faustine et le bel été* (1972). She then acted in **Bertrand Blier**'s *Les Valseuses* (1974), Jean-Louis Bertucelli's *Docteur Françoise Gailland* (1975), and Liliane de Kermadec's *Aloïse* (1975), for which she received her first **César** nomination for Best Supporting Actress. One of her major early roles was in Claude Goretta's *La Dentellière* (1976). For her work therein she earned a César nomination for Best Actress, a British Film Academy Award for Best Newcomer, and Best Foreign Actress at the David di Donatello Awards. Soon after that acclaimed performance, Huppert was named Best Actress at the **Cannes Film Festival** for her title role in **Claude Chabrol**'s *Violette Nozière*. Later in the decade, she acted in **Jean-Luc Godard**'s *Sauve qui peut (la vie)* (1979) and **André Téchiné**'s *Les sœurs Brontë* (1979).

In the 1980s, Huppert won the Volpi Cup at the Venice Film Festival for her performance in Chabrol's *Une Affaire des femmes* (1988). She received César nominations for Best Actress for her interpretations in **Maurice Pialat**'s *Loulou* (1980), **Bertrand Tavernier**'s *Coup de torchon* (1981), and *Une affaire de femmes* (1988). In the same decade, she played leading roles in **Benoît Jacquot**'s *Les Ailes de la colombe* (1980), Joseph Losey's *La Truite* (1982), **Diane Kurys**'s *Coup de foundre* (1983), Blier's *La femme de mon pote* (1983), Godard's *Passion* (1984), **Josiane Balasko**'s *Sac de Nœuds* (1985), and Andrzej Wajda's *Les possédés* (1988). She also appeared in the Anglophone films *Heaven's Gate* (1980), by Michael Cimino, and *Cactus* (1986), by Paul Cox.

In the 1990s, Huppert finally took the César for Best Actress for her performance in Chabrol's *La Cérémonie* (1995). She remained a favorite of Chabrol's and played the title role in his *Madame Bovary* (1991) and a starring role in his *Rien ne va plus* (1997). In the same decade, she played principal roles in Jacques Doillon's *La Vengeance d'une femme* (1990), Werner Schroeter's *Malina* (1991), **Christian Vincent**'s *La Séparation* (1994), Hal Hartley's *Amateur* (1994), **Claude Pinoteau**'s *Les Palmes de M. Schulz* (1996), and three films by Jacquot: *L'Ecole de la chair* (1998), *Pas de scandale* (1998), and *La Fausse suivante* (1999). At the beginning of the twenty-first century, Huppert reaped more awards. She won a second Best Actress award at Cannes and a European Film Award for her work in Michael Haneke's *La pianiste* in 2001. She won Best Actress at the Montreal World Film Festival and the Lumière Award for her artful interpretation in Chabrol's *Merci pour le chocolat* (2000). She also shared a European Film Award and a Silver Berlin Bear for her role in François Ozon's *8 femmes* (2002). Huppert remains an actress in high demand, starring in Patricia Mazuy's *Saint-Cyr* (2000), Schroeter's *Deux* (2002), Raoul Ruiz's *Comédie de l'innocence* (2000), Olivier Dahan's *La Vie promise* (2002), Haneke's *Le Temps du loup* (2003), David Russell's *I Heart Huckabees* (2004), Alexandra Leclère's *Les Sœurs fâchées* (2004), Christophe Honoré's *Ma mère* (2004), and **Patrice Chéreau**'s *Gabrielle* (2005). She also works in the theater, inspiring standing ovations as Hedda Gabler at the Odeon Theater in Paris in 2005. Her range as an actress demonstrates her versatility and talent.

– I –

INDOCHINE (1992). Film. Régis Wargnier's *Indochine* is a somewhat atypical example of the French **heritage film**. The story of Eliane Devries (**Catherine Deneuve**) the owner of a rubber plantation in French Indochina, Camille (Linh Dan Pham), Eliane's adopted daughter, and Jean-Baptiste (Vincent Perez), the lover of both women, *Indochine* is typical of heritage works in its visually stunning representation of a disappeared past. However, it is atypical in that it represents a period of French history generally absent from the national memory—the end of the Empire.

Indochine is structured, more or less, as one long flashback sequence. As the film opens, the scene is completely white. Slowly, the white turns to mist that clears to reveal a Vietnamese funeral while, through voice-over, Eliane explains that it is the funeral of two Vietnamese nobles, whose daughter she has adopted. The veil of mist and the voice-over signal that this scene and everything that follows is flashback and that the French Indochina only exists, in the narrative present, in Elaine's memory.

As this sequence illustrates, the narrative of the film, and by extension the whole of French Indochina, is located in the domain of Eliane's personal memory, thereby completely erasing the point of view of the Indochinese. And since Eliane is played by Catherine Deneuve, probably the most recognizable French actress in the world, it is fairly clear that the perspective we have on the colonial past is that of France itself.

This use of a single point of view also renders the film nostalgic, making it less historical epic than act of memory. Also interesting with regard to the film's use of nostalgia and heritage is the fact that it casts colonization as a form of adoption, wherein France is seen to take possession of the helpless Indochina in order to protect and educate the country. While this is a depiction that would be subject to great historical scrutiny, it is exactly in line with the rhetoric used during Empire to justify colonization, a policy referred to as the "civilizing mission" of colonialism.

Despite all of these nostalgic, seemingly apologist elements, the valorization of colonization in the film is not without nuance. The French are sometimes depicted as brutal and cruel, as when Eliane beats her workers, or when Camille and Jean-Baptiste witness the sale of "prisoners" into what is essentially slavery. Nonetheless, the film tends to look back on the period of Empire with a certain fondness that these moments do not quite negate. The film also foregrounds the Indochinese landscape, presenting it in beautiful, vivid colors that are highly exotic, a presentation that in some ways mirrors the representation of the character of Camille. The film's mise-en-scène is so spectacular, in fact, it often functions to mask the underlying elements of colonial nostalgia. *Indochine*, for all of these reasons, was a highly successful film in France, and it also did very well internationally, even in the United States, where it was awarded an Oscar for Best Foreign Film.

INSTITUT DES HAUTES ÉTUDES CINÉMATOGRAPHIQUES (IDHEC). IDHEC was a Parisian film school founded in 1942 by film director **Marcel L'Herbier**, under the direction of the Occupation government. L'Herbier served as the school's first director. The publicly funded institute taught all aspects of film, from criticism, history, and theory to directing, editing, and production. It was open until 1985, when it was replaced by the Fondation Européenne des Métiers de l'Image et du Son (FEMIS). Former students include **Costa-Gavras**, **Claire Denis**, **Patrice Leconte**, **Louis Malle**, **Alain Resnais**, and **Claude Sautet**.

– J –

JACQUOT, BENOÎT (1947–). Director and screenwriter. In his early teens, Benoît Jacquot visited the **Cinémathèque française**, where he met **Jacques Rivette**, and in fact, he attributes his interest in cinema to the *Nouvelle Vague* or New Wave. Jacquot studied at university, but dropped out to work as an assistant director, most notably for **Marguerite Duras**. He directed television films as well, including a documentary on philosopher Jacques Lacan, who has influenced and commented on his work.

Jacquot's films have been described by the director as "talking films." They often center on a young female protagonist. His first feature film, *L'Assassin musicien* (1976), based on a novel by Fyodor

Dostoevsky, inspired comparisons to **Robert Bresson**, as did his second film, *Les Enfants du placard* (1977). *L'Assassin musicien* stars **Anna Karina**, the New Wave actress Jacquot became fascinated with in his early years. Jacquot cast Brigitte Fossey as the lead for *Enfants du placard*. His third film, *Les Ailes de la colombe* (1981), was adapted from the novel by Henry James and stars **Isabelle Huppert** and Dominique Sanda. *Corps et Biens* (1986) was adapted from a novel by another American writer, James Gunn. In the late 1980s, Jacquot made a few television films before directing *Les Mendiants* (1988), with Sanda as the lead.

In 1990, Jacquot released *La désenchantée*, a film that he says renewed his career. His 1990s films demonstrate a greater interest in making personal connections with his audience. They have also enhanced the acting careers of young actresses, such as Judith Godrèche (in *La désenchantée*) and Virginie Ledoyen, who plays the lead in the critically acclaimed *La Fille seule* (1995). Jacquot has also collaborated with established actresses, such as **Sandrine Bonnaire** in *Le Septième ciel* (1997). He selected Huppert as his lead of *L'École de la chair* (1998), which was nominated for a Golden Palm at **Cannes**, *Pas de scandale* (1999), which was nominated for a Golden Lion at Venice, and *La Fausse suivante* (2000). In 1993, he released a short about his mentor Duras, titled *Écrire*.

In the twenty-first century, Jacquot directed the period films *Sade* (2000), with **Daniel Auteuil**, and *Adolphe* (2002), starring **Isabelle Adjani**. He also directed an adaptation of Giacomo Puccini's opera, *Tosca* (2001). Jacquot continues to enhance the careers of emerging actresses: Isild Le Besco won a Lumière Award for most promising actress in *Sade* and is also the star of Jacquot's *À tout de suite* (2004). In 2005, Jacquot served on the Jury at Cannes.

JASSET, VICTORIN-HIPPOLYTE (1862–1913). Director and film pioneer. Victorin-Hippolyte Jasset, like nearly all early film pioneers, started his career in the theater. His areas of expertise in the theatrical world were costumes and scenery, and he worked in that capacity before becoming a director at the Hippodrome Theater in Paris (which would later be turned into the Gaumont Palace). Jasset entered the cinema in 1906, when **Alice Guy** asked him to do the costumes and scenery for her film, *La Vie du Christ* (1906). He worked

Firmine Richard, Isabelle Huppert, Virginie Ledoyen, Ludivine Sagnier, Danielle Darrieux, Fanny Ardant, Catherine Deneuve, and Emmanuelle Béart in François Ozon's 8 femmes *(2002)*

Juliette Binoche and Michel Piccoli in Leos Carax's Mauvais sang (1986)

Jean Gabin and Arletty in Marcel Carné's Le Jour se lève *(1939)*

Jean-Paul Belmondo and Jean-Luc Godard on the set of Godard's Pierrot le Fou
(1965)

Jean Brochard, Ginette Leclerc, and Pierre Fresnay in Henri-Georges Clouzot's Le Corbeau (1943)

Daniel Auteuil and Isabelle Adjani in Patrice Chéreau's La Reine Margot (1994)

Max Linder with Charlie Chaplin during Linder's 1918 visit to the United States

Yves Montand and Gérard Depardieu in Claude Berri's Jean de Florette *(1986)*

Jeanne Moreau and Brigitte Bardot in Louis Malle's Viva Maria (1965)

for only a brief time at **Gaumont** before being hired on at the newly established **Éclair** studios, where he was paired with veteran film director **Georges Hatot**. Jasset and Hatot collaborated for approximately two years at Éclair, during which time the two produced a number of films, mostly film serials (although only Jasset is credited on most of these). Of these, the most famous are undoubtedly the *Riffle Bill* series, which ran in 1908, the *Nick Carter* series, which ran in 1908 and 1909, and the *Morgan le pirate* series, which ran in 1909. *Nick Carter* was, without a doubt, the most famous of these. Adapted from a dime-store detective serial, Nick Carter became the prototype for the detective film and enjoyed huge popular success. Other films Jasset made for Éclair include *La Fille de la sorcière* (1908), *L'Honneur du corsaire* (1908), *Dragonades sous Louis XIV* (1909), *Fleur empoisonnée* (1909), *Le Vautour de la sierra: le Vautour et l'usurier* (1909), *Le Vautour de la sierra: un marriage mouvementé* (1909), *Le Vautour de la sierra: evasion audacieuse* (1909), and *Ginhara ou fidèlde jusqu'à la mort* (1910).

In 1909, Jasset and Hatot went to North Africa to film and there made a number of films on location. These include *Dans les ruines de Carthage* (1910), *La Résurrection de Lazare* (1910), and *La Reconnaissance de l'arabe* (1910). Jasset returned to Paris in the summer of 1910 and there made *L'Hériodade* (1910) on his own. Jasset also directed independently the *Docteur Phantom* series (1910) for the Société du film négatif studio, newly founded by Hatot. From that point on in his career, Jasset primarily worked alone, apart from a brief collaboration with director Émile Chautard in 1911.

Jasset's success with the serial continued when he created *Zigomar* in 1911. *Zigomar* was a dark, somber, realist depiction of the criminal side of contemporary society. It was a precursor to **Louis Feuillade**'s *Fantômas* and undoubtedly influenced it. *Zigomar* is often seen (as is Feuillade's *Fantômas*) as a precursor to **Réalisme poétique** or poetic realism. *Zigomar* was so successful that it inspired two sequels, *Zigomar contre Nick Carter* (1912), which pit two of Jasset's most famous characters against one another, and *Zigomar peau d'anguille* (1913).

Apart from serials, Jasset was able to direct a number of different types of film. His films include social dramas like *Au pays des ténèbres* (1912), literary adaptations, such as *Le Mystère de Notre*

Dame de Paris (1912), and epic adventures such as *Balaoo* (1912). He also made a female spy film, *Protéa* (1913), which was continued in sequel form after his death. When Jasset died in 1913, he had nearly single-handedly carried the Éclair studios for five years, and established his own reputation as a landmark film director, with a clear, no-nonsense style that had pushed the cinema that much closer to the inevitable dominance of narrative.

JEAN DE FLORETTE **(1986) AND** *MANON DES SOURCES* **(1986).** Films. Arguably two of the best examples of the French **heritage film**, are **Claude Berri's** *Jean de Florette* and its sequel *Manon des sources*. The films recount the saga of Papet (**Yves Montand**) and Ugolin (**Daniel Auteuil**) Soubeyran, members of an old family from the village of Crespin. The two plot to acquire the farm of their neighbor, Jean (**Gérard Depardieu**), a tax collector who has moved from the city to the village. Jean is the son of Florette, a former resident of the village, but is still seen as an outsider. As a result of the plot against him, Jean never discovers the existence of a spring on his property, a spring the Soubeyrans have plugged. Jean's farm ultimately fails, and Jean is killed in a dynamite accident, while attempting to locate a water source on his property.

In the sequel, Manon (**Emmanuelle Béart**), Jean's daughter, takes revenge on the Soubeyrans and the village as a whole, when she finds the hidden source that feeds all of the springs in the village, and blocks it. It is ultimately discovered that Jean was Papet's illegitimate son, and his grief is doubled when Ugolin, distressed over unrequited love for Manon, kills himself.

Both films were enormously popular—in fact, they are two of the most popular films ever made in France, probably precisely because of their connection to heritage. The films offer an idealized representation of the rural past—connections apparent in the choice of subject matter, the mise-en-scène, and in the narrative content. In fact, the films are as much about Provence, rural life, and village culture as they are about Jean and the Soubeyrans. All of these elements were no doubt attractive in a France fearful of globalization, sensing a loss of power and identity with the advent of the European Union, and sometimes panicked by demographic changes in its population prompted by emigration from former colonies.

The films also foreground community and tradition, reassuring themes in a rapidly changing world. They constitute a visually spectacular representation of an important time and place in French cultural heritage, since French identity and regional identity are often linked in the popular sentiment. Moreover, the films are doubly linked to cultural memory, since they are based on a novel and a film by **Marcel Pagnol**, his 1953 film *Manon des sources*, and his 1962 novel *L'Eau des collines*. Therefore, the Berri films function as both literary adaptations of classical texts in French regional literature and cinematic remakes of films that are considered part of classical French cinema.

In addition to the elements of heritage and nostalgia that are present in the films, they feature strong performances by some of the best-known actors in France. Montand and Depardieu were already icons when the films were made, and Auteuil and Béart have gone on to become stars. The success in both cases is linked to their performances in the films. Technically, the films are fairly straightforward with respect to their cinematography and editing, although, as with many other heritage films, they feature high production values.

JEAN VIGO PRIZE. *See* PRIX JEAN-VIGO.

JEUNET, JEAN-PIERRE (1953–). Director and screenwriter. Jean-Pierre Jeunet began filming short animated films with codirector Marc Caro, such as *L'Évasion* (1978) and *Le Manège* (1980), which won a **César** for Best Animated Short. Jeunet won a second César for Best Short Fiction Film for *Foutaises* (1989). With Caro, he directed his first feature, the highly imaginative and futuristic *Delicatessen* (1991), which won Césars for Best First Film and Best Screenplay. His next film, *La cité des enfants perdus* (1995) (codirected with Caro), is remarkable in its innovative special effects. Jeunet later worked with American actors in his direction of the science-fiction film *Alien: Resurrection* (1997). His next film, *Le fabuleux destin d'Amélie Poulain* (2001), was an international blockbuster. It won him Césars for Best Director and Best Film and could be considered one of the later examples of the *cinéma du look*. Jeunet's most recent film to date is the World War II romance *Un long dimanche de fiançailles* (2004), which, like *Amélie,* stars **Audrey Tautou**.

JOANNON, LÉO (1904–1969). Actor, director, and screenwriter. Born Léon Joannen in Aix-en-Provence, Léo Joannon began his career as a screenwriter and film-crew assistant at the end of the silent-film era. He quickly turned his hand to directing, although he continued to write, working on the screenplays for most of his own films. His first film was *Adieu les copains* (1930) and was quickly followed by others, including *Sur la voie du bonheur* (1931), *600 000 francs par mois* (1933), *Bibi la purée* (1934), *Quelle drôle de gosse* (1935), *Train de plaisir* (1936), *Quand minuit sonnera* (1936), *Vous n'avez rien à déclarer* (1937), *Alerte en méditerannée* (1938), which won the Grand Prix du cinéma français, and *L'Emigrante* (1939), starring **Edwige Feuillière**.

The 1930s were really the peak years of Joannon's career. During the 1940s and particularly during the Occupation, he made only a handful of films, no doubt because of his decidedly pacifist politics, which were evident in some of his films. Films from this period include *Caprices* (1942), starring **Danielle Darrieux** and **Albert Préjean**, *Le Camion blanc* (1943), starring Jules Berry, *Lucrèce* (1943), which again starred Feuillière, *Le Carrefour des enfants perdus* (1944), and *Documents secrets* (1945).

Joannon had a bit of a renaissance in the 1950s, during which time he made the Laurel and Hardy feature *Atoll K* (1951) and a number of religious or morally oriented dramas including *Le Défroqué* (1954), which starred **Pierre Fresnay**, *Le Secret de soeur Angèle* (1956), *L'Homme aux clefs d'or* (1956), which again starred Fresnay, and *Le Désert de Pigalle* (1958). In the 1960s, he made a variety of different kinds of film, including the crime films *L'Assassin est dans l'annuaire* (1962), which featured **Fernandel**, and *Les Arnaud* (1967), the war drama *Fort-du-fou* (1963), and the comedy *Trois enfants . . . dans le désordre* (1966).

In addition to writing and directing, Joannon also appeared in a number of films, including his own *Le Défroqué*, *L'Homme aux clefs d'or*, *Le Désert de Pigalle*, and *L'Assassin est dans l'annuaire*, as well as **Pierre Kast**'s *Un amour de poche* (1957). He also tried his hand at producing, producing his two films *Vous n'avez rien à déclarer* (1937) and *Drôle de noce* (1952).

JOUBÉ, ROMUALD (1876–1949). Actor. Romuald Joubé was a stage actor of some renown. He performed at the Odéon under the direction of **André Antoine**, and was in residence at the Comédie Française from 1921 to 1922. Although Joubé's career was spent primarily on the stage, he managed a respectable film career as well. He got his start in the cinema in productions made by **Studio Film d'Art**, but continued making films after the studio closed. In total, Joubé appeared in over forty films over a period of more than thirty years.

Joubé made his debut onscreen in 1910 in **Henri Desfontaines**'s *Shylock*, in which he appeared with **Harry Baur**. That same year, Joubé appeared in **Camille de Morlhon**'s *Polyeucte* (1910), and the following year, he appeared in Georges Denola's *Philémon et Baucis* (1911) and **Albert Capellani** and Desfontaines's *La Momie* (1911). Among Joubé's other silent film performances are de Morlhon's *Brittanicus* (1912), **Henri Pouctal**'s *Serge Panine* (1913) and *Pêcheur d'Islande* (1915), Desfontaines's *La Reine Margot* (1914), *La Forêt qui écoute* (1916), and *Le Dernier rêve* (1916), Capellani's *Les Deux gosses* (1914) and *Marie Tudor* (1917), Antoine's *Les Frères corses* (1917) and *Mademoiselle de la Seglière* (1920), **Abel Gance**'s *J'accuse!* (1919), **Henri Fescourt**'s *Mathias Sandorf* (1920) and *Rouletabille chez le bohemians* (1922), **Jean Kemm**'s *L'Énigme* (1921), **André Hugon**'s *Le Diamant noir* (1922), Henri Étiévant's *La Fille sauvage* (1922), and Raymond Bernard's *Le Miracle des loups* (1924).

Joubé's career more or less failed to survive the advent of sound cinema. He had a handful of minor, some even uncredited, roles in film during the sound era, but was one of those actors who was not able to reestablish his film career in speaking roles. Among the sound films in which Joubé did appear are **Christian-Jacque** and **Sacha Guitry**'s *Les Perles de la couronne* (1937), Gance's sound remake of *J'accuse!* (1938), Émile Couzinet's *Andorra ou les homes d'Airain* (1942) and *Le Brigand gentilhomme* (1943), and Hugon's *Le Chant de l'exilé* (1943).

JOURDAN, LOUIS (1919–). Actor. Born Louis Gendre in Marseilles, Louis Jourdan had a fairly cosmopolitan childhood, spending time in Turkey and England as well as France before studying to become an actor. He was a student of René Simon's at the École dramatique, and made his screen debut in 1939 in **Marc Allégret**'s *Le Corsaire*. Jourdan's screen career was immediately successful, and during the period from the late 1930s until the Nazi Occupation, he was quite busy, appearing in such films as **Henri Decoin**'s *Premier Rendez-vous* (1941), Allegret's *Parade en sept nuits* (1941), *L'Arlésienne* (1942), *La Belle aventure* (1942), *Les Petites du Quai aux fleurs* (1944), and *Félicie Nanteuil* (1945), **Marcel L'Herbier**'s *La Comédie du bonheur* (1942) and *La Vie de bohème* (1945), and **Julien Duvivier**'s *Untel père et fils* (1943).

During the Occupation, Jourdan refused to act in films, at least in those films produced by the Occupation authorities or **Continental Films**. This more or less prevented him from working in France. His other opposition to the Nazi regime—his father was arrested by the Gestapo—also made his position in France somewhat difficult, so, like many actors of the day, he went to the United States.

Although Jourdan was able to work in Hollywood, the roles he found were very different from those he had had on the French screen. In France, Jourdan had been seen as a talented actor, and had therefore played a range of roles in major films, working with the great stars of the day, including **Bernard Blier**, **Michèle Morgan**, **Odette Joyeux**, **Danielle Darrieux**, **Gaby Morlay**, **Micheline Presle**, and **Raïmu**. In Hollywood, he was quickly typecast as the suave European, usually a lover, a type which severely limited the range of his roles. The American films in which he appeared from this period include Alfred Hitchcock's *The Paradine Case* (1947) and Vincent Minelli's *Madame Bovary* (1949). He also starred in **Max Ophüls**'s Hollywood film, *Letter from an Unknown Woman* (1948).

Despite the limitations on his career, Jourdan remained in the United States, working only occasionally in French cinema, most notably in **Jacques Becker**'s *Rue de l'estrapade* (1953), **Claude Autant-Lara**'s *Le Comte de Monte Cristo* (1961), Georges Lampin's *Mathias Sandorf* (1963), Léonard Keigel's *Leviathan* (1962), and **Jean Delannoy**'s *Les Sultans* (1966). Among the other Hollywood films in which he appeared are Jean Negulesco's *Three Coins in the Fountain* (1954), Minelli's *Gigi* (1958), and Walter Lang's *Can-Can* (1960). Since the 1960s, Jourdan has primarily appeared on television and onstage, with only occasional roles in film, and those mostly outside Hollywood.

JOUVET, LOUIS (1887–1951). Actor. Born in Crozon in Brittany, Louis Jouvet trained as a pharmacist but dreamed of becoming an actor. He worked as a pharmacist for a time, while he tried—three times—to gain admission to the Paris Conservatoire d'art dramatique. He finally gave up and studied acting, directing, and all things theatrical in a more hands-on way as an apprentice to Jacques Copeau at the Théâtre du Vieux-Colombier. Despite his lack of formal credentials and his early difficulties, Jouvet went on to become one of the legendary actors of the French stage and screen.

Jouvet made his stage debut in 1910 and his screen debut shortly thereafter, in the 1913 *film d'art* production of *Shylock*. This initial entry into cinema would not be fruitful, as Jouvet abandoned the medium to concentrate all of his energies on his stage career, going on to become director of the Théâtre du Vieux-Colombier.

Jouvet's next foray into cinema would not come for nearly twenty years, during which time he went to the United States to perform onstage, and became director of the Comédie du Champs-Elysées. Jouvet reappeared onscreen in 1933, in *Knock*, a film he codirected. From that point on, Jouvet was a fairly constant presence on the screen and appeared in some of the major films of the period, particularly those associated with *Le Réalisme poétique* or poetic realism. Among the films in which he appeared are Louis J. Gasnier's adaptation of **Marcel Pagnol**'s *Topaze* (1935), **Jacques Feyder**'s *La Kermesse héroïque* (1935), **Jean Renoir**'s *Les Bas-fonds* (1936) and *La Marseillaise* (1938), **Julien Duvivier**'s *Un carnet de bal* (1937), *La Fin du jour* (1939), *La Charette fantôme* (1939), and *Untel père et fils* (1943), **Marcel L'Herbier**'s *Forfaiture* (1937), **Pierre Chenal**'s *L'Alibi* (1937) and *La Maison du Maltais* (1938), **Marcel Carné**'s *Drôle de drame* (1937) and *Hôtel du nord* (1938), Alexander Esway's *Éducation de prince* (1938), **Marc Allégret**'s *L'Entrée des artistes* (1938), **Max Ophüls**'s *L'École des femmes* (1940), Maurice Tourneur's *Volpone* (1941), **Christian-Jacque**'s *Un revenant* (1946), **Henri-Georges Clouzot**'s *Quai des Orfèvres* (1947), **Henri Decoin**'s *Les Amoureux sont seuls au monde* (1948) and *Entre onze heures et minuit* (1949), **Georges Lampin** and **André Cayatte**'s *Retour à la vie* (1949) and *Miquette et sa mère* (1950), and Henri Jeanson's *Lady Paname* (1950).

Considered one of the great stage actors of the last century, Jouvet had a respectable career onscreen as well, although some would argue that his screen career paled before his stage career. Nonetheless,

Jouvet's considerable stage presence translated well on the screen. He was a masterful actor whose forceful performances defined the films he appeared in, although part of his genius was that even with his commanding presence, he never dominated the screen. The roles Jouvet played varied widely. He appeared as aristocrats and police detectives, school teachers and priests. He could play murder mysteries and Molière with equal skill. If it is true that Jouvet's screen career was only a footnote to his great stage career, it is also true that he was one of the great actors of what is considered French cinema's golden age.

JOYEUX, ODETTE (1914–2000). Actress and screenwriter. Odette Joyeux began her career as an actress in the early 1930s. She had smaller roles in films such as Charles de Rochefort's *Le Secret du docteur* (1930) and Jean Tarride's *Le Chine Jaune* (1932), before Jean Choux cast her in his film *Jean de la lune* (1932). Subsequently, Joyeux appeared in **Marc Allégret**'s *Lac aux dames* (1934) and **Gaston Roudès** *Le Chant de l'amour* (1935).

In 1935, Joyeux was cast in **Louis Jouvet**'s production of Jean Giradoux's play *Intermezzo*. It was during her performance in the play that Joyeaux met **Pierre Brasseur**, whom she would later marry. Brasseur went on to cast her in a play of his own, and the two appeared together in Max Neufeld's *Valse éternelle* (1936), Maurice Cammage's *Une femme qui se partage* (1936), and Maurice de Canonge's *Grisou* (1938). During the same period, Joyeux also appeared in **Marie Epstein** and **Jean Benoît-Lévy**'s *Hélène* (1936) and *Altitude 3,200* (1938) and Choux's *La Glu* (1936).

Joyeux went on to appear in several other films during the 1930s and 1940s, including **Claude Autant-Lara**'s *Le Mariage de Chiffon* (1942), *Lettres d'amour* (1942), and *Sylvie et le fantôme* (1946), **Serge de Poligny**'s *Le Baron fantôme* (1943), Allégret's *Les Petites du quai aux fleurs* (1944), **Jean-Paul Paulin**'s *L'Échec au roy* (1945), Gilles Grangier's *Leçon de conduite* (1946), **Jean-Paul Le Chanois**'s *Messieurs Ludovic* (1946), Edmond T. Greville's *Pour une nuit d'amour* (1947), René Le Henaff's *Scandale* (1948), Maurice de Canonge's *Dernière heure, edition spéciale* (1949), **Max Ophüls**'s *La Ronde* (1950), and **Sacha Guitry**'s *Si Paris nous était conté* (1955). *Le Mariage de Chiffon* remains probably Joyeux's best-known role, although it is not clear it was her best role, due to her presence in a number of important films, particularly those by independent directors.

In addition to her contributions as an actress, Joyeux also worked as a screenwriter. Her primary contributions were to television in the 1960s, 1970s, and 1980s, but she did work on films such as Pierre Gaspard-Huit's *La Mariée est trop belle* (1956), Allegret's *L'Amour est en jeu* (1957) and *Sois belle et tais-toi* (1958), and Philippe Agostini's *Rencontres* (1962). Joyeux is also the mother of the actor **Claude Brasseur**.

JUGNOT, GERARD (1951–). Actor, director, screenwriter, and producer. In secondary school Gérard Jugnot befriended Michel Blanc, **Christian Clavier**, and **Thierry Lhermitte**, with whom he would establish the Troupe du Splendid. He debuted in cinema in Jacques Doillon, **Alain Resnais**, and **Jean Rouche**'s *L'An 01* (1973) alongside splendid colleagues Clavier, Lhermitte, and **Josiane Balasko**. He played a minor role in **Bertrand Blier**'s *Les Valseuses* (1974), followed by a leading role alongside Balasko in Francis Fehr's *Pauline et l'ordinateur* (1978). His popularity as a comic actor surged with **Patrice Leconte**'s *Les Bronzés* (1978), an adaptation of a play cowritten by the Splendid Group. He subsequently costarred with **Daniel Auteuil** in Charles Nemes's *Les Héros n'ont pas froid aux oreilles* (1979).

Jugnot's talent for comedy was further demonstrated in Leconte's sequel, *Les Bronzés font du ski* (1979), **Edouard Molinaro**'s *Pour cent briques t'as plus rien* (1982), where he paired again with Auteuil, and Jean-Marie Poiré's *Le Père Noël est une ordure* (1982), another film written by the Splendid group, and Poiré's *Papy fait de la résistance* (1983). He directed and played the lead in his first film, the comedy *Pinot, simple flic*, which was released in 1984. He also directed and starred in *Scout toujours* (1985), *Sans peur et sans reproche* (1988), and *Une époque formidable* (1991), for which he was nominated for a **César** for Best Actor, *Casque bleu* (1994), *Fallait pas!* (1996), *Meilleur Espoir féminin* (2000), and *Monsieur Batignole* (2002).

Although he is well known for his work in comedy, he is an eclectic actor. He was nominated for Césars for Best Actor in Leconte's comedy *Tandem* in 1988, for Best Supporting Actor in Jean-Loup Hubert's war drama *Marthe* in 1998, and for Best Actor in Christophe Barratier' drama *Les Choristes* in 2005. Jugnot directed a remake of **Jean Renoir**'s 1932 classic *Boudu sauvé des eaux*, which originally starred **Michel Simon**, Charles Granval, and Marcelle Hainia. Jugnot's film, titled *Boudu*, was released in 2005 and stars **Gérard Depardieu**, Jugnot, and Catherine Frot. Jugnot also appears in Yves Lavandier's *Oui mais . . .* (2001), Hubert's *Trois petites filles* (2004), Eric Civanyan's *Il ne faut jurer . . . de rien!* (2005), and Leconte's *Les Bronzé 3: Amis pour la vie* (2006).

– K –

KARINA, ANNA (1940–). Actress and director. Born in Denmark as Hanne Karina Blarke Bayer, Anna Karina started her career as a model and then appeared in a Danish short by Ib Schmedes, titled *Pigen og Skoene*. She left for Paris in 1958 and was offered the role of Patricia in **Jean-Luc Godard**'s *À bout de souffle* (1960). She declined the role, however, and it was ultimately played by Jean Seberg. Karina and Godard married in 1961 and remained married until 1967. During that time, she starred in several of his films, including *Vivre sa vie* (1962), *Le Petit soldat* (1963), *Bande à part* (1964), *Alphaville* (1965), *Pierrot le fou* (1965), and *Made in USA* (1966). She won the Silver Berlin Bear for her performance in Godard's *Une femme est une femme* (1961). Through her work with Godard, she became an icon of the *Nouvelle Vague* or New Wave, and worked on other films by New Wave directors, including **Éric Rohmer**'s *Charlotte et son steak* (1961) and **Jacques Rivette**'s *La religieuse* (1966) and *Haut bas fragile* (1995). She also played a small part in **Agnès Varda**'s *Cléo de 5 à 7* (1962).

Karina has appeared in over seventy films, with leading roles in **Michel Deville**'s *Ce soir ou jamais* (1961) and *Zärtliche Haie* (1967), **René Clair**'s *Les Quatre Vérités* (1962), Pierre Gaspard-Huit's *Shéhérazade* (1963), Carl Theodor Dreyer's *Joergen Roos* (1964), Valerio Zurlini's *Des filles pour l'armée* (1965), Jean Aurel's *Lamiel* (1967), Luchino Visconti's *Lo straniero* (1967), André Farwagi's *Le temps de mourir* (1969), André Delvaux's *Rendez-vous à*

Bray (1971), Franco Brusati's *Pane e cioccolata* (1972), **Benoît Jacquot**'s *L'Assassin musicien* (1974), and Jacques Richard's *Ave Maria* (1984). She was nominated for a **César** for Best Supporting Actress in Richard Berry's *Cayenne Palace* (1987). More recently, she plays herself in Thierry Jousse's *Nom de code: Sacha* (2001). She also sings in Jonathan Demme's *The Truth About Charlie* and appears in Berry's *Moi César, 10 ans ½, 1,39 m* (2002). She directed one film, *Vivre ensemble* (1973).

KASSOVITZ, MATHIEU (1967–). Actor, director, and screenwriter. Mathieu Kassovitz made his film debut acting in *Au bout du bout du banc* (1979), a film directed by his father, Peter Kassovitz. He won the **César** for Most Promising Actor for his performance in **Jacques Audiard**'s *Regarde les hommes tomber* in 1995 and was nominated for a César for Best Actor in **Costa-Gavras**'s *Amen* (2002). He delivered a very clever performance in Audiard's *Un héros très discret* and costarred in Jean-Pierre Jeunet's *Le fabuleux destin d'Amélie Poulain* (2001). He had a major English-speaking role in Steven Spielberg's Oscar-nominated film, *Munich* (2005).

In addition to dramatic roles, Kassovitz also does comedy. His roles in his own film, *Métisse* (1993), and in *Amélie* (2001) were somewhat comedic, and he had a fully comic role in Alain Chabat's *Astérix et Obélix: Mission Cléopâtre* (2002). He also appeared in Benoît Delépine and Gustave de Kervern's comic film *Avida* (2006). He once famously quipped that those who say he is a white Spike Lee are saying nothing, since Spike Lee was once called a black Woody Allen. It is true that the influence of both directors is evident in Kassovitz's acting and directing.

Kassovitz began his directing career with shorts such as *Fierrot le pou* (1990), *Cauchemar blanc* (1991), and *Assassins* (1992). To date, he is best known for *La Haine* (1995), which is often associated with *jeune cinéma* and the *cinéma de banlieue*. Simultaneously a contemplation of French discrimination against multiple-generation immigrants and an exposure of police brutality in the working-class suburbs of Paris, *La Haine* won the César for Best Film in 1996, and Kassovitz was named Best Director for *La Haine* at Cannes in 1995. Kassovitz's first feature, *Métisse*, took on the issue of internal discrimination among Parisians of Jewish and African descent, and was also nominated for a César for Best New Film. Both features are important cinematic representations of multicultural France and were influenced by Spike Lee. Kassovitz later directed *Assassin(s)* (1997), and the more conventional thrillers *Les rivières pourpres* (2000) and *Gothika* (2003), a less acclaimed English-language film. He recently began work on a film titled *Babylon A.D.*, scheduled for release in 2007.

KAST, PIERRE (1920–1984). Director, film critic, and screenwriter. After fighting in the French Resistance during World War II, Pierre Kast established the Paris University ciné-club in 1945. He also worked for the **Cinémathèque française** and wrote essays for *Cahiers du cinéma*. In the late 1940s, he worked as an assistant director to **Jean Grémillon**. He also assisted **Jean Renoir** on the film *French Cancan* (1955).

Kast's own directorial debut came in 1949, with the film *Charmes de l'existence* (1949), codirected with Grémillon. Kast went on to make a number of other documentaries on his own, including *Arithmétique* (1951), *Les Femmes du Louvre* (1951), *Je sème à tout vent* (1952), *L'architecte maudit: Claude-Nicholas Ledoux* (1954), and *Le Corbusier, l'architecte du bonheur* (1957).

In the late 1950s, Kast began directing feature-length films. His feature debut, *Un Amour de poche* (1957), reflected Kast's interest in science fiction. His next film, the intellectual *Le Bel Âge* (1960), was cowritten with **Jacques Doniol-Valcroze**, a cofounder of *Cahiers du cinéma*. Kast's portrayals of intellectuals in *La morte-saison des amours* (1961), *Vacances portugaises* (1963), and *Le soleil en face* (1978) have received accolades from arguably elite critics and mixed reviews from popular audiences. His continued passion for science fiction emerged in *Les soleils de l'Ile de Pâques* (1972). He also directed *Un animal doué de déraison* (1976) and *La guérilléra* (1982).

In addition to directing, Kast has also worked as a screenwriter. He wrote the screenplays to his own films, as well as those of Jean-Daniel Pollet's *Une balle au Coeur* (1965) and *Le Maître du temps* (1970) and **Edouard Molinaro**'s *L'Ironie du sort* (1974). He also did some short stints as an actor, appearing in an uncredited role in Molinaro's *La Mort de Belle* (1961) and another in **Claude Lelouch**'s *L'Aventure c'est l'aventure* (1972). Kast was also known as a novelist, and as such was the author of three novels.

KEMM, JEAN (1874–1939). Actor, director, and screenwriter. Born Jules Félix Adolphe Bécheret, Jean Kemm began his screen career as an actor at **Pathé** in 1909. Because of his age at the time he began working in cinema, it is likely that Kemm had previously worked in the theater, although this is uncertain. However, he had a successful screen-acting career, during which he appeared in more than thirty films in a period of less than ten years. He starred in some of the classic silent films by many of the great directors of the day, including Georges Denola's *Chercheurs d'or* (1909), *Le Remords du juge* (1911), *La Gouvernante* (1911), *Le Chef d'œuvre* (1911), *Pauvre père* (1912), *La Porteuse de pain* (1912), *En famille* (1915), and *Le Mot de l'énigme* (1916), **Albert Capellani**'s *Le Signalement* (1910) and *Les Mystères de Paris* (1911), Michel Carré's *L'Homme de peine* (1911), **Georges Monca**'s *Le Petit chose* (1912) and his classic *La Fille des chiffoniers* (1912), Alexandre Devarennes's *La Fille du garde-chasse* (1912), René Leprince's *Le Dédale* (1912), **Camille de Morlhon**'s *Une brute humaine* (1913), *L'Infamie de l'autre* (1913), *Vingt ans de haine* (1914), and *La Vieillesse du père Moreux* (1914).

In 1916, Kemm also began directing as well as acting in films. His first films included *Madeleine* (1916), *Les Deux marquises* (1916), a remake of *Le Dédale* (1917), and *L'Obstacle* (1918), and he also acted in the last of the three. However, after 1918, Kemm devoted himself to directing entirely and did not appear in another film. He made nearly thirty films between 1917 and his death in 1939, and is considered one of the major innovators of the *cinéroman*, or serial drama. Kemm's films include *La Comtesse de Somerive* (1917), *André Cornélis* (1918), which he codirected with Denola, *Le Destin est maître* (1919), *Micheline* (1921), *L'Enigme* (1921), *L'Absolution* (1922), *Hantise* (1922), *La Ferme du Choquart* (1922), *Vidocq* (1922), *L'Enfant Roi* (1923), and *Le Bossu ou le petit Parisien* (1925). Kemm was the first director to bring the literary action hero Le Bossu to the screen and was a master of literary adaptation in general, a number of his films being adaptations of literary texts.

Kemm directed not only silent films, but a number of sound films as well. Among these are *Atlantis* (1930), *Le Juif polonais* (1931), which stars **Harry Baur**, *Amour et discipline* (1933), *Le Coffret de lacque* (1932), which stars **Danielle Darrieux**, *L'Héritier du bal Tabarin* (1933), which stars Duvallès, *Le Barbier de Seville* (1936), codirected with Hubert Boulon, *La Pocharde* (1936), codirected with

Jean-Louis Bouquet, and *Liberté* (1937). In addition to acting and directing, Kemm also worked on the screenplays to both *L'Absolution* (1922) and *Le Bossu* (1925).

KIBERLAIN, SANDRINE (1968–). Actress. Sandrine Kiberlain made her screen debut in Pierre Granier-Deferre's *Cours privé* in 1986. She played minor roles in Francis Huster's *On a volé Charlie Spencer* (1986), **Jean-Paul Rappenau**'s *Cyrano de Bergerac* (1990), and Vera Belmont's *Milena* (1991). Her talent became more apparent in Sophie Fillière's *Des filles et des chiens* (1991), Pascale Bailly's *Comment font les gens* (1992), **Benoît Jacquot**'s television film *Emma Zunz* (1992), and Jean-Pierre Ronssin's *L' Irrésolu* (1993), where she worked alongside her future spouse, Vincent Lindon. She was nominated for a **César** for Most Promising Actress in 1995 for her performance in Éric Rochant's *Les Patriotes*, and later won the award for her work in Laetitia Masson's *En avoir (ou pas)* in 1996. Her work in *En avoir (ou pas)* also won her a Crystal Star at the Brussels International Film Festival. In 1997, she was nominated for a César for Best Supporting Actress in Jacques Audiard's *Un héros très discret*, and in 1998, she was nominated for a César for Best Actress in Jacquot's *Le Septième Ciel*.

Kiberlain subsequently worked for Jacquot on *La Fausse Suivante* (2000). She would work with Masson again in *À vendre*, a performance that earned her a second César nomination for Best Actress in 1999. In 2001, she won Best Actress at the Montreal World Film Festival for her interpretation in **Claude Miller**'s *Betty Fisher et autres histoires*. She also acted in **Edouard Moliaro**'s *Beaumarchais, l'insolent* (1996), Masson's *Je suis venue te dire* (1996) and *Love me* (1999), Pascal Bonitzer's *Rien sur Robert* (1999), Claude Mouriéras's *Tout va bien, on s'en va* (2000), Jeanne Labrune's *C'est le bouquet!* (2002), Pierre Jolivet's *Filles uniques* (2003), Pierre Salvadori's *Après vous* (2003), and Bernard Rapp's *Un petit jeu sans conséquence* (2004).

KIRSANOFF, DIMITRI (1899–1957). Director. Born David Kaplan in Dorpat, Estonia, Dimitri Kirsanoff immigrated to Paris in 1920 with his family. He originally had intended to become a musician and studied music at the École Normale; however, he abandoned his musical studies for the cinema. Kirsanoff's interest in cinema came from his contact with the Parisian avant-garde, and his films would show that influence.

Kirsanoff made his first film, *L'Ironie du destin*, in 1923. This film has been lost. It was followed in 1926 by *Ménilmontant*. The film is set in the Ménilmontant area of Paris, from which it takes its name, and foregrounds the difficulties of life for the city's poor as well as the difference small acts of compassion can make on a human life. It is probably Kirsanoff's best-known film. It embodies avant-garde aesthetics in the predominance of the visual image, in the use of rapid cutting and montage, and in the use of the handheld camera, and in some ways anticipates both the **Nouvelle Vague** or New Wave and neorealism. This film, like most of Kirsanoff's early films, stars his first wife, Nadia Sibirskaïa. It was followed by *Sables* (1927) and *Destin* (1927).

In 1929, Kirsanoff released *Brûmes d'automne*, another experimental film in which a woman reflects on her past. Widely considered a classic of avant-garde cinema, it is one of Kirsanoff's best films, although less well known than *Ménilmontant* (1926). Other Kirsanoff films include *Rapt* (1933), *Les Berceaux* (1935), *Visages de France* (1936), *Jeune fille au jardin* (1936), *La Fontaine d'Aréthuse* (1936), *Franco de port* (1937), *La Plus belle fille du monde* (1938), *Quartier sans soleil* (1939), *Deux amis* (1946), *Fait divers à Paris* (1949), *Arrière-saison* (1950), *Le Témoin de minuit* (1953), *Le Crâneur* (1955), and *Miss Catastrophe* (1957). Most of these later films are unremarkable, with the possible exception of *Rapt*, *Deux amis*, and *Arrière-saison*. It is not surprising that a filmmaker known for his attention to the image might lose his way after the coming of sound. It seems this is what happened to Kirsanoff, with most of the later films being produced with an eye to commercial success rather than avant-garde poetics.

KURYS, DIANE (1948–). Actress, director, producer, and screenwriter. Diane Kurys was born in Lyons, the daughter of Russian Jewish parents who met in a French detention camp during the Occupation. Her father was a French legionnaire and prevented her mother's deportation. Her parents eventually split up, apparently because her father was threatened by her mother's relationship with another woman. Diane lived with her mother and older sister in Paris while her father lived in Lyons. Kurys left home at the age of sixteen to reunite with him, and in her later teens she left France for Israel with Alexandre Arcady, where they lived in a kibbutz. Kurys eventually went back to Paris, where she participated in the protests of May 1968 after planning to study literature at the Sorbonne. Rather than complete her studies, Kurys became an actress in theater, film, and television. She was unhappy with her experience, began writing, and subsequently scripted her first work, which is one of her finest.

One can trace parts of Kurys's youth through her semi-autobiographical films. Kurys's first film, *Diabolo Menthe* (1977), was produced with Arcady through their production company, Alexandre Films. She directed and scripted the film with very little or no directorial training. It won the prestigious **Prix Louis-Delluc**, and its enormous success (it was among the top three best-selling French films in 1977) enabled Kurys to further pursue her directing career. *Diabolo Menthe* narrates the coming of age of two daughters of a single mother—unique characters at the time—who are based on Kurys and her sister. Her portrayal of these formative years has been compared with **François Truffaut**'s *Les quatre-cent coups* (1959). Kurys's next film was the less successful *Cocktail Molotov* (1980), which focuses on young protagonists trying to make it to Paris in May 1968.

Kurys's interest in her mother's past led to what many see as her best film, *Coup de foudre* (1983). It is based on the friendship that seems to have led to her parents' separation, brought to life through excellent performances by **Isabelle Huppert** and **Miou-Miou**. Unfortunately, the two real-life friends died before its opening. *Diabolo Menthe* and *Coup de foudre*, both of which explore female solidarity, are Kurys's most acclaimed films to date. Her *Un homme amoureux* (1987) also gained substantial recognition and was nominated for the Golden Palm at **Cannes**. Her other films include *La Baule-Les Pins* (1990), *Après l'amour* (1992), *À la folie* (1994), *Les enfants du siècle*, a film about George Sand's romance with Alfred de Musset (1999), and *Je reste!* (2003). Kurys is one of France's most well-known **women** directors, though she has resisted being narrowly categorized as such. Instead, she prefers to be remembered simply as a director, and she is indeed ranked among the best.

– L –

LACOMBE, GEORGES (1902–1990). Director. Georges Lacombe began his career in film in 1924 as an assistant to **René Clair**. He worked with Clair on films such as *Les Deux timides* (1929) and *Sous les toits de Paris* (1930), and during the same period, he directed one film of his own, the avant-garde documentary *La Zone* (1928), about garment workers in Paris.

Lacombe began directing on his own in 1930. The following year he made his first feature-length film, *Un coup de téléphone* (1931), starring Colette Darfeuil and Paulette Dubost. From 1931 until 1958, Lacombe worked consistently, directing more than twenty films of various genres. While he is not remembered particularly as one of the great directors or one of the great innovators, he was a solid and fairly popular director whose work was consistent, if rather varied.

Among the films that Lacombe directed are *Ce Cochon de Morin* (1932), adapted from the story by Honoré de Balzac, *La Femme invisible* (1933), *Jeunesse* (1934), *Derrière la façade* (1939), which he codirected with **Yves Mirande**, *Elles étaient douze femmes* (1940), *Le Dernier des six* (1941), which launched the career of director **Henri-Georges Clouzot**, who wrote the screenplay, *Montmartre-sur-seine* (1941), which stars Edith Piaf, *Le Journal tombe à cinq heures* (1942), *L'Escalier sans fin* (1943), *Le Pays sans étoiles* (1946), *Martin Roumagnac* (1946), *La Nuit est mon royaume* (1951), *La Lumière d'en face* (1955), and *Cargaison blanche* (1958).

If Lacombe was not a great director, he was able to draw many of the greatest stars of the day. He worked frequently with **Pierre Fresnay**, for example. Other actors who appear in his films include **Michèle Morgan**, **Michel Simon**, **Jules Berry**, **Pierre Brasseur**, Pierre Renoir, **Brigitte Bardot**, and **Jean Gabin**. Although critics would probably not note their appearances in Lacombe's films as those that defined the careers of these actors, Lacombe was consistently able to give meaningful roles in solid film, and the performances are, therefore, equally solid.

Lacombe retired from cinema in 1958. He made a number of television films in the 1960s and early 1970s. He gave up directing altogether after 1973.

LA FÉE AUX CHOUX (1896). Film. *La Fée aux choux* is arguably the first narrative fiction film ever made. While it has been difficult to put a precise date to the film, many film historians now believe it was made in early 1896, shortly before **Georges Méliès**, who was previously attributed with making the first narrative fiction film, released his first work. **Alice Guy**, the film's director, was, at the time she made the film, the secretary to **Léon Gaumont** and Gaumont et cie was a company that sold photographic equipment. Guy reportedly asked Gaumont's permission to make one or two story films with the company's newly acquired moving picture camera, and *La Fée aux choux* was the first product.

The film is a mere sixty seconds long. It recounts a story, based in folklore, of a woman who gives birth in a cabbage patch. Filmed in continuous shot with a static camera, the film is significant less for its technical innovation than for its use of film as a narrative form. Originally intended to be used as a publicity film to advertise camera equipment, the film prompted Gaumont to move in the direction of film production and to transform itself into **Gaumont Studios**. Guy went on to become head of production at the studio for a number of years, and she is believed to have made several hundred subsequent films.

LA GRANDE ILLUSION (1937). Film. One of the best-known films by legendary director **Jean Renoir**, *La Grande illusion* is a sweeping commentary on war, class, and nationalism. Set during World War I, the film was released just prior to World War II, and it is often seen as anticipating and denouncing the war that was to come. The story of several French prisoners of war, the film focuses on the aristocratic Captain De Boeldieu (**Pierre Fresnay**) and the working-class Lieutenant Marechal (**Jean Gabin**). While in prison camp, the two also befriend a third man, the Jewish Frenchman Rosenthal (**Marcel Dalio**), the son of wealthy bankers.

During the course of the film, the characters attempt escape, but do not, at first, succeed. They are later separated but are reunited when they find they have all been transferred to another camp, this time in a fortress. The camp is commanded by the German aristocrat Von Rauffenstein (Eric Von Stroheim), and during the time the three men are at the fortress, it becomes clear that class affinities tie De

Boeldieu and Rauffenstein, despite their different nationalities. In fact, at one point the two meditate nostalgically on the old order, in which class was the defining pole of identity, and during which the European aristocracies were not divided by national lines. Von Rauffenstein also treats Marechal and Rosenthal with a high degree of humanity and hospitality, which shows that common humanity can supersede class. The three men ultimately attempt escape, but De Boeldieu is shot by Von Rauffenstein and dies.

The film's antiwar sentiment is clear, if not overt. The shooting of De Boeldieu, in particular functions as a critique of war. Von Rauffenstein so regrets his act that he holds a vigil at De Boeldieu's deathbed. The film makes it clear that what unites the two men is more significant than what divides them, and the act of shooting De Boeldieu is depicted as meaningless, although compelled, in the logic of war, by duty. Similarly, when Marechal and Rosenthal hide on the farm of a German war widow, Elsa (Dita Parlo), it is clear that the war and the idea of nation that motivates the war are less real than the human identification that takes place, particularly between Marechal and Elsa. The final comment on the senselessness of war and of the artificiality of the nations that engage in them occurs in the final scene, in which Marechal and Rosenthal cross the border into France—a border that cannot be seen because it is an imaginary construct.

La Grande illusion is firmly rooted in **Le Réalisme poétique** or poetic realism, although its subject matter renders it slightly different from other films of the wave. It shares with these films the presentation of characters from various classes and walks of life, the exploration of the human condition, and a certain pessimism with regard to the ability of individuals to transcend societal convention and so to achieve meaningful relationships with one another. It also shares the chiaroscuro lighting and the impressionistic tendency to use camera work and mise-en-scène to convey fairly abstract human qualities, such as mental and emotional states, and, in this film in particular, the interconnectedness of human beings. The film is widely considered one of the great films of world cinema.

LA HAINE (1995). Film. The second feature film by actor-director **Mathieu Kassovitz**, *La Haine* is a black-and-white film set in the *banlieue* or urban periphery of Paris. A "day-in-the-life" film, *La*

Haine focuses on three young men from the banlieue, Vinz (**Vincent Cassel**), Hubert (Huber Kounde), and Saïd (Saïd Tagmhmaoui). The three protagonists represent different minority groups within the larger French culture: Vinz is Jewish, Hubert is black, and Saïd is *beur* (French of North African origin).

The film follows Vinz, Hubert, and Saïd for twenty-four hours through the streets and buildings of the banlieue, then into the unfamiliar territory of Paris, then back into the banlieue. It chronicles their confrontations with the police, their inability to navigate Paris (literally or figuratively), and their broader inability to move beyond the neighborhood of rent-controlled housing projects, or the *cité*. At the center of the narrative is a .44 magnum that has been lost by the police during riots in the cité. Vinz finds the gun and threatens to use it to seek revenge on the police for the brutal beating of his friend Abdel—the event that had sparked the riots in which the gun was lost. At several points in the film, Vinz comes close to using the gun, but on each of these occasions Hubert manages to dissuade him. Toward the end of the film, Vinz surrenders the gun to Hubert but is shortly afterward shot by the police. The film ends with Hubert in a standoff with the police officer who shot Vinz, as Saïd looks on.

The film attracted a great deal of attention when it was released, in part because it so closely mirrored events that occurred and continue to occur in French society. The film highlights the marginalization experienced by minorities and the descendants of non-European immigrants in France, and it explores the impetus for the riots that have taken place with some frequency in the cities of Paris and other major cities, riots that express the hopelessness and frustration that come from living in a virtual ghetto where crime is rampant and unemployment often reaches rates of 25 percent or more. The film had a great deal of commercial and critical success in France and internationally and is considered a classic of French cinema, as well as a classic example of the ***cinéma de banlieue***.

Beyond its social realism, the film is also striking for its black-and-white cinematography, which recalls the cinematography of earlier film movements such as ***La Nouvelle Vague*** or the New Wave and ***Le Réalisme poétique*** or poetic realism. Like these earlier film movements, *La Haine* explores the reality of being working class in France and inhabiting the urban spaces of the socially marginalized. However, *La Haine* cannot be seen to be a realist film in the classical sense. Some have seen in its camerawork and editing echoes of the *cinéma du look*. While the film is highly stylized, it is less so than most of the look films. However, the use of compressed zooms, unusual tracking shots, aerial photography, and other similar elements do draw constant attention back to the presence of the camera, perhaps asking the viewer to contemplate what the role of visual culture has been in perpetuating social violence.

LANGLOIS, HENRI (1914–1977). Founder of the Cinémathèque Française. Born in 1914 in what was the Ottoman Empire, Henri Langlois moved to Paris as a child. He was an avid film buff from an early age. While in lycée, Langlois, along with his friend, **Georges Franju**, founded a *ciné-club* to help encourage others to love film as much as they did. The two friends would both go on to make significant contributions to French cinema, Franju as a director and Langlois, by virtue of his family's money, to cofound the **Cinémathèque française**, which is one of the most important holdings of films in the country. Because Langlois founded the Cinémathèque française when he did, he was able to amass and preserve a large number of silent films at precisely the moment they were disappearing. Without his intervention, many of the films in its possession today would have been lost. Langlois went on to encourage the creation of other similar archives, as well as a federation of archives throughout the world. Langlois remained the head of the Cinémathèque française until his death in 1977. He was ousted in 1968 for a brief period, in a scandal over his management of the institution, but was reinstated. When he died, it was clear that while he had seen to it that a significant number of films were obtained and archived, he had done little else to assure the integrity of the institution.

L'ASSASINAT DU DUC DE GUISE **(1908).** Film. Directed by **André Calmettes** and **Charles Le Bargy**, both established figures in the world of French theater, *L'Assassinat du Duc de Guise* was the first film released by the short-lived **Studio Film d'Art**. Often classified as the first example of *film d'art* or art cinema, the film was, in fact, the second, as **Pathé**'s film d'art division, the **Société Cinématographique des Auteurs et des Gens de Lettres** (SCAGL), released *L'Arlésienne* (1908) prior to the release of *L'Assassinat du Duc de Guise*. However, the Studio Film d'art film is considered to be of great cinematic importance.

L'Assassinat du Duc de Guise is a historical film that recounts the assassination of Henri de Guise by men on orders from Henri III. The subject had previously been represented in film twice, once by the **Lumière brothers**, and once by Pathé; however, the Film d'art version offers significant innovations over the earlier films. First of all, it is a true narrative film with a recognizable narrative structure. Secondly, the film is heavily influenced by theatrical production, featuring elaborate stage sets and costumes that were unusual in film up to that point. The film also casts established theatrical actors and uses many theatrical conventions in its mise-en-scène, including the use of constructed, enclosed space, framing scenes such that characters enter the scene from off-camera through doors, or exit in a similar fashion. There are also innovations in mise-en-scène in the film. The film uses something approximating deep space in several scenes. It also comes very close to historical realism in its attention to the historical accuracy of the sets and costumes.

The film was also unusual in that it was one of the first films, or perhaps the very first film, to have a musical score composed directly for it. The score for the film was written by composer Camille Saint-Saëns. Through its use of narrative and its development of the shot and framing, the film contributed to the development of narrative cinema. Through its use of high production values, professional actors, theatrically influenced staging, and its musical score, the film contributed to the evolution of film as an art form, not merely an amusing distraction.

L'ATALANTE **(1934).** Film. The last film directed by **Jean Vigo** and the only feature-length film Vigo ever made, *L'Atalante* is the story of Jean and Juliette, played by Jean Dasté and Dita Parlo. The two are young newlyweds who live on a boat called l'Atalante with a man named Le Père Jules, played by Michel Simon, and Jules's son, played by Louis Lefebvre. L'Atalante is a sort of floating utopia, where the two lovers can exist outside the confines of the rest of the world untouched, seemingly, by greed, crass materialism, and the violence of everyday life. Jean is perfectly content with this existence. However, Juliette bores of it after a while and dreams of life in the city. Eventually, she leaves Jean and the boat for life in Paris. Devastated by Juliette's departure, Jean falls into a nearly catatonic depression. At the same time, Père Jules sets out to find Juliette, who discovers that Paris is perhaps not what she expected and longs to return to l'Atalante. The two are ultimately reunited.

The film is known not only for its tragic romance narrative, but also for the strong performances of the actors, for the intensity with which it conveys emotion, and for Boris Kaufman's dreamlike cinematography, which lays somewhere between realism and surrealism. Many film scholars refer to *L'Atalante* as a visual poem, so intense are the images the camera presents. The film, which many regard as one of the greatest films ever made, has ties to *Le Réalisme poétique*, or poetic realism, although not officially classified as part of that wave. It shares with those films the play with light and dark, the poetic quality of its images, the meditation on love and human interaction, as well as a certain degree of pessimism regarding the human condition.

L'Atalante nearly never was. Vigo was hired by **Gaumont** to make the film, which seems puzzling since he was not a commercially oriented director. However, he agreed to make the film but modified it significantly from the popular melodrama Gaumont had intended. Unhappy with the final film, Gaumont reedited it in a move that many film scholars have characterized as butchering it. They also changed the title, releasing it as *Le Chaland qui passe*, and adding a popular song to the narrative. The Gaumont version was a disaster. Vigo died several weeks after finishing the film. Since his death efforts have been made to undo what Gaumont did to the film, but it has not, to date, been restored to its original form. Nonetheless, the film, in re-reedited form, is considered by most critics to be one of the greatest films of all time.

LAUTNER, GEORGES (1926–). Director and screenwriter. Georges Lautner was born in Nice to actress **Renée Saint-Cyr**. He studied law before working as an assistant to directors such as Norbert Carbonnaux. He directed shorts before making his first feature-length film, *La Môme aux boutons* (1958). It was followed by *Arrêtez les tambours* (1960), *Marche ou crève* (1960), *Le Monocle noir* (1961), and *Le Septième juré* (1962), all of which feature **Bernard Blier**. A contemporary of the directors of the *Nouvelle Vague* or New Wave, Lautner opted for more commercial films that followed the French *tradition de qualité*. He is best known for his entertaining detective and crime films, spy parodies, and comedies; several were very successful box-office hits. Lautner's *Les tontons flingueurs,* with **Lino Ventura**, was the third largest grossing film of 1963. He directed a number of films starring **Jean-Paul Belmondo** that would rank among the top five most popular films in France: *Flic ou voyou* was the second biggest French film of 1979; *Le professionel,* too, was the second best-selling film in France in 1981. In 1984, *Joyeuses Pâques* ranked among France's five most commercially successful films of 1984.

Lautner's most prolific period was 1960–1968, when he directed at least one film per year. In addition to the films mentioned above, these include *En plein cirage* (1962), *L'Oeil du monocle* (1962), *Des pissenlits par la racine* (1964), *Le Monocle rit jaune* (1964), *Les Barbouzes* (1964), *Les Bon vivants* (1965), *Galia* (1966), *Ne nous fâchons pas* (1966), *Le Grande sauterelle* (1967), *Fleur d'oseille* (1968), and *Le Pacha* (1968). His films starred some of France's most popular actors of the period, such as Blier, Belmondo, Ventura, **Louis de Funès**, and Mireille Darc. Lautner often worked with the same screenwriters, among them Pierre Laroche, Jacques Robert, and **Michel Audiard**.

Lautner continued his energetic career as a filmmaker into the 1970s. Audiard worked on Lautner's scripts, as did emerging directors **Bertrand Blier** and **Francis Veber.** Blier worked on *Laisse aller, c'est une valse* (1971), and Veber worked on *La Valise* (1973) and *On aura tout vu* (1976). Carbonnaux helped to script Lautner's *Ils sont fous ces sorciers* (1978). France's top stars led the casts of many Lautner's films in the 1970s as well. **Alain Delon** starred in his *Les Seins de glace* (1974) and *Mort d'un pourri* (1977), and **Miou-Miou** starred in *Pas de problème!* (1974). Lautner also directed American actresses Mimsy Farmer and Rita Hayworth in *Road to Salina* (1971). In 1980, Belmondo led the cast of Lautner's *Le Guignolo*, and Miou-Miou acted with Saint-Cyr in *Est-ce bien raisonnable?* (1981) and *Attention! Une femme peut en cacher un autre* (1983). Saint-Cyr is also featured in *Le Cowboy* (1984). **Michel Serrault** and Ugo Tognazzi paired again to make Lautner's 1985 *La*

Cage aux folles 3: 'Elles' se marient. The popular singer Patrick Bruel starred in his *La Maison assassinée* in 1988.

In the 1990s, Lautner directed four films for the big screen: *Présumé dangereux* (1990), *Triplex* (1991), *Room Service* (1992), starring Serrault, and *L'Inconnue de la maison* (1992), featuring Belmondo. He has since directed for French television.

LE BARGY, CHARLES (1858–1936). Actor and director. Charles Le Bargy was one of the great stage actors of the late nineteenth century. He was a member of the Comédie Française from 1880 until 1911 and became a sociétiare of the Comédie Française in 1887. Known for his dramatic capabilities, but equally talented as a comedic actor, Le Bargy's range as well as his talent made him a great theatrical name of his day. He was also an instructor at the Paris Conservatoire d'art dramatique, where he had **Albert Capellani** among his students.

It was because of Le Bargy's great reputation, as well as his talent, that he was recruited by the founders of *Studio Film d'Art* in 1908 to act in and direct films for the fledgling studio, which aspired to bring cinema up from its fairground milieu and place it firmly among the arts. Le Bargy's career in cinema was short. It numbered a total of only six films, but several of these have become classics of the cinema.

L'Assassinat du Duc de Guise (1908) is one such film. Le Bargy codirected the film, which recounts the 1588 assassination of Henri de Guise, with **André Calmettes.** Le Bargy's interpretation of Henri III, on whose orders de Guise is murdered, is considered one of the great performances of the early silent cinema. His next film was *La Tosca* (1909), starring **Sarah Bernhardt** as well as himself, and it was followed by *Le Retour d'Ulyse* (1909), which he codirected with Calmettes. That same year he also acted in Calmettes's film, *La Légende de la Sainte-Chapelle* (1909). This would be Le Bargy's last film for some time, as Studio film d'art went bankrupt in the year of its release, and Le Bargy returned to the stage.

In 1920, however, Le Bargy returned to the screen, this time in front of the camera. He starred in **Louis Mercanton**'s classic silent film, *L'Appel du sang* (1920). Le Bargy made only two films following this performance. In 1928, he had a role in **Gaston Ravel**'s

Madame Récamier, and in 1930 he appeared in **Jacques de Baroncelli**'s *Le Rêve*. Despite his rather brief career, Le Bargy remains one of the pioneers of the early cinema. He is the father of actor Jean Debucourt.

LE CHAGRIN ET LA PITIÉ (1971). Film. **Marcel Ophüls** shot his four-hour documentary, *Le Chagrin et la pitié*, for television in 1969. However, it was banned by government censors and not televised until 1981. The documentary was released in theaters in 1971, and it is one of the only made-for-television documentaries to have had a theatrical release. Ophüls's damning portrayal of France during World War II motivated both the film's censorship and its ultimate success. Because of its fairly explicit depiction of French collaboration with Germany, French Anglophobia, and French anti-Semitism, *Le Chagrin et la pitié* became a landmark film about the German Occupation and one of France's most important documentaries of the twentieth century.

Le Chagrin et la pitié focuses on the memory of the Occupation by the inhabitants of the French city of Clermont-Ferrand, which is located near Vichy. The film is based on interviews conducted in the late 1960s with figures such as a German colonel, leaders of the Resistance, peasants, elites, fascist sympathizers, Jews, British diplomats, and Nazis, including Hitler's interpreter. The film also relies heavily on period newsreel footage and clips from propaganda films.

As part of the *Mode Rétro*, *Le Chagrin et la pitié* presented a direct challenge to France's postwar image of itself. It questions specifically the idea that France was, from the beginning, a nation unified in its resistance to the German Occupation. A number of critics have pointed out that the film's effectiveness was not in its presentation of new ideas, but in its articulation of what French citizens already knew, but had in many ways repressed, about their history.

LE CHANOIS, JEAN-PAUL (1909–1985). Actor and director. Born Jean-Paul Dreyfus, Jean-Paul Le Chanois began his career in the theater, most notably as a playwright. Le Chanois had close associations to the *Groupe Octobre*, which itself had close ties to **Jean Renoir** and to Jacques Prévert, who was a member. Le Chanois's film debut was as an actor in films such as Pierre Prévert's *L'Affaire est dans le* *sac* (1932) and Anatole Litvak's *L'Équipage* (1935), a film on which he also served as an assistant director. The behind-the-scenes work soon captured his full attention, and he all but ceased acting in films, going on to assist in films such as Maurice Tourneur's *Konigsmark* (1935), **Jacques Becker**'s *La Vie est à nous* (1936), Jean Renoir's *La Marseillaise* (1938), and **Max Ophüls**'s *De Mayerling à Sarajevo* (1940), a film in which he also acted.

In 1940, Le Chanois took over the filming of *Une idée à l'eau* (1940), which had been started by Marco de Gastyne. Le Chanois, however, would not make another film for several years, as World War II had started and put a temporary stop to his filmmaking career. In 1946, immediately after the war, Le Chanois made *Messieurs Ludovic* (1946), the first of a number of films, including dramas, melodramas, and a handful of comedies. Examples are *Au coeur de l'orage* (1948); *L'École buissonnière* (1949), starring **Bernard Blier**; *La Belle que voilà* (1950), starring **Michèle Morgan**; *Sans laisser d'adresse* (1951), starring Blier and Danièle Delorme; *Agence Matrimoniale* (1952), starring Blier and Julien Carette; *Papa, maman, la bonne, et moi* (1954), starring Robert Lamoureux and **Gaby Morlay**; *Les Évadés* (1955), starring **Pierre Fresnay**; *Village magique* (1955); *Papa, maman, ma femme et moi . . .* (1956), also starring Lamoureux and Morlay; *Le Cas du Dr Laurent* (1957), starring **Jean Gabin** and Le Chanois's wife, Silvia Montfort; *Les Misérables* (1958), starring Gabin and Blier; *Par-dessus le mur* (1961); *Mandrin* (1962); *Monsieur* (1964); and *Le Jardinier d'Argenteuil* (1966). Le Chanois resumed acting and appeared in several of these later films.

In addition to directing, Le Chanois was an industrious screenwriter. He wrote the screenplays for many of his own films, including *Une idée à l'eau* (1940), *L'École buissonnière*, *La Belle que voilà*, *Agence Matrimoniale*, *Papa, maman, la bonne, et moi*, *Les Évadés*, *Le Cas du Dr Laurent*, and *Les Misérables*. He also wrote screenplays for films by other directors, most notably Tourneur's *La Main du diable* (1943) and *Cécile est morte* (1944), Richard Pottier's *Picpus* (1943), Esway's *L'Idole* (1948), and Jean-Devaivre's *La Dame d'onze heures* (1948) and *Alerte au sud* (1953).

LECLERC, GINETTE (1912–1992). Actress. Born Geneviève Menut, Ginette Leclerc made her screen debut in 1932. That year, she appeared in Pierre Prévert's short film *Le Commissaire est bon enfant* (1932), **Henri Diamant-Berger**'s *L'Enfant du miracle* (1932), and Alexander Korda's *La Dame de chez Maxim*'s (1932), which was the role that really launched her career. The following year she had roles in **Claude Autant-Lara**'s *Ciboulette* (1933), Anatole Litvak's *Cette vieille canaille* (1933), and **Serge de Poligny**'s *L'Étoile de Valencia* (1933), among other films.

Throughout the rest of the decade, Leclerc appeared in film after film, many of them popular or critical successes. She was, however, typecast, and nearly all of her roles were as fallen **women**, calculating women, manipulative women, or worse. Among the other films in which she appeared during the decade were **Marc Allegret**'s *Zouzou* (1934) and *L'Hôtel du libre échange* (1934), **Roger Richebé**'s *Minuit, place Pigalle* (1934), **René Guissart**'s *Dédé* (1934), Pierre Colombier's *L'École de cocottes* (1935), **Jean Kemm**'s *La Pocharde* (1936) and *La Loupiote* (1936), Victor Tourjansky's *La Peur* (1936), René Pujol's *La Peau d'une autre* (1936), *Bach détective* (1936), and *Passé à vendre* (1936), **Pierre Chenal**'s *L'Homme de nulle part* (1937), Léonide Moguy's *Prison sans barreaux* (1938), Autant-Lara's *Le Ruisseau* (1938), **Marcel Pagnol**'s *La Femme du boulanger* (1938), **Abel Gance**'s *Louise* (1939), and Edmond T. Gréville's *Menaces* (1939). Of these, probably the best performance of the decade is that in Pagnol's film, in which Leclerc plays Aurélie Castanier, the frustrated and unfaithful wife of the title. This film is considered one of Pagnol's best and the performance one of Leclerc's best.

Leclerc's career slowed in the 1940s. She managed fewer roles, although it was also the decade that offered her arguably the best role she would have in her career, that of Denise Saillens in **Henri-Georges Clouzot**'s *Le Corbeau* (1943). Instead of a fallen woman in the film, Leclerc plays a character with much more depth, a flawed character certainly, but a warm, human character that is much less flawed than the society which judges her. It is one of the great film roles of all time, and Leclerc plays it beautifully. Her other noteworthy films from the decade include Moguy's *L'Empreinte de Dieu* (1941), **Jacques de Baroncelli**'s *Ce n'est pas moi* (1941), Jean de Limur's *L'Homme qui joue avec le feu* (1942), **André Hugon**'s *Le Chant de l'exilé* (1942), Tourneur's *Le Val d'enfer* (1943), and Jacques Daroy's *Une belle garce* (1947).

Leclerc's career was brought to a standstill at Liberation, at which time she was condemned to a year of prison and forbidden from working for having worked with the Nazi-owned **Continental Films**. Leclerc's decision to work with Continental was not, unfortunately, all that unique. Her sentence, however, was. In any case, like her contemporary, **Arletty**, who was also punished for collaboration, Leclerc's career did not recover. She managed a steady stream of roles, but they were not, for the most part, of the caliber of those she had earlier on. Some of the better films in which Leclerc appears later in her career include Marcello Pagliero's *Un homme marche dans la ville* (1950), **Max Ophüls**'s *Le Plaisir* (1951), **Jean Boyer**'s *Le Chômeur de Clochemerle* (1957), Gilles Grangier's *Gas-oil* (1955) and *Le Cave se rebiffe* (1956), Walerian Borowczyk's *Goto, l'île d'amour* (1968), and René Richon's *La Barricade du Point du Jour* (1978), which was her last film.

LECONTE, PATRICE (1947–). Director and screenwriter. Patrice Leconte studied at the **Institut des Hautes Études Cinématographiques** (IDHEC), worked as a cartoonist for the magazine *Pilote,* and directed shorts before making feature-length films. His first feature films were comedies, beginning with *Les vécés étaient fermés de l'interieur* (1976), which starred Jean Rochefort and **Coluche**. He worked with actors from the Troupe du Splendid— among them **Josiane Balasko**, Michel Blanc, Marie-Anne Chazel, **Christian Clavier**, **Gérard Jugnot**, and **Thierry Lhermitte**—to make *Les bronzés* (1978) and *Les bronzés font du ski* (1979), two comedies about the French Club Med. He won **César**s for Best Film and Best Director for his costume drama, *Ridicule,* in 1997. His feauture *Tandem* (1987), the thriller *Monsieur Hire* (1987), and *Le mari de la coiffeuse* (1990) were nominated for Césars for Best Director and Best Film. He was nominated for a Golden Palm at Cannes for *Monsieur Hire* and for a Golden Palm and an Oscar for Best Foreign Film for *Ridicule.* His other features include *Viens chez moi, j'habite chez une copine* (1981), *Ma femme s'appelle reviens* (1982), *Circulez, y'a rien à voir* (1983), *Les spécialistes* (1985), *Tango* (1993), *Le parfum d'Yvonne* (1994), *Les grands ducs* (1996), *1 chance sur 2* (1998), *La fille sur le pont* (1999), *La veuve de Saint-Pierre* (2000), *Félix et Lola* (2001), *Rue des plaisirs* (2002), *L'homme du train*

(2002), *Confidences trop intimes* (2004), and *Dogora-ouvrons les yeux* (2004), a musical documentary. He revisits his "Bronzés" motif with *Les Bronzés 3: amis pour la vie* (2005).

LE CORBEAU (1943). Film. Directed by **Henri-Georges Clouzot** for the Nazi-operated production company, **Continental Films**, *Le Corbeau* is, perhaps surprisingly, an overtly anti-Occupation film. The film, best classified as a thriller, is the story of a small town plunged into chaos by an unknown citizen who writes poison-pen letters and signs them "Le Corbeau" or "The Raven." The principal target of the anonymous letter writer is the town doctor, Rémy Germain (**Pierre Fresnay**), who is accused in the letters of adultery, performing abortions (illegal under the Nazi Occupation), selling drugs, and cavorting with Denise (**Ginette Leclerc**), a woman of questionable reputation. During the course of the film, the letters begin to denounce other members of the town, ultimately provoking a suicide and portending other equally dark consequences. As a result, the German authorities intervene and, with the help of the local psychiatrist, Michel Vorzay (Pierre Larquey), attempt to identify the writer of the letters. Ultimately, it is discovered that Vorzay is himself the author of the letters.

The film is both timeless and firmly rooted in its historical moment. The writing of anonymous letters to denounce friends and neighbors was common practice during the Occupation, and the motives of the letter writers were very often less than pure. The film openly critiques the practice, questions the motives of those who write such letters, but perhaps more important, points to the hypocrisy of a society that regards such a practice as perfectly acceptable as long as those targeted are of questionable reputation. The film also palpably conveys what it means to live in a society gripped by fear and kept in check by the threat of harm and violence.

The timeless element of the film is in its critique of human and social behavior in general. The village in the film is a community where the veneer of respectability counts for far more than real humanity; where people are judged by how they dress, the way they speak, or their social backgrounds; where individual ambitions count for more than community or humanity. No one in the film is blameless. Nearly all the characters are flawed. However, those who appear—on the surface—to be worthy of condemnation ultimately prove less corrupt and tainted than the society that stands in judgment of them.

The film features consistently strong performances by its cast. It is considered a classic for its ability to convey this moral ambiguity of the human condition in such nuanced terms. Also highly noteworthy is the use of the thriller genre to explore complex social questions, which has led the film to be regarded as one of the greatest thrillers ever made. It is also recognized for its use of film noir elements, including the symbolically charged use of light and dark, and the often near-expressionistic representations of the dark side of human reality.

LE FABULEUX DESTIN D'AMÉLIE POULIN (2001). Film. **Jean-Pierre Jeunet**'s *Le fabuleux destin d'Amélie Poulin* tells the fictional story of the childhood and young adulthood of its eponymous heroine, Amélie (**Audrey Tautou**). Amélie's mother homeschools her because she is misdiagnosed with a heart condition. The "heart condition" is merely the fluttering of her heart when her father, a doctor, finally touches her. As a result, Amélie is cloistered from the outside world and has little contact with her parents. She therefore retreats into her imagination.

Amélie's life changes as a result of the announcement of the death of Princess Diana. It is not the princess's death that produces the change, however, but her discovery of a child's hidden box of toys and photos she finds after she drops a bottle upon hearing the news. Amélie manages to find the owner of the box, who is reunited with his childhood treasures. She then decides to help her neighbors and coworkers find happiness. She also becomes fascinated with a man named Nino (**Mathieu Kassovitz**), but Amélie is unable to bring herself close to him until the film's conclusion.

A number of critics have commented on Jeunet's technological manipulation of images in producing the Parisian landscapes presented in the film. The monuments, subways, and Montmartre cafés are all uniquely pleasing to the eye in a way that is almost unreal. The city is devoid of traffic or graffiti, and even the mendicants in the city seem to be in high spirits. Jeunet has expressed his admiration for the images of Paris in the 1940s and '50s, and the film suggests nostalgia for an earlier time. Jeunet's title echoes that of **Sacha Guitry**'s films *Le Destin fabuleux de Désirée Clary* (1942) as well as **Claude Autant-Lara**'s *Occupe-toi d'Amélie* (1949). One could also consider *Le fabuleux destin d'Amélie Poulin* as a late example of the *cinéma du look,* one that similarly employs brilliant colors (especially the matching colors of characters' outfits with their surroundings), advertising techniques, and stories of youthful romance. It is perhaps worth noting that Dominique Pinon, who plays the character Joseph, also played the role of Le Curé in **Jean-Jacques Beineix**'s landmark *look* film, *Diva* (1981).

Although *Le fabuleux destin d'Amélie Poulin* is a light romance it bears certain similarities to **François Truffaut's** *Les 400 coups* (1959). Amélie's alienation from her parents could be compared to Antoine Doinel's isolation, and the settings of the two films are similar. The character of Suzanne in the film is played by Claire Maurier, the same actress who interpreted the role of Antoine's mother in *Les 400 coups*. Just as Antoine seeks pleasure in the cinema, Amélie substitutes interpersonal communication with fantasy and television. Just as Amélie's father is fixated on his missing gnome, Antoine's father is preoccupied with his lost Michelin Guide. Despite the similarities, however, the films have starkly different conclusions. After her life is changed by the discovery of someone else's hidden childhood treasures, Amélie reunites families, successfully plays cupid to lonely customers of Les Deux Moulins, and provides an ailing painter's link to the outside world. Finally, Amélie engages in her own romance with a man who has previously been obsessed with discarded photos. Jeunet's film is, of course, far more romantic and optimistic than Truffaut's, and although Jeunet's film, like Truffaut's, was shot on location, the images in the film are polished and enhanced.

Despite some critical reactions to the film's artificial rendering of Paris, *Le fabuleux destin d'Amélie Poulin* was a triumph for French cinema. It sold over 8 million tickets in France, went on to become an international blockbuster, and was among the top-selling films in Great Britain and one of the top-performing international films in the United States. It won Best Film and Best Director at the **César Award**s and made Tatou an international star. It also marked the return to France of Jeunet, who had directed the American film *Alien: Resurrection* (1997) a few years before.

LEFEBVRE, JEAN (1922–2004). Actor. Jean Lefebvre made his screen debut in Maurice Cam's *Bouquet de joie* (1952). He went on to make films over a period of more than thirty years. Although he is often best remembered for his comic films, he played in a number of dramatic films and romantic films including Jean Stelli's *Une fille sur la route* (1952), Maurice de Canonge's *L'Amour toujours l'amour* (1952), **Henri-Georges Clouzot**'s *Les Diaboliques* (1955), Gilles Grangier's *Gas-Oil* (1955), **Roger Vadim**'s *Et Dieu . . . créa la femme* (1956), Richard Pottier's *La Châtelaine du Liban* (1956) and *Tabarin* (1958), Yves Allegret's *Quand la femme s'en mêle* (1957) and *La Fille de Hamburg* (1958), André Berthomieu's *En légitime défense* (1958), and a number of Raoul André films, including *Cherchez la femme* (1955), *L'Homme et l'enfant* (1956), and *La Polka des menottes* (1957).

Lefebvre's early comic roles were in films such as Michel Boisrond's *Cette sacrée gamine* (1956), Raymond Bernard's *Le Septième commandement* (1957), and **Marc Allegret**'s *Un drôle de dimanche* (1958). However, it was not until the 1960s that he began doing comic films with any regularity. He went on to appear in Jean Chérasse's *La Vendetta* (1961) and *Un clair de lune à Maubeuge* (1962), Robert Dhéry's *La Belle Américaine* (1961) and *Allez France!* (1964), **Philippe de Broca**'s *Les Veinards* (1962), Girault's *Faites sauter la banque!* (1963), *Le Gendarme de St. Tropez* (1964), *Le Gendarme à New York* (1966), and *Le Gendarme se marie* (1968), **Yves Robert**'s *Bébert et l'omnibus* (1963), Jean Boyer's *Relaxe-toi chérie* (1964), **Jean-Paul Le Chanois**'s *Monsieur* (1964), **Georges Lautner**'s *Les Tonton flingueurs* (1963), *Les Bons vivants* (1965), codirected with Grangier, *Ne nous fâchons pas* (1966), *Quelques messieurs trop tranquilles* (1973), *Pas de problème* (1975), and *Ils sont fous ces sorciers* (1978), **Léo Joannen**'s *Trois enfants . . . dans le désordre* (1966), Robert Lamoureux's *Mais où est donc passé la septième compagnie* (1973), *On a retrouvé la septième compagnie* (1975), and *La septième compagnie au clair de lune* (1977). He also appeared in numerous television films and television series.

LEFÈVRE, RENÉ (1898–1991). Actor and screenwriter. René Lefèvre made his screen debut at the end of the silent era in René Hervil's *Knock ou le triomphe de la médécine* (1925). This was followed by roles in **Julien Duvivier**'s *Le Mariage de Mademoiselle Beulemans* (1927) and *Le Tourbillon de Paris* (1928), Hervil's *Le Ruisseau* (1928), André Berthomieu's *Pas si bête* (1928), *Ces Dames* *aux chapeaux verts* (1929) and *Rapacité* (1929), and **Roger Lion**'s *Un soir au cocktail's bar* (1929).

In 1931, Lefèvre was cast in the lead in **René Clair'**s *Le Million* (1931). He went on to appear in Jean Boyer and Max Neufeld's *Monsieur, Madame et Bibi* (1932), Alexandre Ryder's *L'Âne de Buridan* (1932), **André Hugon**'s *La Paix chez soi* (1933), Jean de Limur's *Paprika* (1933) and *Petite peste* (1938), Yvan Noé's *Mes tantes et moi* (1936), **Jean Renoir**'s *Le Crime de Monsieur Lange* (1936), and Maurice Keroul and **Georges Monca**'s *Le Choc en retour* (1937). He also had supporting roles in such films as Berthomieu's *La Femme idéale* (1933), Pierre Billon's *La Piste du sud* (1938), and **Jean Grémillon**'s *Gueule d'amour* (1937). *Le Million* and *Le Crime de Monsieur Lange* both became classics of French cinema and are regarded as two of Lefèvre's best performances. As in the character he plays in these two films, Lefèvre's roles tended to be quiet, timid men who expressed themselves or their emotions with difficulty.

Lefèvre continued to act in the 1940s and 1950s, but he made only a handful of films and was again relegated to supporting actor. He appeared in such films as **Robert Vernay**'s *La Femme que j'ai la plus aimée* (1942), Albert Valentin's *A la belle frégate* (1943), Yves Allegret and Jean Choux's *La Boîte aux rêves* (1945), Alexander Esway's *Le Bataillon du ciel* (1947), **Louis Daquin**'s *Le Point du jour* (1949) and *Bel Ami* (1957), **Jacqueline Audry**'s *La Garçonne* (1957), *C'est la faute d'Adam* (1958), and *Le Secret du Chevalier d'Éon* (1959), Jules Dassin's *Celui qui doit mourir* (1957), and Marc Allegret's *Sois belle et tais-toi* (1958).

During the same period, Lefèvre tried his hand at both screenwriting and directing. He wrote the story upon which **Georges Lacombe**'s *Les Musiciens du ciel* (1940) was based, and he also contributed to the screenplay. He also worked on the screenplays for Marc Allegret's *Parade en sept nuits* (1941), *Opéra-Musette* (1942), a film he codirected with Claude Renoir and in which he starred, and Duvivier's *Sous le ciel de Paris* (1951), and cowrote the screenplay for Denys de la Patellière's *Rue des Prairies* (1959) with **Michel Audiard**. Lefèvre retired from cinema and television in the early 1980s.

LELOUCH, CLAUDE (1937–). Cinematographer, director, producer, and screenwriter. Claude Lelouch began his career by forming his own production company, Les Films 13, in 1960. He went on to produce his own films, the first feature being *Le propre de l'homme* (1961), in which he also stars. Lelouch is best known for his film *Un homme et une femme* (1966), which won a Golden Palm at **Cannes** and an Oscar for Best Foreign Film and Best Original Screenplay. He was awarded Best Director at the Montreal World Film Festival for *Tout ça . . . pour ça!* (1993). He directed, among other films, *Vivre pour vivre* (1967), *Un homme qui me plaît* (1969), *Le voyou* (1970), *Smic Smac Smoc* (1971), *Toute une vie* (1974), *À nous deux* (1979), *Les Uns et les autres* (1981), *Un homme et une femme, 20 ans déjà* (1986), *Happy New Year* (1987), *Les Misérables* (1995), and *And Now . . . Ladies and Gentlemen* (2002). He also directed the French segment for the internationally codirected film, *11'9"01* (2002).

LEPRINCE, RENÉ (1876–1929). Actor, director, and screenwriter. René Leprince began his career in the Parisian café-concerts. He joined **Pathé** in about 1908, acting in and directing films. In the early years, Leprince was primarily an actor appearing in such films as **Yves Mirande**'s *Octave* (1909), in which **Harry Baur** also appeared; **Georges Monca**'s *Le Chien de Montargis* (1909); Michel Carré's *La Peau de Chagrin* (1909), in which he appeared with **Stacia Napierkowska**, Paul Capellani, and **Henri Desfontaines**; **Albert Capellani**'s *La Vengeance de la morte* (1910) and *La Mort du duc d'Enghien* (1912); Georges Denola's *Par un jour de carnaval* (1910), in which he appeared with Maria Fromet; **Camille de Morlhon**'s *Fouquet, l'homme au masque de fer* (1911); and **Ferdinand Zecca**'s *La Fièvre de l'or* (1912), which Leprince codirected.

Leprince may have directed a film called *La Princesse noire* (1908), but he did not seriously turn his attention to directing until 1910 or 1911. After that time, he directed more than fifty films over a period of approximately twenty years, working right up to the time of his death. Films directed by Leprince include *Le Visiteur* (1911), codirected with Capellani; *Le Stigmate* (1911); *Josette* (1912); *Le Lys de la mansarde* (1912), codirected with Monca; *Le Club des élégants* (1912); *L'Amour plus fort que La Haine* (1912); *Le Miracle des fleurs* (1912); *Le Roi de l'air* (1913) and *L'Étoile du génie* (1914), both codirected with Zecca; *Sacrifice fraternel* (1915); *La Vie d'une reine* (1917); *La Force de la vie* (1920); *Vent debout* (1923); *Le Vert galant* (1924), starring **Joë Hamman**; *L'Enfant des Halles* (1924); *Mylord l'Arsouillle* (1925); *Fanfan-la-tulipe* (1925); *Titi, premier roi des gosses* (1926); *Princesse Masha* (1927); and *La Tentation* (1929), which was finished by **Jacques de Baroncelli** as Leprince died while it was being filmed.

Leprince directed the Comédie Française actor René Alexandre in a number of films, including *Les Martyrs de la vie* (1912), *La Revanche du passé* (1912), *Le Roi du bagne* (1913), codirected with Maurice Mahut, *La Leçon du gouffre* (1913), and *Les Larmes du pardon* (1919). He also directed several **Max Linder** films, including *Max et Jane veulent faire du théâtre* (1912), *Max, Jockey par amour* (1913), *Max dans les airs* (1914), and *Max devrait porter des bretelles* (1917). All of these were codirected with Linder, although Leprince did direct one or two Max films on his own.

LES ENFANTS DU PARADIS (1945). Film. Directed by **Marcel Carné** near the end of the German Occupation of France, *Les Enfants du paradis* is often considered the last film, or one of the last films, of *Le Réalisme poétique* or poetic realism. The film tells the story of the star-crossed lovers Garance (**Arletty**) and Baptiste (**Jean-Louis Barrault**). Garance is an actress, Baptiste a mime, and they are kept apart by circumstance and a variety of others, including the actor Fredéric Lemaître (**Pierre Brasseur**), the criminal and dandy Lacenaire (Marcel Herrand), the count Edouard (Louis Salou), and a host of other characters who collectively represent a mosaic of nineteenth-century France, the period during which the film is set.

Widely regarded as one of the greatest films of all time, *Les Enfants du paradis* is a highly complex film that meditates on class, gender, individual freedom, the role of art, and most of all, love. The title of the film refers to the least expensive seats in the theater in France, evoking both the theater and narrative representation and the poor and working classes of the city. Both theater and the working class figure prominently in the film, which explores the nature of life for those at the lower end of the class system, and which consistently uses the theater to comment on the reality it depicts. The theater is also a metaphor for the film itself, which is also commenting on the nature of human existence.

Typically of films associated with poetic realism, *Les Enfants du paradis* is rather dark in its assessment of the possibility for real love in the human world. Garance and Baptiste never come together, despite the fact that they truly love one another. Nonetheless, the film celebrates love as a beacon of light, like the theater, in an otherwise difficult existence. Like other films associated with poetic realism, the film focuses on the poor and the working classes and represents those parts of the city associated with such groups.

Apart from the narrative, the film is hailed for the brilliant performances of its star-studded cast. It is often considered Arletty's best performance, and Barrault's semisilent performance is one of the legendary roles of the cinema. Moreover, the film is also remarkable in its realist and yet dreamlike camera work that captures the everyday world, and yet transcends it. The production of the film is also of some interest. It has one of the most elaborate soundstages ever constructed. This is particularly remarkable given that the film was made under the difficult economic conditions of the Occupation. Officially, Carné had to collaborate with the Vichy-era censor. In reality, he worked semi-independently, making the film at Studios de la Victorine in Nice, instead of at the German-owned **Continental Films**. He also utilized cast and crew members who were officially forbidden from working in the cinema, either because they were Jews or members of the Resistance. The best-known of these is Alexander Trauner, who designed the film's legendary sets. Carné is also famous for having hidden certain reels from the Germans, fearful they would be censored and hopeful that the Liberation would come, as it did, before he finished the film.

It is almost fitting that the film heralded the Liberation, as liberation is one of its central motifs. Love and theater are both forms of liberation celebrated by the film (as is, by implication, the cinema). Arletty's Garance is, for the time, also a rather liberated **woman**, who refuses to be held back or held down by men. Her character is one of the most interesting female characters in cinema of the 1930s and 1940s, and some critics have seen her as not just an argument for women's liberation, but an attempt to undermine conventional gender roles altogether.

LES QUATRE CENTS COUPS (1959). Film. *Les Quatre cents coups* was the first feature-length film by director **François Truffaut**. An important contribution to la *Nouvelle Vague*, or the New Wave, it narrates the troubles of Antoine Doinel (Pierre Léaud), a young teenager. The actor Léaud would later be cast in Truffaut's Antoine Doinel cycle, which includes the segment *Antoine et Colette* (1962), *Baisers volés* (1968), and *Domicile conjugal* (1970). Léaud, whose life resembles the details of Truffaut's own life, has often been perceived as Truffaut's cinematic double.

In the opening sequence of *Les Quatre cent coups*, Antoine is caught during class with a picture of a pinup model in a bathing suit. He is ordered to stand against the wall, where he writes words that challenge the teacher's authority. Antoine goes home to his parents, who do not hide their wishes to send the boy away. Antoine skips school the next day and spies his mother (Claire Maurier) kissing a lover. Later at school, he blames his truancy on his mother's death. The adults are aghast at the lie. Antoine runs away from home temporarily. He and his friend René (Patrick Auffay) steal a typewriter. When Antoine is caught, his father (Albert Rémy) asks the police to do something. The authorities and parents agree to send Antoine to reform school, where he resides briefly before he escapes to the sea. Antoine's face is captured onscreen in Truffaut's famous concluding freeze-frame.

Les Quatre cents coups is almost certainly an autobiographical film, although Truffaut altered certain details about his past. The film was shot in neighborhoods where Truffaut spent his childhood and echoes his early experiences as an unwanted child. Like Antoine, Truffaut loved the cinema, skipped school, and engaged in theft. He was sent to reform school in Villejuif but was rescued by film critic **André Bazin**, to whom the film is dedicated. Like his character Antoine, Truffaut himself often challenged the authority figures around him. As a critic and filmmaker Truffaut would also be known for questioning the received order. He is, for example, well known for his critiques of the established French *tradition de qualité*, or tradition of quality.

Les Quatre cents coups does not, however, constitute a break with all film tradition. Scholars have frequently asserted that the film marks a certain return to the ***réalisme poetique***, or poetic realism of earlier French cinema, specifically in its representation of the working classes, and its foregrounding of the Parisian landscape. The film was one of France's official selections at the 1959 **Cannes Film Festival**, despite the fact that Truffaut had been banned from the festival a year earlier for his written attacks on the French film industry. Truffaut took the award for Best Director, and his film brought in an estimated 450,000 spectators upon its release, making it the New Wave's first big triumph at the French box office.

***LES VACANCES DE MONSIEUR HULOT* (1953)**. Film. In the opening credits to **Jacques Tati**'s *Les Vacances de Monsieur Hulot,* the audience is invited to relax, take a seat behind the camera, and abandon any hopes of finding a plot. What follows is a humorous series of adventures and blunders of the lead character, Monsieur Hulot, played by Tati himself. Hulot, a creation of Tati based on his personal acquaintances, spends his summer vacation at the beach among other tourists, several of whom are British. With a signature gait in which he angles forward, seemingly on the balls of his feet, he creates disorder wherever he wanders. He is positioned as a curious outsider who is oblivious to the disruption and trouble he inadvertently causes. The cinematic gags that result are reminiscent of classic silent films like those featuring **Max Linder** or **Romeo Bosetti**, but Tati's film diverges from the classics in significant ways.

Although Tati uses comic gags from silent cinema, he infuses his work with unusual sounds that call attention to themselves, such as the muffled drone of the train station loudspeaker, or the odd chord of a swinging door. The sounds in the film take on a life of their own, often emerging independently of the images and creating their own story. Hulot is the main character, yet utters only one line—"Hulot, Monsieur Hulot"—and even this is muffled by his pipe. Furthermore, the conversations of the tourists are heard off-screen and do not always correspond to the action. Viewers must construct their own meaning as Tati plays with audience expectations of sound, image, and narrative.

Critics have noted that while Tati's film abandons conventional uses of narrative, characterization, and sound, it is by no means devoid of meaning. The character Hulot, who emerged with *Les Vacances de Monsiuer Hulot* and later appeared as the leading figure in Tati's *Mon Oncle* (1958), *Playtime* (1967), and *Trafic* (1971), brings with him satiric commentaries on modernity, especially the uniformity of modern life brought upon by mass-produced household gadgets. Impressively, Tati managed to craft this commentary partly through the use of bizarre and inscrutable sounds. A radio broadcast in the hotel announces that industrial production has remained stagnant and that authorities have rejected the call for a shorter working week. The announcement is drowned out by the festive, albeit deafening, music of Hulot's record player, though one registers that the demand for increased productivity threatens the delightful frivolity of Hulot's vacations. If sounds in the film can be associated with sounds in reality, those real sounds seem to be mocked through their distortion, creating satire that ultimately must be constructed by the spectator. Hulot, in his old, sputtering car that is passed by newer, sleeker, and faster models, seems to arrive from a different time, a time perhaps when people expected that modern inventions would make life more enjoyable. His attempts to employ new devices often end in chaos, but his spontaneous blunders are welcome alternatives to the predictability of the modern world around him.

LES VALSEUSES (1974). Film. *Les Valseuses* was directed by **Bertrand Blier**, who adapted the film from his own novel. It narrates the journeys of two troublemakers in their twenties, Jean-Claude (**Gérard Depardieu**) and Pierrot (**Patrick Dewaere**). After they chase a woman with their grocery cart and then harass her, the two steal a car to take a joy ride. Upon their return, the owner of the car flaunts his date, Marie-Ange (**Miou-Miou**), and shoots Pierrot in the testicle. The two then take the car, force a doctor to take care of Pierrot, steal the doctor's money, and run away from police by stealing bikes and cars or jumping on trains. Pierrot vows to tamper with the car to enact his revenge on the owner.

The pair later breaks into a seaside vacation home during the offseason, where Jean-Claude washes and shampoos Pierrot. Jean-Claude tells Pierrot that he finds him desirable, but Pierrot refuses his advances. They reunite with Marie-Ange and subsequently charm a recently released prisoner named Jeanne (**Jeanne Moreau**). They locate Jeanne's son, Jacques (Jacques Chailleux). Jean-Claude, Pierrot, and Marie-Ange later steal a car from a family and take the daughter Jacqueline (**Isabelle Huppert**) with them, at Jacqueline's request. They drive off in the stolen car, heading nowhere in particular. Later, it is suggested that they may be traveling in the very car that Pierrot had altered so that it would crash.

Like the director **Patrice Leconte**, Blier collaborated with actors experienced in the *café-théâtres* of Paris, such as Dewaere, Miou-Miou, and **Gérard Jugnot**, who plays a small role in the film. *Les Valseuses* was the second most commercially successful French film in 1974, just after Just Jaeckin's soft-porn feature, *Emmanuelle*. Like the films of the *Nouvelle Vague* or New Wave that preceded it and the films of the *cinéma du look* afterward, *Les Valseuses* was a film targeted to youth in society. This is evident in its fast pace, its overt sexual content, and its antiestablishment narrative.

Some of this film's material alarmed early reviewers, who found the film shocking and grotesque. Since then, many critics and scholars have found more depth to the film, frequently commenting on its questioning of gender roles, both male and female. Those critics who focus on Blier's representation of masculinity point to the relationship between the wounded, emasculated Pierrot, who insists on heterosexuality, and the overtly bisexual Jean-Claude. Much has also been written about the film's apparent misogyny, particularly in the first half of the film in which the two protagonists derive pleasure by insulting and harassing women.

Blier's apologists counter that Marie-Ange refuses to play the role of the victim and forces the men to question their own masculinity. This reading, they argue, is supported by the sexual contact between Marie-Ange and the two protagonists, who fail to satisfy her sexually, although a fairly virginal Jacques has no trouble in this area. Furthermore, Blier clearly mocks his protagonists' overblown conceptions of their own masculinity, both through their failed sexual exploits and their disastrous imitations of film antiheroes. By extension, the entertainment the men glean at the expense of the women characters can also be viewed as a critique of their immaturity, though it is unclear whether the discomfort of the women is supposed to have a comic effect. In any case, Blier most likely intends to rattle his spectators and shake them into questioning received ideas and roles. For some, *Les Valseuses* was seen as a threat to conventional morals, and for others it is a commentary on post–May 1968 rebellious youth.

Les Valseuses also invites comparisons to New Wave films, especially **Jean-Luc Godard**'s *À bout de souffle* (1960) and *Pierrot le fou* (1965) and **François Truffaut**'s *Jules and Jim* (1962). There are various differences between Blier's film and those of the New Wave however. Where New Wave films often center on problematic love relationships, in *Les Valseuses* there is no time to stop for love. Blier also focuses on the male couple, whereas the New Wave tends to focus on heterosexual, individualistic antiheroes and their relationships with women. The suicide of Jeanne, played by the New Wave icon Moreau, also seems to evoke the violent finale of the New Wave of the 1960s, and Moreau actually starred earlier in Truffaut's *Jules and Jim*.

LES VAMPIRES (1915). *See FANTÔMAS* (1913–1914) and *LES VAMPIRES* (1915).

L'HERBIER, MARCEL (1888–1979). Director and producer. Born into a prominent bourgeois family, Marcel L'Herbier studied law and then sought to pursue a career in music or literature. He ultimately decided on literature, partly through exposure to the literary world as a result of a circle of influential friends that included the poet Maurice Maeterlinck. He published a novel and a play before serving in the army in World War I.

It was in the army that L'Herbier was first exposed to film, as he was assigned to the *Service Cinématographique de l'Armée*, the military's film production service. Nonetheless, it is reported that he remained unimpressed with cinema until the actress **Musidora** took him to see Cecile B. DeMille's *Forfaiture* (1915). This apparently transformed L'Herbier's life, and he decided to devote himself entirely to the cinema.

L'Herbier made two independent films, *Phantasmes* (1917), which remained unfinished, and *Rose-France* (1918), before signing on at **Gaumont** in 1919. While at Gaumont, he made eight films: *Le Bercail* (1919), *Rose-France* (1919), *Le Carnaval des vérités* (1920), *L'Homme du large* (1920), *Prométhée . . . banquier* (1921), *Villa Destin* (1921), *Eldorado* (1921), and *Don Juan et Faust* (1922). In 1923, he founded his own production company, Cinégraphic, for which he made an additional six silent films: *L'Inhumaine* (1924), *Feu Mathias Pascal* (1926), *Le Vertige* (1927), *Le Diable au coeur* (1928), his great film *L'Argent* (1928), and *Nuits de princes* (1929). In addition to L'Herbier's own films, Cinégraphic also produced two films by **Jacque Catalain**, *Le Marchand de plaisirs* (1922) and *La*

Galerie des monstres (1924). Catalain also starred in a number of L'Herbier's own films.

As a silent-film director, L'Herbier was a master. An artisan of the visual image, he demonstrated evident avant-garde tendencies, probably as a result of his literary background, and almost certainly as a result of a connection to **Louis Delluc** (Delluc's wife Eve Francis appears in a number of L'Herbier's films). His films tend to be expressionistic and highly dramatic, and in true avant-garde form, images often convey elements such as emotion, mental state, and even moral state, which typically lie outside of the visual realm. L'Herbier is also often credited with bringing the early cinema to maturity visually, expanding the potential of elements such as lighting, costume, frame, and image to convey symbolic meaning. He was a master of literary adaptation, adapting works by Honoré de Balzac, Émile Zola, and Luigi Pirandello, among others, and maintaining in his adaptations something of the poetry of these literary works. In addition to directing, he wrote the screenplays for most of his films.

L'Herbier transitioned to sound cinema at the end of the 1920s. His first sound films were *L'Enfant de l'amour* (1930), *La Femme d'une nuit* (1930), *Le Mystère de la chambre jaune* (1930), *Le Parfum de la dame en noir* (1931), and *L'Épervier* (1933). In general, these films relied heavily on the same visual style as the silent films, although this seems sometimes out of place in a sound film. The acting is, as in many early sound films, a bit stilted. In general, these are not considered among L'Herbier's best. The exception to this is *Le Parfum de la dame en noir* (1931), a film that fully incorporated sound into an avant-garde poetics.

By the middle of the 1930s, L'Herbier seemed to have found his stride. He retained much of his expressionist lighting and use of décor, but was able to work these elements into the developments in narrative form that the addition of sound brought on. Films such as *Le Bonheur* (1934), which starred **Charles Boyer** and **Gaby Morlay**, *La Route impériale* (1935), *Veille d'armes* (1935), *Les Hommes nouveaux* (1936), starring **Harry Baur** and Gabriel Signoret, *La Porte du large* (1936), *La Citadelle du silence* (1937), *La Tragédie impériale* (1938), starring Baur and Marcelle Chantal, *Adrienne Lecouvreur* (1938), starring Yvonne Printemps and **Pierre Fresnay**, and *Entente Cordial* (1939), were largely critical and popular successes. Many of these films are considered some of the best films made during the decade.

In the 1940s, L'Herbier continued to make films. *Histoire de rire* (1941), *La Nuit fantastique* (1942), *L'Honorable Catherine* (1943), one of **Edwige Feuillière**'s best films, and *La Comédie du bonheur* (1943), were all successes, as were postwar pictures such as *La Vie de bohème* (1945) and *L'Affaire du collier de la reine* (1946). During this decade, L'Herbier turned more to comedy in his films, where drama had been his preferred form in earlier days.

It was during the 1940s that L'Herbier also devoted a great deal of time to developing the cinema as an art form. He founded the **Institut des Hautes Études Cinématographiques** (IDHEC) film school in 1943, under the direction of the Nazi occupying forces, and he served as its first director. He also served on the boards of numerous technical associations. L'Herbier had long written and theorized on the cinema in various newspapers, magazines, and pamphlets, but in 1946, he published an anthology of writings on the cinema titled *Intelligence du cinématographe*. He also founded the film section of *Le Monde* in the 1950s, a period during which he began experimenting in made-for-television films. If some of his films seem a bit stuffy or overly obtuse to a contemporary audience, L'Herbier is still considered and remembered among film critics and filmophiles as one of the great directors of the silent-film era and of the prewar sound era, as well as an important figure in the evolution of film itself.

LHERMITTE, THIERRY (1952–). Actor, producer, and screenwriter. Thierry Lhermitte was one of the founders of the Troupe du Splendid with **Patrice Leconte**, **Josiane Balasko**, and Michel Blanc. Early in his acting career he appeared in Jacques Doillon's *L'An 01* (1973), **Bertrand Blier**'s *Les Valseuses* (1974), and **Bertrand Tavernier**'s *Que la fête commence* (1975). He also collaborated with Balasko, Blanc, and others on the script of Patrice Leconte's *Les Bronzés* (1978) and *Les Bronzés font du ski* (1979), and he appeared with all of them in the films. Lhermitte later collaborated with Balasko on the script for Jean Marie-Poiré's *Les hommes préfèrent les grosses* (1981) and *Père Noël est une ordure* (1982). He appeared in both films.

Lhermitte was also a favorite of director Claude Zidi, who cast him in a number of films including *Les Ripoux* (1984), *Les Rois du gag*

(1985), *Ripoux contre Ripoux* (1990), *La Totale* (1991), and *Ripoux 3* (2003). He played key roles in Jean-Loup Hubert's *L'année prochaine . . . si tout va bien* (1981), Blier's *La femme de mon pote* (1983), Leconte's *Tango* (1993), Michel Blanc's *Grosse fatigue* (1994), Francis Veber's *Le Diner de cons* (1998) and *Le Placard* (2001), Pierre-Olivier Scotto's *Le Roman de Lulu* (2001), Jean Becker's *Effroyables jardins* (2003), Patrick Timsit's *L'Américaine* (2004), and Balasko's *L'Ex-femme de ma vie* (2005).

LINDER, MAX (1883–1925). Actor, director, and screenwriter. Born Gabriel Maximilien Leuvielle in 1883, Max Linder, as he would be known onscreen, was attracted to theater from a young age. He began to seriously study theater at the age of seventeen and then went to Bordeaux to become an actor. In 1904, he moved to Paris where he became a star of the Parisian theater and of the café-concerts. Because of his connection to other theater and café-concert performers and managers turned cinema pioneers (**Ferdinand Zecca**, **Gaston Velle**, and **Lucien Nonguet** among them) Linder was hired on at **Pathé** in 1905. He was already something of a star at that time, since he was one of the more popular of the Parisian performers. In fact, he was unwilling to fully commit to cinema at first, acting by day for Pathé under the assumed name Max Linder, and continuing live performances at night under his real name. However, it was in cinema that Linder would truly become a star, in many ways the first film star, with one of the first truly developed and recognizable characters in cinema, the eponymous Max, and by 1908, Linder was working so much at Pathé he was forced to give up the theater altogether.

The character of Max was not an immediate creation at Pathé. Linder's first films, mostly under the direction of Louis J. Gasnier, featured him in various comic roles, although the elements of Max, the look of the refined gentleman, the comedy that derives from a combination of bad luck and hedonism, are there. Linder's first credited role in *La Première sortie d'un collégien* (1905) already contained some of these elements, which were no doubt holdovers from his live performances in the café-concerts. These comedic traits or signatures become progressively more evident in the early films such as *Le Pendu* (1906) and *Idée d'Apache* (1906).

The character Max, a dandy in a top hat and a bit of a cad, made his debut in the 1907 film *Les Débuts d'un patineur*. Between 1907 and 1916, Linder would be a constant presence on the screen, both in France and abroad, making him one of the first truly international film stars. Among the most celebrated of his *Max* films are *La Très moutarde* (1908), *En bombe* (1910), *Max fait du ski* (1910), *Les Débuts du Max au cinéma* (1910), *Max dans les Alpes* (1910), *Max prend un bain* (1910), *Max a trouvé une fiancée* (1910), *Champion de boxe* (1911), *Max a un duel* (1911), *Max lance la mode* (1912), *Bandit par amour* (1912), *Une nuit agitée* (1912), *Max et les femmes* (1912), *Max toreador* (1913), *Max professeur de tango* (1913), *Max fait de la photographie* (1913), *Max et la statue* (1913), *N'embrassez pas votre bonne* (1914), *La Médaille de sauvetage* (1914), *Max et sa belle-mère* (1914), *L'Idiot qui se croit Max* (1914), *Le Sosie* (1915), and *Max et l'espion* (1916).

While Linder's Max was undoubtedly the best known and one of the most influential of the comic characters of the silent-film era, he was not the first. **André Deed's** Boirieau and **Roméo Bosetti's** Roméo had both already appeared in film before Linder arrived on the scene, as it were. However, both Boireau and Roméo remain fairly two-dimensional. Both are representative of "the fool" type character typically found in common burlesque, and both lack the distinctive character traits that made Max so memorable. Moreover, there is a move toward subtlety and sophistication of performance in Linder's comic performances, a differentiation between what is needed onstage and what onscreen. It is this comic subtlety, no doubt, that would influence later screen comics, such as Charlie Chaplin, and it is completely absent from the performances of either Deed or Bosetti.

During the same period, Linder made a number of other films in which he did not appear as Max and sometimes did not even perform a comic role. Many of these films also rank among the classics of silent film. These include *La Légende de Polichinelle* (1907) under the direction of **Albert Capellani**, *Un drame à Seville* (1907) under the direction of André Heuzé, *C'est Papa qui a pris la purge* (1907) under the direction of **Louis Feuillade,** *Le Voleur mondain* (1909) in which Linder incarnates Arsène Lupin, gentleman thief, *Le Serment d'un Prince* (1910), and *Le Petit café* (1919). During the same period,

Linder moved from simply acting in films to writing and directing as well, and from 1911 on, he would write and/or direct many of the films in which he appeared.

If the early part of Linder's career seemed to unfold like a fairy tale, the latter part played out more like a tragedy. In 1914, at the height of his career, Linder was called to the front to fight in World War I. Early in his tour of duty, he was involved in a gas and shrapnel attack in which he nearly died. He was dismissed from the army and sent home, where he managed to recover, but not fully. He was plagued from that point on with chronic health problems and depression.

Linder, who was determined to be a truly international star, was never quite able to break into the American market. Hollywood by that time was the center of the film world (in part due to the war in Europe). Linder made two very unsuccessful attempts to break into the U.S. market, the first in 1916, during which time he signed a contract with Chicago-based Essaney Studios (where Chaplin had been filming) to make a series of films. Linder made only three, *Max in a Taxi* (1916), *Max Comes Across* (1917), and *Max Wants a Divorce* (1917). With the success of these three much less than hoped for, and Linder's health in crisis, he returned to France without the big break he had looked for.

Linder's second attempt came in 1921. After grappling with the realization that the interruption in his career caused by the war had severely jeopardized his popularity in France, Linder again sought to relocate to Hollywood. He again made three films, *Be My Wife* (1921), *Seven Years' Bad Luck* (1922), and *The Three Must Get Theirs* (1922), a spoof on the *Three Musketeers*. While the films were successful, they did not lead to a contract, as Linder had hoped. His health was again deteriorating, and he had to return to France unable to enjoy the success of those films.

Linder recovered again and made every effort to continue his career. He made *Au Secours* with **Abel Gance** in 1924, but a series of disputes between the two meant the film was not released. In 1925, presumably depressed over his declining health and failing career, Max Linder committed suicide with his nineteen-year-old wife. The two left behind a daughter, Maude Max Linder.

From the time of his death until the present, Max Linder was more or less forgotten. His comic style had influenced Chaplin (who called him "the professor") and his jokes and storylines had been recycled by everyone from Chaplin to the Marx Brothers. Yet no one even remembered that he had existed. The recent release of some of his films on video and DVD has, to some degree, counteracted the effects of this public amnesia, as has the growing scholarly interest in silent film. Still, with so much time elapsed between the glory days and the present, it is likely we will never fully appreciate what a star Linder was in his prime.

LION, ROGER (1882–1934). Director, producer, and screenwriter. Born Roger Juda, Roger Lion went on to a career in cinema that lasted three decades. Lion began his career at **Gaumont** as a technical assistant. It was at Gaumont that he began working as a director with his film *La Petite Bretonne* (1914). However, he made the bulk of his silent films with **Éclair**, where he went in 1914. At Éclair, Lion made a number of films, including *Agence cacahouète* (1915), starring **Raïmu**, *A qui la femme* (1915), *Français! N'oubliez jamais* (1916), codirected with Robert Boudrioz, *Les Deux giffles* (1916), *Quand Madelon* (1917), *Ma femme est folle* (1917), *Le Prince Plouf* (1917), *Ma femme est folle* (1917), *Pour faire plaisir* (1918), *La Flamme cachée* (1918), codirected with **Musidora**, *Dagobert, le fils à son père* (1919), *L'Éternel féminin* (1921), and probably several films for which he is not credited. During the same period, he founded the *Société des Auteurs de Films*.

Lion went to Portugal in 1922 and remained there until 1924. While in Portugal, he made the films *A Seria de Pedra* (1923), *Os Ohlos de Alma* (1923), and *Aventuras de Agapito* (1924), and produced films for other directors. He was instrumental in the development of Portuguese cinema, along with fellow Frenchmen Georges Pallu and Maurice Mariaud. Lion returned to France after two years and resumed his French film-directing career, making such films as *La Fontaine des amours* (1924), *J'ai tué!* (1924), as well as *La Clé de voûte* (1925), *Les Fiançailles rouges* (1926), *Jim la houlette, roi des voleurs* (1926), codirected with Pierre Colombier, *Le Chasseur de chez Maxim's* (1927), *La Venenosa* (1928), *La Nuit est à nous* (1929), *Un soir au cocktail's bar* (1929), and *L'Appel de la chair* (1929), codirected with Henry Roussel. Several of Lion's films feature the actor **Jean Murat**. In addition to directing, Lion also wrote or cowrote many of the screenplays for his films.

In the 1930s, Lion made a number of successful feature films with sound. Some of his most interesting sound films, however, were not feature films, but documentaries. These included *La Raïs* (1930), *Messaoud Habib* (1930), *Grégor et ses Grégoriens* (1930), *La Fille de Roland* (1930), and *Ghanili Dour* (1932). All of these featured musical performances, a subject Lion had filmed during the silent era, but which he could obviously better treat in sound film. His other sound films include *La Place est bonne!* (1930), *Le Lit conjugal* (1931), *Allô . . . Allô* (1931), *Y'en a pas deux comme Angélique* (1931), *Direct au coeur* (1932), codirected with Antoine Arnaudy who also stars in the film, *Le Couché de la mariée* (1933), and *Trois balles dans la peau* (1933).

Lion's filmmaking style was somewhat avant-garde. He had a tendency to play with genre, as with *Jim la houlette, roi des voleurs*, which mixes elements of film noir and romantic comedy. In addition, some of his films showed characteristics of later avant-garde movements. For example, *Un soir au cocktail's bar* is a snapshot of life in a bar, and although it is a narrative film, it is shot in documentary style, making it something of a precursor to both the **Nouvelle Vague** or New Wave and *cinéma vérité*. This documentary tendency is, of course, also present in Lion's musical films. There is another way in which documentary functions as a motif in Lion's films, as several of them feature the camera as voyeur. This is evident in *Un soir au cocktail's bar*, and other examples include *Le Chasseur de chez Maxim's* (1927), which reveals the secret nightlife of an average citizen, and *L'Appel de la chair* (1929), which centers on a secret passion a man has for his stepmother. Lion was virtually unknown until quite recently, as most of his films had been thought lost. Some of his films have recently been recovered, as a result of a collaborative effort by the French and the Portuguese, and he has received more attention as a result.

LODS, JEAN (1903–1974). Director. Jean Lods was born in Paris and decided on a career in film from a very early age. He studied at the Conservatoire of Strasbourg before beginning work on his own. Most of Lods's early work as a filmmaker was in short, avant-garde films that walked the line between impressionism and documentary. Among these short films were titles such as *24 heures en 30 minutes* (1928), *Champs-Élysées* (1929), *La Vie d'un fleuve: La Seine* (1931),

264 • LOUIS DELLUC PRIZE

and *Le Mile de Jules Ladoumègue* (1932). He also made the film *Histoire d'une ville, Odessa* (1934) during a trip to Russia; however that film has been lost.

In addition to his avant-garde poetics, Lods had a passion for things political. He made the overtly political *La Marche de la faim* (1929) relatively early in his career. His only feature-length film, *L'Équipe* (1930), was also a politically oriented proletarian film. He was also a member of the *Association des Écrivains et des Artistes Révolutionnaires* (AEAR), which had as stated goals the advancement of a proletarian and naturalist esthetics in literature and film. Other members included Louis Aragon, Luis Buñuel, Jean Giono, **Jean Vigo**, **Léon Moussinac**, and Yves Allegret.

Lods's interest in things political led him to make a series of documentaries on politically or culturally iconic figures. Included in this series are the films *Aristide Maillol* (1943), about the French sculptor, *Hommage à Albert Einstein* (1955), on the great scientist, *Henri Barbusse* (1958), on the writer and fellow AEAR member, *Jean Jaurès* (1959), on the assassinated Socialist politician, and *Stéphane Mallarmé* (1960), on the avant-garde poet. Apart from directing, Lods also had a bit part in **Claude-Autant Lara**'s film *Ciboulette* (1933).

In addition to his filmmaking, Lods influenced the direction of French cinema through his friendship with Vigo and through his involvement in *ciné-clubs*, which were central to creating an appreciation for the form and to influencing film aesthetics. Vigo, it is said, was inspired to make his classic film ***L'Atalante*** (1934) during a trip down the Seine with Lods while he was filming *La Vie d'un fleuve: La Seine* (1931). He was also instrumental in introducing the French public to Soviet film through the founding of the ciné-club, *Les Amis de Spartacus,* which was devoted to the purpose. The club was founded by Lods in 1927, along with his brother-in-law, the film critic and theorist **Léon Moussinac**. Lods also served to inspire other filmmakers through his devotion to the teaching of the art form. He helped found the **Institut des Hautes Études Cinématographiques** (IDHEC) with fellow director **Marcel L'Herbier**. He also served as the head of instruction at the IDHEC from 1943 until 1952.

LOUIS DELLUC PRIZE. *See* PRIX LOUIS-DELLUC.

LUMIÈRE, AUGUSTE (1862–1954). Cinematographer and film pioneer. The elder brother of **Louis Lumière**, Auguste Lumière assisted Louis in the development of the *cinématographe*, the first film camera, and aided him in the founding and running of the Studios Lumières as well as the Lumière's photographic and filmmaking business. Auguste was not, however, the filmmaker or the technical genius his brother was. Rather, he served as a steady right-hand man in the operations.

LUMIÈRE, LOUIS (1864–1948). Cinematographer, director, and film pioneer. Louis Lumière was the youngest son of Antoine and Jeanne-Joséphine Lumière. His brother **August Lumière** was the eldest. Antoine Lumière was a painter turned photography equipment supplier, so Lumière and his brother Auguste literally grew up around photographic equipment. It is no surprise then that Louis and his brother both showed an early interest in the image and the process of capturing and reproducing images, but it was Louis Lumière who showed the most promise as an innovator of the technology associated with photography. He had, perhaps, more time to devote to such research, since in his late teens he, unlike his brother, dropped out of the technical school in which their father enrolled them. Lumière then spent his time examining and tinkering with his father's photographic equipment and along the way developed a new process for making photographic film plates. His work was immediately recognized and he won a Grand Prix for his innovations in the realm of visual recording at the Paris Exposition of 1889.

As a result of Lumière's discovery, the family moved to Lyon, where Antoine opened a factory in order to manufacture and sell the film plates Louis had designed. This factory subsequently became the largest manufacturer of photographic plates and film stock in France. The brothers' initiation into the world of moving pictures came in 1894, when they witnessed a demonstration of Thomas Edison's recently invented Kinetoscope, a peephole camera and projector that was a precursor to the modern film camera. Enthralled by the possibility of capturing and projecting moving images with a camera, the brothers set out to create a device of their own, which, unlike Edison's, would project such images outward onto a screen, rather than inward. Thus their vision was for an inherently communal viewing experience, whereas Edison's was necessarily individual.

In 1895, the brothers succeeded in developing their own camera and projector, which they called the ***Cinématographe,*** the device for which the cinema is named. The Lumières's *Cinématographe* had other distinctions from Edison's machine, most notably, where Edison's device relied upon the continuous movement of images through the device, the Lumière brothers were able to apply the principle of intermittent motion to their machine, thereby allowing the film to flow more smoothly through the device. Other important differences between the two devices included the number of images screened per second of viewing (the Kinetograph required forty-eight images per second to the *Cinématographe*'s sixteen) and the size of the machines (Edison's was large and stationary, whereas the Lumière brothers' was small and portable). These and other innovations permitted the *Cinématographe* to be taken out of a studio and used on location anywhere.

The brothers made some twenty short films, each about one minute long and most documenting daily activities around their house, and gave demonstrations and screenings to various learned and photography groups. By late 1895, however, enough interest had been generated in the Lumière invention that a public screening was arranged in Paris on 28 December 1895. The brothers screened the twenty short films of their own making, and the success of this showing was such that the cinema became an overnight sensation. They then engaged a number of cameramen and sent them out around the world to film happenings and events that might be of interest to the film public with the intention of marketing these films directly for public consumption. The event films, or *actualités,* constituted the first film genre.

Louis Lumière was far more involved in the filmmaking end of the business than Auguste, and it was he who made the first commercially released film by the Lumière company, *La Sortie de l'usine,* in late 1895. This film is interesting not only because of its director, but also because of its substance. The Lumière vision of cinema is often said to have been one of a means of documenting reality, very different from the narrative cinema that dominates today. This reputation stems from the Lumières's interest in the *actualités* or reality films. However, it is also true that Lumière recognized very early the potential of film to represent or re-create reality. Among the first twenty films made by Lumière, there is one comic skit, *L'Arroseur arosé* (*Watering the Gardener*). More important, however, the film *La Sortie de l'usine*, often taken for a documentary, is also a fiction in that Lumière staged the entire exit by having his own workers pretend to leave his factory precisely so he could film it.

The Lumière brothers' contribution to cinema, therefore, was not limited to technical devices or processes, or to the collective nature of the viewing experience. They recognized film's double capacity to capture reality and to supplant it—the two dominant directions the modern cinema would take. Although they are less recognized for this latter contribution, it is an important one.

After several years, when they had built up enough interest in the cinema to have a reliable market for their equipment and film stock, the Lumière brothers gave up filmmaking altogether to concentrate on sales and marketing. This is perhaps explained by the brothers' belief that the cinema was a passing craze that would eventually die out. It may also be that once they had provided the equipment, they were able to yield the way to more creative and artistic filmmakers, such as **Alice Guy** and **Georges Méliès**, who witnessed their film screenings and were inspired to the point of becoming filmmakers themselves. Their studio also yielded to the more commercially successful studios like **Pathé** and **Gaumont**, which were already becoming dominant. Whatever the case, neither Louis nor Auguste ever made another film, although they did make themselves quite rich selling their invention to the world.

– M –

MACHIN, ALFRED (1877–1929). Cinematographer, director, producer, and screenwriter. Alfred Machin began his career as a photographer and in that capacity worked for the magazine *L'Illustration*. In 1905, however, he exchanged still photography for the cinema and was hired as a cameraman at **Pathé**. Machin worked for several years as a cameraman, but by 1908, he had moved into cinematography, directing, and screenwriting. As a cinematographer he made more than thirty films, all of which he also directed. In addition, Machin directed numerous films that utilized a third-party cinematographer. In total, Machin made 120 films, some documentary and some narrative, but nearly all of them having some connection to animals. He also wrote or collaborated on the screenplays of more than forty of the films he directed. Although he was one of the most popular filmmakers of his time, Machin has, for the most part, been ignored by film historians.

Machin worked as a cinematographer at Pathé from 1908 until 1922. His first film assignments at Pathé were animal films called *films à chasse* or hunting films. Among these were *La Chasse à l'hippopotame sur le Nil bleu* (1908), *La Chasse à la panthère* (1909), *La Chasse à la girafe en Ouganda* (1910), *En Egypte, élevage des autruches* (1910), and *La Chasse aux éléphants sur les bords du Nyanza* (1911). While in Africa Machin did other types of documentary as well, including *Les Chillouks, tribu de l'Afrique centrale* (1910), *Moeurs et coutumes des Chillouks* (1910), *Comment une lettre nous parvient des grands lacs de l'Afrique centrale* (1911), and *Le Cinéma en Afrique* (1911).

In 1909, he made a detour from his African trip and was sent to Holland in order to promote film production there. While in Holland, Machin made a number of documentaries including *Enfants de Holland* (1909) and *Coiffures et types de Holland* (1909), and he also made his first narrative film, *Le Moulin maudit* (1909). Following this narrative film, Machin managed a few others amid his documentary projects. These include *Soyez donc charitables* (1911), *Parfum troublant* (1911), *Little Moritz, soldat d'Afrique* (1911), *Babylas vient d'heriter une panthère* (1911), *L'Aeroplane de Fouinard* (1911), *Madame Babylas aime les animaux* (1911), *Little Moritz chasse les grands fauves* (1911), and *La Peinture et les chochons* (1912). As is apparent from the titles of several of these films, Machin introduced animals into the narratives of fiction films, and he was, in that respect, a pioneer of animal films.

Late in 1911, Machin returned to Holland to establish a Pathé subsidiary. He then went to Belgium and founded a Pathé studio in that country. Both Belgium and Holland consider Machin as the founder of their respective film industries. During the same period, Machin also directed. While he continued to make documentaries and comic films, he also developed a more serious filmmaking style during this period. Some of the films between 1912 and the start of World War I in 1914 are considered among his best, thematically and artistically. Machin experimented with the superimposition of images and created a series of mature films from the standpoint of both style and depth. Among the films from this period are *L'Âme des moulins* (1912), *La Fleur sanglante* (1912), *L'Or qui brûle* (1912), *Le Baiser de l'empereur* (1913), *L'Agent Rigolo et son chien policier* (1913), *L'Hallali* (1913), *Voyage et grandes chasses en Afrique* (1913), *Au ravissement des dames* (1913), *La Fille de Delft* (1914), and *Maudite soit la guerre* (1914). Among these, *L'Or qui brûle* (1912) and *Maudite soit la guerre* (1914) are considered to be his best films.

During the war, Machin served as a reporter and photographer for Pathé. He was one of the founders of the *Service cinématographique de l'armée*, and he spent the war serving as a photojournalist and documentary filmmaker, capturing images of the war. He made more than twenty documentary films on the subject of the war, including *Notre cavalrie d'Afrique au front* (1915), *Le Drapeau des chasseurs d'Artois* (1915), *Avec nos soldats dans les forêts d'Argonne* (1915), *Monuments historiques d'Arras, victimes de la barberie allemande* (1916), *Le Service de santé aux armées* (1916), and *Dressage de chiens sentinelles* (1916).

After the war, Machin returned to Pathé, where he again began making narrative films, predominantly comedies. His first postwar film was *Suprême sacrifice* (1919), which he codirected with Armand du Plessy. This was followed by *Une nuit agitée* (1920), *On attend Polochon* (1920), and *Serpentin fait de la peinture* (1922).

In 1922, Machin left Pathé and opened his own studio, Les Studios Nice Machin, at the site of the former Pathé studio in Nice. There he continued to make films and to work with animals. He remained at that studio and worked independently until the end of his career, which coincided with the end of the silent era. Among these last films are *Pervenche* (1922), *Bête . . . commes les hommes* (1922), *Moi, j'accuse* (1923), *L'Enigme du Mont Agel* (1924), *Les Heritiers de l'oncle James* (1924), *Le Coeur des gueux* (1925), *Le Manoir de la peur* (1927), and *Black and White* (1929), his last known film.

MALLE, LOUIS (1932–1995). Director. Louis Malle was born into a wealthy family who owned the Béghin sugar dynasty. He studied at the **Institut des Hautes Études Cinématographiques** (IDHEC), and during his student years codirected his first major work, *Le monde du silence* (1956), with Jacques Yves Cousteau. The underwater documentary won a Golden Palm at **Cannes** and an Oscar for Best Documentary. He later worked as an assistant director for **Robert Bresson** on his 1956 film, *Un condamné à mort s'est échappé*. Bresson's film was funded by the Malle family's production company, Nouvelles Editions de Films. The company produced Malle's own first feature film, *Ascenseur pour l'échafaud*, which won the **Prix Louis-Delluc** in 1957. The film's cinematographer was Henri Decae, who would work with Malle on several of his early films, and the film starred **Jeanne Moreau**, who would also play the lead in Malle's 1958 *Les Amants*, a film that received both acclaim and censorship for its explicit sexual content and its then controversial and groundbreaking portrayal of a **woman**'s sexual pleasure. In the United States, the question of whether *Les Amants* was pornographic went all the way to the Supreme Court.

Although there are similarities between the film aesthetics and daring of Malle and his contemporaries in the *Nouvelle Vague* or New Wave, Malle distanced himself from the New Wave. Unlike the other directors of the New Wave, Malle was not a *Cahiers du cinéma* critic, was skeptical about the idea of a New Wave, and had a rather ample film budget. Nevertheless, the directorial successes he received during his youth in the late 1950s, his use of amoral, antiheroic protagonists, his employment of settings outside of the studio, and his portrayals of characters associated with the Algerian War have led several observers to make parallels.

Malle's feature films in the early 1960s were generally popular successes. These include *Zazie dans le métro* (1960), *Vie privée* (1962), and *Viva Maria* (1965). *Vie privée* is a portrayal of its leading actress, international film star **Brigitte Bardot**. *Viva Maria* brought together Moreau and Bardot—two actresses who are also linked to the New Wave. Malle's *Le feu follet* (1963) stars Maurice Ronet, a right-wing actor whose friendship with Malle raised questions about his seemingly fluctuating political ties, as did his relationship with right-wing novelist Roger Nimier, who worked on the script of *Ascenseur pour l'échafaud*.

Malle later codirected a film in three parts with directors **Roger Vadim** and Federico Fellini, titled *Histoires extraordinaires* (1967).

Malle's sketch, *William Wilson*, costarred Bardot and **Alain Delon**. Malle subsequently declared that he had grown weary of commercial filmmaking and accepted an opportunity to travel to India, where he shot the documentaries *Calcutta* (1968) and *L'Inde fantôme* (1968). Critics trace Malle's increased politicization to his journey to India and to the events in France of May 1968. Malle, who served on the 1968 **Cannes** jury, supported the suspension of the Festival along with **Jean-Luc Godard**, **François Truffaut**, and others.

In the 1970s and 1980s, Malle continued to direct provocative films. His portrayal of an incestuous relationship between mother and son in *Le souffle au coeur* (1971) attempted to challenge conventional notions of sexuality. He would again face censorship with *Pretty Baby* (1978), a film featuring then child actress Brooke Shields, set in a brothel in New Orleans. In addition to challenging the status quo with his representations of sexuality, Malle's portrayals of French collaboration with the Nazis sparked debates concerning the myth of France's unified resistance to the Occupation. *Lacombe Lucien* (1974) has been noted for its disturbingly neutral representation of French collaborators and is often included among works belonging to the **Mode Rétro**. Patrick Modiano, an author considered pivotal to reorienting discussions about the French role in the Holocaust, wrote the screenplay for the film.

Malle's autobiographical feature ***Au revoir les enfants*** (1987) depicts the director's childhood friendship with a Jewish boy who was tragically taken from his school by the Gestapo and sent to a concentration camp. It recognizes heroic acts of French resistance while also foregrounding the alliances some French citizens made with German Nazis. The film won seven **César** Awards (including Best Director, Film, and Screenplay), the Prix Louis-Delluc, the Golden Lion at Venice, and Best Director at the British Film Academy Awards. Several critics have asserted that *Au revoir les enfants*, Malle's most acclaimed film, provides a window into the formative experiences that most poignantly shaped Malle's art.

In the late 1970s, Malle began directing English-language feature films in the United States, which include *Pretty Baby*, *Atlantic City USA* (1980)—both featuring actress Susan Sarandon—*My Dinner with André* (1981), *Crackers* (1984), and *Alamo Bay* (1985). He also directed documentaries—*God's Country* (1986) and *And the Pursuit of Happiness* (1987)—during his sojourn in Hollywood. *My Dinner with André*, a film that focuses on the conversations of two protagonists, was remarkable for its rejection of spectacle and fast action that characterized many of the films of his American colleagues.

In the 1990s, Malle directed his last French film, *Milou en mai* (1990), based on Anton Chekhov's *The Cherry Orchard*. His final work was an Anglophone film set in New York, *Vanya on 42nd Street* (1994). It, too, took its inspiration from Chekhov. In this film, Malle blends documentary and feature filmmaking as he recounts the lives of actors rehearsing for a production of the play *Uncle Vanya*.

If any consistencies can be observed in Malle's work, it may be his films' provocative elements. His ideas, whether they be related to national history, gender, sexuality, or bourgeois morality are difficult to classify and challenging to interpret. In many of his films, his characters are at one and the same time sympathetic and disturbing, representative of the tendency of human relationships to defy simplified descriptions. His ability to inspire continued debate in France and elsewhere is perhaps one of his most enduring legacies.

MANON DES SOURCES (1986). *See JEAN DE FLORETTE* (1986) AND *MANON DES SOURCES* (1986).

MARAIS, JEAN (1913–1998). Actor. Born Jean Alfred Villain-Marais in Cherbourg, Jean Marais dreamed of becoming an actor from an early age. Marais left school at the age of fourteen. He had been a weak student in any case. He went to work for a photographer and studied acting with Charles Dullin. Marais's introduction to cinema came through Dullin, who introduced him to **Marcel L'Herbier**. Marais had a series of mostly minor supporting roles in several films in the 1930s, but most, apart from L'Herbier's films, were fairly insignificant. Among the films in which Marais appeared in this early part of his career were L'Herbier's *L'Epervier* (1933), *Le Scandale* (1934), *L'Aventurier* (1934), *Le Bonheur* (1934), *Les Hommes nouveaux* (1936), and *Nuits de feu* (1937), Jean Tarride's *Étienne* (1933), Victor Trivas's *Dans les rues* (1933), and **Henri Decoin**'s *Abus de confiance* (1938). He also had an uncredited role in **Marcel Carné**'s *Drôle de drame* (1937).

The turning point in Marais's career came in 1937, the year he met **Jean Cocteau**. The two men formed an instant bond, and Marais would go on to be Cocteau's companion for a number of years. Cocteau cast Marais in a number of his stage plays, most notably *Oedipe-Roy* in 1937. Thereafter, Marais's screen career also took a turn for the better. He had fairly significant roles in **Jacques de Baroncelli**'s *Le Pavillon brûle* (1941) and Roland Tual's *Le Lit à colonnes* (1942). However, he never gave up the stage, continuing to act in theater throughout his life.

Marais's real breakthrough film roles, however, also came through Cocteau, specifically in films which Cocteau either directed or for which he wrote the screenplays. These films include **Jean Delannoy**'s *L'Éternel retour* (1943), Cocteau's *La Belle et la bête* (1946), *L'Aigle à deux têtes* (1948), *Les Parents terribles* (1948), *Coriolan* (1950), and *Orphée* (1950), and Pierre Billon's *Ruy Blas* (1948). Marais also had other roles during this period, including in **Christian-Jacques**'s *Voyage sans espoir* (1943) and *Carmen* (1945), Henri Calef's *Les Chouans* (1947), Delannoy's *Aux yeux du souvenir* (1948) and *Le Secret de Mayerling* (1949), and **René Clément**'s *Le Chateau de verre* (1950).

By the 1950s, Marais was a veritable icon of the cinema. He was highly sought after as a leading man, embodying masculinity, strength, and physical beauty. He starred in such films as Yves Allegret's *Les Miracles n'ont lieu qu'une fois* (1951), **Roger Richebé**'s *Les Amants de minuit* (1953), **Georges Lacombe**'s *L'Appel du destin* (1953), Decoin's *Dortoir des grandes* (1953), **Marc Allegret**'s *Julietta* (1953) and *Futures vedettes* (1955), **Sacha Guitry**'s *Si Versailles m'était conté* (1954), *Si Paris nous était conté* (1954), and *Napoléon* (1955), **Robert Vernay**'s *Le Comte de Monte Cristo* (1955), **Jean Renoir**'s *Elena et les hommes* (1956), **Pierre Kast**'s *Un amour de poche* (1957), Clément Duhour's *La Vie à deux* (1958), Georges Lampin's *La Tour, prends garde!* (1958), and Delannoy's *La Princesse de Clèves* (1960), a film for which Cocteau wrote the screenplay.

In the 1960s, Marais starred in a series of adventure films, starting with **André Hunébelle**'s *Le Bossu* (1960). He made a terrific swashbuckler, and these films added a new dimension to his already impressive career. Among the other adventure films in which he appeared were Hunébelle's *Le Capitan* (1960), *Le Miracle des loups* (1961), and *Les Mystères de Paris* (1962), Pierre Gaspard-Huit's *Le Capitaine Fracasse* (1961), Decoin's *Le Masque de fer* (1962), Christian-Jacques's *Le Gentleman de Cocody* (1964) and *Le Saint prend l'affût* (1966), and Gilles Grangier's *Train d'enfer* (1965). Other films in which Marais appeared include **Abel Gance**'s *Austerlitz* (1960), Claude Boissol's *Napoléon II, l'aiglon* (1961), and Robert Thomas's *Patate* (1964). Marais also appeared in the remake of **Louis Feuillade**'s legendary series *Fantômas* (1964) and its sequels *Fantômas se déchaîne* (1965) and *Fantômas contre Scotland Yard* (1967), all directed by Hunébelle.

The year 1970 brought Marais one of his last great roles, that of the king to **Catherine Deneuve**'s queen in **Jacques Demy**'s *Peau d'âne* (1970). Thereafter, Cocteau went into semiretirement, spending time on painting and sculpting, his other great loves. He made the occasional appearance in television productions but rarely appeared onscreen. Exceptions are his appearances in Demy's *Parking* (1985), Willy Rameau's *Lien de parenté* (1986), Jérôme Foulon's *Les Enfants du naufrageur* (1992), and **Claude Lelouch**'s *Les Misérables* (1995). His final film role was in Bernardo Bertolucci's international multilanguage film *Stealing Beauty* (1996). When Marais died in 1998, the world mourned a great icon of cinema, and France mourned one of the last living links to what it considers French cinema's golden age.

MARCHAL, GEORGES (1920–1997). Actor. Born Georges Louis Lucot in Nancy, Georges Marchal became one of the most prominent leading men of the 1940s and 1950s. He was a star on a par with **Jean Marais** and, like Marais, was in demand as much for his looks as for his acting ability. He had a film career spanning five decades, during the course of which he appeared in more than sixty films.

Marchal made his screen debut in an uncredited role in **Henri Decoin**'s *Premier rendez-vous* (1941). He quickly moved to supporting roles and then leading roles, appearing in such films as Roland Tual's *Le Lit à colonnes* (1942), Jean de Limur's *L'Homme qui joue avec le feu* (1942), **Jean Grémillon**'s *Lumière d'été* (1943), Pierre Billon's *Vautrin* (1944), **Jean-Paul Paulin**'s *Échec au roy* (1945), **Jacques de Baroncelli**'s *Fausse alerte* (1945), Yves Allegret's *Les Démons de l'aube* (1946), **Serge de Poligny**'s *Torrents* (1947) and *La Soif des* *hommes* (1949), Léonide Moguy's *Bethsabée* (1947), André Zwa-boda's *La Septième porte* (1948), Christian Stengel's *La Figure de proue* (1948), Jean Stelli's *La Voyageuse inattendue* (1949) and *Dernier amour* (1949), Jacques Daroy's *La Passagère* (1949), and Decoin's *Au grand balcon* (1949).

The peak of Marchal's career was the 1950s, during which time he had lead roles in more than twenty films. His forte seemed to be the costume drama and swashbuckling adventure, or at least that was the type of role he primarily played. Among the films in which he starred are **Marcel L'Herbier** and Paolo Moffa's *Les Derniers jours de Pompei* (1950), Gilles Grangier's *Le Plus joli péché au monde* (1951) and *Jupiter* (1952), Carmine Gallone's *Messalina* (1951), Henri Calef's *Les Amours finissent à l'aube* (1953), **André Huné-belle**'s *Les Trois mousquetaires* (1953), **Sacha Guitry**'s *Si Versailles m'était conté* (1954), Georges Combray's *La Contessa di Castiglione* (1955), Raoul André's *Cherchez la femme* (1955), René Jolivet and Ricardo Muñoz Suay's *Les Aventures de Gil de Santillane* (1956), Maurice Cloche's *Marchands de filles* (1957) and *Les Filles de nuit* (1958), Edmont T. Grevilles's *Quand sonnera minuit* (1958), and **Abel Gance**'s *Austerlitz* (1960), as well as a number of Spanish and Italian films.

In addition to his other work, Marchal also starred in several films by Luis Buñuel, who was his close friend. His Buñuel films include *Cela s'appelle l'aurore* (1955), *La Mort en ce jardin* (1956), *Belle de jour* (1967), and *La Voie lactée* (1969). Apart from the Buñuel films, Marchal only acted in a handful of films in the 1960s, most of them outside of France. By the 1970s, Marchal was working primarily in television, with the notable exception of Nina Companéez's *Faustine et le bel été* (1972) and **Benoît Jacquot**'s *Les Enfants du placard* (1977), his final film. Marchal continued acting in television until 1989, at which point he formally retired.

MAREY, ÉTIENNE-JULES (1830–1904). Film pioneer. Étienne-Jules Marey was a French physiologist, member of the Academy of Medecine, and a professor at the Collège de France. Marey developed several important devices for the study of human physiology, including a device to register pulse and blood pressure. His primary interest, however, was in developing the means to use photography to capture and represent movement. He developed several techniques and inventions that would pave the way for the invention of the film camera. One of Marey's contributions was his "tambour," a kind of pressure sensor that could be used to register movement. Marey attached the device to the hoofs of a horse to register the movement of the hooves. In so doing, he discovered that all representations of a horse in motion made up to that time were incorrect. This discovery led William Muybridge to develop his zoopraxiscope in order to be able to accurately photograph and represent a horse's movement. Marey applied his technology to a motion-sensing suit that he used to capture human motion.

Marey was, in turn, inspired by Muybridge to develop a way to capture movement in a single frame. He developed a technique for exposing multiple images on the same rotating plate through the use of a slotted shutter. This allowed for the photographic image to represent the photographed movement. He called these images *chronophotographes*. He developed a photographic gun in 1882 with a rotating photographic plate. The gun enabled the user to rapidly photograph a moving object with a quick succession of images. This allowed for the photography of the movement of birds, something that had not previously been possible. In 1887, he developed a rudimentary film camera using George Eastman's recently developed silver bromide film. This camera was a direct predecessor to **Auguste** and **Louis Lumière**'s *cinematographe*. A significant difference between Marey's invention and that of the Lumières is that Marey's device did not use transparent film and the film was not notched. He was not, therefore, able to accurately capture continuous motion because of an unresolved issue with continuous feed of the film and with the continuity of the time of exposure and the distance between images. In 1894, Marey also invented a slow-motion camera.

MARIUS **(1931),** *FANNY* **(1932), AND** *CÉSAR* **(1933).** Films. These three films, all connected to **Marcel Pagnol**, are some of the most beloved French films of all time. *Marius* (1931) was codirected by Pagnol and Alexander Korda, *Fanny* (1932) was directed by **Marc Allegret**, and *César* (1936) was directed by Pagnol himself. All three films were based on successful stage plays. Together they tell the story of the ill-fated romance between Marius (**Pierre Fresnay**) and

Fanny (**Orane Demazis**). In *Marius*, the eponymous hero is the son of César (**Raïmu**), a tavern-owner in Marseille. He has no taste for the family business and dreams of running away to become a sailor. Fanny is promised to the much older Panisse (Fernand Charpin), but dreams of Marius. Marius and Fanny spend one night together, and then Marius goes to sea.

Fanny continues the story. Fanny finds herself pregnant by Marius, who is away for five years and completely unaware of the situation. Fanny has to decide what to do. She consults numerous people in her life, including César and Panisse, who offers to marry Fanny and raise the child as his own. This is ultimately what she chooses to do. In *César*, we see the resolution of the situation. Panisse dies without telling his son, Césariot (André Fouché), that his real father is Marius. After Panisse's death, Césariot discovers the truth. He seeks out Marius, who has long since returned from sea and works as a mechanic. Posing as a reporter, Césariot attempts to learn about Marius. Due to a series of miscommunications, Césariot comes to believe that Marius is a criminal, and he resolves to have nothing to do with him. In the end, however, the truth comes out and reconciliation occurs.

To the contemporary viewer, these films might seem a bit dated in their staging, as they are, in many ways, filmed staged plays. Pagnol, in fact, viewed cinema (at least sound cinema) as a means of fixing theatrical productions forever in time and transmitting them to a larger audience than the theater permitted. He evolved a theory of mise-en-scène that consisted of an attempt to reproduce the theater on the screen. The *Trilogie marseillaise* constituted his first serious effort at putting that theory into practice.

Beyond their connection to Pagnol and his plays, the films mark the origin of a sort of provincial cinema in France that would influence filmmaking up to the present day. The evocation of life in Marseille in these three films is highly romantic and perhaps already even a bit nostalgic, since at the time they were made, the way of life they represented was already disappearing. The films also romanticize the Marseille accent, which was, until that point, looked down upon. Pagnol films have come over time to represent a rural, pastoral, and iconic France. These three films in particular hold a special place in French film history. Other Pagnol films have been remade in France, but no one has touched these, the originals being alive and well in film history and memory.

MARKER, CHRIS (1921–). Director and screenwriter. Born Christian François Bouche-Villeneuve, filmmaker Chris Marker is probably one of the best-known and most widely respected documentary filmmakers in the world. He is also one of the few documentary filmmakers to be considered an **auteur**, so individual is his filmmaking style, at once classical and avant-garde, influenced by the ideals of political engagement in French literature from Jean-Paul Sartre onward, and underpinned by an interest in philosophy and the workings of memory. Marker's documentaries have dealt with topics as far-ranging as American hegemony, Africa, and the Internet. In recent years, he has grown fairly postmodern in his filmmaking style, experimenting with possibilities for multimedia, the Internet, and filmmaking.

Marker was awarded a Golden Berlin Bear for Best Feature-Length Documentary for *Description d'un combat* in 1961. His documentary, *Le joli mai*, won Best First Film at the Venice Film Festival in 1963. He won the **Prix Jean-Vigo** for Best Short Film for his 1953 documentary *Les statues meurent aussi* (with **Alain Resnais**)—a film that was banned from commercial cinema for ten years—and won the prize again in 1963 for the short *La Jetée*. His documentary *Cuba Si!* (1960) was also banned. In 1983, he won a **César** for Best Short Documentary for *Junkopia*. He often traveled abroad to make documentaries; *Si j'avais quatre Dromadaires* (1966) features photographs from over twenty countries. He produced and codirected the documentary *Loin du Viet-nam* (1967). His first independently directed film was *Dimanche à Pékin* (1955).

MATHOT, LÉON (1886–1968). Actor and director. Léon Mathot began his career at **Pathé** studios near the turn of the century. He started as an actor and quickly became a veritable star, something that was unusual at that time. Over the course of the silent era, Mathot appeared in more than forty films, including **Georges Hatot** and André Heuzé's *La Course à la perruque* (1906), **Henri Andréani**'s *La Légende des chevaliers d'Algabert* (1912), *Les Rivaux d'Arnheim* (1912), and *Le Pont fatal* (1914), **Alfred Machin**'s *La Dramatique* *passion d'Algabert et d'Elisabeth de Rodembourg* (1912) and *Le Secret de l'acier* (1912), **Camille de Morlhon**'s *Sous l'uniforme* (1915), **Abel Gance**'s *Fioritures* (1916), *Les Gaz mortels* (1916), *La Zone de la mort* (1917), *Le Droit à la vie* (1917), and *Barberousse* (1917), Maurice Mariaud's *Nemrod et cie* (1916), **Henri Pouctal**'s *Volonté* (1917), his series *Le Comte de Monte Cristo* (1918), and his film *Travail* (1920), Charles Burguet's *La Course du flambeau* (1918), **Gaston Ravel**'s *La Maison d'argile* (1918), Edouard-Émile Violet's *Papillons* (1920), René Hervil's *L'Ami Fritz* (1920), and **René Leprince**'s *L'Empereur des pauvres* (1922), *tre ou ne pas être* (1922), *Jean d'Aggrève* (1922), and *Mon oncle Benjamin* (1923).

Later in his silent career, Mathot moved from more mainstream film to avant-garde cinema. He starred in **Jean Epstein**'s *Coeur fidèle* (1923) and *L'Auberge rouge* (1923), as well as in **Germaine's Dulac**'s *Le Diable dans la ville* (1924). Other late films include Henri Étiévant's *La Nuit de la revanche* (1924), Marco de Gastyne's *La Blessure* (1925), **André Hugon**'s *Yasmina* (1926), and **Henri Diamant-Berger's** *Rue de la paix* (1926). He also appeared in a small number of sound films, including **Henri Fescourt**'s *La Maison de la flèche* (1930) and Hervil and **Louis Mercanton**'s *Le Mystère de la villa rose* (1930).

In the late 1920s, Mathot began directing as well as acting. His first film was *Celle qui domine* (1927), codirected with Carmine Gallone, and it was a film in which Mathot also starred. Other Mathot films include *Dans l'ombre du harem* (1928), codirected with André Liabel; *Le Refuge* (1930); *La Bande à Bouboule* (1931); *Embrassez-moi* (1932); *Bouboule 1er roi nègre* (1933); *Le Comte Obligado* (1934); *La Mascotte* (1935), starring Lucien Baroux; *Les Loups entre eux* (1936), starring **Jules Berry** and Gina Manès; *L'Ange du foyer* (1936); *L'Homme à abattre* (1937), starring Berry and **Viviane Romance**; *Chéri-Bibi* (1937), starring **Pierre Fresnay**, **Jean-Pierre Aumont**, and Colette Darfeuil; *Le Révolté* (1938), starring Pierre Renoir and **René Dary**; *Le Collier de chanvre* (1940); *Cartacalha, reine des gitans* (1942), also starring Romance; *Forte tête* (1942), starring Dary; *L'Homme sans nom* (1943), starring Jean Galland; *La Route du bagne* (1945), also starring Romance; *La Danseuse de Marrakech* (1949); and *Mon gosse de père* (1953), his final film.

In general, Mathot has been remembered more as an actor than as a director. His popularity and his range on the screen are one reason the films in which he acted are more memorable than those he directed. What is more, he was fortunate, as an actor, to work with some of the great directors of the silent era. As a director, Mathot tried his hand at comedy and drama and was able to work with some of the best actors of the day. His films were relatively successful during their release. However, with relatively few exceptions, they have been forgotten.

MAXUDIAN (1881–1976). Actor. Born Max Algop Maxudian in Smyrna in what is now Turkey, Maxudian, who was of Armenian, not Turkish, origin, moved with his family to France in 1893. He began his acting career on the stage, appearing at the Grand Guignol and the Odéon theaters. It was reportedly **Sarah Bernhardt**, with whom Maxudian often worked, who interested Maxudian in the cinema, when she herself began to appear in films.

Maxudian's silent career was fairly prestigious. He appeared largely in *Film d'art* productions and was quite often the lead actor in the films in which he appeared. He made his screen debut in **Henri Desfontaines** and **Louis Mercanton's** *Les Amours de la reine Élisabeth* (1912), a film in which he appeared opposite Bernhardt. He also starred in Desfontaines and Mercanton's *Adrienne Lecouvreur* (1913), also opposite Bernhardt, as well as their film *Anne de Boleyn* (1913). Other silent films in which he starred include Mercanton and René Hervil's *Le Tablier blanc* (1917) and *Bouclette* (1918), Jean Hervé's *Le Pauvre village* (1917), Mercanton's *Phroso* (1922) and *Venus* (1929), Charles de Marsan and Charles Maudru's *Les Premières armes de Rocambole* (1923), **Abel Gance's** *La Roue* (1923) and *Napoléon* (1927), Rex Ingram's *The Arab* (1924), Henry Roussel's *La Terre promise* (1925), and **Jacques de Baroncelli's** *Le Réveil* (1925). Maxudian was also a particular favorite of director **Roger Lion**. He appeared first in Lion's Portuguese films *A Sereia de Pedra* (1923) and *Os Olhos da Alma* (1924). He went on to appear also in Lion's *La Fontaine de l'amour* (1924), *J'ai tué!* (1924), and *La Clé de voûte* (1925), *Un soir au cocktail's bar* (1929), *La Nuit est à nous* (1929), and *L'Appel de la chair* (1929).

Beginning during the silent era and continuing on into the sound era, Maxudian, like his contemporary, **Marcel Dalio**, began to be typecast as the foreigner, the Arab, or the Jew, and sometimes, therefore, the villain of the piece. It is probably also the case, as it was with Dalio, that he was a much better actor than many of the roles afforded him would suggest. This trend to typecast him began in the silent era but continued long into his performances in sound films.

During the 1930s and 1940s, Maxudian appeared in more than thirty films, including **Gaston Ravel**'s *L'étranger* (1930), **Henri Fescourt**'s *La Maison de la flèche* (1930), Charles de Rochefort's *Le Secret du docteur* (1930), Pierre Billon's *Nuits de Venise* (1931) and *Bourrasque* (1935), Gabriel Rosca's *Rocambole* (1932), Lion's *Direct au coeur* (1932), codirected with Arnaudy, and his *Trois balles dans la peau* (1933), Leo Mittler's *La Voix sans visage* (1933), **Julien Duvivier**'s *Golgotha* (1935), Viktor Tourjansky's *Les Yeux noirs* (1935) and *Puits en flammes* (1936), René Pujol's *Passé à vendre* (1936), Maurice de Canonge's *Un soir à Marseille* (1937), **André Hugon**'s *La Rue sans joie* (1938), and **Dimitri Kirsanoff**'s *L'Avion de minuit* (1938).

Maxudian's career more or less ended during the 1940s. After the Occupation, he was not permitted to act in film because of his foreign origin. After Liberation, he appeared in a handful of films, including **Claude Autant-Lara**'s *Le Diable au corps* (1946), Raymond Leboursier's *Le Furet* (1949), and Francis Campaux's *Ronde de nuit* (1949). However, he was not able to recapture the momentum his career had had prior to the war. He retired from the screen in 1950.

MELCHIOR, GEORGES (1889–1944). Actor. Georges Melchior was one of the great screen actors of the silent era. He began his career at **Pathé**, where he appeared in **Albert Capellani**'s *L'Envieuse* (1911), but he went almost immediately to rival **Gaumont**, where he remained for a number of years. While at Gaumont, Melchior worked closely with **Louis Feuillade**, appearing in such films as *L'Attrait du bouge* (1912), *Le Maléfice* (1912), *Le Valet de coeur* (1913), *Un drame au Pays Basque* (1913), *S'affranchir* (1913), *L'Agonie de Byzance* (1913), *Les Millions de la bonne* (1913), *La Marche des rois* (1913), *La Rencontre* (1914), *La Petite Andalouse* (1914), *Manon de Montmartre* (1914), *Les Lettres* (1914), *Pâques rouges* (1914), and Feuillade's legendary ***Fantômas*** series (1913–1914), in which Melchior played journalist Jérome Fandor alongside Edmond Bréon and **René Navarre**.

Beyond his work with Feuillade, Melchior was also a favorite of director René Le Somptier who cast him in *Grand-maman* (1912), *Fleur fanée . . . coeur aimé* (1913), *Un drame de l'air* (1913), *Le Pressentiment* (1914), *Le Monde renversé* (1914), *La Fille du caissier* (1914), *Chef d'école* (1914), *Le Pont des enfers* (1916), and *Aubade à Sylvie* (1917). Other films in which he appeared at Gaumont include **Henri Fescourt'**s *L'Amazone masquée* (1912), *Les Deux médaillons* (1913), *Le Départ dans la nuit* (1913), and *La Voix qui accuse* (1913), and **Gaston Ravel**'s *L'Amoureuse aventure* (1914).

Melchior left Gaumont in 1917 and went out on his own. He appeared in a number of other silent films, including René Hervil and **Louis Mercanton**'s *Mères françaises* (1917), **Jacques Feyder**'s classic silent film *L'Atlantide* (1920), **Julien Duvivier**'s *Les Roquevillard* (1922), **Gaston Roudès**'s *Le Lac d'argent* (1922), *Les Rantzau* (1923), *Le Petit moineau de Paris* (1923), and *La Maison au soleil* (1928), Donatien's *Mon curé chez les riches* (1925), *Florine, la fleur du Valois* (1926), and *Au revoir et merci* (1927), codirected with Pierre Colombier, Léon Abrams and Mercanton's *La Voyante* (1923), Le Somptier's *La Forêt qui tue* (1925) and *Le P'tit Parigot* (1926), Jean Choux's *La Terre qui meurt* (1926), Guiseppe Guarino's *Le Marchand de bonheur* (1926) and *Casque blanche . . . Toque noire* (1927), **André Hugon**'s *La Vestale du Gange* (1927), Marcel Dumont and Roudès's *La Dédale* (1927), Mario Nalpas and Henri Étiévant's *La Sirène des tropiques* (1927), and Georges Pallu's *La Petite soeur des pauvres* (1928).

Melchior attempted to transition into sound film in the 1930s, but he was never the actor in a sound film that he was on the silent screen. He had roles in a handful of films, including Jean Godard's *Pour un soir . . .!* (1931), Pallu's *La Vierge du rocher* (1932), Charles-Félix Tavano's *Le Billet de logement* (1932), Maurice Champreux's *Le Grand bluff* (1933), and **Marcel L'Herbier**'s *La Citadelle du silence* (1937), which was his final film.

MÉLIÈS, GEORGES (1861–1938). Cinematographer, director, and film pioneer. Georges Méliès's first exposure to the cinema coincided exactly with the world's first exposure. On 28 December 1895, Méliès, a magician and the director of the Théâtre Robert Houdin in Paris, was one of thirty-four guests invited to witness **Auguste** and **Louis Lu-**

mière's unveiling of their new moving pictures. For Méliès the honor was extended as a courtesy, since Antoine Lumière, the father of the two filmmakers, had a photography studio just above Méliès's theater. The experience of seeing pictures "brought to life" on the screen was, for Méliès, a life-altering moment. Always interested in illusions and in the ability to make an audience see things that were not there, Méliès was attracted to the power of illusion offered by the cinema, and he immediately determined to make films of his own.

Méliès thus became one of the pioneers of the new medium called the cinema. Méliès had an interest in the potential of photography to create such moving pictures prior to the Lumière screening. He had studied photographs of motion, such as Edweard Muybridge's "Animal Locomotion" photographs. He had also independently experimented with slide projection and magic lanterns in his magic act. Immediately upon seeing what the Lumière brothers had accomplished, Méliès set about trying to obtain his own version of their film camera (the *cinématographe*). He first attempted to buy one from the Lumières, who refused. Méliès then managed to purchase a film projector that was a copy of Thomas Edison's projector, the kinetoscope. He made modifications and improvements to the technology and, in 1896, produced his own camera-projector combination, which he called the *kinetographe* and in the same year, made his first film.

The French film critic **Georges Sadoul** credited Méliès with being the first narrative film director. That credit more properly belongs to **Alice Guy**, who produced a narrative film some months before Méliès. Nonetheless, Méliès was the second, and the first male narrative film director.

In 1897, Méliès built the first full-scale film studio at his family's estate in Montreuil and founded his production company, Star-Film, with the help of his daughter, Georgette. Over the course of his lifetime, Méliès made well over 150 films at Star, most starring himself and the actress Jehanne d'Alcy, who was his mistress and later his second wife. He also produced many films starring Bleuette Bernon. He pioneered several of the effects that have become the building blocks of contemporary cinema. Among these are the use of multiple exposure, splicing, the dissolve, the matte shot, tracking, and montage. He also was one of the first filmmakers to experiment with staging of shots and scenes as well as with ways of linking shots together to create a narrative.

Méliès's work was enormously popular during the early part of his career. More significantly, with respect to the standing of his work during his own lifetime, Méliès was one of the only early filmmakers who was invited to produce films to be shown in tandem with theater and stage productions, an indication that his films were considered as much art as entertainment. Still, despite all of these contributions to cinema, early critics and film scholars often regarded Méliès a peripheral figure whose filmmaking was overly simplistic, and the impact of his work has often been dismissed.

The somewhat peripheral position Méliès has in film history is probably due, in part, to the way in which he made films. He was a very independent figure among the film pioneers, and he did not move stylistically or thematically in the same direction as others like **Charles Pathé** or **Léon Gaumont**. Most other early filmmakers began by making "real life" and historical event films and then gradually moved into producing narrative films, including comedies and melodramas. Méliès primarily produced single-scene films and was not as interested in moving in the direction of full-length narrative films. His interest derived from film's capacity to show the viewer things that do not exist, and for that reason he is primarily remembered for his "trick" films, or *trucs*, which were centered around magic tricks or the use of special effects. These include *The Conjuring of a Woman at the House of Robert Houdin, Magician* (1896), *Illusions fantasmagoriques* (1898), *Le Repas fantastique* (1900), *L'Homme à la tête en caoutchouc* (1901), *Illusions funambulesques* (1903), and *Les Cartes vivantes* (1904). He is equally well known for his fantasy or fairy tale films, or *féeries*, most notably *Cendrillon* (1899), *Le Petit chaperon rouge* (1901), *Au royaume des fées* (1903), and *La Fée libellule* (1908).

Méliès became a victim of the progressive commercialization of cinema. He was a filmmaker who assumed total creative control over each of his films himself, rather than enlisting others to make films for his company (as with Pathé and Gaumont). This meant that he was not able to produce as many films in a year as the more commercialized operations and also that his films were more expensive to distribute, thus limiting the number of venues where they were shown. By 1911, this refusal to commercialize forced Méliès to sell his films to Charles Pathé in order to find the financing to work. He made his last films in 1912, although since Pathé had control over the final product, many of these were cut down from Méliès's original versions. He was gradually forced to sell off his studio, and even the Théatre Robert Houdin was bulldozed to make way for a road construction project.

Nearly penniless, Méliès supported himself by doing theatrical revues. His income was supplemented from the sales of a toy store owned by his second wife (and former mistress) Charlotte Stéphanie Faës (Jehanne D'Alecy). The two lived in relative obscurity until 1926, until film journal editor Léon Druhot stumbled upon Méliès and attempted to draw attention to his plight. He was embraced by the avant-garde movement, most particularly the surrealists, who saw parallels to their own work in his, and he finished his life quietly making publicity films and admired by a small but faithful entourage.

Some twenty years after his death, his role as a pioneer in film history was finally recognized, and his contribution to the technical development of film, particularly special effects, was acknowledged. Recently, film scholars have become newly interested in Méliès and his work. Since many of Méliès's films still survive (as a result of his early foray into the American film market), there has been ample opportunity to study his filmmaking. Such scholars see a certain "modernity" in his filmmaking, a style and vision that was generations ahead of his peers.

Although Méliès is still best remembered for his trick films and his féeries, his work comprised a significant range. He is regarded as one of the fathers of the modern horror film, and some his films, including, *Le Manoir du diable*, (1896) *La Damnation de Faust* (1898), *Barbe-bleue* (1901), and *L'Homme mouche* are considered early classics of the genre. He is also the undisputed founder of the science-fiction genre, and films such as *La Lune à un mètre* (1898), *Le Voyage dans la lune* (1902), *Le Voyage à travers l'impossible* (1904), and *20000 lieues sous les mers* (1907) are also considered early classics.

He could, when the spirit moved him, be much more serious. His catalog includes biopics such as *Jeanne d'Arc* (1899), and literary adaptations such as *Faust et Marguérite* (1897) and *Les Aventures de Robinson Crusoe* (1902). His 1899 film *L'Affaire Dreyfus* was an overtly political film on the Dreyfus Affair, produced at a time when the political ramifications for questioning the government's position on Dreyfus was still quite dangerous, and indeed, Méliès did suffer for a time from negative fallout from the film. All in all, Méliès was a brilliant visionary of the early cinema, and like many such visionaries, it is likely that his true impact may never be fully recognized.

MÉLIÈS PRIZE. *See* PRIX MÉLIÈS.

MELVILLE, JEAN-PIERRE (1917–1973). Director, producer, and screenwriter. Born Jean-Pierre Grumbach in Paris in 1917, Jean-Pierre Melville would only make thirteen films in his career. Nonetheless, like **Robert Bresson** and **Max Ophüls** (who were both his contemporaries) his influence on French cinema and cinema in general is disproportionate to his output. He was, without overstating the facts, a legend and he was so in his own time. He was a pivotal influence on the filmmakers of the *Nouvelle Vague* or New Wave, and he was central in changing the direction of French cinema in the postwar era and particularly the 1960s.

Melville had no formal training in cinema. Like the early pioneers, he was self-taught. There is even a famous story about him beginning to make films on a **Pathé** home movie camera when he was a very small child. He was also driven by a passion for the cinema itself. He was an avid lover of Hollywood film, particularly film noir and the Western, and the influence of Hollywood is evident in his own films. He came to professional filmmaking after World War II. He first served in the French forces, then in the English forces, having fled the German invasion. He then served as an undercover agent in the Resistance forces. Melville was his covert name as a Resistance agent. He chose the name himself as an expression of admiration for the American author. It was the name he would use in cinema.

When Melville began making films just after the war, he was denied membership in the French filmmaking union. Typical of the way he would conduct himself throughout his career, he set up on his own, at his own "studio" and created his own production company in order to produce his own films. His first film was a short titled *24 heures dans la vie d'un clown* (1946), and it was followed by the feature-length *Le Silence de la mer* (1947). This film, which many consider exceptional for its exploration of French collaboration with Nazi Germany, was made during that brief period after the war that preceded the national silence on the subject. It was seen and admired by **Jean Cocteau**, who invited Melville to direct the film adaptation of *Les Enfants terribles* (1950). Melville followed his work with Cocteau by directing the film *Quand tu liras cette lettre* (1953), the story of a young woman torn between taking religious vows and taking care of her family. These early films tend to be forgotten in many analyses of Melville because they are not the gangster films for which he is typically remembered.

The first of the better-known Melville films is *Bob le flambeur* (1955). The film tells the story of a retired gangster, plagued by gambling debts, who agrees to hold up a casino. It introduced Melville's own blend of noir and moral tale, dispassionately recorded through a very neutral and distant camera. The film was followed by *Deux hommes de Manhattan* (1958), *L'Aîné des Ferchaux* (1962), *Le Doulos* (1962), *Landru* (1962), *Le Deuxième souffle* (1966), *Le Samouraï* (1967), which won the **Prix Louis-Delluc**, *Le Cercle rouge* (1970), and *Un Flic* (1972), all of which are in the same vein.

In the middle of these, however, Melville would return to the war. *Léon Morin, Prêtre* (1961), often considered a pivotal film in Melville's career, and *L'Armée des ombres* (1969) are both wartime dramas that deviate from Melville's general pattern of using gangster-type plots as vehicles. However, the films are similar in tone and in theme to many of Melville's other films. This very fact suggests that what is at the heart of Melville's standing as an **auteur** is less the form of his films than both his filmmaking style and the philosophical substance of his films.

It is difficult to classify Melville's work with respect to movement or period. His films may have influenced the *Nouvelle Vague*, but he preceded it and he always remained deliberately aloof from it. He was also deliberately and consciously out of step with most of the other filmmakers of the day. He is, rather, one of a handful of fiercely independent filmmakers such as Ophüls, Bresson, and **Jacques Becker,** all of whom were making films in the 1950s and 1960s, and all of whom helped move French cinema away from the formulaic comedies and melodramas the major studios were producing and more toward an independent, author-centered cinema in the spirit of the cinema of the 1930s.

MÉMOIRES D'IMMIGRÉS: L'HÉRITAGE MAGHRÉBIN (1997).

Film. Hailed as *the* film on immigration in France, *Mémoires d'immigrés* is a three-part documentary by filmmaker Yamina Benguigui, who is herself the daughter of Algerian immigrants. The film was originally made for television by Canal Plus; however, the documentary was so successful it was released theatrically, making it one of the few made-for-television films to be released in theaters. The film is of enormous historical significance, since it was one of the first films to commit France's history of immigration from former colonies to film, and the first documentary to do so.

Mémoires d'immigrés is structured in triptych. The first part, "Les Pères" or "The Fathers," focused on the men who came to France to work, starting at the beginning of the twentieth century. The men are interviewed primarily in or near the places they worked in order to foreground the experiences of immigrants in the world of work, but also to draw attention to the industries in which immigrants have made a significant contribution. These include mining, construction, and manufacturing. The film also relies on close-ups to emphasize the personal nature of the experiences recounted, but longer shots are used to document places of work. Also interviewed are various members of the government who recount recruitment efforts and the attitudes of policy makers toward immigrants. These interviews suggest that the French government considered little but issues of demand for labor in building its immigration policy.

The film also shows, briefly, the living conditions in which men were housed, drawing attention to the general lack of interest on the part of France in the welfare of those who came to work. Woven in among interviews is archival footage taken from earlier periods, notably the 1950s and 1960s, showing immigrants attempting to integrate into the larger culture.

The second part focuses on "Les Mères" or "The Mothers" and looks at the experience of women in the history of immigration. Specifically it focuses on the "family reunification" policies that allowed men in France to reunite with their families. The women in this part are filmed largely in their homes, drawing attention both to the sphere in which they predominantly found themselves and to the commonalities that unite women of Maghrebian origin with women in France.

The third part focuses on "Les Enfants" or "The Children" and looks at the experience of those of Maghrebian origin born and brought up in France. The section documents the *banlieue* and the rent controlled housing projects or HLMs in which many immigrants reside. It also recalls the *bidonvilles*, or shanty towns, that preceded them. This part emphasizes the stories of everyday people and also highly visible people such as the writer Mounsi, and the writer and sociologist Azouz Begag, who is the current minister of equal opportunities.

As noted, the film has been hailed for bringing the history of immigration into the public sphere and for personalizing the experience of immigration, bringing it out of the realm of statistics and political polemic and rendering it a lived and living experience, a part of history and memory. It has been one of the most successful documentaries of all time.

MERCANTON, LOUIS (1879–1932). Director. Born in Switzerland, Louis Mercanton came to France to work in the theater and then the cinema. He began his career with **Éclair** studios as a director and screenwriter, where he worked on the screenplay to **Henri Desfontaines**'s *Shylock* (1910), starring **Harry Baur**, and *Les Amours de la reine Élisabeth* (1912), starring **Sarah Bernhardt**, and he also codirected *L'Assassinat d'Henri III* (1911), *Anne de Boleyn* (1913), and *Adrienne Lecouvreur* (1913), all with Desfontaines. In addition to his collaboration with Desfontaines, Mercanton directed *Le Spectre du passé* (1913), *Vendetta* (1914), *Jeanne Doré* (1915), *Le Tournant* (1916), *Manuella* (1916), *Le Tablier blanc* (1917), *La P'tite du sixième* (1917), *Oh! Ce baiser!* (1917), *Midinettes* (1917), *Mères françaises* (1917), *Le Torrent* (1917), *Un roman d'amour et d'aventures* (1918), *Bouclette* (1918), *Aux jardins de Murcie* (1923), and *Sarati, le terrible* (1923), all with René Hervil.

In 1919, Mercanton began directing and producing independently. His first independent film, *L'Appel du sang* (1919), was a hit, and he went on, during the silent era, to direct such films as *Miarka, fille à l'ours* (1920), *L'Homme merveilleux* (1922), *Phrose* (1922), *Les Deux gosses* (1924), *La Petite bonne du palace* (1926), *Monte Carlo*

(1926), *Cinders* (1926), *Croquette* (1927), and *Venus* (1929), and also produced both *Miarka, la fille à l'ours* (1920) and *Venus* (1929). He also codirected *La Voyante* (1924) with Léon Abrams.

Mercanton's career extended only a few years into the sound era. Nonetheless, he managed to direct more than thirteen films in a period of three years. His sound films include the English-language films *The Nipper* (1930), *These Charming People* (1931), and *A Man of Mayfair* (1931), as well as the French films *La Lettre* (1930), based on the play by Somerset Maugham and starring Paul Capellani, *Le Mystère de la villa rose* (1930), again, codirected with Hervil and a classic of early sound cinema, *Chérie* (1930), codirected with actress Mona Goya who also starred in the film, *Marions-nous* (1931), *Il est charmant* (1932), and *Cognasse* (1932), his final film.

METZ, CHRISTIAN (1931–). Film theorist. Christian Metz is a prominent film theorist whose seminal essay in 1964, "Le cinéma: langue ou langage?" is considered a landmark in modern film theory. Metz is well known for his categorization of film sequences, or syntagmas, in his essay "Grande Syntagmatique." His two books, *Language and Cinema* and *Film Language: A Semiotics of the Cinema*, based on essays he wrote in the 1960s, were published in English translation in 1974 and have influenced scholars and students of film and media studies internationally. His *Psychoanalysis and Cinema: The Imaginary Signifier* was published in English in 1982. The original French version appeared in 1977. Metz's theories are influenced by structuralist thinkers such as Ferdinand de Saussure and psychoanalysts such as Sigmund Freud and Jacques Lacan. He has been instrumental in creating the idea that film is a language, whose parts, including shots, camera angles, transitions, and montage, communicate messages to the spectator.

MILLER, CLAUDE (1942–). Actor, director, producer, and screenwriter. Claude Miller studied at the **Institut des Hautes Études Cinématographiques** (IDHEC) before becoming an assistant to **Marcel Carné**, **Robert Bresson**, **Jacques Demy**, and **Jean-Luc Godard**, among others. He worked as production manager for **François Truffaut**, who is often viewed as Miller's mentor. He was nominated for a **César** for Best Director for his first three features, *La Meilleure* *façon de marcher* (1976), *Dîtes-lui que je l'aime* (1977), and the thriller *Garde à vue* (1981). He won a César for Best Screenplay for *Garde à vue* in 1982, and it was later remade in Hollywood as *Under Suspicion* (2000).

Miller also received nominations for Best Director for his fifth and sixth films, *L'effrontée* (1985)—which won the **Prix Louis-Delluc**—and *La petite voleuse* (1988), which he completed for Truffaut after his death in 1984. *La classe de neige* (1998) won the Jury Prize at the **Cannes Film Festival** in 1998. Miller was nominated for a Golden Palm at Cannes and a César for Best Director for *La petite Lili* (2003). He also directed *Mortelle randonée* (1983), *L'accompagnatrice* (1992), *Le sourire* (1994), and *Betty Fisher et autres histoires* (2001).

MILTON, GEORGES (1888–1970). Actor. Georges Milton was born Georges Désiré Michaud. He began his career in the Parisian café-concerts and was reportedly encouraged by Maurice Chevalier. Milton was primarily a singer. He had a great deal of success singing popular songs and was a star in the interwar years. He began his film career in the silent era, appearing in **Henri Diamant-Berger**'s *Gonzague (*1922), but since he could not sing in silent film, he left screen acting largely for the advent of sound.

Milton returned to the screen in the 1930s and had a fair degree of popular success during that decade and the one that followed. He appeared in such films as Pierre Colombier's *Le Roi des resquillers* (1930) and *Le Roi du cirage* (1931), **Léon Mathot**'s *La Bande à Bouboule* (1931), *Embrassez-moi* (1932), *Nu comme un ver* (1933), *Bouboule 1er, roi nègre* (1933), and *Le Comte Obligado* (1934), **André Hugon**'s *Famille nombreuse* (1934) and *Gangster malgré lui* (1935), Marc Didier's *Le Billet de mille* (1934), **Abel Gance**'s *Jérôme Perreau héros des barricades* (1935), Jacques Hossin's *Les Deux combinards* (1937) and *Le Prince Bouboule* (1939), and Robert Hennion's *Ploum ploum tra la la* (1947) and *Et dix de der* (1948). Primarily a comic actor, Milton is best known for his incarnation of the comic figure Bouboule.

MIOU-MIOU (1950–). Actress. Born Sylvette Herry, Miou-Miou (the stage name was given to her by French comedian **Coluche**) began her career in the early 1970s. She had bit parts in films such as **Georges Lautner**'s *Quelques messieurs trop tranquilles* (1973), Gérard Pirès's *Elle court, elle court la banlieue* (1973), and **Gérard Oury**'s *Les Aventures de Rabbi Jacob* (1973), before being cast in **Bertrand Blier's** *Les Valseuses* (1974). The film became a French classic, and Miou-Miou instantly became a star. She made more than sixteen films in the 1970s alone, including Lautner's *Pas de problème!* (1975) and *On aura tout vu* (1976), Jean-Pierre Blanc's *D'amour et d'eau fraîche* (1976), Alain Tanner's *Jonas qui aura 25 ans en l'an 2000* (1976), and **Claude Miller**'s *Dîtes-lui que je l'aime* (1977), in which she played opposite **Gérard Depardieu**, her costar in *Les Valseuses*. In 1979, she appeared in *La Dérobade*, a film for which she won a **César** for Best Actress.

Miou-Miou continued to be a star in the 1980s. She appeared in a number of films, including Yves Boisset's *La Femme flic* (1980) and *Canicule* (1984), Lautner's *Est-ce bien raisonnable?* (1981) and *Attention! Une femme peut en cacher une autre* (1983), Michel Drach's *Guy de Maupassant* (1982), **Bertrand Blier**'s *Tenue de soirée* (1986), and **Michel Deville**'s *La Lectrice* (1988). In 1983, she gave what was considered one of her best performances in Diane Kurys's semi-autobiographical film, *Coup de foudre*. This gained her a great deal of international attention, as the film was nominated for an Academy Award for Best Foreign Film. She became known as an actress well suited to play atypical **women**, frail and helpless on the surface, yet who are capable of uncommon strength. Her 1988 performance in *La Lectrice* is a case in point.

In the 1990s, Miou-Miou continued to appear regularly in film. She had a number of acclaimed roles, most notably in **Louis Malle**'s *Milou en mai* (1990), **Patrice Leconte**'s *Tango* (1993), **Claude Berri's** epic version of Émile Zola's *Germinal* (1993), and Anne Fontaine's *Nettoyage à sec* (1997), a role written for her. The decade also marked something of a slowdown in her film career, as she redirected her energies toward political activism. She has continued to act but reduced her schedule from the four to five films per year she once did. Since 2000, she has appeared in several films, including Claude Mouriéras's *Tout va bien, on s'en va* (2000), Dominique Cabrera's *Folle embellie* (2004), and Berri's *L'Un reste, l'autre part* (2005). Her most recent films are Michel Gondry's *The Science of Sleep*

(2006), Gérald Hustache Mathieu's *Avril* (2006), and Thierry Klifa's *Le Héros de la famille* (2006). Director Anne Fontaine once called Miou-Miou "the most popular actress of her generation." Fontaine's characterization is for the most part true, since, even in semiretirement, Miou-Miou remains one of the most widely recognized of French screen actresses.

MIRANDE, YVES (1875–1957). Actor, director, and screenwriter. One of the great screenwriters of French cinema, Yves Mirande had a career that began in the silent-film era and lasted until just before his death. Mirande actually began his career in the theater, writing popular plays in what the French term the *théâtre du Boulevard*. He got his start in cinema as a result of the demand to adapt his plays for the screen, and he went on to become a major screenwriter and occasional director.

During the silent era, a number of films were based on Mirande's plays, including **Léonce Perret**'s *La Tournée des grands ducs* (1909), **André Hugon**'s *Le Chignon d'or* (1916), starring **Harry Baur** and **Mistinguett**, **Roger Lion** and Nicolas Rimsky's *Le Chasseur de chez Maxim's* (1927), Robert Péguy's *Embrassez-moi* (1928), and Robert Boudrioz's *Trois jeunes filles nues* (1929).

The 1930s and 1940s were the peak of Mirande's screenwriting years, and it was during this period that he began working directly on screenplays rather than simply allowing his theatrical plays to be adapted for the screen. Mirande's work during the period was largely in popular films. He did not work in the more avant-garde tradition, or in the vein of *Le Réalisme poétique* or poetic realism, although he did work with both **Julien Duvivier** and **Jacques Feyder**. Among the films for which Mirande wrote the screenplays are Feyder's *Si l'empereur savait ça* (1930) and *Oympia* (1930), Robert Wyler's *Papa sans le savoir* (1931) and *La Merveilleuse journée* (1932), which Mirande codirected, **René Guissart**'s *La Chance* (1931), *Tu seras duchesse* (1932), *Ménilmontant* (1936), and *À nous deux, madame, la vie* (1936), which Mirande codirected, **Léon Mathot**'s sound remake of *Embrassez-moi* (1932), Pierre Colombier's *Charlemagne* (1933), Marc Didier's *Le Billet de mille* (1934), **Léo Joannen**'s *Quelle drôle de gosse* (1935) and *Le Train de plaisir* (1936), Edmond T. Greville's *Princesse Tam Tam* (1935), Duvivier's *Un carnet de bal* (1937), Jean

Boyer's *Circonstances attenuantes* (1939), **Georges Lacombe**'s *Derrière la façade* (1939), which Mirande codirected, and *Elles étaient douze femmes* (1940), Hugon's *Moulin Rouge* (1940), **Robert Vernay**'s *La Femme que j'ai la plus aimée* (1942), **Jacques de Baroncelli**'s *Soyez les bienvenus* (1942), and René Le Henaff's *Des jeunes filles dans la nuit* (1943).

In addition to codirecting, Mirande directed and wrote several films, including *Baccara* (1935), *Sept hommes, une femme* (1936), *Messieurs les ronds de cuir* (1936), *Café de Paris* (1938), *Paris-New York* (1940), and *Moulin Rouge* (1941). He also made a satirical film titled *L'An 40* in 1941, but that film was banned by the government after only one screening. Mirande also tried his hand at acting with a few small roles in Karl Anton's *Le Chasseur de chez Maxim*'s (1933), Lacombe's *Derrière la façade* (1939), and Raymond Leboursier's *Les Petits riens* (1942). Mirande's material was still being produced in the cinema long after his death. The most recent example of a film using his work was Claude Vital's remake of *La Merveilleuse journée* (1980).

MISTINGUETT (1872–1956). Actress. Born Jeanne Bourgeoise, Mistinguett aspired to be a performer from an early age. She made up her stage name as a child and made her theatrical debut in 1895 while not much more than a child. Mistinguett had a long career in the Parisian theater and café-concerts. She was one of the great stars of French cabaret and had a successful career as a recording artist. She was known throughout the world and was probably the most famous female entertainer of the day. She came to the screen with the intent of making herself a film star.

Mistinguett appeared in more than forty films during her career. She made her screen debut in the starring role in Henri Burguet's silent film *L'Empreinte ou la main rouge* (1909), in which she starred opposite Max Dearly, with whom she had worked in the music halls and the theater. Other films in which Mistinguett starred include the uncredited films *Ce bon docteur* (1909), *L'Enlèvement de Mademoiselle Biffin* (1909), *Un mari qui l'échappe belle* (1909), *L'Oubliée* (1912), *Léocadie veut se faire mannequin* (1911), and *La Fiancée recalcitrante* (1909). She appeared in several films directed by **Albert Capellani**, including *La Vagabonde* (1911), *L'Épouvante* (1911), *La Glu* (1913), the four-part series *Les Misérables* (1913), and *Fleur de pavé* (1909), codirected with Michel Carré. She also appeared in Georges Denola's *Zizi la bouquetière* (1910), *La Ruse de Miss Plumcake* (1911), *La Bonne à tout faire* (1911), *La Moche* (1912), and *La Folle de Penmarch* (1912) and **Georges Monca**'s *Les Timidités de Rigadin* (1910), *Agence Alice ou la sécurité des ménages* (1910), *La Cabotine* (1911), *Le Coup de foudre* (1912), *Bal costumé* (1912), *La Vocation de Lolo* (1912), *Une bougie recalcitrante* (1912), and *La Valse renversante* (1914). Other silent films she appeared in include **André Hugon**'s *La Chignon d'or* (1914), *Sous la menace* (1916), *Fleur de Paris* (1916), *Mistinguette détective* (1917), and *Mistinguette détective II* (1917) and **Henri Diamant-Berger**'s *Une soirée mondaine* (1917). Mistinguett was known for her legs and her stage routines, and several of the films in which she appeared featured both.

Mistinguett more or less disappeared from the screen from 1917 until 1928, when she had a small role in Berthe Dagmar and **Jean Durand**'s *Île d'amour* (1928). She had only two roles in speaking films. She appeared in **Christian-Jacque**'s *Rigolboche* (1936) and the Italian film *Carosello del varietà* (1955), her final film. Mistinguett was nearly as famous for her love life as she was for her performance career. She was reputed to have been the mistress of the king of Spain and Prince Edward, the future Edward VII of England. She was also the longtime companion of the much younger Maurice Chevalier, her costar at the Folies-Bergères. She remains a legend of the French music-hall and the silent screen.

MITRY, JEAN (1907–1988). Actor, director, and film historian. Jean Mitry was attracted to a career in cinema out of a sheer love of the medium. As a young man, he had attended *ciné-clubs*, and in 1928, he worked as an assistant director to **Pierre Chenal**. Mitry went on to direct. His films include *Pacific 231* (1949) and *Énigme aux Folies-Bergère* (1959). He also went on to try his hand at acting, appearing in Jean Renoir's *La Nuit du carrefour* (1932), and at screenwriting, writing the dialogue for Pierre Weill's *Trois dans un moulin* (1936).

Ultimately Mitry would decide that sharing his passion for the cinema was his calling. He became a professor at the **Institut des Hautes Études Cinématographiques** (IDHEC) when it was founded in 1945. He also cofounded the *Cinémathèque Française* with **Henri Langlois** and **Georges Franju**. Perhaps Mitry's most important contribution to film, however, is his enormous film history, titled *Filmographie universelle*. He also published a theoretical work on the cinema, titled *Esthétique et psychologie du cinéma*. Mitry died in 1988.

MOCKY, JEAN-PIERRE (1929–). Actor, director, producer, and screenwriter. Jean-Pierre Mocky was born Jean-Paul Adam Mokiejewski in Nice. His screen-acting debut was in Jeff Musso's *Vive la liberté* in 1944. Afterward, he had a number of small roles in films such as Pierre Billon's *L'Homme au chapeau rond* (1946), Jean Stelli's *La Cabane aux souvenirs* (1947), and Jean Dréville's *Les Casse-pieds* (1948). He also had an uncredited part in **Jean Cocteau**'s *Orphée* (1950). Mocky later acted in French and Italian films, including Michelangelo Antonioni's *I Vinti* (1953), Giorgio Bianchi's *Graziella* (1954), Francesco Maselli's *Gli sbandati* (1955), **Robert Vernay**'s *Le Compte de Monte-Cristo* (1955), and Gilles Grangier's *Le rouge est mis* (1957).

In the late 1950s, Mocky branched out from acting to try his hand at directing. His first film was *La tête contre les murs* (1958), in which he appeared and for which he also cowrote the script. Under the orders of the producers, the film was completed by director Georges Franju. After *La tête contre les murs,* Mocky acted only in his own films with a few notable exceptions. He appeared in **Jean-Luc Godard**'s *Prénom Carmen* (1983) and Godard's television film *Grandeur et décadence d'un petit commerce de cinéma* (1986).

Mocky's first completed film as a director was *Les Dragueurs* (1959), with **Charles Aznavour** and Jacques Charrier. It was followed by *Un couple* (1960), starring Francis Blache, who played principal roles in Mocky's *Snobs* (1961), *La grande lessive* (1968), and *L'Étalon* (1969). *Les vièrges* (1962) also featured Aznavour and French playwright and actor Jean Poiret. Mocky began a fruitful collaboration with the beloved comic actor **Bourvil** in *Un drôle de paroissien* (1963), which was nominated for a Golden Berlin Bear. Bourvil also starred in *La grande frousse* (1964), *La grande lessive*, and *L'Étalon*. Another megastar of French comedy, **Fernandel**, would lead the cast of Mocky's *La Bourse et la Vie* (1965) with Poiret.

Mocky's early career was defined in part by his work with famous comedians. In his later career he would become known for his black humor. In the 1970s and beyond, Mocky worked continuously with Jean Poiret and with actors Jacques Dufhilo, **Richard Bohringer**, and especially Michel Serrault. Serrault would lead in Mocky's *Les Compagnons de la Marguerite* (1966), *L'Ibis rouge* (1975), *Le Roi des bricoleurs* (1977), *À mort l'arbitre!* (1983), *Le Miraculé* (1986), *Ville à vendre* (1991), *Bonsoir* (1993), *Le Furet* (2003), and *Grabuge!* (2005).

During the 1970s, Mocky began taking major roles in many of his films, among them *Solo* (1970), *L'Albatros* (1972), *L'Ombre d'une chance* (1974), *Un linceul n'a pas de poches* (1975), *Le piège à cons* (1979), *La Machine à découdre* (1985), *Mocky Story* (1991), *Le Mari de Leon* (1992), *Vidange* (1997), *La Candide Madame Duff* (1999), *Tout est calme* (1999), *Le Glandeur* (2000), *La Bête de miséricorde* (2001), and *Les Araignées de la nuit* (2001). Mocky's *Litan* won the Clavell de Plata at the Catalonian International Film Festival in 1982. His *Le Miraculé* was nominated for a Golden Berlin Bear in 1987.

MODE RÉTRO. The **Mode Rétro** is a name given to a trend in films made in the late 1960s and early 1970s on the subject of the Nazi Occupation of France in World War II. The mode was a tendency to deal openly with the issue of the Occupation and with French collaboration with the Occupation. It is interesting in that it lasted only for a few short years, and it ran in direct contrast to the dominant mode of writing, thinking, and filming about the Occupation, called *resistancialisme* by historian Henry Rousso.

Resistancialisme is the name given to the French tendency to depict resistance to the Nazis as the standard mode adopted by the French, and this view of the Occupation was inaugurated by none other than Charles de Gaulle on the eve of the Liberation. Films seen as belonging to the **Mode Rétro** include **Marcel Öphuls**'s *Le Chagrin et la pitié* (1968), which some critics have seen as inaugurating the trend and **Louis Malle**'s *Lacombe Lucien* (1971). **François Truffaut**'s *Le Dernier métro* (1980) is seen by some critics as the last film of the mode rétro and by others as the first film to shift the trend back toward representations of resistance. A very late example of this sort of film is Jacques Audiard's *Un héros très discret* (1996), which was made

just before the trial of Maurice Papon for war crimes and collaboration. That trial arguably put a final end to resistancialisme. A parallel
mode has been seen to exist in literature from the same period.

MOLINARO, ÉDOUARD (1928–). Director and screenwriter.
Edouard Molinaro began his filmmaking career in the 1950s. A contemporary of the directors of the *Nouvelle Vague* or New Wave,
Molinaro seemed little influenced by the aesthetics and poetics of
these directors and is often considered to be a commercial filmmaker
rather than a New Wave **auteur**. His first film was *Les Alchimistes*
(1957), and it was followed by *Le dos aux murs* (1958), featuring
Jeanne Moreau and **Gérard Oury**, and *Des femmes disparaissent*
(1959), starring Robert Hossein.

Molinaro is best known for his internationally successful film *La
Cage aux folles*, which was France's best-selling film in 1978. Based
on a play by Jean Poiret and starring Michel Serrault alongside Italian actor Ugo Tognazzi, *La Cage aux folles* is frequently cited in
studies of cinematic representations of homosexuality, camp, and
comedy. It was nominated for an Oscar in 1980 and was remade in
Hollywood as *The Birdcage*. Its sequel, *La Cage aux folles 2* (1980),
was also very popular.

Molinaro has directed a number of other French blockbusters, in-
cluding *Oscar* (1967), starring the beloved comic actor **Louis de
Funès**, *Hibernatus* (1969), also with de Funès, *Mon oncle Benjamin*
(1969), and *L'Emmerdeur* (1973). Although not a member of the
New Wave, he collaborated with several of its icons. He codirected
Les Sept Péchés capitaux with **Claude Chabrol**; **Jean-Claude Brialy** starred in his *Arsène Lupin contre Arsène Lupin* (1962) and *La
Chasse à l'homme* (1964); and **Brigitte Bardot** played the lead in
Une ravissante idiote (1964). However, he has repeatedly expressed
dissatisfaction with these films and seems to wish not to be defined
by commercial success.

Molinaro worked with some of France's best-known actors, among
them Serrault, who played in *La Cage aux folles*, *La Cage aux folles
2*, *Quand passent les faisans* (1965), and *La Liberté en croupe*
(1970). He has also worked with **Lino Ventura** in films such as *Un
témoin dans la ville* (1959). **Annie Girardot** starred in *La Mandarine*
(1971) and *Cause toujours . . . tu m'intéresses!* (1979). **Daniel Au-**

teuil acted in *Pour cent briques t'as plus rien* (1982), *Palace* (1985), and *L'Amour en douce* (1985). **Claude Brasseur** starred in *Palace* and *Le Souper* (1992). Molinaro directed an American film, *Just the Way You Are* (1984), starring Kristy McNichol. His most recent films for the cinema to date are the **heritage film** *Beaumarchais l'insolent* (1995) and *Le Mal de mère* (2001).

MONCA, GEORGES (1888–1940). Actor, director, and screenwriter. Georges Monca began his career in the theater. He was an established actor who went on to become the director of the Théâtre de la République. Monca was recruited by **Pathé** in 1908 to act in and direct films for the studio; however, he quickly gave up screen acting to focus on directing. He made nearly three hundred films during the course of a career that spanned five decades. Nearly all of his films were done in the silent era, and although Monca is probably best remembered for his comedies, he directed a wide array of films.

Early in his directing career, Monca worked on the legendary Boireau *burlesque* series, when he codirected *Les Apprentisages de Boireau* (1907) with **Albert Capellani**. The film starred the legendary comic actor **André Deed**. This experience probably led Monca to try to resurrect the *Boireau* series after Deed left Pathé for Italy. He directed three episodes, *Boireau—deux vieux amis de collège* (1908), *Boireau—Consentement forcé* (1908), and *Boireau a mangé de l'ail* (1908), all featuring Paul Berthot in the title role. However, the public was not receptive to the series without its star.

Monca was also responsible for the highly successful *Rigadin* comic series, which ran from 1909 until 1919, and which starred comic actor **Charles Prince**. There were more than one hundred films made in the *Rigadin* series, including *Rigadin* (1909), *Rigadin et ses fils* (1911), *Rigadin a perdu son monocle* (1911), *Rigadin aux Balkans* (1912), *Rigadin et la poudre de l'amour* (1912), *Rigadin veut faire du cinéma* (1913), *Rigadin Napoléon* (1913), *Rigadin mauvais ouvrier* (1914), *La Nuit de noces de Rigadin* (1914), *Le Divorce de Rigadin* (1915), *Rigadin n'est pas un espion* (1915), *L'Or de Rigadin* (1916), *Rigadin, méefie-toi des femmes* (1916), *Les Deux Rigadins* (1917), *L'Épervier de Rigadin* (1918), *Rigadin a fait un riche mariage* (1918), *La Femme de Rigadin* (1918), and *Rigadin dans les Alpes* (1919).

Monca also did a number of very successful films featuring French music-hall diva **Mistinguett**. Monca's Mistinguett films include *Agence Alice ou la sécurité des ménages* (1910), *Le Clown et le pacha* (1911), *L'Abîme* (1911), *La Cabotine* (1911), *Le Coup de foudre* (1912), *Bal costumé* (1912), *La Vocation de Lolo* (1912), *Une bougie recalcitrante* (1912), and *La Valse renversante* (1914).

Other films Monca directed include *Un monsieur qui suit les dames* (1908); *Le Soulier trop petit* (1909), starring **Max Linder**; *Les Deux orphelines* (1909); *Jim Blackwood jockey* (1909); *Les Femmes collantes* (1910); *La Cigale et la fourmi* (1910); *Le Secret du passé* (1911); *La Fille des chiffonniers* (1912), starring **Jean Kemm**; *Le Petit chose* (1912); *Trois femmes pour un mari* (1913); *La Goualeuse* (1914), codirected with Alexandre Devarennes; *En Famille* (1915); *Le Malheur qui passe* (1915), starring Gabrielle Robinne; *Le Mot de l'énigme* (1916); *La Mort du duc d'Enghien* (1916); *La Proie* (1917); *Les Feuilles tombent* (1917); *Chantelouve* (1921); *Judith* (1921); *Altemer le cynique* (1924); *L'Ironie du sort* (1924); and *Autour d'un berceau* (1925) and *Le Chemineau* (1926), both codirected with Maurice Kéroul.

In addition to directing during the silent era, Monca also acted in several films, including **Lucien Nonguet**'s *Victime de sa probité* (1908) and *Le Roman d'un malheureux* (1908), Capellani's *Riquet à la houppe* (1908), and his own *Le Sourire de Rigadin* (1916). He also wrote the screenplays for a number of the films he directed.

Monca made only a handful of sound films. He was one of the masters of the silent film and found it difficult to adapt to the use of sound. His sound films include *La Chanson du lin* (1931), *La Roche aux mouettes* (1933), *Une nuit de noces* (1935), codirected with Kéroul, *Trois jours de perm'* (1936), and *Le Choc en retour* (1937), his final film, which was also codirected with Kéroul.

MONTAND, YVES (1921–1991). Actor. Yves Montand was born Ivo Levi in Monsumano, Italy. His parents were antifascist and migrated to Marseille. Montand left school at the age of eleven and held a number of working-class jobs, including factory worker and docker. He became a singer in the night clubs of Marseille when he was in his late teens and then moved to Paris, where he sang at the Moulin Rouge. There he met Edith Piaf, who would become one of his mentors and legendary lovers. He appeared with Piaf in Marcel Blistène's film, *Étoile sans lumière*, in 1946. That same year, he had a supporting role in **Marcel Carné**'s *Les Portes de la nuit* (1946).

During the late 1940s, Montand was in the United States with actress **Simone Signoret**, whom he married, and who would remain his partner until her death in 1985. He returned to France, became a very popular music-hall singer, and developed a parallel acting career. His breakthrough role was in **Henri-Georges Clouzot**'s *Le Salaire de la peur* (1953). He went on to appear in **Sacha Guitry**'s *Napoléon* (1954) and **Claude Autant-Lara**'s *Marguerite de la nuit* (1955).

During the 1950s and 1960s, Montand and Signoret worked in between France and Hollywood. They were turned away from the United States during the McCarthy era, because of their leftist political leanings, but Montand later returned to perform as a singer in New York. He went from Broadway to Hollywood and costarred with Marilyn Monroe in George Cukor's *Let's Make Love* (1960). He also had a notorious affair with Monroe. Montand led the casts of subsequent Hollywood films. He costarred with Ingrid Bergman in Anatole Litvak's *Goodbye Again* (1961) and with Shirley MacLaine in Jack Cardiff's *My Geisha* (1962).

Montand's international reputation was established through his collaboration with **Costa-Gavras**, notably in the film *Compartiment tuers* (1964), *Z* (1969), and *L'Aveu* (1970). He also worked with **Alain Resnais** on *La Guerre est finie* (1966), with **Claude Lelouch** on *Vivre pour vivre* (1967), with Vincente Minnelli in *On a Clear Day You Can See Forever* (1970), with **Gérard Oury** on *La folie des grandeurs*, and with **Jean-Luc Godard** on *Tout va bien* (1972). He also had a supporting role alongside fellow icons **Alain Delon** and **Bourvil** in **Jean-Pierre Melville**'s *Le Cercle rouge* (1970).

In addition to his work with Costa-Gavras, Montand was also a favorite of director **Claude Sautet**. He appeared in a number of Sautet's films, beginning with *César et Rosalie* (1972), which also starred Signoret. He also played principal roles in Sautet's *Vincent, François, Paul et les autres* (1974). Other films in which he appeared include **Alain Corneau**'s *La Menace* (1977) and Joseph Losey's *Les Routes du sud* (1978). He received a **César** nomination for Best Actor in **Henri Verneuil**'s 1979 film *I comme Icare*. In 1979, he also starred in Costa-Gavras's *Clair de femme* with Signoret.

In the 1980s, Montand appeared less frequently in films. Nevertheless, he delivered several acclaimed performances and remained a French icon. In 1984, he received a second César nomination for Best Actor in Sautet's *Garçon!* He received critical acclaim for his work in **Claude Berri**'s *Jean de Florette* (1986) and its sequel *Manon des sources* (1986). He served as president of the **Cannes Film Festival** Jury in 1987. He also played himself in **Jacques Demy**'s *Trois places pour le 26* (1988), which perhaps points to his status in French culture. He also appeared in Jacques Deray's *Netchaïev est de retour* (1991). Montand died during the shooting of **Jean-Jacques Beineix**'s *IP5 : l'île aux Pachydermes* (1992).

MOREAU, JEANNE (1928–). Actress, director, and screenwriter. Jeanne Moreau was born in Paris, the daughter of a French father and British mother. She studied at the Conservatoire d'art dramatique in Paris with Denis d'Inès. She became a stage actress at the Festival d'Avignon, where she worked under theater director Jean Vilar and with actor **Gérard Philipe**. She also acted at the Comédie-Française and the Théâtre National Populaire. Moreau debuted in cinema in Jean Stelli's *Dernier amour* (1949). Some of her early leading roles were in **Jacques Becker**'s acclaimed *Touchez pas au grisbi* (1954), Jean Dréville's *La Reine Margot* (1954), Gilles Grangier's *Gas-oil* (1955), and **Edouard Molinaro**'s *Le Dos au mur* (1957). Her career as an art-house film star and her image as a femme fatale were launched with her performance in **Louis Malle**'s *Ascenseur pour l'échafaud* (1957). She also starred in Malle's *Les Amants* (1958) and acted again with Gérard Philipe in **Roger Vadim**'s *Les liaisons dangereuses* (1959).

In 1960, she won Best Actress at the **Cannes Film Festival** for her performance in Peter Brook's *Moderato Cantabile*. In that decade Moreau became famous for her seductive, intellectual persona in films by *Nouvelle Vague* or New Wave and **auteur** directors. Some of her most memorable starring roles were in **François Truffaut**'s *Jules et Jim* (1962) and *La mariée était en noir* (1968), Joseph Losey's *Eva* (1962), **Jacques Demy**'s *La Baie des anges* (1963), and Luis Buñuel's *Le journal d'une femme de chambre* (1964). She is also a singer and performed the theme song for *Jules et Jim*, titled "Le Tourbillon de la vie." She played a singer in **Jean Renoir**'s television film, *Le petit théâtre de Jean Renoir*. Moreau furthered her international prestige in Michaelangelo Antonioni's *La Notte* (1960), Orson Welles's *The Trial* (1962) and *Chimes at Midnight* (1965), and John Frankenheimer's *The Train* (1964), among others. She costarred with Welles in his *Immortal Story* (1967). She worked again with Malle in *Le feu follet* (1963) and *Viva Maria* (1965); the latter costarred **Brigitte Bardot**. Critics have contrasted Moreau's cerebral allure and professional expertise with Bardot's supermodel status. Indeed, although Bardot was a role model for **women** who wished to express their sexuality freely, her fame hinged largely on her beauty. Moreau was the ultimate model, being at once freely seductive, independent, adventurous, and smart.

In the 1970s, Moreau played significant parts in **Marguerite Duras**'s *Nathalie Granger* (1972), **Bertrand Blier**'s *Les Valseuses* (1973), **André Téchiné**'s *Souvenirs d'en France* (1975), and Joseph Losey's *Monsieur Klein* (1975). She also acted with Robert De Niro and Tony Curtis in Elia Kazan's *The Last Tycoon* (1975). Moreau headed the jury at Cannes in 1975. In 1976, she made her directorial debut with the feature *Lumière*, which she scripted. Later in the decade, she directed and coscripted *L'Adolescent* (1978). It was nominated for a Golden Berlin Bear. In the 1980s, Moreau directed one documentary—*Lillian Gish*—in 1984. She played leading roles in Losey's *La Truite* (1982) and **Michel Drach**'s *Sauve-toi, Lola* (1986) and was nominated for a **César** for Best Actress in **Jean-Pierre Mocky**'s *Le Miraculé* (1987). In 1992, she won the César for Best Actress in Laurent Heynemann's *La Vieille qui marchait dans la mer*.

Moreau continued to enchant film audiences throughout the 1990s and beyond. Her role as Amande in **Luc Besson**'s *Nikita* (1990) recalled the character of Catherine in Truffaut's *Jules et Jim* (1962), the film for which she is best known. She provided the voiceover for Jean-Jacques Annaud's *L'amant* (1992), a film adapted from Duras's novel. She would later play Duras in Josée Dayan's *Cet amour-là* (2001). She had much in common with Duras, who was, herself, something of a sultry intellectual, a type that is a bit uncommon in the cinema. Moreau also played principal roles in Theo Angelopoulos's *The Suspended Step of the Stork* (1991), Guy Jacques's *Je m'appelle Victor* (1993), and Ismail Merchant's *The Proprietor* (1996).

More recently, Moreau appeared in François Ozon's *Le Temps qui reste* (2005) and Serbian director Ahmed Imamovic's *Go West* (2005). She is expected to appear in Zoe R. Cassavetes's film *Broken English*, scheduled for release in 2007. Moreau was awarded a Career Golden Lion at Venice in 1992, an honorary César for her life's work in 1995, an honorary Golden Berlin Bear in 2000, and an honorary Golden Palm at Cannes in 2003. She has performed in over one hundred films.

MORGAN, MICHÈLE (1920–). Actress. Born Simone Roussel near Paris, Michèle Morgan aspired to become an actress from an early age. She studied drama with René Simon in Paris and found bit parts in films. Among her early and largely uncredited roles were parts in **René Guissart**'s *Une fille à papa* (1935), Yvan Noé's *Mademoiselle Mozart* (1935) and *Gigolette* (1936), Léonide Moguy's *Le Mioche* (1936), and Robert Siodomak's *La Vie parisienne* (1936).

Morgan's big break came in 1937, when **Marc Allegret** cast her opposite **Raïmu** in his film *Gribouille* (1937). Her reputation was cemented the following year when she starred opposite **Jean Gabin** in **Marcel Carné**'s *Le Quai de brumes* (1938). The film has long been considered one of her best and best known. With these two films, in particular, Morgan, a classic beauty and a talented actress, became an international star, and she went on to become one of the great actresses of French cinema. Her film career ultimately spanned five decades.

During the late 1930s and 1940s, Morgan's star continued to rise. She appeared in many of the period's most significant films, including Allegret's *Orage* (1938), opposite **Charles Boyer**, Maurice Gleize's *Le Récif de corail* (1938), opposite Gabin, **Jacques Feyder**'s *La Piste du nord* (1939), Albert Valentin's *L'Entraîneuse* (1940), **Georges Lacombe**'s *Les Musiciens du ciel* (1940), opposite **Michel Simon**, **Jean Grémillon**'s *Remorques* (1941), again with Gabin, **Julien Duvivier**'s *Untel père et fils* (1943), alongside Raïmu and **Louis Jouvet**, and **Jean Delannoy**'s *La Symphonie pastorale* (1946) and *Aux yeux du souvenir* (1948), opposite **Jean Marais**.

Morgan also went to Hollywood during this period; however, she was not able to command the respect in Hollywood films that she did in French films. She appeared in a handful of English-language roles in such films as Lewis Milestone's *My Life with Caroline* (1941), Robert Stevenson's *Joan of Paris* (1942), Michael Curtiz's *Passage to Marseille* (1944), alongside Humphrey Bogart, Arthur Ripley's *The Chase* (1946), and Carol Reed's *The Fallen Idol* (1948). Ultimately, Morgan gave up on Hollywood and returned to France.

The 1950s were still peak years in Morgan's career. She appeared in more than twenty films during the decade. Among the best known are Allegret's *Maria Chapdelaine* (1950), **René Clément**'s *Le Château de verre* (1950), Grémillon's *L'Étrange Madame X* (1951), Delannoy's *La Minute de vérité* (1952), *Obsession* (1954), and *Marie-Antoinette reine de France* (1956), **Christian-Jacque** and De-lannoy's *Déstinées* (1954), **Sacha Guitry**'s *Si Paris nous était conté* (1955) and *Napoléon* (1955), **René Clair**'s *Les Grandes manœuvres* (1955), Denys de la Patellière's *Retour de manivelle* (1957), **André Cayatte**'s *Le Miroir à deux faces* (1958), **Henri Verneuil**'s *Maxime* (1958), Robert Hossein's *Les Scélérats* (1959), and **Henri Decoin**'s *Pourquoi viens-tu si tard?* (1959). In addition, Morgan did several international films, particularly in Italy and Germany.

Although her career was in slowdown by the 1960s, Morgan managed to find roles in a number of films, including Alex Joffé's *Fortunat* (1960), Verneuil's *Les Lions sont lâchés* (1961), Philippe Agostini's *Rencontres* (1962), **Gérard Oury**'s *Le Crime ne paie pas* (1962), **André Hunébelle**'s *Méfiez-vous, mesdames!* (1963), **Claude Chabrol**'s *Landru* (1963), Hossein's *Les Yeux cernés* (1964), and **Michel Deville**'s *Benjamin* (1968). She had only one film role in the 1970s, in Chabrol's *Le Chat et la souris* (1975). In the 1980s and 1990s, Morgan worked primarily in television, and she did not have a single credited role in a French film. She retired from the screen in 1999.

MORLAY, GABY (1893–1964). Actress. Born Blanche Fumoleau, Gaby Morlay began her career during the silent-film era and established herself as an actress with staying power, building a career that lasted five decades. In 1915, she was hired on at **Pathé**, where she made her name starring opposite **Max Linder** in his *Max* films. She appeared in such Linder films as *Le Vacance de Max* (1913), *Le 2 août, 1914* (1914), and *Max dans les airs* (1914). Morlay was such a hit that she was granted her own eponymous series, including such films as *Gaby en auto* (1917), *Pour épouser Gaby* (1917), and *Le Chevalier de Gaby* (1920), all directed by Charles Burguet. She also went on to appear in more than twenty other silent films including René Le Somptier's *Les Épaves de l'amour* (1917), Burguet's *Au paradis des enfants* (1918), *La Mendiante de Saint-Sulpice* (1922), and *Faubourg Montmartre* (1924), Bernard-Deschamps's *L'Agonie des aigles* (1922), **Louis Feuillade**'s *Le Fils du filibustier* (1922), Pierre Colombier and **Roger Lion**'s *Jim la houlette, roi des voleurs* (1926), and **Jacques Feyder**'s *Les Nouveaux messieurs* (1929).

Morlay easily made the transition from silent to sound cinema. In fact, the peak of her career was the period dating from the beginning of sound cinema to the Liberation. Her first speaking roles were in films such as Maurice Tourneur's *Accusée, levez-vous* (1930) and *Maison de danses* (1931), **Léonce Perret**'s *Après l'amour* (1931), and Raymond Bernard's sound remake of *Faubourg Montmartre* (1931). She appeared in nearly fifty other films during the period, including Perret's *Il était une fois* (1933), **Abel Gance** and Fernand Rivers's *Le Maître de forges* (1933), Marc Didier's *Le Billet de mille* (1934), **Marcel L'Herbier**'s *Le Scandale* (1934), *Le Bonheur* (1934), *Nuits de feu* (1937), *La Mode rêvée* (1939), and *Entente cordiale* (1939), Tourneur's *Samson* (1936), Colombier's *Le Roi* (1936), Viktor Tourjansky's *La Peur* (1936), Félix Gandéra's *Les Grands* (1936), **Marc Allegret**'s *Les Amants terribles* (1936) and *L'Arlésienne* (1942), Jean Dréville's *Les Nuits blanches de Saint-Petersbourg* (1937), **Sacha Guitry**'s *Quadrille* (1938) and *Le Destin fabuleux de Désirée Clary* (1942), **Georges Lacombe** and **Yves Mirande**'s *Derrière la façade* (1939), **Léon Mathot**'s *Le Bois sacrée* (1939), Lacombe's *Elles étaient douze femmes* (1940), Mirande's *Paris-New York* (1940), **Jean Delannoy**'s *Le Diamant noir* (1941), Jean Stelli's *Le Voile bleu* (1942) and *L'Enfant de l'amour* (1944), René Le Henaff's *Des jeunes filles dans la nuit* (1943), and Yvan Noé's *La Cavalcade des heures* (1943).

After the Liberation, Morlay was investigated for collaboration with the Nazis. This was less from anything she may have personally done than for the fact that she had long been involved with the politician Max Bonnafous, who served in the Vichy government. Morlay and Bonnafous later married, and her career survived the scandal. She remained an important actress for the remainder of the 1940s and much of the 1950s. Among the films in which she appeared are André Zwaboda's *Farandole* (1945), Maurice de Canonge's *Dernier métro* (1945), Allegret's *Lunegarde* (1946), Stelli's *Mensonges* (1946), **Henri Decoin**'s *Les Amants du pont Saint-Jean* (1947), **Jacqueline Audry**'s *Gigi* (1949) and *Mitsou* (1956), Charles Félix-Tavano's *Ève et le serpent* (1949), **André Hunébelle**'s *Millionnaires d'un jour* (1949) and *Les Collégiennes* (1957), **Max Opüls**'s *Le Plaisir* (1952), Guitry's *Si Versailles m'était conté* (1954), **Jean Grémillon**'s *L'Amour d'une femme* (1954), **Jean-Paul Le Chanois**'s *Papa, maman, la bonne et moi . . .* (1954) and *Papa, maman, ma femme et moi . . .* (1956), **Robert Vernay**'s *Les Lumières du soir* (1956), Georges Lampin's *Crime et châtiment* (1956), Léonide Moguy's *Donnez-moi ma chance* (1957), André Berthomieu's *Sacrée jeunesse* (1958), and **Pierre Schoendoerffer**'s *Ramuntcho* (1959).

In addition to her work in France, Morlay spent a good deal of time, particularly during the 1950s, in Italy, where she made a number of films. Her career did not extend much beyond the 1950s in either country, however. She appeared in only two films in the 1960s, Alex Joffé's *Fortunat* (1960) and Le Chanois's *Monsieur* (1964), which was her final film before dying of cancer.

MORLHON, CAMILLE DE (1869–1952). Director, film pioneer, and producer. Born Louis Camille de la Valette de Morlhon to an aristocratic family, Camille de Morlhon began his career as a playwright. He had a fair degree of success in the theater, writing largely comedies. He met **Léon Gaumont** through their mutual interest in automobiles, and it was Gaumont who encouraged Morlhon to consider the cinema. Morlhon wrote and directed the film *Sous l'uniforme* for **Gaumont Studios** in 1908. However, the studio found the film too politically charged since it seemed to evoke the Dreyfus Affair, and Morlhon left and went to **Pathé**. Originally, Pathé hired Morlhon to do literary adaptations. However, he soon developed a *film d'art* style of directing, and his subjects moved beyond simple literary adaptation to classically influenced historical films and orientalist dramas. He also did the typical farcical comic films that were popular at the time. Morlhon went on to make more than 150 silent films, and he was one of the most significant of the early film directors. Many of his silent films were later remade by other directors during the sound era.

While at Pathé, Morlhon made such films as *Quand l'amour veut* (1908), *Un tic gênant* (1908), *Benvenuto Cellini* (1908), *Le Roman de l'écuyère* (1909), *Conscience de miséreux* (1909), *La Récompense d'une bonne action* (1909), *Le Fer à cheval* (1909), *Cœur de Gavroche* (1909), *Mater Dolorosa* (1909), *La Belle Niçoise* (1909), *Mademoiselle Faust* (1909), *Olivier Cromwell* (1909), *La Gueuse* (1909), *L'Affaire du collier de la reine* (1910), *Le Spectre du passé* (1910), *Une aventure secrète de Marie-Antoinette* (1910), *Cagliostro* (1910), codirected with **Gaston Velle**, *Le Tyran de Jérusalem* (1910), *Une intrigue à la cour d'Henri VIII* (1911), *Une conspiration sous Henri III* (1911), *Britannicus* (1912), *Vengeance Kabyle* (1912), *La Haine de Fatimeh* (1912), *Un mariage sous Louix XV* (1912), and *Le Fils prodigue* (1912).

Morlhon left Pathé in 1912 to found his own production company, Valetta films. He went on to direct such films as *La Calomnie* (1913), *Don Quichotte* (1913), *L'Usurier* (1913), *Le Faux père* (1915), *Sous l'uniforme* (1915), *La Marchande de fleurs* (1915), *Cœur de Gavroche* (1916), *Le Secret de Geneviève* (1916), *Fille d'artiste* (1916), *Marise* (1917), *Miséricorde* (1917), *Expiation* (1918), *Simone* (1918), *L'Ibis bleu* (1919), *Une fleur dans les ronces* (1921), and *Tote* (1923). Although produced independently, these later films were still distributed by Pathé.

The war put a virtual end to Morlhon's film production. When he resumed directing, it was after the arrival of sound. He did not, however, have much success with sound film and made only one film, *Roumanie, terre d'amour* (1930). At that point, he gave up the cinema and went into radio, writing and producing radio plays, seeming to do better with sound but no image than with sound and image.

In addition to directing, Morlhon wrote the screenplays for nearly all of his films. In his capacity as a screenwriter, he had a significant impact on the film industry. He actively lobbied for author's rights to films, and in 1917, he founded *La Société des Auteurs de Films* to help screenwriters obtain the rights to their work.

MOULOUDJI (1922–1994). Actor. Born in Paris to an Algerian Kabyle father and a French mother, Marcel Mouloudji grew up in a working-class household. His mother was an alcoholic who had to be institutionalized, and Mouloudji was raised by his father. Through his father's connections to the Communist Party, Mouloudji was introduced to the *Groupe Octobre*, and it was through that group that he came to the theater and then the cinema.

Mouloudji began his career on the stage, working with Jacques Prévert and **Jean-Louis Barrault**, whom he had met through the Groupe Octobre. He got his first film role in 1936, when Prévert introduced him to **Marcel Carné**, who then cast him in his film *Jenny* (1936). That same year, Mouloudji also appeared in **René Guissart**'s *Ménilmontant* (1936) and Jacques Daroy's *La Guerre des gosses* (1936). He went on to become an established supporting actor, appearing in more than thirty films during the 1930s, 1940s, and 1950s. He worked frequently with director **Christian-Jacque**, appearing in *À Venise, une nuit* (1937), *Les Disparus de Saint-Agil* (1938), *Le Grand élan* (1939), *L'Enfer des anges* (1941), *Premier bal* (1941), and *Boule de suif* (1945). Probably his best-known role is in André Cayatte's *Nous sommes tous des assassins* (1952). He also worked with Cayatte on the film *Justice est faite* (1950).

Among the other films in which Mouloudji appeared are Alexandre Ryder's *Mirages* (1937), **Serge de Poligny**'s *Claudine à l'école* (1937), **Henri Decoin**'s *Les Inconnus dans la maison* (1942), Jean Dréville's *Les Roquevillard* (1943) and *Les Cadets de l'océan* (1945), André Berthomieu's *Ange de la nuit* (1944), Alexander Esway's *Le Batallion du ciel* (1947), **Jean Delannoy**'s *Les Jeux sont faits* (1947), **Henri Calef**'s *Bagarres* (1948) and *Les Eaux troubles* (1949), **Henri Diamant-Berger**'s *La Maternelle* (1949), **Sacha Guitry**'s *La Vie d'un honnête homme* (1953), **Maurice de Canonge**'s *Boum sur Paris* (1954), Decoin, Delannoy, and Ralph Habib's *Les Secrets d'alcove* (1954), Pierre Billon's *Jusqu'au dernier* (1957), and **Pierre Chenal**'s *Rafles sur la ville* (1958). Like other actors such as **Marcel Dalio**, Mouloudji's origins likely kept him from becoming a more prominent actor. He was often typecast as the Jew or the criminal. He was a talented actor, and in another era he might have had lead roles.

In addition to acting, Mouloudji was also a talented singer. Although he first became interested in singing during the Occupation, when forced to flee to the *Zone Libre* in the South of France he did not establish himself in the field until the 1950s. He wrote and recorded numerous songs and became quite successful. In 1980, a performance of him singing at the Olympia was broadcast on French television. Although he did not appear in film after 1960, Mouloudji did continue to act in the theater. He is the father of actress and singer Annabelle Mouloudji.

MOUSSINAC, LÉON (1890–1964). Film critic, historian, and theorist. A childhood friend of avant-garde filmmaker **Louis Delluc**, Léon Moussinac went on to become a significant film critic and film theorist. Known for his ties to the Communist Party, Moussinac was significant in introducing the French public to Russian film through his *ciné-club*, *Les Amis de Spartacus*, which he cofounded with his brother-in-law **Jean Lods**. Moussinac also introduced the French public to the writings of several Russian film theorists, most notably Sergei Eisenstein. Through his own writings in magazines and in his essays *Naissance du cinéma* (1925), *Le Cinéma soviétique* (1927), *Panoramique du cinéma* (1928), *L'Âge ingrat du cinéma* (1946), and *Sergei Eisenstein* (1963), he promoted a socially engaged cinema grounded in avant-garde poetics.

Moussinac had originally intended to be a writer, but after service in World War I, he began to focus his attention on the cinema. In 1920, he founded the cinema section of the respected literary magazine *Le Mercure de France* and was the primary contributor to that section until 1928. In 1932, he also created a special cinema supplement to the left-leaning newspaper *L'Humanité*. He also founded his own film journal, *Cinéa*. After World War II, Moussinac became closely involved in the teaching of cinema through his involvement with various French film schools, including the **Institut des Hautes Études Cinématographiques** (IDHEC). He served as the director of IDHEC from 1947 until 1949. The ***Prix Léon-Moussinac***, given annually to the best foreign film, is named for him.

MOUSSINAC PRIZE. *See* PRIX LÉON-MOUSSINAC.

MURAT, JEAN (1888–1968). Actor. Born in the picturesque town of Périguex, Jean Murat went on to become a matinee idol of the 1930s. He began his career near the end of the silent era, appearing in such films as **Jean Legrand**'s *Souvent femme varie* (1923), **Roger Lion**'s Portuguese film *Os Ohlos da Alma* (1924), as well as Lion's *La*

Fontaine des amours (1924), *Les Fiançailles rouges* (1926), and *La Nuit est à nous* (1929), **Henri Andréani**'s *L'Autre aile* (1924), Maurice Champreux and **Louis Feuillade**'s *Le Stigmate* (1924), **Jacque Catelain**'s *La Galerie des montres* (1924), **Jacques Feyder**'s *Carmen* (1926), **René Clair**'s *La Proie du vent* (1927), **Jacques de Baroncelli**'s *Le Duel* (1928), **Julien Duvivier**'s *La Divine croisière* (1929), and **Louis Mercanton**'s *Venus* (1929). He also appeared in a number of German-made films.

It was during the sound era, however, that Murat came into his own as an actor. He had little trouble transitioning to sound film, and he suddenly found himself cast as a lead actor rather than a supporting actor. Ironically, however, this had less to do with his voice than his looks. In 1930, he appeared in **Marcel L'Herbier**'s *La Femme d'une nuit* (1930) along with Antonin Artaud. The following year, he appeared in René Barberis's *Un trou dans le mur* (1931) and had starring roles in André-Paul Antoine's *La Folle aventure* (1931), Wilhelm Thiele's *Dactylo* (1931), and Hanns Schwarz and Max de Vaucorbeil's *Le Capitaine Craddock* (1931).

Murat was a leading man from 1932 until well into the 1940s. He appeared in a variety of films ranging from avant-garde productions to mystery films to romantic comedies. He starred in such films as Baroncelli's *Le Dernier choc* (1932), Kurt Gerron and Roger Le Bon's *Stupéfiants* (1932), André Berthomieu's *Mademoiselle Josette, ma femme* (1933), **Jean Epstein**'s *L'Homme à l'hispano* (1933) and *La Châtelaine du Liban* (1934), Feyder's *La Kermesse héroïque* (1935), **Christian-Jacque**'s *La Sonnette d'alarme* (1935), Anatole Litvak's *L'Équipage* (1935), Raymond Bernard's *Anne-Marie* (1936) and *J'étais un aventurier* (1937), **Pierre Chenal**'s *Les Mutinés d'Elseneur* (1936), **Léon Mathot**'s *L'Homme à abattre* (1937), Maurice de Canonge's *Le Capitaine Benoît* (1938), Jean de Limur's *Le Père Lebonnard* (1939), Richard Pottier's *Mademoiselle Swing* (1942), Jean Choux's *La Femme perdue* (1942), **Jean Delannoy**'s *L'Éternel retour* (1943), and Henri Calef's *Bagarres* (1948).

In the 1950s, Murat returned to supporting actor status. Nonetheless, he was able to find roles in several significant films. He appeared in Jean Stelli's *La Nuit est à nous* (1953), Jean-Devaivre's *Alerte au sud* (1953), **Jacqueline Audry**'s *Huis clos* (1954), **Sacha**

Guitry's *Si Versailles m'était conté* (1954), **Marc Allegret**'s *L'Amant de Lady Chatterly* (1955), **Jean-Paul Le Chanois**'s *Les Misérables* (1958), and Denys de la Patillière's *Les Grandes familles* (1958), among others. Murat had only a handful of roles in the 1960s. He appeared in **Philippe de Broca** and **Claude Chabrol**'s *Les Sept péchés capitaux* (1962), Andrew Marton's *It Happened in Athens* (1962), and two Italian films, Daniel d'Anza's *I Piaceri des sabato notte* (1960) and Carlo Campogalliani and Piero Pierotti's *Il Ponte dei sospiri* (1964). Murat retired from the screen in 1964. He was married to the actress Annabella.

MUSIDORA (1889–1957). Actress, director, and screenwriter. Born Jeanne Roques in Paris in 1889, Musidora got her start on the stage. She was a successful cabaret performer before making her debut in cinema in Raphaël Clamour's *Les Misères de l'aiguille* (1913). She was almost immediately afterward lured to **Gaumont,** where she made films almost exclusively under the direction of **Louis Feuillade**. She appeared in Feuillade's *Le Calvaire* (1914), *Severo Torelli* (1914), *Le Sosie* (1915), *Union sacrée* (1915), and *Les Fiançailles d'Agénor* (1916), among other films. Of course, her most famous films with Feuillade are those in the series *Les Vampires*, made from 1915 to 1916, a series of which Musidora's character, Irma Vep, was the undisputed star. She also starred in Feuillade's *Judex* series, which ran in 1917. She also starred in **André Hugon**'s *Les Chacals* (1917), *Johannès fils de Johannès* (1918), and *Mademoiselle Chiffon* (1919), among other films.

Musidora's influence on the cinema cannot be measured in terms of the mere number of films in which she appeared. Her role as Irma Vep in Feuillade's *Les Vampires* (1915) was an important precursor to the femme fatale, and she was one of the first obviously sexual and sexualized **women** to appear onscreen. That she often portrayed powerful, independent, working women is not insignificant, nor is the fact that her characters were inscribed as overtly threatening to the social order. Musidora often embodied onscreen the growing unease over the rapid changes in society as a result of modernity—the place of woman in society being central to those changes. She marks the beginning of a long trajectory of the exploration of these issues in cinema.

Although she is not credited, it seems Musidora also contributed to the screenplays of several of the films in which she appeared. She also turned her hand to directing, making *Pour Don Carlos* (1920) and *Soleil et ombre* (1922), with Jacques Lasseyne, and directing *Vincenta* (1919) and *La Terre des taureaux* (1924) among other films. She disappeared from the screen in the 1920s, perhaps a victim of sound. She spent her time after cinema writing (she published two novels and a play) and publishing her memoirs. In 1951, she directed and appeared in *La Magique de l'image*, a retrospective on silent film dedicated to Feuillade.

– N –

NAPIERKOWSKA, STACIA (1886–1945). Actress and director. Born Renée Claire Elisabeth Napierkowska in Paris of Polish parents, Stacia Napierkowska went on to become one of the great actresses of silent film. She was trained in classical dance and theater and performed on the stage before making her film debut. Napierkowska was hired on at **Pathé** in 1908. She made her film debut in Henri Burguet's *L'Empreinte ou la main rouge* (1908) alongside other theatrical stars like **Mistinguett** and Max Dearly.

Napierkowska was a favorite of director **Albert Capellani**, who cast her in several of his films, including *L'Arlésienne* (1909), *La Peau de chagrin* (1909), *Lucrèce Borgia* (1909), *L'Assomoir* (1909), *La Zingara* (1910), *Tristan et Yseut* (1911), *Notre Dame de Paris* (1911), *Les Mystères de Paris* (1911), and *Un amour de La Du Barry* (1912). She also worked frequently with director **René Leprince**, starring in his films *La Légende des tulipes d'or* (1912), *Le Reprouvé* (1912), *Le Miracle des fleurs* (1912), and *Les Martyrs de la vie* (1912).

Among her other films at Pathé are the uncredited *Le Fils du saltimbanque* (1908), Charles Esquier's *La Fille du saltimbanque* (1909), Michel Carré's *L'Oeuvre de Jean Serval* (1909), **Ferdinand Zecca** and **Henri Andréani**'s *Cléopatre* (1910) and *La Tragique aventure de Robert le taciturne, duc d'Aquitaine* (1910), Andréani's *La Messaline* (1910), **Gaston Velle**'s *Le Charme des fleurs* (1910), *Au temps des pharaons* (1910), Velle and **Camille de Morlhon**'s

Cagliostro, aventurier, chimiste et magicien (1910), Morlhon's *Semiramis* (1911), Zecca and Leprince's *La Fièvre de l'or* (1912), and Leprince and Maurice Mahut's *Le Roi du bagne* (1913).

Napierkowska appeared alongside Pathé's great star **Max Linder** in a number of his Max films, including *Amour tenace* (1912), *Max veut grandir* (1912), *Max et la fuite de gaz* (1912), *Max émule de Tartarin* (1912), *Max lance la mode* (1912), *Max peintre par amour* (1912), *Max escamoteur* (1912), *Une nuit agitée* (1912), *Entente cordiale* (1912), *Un mariage au téléphone* (1913), and *Max toréador* (1913). She also did several films for **Gaumont** during the period between 1910 and 1915. She worked with **Louis Feuillade** on *Le Festin de Balthazar* (1910) and his landmark series *Les Vampires* (1915). She also appeared in her friend **Germaine Dulac**'s film *Venus victrix* (1916).

From 1915 until 1920, Napierkowska worked exclusively in Italy. There she made nearly twenty films and was the star of them all. She also directed one film, *L'Héritière de la manade* (1917). She returned to France in 1920 to star in **Jacques Feyder**'s legendary silent film *L'Atlantide* (1920), which is probably her most famous role. After *L'Atlantide*, she appeared in Henri Étiévant's *La Fille de Camargue* (1921), Théo Bergerat's *La Douleureuse comédie* (1921), Marco de Gastyne's *Inch'Allah* (1922), Albert-Francis Bertoni's *Les Frères Zemganno* (1925), and Fred LeRoy Granville's *Le Berceau de dieu* (1926). Napierkowska retired from the screen in 1926 after having appeared in more than eighty films.

NAPOLÉON VU PAR ABEL GANCE **(1927).** Film. Directed by Abel Gance, this sweeping biopic of Napoléon Bonaparte was a silent film that ran six hours and forty minutes at the time of its release in April 1927. Immediately hailed as a classic, the film nearly bankrupted the studio company that produced it. Apart from its heroic depiction of one of France's great heroes, the film has passed into legend because of the technical and cinematic innovations used in making the film, innovations that have had a lasting impact on the direction of cinema.

The film depicts Bonaparte's life from boyhood through his early career. It was intended to be the first in a series of four films, but it was so expensive Gance could never find funding for the other parts. Much of the expense went to cover Gance's numerous technological innovations, which range from the use of the moving camera (mounted on horseback during a battle scene) to the use of Polyvision, a system of filming that involved the use of three cameras working simultaneously. In projection, Polyvision required a three-screen panoramic projection system in order to show what each of the cameras had filmed.

Gance shot the film on location in Corsica, France, and Italy and includes spectacular battle scenes that employed thousands of extras. In addition to the grandeur of the subject and the numerous technical innovations employed by Gance, *Napoléon* is considered a classic because of the epic mode in which it was filmed. His camerawork is highly impressionistic, relying on techniques such as montage to convey the historical spirit (a Republican spirit in Gance's vision) of the future emperor. Many, however, including such prominent critics as **Léon Moussinac**, were troubled by Gance's glorification of the emperor. Such critics regard the film as romanticizing totalitarianism.

Criticism aside, the film was largely overlooked for decades because it happened to be released the same year synchronized sound came to the cinema, at which point silent film was all but forgotten. Interest in the film in recent years, however, has been running high. It was reedited in the 1970s by film historian Kevin Brownlow and screened in reedited form for the first time in 1981. The restoration reportedly took ten years to complete, and the Brownlow version is one of the most complete to be released since the original cut. A second re-edition of *Napoléon* was done with the backing of Francis Ford Coppola. This version features a score written by Coppola's father. It seems Coppola had originally backed Brownlow's version but refused to allow it to be released without his father's score. The shorter Coppola version of the film has also been released.

NATAN, BERNARD (1886–1942). Producer. Born Nathaniel Tanenzapf in Jassy, Romania, Bernard Natan came to France at the age of twenty. He found a job working as a projectionist in a movie theater, and it was this that sparked his interest in the cinema. In 1910, Natan embarked on the first in a series of ventures designed to gain access to the French film industry. He and several friends formed a small production company called Ciné Actualités, but it produced only a small number of films. In 1913, Natan opened a film processing company called Rapid Films. This venture was more successful, and the company became one of the major film processors in France.

Natan's entrepreneurial drive was interrupted in 1914 when he volunteered to serve in World War I, despite having no obligation to do so (he still held Romanian citizenship). He served from 1914 until 1918 and was decorated with the Croix de guerre. Upon being discharged, Natan set about expanding Rapid Films, acquiring space for the operation and adding editing and producing capacity. He also became a naturalized French citizen in 1921. In 1924, he again ventured into full-scale film production, this time with more success. He formed the production company Les Productions Natan with director **Henri Diamant-Berger** and with John Maxwell. The company produced a number of films, including Henry Roussel's *Destinée* (1925), **Marco de Gastyne**'s *La Châtelaine du Liban* (1926), *La Merveilleuse vie de Jeanne d'arc* (1929), and *La Madone des sleepings* (1927), codirected by Maurice Gleize, **Léonce Perret**'s *La Femme nue* (1926) and *Printemps d'amour* (1927), Maurice Champreux's *Les Cinq sous de Lavarède* (1927), and Diamant-Berger's *Éducation de prince* (1927).

In 1928, Natan undertook his most ambitious venture. He acquired a controlling interest in **Pathé Studios**, which **Charles Pathé** had begun progressively selling off. It seems, although it is not certain, that Pathé had sought the buyout by Natan in order to fend off a financial crisis or a foreign takeover. Natan merged Pathé with Rapid Films and added the assets and facilities of Productions Bernard Natan. He also began buying up cinemas and cinema chains in order to centralize film distribution. Natan changed the name of the studio from Pathé to **Pathé-Natan**, keeping the old prestige but announcing a new era.

As the studio's managing director, Natan turned Pathé into the most significant studio and production and distribution company in France. He also ushered Pathé into the era of sound, producing the first sound films in France. Pathé-Natan was highly successful. Natan was forward looking and he began to acquire radio outlets in order to expand Pathé-Natan's audience as well as to experiment with television. However, the financial problems he had inherited when he bought out Pathé, legal issues related to the sale of the studio, and the crash of the stock market led to some financial problems and particularly cash-flow problems. These problems were heightened by financial problems at the bank that had financed the takeover and expansion. These issues caught the attention of Charles Pathé himself, who was under investigation for the processes by which he had sold Pathé. The company was publicly held, and Pathé may not have given shareholders their fare share. This provoked lawsuits by the shareholders, and Pathé, partly to defend himself and partly, it seems, to regain control of the studio, began a campaign of lies and misinformation against Natan. Thus began what is almost certainly one of the darkest episodes in French cinema history.

Pathé, and perhaps several investors, sought to forcibly wrest control of the studio from Natan. Pathé, it seems, also sought to shift blame for his own mismanagement to the studio's new controlling partner. In order to achieve these aims, he and his associates began a long and very nasty, clearly anti-Semitic propaganda campaign against Natan. Among the nasty lies spread through the press and elsewhere was the rumor that Natan had been embezzling large sums of money from the studio and that the studio was, therefore, insolvent. Despite the fact that there was no truth to any of these claims, the French government put the studio in receivership. Natan was driven out of the company, and ownership was given to the investors of a group called the Société Nouvelle Pathé Cinéma.

Natan attempted to continue producing films on his own. He managed to produce several films, most notably **Pierre Chenal**'s *La Maison du Maltais* (1938) and Bernard's *Cavalcade d'amour* (1940). However, in the end, the campaign against Natan cost him more than his reputation and more than his studio. It cost him his life. He was arrested in 1938, tried and convicted on the accusations leveled against him by Pathé and his associates, convicted, stripped of his citizenship, turned over to the Nazis, and sent to Auschwitz, where he died in 1942. This all occurred despite the fact that the review of the finances of Pathé-Natan disproved all of the charges against Natan and demonstrated that the studio had always been profitable. Long after Natan's death, however, the idea persisted that he was a criminal and an embezzler and that he had nearly run the studio into the ground, only to have it saved by its founder and his associates. It is only in very recent years that Natan's true contributions have been recognized and that the process of clearing his name was begun.

NATANSON, JACQUES (1901–1975). Director and screenwriter. Born in Asnières, Jacques Natanson started his career as a playwright and went on to become one of the most popular screenwriters of the 1930s, 1940s, and 1950s. Natanson's plays were largely popular in the vein of the *comédie du boulevard*, and he brought something of that with him to the screen. He started working in film in the early 1930s, cowriting on such films as Carmine Gallone's *Un soir de rafle* (1931) and Augusto Genina's *Ne sois pas jalouse* (1932). Natanson worked on the screenplays of more than thirty films, including Pierre Billon and Kurt Gerron's *Une femme au volant* (1933), Jean de Limur's *Paprika* (1933), Viktor Tourjansky's *L'Ordonnance* (1933) and *Les Yeux noirs* (1935), Alexis Granowsky's *Les Nuits muscovites* (1934) and *Tarass Boulba* (1936), **Jacques de Baroncelli**'s *Michel Strogoff* (1935), **Marcel L'Herbier**'s *Forfaiture* (1937), **Max Ophüls**'s *De Mayerling à Sarajevo* (1940), *La Ronde* (1950), *Le Plaisir* (1952), and *Lola Montès* (1955), Richard Pottier's *Vertige* (1947), and Ralph Habib's *La Rage au corps* (1954).

In addition to screenwriting, Natanson also tried his hand at directing. He made four films in total. The first was *La Fusée* (1933), and it was followed by *Maître Bolbec et son mari* (1934), *Le Clown Bux* (1935), and *Les Gais lurons* (1936). His success as a director was not spectacular, and he focused his efforts on writing after 1936.

Natanson has the distinction of being an artistic screenwriter with popular appeal. Several of the films he worked on can well be considered avant-garde, most notably those of Ophüls. However, a number of the films he worked on were also successful with audiences. The French writer Colette, who was popular and literary herself, once said of Natanson that he was one of the most gifted writers of his generation. That reputation has held.

NAVARRE, RENÉ (1877–1968). Actor and director. Born in Limoges, René Navarre became one of the great stars of silent film. He got his start at **Gaumont** in 1911, and from the beginning he worked closely with **Louis Feuillade**. He starred in more than sixty films at Gaumont, and nearly all were directed by Feuillade. Among the Feuillade films in which Navarre appeared were *La Vie telle qu'elle est* (1911), *Quand les feuilles tombent* (1911), *Le Poison* (1911), *Aux lions les Chrétiens* (1911), *André Chenier* (1911), which Feuillade codirected with **Étienne Arnaud**, *Les Vipères* (1911), *Le Mort vivant* (1912), *L'Anneau fatale* (1912), *L'Homme de proie* (1912), *La Hantise* (1912), *Un scandale au village* (1913), codirected with Maurice Mariaud, *Les Audaces de coeur* (1913), codirected with **Léonce Perret**, *Erreur tragique* (1913), *Le Secret du forçat* (1913), *Le Revenant* (1913), *Le Guet-apens* (1913), *L'Écrin du rajah* (1913), *La Gardienne du feu* (1913), *La Petite Andalouse* (1914), *Le Diamant du sénéchal* (1914), *Manon de Montmartre* (1914), *Pâcques rouges* (1914), and *Le Calvaire* (1914).

Without any doubt, however, Navarre's most famous role was in Feuillade's *Fantômas* series, which ran in 1913 and 1914. Navarre played the title character, and in many ways he was Fantômas, bring to life the slippery evil genius mastermind of a diabolical criminal gang. Given the longstanding reputation of the *Fantômas* series as one of the classics of the silent cinema and one of the most important and influential film series ever made, it is not an exaggeration to say that Navarre himself passed into legend with his role in *Fantômas*.

Navarre left Gaumont in 1915, the year in which he was mobilized for service in World War I. He was discharged shortly after, at which point he founded his own production company, Films René Navarre, for which director **Henri Diamant-Berger** and director and producer Serge Sandberg both directed films. Navarre, himself, also tried his hand at directing during this period, making such films as *Le Document secret* (1918), *Tue la mort* (1920), *Le Sept de trèfle* (1921), *La Reine lumière* (1921), *L'Homme aux trois masques* (1921), and *L'Aiglonne* (1921).

Navarre also returned to acting, appearing in more than twenty films between 1918 and 1946, including **Jean Kemm**'s *Vidocq* (1922), **Gaston Ravel**'s *Le Gardien du feu* (1924), Mariaud's *Mon oncle* (1925), Luitz-Morat's *Jean Chouan* (1926), in which he starred, Maurice Champreux's *Judex 34* (1934), Diamant-Berger's *Arsène Lupin, détective* (1935), **Léon Mathot**'s *Chéri-bibi* (1937), Jean Dréville's *Son oncle de Normandie* (1938), Pierre Caron's *Bécassine* (1940), and Maurice de Canonge's *Les Trois tambours* (1946). During this second phase of his career, Navarre was primarily a supporting actor. Like many other silent film-era actors, he found it difficult to maintain his profile in a medium that had changed dramatically.

NEW WAVE. *See* NOUVELLE VAGUE/NEW WAVE.

NONGUET, LUCIEN (1868–?). Director. Lucien Nonguet was a stage manager in the Parisian theater before he came to cinema, no doubt through his connections to former theatrical personalities like **Ferdinand Zecca** (both had ties to the Théâtre de l'Ambigu). Nonguet was hired on at **Pathé** as a director and assistant to Zecca in 1901, and the two began a series of important collaborations. The first of these was *Quo Vadis* (1901) based on the novel by Henryk Sienkiewicz, and this was shortly followed by the much lighter and more magical *féerie, La Belle au bois dormant,* in 1902. The best known of the Zecca/Nonguet collaborations is the silent-film classic *La Vie et la passion de Jésus Christ* (1905), which presents the life of Christ in a series of epic tableaux.

Nonguet also made a number of films at Pathé working on his own. When working alone, he seemed to prefer either historical reconstructions or reconstructed *actualités*, and both types of films have similar characteristics. They are composed of a series of tableaux, they are filmed in long shots with no camera movement, and they are often based on photographs or paintings of the events depicted. Nonguet's historical films include *La Révolution en Russie* (1905), *Le Saint Barthélémy* (1905), on the infamous massacres during France's wars of religion, and the grand *Épopée Napoléonéenne* (1903), a sweeping, two-part epic of the life of Napoleon. *The Épopée Napoléonéenne* is of particular interest not only because of its popular success, but also because it seems to have been the model upon which Nonguet's later histories and actualités were based, and indeed upon which many Pathé histories and actualités were based.

Nonguet divided the film into two parts, one consisting of five tableaux depicting Napoleon's early life and childhood and the second composed of ten tableaux depicting his rise to power and the Empire. The tableaux are based on paintings of Napoleon by Jacques-Louis David, Horace Vernet, and others. It seems that Pathé composed the film so that the entire thing could be shown together or that any of the component tableaux or any combination of them could be shown separately, therefore maximizing the commercial potential of what must have been a rather expensive film to make. This structure was used again with *La Vie et la Passion de Notre Seigneur Jé-sus Christ* (1907) by Zecca.

An interesting exception to this trend in the historical reconstructions is *La Révolution en Russie,* which blends fictional scenes with real documentary footage, and features some variations in shot. This is a slightly later film, and it may show the influence of experimentation within the cinema as it began to evolve toward narrative.

In addition to reconstructed histories and actualities, Nonguet also made several burlesque films near the end of his film career, including films with silent-film icon **Max Linder**. These include *Idée d'Apache* (1906) and *Les Débuts du Max au cinéma* (1908). Nonguet also had a number of collaborations with other Pathé directors, most notably his 1908 collaboration with **Albert Capellani** on the remake of *La Belle au bois dormant*. Nonguet left Pathé in 1910 and went to work for **Éclair**. He made a handful of films with that studio and disappeared from view in 1920. His precise date of death is not known.

NOUVELLE VAGUE/NEW WAVE. The term "New Wave" or "*Nouvelle Vague*" in French refers to films made by a group of French directors during the 1960s and early 1970s. Typically included in the category of New Wave directors are **Jean-Luc Godard**, **Alain Resnais**, **Claude Chabrol**, **Jacques Rivette**, **Eric Rohmer**, **François Truffaut**, and **Agnès Varda**. **Louis Malle** is associated with the group and sometimes cited as a New Wave director. This group, particularly Godard, Rivette, Rohmer, and Truffaut, cultivated ideas about the cinema that were heavily influenced by French critic **André Bazin** and their work with him on the French film journal *Les Cahiers du cinéma*. Specifically, they inherited from Bazin and their time at the *Cahiers du cinéma* a disdain for films produced in France during the 1940s and 1950s—a cinéma that they termed the "*cinéma de papa*," a derogatory term for the *tradition de qualité* they considered stale, formulaic, tied to high production values, overly glossy, and downright dull.

For the New Wave directors, the filmmaker was an "**auteur**" or an author who created the film from nothing, and they believed that the work of individual filmmakers ought to display strong, distinctive characteristics that labeled their films as their own. They held up the films of earlier French film directors such as **Jean Vigo** and **Jean Renoir**, the Italian director Roberto Rossellini, and the British director Alfred Hitchcock as examples of auteurs.

In the beginning, the New Wave critics (as they were then) expressed their ideas about film in writing; however, in the late 1950s, as a result of new film subsidies offered by the French government, they turned to cinema as a means of demonstrating their vision of a new French cinema, and the New Wave of French cinema was born. Typically, the first films cited as New Wave are Claude Chabrol's *Le Beau Serge* and François Truffaut's *Les Quatre Cent Coups*, both in 1959, and Jean-Luc Godard's *A Bout de souffle* (1960). Some critics also point to **Agnès Varda**'s *La Pointe Courte* (1956; shot in 1954) as an important precursor to the New Wave. These were closely followed by films from the other New Wave directors, as well as new films by Truffaut and Godard.

There are certain shared narrative characteristics among the films considered New Wave. One is the influence of French existentialist philosophy. Nearly all of the New Wave films are character centered and feature a character most properly described as an antihero. These films focus on the alienation and marginalization experienced by the protagonist as he (or she) moves through a dysfunctional world in which he or she has no place. These films often end with the death of the protagonist, or at least with an ambiguous reference to that death. The films also share certain production characteristics. In keeping with their dislike of studio-produced films, the New Wave directors typically shot on location, quite often outside and frequently in locales that would not be considered worthy of filming in an industry dominated by high production values. The streets of working-class neighborhoods in Paris were a common choice for these directors. In this respect, the New Wave reflects the influence of a filmmaking practice that dates back to the silent films of **Louis Feuillade**, extends to *Le Réalisme poétique* or poetic realism, and is continued after the New Wave in the *cinéma de banlieue*. In addition to the interest in filming the city, there is also a tendency to avoid the seamless narration and invisible editing practices common to a more traditional narrative cinema.

Because the New Wave directors often relied on handheld cameras, they were able to draw attention to the presence of the camera by filming with a free camera that produced shaky, destabilized images. They also used unusual cuts and tracking shots that also point back to the presence of the camera. Quite often the actors and actresses played on the screen in such a way as to seem uncomfortable, often as though they were acting, or else they would improvise scenes not directly included in the film's screenplay. In Godard's work in particular such characteristics are evident, and he encouraged them often by not allowing the actors to know how the plot unfolded, or by not giving them a script at all.

Together, the New Wave directors made some forty to fifty films in a period of about five years. Truffaut, Godard, Chabrol, Rivette, and Rohmer alone made thirty-two films between 1959 and 1966. By 1966, which typically marks the end of the New Wave, the experimental filmmaking techniques of the New Wave had so permeated French cinema that most French film production at the time reflected some or all of the New Wave characteristics. At about the same time, many of the New Wave directors themselves began to move in different directions, and their films, therefore, became more different than alike. In this respect, the New Wave cannot really be said to have ended or disappeared in 1966. It is rather that the theory and technique behind the New Wave became absorbed into dominant filmmaking practice and therefore ceased to be new.

Apart from the technical and stylistic innovations attributed to the New Wave, the movement also made several other contributions to the development of French cinema. It has been convincingly argued, for example, that the New Wave films were very strongly influenced by a deep sense of political engagement during a period when censorship prevented direct political criticism (particularly about the ongoing Algerian War). Many have seen veiled references to that conflict and to the violence it engendered in the works of directors such as Godard. In this respect, the New Wave reinitiated the politically engaged cinema that had been abandoned by many French directors of the late 1940s and 1950s. What is more, the New Wave directors created a much more intellectually engaged cinema that removed film from the realm of popular entertainment and elevated it to the level of social and political debate, and most important art. In that respect, these directors are in many ways responsible for the privileged status film still enjoys in French culture.

– O –

OGIER, BULLE (1939–). Actress. Bulle Ogier was born Marie-Thérèse Thielland in Boulogne-sur-Seine. Her mother was a painter and her father a lawyer. She was a leading stage actress and pioneer, with Marc'O, of Parisian café-théâtres. She debuted in cinema in Marc'O's *Les Idoles* (1964). In the 1960s, she also acted in Jacques Baratier's *Piege* (1968), René Allio's *Pierre et Paul* (1969), and **Jacques Rivette**'s *L'Amour fou*. In the 1970s, she was noted for her work with Rivette in his *Out One: Noli mi tangere* (1971), *Out One: Spectre* (1972), *Céline et Julie vont en bateau* (1974), and *Duelle* (1976). She coscripted *Céline et Julie vont en bateau* and would later collaborate on the script of Rivette's *Le Pont du Nord* (1980).

Bulle acted three times under director **Marguerite Duras** in her *Des journées entières dans les arbres* (1977), *Le Navire night* (1979), and *Agatha et les lectures illimitées* (1981). She also appeared in films by her partner, Barbet Schroeder, including *La Vallée* (1972), *Maîtresse* (1976), and later *Tricheurs* (1984). Also in the 1970s, her career was enhanced by her roles in Louis Buñuel's *Le Charme discret de la bourgeoisie* (1972), **Claude Lelouch**'s *Mariage* (1974), **André Téchiné**'s *Pauline s'en va* (1975), and **Philippe Garrel**'s *Un ange passe* (1975).

In the 1980s, Ogier worked with emerging directors and in television productions in addition to collaborating with established cinéastes. She performed in Rivette's *Le Pont du Nord* and *La Bande des quatre* (1988), Robert Pansard-Bresson's *Le Rose et le blanc* (1980), Edouardo de Gregorio's *La Mémoire courte* (1982) and *Aspern* (1984), Raoul Ruiz's *Voyage autour d'une main* (1985), Manoel de Oliveira's *Mon cas* (1986), and Luc Bondy's *Terre étrangère* (1988). In 1984, she suffered from the tragic death of her daughter, actress Pascale Ogier, who died at the age of twenty-four after winning Best Actress at the Venice Film Festival for her role in **Éric Rohmer**'s *Les Nuits de la plein lune*.

In the 1990s and after, Ogier remains an energetic actress, appearing often in films by Europe's newer directors. She played in Xavier Beauvois's *Nord* (1991), Caroline Champetier's *Le Sommeil d'Adrian* (1993), Marion Vernoux's *Personne ne m'aime* (1993), Emmanuelle Cuau's *Circuit Carole* (1994), Marco Nicoletti's *Tout va mal* (1995), Olivier Assayas's *Irma Vep* (1995), Werner Schroeter's *Deux* (2001), Julie Lopes-Curval's *Bord de mer* (2001), Jean-Paul Civeyrac's *Toutes ces belles promesses* (2002), Olivier Vinuesa's *Le Mal de mer* (2004), Rivette's *Ne touchez pas la hache* (2006), and de Oliveira's *Belle toujours* (2006). She was nominated for a **César** Award for Best Supporting Actress in **Tonie Marshall**'s *Venus beauté (institut)* in 2000.

OPHÜLS, MARCEL (1927–). Director. Marcel Ophüls was born Marcel Oppenheimer in Frankfurt-am-Main, Germany, the son of director **Max Ophüls** and actress Hilde Wall. The family migrated to Paris in the early 1930s, and Marcel took French citizenship in 1938. He moved to the United States in the 1940s when his father was in exile and went to high school in Hollywood. In the mid-1940s, he worked for a theater unit in Tokyo during the American occupation of Japan. Ophüls returned to France in 1950 and studied philosophy at the Sorbonne. He worked as an assistant to several directors, including John Huston, Anatole Litvak, and his father. He directed his first short, the biographical *Matisse ou Le talent du bonheur*, which was released in 1960. He directed a few fiction films in the 1960s, including the sketch "Münich" for the film *L'amour à vingt ans* (1962). He also directed the comedy *Peau de banane*, starring **Jeanne Moreau** and **Jean-Paul Belmondo** (1964). His next feature was the action film *Feu à volonté* (1965), starring Eddie Constantine.

Above all, Marcel Ophüls is known for his historical documentaries. His famous and controversial ***Le chagrin et la pitié*** (1969) casts a critical lens on Occupied France. It was initially created for television yet was banned but circulated in cinema houses. Ophüls also directed the documentaries *A Sense of Loss* (1972), about Northern Ireland, and *The Memory of Justice* (1976), a documentary about the Nuremburg trials and simultaneously an investigation into French and American military activities in Algeria and Vietnam. He also worked for ABC and CBS News and taught at Princeton University. He resumed his directing career with a documentary about Klaus Barbie, *Hôtel Terminus* (1988). It won the Fédération Internationale de la Presse Cinématographique (FIPRESCI) Prize at **Cannes** in 1989 and the Oscar for Best Documentary in 1989. He subsequently directed *November Days* (1991), about Germany's reunification, and *Veillées d'armes: Histoire du journalisme en temps de guerre* (1994).

OPHÜLS, MAX (1902–1957). Director, producer, and screenwriter. Born Max Oppenheimer in Saarbrüken, Germany, Max Ophüls began his career on the stage. He started as an actor, and then went into directing theater, before becoming interested in cinema in the 1930s. He adopted the stage name "Ophüls" because it was an aristocratic name, no doubt to disguise his Jewish origins. The name was accepted to such a degree that members of the Ophüls family once contacted Ophüls to inquire to which members of the family he was related.

Ophüls began his film career assisting director Anatole Litvak on such films as *Nie wieder Liebe* (1931). He began directing on his own in 1931 while still in Germany. And he made a handful of German films before fleeing Germany for France in 1933. His German films include *Die Verliebte Firme* (1931), *Dann schon lieber Lebertran* (1931), *Die Verkaufte Braut* (1932), and *Liebelei* (1933), probably the best of the German films. These early films, predominantly comedies, already show some of the tendencies associated with Ophüls later in his career. There is a penchant for period pieces, an interest in music and art, a tendency to play with genre, an extreme attention to detail, particularly as regards staging and setting, and a careful focus on the visual. *Liebelei* (1933), which was actually released after Ophüls fled Germany, also introduces the theme of impossible love, which characterizes many of Ophüls's later films. Although *Liebelei* was released in Nazi Germany due to audience demand, Ophüls's name, aristocratic or not, was deleted from the credits since he was Jewish.

In France, Ophüls immediately took up directing, making the films *On a volé un homme* and *Une histoire d'amour* in 1933. He also made *Divine* (1935), *La Tendre ennemi* (1936), *Yoshiwara* (1937), *Werther* (1938), *Sans lendemain* (1939), and *De Mayerling à Sarajevo* (1940), as well as the shorts *Valse brillante de Chopin* (1936) and *Ave Maria* (1936), before fleeing France for the United States ahead of the Nazi Occupation. Ophüls also started an adaptation of Molière's *L'École des femmes* but had to abandon the film because leading man **Louis Jouvet** walked out on the project. In addition, he made *La Signora di tutti* (1934) in Italy and *Komedi om geld* (1936) in the Netherlands. While most of these films are solid works, none of them approaches what Ophüls would achieve in his second French filmmaking career after the war. Many of Ophüls's characteristic traits are present in these films, but the avant-garde spirit that dominates the later films is still not quite developed.

Ophüls had a turbulent time in Hollywood. He again set about working in cinema but had more trouble establishing himself than he had in France. He was hired by Howard Hughes to make the film *Vendetta*, and he had made most of the film when Hughes fired him in 1946. Preston Sturges, who also was hired as director, quit, and the film was finished by Mel Ferrer and released in 1950. Although Ophüls had directed all but a handful of scenes, including the ending of the film, his name appeared nowhere on the credits. The next year he made *The Exile* (1947), starring Douglas Fairbanks Jr. This film exhibits many of Ophüls's signature traits, including period setting and impossible love. Also evident is the beginning of Ophüls's visual style, marked by expressionistic use of the camera and particularly camera movement. Ophüls's next film was *Letter From an Unknown Woman* (1948), the first film to reflect his mature filmmaking style. It was probably the best of his Hollywood films. His final Hollywood films were *Caught* (1949) and *The Reckless Moment* (1949), both of which feature James Mason.

Subsequently Ophüls returned to France. This last stage of his career is considered his most artistically sophisticated, although by this point, Ophüls's style was so advanced it would take film critics and the filmgoing public a decade to catch up. His first film back in France was *La Ronde* (1950), an exploration of love and sex in turn-of-the-century Vienna. Featuring an all-star cast that included **Simone Signoret** and **Serge Reggiani**, the film, which uses a carousel as its visual and thematic center, was avant-garde but in a fairly mild way. It was a success, and was nominated for two Oscars and a British Academy of Film and Television Arts (BAFTA) award. The film also expanded Ophüls's exploration of love to include an exploration of sex versus love, a theme that would recur in all of his later films.

His next French film was *Le Plaisir* (1952), a sketch film featuring three related stories adapted from Guy de Maupassant's writings. The film also featured a star-studded cast, including **Pierre Brasseur**, **Danielle Darrieux**, **Jean Gabin**, **Ginette Leclerc**, and **Gaby Morlay**. Here, the exploration of sexual pleasure was more evident even than in *La Ronde*, as it formed the center of the film. It was followed by *Madame de . . .* (1953), starring Darrieux and **Charles Boyer**, another exploration of love, this time focusing on secrets kept. This is probably the weakest of Ophüls's late films.

Ophüls's final, completed film was *Lola Montès* (1955), starring **Martine Carol** in the title role. Based on the life of a nineteenth-century performer and courtesan, the film was boldly experimental in its use of color, its mixture of languages, its subject matter, and its camerawork. It was an extremely expensive film to make, and it was so ahead of its time that audiences did not understand it, critics did not like it, and it was an enormous commercial failure. The film nearly ruined Carol's career, and it might have been a black mark on Ophüls's legacy but for the fact that critics in later years, the critics associated with the *Nouvelle Vague* or New Wave, found an avant-garde spirit to the film that they felt lacking in almost all other films made in the 1950s. The film has passed into legend. Although it was by any standard a disaster when it was made, it has since become regarded as one of the great French films.

Ophüls had intended to make another film, *Les Amants de Montparnasse*, detailing the life of the artist Amedeo Modigliani. He died, however, while the film was being made, and it was finished by one of the other avant-garde directors of the day, **Jacques Becker**, and released in 1958. In addition to directing, Ophüls wrote or contributed to the screenplays of nearly every film he made. He was such a perfectionist that he even worked as cameraman on several of the films. He also produced one film, *Le Plaisir* (1952), although he is not credited in that regard. In addition to his own contributions to cinema, Ophüls was the father of filmmaker **Marcel Ophüls**.

– P –

PAGE, LOUIS (1905–1990). Cameraman and cinematographer. Born in Lyon, Louis Page began his career as a painter before turning to the cinema. He got his start in film as an assistant to **Jean Cocteau**

on the film *Le Sang d'un poète* (1930). Afterward he turned away from directing to cinematography, no doubt because of his ability to influence the visual elements of a film, and he is, in fact, known for his highly focused, nearly poetic film images. He is associated with **Le Réalisme poétique** or poetic realism of the 1930s, since he was the cinematographer for a number of directors associated with the movement. Page also worked with directors not associated with that movement, although nearly all of the directors with whom he worked in the 1930s had a strong interest in visual poetics. Among the 1930s films to which he contributed were **Marcel L'Herbier**'s *Le Parfum de la dame en noir* (1931), **René Clair**'s *Le Quatorze Juillet* (1933), **Jacques Feyder**'s *La Kermesse héroïque* (1935), Léonide Moguy's *Le Mioche* (1936), Pierre Billon's *Courrier sud* (1936) and *La Bataille silencieuse* (1937), **Jacques Becker**'s *La Vie est à nous* (1936), **Marcel Carné**'s *Drôle de drame* (1936) and *Le Quai de brumes* (1938), and **Pierre Chenal**'s *L'Affaire Lafarge* (1938).

In the 1940s, Page worked on far less well-known films; however his focus remained independent films, often with the same directors he had worked with in the 1930s. He also began to work on more commercially oriented films, particularly during the postwar period. Among those to which he contributed were Billon's *Le Soleil a toujours raison* (1943), **Jean Grémillon**'s *Lumière d'été* (1943), *Le Ciel est à vous* (1944), and his D-Day documentary *Le 6 Juin, à l'aube* (1945), **Marc Allegret**'s *L'Arlésienne* (1942) and *Félicie Nanteuil* (1945), André Malraux's *L'Espoir* (1945), André Zwoboda's *François Villon* (1945), **Christian-Jacque**'s *Sortilèges* (1946) and *Un revenant* (1946), **Georges Lacombe**'s *Le Pays sans étoiles* (1946), Marel Blistène's *Macadam* (1946), **René Clément**'s *Au-delà des grilles* (1949), and André Cayatte, Jean Dréville, **Henri-Georges Clouzot**, and Georges Lampin's *Retour à la vie* (1949).

During the 1950s and 1960s, Page worked largely in the popular cinema. The 1950s, in any case, are not known for having produced avant-garde cinema and Page was not associated with **La Nouvelle Vague** or the New Wave, the avant-garde movement of the 1960s. He did contribute to several well-known detective and crime films during the period, probably since the force and focus of his images lent themselves well to those genres. He worked, for example, on Gilles Grangier's *Le Rouge est mis* (1957), *Le Désordre de la nuit* (1958), and *Maigret voit rouge* (1963), **Jean Delannoy**'s *Maigret tend un piège* (1958) and *Maigret et l'affaire Saint-Fiacre* (1959), **Henri Verneuil**'s *Mélodie en sous-sol* (1963), and Alex Joffé's *La Grosse caisse* (1964).

Page's other focus during these decades was on drama, although he did do the occasional comedy. Films on which he worked include Lampin's *Les Anciens de Saint-Loup* (1950), **Louis Daquin**'s *Maître après Dieu* (1951), Grémillon's *L'Étrange Madame X* (1951) and *L'Amour d'une femme* (1954), Lacombe's *La Lumière d'en face* (1955), Verneuil's *Des gens sans importance* (1955) and *Le Président* (1961), Allegret's *En effeuillant la marguerite* (1955), Denys de La Patellière's *Les Grandes familles* (1958) and *Rue des Prairies* (1959), Gangier's *Archimède, le clochard* (1959) and *Le Cave se rebiffe* (1961), Delannoy's *Le Baron de l'écluse* (1960), **Jean-Paul Le Chanois**'s *Monsieur* (1964), and Pierre Prévert's *À la belle étoile* (1966), which was Page's final film. It is interesting to note that many of the films on which Page worked featured the great actor **Jean Gabin**, and it is, for the most part, Page's chiseled images of Gabin that have passed into memory.

PAGNOL, MARCEL (1895–1974). Director, producer, and screenwriter. Born in Aubagne along the southern coast of France, Marcel Pagnol would become one of the writers and filmmakers most closely associated with his native region of Provence. He was the son of a teacher, and despite the fact that his mother did not allow him to read until the age of six, he became an avid reader, interested early in all things literary. He began writing plays at the age of fifteen, and continued to do so through his university studies and his early career as a teacher himself.

Pagnol abandoned teaching and devoted himself to the theater upon moving to Paris in 1922. He quickly achieved success in the Parisian theater, as his loving regionalism appealed to Parisian audiences. It was in the theater that he cultivated his relationships with many of the actors he would work with in cinema, including **Raïmu** and **Orane Démazis**. He was not, at that point, interested in cinema since he had, according to his writings, never been a fan of silent film.

When sound came to film, however, Pagnol changed his mind. He saw in the sound cinema an opportunity to film the theater and thereby to preserve it and distribute it to a much wider audience. He founded his production company, Films Marcel Pagnol, in 1931, just after the arrival of sound cinema in France. Although **Gaumont** functioned as the distributor for Pagnol's films, Pagnol created his own production company in order to guarantee the total control he desired in making films.

Pagnol's first film, *Marius* (1931), codirected with Alexander Korda, was a direct adaptation of one of his plays and the first in a trilogy. It is probably the only film that attains the standard of filmed play that Pagnol laid out for the cinema. It is shot largely indoors, although there are scenes of the Bay of Marseille that are quite important. There is very little camera movement and no displacement from set to set within a scene. Only in the later film based on this trilogy, *César* (1936), does this standard break down, and Pagnol moves progressively to the foregrounding of the outdoors, a characteristic for which he became known. The second film in the trilogy, *Fanny* (1932), was not directed by Pagnol but by **Marc Allegret**. Pagnol cast **Pierre Fresnay** in the title role of *Marius*, alongside Raïmu and Demazis, and the film launched the film careers of all three.

Pagnol made numerous films during the 1930s, 1940s, and 1950s. They were primarily based on his own writings, including *Merlusse* (1933), *Cigalon* (1935), *Topaze* (1936), *César, Le Schpountz* (1938), *La Fille du puisatier* (1940), *La Prière aux étoiles* (1941), *La Belle meunière* (1948), the remake of *Topaze* (1951), which starred **Fernandel**, and *Manon des sources* (1953). Alternatively, Pagnol adapted the works of other writers, many associated with Provence. These include *Joffroi* (1933), *Angèle* (1934), *Regain* (1937), and *La Femme du boulanger* (1938), all adapted from works by Jean Giono; *Le Gendre de Monsieur Poirier* (1933), adapted from a play by Émile Augier; and *Les Lettres de mon moulin* (1954), adapted from the works of Alphonse Daudet. He also directed one television film, *Le Curé de Cucugnan* (1967).

In addition to his directing, Pagnol also collaborated on a number of films made by other directors. He wrote or collaborated on the screenplays for films such as **Roger Lion**'s *Direct au coeur* (1932), **Roger Richebé**'s *L'Agonie des aigles* (1933), Louis J. Gasnier's *Topaze* (1933), which starred **Louis Jouvet**, **Robert Vernay**'s *Arlette et l'amour* (1943), Raymond Leboursier's *Naïs* (1945), which also stars Jacqueline Pagnol, Jean Boyer's *Le Rosier de Madame Husson* (1950), and **Henri Verneuil**'s *Carnaval* (1953). Pagnol produced every film he personally made.

A number of Pagnol's films were also remade in other languages. In 1933, Mario Almirante made an Italian version of *Fanny*. Harry d'Abbadie d'Arrast adapted *Topaze* for Hollywood, the same year that Gasnier made his French version. James Whale collaborated with Preston Sturges to make *Port of Seven Seas* (1938), based on the *Marius* trilogy. Peter Sellers made *Mr. Topaze* (1961), based on *Topaze*, and Joshua Logan made *Fanny* (1961), starring Leslie Caron, **Charles Boyer,** and Maurice Chevalier. The Japanese film *Umineko no minato* (1942) and the Hungarian film *Bukfenc* (1993) are also based on Pagnol's work. The Hollywood remakes in particular gave Pagnol a great deal of discomfort, as Hollywood actively sought to change the stories to make them conform to the Hollywood censor, which took issue with stories about pregnant, unmarried women. Of course, Pagnol is not Pagnol without the pregnant, unmarried woman.

Pagnol also wrote a great deal about the cinema, although his critical writings have not had the force or staying power of his filmmaking. Perhaps this is because his theories are often at odds even with his own practice. Despite the fact that Pagnol was almost certainly an **auteur** in the very sense of the word, he was not, himself, convinced of the existence of such a thing as auteur in the cinema and he never considered himself one, although he retained legendary control over every film he every made. The early auteur theorists, who believed in such a concept, also did not consider Pagnol an auteur, although this is probably because they did not like his films. He advocated quite frequently a theatrical orthodoxy in filmmaking, once postulating that the cinema "should confine itself to photographing theater." This was a practice, however, which he himself progressively rejected. Pagnol was also fairly critical of silent film, although there are certain similarities between his filmmaking and the early efforts of the proponents of *film d'art*. He founded the literary journal *Les Cahiers du Sud* and the film journal *Les Cahiers du Film*, and it was in the latter that many of his writings on the cinema appear.

Pagnol has iconic standing in French film history and cultural memory. He was the first filmmaker to become a member of the Académie Française, which says a great deal about his status. He is closely associated with the 1930s, considered the golden age of French cinema, and with the *tradition de qualité*. He is also linked to French regional identity because of the way in which his films lovingly evoke southern France. In recent years he also became associated with nostalgia, because his films have often been remade into very successful **heritage films**, which nostalgically evoke a disappeared France. It is perhaps worth noting that most of Pagnol's original films were, themselves, nostalgic, because the world they presented was disappearing even when Pagnol made them. Among the heritage works based on Pagnol's writings or films are **Claude Berri**'s *Jean de Florette* (1986) and *Manon des sources* (1986), starring **Daneil Auteuil**, **Emmanuelle Béart**, **Gérard Depardieu**, and **Yves Montand**, and **Yves Robert**'s *La Gloire de mon père* (1990) and *Le Château de ma mère* (1990). Gérard Oury also remade *Le Schpountz* in 1999; however, it is difficult to consider this a heritage work, particularly since Oury cast Smaïn, an actor of North African origin, in the lead. A number of Pagnol's works have also been remade for French television.

PAINLEVÉ, JEAN (1902–1989). Director and producer. The son of the mathematician and French prime minister, Paul Painlevé, Jean Painlevé studied biology and medicine and became a scientist. Painlevé began experimenting with cinema in the early 1920s while studying at the Sorbonne. He made his first film, *L'œuf d'épinoche* (1925), for a presentation he made at the French Academy of Sciences. He was a friend of director René Sti, who fueled his interest in the medium, and one of his early films, *Mathusalem* (1927), features avant-garde writer and actor Antonin Artaud. It should be clear from this fact that, in addition to his scientific background, Painlevé had a strong interest in the avant-garde. He went on to make more than two hundred films, most of which center around issues of life or death in the natural world, and many of which feature the ocean or its inhabitants. Some films are less focused on specific animals and are more purely theoretical in their subject matter. Many also have a decidedly surrealist aspect, which is not surprising since Painlevé was closely associated with the early surrealist movement.

Painlevé's films include *La Daphnie* (1927), *Hyas et stenorinques* (1927), *La Pieuvre* (1927), *Mobile de Calder* (1929), *Pantopodes*

(1929), *Caprelles* (1929), *Les Crabes* (1930), *Crevettes* (1930), *Ruptures de fibres* (1931), *Électrophorase de nitrate d'argent* (1932), *L'Hippocampe* (1934), *Corèthre* (1935), *Vie dessous l'eau* (1935), *La Quatrième dimension* (1936), *Microscopie à bord d'un bâteau de pêche* (1936), *Voyage dans le ciel* (1937), *Images mathématiques de la lutte pour la vie* (1937), *Solutions françaises* (1939), *Le Vampire* (1945), *Jeux d'enfants* (1946), *Notre planète la Terre* (1946), *Œuvre scientifique de Pasteur* (1947), *Assassins d'eau douce* (1947), *Écriture de la danse* (1947), *La Chirurgerie correctrice* (1948), *Étourneaux* (1950), *Halammohydra* (1952), *Les Oursins* (1954), *Eleutheria* (1955), *Miscellanées* (1955), *Les Danseuses de la mer* (1956), *L'Astérie* (1958), *Les Alpes* (1958), *Descente de la mer en accéléré* (1960), *Seiche, étoile de mer, coquille saint-jacque* (1960), *Comment naissent des méduses* (1960), *La Crevette* (1963), *Amours de la pieuvre* (1965), *Diatomées* (1968), *Les Tarets* (1969), *Limaille* (1970), *Acera ou le bal des sorcières* (1972), *Énergie et dynamique des photons* (1974), *Les Homards* (1975), and *Cristaux liquides* (1978). He also made one animated film, *Barbe bleue* (1938).

Although often classified as documentaries, Painlevé's films are not documentaries in the typical sense, as they are often less scientific than poetic, and there is as much and sometimes more attention given to the visual impact of the films as there is to pedagogical value. Many of his films have a decidedly surrealist quality, and in typical surrealist fashion, there are often metaphorical and allegorical allusions to issues that lie outside the film. For example, both *Le Vampire* and *Assassins d'eau douce* reference fascism and Nazism and the brutality of World War II. Painlevé contributed to Georges Franju's celebrated documentary *Le Sang des bêtes* (1946), which was also a covert exploration of the Occupation and the war.

In addition to the visual qualities, there is also a decidedly avant-garde aspect to the soundtracks of Painlevé's films. These often feature counterintuitive samples from popular music that serve as a commentary on the images on the screen.

Painlevé's films, with the exception of *L'Hippocampe*, which was distributed by **Pathé-Natan**, were not widely seen by the public. In fact, for many years his work was largely ignored. However, in recent years, interest in his films has been growing, and there have been several important museum exhibits and screenings featuring his work.

In addition to his own filmmaking, Painlevé was actively involved in the cultural promotion of cinema. He was the general director of cinema for the French government from 1944 to 1945, and he served as president of the French Federation of *ciné-clubs* from 1946 to 1956. Painlevé was also a producer and in 1930 he founded the production company Documents Cinématographiques. The company produced all of Painlevé's own films and is still in existence.

PARNALAND, AMBROISE-FRANÇOISE (1854–1913). Film pioneer and producer. An accountant by trade, Ambroise Parnaland was also an amateur inventor and someone with a keen interest in all things technological. Among Parnaland's inventions were several film cameras including the Phototheagraphe and the Cinepar, both patented in 1896. As a result of his interest in photography and motion photography in particular, Parnaland founded the company Parnaland Frères in 1895. Initially, the company sold cameras, most notably the Cinepar, but eventually Parnaland branched into film production. The studio made a number of films, including *La Malle et l'auvergnat* (1900), *Grosse tête de Pierrot* (1900), and *En passant l'octroi* (1901).

Parnaland Frères was, however, plagued almost from the beginning. The company used a "P.F." logo that was identical to that used by **Pathé Frères**, which caused confusion. In addition, the company distributed films Parnaland had taken of Parisian surgeon Dr. Eugène-Louis Doyen performing surgery without Doyen's permission. The ensuing legal action forced Parnaland to reorganize his company, and it was eventually re-created as **Éclair** studios in 1907. Parland himself was not long at Éclair. His partner in the reorganization venture, the lawyer Charles Jourjon, forced Parnaland out of the company in short order. Parnaland went back to selling photographic equipment but without much success. By 1912, he had given up on all things photographic and had gone back to being an accountant.

PATHÉ, CHARLES MORAND (1863–1957). Film pioneer, producer, and studio director. Charles Pathé was born in Paris in 1863, the youngest of four sons. His family owned a butcher's shop in which he worked as a child. As a young man, Pathé became determined to do whatever he had to get rich. He served in the military, went abroad to South America in search of business opportunities, and tried his hand at selling wine. None of these efforts amounted to much of anything. What changed the course of Pathé's life was a chance discovery, that of the phonograph. In 1894, while visiting a fair in Vincennes near Paris, Pathé witnessed a demonstration of the Edison Talking Machine phonograph. Immediately struck with the commercial potential of such a device, Pathé bought one himself. He put it to use right away, becoming an itinerant performer of sorts, traveling with fairs and circuses, demonstrating the phonograph to audiences who paid an entry fee to hear it.

Pathé decided that demonstrating phonographs would never make him rich so he decided to sell them. In 1895, he had copies made of the Edison model, without any real second thought about the ethical implications of such a thing, and opened a shop to sell phonographs. The following year, Pathé was taken by another of Edison's ideas— the kinetoscope, a precursor to the movie camera. Pathé made an agreement with inventor Henry Joly to copy and "improve" the kinetoscope into a film camera the two called the *Photozootrope*. And in 1896, in partnership with his three brothers, Émile, Jacques, and Théophile, he established the **Société Pathé Frères**, a company dedicated to making and marketing film cameras, film stock, and phonographs and making films.

A studio was built in Vincennes, where Pathé had discovered the phonograph, to house the filmmaking part of the business. In 1897, backed by electric equipment manufacturer Claude Grivolas, the company became the Compagnie Générale de Cinématographes, Phonographes et Pellicules (Anciens Établissements Pathé Frères), and in 1898 the phonograph division and the film division were split, with Émile in charge of phonographs and Charles in charge of film. In the same year, Pathé hired on **Ferdinand Zecca** as head of film production for the company, allowing him to attend to what he knew best, commercialization. His legacy would be best expressed in an expression he often used himself: "I did not invent cinema, but I industrialized it." With Zecca firmly at the creative helm, that is precisely what Pathé set about doing.

The Pathé model was aggressive, formulaic, efficient, and highly successful. Under Zecca, Pathé hired numerous other screenwriters and directors including Louis Gasnier, **Gaston Velle**, and **André Heuzé.** It was the job of these directors and writers to quickly develop and film formulaic but effective films (often copied from **Gaumont** or British cinemas) designed to conform to audience demands. The studios produced many farces and chase films, for example, which were very easy to write and produce in a short period of time. The model was so successful that in 1902 a new much larger film studio was built at Vincennes and two new factories were built to process and film stock.

In 1906, Pathé began to move toward permanent cinemas for film exhibition, and in 1907 the company began renting film prints instead of selling them, melting down and reusing film stock when films were no longer wanted. Pathé's films, therefore, were produced faster and more cheaply than any of their competitors, which quickly positioned them as the giant of the film industry. In 1908 Pathé also began to open international offices, most with full production and distribution capacity in places like the United States, Spain, Italy, and Great Britain. This gave Pathé prominence in both the French and global markets. In 1912 mechanical colorization of films was perfected at the Pathé plants, which again gave the studio a great cost advantage over its competitors. Industrialization was indeed the key to the Pathé vision.

During the years Pathé was head of the studio and Zecca was head of production, Pathé was one of the dominant production companies in the world. It produced films by such directors as **Roméo Bossetti**, **Albert Capellani**, **Segundo de Chomon**, **Henri Diamant-Berger**, **Jean Epstein**, **André Hugon**, **Max Linder**, **Alfred Machin**, **Camille de Morlhon**, **Georges Monca**, **Lucien Nonguet**, and **Henri Pouctal**. The studio also represented such early film stars as Bossetti, **André Deed**, Charles Dullin, Henri Étiévant, Jean Garat, Louis Lagrange, Linder, Léontine Massart, **Léon Mathot**, **Mistinguett**, **Stacia Napierkowska**, **Charles Prince**, Gabrielle Robinne, and Gabriel Signoret. It pioneered narrative film during the silent era and specialized in genres like the historical epic, the comedy, including the burlesque and the chase film, and the melodrama. It was also a driving force in the creation of *film d'art*. It dominated, at one time, in the newsreel area with its *actualités*. And it had locked in distribution deals with major distributors.

Pathé might have remained a dominant force in world cinema but for the combination of several forces. First of all, film production and sales ground to a halt in the last years of World War I. This had cata-strophic consequences for the French film industry as a whole and for the European film industry as well. Secondly, the arrival of sound cinema required a huge up-front expense in order to convert produc-tion equipment and standing cinemas so that they would accommo-date talking pictures. Finally, the collaboration and collusion of American studios to dominate world production was beginning to take effect, and it became extremely difficult for any studio outside of the Hollywood cartel to maintain a foothold in the global cinema marketplace. To add insult to injury, Kodak film, with which Pathé had an agreement to market blank film in Europe, gave up production of that film, and Pathé saw what had been a sizeable investment sim-ply disappear. With the exception of the Pathé news bulletin, the Pathé News (an English-language version of Pathé's *Journal*), Pathé was forced to pull out of nearly all of its foreign markets in order to concentrate on keeping the French parent company solvent.

In 1929, in the midst of a financial crisis and possible fraud, Charles Pathé was forced to sell his shares in the company. Pathé claimed he found the new owner, **Bernard Natan**, overbearing and egomaniacal and he withdrew from the business shortly thereafter. The truth, however, is much more complex. Pathé, it seems, was guilty of mismanagement and probably fraud and he was forced out of the studio.

The new **Pathé-Natan** lasted ten years, and became the most sig-nificant studio, production company, and film distributor in France. However, Pathé, seeking to shift blame for his own misdeeds and try-ing to wrest control of the studio away from Natan, began a vicious propaganda campaign, and the result was that Natan was forced out of the studio, arrested, and sent to Auschwitz, where he died in 1942.

The studio was put in receivership and reformed in 1944 under the name Société des établissements Pathé-Cinema. Since that time, largely as a result of the changes Natan made and through an invest-ment in quality film productions, in well-conceived coproductions, and particularly through an investment in cinemas, the company flourished. It remained in its reorganized form until it was bought out in 1992. All charges against Pathé were ultimately dropped, although a review of the facts and finances of the company suggest that he was guilty of fraud and mismanagement and that Natan was guilty only of being an easy target. Pathé himself escaped all charges. He lived quietly until his death.

PATHÉ-NATAN. Pathé-Natan was the name given to **Pathé Studios** in 1928 after its takeover by film producer **Bernard Natan** and its merger with Natan's companies Rapid Films and Productions Bernard Natan. Natan obtained control of the company by buying out the interest of founder **Charles Pathé** who sold his shares in order to fend off a financial crisis or a foreign takeover. Under Natan's direction, the studio underwent a massive transformation that expanded its studio and production facilities, its editing capability, and its distribution network. It also began a large buyout of cinemas and theater chains in order to guarantee distribution. The studio became larger, more centralized, and more efficient. It also reintroduced several of its products, including the Pathé *Journal*, which had been shut down in 1927.

Under Natan's direction, Pathé-Natan became the most significant studio and production and distribution company in France. Between 1929 and 1936, when Natan was forced out of the company, the studio produced more than seventy feature-length films, including **André Hugon**'s *Les Trois masques* (1929), *La Tendresse* (1930), *Le Marchand de sable* (1931), and *La Croix du sud* (1931), Marco de Gastyne's *La Belle garce* (1930), Pierre Colombier's *Le Roi des resquilleurs* (1930), *Le Roi du cirage* (1931), *Charlemagne* (1933), and *Théodore et cie* (1933), Jean de Limur's *Mon gosse de père* (1930), **Jacques de Baroncelli's** *L'Arlésienne* (1930), Fyodor Otzep's *Les Frères Karazamoff* (1931) and *Amok* (1934), **Léonce Perret**'s *Après l'amour* (1931) and *Enlevez-moi* (1932), Maurice Tourneur's *Les Gaietés de l'escadron* (1932), *Au nom de la loi* (1932), *Les Deux orphelines* (1933), and *Königsmark* (1935), **René Clair**'s *Le Dernier milliardaire* (1934), Raymond Bernard's *Les Misérables* (1934), **Marcel L'Herbier**'s *Le Bonheur* (1934), and Anatole Litvak's *L'Équipage* (1935).

In 1936, Pathé, probably in order to extricate himself from the problems of his own mismanagement, began a campaign against Natan. The studio was suffering from various financial problems inherited from the Pathé era. There were also various legal issues related to the sale of the studio, and the crash of the stock market led to some financial problems and particularly cash-flow problems. These problems were heightened by financial problems at the bank that had financed the takeover and expansion.

Natan was accused of mismanagement and of embezzling large sums of money from the studio. The studio was declared insolvent, despite the fact that the records show that it was operating in the black. Natan was driven out of the company, despite the fact that there seems to have been no merit to the charges against him. He was, it seems, a victim of anti-Semitism. The company was put in receivership and ownership was given to the investors of a group called the *Société Nouvelle Pathé Cinéma*.

PATHÉ STUDIOS. *See* SOCIÉTÉ PATHÉ FRÈRES.

PAULIN, JEAN-PAUL (1902–1976). Director, producer, and screenwriter. The son of sculptor Paul Paulin, Jean-Paul Paulin was a childhood friend of **Jean Renoir**, as his father was the friend of Renoir's father, Auguste Renoir. It was in part because of his connection to Renoir that Paulin became interested in the cinema.

Unlike Renoir, Paulin did not begin experimenting with film until the arrival of sound. He made his first feature film, *La Femme nue*, in 1932, a remake of **Léonce Perret**'s 1926 silent film. He went on to direct seventeen other films and to produce two others. The peak of Paulin's film career was the 1930s, during which time he also made *Pas besoin d'argent* (1933), starring **Claude Dauphin** and Lisette Lanvin, *L'Abbé Constantin* (1933), again with Dauphin and Léon Bélières and **Françoise Rosay**, *L'Esclave blanc* (1936), which was made from a script written by Carl Theodor Dreyer, *Les Filles du Rhône* (1937), starring Annie Ducaux and Madeleine Sologne, *La Danseuse rouge* (1937), *Le Chemin de l'honnneur* (1939), starring Henri Garat and **Renée Saint-Cyr**, and *Trois de Saint-Cyr* (1939). His focus during the decade was primarily on literary adaptation or on intrigue or adventure films.

During the 1940s, Paulin continued to make films. He directed *La Nuit merveilleuse* (1940) with an all-star cast that included **Fernandel**, Jane Marken, Madeleine Robinson, and Charles Vanel; *Cap au large* (1942), featuring Robert Lynen and Mila Parély; *L'Homme qui vendit son âme* (1943); *Échec au roy* (1945), starring Lucien Barroux and **Odette Joyeux**; *La Nuit de Sybille* (1947), again starring Baroux; *Le Château de la dernière chance* (1947), starring Robert Dhéry and Julien Carette; *La Voix du rêve* (1948), again starring Saint-Cyr; *Voyage à trois* (1949); and *L'Inconnue no 13* (1949), starring Mady Berry and **René Dary**. There cannot be said to be a dominant trend among these films, although it is noteworthy that Paulin experimented with comedy as well as drama, which he had not done in the 1930s.

In the 1950s, Paulin made only one film, *Folie Douce* (1950), although he produced both Paul Mesnier's *Poil de Carotte* (1952) and Jean Boyer's *J'Avais sept filles* (1954). He gave up the cinema after 1954 and has been more or less forgotten. While it is true that his filmmaking was uneven and some of his films seem a bit propagandistic, there are some interesting films among those he made. Those who know his work consider *La Femme nue*, *L'Esclave blanc*, *Les Filles du Rhône*, *La Nuit merveuilleuse*, and *Cap au large* to be the best.

PERRET, LÉONCE (1880–1935). Actor, director, film pioneer, and screenwriter. Born in Poitou-Charentes, Léonce Perret aspired to become an actor from a young age. He began his career on the stage in the popular theater, but as the cinema emerged Perret became more interested in that medium. He was hired on at **Gaumont** in 1909, as an actor, director, and screenwriter, and he went on to become one of the most prolific directors at the studio. Over the course of his career, Perret directed nearly three hundred films, acted in nearly one hundred, and wrote the screenplays for more than thirty. He was one of the early innovators of the cinema, and he worked in a wide range of genres, from burlesque to drama, to tableaux films, to war films, to romantic comedy.

From 1909 until 1916 Perret acted and directed. He is known for his penchant for alluring actresses, and he either launched or established the careers of several, including Yvette Andreyor, **Renée Carl**, Fabienne Fabrèges, Jeanne Marie-Laurent, Suzanne Le Bret, and Suzanne Grandais. Andreyor appears in such films as *Dans la vie* (1911), *La Paix du vieil ermite* (1911), *L'Amour qui tue* (1911), and *Les Blouses blanches* (1912). Carl appears in such films as *La Fille de Jephté* (1910), *Le Gardien de la Camargue* (1910), *Dans la vie* (1911), and *Le Fils de la Sunamite* (1911). Fabrèges appears in such films as *Le Portrait de Mireille* (1910), *Mimosa* (1910), *Le Rendez-vous* (1910), *Le Lys brisé* (1911), *Tu t'en iras jeunesse* (1911), *Les Blouses blanches* (1912), as well as a number of propagandistic, nationalist war films made during World War I, including *L'Angélus de la victoire* (1916) and *Marraines de France* (1916). Le Bret had roles in *Léonce et les écrevisses* (1913), *Léonce à la campagne* (1913), *Les Fiancés de l'air* (1913), and *L'Ange de la maison* (1913). Grandais appears in such films as *Le Moïse du moulin* (1911), *Le Chrysanthème rouge* (1912), *Les Blouses blanches* (1912), *Graziella la gitane* (1912), *La Lumière et l'amour* (1912), *L'Apollon de roches noires* (1913), and *L'Esclave de Phidias* (1917). Marie-Laurent appears in *Le Cheveau blanc* (1910), *La Fille de Jephté* (1910), *Petite mère* (1910), and *Noël de grand-mère* (1910). Perret's wife, Valentine Petit, also appears in a number of his films from the period, including *Monsieur Prud'homme s'émancipe* (1910), *La Petite Béarnaise* (1911), *Titine et Totor* (1911), *L'Express matrimonial* (1912), *Un coq en pâte* (1912), and *Sur les rails* (1912).

Perret promoted actors as well as actresses. Among his preferred were Paul Manson, who appears in such films as *L'Heure du rêve* (1915), *L'X noir* (1916), *La Fiancée du diable* (1916), and *Les Poilus de la revanche* (1916). Another favorite was Émile Keppens, who appeared in *Sur les rails* (1912), *Les Mystères des roches de Kador* (1912), *Au fond du gouffre* (1913), and *Les Épingles* (1913). Louis Leubas also appeared frequently in films such as *Main de fer contre la bande aux gants blancs* (1912), *La Force de l'argent* (1913), *L'Enfant de Paris* (1913), and *La Voix de la patrie* (1914). Of course, Perret appeared in many of the films he directed, including *Le Rendez-vous* (1910), *Jour d'échéance* (1910), *Monsieur Prud'homme s'émancipe* (1910), *Dans la vie* (1911), *La Paix du vieil hermite* (1911), *Les Béquilles* (1911), and the films in the Léonce series, which ran from 1912 until 1916.

In addition to acting in his own films, Perret appeared in several films directed by **Louis Feuillade**, with whom he sometimes collaborated as director. Feuillade films in which Perret appears include *Judith et Holopherne* (1909), *Esther* (1910), *Le Festin de Baltazar* (1910), and *André Chenier* (1912). Perret also frequently cast actors most often associated with Feuillade, including **René Navarre**, **René Cresté**, and Edmond Bréon.

After 1916, Perret no longer acted and focused entirely on directing and screenwriting. That year he made several pronationalist war films, including *L'Angélus de la victoire* (1916) and *Marraines de France* (1916), as well as a number of other films, including the mystery films *L'X noir* (1916) and *Le Mystère de l'ombre* (1916), the romantic comedies *Les Bobines d'or* (1916) and *Le Printemps du coeur* (1916), the comedies *Les Armes de la femme* (1916) and *Le Roi de la montagne* (1916), and the dramas *L'Empreinte du passé* (1916) and *Le Retour du passé* (1916). The snapshot of films made in just one year gives some idea of the diversity of the types Perret made during his career.

In 1917, Perret left Gaumont and went to Hollywood, where he remained and worked for a number of years. His diverse filmmaking interests did not change, and he filmed in a number of different genres as he had done in France. Among the films he made while in the United States were the crime films *The Silent Master* (1917) and *The Empire of Diamonds* (1920), the dramas *The Mad Lover* (1917) and *The Money Maniac* (1921), the comedies *The Accidental Honeymoon* (1918) and *The Million Dollar Dollies* (1918), the mystery *The Thirteenth Chair* (1919), the adaptation *Koenigsmark* (1923), which was his most successful Hollywood film, and the classic historical drama *Madame Sans-Gêne* (1924), which was a cross-cultural coproduction. He also made a war film while in Hollywood, *Lest We Forget* (1918), and it had the same air of propaganda as his previous war films. Perret produced several of his American films, adding producer to his resume.

Perret returned to France in 1925 and resumed making films there. His later films include the late silent films *La Femme nue* (1926), *Le Printemps de l'amour* (1927), *Morgane la sirène* (1928), and *La Danseuse d'orchidée* (1928). He also made several sound films, including *Quand nous étions deux* (1930), *Après l'amour* (1931), *Enlevez-moi* (1932), *Il était une fois* (1933), and *Les Deux couverts* (1935), written by **Sacha Guitry**. *Les Deux couverts* was Perret's final film, as he died the year it was released. Several of these later films starred another female star, **Gaby Morlay**. Like many early silent directors, Perret was ignored until fairly recently, when interest in his work and his role in the evolution of cinema has emerged. He was one of the most prolific directors of the silent period, and some of his early sound films are also quite interesting. Although he is not known specifically for innovating a particular genre, the mere range of his films is sufficient to establish his centrality to the evolution of early cinema. Many of his films still exist and in recent years a number of them have been restored, which suggests that interest in his diverse body of work will likely continue.

PHILIPPE, GÉRARD (1922–1959). Actor and director. Born in **Cannes**, Gérard Philippe wished to pursue acting, despite his parents' desire that he become a lawyer. He took private lessons and eventually, with encouragement, applied to the Conservatoire d'art dramatique in Paris. He began his career on the stage, where he was acclaimed as a talented dramatic actor. He acted onstage for much of his career, and in 1951, he became a member of the Théâtre National Populaire. However, the cinema caught his attention, and he made his screen debut in **Marc Allegret**'s *Les Petites du Quai aux fleurs* (1944) and went on to small roles in such films as Yves Allegret and Jean Choux's *Les Boîtes aux rêves* (1945), **Alain Resnais**'s *Ouvert pour cause d'inventaire* (1946), Georges Lampin's *L'Idiot* (1946), and **Georges Lacombe**'s *Le Pays sans étoiles* (1946), before landing the role that would make him a film star, the part of François Jaubert in **Claude Autant-Lara**'s adaptation of Raymond Radiguet's *Le Diable au corps* (1947).

From 1947 until the end of his life, Philippe was one of the major film stars of French cinema, a screen idol who was arguably the most popular actor of his time. Film audiences adored him for his striking features and his charm, and directors loved him for his well-developed and understated acting style, his range as a performer, and his ability to become whatever character he played. He appeared opposite some of the most prominent leading ladies of the 1940s and 1950s, including **Simone Signoret**, **Michèle Morgan**, **Danielle Darrieux**, **Jeanne Moreau**, and **Martine Carol,** and starred alongside some of the great stars of the cinema.

Philippe appeared in such films as **Christian-Jacque**'s *La Chartreuse de Parme* (1948), *Souvenirs perdus* (1950), and *Fanfan la Tulipe* (1952), **Marcel Carné**'s *Juliette ou la clef des songes* (1950), **Max Ophüls**'s *La Ronde* (1950), **René Clair**'s *La Beauté du diable* (1950), *Les Belles de nuit* (1953), and *Les Grandes manœuvres*

(1955), Yves Allegret's *Les Orgeuilleux* (1953) and *La Meilleure part* (1956), **Sacha Guitry**'s *Si Versailles m'était conté* (1954) and *Si Paris nous était conté* (1955), **René Clément**'s *Monsieur Ripois* (1954), Autant-Lara's *Le Rouge et le noir* (1954) and *Le Joueur* (1958), **Julien Duvivier**'s *Pot-Bouille* (1957), **Jacques Becker**'s *Les Amants de Montparnasse* (1958), Clément Duhour's *La Vie à deux* (1958), **Roger Vadim**'s *Les Liaisons dangereuses* (1959), and Luis Buñuel's *La Fièvre monte à El Pao* (1959), which was Philippe's last film.

In addition to acting, Philippe directed one film, *Les Aventures de Till l'Espiegle* (1956), in which he also starred. He also narrated several documentaries, including *Les Fêtes galantes* (1950), a documentary about the painter Jean-Antoine Watteau, and *Saint-Louis, angle de la paix* (1951). He would, no doubt, have had a much longer career but for his untimely death from liver cancer just short of his thirty-seventh birthday. Philippe was married to Nicole Fourcade, who took the name Anne Philippe after their marriage. She published two books about him after his death.

That Philippe played roles as diverse as the gullible but heroic Fanfan in Christian-Jacque's *Fanfan la Tulipe*, the philandering André Ripois in Clément's *Monsieur Ripois*, and the downright despicable Valmont in Vadim's *Les Liaisons dangereuses* is a testament to his range as an actor and serves as evidence that his popularity was not due entirely to his good looks. Nonetheless, it is true that Philippe's place in film legend has, at least in part, been rooted in his embodiment of youthful masculinity in an age that many look back on nostalgically. Philippe, like other stars who have died tragically, became an image of perpetual youth linked to an era now remembered as glorious. Like such stars, this peculiar position as youth and beauty frozen in time was assured by his death, and his status as a cultural icon, not surprisingly, has only increased in the years since he died. His image has appeared on commemorative postage stamps and coins, and he has a film festival named after him. It is unlikely that his reputation in French culture or film history will diminish. Rather, like Marilyn Monroe or Princess Diana, it is more likely that Philippe's appeal will increase with each year that passes.

PICCOLI, MICHEL (1925–). Actor, director, producer, and screenwriter. Michel Piccoli was born Jacques Daniel Michel Piccoli in

Paris. His mother was a pianist and his father a violinist. He studied drama under Andrée Bauer-Thérond and René Simon and later worked simultaneously as a stage and film actor. He debuted in cinema with a small role in **Christian-Jacque**'s 1945 film *Sortilèges*, followed by a more substantial part in **Louis Daquin**'s 1949 *Le point du jour*. Damien cast Piccoli in another film that same year, titled *Le parfum de la dame en noir*. In the early 1950s, Piccoli appeared in three short films by director Paul Paviot and acted a second time for Christian-Jacque in a segment of the film *Destinées* (1954). Piccoli played minor roles in a number of films by major French directors in the mid-1950s, including **Jean Renoir**'s *French Cancan* (1955), **René Clair**'s *Les Grands Maneouvres* (1955), **Alexandre Astruc**'s *Les Mauvaises rencontres* (1955), **Jean Delannoy**'s *Marie-Antoinette Reine de France* (1955), and **Raymond Rouleau**'s *Les Sorcières de Salem* (1956). He played a supporting role in Christian-Jacque's 1957 *Nathalie* and acted for the first time for Louis Buñuel in *La mort en ce jardin* (1956).

Piccoli's major performances began in the 1960s with his starring role beside **Brigitte Bardot** in **Jean-Luc Godard**'s *Le Mépris* (1963). He provided a voiceover for the *Nouvelle Vague* or New Wave forerunner, **Agnès Varda**, in her *Salut les cubains* (1963), and he later delivered leading roles in Varda's *Les Créatures* (1966), **Roger Vadim**'s *La Curée* (1966), and Buñuel's *Belle de jour* (1967). In 1965, he played the title role in Marcel Bluwal's popular television film, *Dom Juan ou le festin de Pierre*, a role that increased his popular appeal. In the same decade, Piccoli had supporting roles in **Constantin Costa-Gavras**'s *Compartiment tueurs* (1965) and *Un homme de trop* (1967), **Alain Resnais**'s *Le guerre est finie* (1966), Buñuel's *Le journal d'une femme de chambre* (1964) and *La Voie lactée* (1969), **Jacques Demy**'s *Les Demoiselles de Rochefort* (1967), and Alfred Hitchcock's *Topaz* (1969). He also starred opposite **Catherine Deneuve** in Alain Cavalier's *La Chamade* (1968). He started acting for Italian director Marco Ferreri in *Dillinger è morto* (1969). His fame would later soar with his performance in Ferreri's provocative and challenging *La grande bouffe* (1973).

In 1970, Piccoli began another fruitful collaboration with director **Claude Sautet** in *Les choses de la vie* (1970), where he costarred with **Romy Schneider**. In addition, he played significant parts in **Claude**

Chabrol's *La Décade prodigieuse* (1971), Yves Boisset's *L'Attentat* (1972), **Michel Deville**'s *La Femme en bleu* (1973), Claude Faraldo's *Themroc* (1973), Chabrol's *Les noces rouges* (1973), Sautet's *Vincent, François, Paul, et les autres* (1974), Jacques Ruffio's *Sept morts sur ordonnance* (1975), Sautet's *Mado* (1976), **Bertrand Tavernier**'s *Des enfants gatés* (1977), and Francis Girod's *L'État sauvage* (1978). Piccoli began producing in the 1970s. His films as producer include *Themroc* and *L'État sauvage*. In the same decade, Piccoli published a memoir titled *Dialogues égoïstes* (1976).

In 1980, Piccoli won his first major award for Best Actor at the **Cannes Film Festival**. The award was for his work in Marco Belloccio's *Salto nel vuoto*. Also in 1980, Piccoli acted in **Louis Malle**'s American feature, *Atlantic City*. In 1982, he won a Silver Berlin Bear for his interpretation in Pierre Granier-Deferre's *Une étrange affaire*. Piccoli also gave memorable performances in Godard's *Passion* (1982) and Demy's *Une chambre en ville* (1982). Later in the decade, he played starring roles in **Claude Lelouch**'s *Viva la vie!* (1984), **Leos Carax**'s *Mauvais sang* (1986), and Malle's *Milou en mai* (1989).

Piccoli also tried his hand at directing, making his debut with a segment for the film *Contre l'oubli* (1991). He followed with the short *Train de nuit* (1994) and his first feature film *Alors voilà* (1997). Also in the 1990s, Piccoli starred in **Jacques Rivette**'s *La Belle Noiseuse* (1991). He costarred with Deneuve again in both Raoul Ruiz's *Généalogies d'un crime* (1997) and Manoel de Oliveira's *Je rentre à la maison* (2001). Piccoli directed and scripted *La plage noire* (2001), starring Dominique Blanc, and *C'est pas tout à fait la vie dont j'avais rêvé* (2004). Piccoli is one of France's most inventive and prolific entertainers. His energetic film career includes performances in more than two hundred television and cinema films.

PINOTEAU, CLAUDE (1925–). Director and screenwriter. Claude Pinoteau was born in Boulogne-sur-Seine. He began his career in cinema in the early 1950s as an assistant director to such filmmakers as **Jean Cocteau, Henri Decoin, Jean-Pierre Melville, Max Ophüls,** and **Henri Verneuil.** Among his credits as assistant director are such films as Melville's *Les Enfants terribles* (1950), Cocteau's *Orphée* (1950), which stars **Jean Marais**, Gilles Grangier's *L'Amant de* *paille* (1951), Decoin and **Jean Delannoy**'s *Les Secrets d'Alcove* (1952), which stars **Bernard Blier**, **Jeanne Moreau,** and **Martine Carol**, Ophüls's *Lola Montès* (1955), which also stars Carol, Verneuil's classic film *Mélodie en sous-sol* (1963), which stars **Jean Gabin** and **Alain Delon**, and **Claude Lelouch**'s *L'Aventure, c'est l'aventure* (1972), which stars **Lino Ventura** and Jacques Brel.

In the late 1960s, Pinoteau began working as a screenwriter as well as an assistant director. He contributed to the scripts for such films as Lelouch's *Un homme qui me plaît* (1969) and *Le voyou* (1970). Fairly early in his career, Pinoteau transitioned to directing. His first films were shorts, but he went on to release his first feature-length film *Le silencieux*, starring Ventura, in 1973. Actress **Isabelle Adjani** received one of her first major roles in Pinoteau's second feature, *La gifle* (1974), which won the prestigious **Prix Louis-Delluc**.

Following *La gifle*, Pinoteau released *Le grand escogriffe* (1976) and *L'homme en colère* (1979). Both were fairly successful; however, the director's biggest commercial success to date is *La boum* (1980), which sold more movie tickets than any other French film released during the same year. *La boum* starred Sophie Marceau, **Claude Brasseur**, and Brigitte Fossey. Director and screenwriter Danièle Thompson collaborated on the script, as she would for some of his later films, including the sequel *La Boum 2*, which was one of the top five French films of 1982. Pinoteau later directed *La Septième cible* (1984), which also featured Ventura. Marceau starred again in *L'étudiante* (1988), a film focusing on light youthful themes. Vincent Perez, a popular actor with young audiences, led the cast of *La neige et le feu* (1991). Pinoteau's *Cache cash* (1994) similarly features youthful protagonists; this time they are two young boys. His *Les palmes de M. Schutz* (1997), adapted from the play about Marie and Pierre Curie by Jean-Noël Fenwick, stars **Isabelle Adjani**, **Charles Berling**, and **Philippe Noiret**.

PISIER, MARIE-FRANCE (1944–). Actress, director, and screenwriter. Marie-France Pisier was born in Dalat, Vietnam, which was then part of French Indochina, where her father was a colonial official. She moved to Paris with her family at the age of twelve and subsequently studied law and political science. She first ventured into cinema at the age of seventeen opposite Jean-Pierre Léaud in

François Truffaut's sketch "Antoine et Colette" for the film *L'Amour à vingt ans* (1962). She later played leading roles alongside actor and director Robert Hossein in three of his films: *La Mort d'un tuer* (1963), *Les Yeux cernés* (1964), and *Le Vampire de Düsseldorf* (1965).

Pisier worked for some of France's most acclaimed **auteurs**, among them **Alain Robbe-Grillet** in *Trans-Europ-Express* (1966), Truffaut in *Baisers volés* (1968), **Jacques Rivette** in *Céline et Julie vont en bateau* (1974), and **André Téchiné** in *Souvenirs d'en France* (1975), *Pauline s'en va* (1975), *Barocco* (1976), and *Les Soeurs Brontë* (1979). Pisier costarred in Truffaut's last Antoine Doinel film, *L'Amour en fuite* (1979). In the 1970s she expanded her filmmaking career to include screenwriting. She went on to work on the scripts of **Jacques Rivette**'s *Céline et Julie vont en bateau* (1974) and Truffaut's *L'Amour en fuite* (1979).

In the meantime, Pisier's acting career remained her mainstay. She won her first César for Best Supporting Actress in **Jean-Charles Tachella**'s *Cousin, Cousine* (1976) and a second César for Best Supporting Actress in *Barocco* (1977). In the late 1970s, she entered English-language cinema with the leading role in Charles Jarrott's *The Other Side of Midnight* (1977). She also played in the French and English film, *French Postcards* (1979), directed by Willard Huyck. She costarred with **Nouvelle Vague** or New Wave icon **Jean-Paul Belmondo** in **Henri Verneuil**'s *Le Corps de mon ennemi* (1976) and in Gérard Oury's very successful adventure film, *L'As des as* (1982).

In the early 1980s, Pisier maintained a strong international presence. She landed a leading role in **Francis Girod**'s *La Banquière* (1980), starred in Hungarian director George Kaczender's Anglophone *Chanel solitaire* (1981), acted in Moroccan director Moumen Smihi's *44 ou les Récits de la nuit* (1981), played in American director Paul Williams's *Miss Right* (1982), costarred in German director Hans Geissendörfer's *Der Zauberberg* (1982), acted in **Roger Vadim**'s *The Hot Touch* (1982), and played a key role in **Yves Boisset**'s *Le Prix du danger* (1982).

Pisier also wrote several novels, one of which, *Le Bal du gouverneur*, she adapted for the screen in 1990. *Le Bal du gouverneur* (1990) also marked Pisier's debut as a director. Like director **Claire**

Denis, Pisier built on her experiences in France's former colonies. Her second film was *Comme un avion* (2002), in which she also stars. Pisier continues to act in films, among them Raoul Ruiz's *Le Temps retrouvé* (1999), Yamina Benguigui's *Inch'Allah Dimanche* (2001), Laurence Ferreira Barbosa's *Ordo* (2003), and Christophe Honoré's *Dans Paris* (2006).

POETIC REALISM. *See* RÉALISME POÉTIQUE.

POIRET, JEAN (1926–1992). Actor, director, and screenwriter. Jean Poiret was born in Paris. He debuted as a stage actor at the Théâtre de l'Athénée and later performed in music halls with **Michel Serrault**. One of his first appearances in cinema was in **Michel Boisrond**'s *Cette sacrée gamine* (1956), a film starring **Brigitte Bardot** that also featured Serrault in a small role. Poiret and Serrault played small and supporting roles in Roger Pierre and Jean-Marc Thibault's *La Vie est belle* (1956), Jean Boyer's *La Terreur des dames* (1956), Maurice Cloche's *Adorables demons* (1957), Philippe Agostini's *Le Naïf aux quarante enfants* (1958), Raoul André's *Clara et les méchants* (1958), Boyer's *Nina* (1959), Jean Berry's *Oh! Qué mambo* (1959), **Henri Diamant-Berger**'s *Messieurs les ronds de cuir* (1959), and Clément Duhour's *Vous n'avez rien à déclarer?* (1959). Poiret costarred with Serrault in Cloche's short film *Ça aussi c'est Paris* (1957) and in **Sacha Guitry**'s *Assassins et voleurs* (1957).

In the 1960s, Poiret played alongside Serrault in several films, among them Raymond Bailly's *Ma femme est une panthère* (1960), Norbet Carbonnaux's *La Gamberge* (1962), Boisrond's *Comment réussir en amour* (1962), Jacques Pintoeau's *Durs à cuire* (1964), Jacques Poitrenaud's *La Tête du client* (1965), Rigaud's *Les Baratineurs* (1965), and André's *Le Grande bidule* (1967), *Ces messieurs de la famille* (1967), and *Ces messieurs de la gâchette* (1969). Poiret acted in films without Serrault, such as Pierre Chevalier's *Auguste* (1961), Boyer's *C'est pas moi, c'est l'autre* (1962), and Roland Quignon's *Aux frais de la princesse* (1969). He was a favorite of director **Jean-Pierre Mocky**, acting in *Les Vièrges* (1963), *Un drôle de paroissien* (1963), *La Grande frousse* (1964), *La Bourse et la vie* (1966), and *La Grande lessive* (1968). In the 1970s, Poiret played in Marcel Camus's *Le Mur de l'Atlantique* (1970) and again alongside Serrault in Pierre Tchernia's *La Guele de l'autre* (1979), for which he wrote the script.

Poiret is perhaps best known internationally as the author of *La Cage aux folles*, first a stage play in 1973 for the Théâtre du palais royal. It became the famous 1978 film directed by **Edouard Molinaro** that starred Serrault. Poiret's work on the script brought him an Oscar nomination. He worked on the scripts of other films, including Michel Drach's *La Bonne occase* (1964), Molinaro's *La Cage aux folles II* (1980), and **Georges Lautner**'s *Joyeuses Pâques* (1984). In the 1980s, Poiret would pair again with Serrault in **Jean Yanne**'s *Liberté, égalité, choucroute* (1985) and Mocky's *Le Miraculé* (1987). He played leading roles in **Claude Chabrol**'s *Poulet au vinaigre* (1985) and *Inspecteur Lavardin* (1986), Gérard Krawczyk's *Je hais les acteurs* (1986), and Francis Girod's *Lacenaire* (1990). He later appeared in German director Christoph Böll's *Sisi und der Kaiserkess* (1991). Poiret directed one film, *Le Zèbre* (1992), which he also scripted. It was nominated for a **César** for Best First Film.

POIRIER, LÉON (1884–1968). Director and producer. Born Louis Marie Léon Poirier, Léon Poirier was the nephew of impressionist painter Berthe Morisot. Poirier had early artistic ambitions himself, and he began his career in the theater, where he produced plays and managed theaters before opening his own theater, the Théâtre des Champs-Elysées in 1913. The Théâtre featured performances of the Ballets russes, among other things, but had to close for financial reasons. He was hired on at **Gaumont** in 1913 to direct films and write screenplays, and he remained there in that capacity until he enlisted in the army to serve in World War I. Films directed by Poirier from the period 1913 to 1919 include *Le Nid* (1914), *Le Trèfle d'argent* (1914), *Le Jugement des pierres* (1914), *Monsieur Charlemagne* (1914), *Cadette* (1914), *Ces desmoiselles Perrotin* (1914), *L'Amour passé* (1914), and *L'Aventure de la petite duchesse* (1914).

In 1919, Poirier returned to Gaumont and replaced **Louis Feuillade** as head of production. Like Feuillade, he continued to direct, although he never matched Feuillade in terms of number of films made, diversity of films made, or significance of films made. He left Gaumont in the mid-1920s to pursue directing independently. Poirier's later films include *Âmes d'orient* (1918), *Le Penseur* (1920),

Narayana (1920), *L'Ombre déchirée* (1921), *Jocelyn* (1922), *Geneviève* (1923), *L'Affaire du courrier de Lyon* (1923), *La Brière* (1924), *Verdun, visions d'histoire* (1924), *Le Coffret de Jade* (1929), *Cain: aventure des mers exotique* (1930), *La Voie sans disques* (1933), *L'Appel du silence* (1936), *Soeur d'armes* (1937), *Brazza, ou l'épopée du Congo* (1940), *Jeannou* (1943), and *La Route inconnue* (1949).

For the most part, Poirier had a unique style of directing that has been seen as symbolist or impressionist. His work included literary adaptations, such as *Jocelyn* (1922) and *L'Affaire du courrier de Lyon* (1923), and these films might be seen as a continuation of the ***film d'art*** tradition. His war film *Verdun, visions d'histoire* is also highly impressionistic. Some of his work also had nationalist tendencies. *L'Appel du silence*, a biopic about Charles de Foucauld, and *Brazza, ou l'épopée du Congo* are orientalist films that portray Africa through a highly exotic gaze and that glorify conquest and empire. *Jeannou*, his very controversial film, is overtly Pétainist.

Probably Poirier's most significant Africa film was not a narrative film but a documentary. *La Croisière noire* (1926) documented a continental North-South car rally, undertaken to bolster public support for France's colonial enterprise. Poirier rode with the Citroën team during the rally and "captured" Africa along the way. The film is also highly orientalist and seemingly propagandistic. It was an enormous success, and the images of Africans in it influenced fashion and home décor for years afterward. From that point of view, also, the film was a success in that it accomplished the mission it had been given.

Poirier retired from the cinema in 1949, after making *La Route inconnue* (1949), a semimystical film about the three major religions. The film was not a success and probably prompted Poirier's retirement. Critical opinion of Poirier's work since his retirement has been mixed. There are some who see him as a great and innovative filmmaker and who put aside the political criticisms of his work as either misguided or irrelevant. Others, however, do not see great artistic merit to Poirier's films and find the content and point of view to be sufficiently problematic to override any artistic merit that might be argued. Time will tell where Poirier ultimately falls in the canon of French cinema.

POLIGNY, SERGE DE (1903–1983). Director. Serge de Poligny began his career in cinema as a set decorator for Paramount Studios in France. He ultimately became interested in directing and went on to direct nearly twenty films over a period of twenty years. Poligny made his directorial debut in 1932 with the film *Une brune piquante* (1931). The following year he made *Vous serez ma femme* (1932), *Coup de feu à l'aube* (1932), and *Les As du turf* (1932), the film that really established his reputation. His subsequent films include *Rivaux de la piste* (1933), starring **Albert Préjean**, *L'Étoile de Valencia* (1933), starring **Jean Gabin**, *Un de la montagne* (1934), *L'Or* (1934), codirected with Karl Hartl and starring Pierre Blanchar, *Retour au paradis* (1935), starring **Claude Dauphin**, *Johnny, haute-couture* (1935), *La Chanson du souvenir* (1936), codirected with Douglas Sirk, *Claudine à l'école* (1937), starring Pierre Brasseur, *Le Veau gras* (1939), starring Elvire Popesco, *Le Baron fantôme* (1943), *La Fiancée des ténèbres* (1945), starring **Pierre Richard-Willm** and Jany Holt, *Torrents* (1947), *La Soif des hommes* (1949), *Cap d'Alger* (1952), and *Les Armes de la paix* (1954).

It is difficult to identify a common theme in de Poligny's films. This is partly because several of the films he made, notably *Coup de feu à l'aube*, *Vous serez ma femme*, *Rivaux de la piste*, and *L'Étoile de Valencia*, were French versions of German films, essentially remakes. Among those films that de Poligny authored, including *Retour au paradis*, *Le Veau gras*, *Le Baron fantôme*, *La Fiancée des ténébres*, and *La Soif des hommes*, there are common elements. There are, in several of the films, the use of fantasy or myth and a somewhat gothic overtone. There is also an underlying theme of domination as there are films dealing with the crusades against the Cathares in France and two dealing with colonization and colonialism. What links all the films is de Poligny's visual style, which was mesmerizingly poetic. Some critics, in fact, regard de Poligny as a forgotten **auteur** of French cinema's golden age.

POSITIF. The principal rival to *Les Cahiers du cinéma*, *Positif* is a film journal founded in 1952 by Bernard Chardère. The journal has had a long and fairly prestigious run. Its critical view is often at odds with that of *Les Cahiers du cinéma*. It did not embrace the *Nouvelle Vague* or New Wave at all, for example, but rather condemned it, as may be expected from a journal that has also criticized the entire notion of the **auteur**. The journal is put out by a committee of unpaid writers, many of whom are filmmakers themselves. Most notable among them is Michel Ciment. The journal, in general, is defined by a strong sense of political engagement, and it has often featured critiques of films rooted almost entirely in what the critics perceive as an irresponsible social message. Many of the critics at *Positif* have inherited a vision of cinema and film poetics that belongs to an older generation, such as that of **Louis Delluc**, to whom it once devoted an edition, and the surrealist movement, although there is a fair range to the writings presented over the history of the journal.

POUCTAL, HENRI (1856–1922). Actor, director, film pioneer, and screenwriter. Like many film pioneers, Henri Pouctal began his career in the theater. He worked as an actor principally before being hired on at *Studio Film d'art* in 1908. In the beginning, Pouctal worked as both an actor and director. He acted in such films as **André Calmettes** and **Henri Desfontaines**'s *Résurrection* (1910) and *Jésus de Nazareth* (1911) and Calmettes's *L'Écharpe* (1910), *Le Chevalier d'Essex* (1911), and *La Dame aux Camélias* (1912). Pouctal codirected the two later films.

Pouctal began directing in 1910, and by 1912 had devoted himself entirely to directing. He went on to make more than seventy films over a period of approximately ten years. Among films he directed are *Vitellius* (1911), *Werther* (1911), *Madame Sans-Gêne* (1911), *Camille Desmoulins* (1911), and *Les Trois mousquetaires* (1912), the last two codirected with Calmettes, *Le Saltimbanque* (1912), *Blanchette* (1912), *Le Trait d'union* (1913), which stars **Jacques Feyder**, *Frères ennemis* (1913), *Colette* (1913), *La Rose rouge* (1914), *Le Légionnaire* (1914), *L'Heure tragique* (1914), *Pêcheur d'islande* (1915), *L'Homme masqué* (1916), *Chantecoq* (1916), *Debout les morts!* (1916), *Le Roman d'un spahi* (1917), the eight-part serial *Le Comte de Monte-Cristo* (1918), *Travail* (1920), and *Gigolette* (1921). As may be expected from his *film d'art* connections, Pouctal worked predominantly with literary adaptation, although he did other types of film. Pouctal worked with actors such as **Léon Mathot** and Camille Bert and was once hailed as one of the great directors of silent film by **Louis Delluc**.

PRÉJEAN, ALBERT (1893–1979). Actor. One of the great actors of the early cinema, Albert Préjean began his career in film in 1921 after being discharged from military service. He had no theatrical training and was one of the first actors to make his career entirely in the cinema. His career spanned silent and sound film, and he appeared in more than ninety films over a period of forty years, during which time he worked with many of the great directors of the day.

Préjean made his film debut in **Henri Diamant-Berger**'s *Les Trois mousquetaires* (1921). During the silent era, he went on to appear in Diamant-Berger's *Gonzague* (1922), starring Maurice Chevalier, *Le Roi de la vitesse* (1923), and *Éducation de Prince* (1927), Raymond Bernard's *Le Miracle des loups* (1924) and *Le Joueur d'échec*s (1927), **René Clair**'s *Paris qui dort* (1925), *Le Fantôme du Moulin rouge* (1925), *Le Voyage imaginaire* (1926), and *Un chapeau de paille* (1927), Henri Chomette's *Le Requin* (1929), and **Jacques Feyder**'s *Les Nouveaux messieurs* (1929). It was really Préjean's work with Clair during the silent era that established him as an actor and also established the persona he would often portray onscreen, a sort of hapless everyman, defined by an optimism and caught up in the wonder of the world. This combination rendered many of Préjean's characters endearing and very human.

During the sound era, Préjean continued to be a force onscreen and appeared in starring roles through the 1930s and 1940s. He appeared in such films as Clair's *Sous les toits de Paris* (1930), **Serge de Poligny**'s *Les Rivaux de la piste* (1932), **Henri Decoin**'s *Les Bleues du ciel* (1933), Pierre Colombier's *Théodore et Cie* (1933), Jean de Limur's *L'Auberge du petit dragon* (1934), Félix Gandara's *Le Secret d'une nuit* (1934), **Julien Duvivier**'s *Le Pacquebot Tenacity* (1934), **René Guissart**'s *Dédé* (1934), Robert Siodmak's *La Crise est finie* (1934) and *Mollendard* (1938), **Léo Joannen**'s *Quelle drôle de gosse!* (1935), Edmond T. Gréville's *Princesse Tam-Tam* (1935), **Marcel Carné**'s *Jenny* (1936), **Christian-Jacque**'s *À Venise, une nuit* (1937), Carl Lamac's *Place de la Concorde* (1937), Pierre Billon's *Piste du sud* (1938), **André Hugon**'s *La Rue sans joie* (1938), Maurice Cloche's *Nord Atlantique* (1939), Jean Stelli's *Pour le maillot jaune* (1939) and *L'Or du Cristobal* (1940), codirected by **Jacques Becker** and **Jean Renoir**, André Cayatte's *Au bonheur des dames* (1943), and Richard Pottier's *Les Caves du 'Majestic'* (1945).

During the 1930s and 1940s, Préjean was one of the preferred leading men of the cinema, and he was often cast opposite **Danielle Darrieux**. He also appeared opposite **Françoise Rosay**, Elvire Popesco, and Dita Parlo. During the 1950s, his career waned a bit and he appeared in supporting roles in a much smaller number of films. Most of the films in which he appeared were fairly insignificant. He made his last film appearance in 1962 in Jean-Louis Richard's *Bonne chance, Charlie* (1962). He is the father of actor Patrick Préjean.

PRESLE, MICHELINE (1922–). Actress. Micheline Presle made her screen debut in 1937. She had small roles in Pierre Caron's *La Fessée* (1937), Jean de Limur's *Petite peste* (1938), and Christian Stengel's *Je Chante* (1938) before being "discovered" by director Georg Wilhelm Pabst, who cast her in a leading role in his film *Jeunes filles en détresse* (1939). Presle went on to appear in more than one hundred films after that, including films on both sides of the Atlantic. She has also worked extensively in television. She is one of the most prolific actresses ever to have worked in French cinema.

In the 1930s and 1940s, Presle appeared in such films as **George Lacombe**'s *Elles étaient douze femmes* (1940), **Marc Allegret**'s *Parade en sept nuits* (1941), *La Belle aventure* (1942), and *Félicie Nanteuil* (1945), **Marcel L'Herbier**'s *La Nuit fantastique* (1942), **Jacques de Baroncelli**'s *Fausse alerte* (1945), **Christian-Jacque**'s *Boule de suif* (1945), **Claude Autant-Lara**'s *Le Diable au corps* (1946), and **Jean Delannoy**'s *Les Jeux sont faits* (1946). She went to Hollywood in the early 1950s after marrying American actor and producer William Marshall. She spent two years working in Hollywood, where she appeared in such films as Jean Negulesco's *Under My Skin* (1950) and Marshall's *The Adventures of Captain Fabian* (1951) but returned to making films in France when the American response was lukewarm.

Presle's career seemed only to reach another high point in France in the 1950s. She starred in such films as Raymond Bernard's *La Dame aux Camélias* (1953), **Sacha Guitry**'s *Si Versailles m'était conté* (1954) and *Napoléon* (1955), Pierre Gaspard-Huit's *La Mariée est trop belle* (1956) and *Christine* (1958), and **André Hunébelle**'s *Treize à table* (1956). Her career went from strength to strength, and she appeared in a number of films in the 1960s and 1970s including Delannoy's *Le Baron de l'écluse* (1961), **Philippe de Broca** and **Claude Chabrol**'s *Les Sept péchés capitaux* (1962), **Julien Duvivier**'s *Le Diable et les dix commandements* (1962), Raoul Lévy's *Je vous salue, mafia!* (1965), **Jacques Rivette**'s *La Religieuse* (1966), de Broca's *Roi de coeur* (1966), Allegret's *Le Bal du comte d'Orgel* (1970), **Jacques Demy**'s *Peau d'âne* (1970), Christian-Jacque's *Les Pétroleuses* (1973), and Claude d'Anna's *Trompe l'oeil* (1975).

During the late 1970s and 1980s, Presle worked predominantly in television. Those film roles she had were in fairly insignificant films. Some exceptions were her roles in Chabrol's *Le Sang des autres* (1984), Gérard Frot-Coutaz's *Beau temps mais orageux en fin de journée* (1986), and **Alain Resnais**'s *I Want to go Home* (1989). Presle has acted in a fair number of films in the last two decades. Among her other roles, she has appeared in Alexandre Jardin's *Fanfan* (1993), her daughter **Tonie Marshall**'s *Pas très catholique* (1994), *Enfants de salaud* (1996), *Vénus beauté (institut)* (1999), and *France boutique* (2005), **Claude Lelouch**'s *Les Misèrables* (1995), Danièle Dubroux's *Le Journal du séducteur* (1996), **Gérard Jugnot**'s *Fallait pas!* (1996), Francis Girod's *Mauvais genre* (2001), and Merzak Allouache's *Chouchou* (2003). Presle has acted in a wide variety of genres, but she is a particularly good comic actress.

PRINCE, CHARLES (1872–1933). Actor and director. Born Charles Prince Seigneur, Prince, as he would be known onscreen, signed on at **Pathé** studios in 1908 and went on to become one of the great comic stars of the silent screen. Prince's best-known screen character was Rigadin, and he appeared in a series of comic films that ran between 1909 and 1918 and included such titles as *Rigadin* (1909), *Rigadin face à Napoléon* (1910), *Rigadin débute au music-hall* (1911), *Rigadin aux Balkans* (1912), *Rigadin président de la République* (1913), *Rigadin veut faire du cinéma* (1913), *Rigadin et l'homme qui l'assassina* (1914), *Un marriage à la baïonette* (1915), *Rigadin et les deux dactylos* (1916), *Une nuit tragique de Rigadin* (1917), *Rigadin a fait un riche marriage* (1918), *La Femme de Rigadin* (1918), *Rigadin et le code de l'honneur* (1919), and *Rigadin dans les Alpes* (1919). All told, there were more than one hundred films in the *Rigadin* series. All films in the series were directed by **Georges Monca**.

The *Rigadin* series accounted for most of Prince's contribution to the cinema. It was internationally very successful, although the character appeared under different names in different countries. The series was called the *Moritz* series in Germany, the *Tartufini* series in Italy, and the *Whiffles* series in England, for example. Prince also appeared in a number of other silent films including Monca's *Le Contrôleur des wagon-lits* (1913), *La Mariée recalcitrante* (1916), *Les Femmes collantes* (1920), *Chouquette et son as* (1920), all which Prince codirected, Monca's *Un monsieur qui suit les dames* (1908), *L'Armoire normande* (1908), *Ce que femme veut* (1909), *Le Bon roi Dagobert* (1911), *Les Surprises du divorce* (1912), *Le Roi Koko* (1913), *Monsieur le directeur* (1913), and *Les Fiancés héroïques* (1915), Charles Esquier's *Sanatorium pour maigrir* (1909), **Albert Capellani** and Michel Carré's *Fleur de pavé* (1909), Yves Mirande's *Le Petit qui a faim* (1909), Henri Germain's *La Malle du peintre* (1910), and Robert Péguy's *Embrassez-moi* (1928). He also starred in and directed *Si jamais je te pince* (1920). In terms of his box-office success, Prince was the only comic star during the silent era to rival Pathé's other great star, **Max Linder**. His comedy, however, was much more in the vein of **Romeo Bossetti** and **André Deed** than that of Linder, who had an air of elegance to his slapstick.

Prince appeared in a handful of sound films before his death. These include Joe Francis and Jean Toulot's *Le Tampin du Capiston* (1930), Péguy and Erich Schmidt's *Son altesse l'amour* (1931), Maurice Toureur's *Partir* (1931), Pierre Colombier's *Sa meilleure cliente* (1932), Alexandre Ryder's *L'Âne de Buridan* (1932), and Maurice Cammage's *Le Coq du régiment* (1933), his final film. Prince had supporting roles in these films, and it is for his work during the silent era that he is best remembered.

PRIX JEAN-VIGO/JEAN VIGO PRIZE. Founded in 1951 by Claude Aveline, this annual award is named after the director **Jean Vigo**. It emphasizes originality and is often granted to emerging directors. After 1960, it was decided that two awards would be given each year, one for feature-length film and one for short film. Films that have received the prize include **Alain Resnais** and **Chris Marker**'s *Les Statues meurent aussi* (1954), Resnais's *Nuit et brouillard* (1956), **Claude Chabrol**'s *Le Beau Serge* (1959), **Jean-Luc Go-**

dard's *À bout de souffle* (1960), Ousmane Sembene's *La Noire de . . .* (1966), Mehdi Charef's *Le Thé au harem d'Archimède* (1985), and Cédric Kahn's *Trop de bonheur* (1994).

PRIX LÉON-MOUSSINAC/MOUSSINAC PRIZE. The Prix-Léon Moussinac is the critics' prize for the best foreign film of the year. Established in 1967, the award is named for theorist **Léon Moussinac**. Past winners include Roman Polanski's *Rosemary's Baby* (1969), Federico Fellini's *Fellini-Roma* (1972), David Lynch's *Elephant Man* (1981), Ingmar Bergman's *Fanny and Alexander* (1983), Wim Wenders's *Paris, Texas* (1984), Mike Leigh's *Secrets and Lies* (1996), and Roberto Benigni's *Life is Beautiful* (1998).

PRIX LOUIS-DELLUC/LOUIS DELLUC PRIZE. The Prix Louis-Delluc is the film critics' prize for best French film, with a particular emphasis on cinematography. It was established in 1937 by Maurice Bessy and Marcel Idzkowski. The prize is named for filmmaker **Louis Delluc**. The prize is awarded the second Thursday of December each year. Past winners include **Jean Renoir**'s *Les Bas-fonds* (1937), **Marcel Carné**'s *Quai des brumes* (1939), **Jean Cocteau**'s *La Belle et la bête* (1946), **Jacques Becker**'s *Rendez-vous de juillet* (1949), **Jacques Tati**'s *Les Vacances de Monsieur Hulot* (1953), **Henri-Georges Clouzot**'s *Les Diaboliques* (1954), **René Clair**'s *Les Grandes manoeuvres* (1955), **Louis Malle**'s *Ascenceur pour l'échafaud* (1957), **Jean Rouch**'s *Moi, un noir* (1958), **Jacques Demy**'s *Les Parapluies de Cherbourg* (1963), **Jean-Paul Rappeneau**'s *La Vie de château* (1965), **Bertrand Tavernier**'s *L'Horloger de Saint-Paul* (1973), **Diane Kurys**'s *Diabolo menthe* (1977), **Alain Corneau**'s *Tous les matins du monde* (1991), **André Téchiné**'s *Les Roseaux sauvages* (1994), and **Alain Resnais**'s *On connaît la chanson* (1997). No award was given during the period of the Nazi Occupation of France, from 1940 to 1944.

PRIX MÉLIÈS/MÉLIÈS PRIZE. The Prix Méliès is a critics' prize that rewards the best French film or French coproduction of the year. Founded in 1946, the prize is named for pioneer filmmaker **George Méliès**. Past winners include **René Clément**'s *La Bataille du rail* (1946), **René Clair**'s *Le Silence est d'or* (1947), **Claude**

Autant-Lara's *Le Rouge et le noir* (1954), **Jacques Tati**'s *Mon oncle* (1958), **Alain Resnais'** *Hiroshima mon amour* (1959), **François Truffaut**'s *Les Quatre cents coups* (1959), **Jacques Demy**'s *Les Parapluies de Cherbourg* (1964), **Eric Rohmer**'s *Ma nuit chez Maud* (1969), **Louis Malle**'s *Lacombe Lucien* (1974), **Bertrand Tavernier**'s *Coup de torchon* (1981), **Agnès Varda**'s *Sans toit ni loi* (1985), **Jacques Rivette**'s *La Belle noiseuse* (1991), and **Jean-Pierre Jeunet**'s *Le Fabuleux Destin d'Amélie Poulanc* (2001).

– R –

RAÏMU (1883–1946). Actor. Born Jules Auguste Muraire in Toulon in southern France, Raïmu went on to become one of the most beloved character actors in French cinema. He began his career on the stage in Toulon, performing in local café-concerts, quite often doing impressions. His success in that milieu attracted the attention of **Sacha Guitry**, who brought him to Paris and put him to work in the theater. Raïmu went on to perform in the Folies Bergères as well as the Comédie Française.

Although Raïmu is best remembered as a screen star, it was the theater that launched his film career. He had tried his hand at screen acting during the silent era, appearing in films such as the uncredited *Le Fumiste* (1912) and **Henri Desfontaines**'s *L'Homme nu* (1913). However, it was through his role in **Marcel Pagnol**'s stage play, *Marius*, that Raïmu finally caught the attention of the cinema. In 1929, Pagnol apparently invited Raïmu to appear in his production of *Marius* (1931), offering him the role of Panisse, Fanny's hapless suitor. However, Raïmu seems to have seen a better match in the role of César, Marius's father, and it was that role he requested. He played César onstage and then onscreen in Pagnol and Alexander Korda's adaptation of the play in 1931. He went on to reprise the role in **Marc Allegret**'s adaptation of *Fanny* (1932) and Pagnol's adaptation of *César* (1936), and it is probably the role with which Raïmu is most closely associated.

In addition, Raïmu went on to appear in a number of other memorable roles in various other films. He worked again with Pagnol, appearing in *La Femme du boulanger* (1938) and *La Fille du puisatier*

(1940). He was also a particular favorite of Allegret, who cast him in *Mam'zelle Nitouche* (1931), *Le Blanc et le noir* (1931), *La Petite chocolatière* (1932), *Gribouille* (1937), *Parade en sept nuits* (1941), and *L'Arlésienne* (1942). In addition to his close association with Pagnol, Raïmu was associated with **Le Réalisme poétique** or poetic realism. In addition to his work with Allegret, he also appeared in **Julien Duvivier**'s *Un carnet de bal* (1937) and *Untel père et fils* (1943).

For obvious reasons, Raïmu worked with southern director **André Hugon**, appearing in such films as *Gaspard de Besse* (1935) and *Le Héros de la Marne* (1939). In addition, Raïmu also worked with Tourneur on *Les Gaiétés de l'escadron* (1932), Pierre Colombier on *Charlemagne* (1933), *Théodore et Cie* (1933), *Le Roi* (1936), and *Les Rois du sport* (1937), Raymond Bernard on *Tartarin de Tarascon* (1934), **Roger Richebé** on *J'ai une idée* (1934) and *Minuit place Pigalle* (1934), **André Berthomieu** in *Le Secret de Polichinelle* (1936), *La Chaste Suzanne* (1937), and *Les Nouveaux riches* (1938), Guitry in *Faisons un rêve* (1937), **Jean Grémillon** in *L'Étrange Monsieur Victor* (1937), **Christian-Jacques** and Guitry in *Les Perles de la couronne* (1937), **Léo Joannen** in *Vous n'avez rien à déclarer* (1937), Fernand Rivers in *Le Fauteuil 47* (1937), Jean Boyer in *Noix de coco* (1939), Jeff Musso in *Dernière jeunesse* (1939), Alexander Esway in *Monsieur Brotonneau* (1939) and *L'Homme qui cherche la vérité* (1940), **Georges Lacombe** in *Monsieur La Souris* (1942), **Henri Decoin** in *Les Bienfaiteurs* (1942) and *Les Inconnus dans la maison* (1942), Raymond Leboursier in *Les Petits riens* (1942), and René Le Henaff in *Le Colonel Chabert* (1943) and *Les Gueux au paradis* (1946). Orson Welles once called Raïmu the greatest French actor who ever lived. While some would, no doubt, dispute that assessment, the range of roles Raïmu played, from duped husband to jovial mercurial barkeeper to tough prosecutor, seems to give credence to that judgment. However, for many filmgoers throughout the world, it is the barkeeper that stole the show.

RAPPENEAU, JEAN-PAUL (1932–). Director and screenwriter. Rappeneau started as an assistant to Raymond Bernard and Jean Dréville. He worked as a screenwriter for **Yves Robert**, **Louis Malle**, and **Phillippe de Broca**. His most successful feature to date is the

heritage film *Cyrano de Bergerac* (1990), an adaptation of Edmond Rostand's nineteenth-century play. The film won ten **César Award**s, including Best Director, Best Film, Best Actor (**Gérard Depardieu**), and Best Cinematography. It later received a "César of Césars" at the twentieth anniversary of the César Awards in 1995. Rappeneau's first film was a short titled *Chronique provinciale* (1958). His feature debut, *La vie de château* (1966), starred **Catherine Deneuve** and won the **Prix Louis-Delluc**. Rappeneau has often worked with major French celebrities including **Jean-Paul Belmondo** in *Les mariés de l'an II* (1971), **Yves Montand** and Deneuve in *Le sauvage* (1975), **Isabelle Adjani** and Montand in *Tout feu, tout flamme* (1982), **Juliette Binoche** in the heritage film *Le hussard sur le toit* (1995), and Adjani and Depardieu in *Bon voyage* (2002). *Le sauvage*, *Le hussard sur le toit* and *Bon voyage* were all nominated for Césars for Best Director, and *Le hussard sur le toit* was also nominated for Best Film.

RAVEL, GASTON (1878–1958). Director, producer, and screenwriter. Born in Paris, Gaston Ravel was primarily a silent-film-era director. He began his career at **Gaumont** under the direction of **Louis Feuillade** and began making films in 1914. Ravel went on to make at least thirty silent films, many of them starring Gaumont actors such as Yvette Andreyor, Louise Lagrange, **Léon Mathot**, **Georges Melchior**, Claude Mérelle, **Musidora**, **René Navarre**, and Jean Signoret. His early Gaumont films include *Saint-Odile* (1914), *La Fille aux pieds nus* (1914), *La Petite refugiée* (1914), *Autour d'une bague* (1915), *Triple entente* (1915), *Fille d'Eve* (1916), *La Femme inconnue* (1916), *L'Homme qui revient de loin* (1917), *Du rire aux larmes* (1917), *La Geôle* (1918), and *La Maison d'argile* (1918). Ravel also codirected several films with **Jacques Feyder** including *Des Pieds et des mains* (1915) and *Monsieur Pinson policier* (1916).

In 1919, Ravel left France for Italy to work in the emerging Italian cinema. He made several films in Italy between 1919 and 1922, including *Cosmopolis* (1920) and *Saracinesca* (1921), codirected with Augusto Camerini. In late 1921, Ravel returned to France and resumed directing. His later silent films include *À l'ombre du Vatican* (1922), *Tao* (1923), starring **Joë Hamman**, *Ferragus* (1923), *Jocaste* (1924), *Le Gardien du feu* (1924), *Chouchou poids plume* (1925), *L'Avocat* (1925), *Amour, délice, et orgues* (1925), *Le Roman d'un* *jeune homme pauvre* (1926), *Le Fauteuil 47* (1926), and *Le Bonheur du jour* (1927). He also codirected several films with Tony Lekain, including *On ne badine pas avec l'amour* (1924), *Madame Récamier* (1928), and *Figaro* (1929).

Ravel made only a handful of films during the sound era, although his 1929 film, *Le Collier de la reine*, which stars Marcelle Chantal, was one of the first sound films in French. His other sound films include *L'Étrangère* (1931), *Monsieur de Porceaugnac* (1932), *Le Rosaire* (1934), and *Fanatisme* (1934), all codirected with Lekain. Ravel predominantly worked with literary adaptation, adapting works ranging from Greek tragedy to Pierre de Beaumarchais to Honoré de Balzac. However, some of his films, most notably *Des Pieds et des mains*, have also been seen as avant-garde experiments in comedy and the absurd. In addition to directing, Ravel wrote the screenplays for several of his films and self-produced his film *Chouchou poids plume* (1925). He gave up the cinema after 1934.

RÉALISME POÉTIQUE/POETIC REALISM. *Réalisme poétique* or poetic realism is a name given to a trend or current in French cinema starting in the 1930s and leading to the Nazi Occupation. It is often called a movement or school, but it was less coherent than either of those terms might suggest. Sometimes referred to as "populist" cinema, poetic realism was influenced and to some degree inspired by the political ideas of the Front Populaire, and indeed, several filmmakers associated with the current were members of the party. While it is not a coherent movement, there are several underlying tendencies that unite the films associated with poetic realism. First of all, as the name suggests, these were realist, often darkly realist, films, sometimes adapted from the works of realist writers, sometimes written for the screen. Secondly, in a more naturalist vein, directors associated with the current had a strong interest in the working classes, and working-class characters figure prominently in these films. Thirdly, the films associated with the current often use stark images and chiaroscuro lighting, where light and dark take on symbolic effect. Finally, the films depict Paris or some other large city. They focus on working-class areas, notably the *banlieues*. In that regard, the current followed on from the influence of early directors such as **Louis Feuillade** and **René Clair**, and would influence later French waves, including the *Nouvelle Vague* or New Wave and the *cinéma de banlieue*. Many critics also feel that the current influenced both Italian neorealism and American film noir. One difference from both the later and earlier currents is that, although the films associated with poetic realism feature the city, they were typically shot on sound stages and in studios.

Directors whose films exhibit characteristics associated with poetic realism include **Marce Carné**, **Pierre Chenal**, **Julien Duvivier**, **Jean Grémillon**, and **Jean Renoir**. Some of the best-known films associated with the current include Grémillon's *La Petite Lise* (1930), *Guele d'amour* (1937), and *Remorques* (1939), Chenal's *La Rue sans nom* (1933), *Le Dernier tournant* (1933), and *Crime et chatîment* (1934), Carné's *Le Quai de brumes* (1938), *L'Hôtel du nord* (1939), and *Le Jour se lève* (1939), Duvivier's *La Bandera* (1935), *La Belle équipe* (1936), and *Pepé le Moko* (1937), and Renoir's *La Grande illusion* (1937), *La Bête humaine* (1938), and *La Règle du jeu* (1939). The actor most closely associated with poetic realism is **Jean Gabin**, who starred in many of the films cited as examples. Although a later director, **Jacques Becker** also shows tendencies derived from poetic realism. **Marc Allegret** also shows some characteristics of poetic realism in his works, and his brother, Yves Allegret, has been seen as having revived certain aspects of the vein after the war. **Jacques Feyder** is considered an important influence on the current, although only his *La Kermesse héroïque* (1935) is typically named among films belonging to the vein. Some critics point to the influence of **Jean Vigo**, who is also sometimes included in the list of poetic realism directors.

REGGIANI, SERGE (1922–2004). Actor. Serge Reggiani was born in Reggio Emilia, Italy. His parents fled the fascist regime and migrated to France in the early 1930s. He studied at the Conservatoire des arts cinématographiques and the Conservatoire d'art dramatique in Paris. One of Reggiani's early significant stage roles was under the direction of **Jean Cocteau** in his play *Les Enfants terribles*. Reggiani first appeared onscreen in an uncredited role in *Les Disparus de Saint-Agil* (1938), directed by **Christian-Jaque**. He later acted in **Louis Daquin**'s *Le Voyageur de la Toussaint* (1942), **Léo Joannon**'s *Le*

Carrefour des enfants perdus (1944), Marcel Blistene's *Etoile sans lumière* (1945), and André Zwoboda's *François Villon* (1945). His breakthrough role arrived in 1946 with **Marcel Carné**'s *Les Portes de la nuit*. His popularity rose with his performances in **Henri-Georges Clouzot**'s *Manon* (1949), André Cayatte's *Les Amants de Vérone* (1949), **Max Ophüls**'s *La Ronde* (1950), and especially in **Jacques Becker**'s *Casque d'or* (1951).

Reggiani engaged in parallel careers in French and Italian cinemas. He costarred with **Jean-Paul Belmondo** in **Jean-Pierre Melville**'s *Le Doulos* (1962) and further developed his film career in Luigi Comencini's *Tutti a casa* (1960), Luchino Visconti's *Il Gattopardo* (1963), Gérard Calderon's *Le Bestiaire d'amour* (1963), Robert Enrico's *Les Aventuriers* (1966), and Melville's *L'Armée des ombres* (1969).

Also in the 1960s, Reggiani developed a very successful singing career. He released his first album in 1965 and another in 1967, which was a large success. In addition, he acted in the theater, receiving accolades for his principal role in Jean-Paul Sartre's play *Les séquestrés d'Altona*. In the 1970s, Reggiani continued to balance his music and film careers. He starred in Enrico's *Les Caïds* (1972), **Claude Sautet**'s *Vincent, François, Paul et les autres* (1974), and **Claude Lelouch**'s *Le Chat et la souris* (1975). He acted with fellow singer-actor Jacques Dutronc in Lelouch's *Le Bon et les méchants* (1975). Soon after, he starred with Dutronc and **Isabelle Adjani** in Jacques Ruffio's *Violette et François* (1977).

In 1980, Reggiani appeared in Ettore Scola's *La Terrazza* (1980). That same year, he suffered as a result of the suicide of his son Stéphan. After a few years, he returned to the screen in a number of European features, such as Theo Angelopoulos's *O Melissokomos* (1986), **Léos Carax**'s *Mauvais sang* (1986), and Lelouch's *Il y a des jours . . . et des lunes* (1989). He also became a painter and continued to record songs. The following decade he acted in Josée Dayan's *Plein fer* (1990), Aki Kaurismäki's *I Hired a Contract Killer* (1991), Pierre Granier-Deferre's *Le Petit garçon* (1993), and Mario Gas's *Le Pianiste* (1997). His starred for his son, director Simon Reggiani, in the short *Zani* (1991) and the feature *De force avec d'autres* (1992). This beloved actor's last appearance on the big screen was in 1997 in Gérard Krawczyk's *Héroïnes*.

RENAUD, MADELEINE (1900–1994). Actress. Madeleine Renaud was one of the great stage actresses of the past century, and she was also a prominent screen actress. She studied drama at the Paris Conservatoire d'art dramatique, and then entered the Comédie Française in 1921. She remained in residence at the Comédie Française until 1946, at which point she left to form her own theatrical company with her husband, actor **Jean-Louis Barrault**. The company, called the Compagnie Renaud-Barrault, was a very successful independent troupe and was associated with the Théâtre de l'Odéon, among other theaters.

Renaud made her screen debut during the silent era, appearing in René Leprince's *Vent debout* (1923) and Jean Choux's *La Terre qui meurt* (1926). However, Renaud did not have much success on the screen until the arrival of sound, at which point she became a sought-after screen actress. Among the films in which she appeared during the 1930s and 1940s are **Henri Fescourt**'s *Serments* (1931), Choux's *Jean de la lune* (1931), Harry Lachman's *Mistigri* (1931) and *La Belle marinière* (1932), **René Guissart**'s *Primerose* (1933), **André Hugon**'s *Boubouroche* (1933), Curtis Bernhardt's *Le Tunnel* (1933), **Jean Benoît-Lévy** and **Marie Epstein**'s *La Maternelle* (1933) and *Hélène* (1936), Pierre Caron's *Les Demi vièrges* (1936), Jean Dréville's *Les Petites alliées* (1936), **Jean Grémillon**'s *L'Étrange Monsieur Victor* (1937), *Remorques* (1941), *Lumière d'été* (1943), and *Le Ciel est à vous* (1944), and **Georges Lacombe**'s *L'Escalier sans fin* (1943).

Renaud did not act onscreen during the Nazi Occupation and, in fact, she was absent altogether from 1944 until 1952, when she appeared in **Max Ophüls**'s *Le Plaisir*. She appeared only occasionally in film after that, since her theatrical career took up most of her time. Her later films include Philippe Agostini's *Le Dialogue des Carmélites* (1960), Ken Annakin and Andrew Marton's *The Longest Day* (1962), **Philippe de Broca**'s *Le Diable par la queue* (1969), **Edouard Molinaro**'s *La Mandarine* (1972), **Marguerite Duras**'s *Des Journées entières dans les arbres* (1976), and Francesca Comencini's *La Lumière du lac* (1988), her final film, in which she appeared with Barrault.

RENOIR, JEAN (1894–1979). Actor, director, producer, and screenwriter. Arguably one of the most significant French filmmakers ever,

Jean Renoir was the second son of renowned painter Pierre-Auguste Renoir. Interested in the image from a very early age, Renoir had an equal fascination with literature and the theater, which he first experienced in the form of Guignol, a puppet show. Renoir's interest in cinema was sparked after his service in World War I, when he and his first wife, Catherine Hessling, spent time watching films. Renoir apparently had a desire to make a film star out of Hessling, who had been one of his father's models.

Indeed, nearly all of Renoir's early films feature Hessling quite prominently. These include *Une vie sans joie* (1924), *La Fille de l'eau* (1925), *Nana* (1926), *Sur un air de Charleston* (1927), *Marquitta* (1927), *La Petite marchande d'allumettes* (1928), and *Tire-au-flanc* (1928). Renoir made two other silent films, *Le Tournoi dans la cité* (1928) and *Le Bled* (1929). What unites all of these silent films, despite their wide array of topics, is the predominance of image and the experimentation with form. It is almost natural for a silent filmmaker to be preoccupied with the visuals of films since there was not yet sound. And yet Renoir, even early on, demonstrated an awareness of the symbolic potential of the film image that was well beyond that of his peers. There were early experiments in the light-dark contrasts that would characterize the later wave of *Le Réalisme poétique* or poetic realism, with which Renoir would be associated. Moreover, there is evident in these silent films a type of impressionism that some have said united elements of his father's philosophy of the image with the poetics of the German avant-garde. All of these films are still in existence with the exception of *Marquitta* (1927), which is believed lost.

If Renoir established his reputation during the silent era, it is typically his early sound films that are remembered as his greatest works. Among these, *La Chienne* (1931), *Boudu sauvé des eaux* (1932), *Le Crime de Monsieur Lange* (1936), *Une partie de campagne* (1936), *La Grande illusion* (1937), *La Marseillaise* (1938), *La Bête humaine* (1938), and *La Règle du jeu* (1939) are all considered masterpieces. Renoir's other films from the 1930s include *On purge bébé* (1931), *Chotard et Cie* (1932), *La Nuit du carrefour* (1932), *Madame Bovary* (1933), *Toni* (1935), *Les Bas-fonds* (1936), and *La Vie est à nous* (1936), which Renoir later disavowed.

La Chienne is one of the first Renoir films to interrogate human nature and the interaction between flawed human beings and an equally or perhaps more flawed social system. It is the story of an aging man, Legrand, who wishes to be a great painter, and it recounts his chance meeting with Lulu, the girlfriend of a thug and con artist. The film depicts Legrand's subsequent involvement with Lulu and the misery this adulterous relationship brings to all involved. The central preoccupation of the film is one of flawed people in a fundamentally flawed society, and it repeats everywhere in Renoir's other films.

Boudu sauvé des eaux is the story of a good Samaritan who rescues a homeless man from the Seine and who is then left to deal with the man he has saved, who turns out to be very different than the helpless innocent the man had imagined. *Une partie de campagne* is the story of a petit-bourgeois family's Sunday picnic. However, the film, which features stunning visuals that reproduce paintings from Fragnonard and Renoir, is a merciless critique of social class and the interaction between class and gender. The critical exploration of class and gender is not quite so brutal as it is in the later film *La Règle du jeu*, the story of a weekend hunting party at a stately country house, but it is nonetheless quite dark. *La Bête humaine*, about love and betrayal and life in the working classes, is equally dark, but one could expect little else from a film adapted from the novel by Émile Zola. *La Grande illusion* is a somber, pensive, visually stunning reflection on the utter senselessness of war, and it is set against an exploration of the potential breakdown of class relations in the context of such destabilizing events as war. It is both hopeful and dark at the same time and widely considered perhaps the greatest film Renoir ever made.

Against these somber, yet always meditative explorations of the human condition, Renoir created films such as *Le Crime de Monsieur Lange*, which presents the murder of the despicable owner of a printing shop and the formation of a workers' cooperative in the shop after his death. There is again the hope and darkness, although the formation of the workers' cooperative has often been read as the hopeful looking toward the Front Populaire in France. The film is also significant for its casting of all the members of the **Groupe Octobre**. There is also *La Marseillaise*, which is both homage to the Revolution and a warning that the victories of that revolution could well be lost. This is Renoir from the period in French film associated with *Le*

Réalisme poétique. Renoir's gaze in the films from the 1930s is clear-sighted and critical, hopeful and poetic, light and dark at the same time. The poetry of his images and his play with genre and structure contrast with the often somber realism of the camera's gaze. The great **Jean Gabin** was the star of most of Renoir's films from this period, although Renoir also cast **Marcel Dalio** in several of them. He was one of the few directors to make full use of Dalio's great talent.

Jean Renoir also began work on *Tosca* (1941), which was being made in Italy as war broke out. The film was finished without Renoir, who returned to France, but ultimately left again as France surrendered to the Nazis. Renoir spent the war years in Hollywood, where he made films in English, including *Swamp Water* (1941), *The Amazing Mrs. Holliday* (1943), *This Land is Mine* (1943), *Salute to France* (1944), *The Southerner* (1945), *Diary of a Chambermaid* (1946), *The Woman on the Beach* (1947), and *The River* (1951). While these films are almost universally seen as less coherent and less forceful than Renoir's French films, they are, nonetheless, solid works that exhibit many of Renoir's filmmaking characteristics. They deal with pressingly realist social issues, from adoption, to Occupation and resistance, to dirt farming, to colonial class politics. They are visually stunning, and they are bittersweet explorations of the human condition. The films have different strengths, although it is worth noting that **André Bazin** was quite taken with *Diary of a Chambermaid*, which he classified as a burlesque tragedy, and which he considered the best of Renoir's Hollywood films.

Renoir returned to France in 1951 and resumed making films there, although he ultimately renounced his French citizenship and became an American citizen. His later films include *Le Carrosse d'or* (1953), a French-Italian coproduction; *French Cancan* (1955), a musical film set in the Moulin Rouge; *Eléna et les hommes* (1956), the story of a pre–World War I love triangle involving a Polish countess; *Le Testament du Docteur Cordelier* (1959), a retelling of the Jekyl and Hyde story; *Le Déjeuner sur l'herbe* (1959), another painting-inspired exploration of class and gender roles but in a completely different era than that of *Une partie de campagne* (1936); and *Le Caporal épingle* (1962), another exploration of the experiences of prisoners of war. As may be evident, several of these later films directly revisit the themes of Renoir's early films and the visual style remains largely unchanged, although the dominance of color film by this time gives a different dimension to the images on the screen, which become more realist and less poetic. If these films are not quite the equals of the films of the 1930s, it must, nonetheless, be pointed out that no serious critic anywhere ever accused Renoir of ever making a bad film.

In addition to directing, Renoir wrote or contributed to the screenplays of nearly all of his films. He also acted in a good many of them, including *Une vie sans joie*, *Une partie de campagne*, *La Vie est à nous*, *La Bête humain*, and *La Règle du jeu*. He also appeared in films by other filmmakers, including Alberto Cavalcanti's *Le Petit chaperon rouge* (1930) and Roberto Rosselini's *L'Amore* (1948). Probably Renoir's most memorable performances in film were as the wolf in Cavalcanti's *Le Petit chaperon rouge* (1930) and as Octave in *La Règle du jeu* (1939). Renoir also produced several of his own films including *Une vie sans joie*, *La Fille de l'eau*, *Nana*, *Le Crime de Monsieur Lange*, *La Marseillaise*, *This Land is Mine*, and *The River*.

Renoir retired from the cinema in 1962. He was, even during the 1930s, considered one of the greatest directors to make films. However, it was about the time of his retirement that he was elevated to the status of legend, as many of the filmmakers of the **Nouvelle Vague** or New Wave, inspired, no doubt, by their mentor Bazin, rediscovered Renoir's films. **Alain Resnais**, in particular, was extremely moved by Renoir's films, but all of the directors associated with the movement hailed Renoir as the type of filmmaker in whose footsteps they followed. Renoir's reputation since that time has held fast, and he is regarded as one of the greatest directors ever to make films.

RESNAIS, ALAIN (1922–). Cinematographer, director, and editor. Alain Resnais began experimenting with filmmaking at the age of fourteen. He studied film at the **Institut des Hautes Études Cinématographiques** (IDHEC) before becoming a filmmaker. While there, he took courses with the avant-garde filmmaker and theorist **Jean Epstein**. Epstein's theories, particularly those concerning film's capacity to render the mental life of a character or an age, seem to have resonated quite strongly with Resnais, and his filmmaking style would show the influence of Epstein's work.

Resnais's first film was the short documentary *Van Gogh* (1948), which won an Academy Award. It was followed by the shorts *Gaugin* (1950) and *Guernica* (1950). He continued to focus on the fine arts in *Les statues meurent aussi* (1953), a documentary about African art that earned him the **Prix Jean-Vigo**. The short *Toute la mémoire du monde* (1956), a documentary on France's Bibliothèque Nationale, is an early example of Resnais's long-term interest in the complexities of memory, evidence of the influence of Epstein. His renowned documentary on the Holocaust, *Nuit et brouillard* (1955), has been lauded for its rich contemplation of human memory and trauma, as is his most famous feature film, *Hiroshima mon amour* (1959), which was based on the script by the novelist and filmmaker **Marguerite Duras**. These two films together point to the particular way in which memory and mental life have been rendered in Resnais's work, through an exploration of war and the mental traces it leaves, from trauma and repression to the process of memorialization. Resnais's innovative use of fragmented narrative, montage, and interspersed documentary footage in *Hiroshima mon amour* are a case in point, and the film attracted wide critical attention and sparked his association with the New Wave. The film won the Film Writers Award at **Cannes**, though it was initially excluded from the program for political reasons.

Alain Robbe-Grillet, one of the inventors of *le nouveau roman* (the "new novel"), scripted Resnais's second feature, *L'Année dernière à Marienbad* (1961), which won a Golden Lion at Venice. This film is also influenced by Epstein's theories as it attempts to represent the effects of psychological trauma on film. While the role of war is not evident in this film, some critics, Lynn Higgins among them, have argued that the film is about the Algerian War, which functions as the ultimate repressed trauma so repressed the viewer never actually gets to it. It may also be worth noting that the film was made in a climate of censorship.

Resnais's third feature, *Muriel ou le temps d'un retour* (1963), reiterates the theme of memory and explores the way in which the past encroaches on the present and points to the other theme in Resnais's films—that of war. Like **Jean-Luc Godard**'s *Le petit soldat* (1963), it recalls French practices of torture during the Algerian War.

Resnais later directed *La guerre est finie* (1966), the sketch "Claude Ridder" for *Loin du Vietnam* (1967), *Je t'aime, je t'aime*

(1968), the sketch "Wall Street" for *L'an 01* (1973), and *Stavinsky* (1974). Resnais won **César**s for Best Film and Best Director for his English-language film *Providence* (1977), then won the Grand Prize of the Jury at **Cannes** for *Mon oncle d'Amérique* (1980). He also directed *La vie est un roman* (1983), *L'amour à mort* (1984), *Mélo* (1986), and *I want to go home* (1989). Resnais won Césars for Best Film and Best Director for the two-part film, *Smoking/No Smoking* (1993), and a César for Best Film for the musical comedy *On connaît la chanson* (1997). His latest film to date is another musical, *Pas sur la bouche* (2003). He is considered one of France's major **auteurs**.

REVUE DU CINÉMA. *La Revue du cinéma* was a film journal founded in the 1920s, for which critics such as **Jean Epstein** and **Louis Delluc** wrote. It was revived in the postwar era by **Jean-Georges Auriol** and **Jacques Doniol-Valcroze** and influenced other journals, most notably *Les Cahiers du cinéma*.

RICHARD, PIERRE (1934–). Actor, director, and screenwriter. Pierre Richard was born Pierre Defays in Valenciennes. He studied drama under Jean Vilar at the Centre Dullin. He later wrote sketches for cabarets in which he performed solo or with Victor Lanoux. His first appearance as a film actor was in an uncredited role in **Jaques Becker**'s *Les Amants de Montparnasse* (1958). He played a small role in **Yves Robert**'s *Alexandre le Bienheureux* (1967) and would later star in Robert's hit *Le Grand Blond avec une chassure noir* (1972), *Le Retour du grand blond* (1974), and *Le Jumeau* (1984).

In 1970, Richard branched out into directing. His first feature film was *Le distrait* (1970), a film in which he played the leading role. He went on to direct such films as *Les malheurs d'Alfred* (1972), *Je sais rien, mais je dirai tout* (1973), *Je suis timide . . . mais je me soigne* (1978), *C'est pas moi, c'est lui!* (1980), *On peut toujours rêver* (1991), and *Droit dans le mur* (1997). He also starred in all of these films.

In the 1970s and 1980s, Richard was one of France's most popular comic actors. He starred in **Claude Zidi**'s highly successful comedies *La Moutarde me monte au nez* (1974) and *La Course à l'échalote* (1976) and Gérard Oury's blockbuster *La Carapate* (1978) and *La parapluie* (1980). He also costarred with **Gérard Depardieu** in Francis Veber's *La chèvre* (1981), *Les compères* (1983), and *Les fugitifs* (1986), all of which were among the top French films in the year of their release. These films and others made Richard an international star. Later in the 1980s, Richard starred in Moshé Mizrahi's *Mangeclous* (1988) and **Edouard Molinaro**'s *À gauche en sortant de l'ascenseur* (1988).

In the 1990s, Richard played leading roles in Jean-Louis Leconte's *Bienvenue à bord* (1990), Yves Hanchar's *La Partie d'échecs* (1994), Marco Pico's *La Cavale des fous* (1993), and Georgian director Nana Djordjadze's multilingual film *A Chef in Love* (1997). More recently, Richard played in Catherine Corsini's *Mariées mais pas trop* (2003) and starred in Damien Odoul's *En attendant le déluge* (2003). He has also done a number of television films.

RICHARD-WILLM, PIERRE (1895–1983). Actor. Born Pierre Richard, Pierre Richard-Willm made his screen debut at the beginning of the sound era and went on to become one of the dashing leading men of the 1930s and 1940s, appearing in nearly forty films. Richard-Willm debuted in Alberto Cavalcanti's *Toute sa vie* (1930) and went on to appear in Cavalcanti's *Les Vacances du diable* (1931), Alexandre Ryder's *Un soir au front* (1931), Henri Chomettes and Robert Siodmak's *Autour d'une enquête* (1931), Pierre Billon and Carl Lamac's *La Fille du régiment* (1933), **Marcel L'Herbier**'s *L'Épervier* (1933), *La Route impériale* (1935), *La Tragédie impériale* (1938), and *Entente cordiale* (1939), Jean de Marguenat's *Le Prince Jean* (1934), Billon's *La Maison dans la dune* (1934), *Courrier sud* (1936), and *L'Argent* (1936), **Jacques Feyder**'s *Le Grand jeu* (1934) and *La Piste du nord* (1939), Tony Lekain and **Gaston Ravel**'s *Fanatisme* (1934), Alexis Granowsky's *Les Nuits muscovites* (1934), **Julien Duvivier**'s *Un carnet de bal* (1937), **Marc Allegret**'s *La Dame de Malacca* (1937), and **Max Ophüls**'s *Werther* (1938), among other films.

Richard-Willm's career showed signs of slowing during the 1940s, as he appeared in fewer films although typically in the lead role. He acted in such films as **Jacques de Baroncelli**'s *La Duchesse de Langeais* (1942), André Berthomieu's *La Croisée des chemins* (1942), **Robert Vernay**'s *Le Comte de Monte Cristo* (1943), **Serge de Poligny**'s *La Fiancée des ténèbres* (1945), Christian Stengel's

Rêves d'amour (1947), and Louis Cuny's *Le Beau voyage* (1947). He played in a wide array of films of different types. He was a dramatic, not a comic, actor. Probably because of his striking good looks and his elegance of presentation, he quite often played military men and aristocrats. He retired from the cinema in 1947 and devoted the rest of his career to the theater.

RICHEBÉ, ROGER (1897–1989). Director, producer, and screenwriter. Born in Marseille, Roger Richebé was lured into the cinema by a commercial venture of his father's to finance cinema houses. Not content to simply screen films, Richebé began directing and producing. As a director Richebé made nearly twenty films during the 1930s, 1940s, and 1950s. He made his first film, *L'Agonie des aigles*, in 1933, and went on to direct *Minuit place Pigalle* (1934), *L'Habit vert* (1937), *Prisons de femmes* (1938), *La Tradition de minuit* (1939), *Madame Sans-Gêne* (1941), *Les J3* (1946), *Monseigneur* (1949), *Les Amants de minuit* (1953), *Élisa* (1957), and *Que les hommes sont bêtes* (1957), among other films. In addition to directing, he wrote the screenplays for a number of his own films and worked on the screenplay for **Abel Gance**'s *Austerlitz* (1960).

In 1930, Richebé created a joint production company with Pierre Braunberger, Les Établissements Braunberger-Richebé. The venture lasted a few years before Richebé formed his own production company, Les Films Roger Richebé. He also coproduced with **Marcel Pagnol**. Among the films Richebé produced either independently or in collaboration were **Marc Allegret**'s *Mam'zelle Nitouche* (1931), *Le Blanc et le noir* (1931), *Fanny* (1932), codirected with Pagnol, and *La Petite chocolatière* (1932), **Jean Renoir**'s *La Chienne* (1931), Maurice Tourneur's *Königsmark* (1935), **Marcel L'Herbier**'s *Forfaiture* (1937), his own *Madame Sans-Gêne* (1941), *Monseigneur* (1949), and *Les Amants de minuit* (1953), **Georges Lacombe**'s *Monsieur La Souris* (1942), **Robert Bresson**'s *Les Anges du péché* (1943), **Christian-Jacque**'s *Voyage sans espoir* (1943), and **Henri Decoin**'s *Clara de Montargis* (1951). He retired from the cinema in 1960.

RIVETTE, JACQUES (1928–). Director, critic, and screenwriter. Before becoming a member of French cinema's famous *Nouvelle Vague* or New Wave, Jacques Rivette assisted other greats of the cinema, particularly **Jean Renoir** and **Jacques Becker**. He wrote the short films *Aux quatre coins* (1949), *Le quadrille* (1950), and *Le divertissement* (1952) and contributed to *Gazette du cinéma* before moving to **Cahiers du cinéma**. He took over the editorship of *Cahiers du Cinéma* from **Éric Rohmer** from 1963 to 1965.

Rivette began directing during the 1950s. His first short, *Le coup du berger* (1956), was produced by fellow New Wave director **Claude Chabrol**, who allowed Rivette to use his apartment as a setting. Rivette began filming his first feature-length film, *Paris nous appartient*, in 1959, although it took him two years to make it because of funding issues so the film was not released until after Chabrol's *Le beau Serge* (1959), Truffaut's *Les Quatre cents coups* (1959), or several other New Wave films. The film is the story of a group of actors trying to stage a Shakespearian play. It captures Parisian street life in a way that is reminiscent of **Louis Feuillade** and *Le Réalisme poétique* or poetic realism, and it is decidedly modern in its themes of alienation and disconnection. Rivette's work was admired by **François Truffaut** who gave a silent nod to Rivette in his film *Les Quatre cents coups* (1959). When the protagonist of Truffaut's film, Antoine Doinel, goes to the movies with his parents in Truffaut's film, it is Rivette's *Paris nous appartient* that is playing. The film was still in production at the time.

Rivette's second film was *La religieuse* (1967), based on the novel by Denis Diderot. The story of an aristocratic woman forced into the church against her will, the film was censored for its depiction of the church and of oppressive institutions in general. His third feature, *L'amour fou* (1969), returned to the play within the film structure of his first film and centers on the production of Racine's *Andromaque*. It was followed by *Out one: noli me tangere* (1971), based on a work by Honoré de Balzac. The original version of the film runs over twelve hours; however, it was cut and edited down to 255 minutes and released as *Out one: spectre* (1974). It features several New Wave icons, including the critic and director **Jacques Doniol-Valcroze**, the actor Jean-Pierre Léaud, the director **Éric Rohmer**, and the producer/actor **Barbet Schroeder**. This film also features themes of alienation and is centered around a story within a story.

Rivette's next film, *Céline et Julie vont en bateau* (1974), offers perhaps the most mature interrogation of storytelling and relationship between narrative and reality. The film is the story of two women who enter a house where the same narrative repeats over and over. It centers on the ultimately successful, although trying, efforts of the two women to change the course of the narrative. The film received wide critical acclaim and is noteworthy because Rivette gave scriptwriting and script-altering power to the actresses in the film, Juilet Berto, Dominque Labourier, **Bulle Ogier**, and **Marie-France Pisier**, an act which replicates the function they perform within the film. Rivette's subsequent films were *Noroît* (1975), *Duelle* (1976), *Le pont du Nord* (1982), *Merry-go-round* (1983), *L'amour par terre* (1984), *Hurlevent* (1985), and *La bande des quatre* (1989).

Rivette's first film of the 1990s, *La belle noiseuse* (1991), won the Grand Prize of the Jury at **Cannes** and was nominated for a Golden Palm and a **César** for Best Film. Still concerned with representation, this film moves away from storytelling to painting. It is the story of an artist who has lost his muse only to rediscover her in a young model, much to the chagrin of his wife. The film stars **Emmanuel Béart**, **Michel Piccoli**, and Jane Birkin. Rivette's next film was the two-part narrative about Joan of Arc, *Jean la pucelle* (1994), and it was followed by *Haut bas fragile* (1995), *Secret défense* (1998), *Va savoir* (2001), and *Histoire de Marie et Julien* (2003).

ROBERT, YVES (1920–2002). Actor, director, producer, and screenwriter. Yves Robert was born in Saumur, France. He worked in the theater before debuting in cinema in René Lucot's *Les Dieux du dimanche* (1948). He subsequently acted in **Marcel Carné**'s *Juliette ou la Clef des songes* (1950), Maurice Labro's *Le Tampon du Capiston* (1950), and Jean Anouilh's *Deux sous de violettes* (1951). In 1951, Robert made his directorial debut with the short *Les bonnes manières* (1951). His debut feature film was *Les hommes ne pensent qu'à ça* (1954), which featured **Louis de Funès**. Robert continued to act while working on his directing career. In the 1950s, he appeared in **Marc Allégret**'s *Futures Vedettes* (1955), **René Clair**'s *Les grandes maneouvres* (1955), and **Claude Autant-Lara**'s *La Jumente verte* (1959).

Robert's second feature was *Ni vu, ni connu* (1958), which also starred de Funès. It was followed by *Signé Arsène Lupin* (1959) and *La famille Fenouillard* (1961). His directing career soared with his *La guerre des boutons* (1962), starring Jacques Dufilho. The film was the largest grossing film in France in 1962 and among the top ten most successful French films in the latter part of the twentieth century. It also won the **Prix Jean-Vigo**. *La guerre des boutons* was also the first feature produced by Robert's company La Guéville, which he established with his wife, actress Danièle Delorme. Also in the 1960s, Robert directed *Bébert et l'omnibus* (1963), *Les copains* (1965), *Monnaie de singe* (1966), *Alexandre le bienheureux* (1968), and *Clérambard* (1969).

In the 1970s, Robert directed some of France's most popular comedies. *Le grand blond avec une chaussure noire* was among France's five top-selling films of 1972. It was coscripted with Francis Veber and starred **Pierre Richard**. The film won the Silver Berlin Bear and was remade in Hollywood as *The Man with One Red Shoe* (1985), starring Tom Hanks. Robert directed a sequel, *Le retour du grand blond* (1974), also coscripted with Veber. Robert's *Un éléphant ça trompe énormément* (1976) and *Nous irons tous au paradis* (1977) were both among France's most successful films in the years they were released. Both were coscripted with Jean-Loup Dabadie. He also directed *Salut l'artiste* (1973) and *Courage fuyons* (1979). He had only one major role during the 1970s, in **Claude Berri**'s *Le cinéma de papa* (1970). Interestingly, some of Robert's later films would be compared with Berri's.

In the 1980s, Robert played principal roles in **Claude Sautet**'s *Un mauvais fils* (1980) and *Garçon!* (1983). He directed a single film in that decade, *Le jumeau* (1984). As a director, he is most famous for the films that followed, *La Gloire de mon père* (1990) and *Le Château de ma mère* (1990). Both films were based on **Marcel Pagnol**'s memoirs, *Souvenirs d'enfance*. Shot in Provence, the films have been classified as nostalgic **heritage films** and compared to the Pagnol films of **Claude Berri**. Robert's last two films as director were *Le bal des casse-pieds* (1992) and *Montparnasse-Pondichéry* (1994), both of which starred **Miou-Miou**.

Robert continued to act in the 1990s. He played a lead role in *Montparnasse-Pondichéry*, and he also appeared in **Coline Serreau**'s *La Crise* (1992) and Jean-Denis Robert's *Sortez des rangs* (1995). His last film as an actor was Gilles Bourdos's *Disparus* (1998).

ROBIN, DANY (1927–1995). Actress. Dany Robin originally intended to be a dancer. She studied ballet and even danced professionally before studying drama at the Paris Conservatoire d'art dramatique. She made her screen debut in 1946, appearing in **Marc Allegret**'s *Lune-garde*, and she went on to appear in more than fifty films during the 1940s, 1950s, and 1960s. Among the films in which Robin appeared are **Marcel Carné**'s *Les Portes de la nuit* (1946), **René Clair**'s *Le Silence est d'or* (1947), **Henri Decoin**'s *Les Amoureux sont seuls au monde* (1948), Gilles Grangier's *Jupiter* (1952), **Julien Duvivier**'s *La Fête à Henriette* (1952), **Roger Richebé**'s *Les Amants de minuit* (1953), **André Hunébelle**'s *Cadet-Rouselle* (1954) and *Les Mystères de Paris* (1962), **Sacha Guitry**'s *Napoléon* (1955), **Jacqueline Audry**'s *L'École des cocottes* (1958) and *Le Secret du Chevalier d'Éon* (1959), **Jean-Paul Le Chanois**'s *Mandrin* (1962), and Alfred Hitchcock's *Topaz* (1969), her last film. A solid actress who was as capable of doing comedy as drama, Robin was also one of the bombshells of French cinema.

ROHMER, ERIC (1920–). Director, film critic, and screenwriter. Eric Rohmer was born Jean-Marie Maurice Schérer. He began his professional life as a teacher and novelist and in cinema circles as a film critic. Before gaining acclaim for his participation in the ***Nouvelle Vague*** or New Wave, he published the novel *Elizabeth, ou les vacances* (1946) under the pseudonym Gilbert Cordier. He wrote influential essays on film, including "Le Cinéma, art de l'espace" (1948) "Pour un cinéma parlant" (1948) in *Les temps modernes*, and "Celluloid et le marbre" (1955). His criticism was published in both ***Revue du cinéma*** and ***Cahiers du cinéma***.

Rohmer also actively attended *ciné-clubs*, such as the *Ciné-club du Quartier Latin* and *Objectif 49*. He was a cofounder in the early 1950s of *Gazette du cinéma*, a short-lived publication that featured articles by **Jacques Doniol-Valcroze**, **Alexandre Astruc**, **Jean-Luc Godard**, **François Truffaut**, and **Jacques Rivette**, among others. In 1957, he published the book *Hitchcock* with **Claude Chabrol**. He also replaced **André Bazin** as editor in chief for *Cahiers du cinéma* from 1957 to 1963. Though considered a member of the New Wave, Rohmer's career was rather distinct. He was about a decade older than his colleagues and arguably more conservative.

Rohmer directed his first short, *Journal d'un scélèrat*, in 1950. From there, he began a period of collaboration with other New Wave directors. He also directed *Bérénice* (1954), *Tous les garçons s'appellent Patrick* (1957), and *Véronique et son cancre* (1958). Chabrol produced Rohmer's feature debut, *Le signe du lion* (1959), an important, albeit less commercially successful, New Wave film. It was followed by *Charlotte et son steak* (1960), which was adapted from a short film by Godard and that starred the director. Although Rohmer is now recognized as a key figure in the New Wave, his films were somewhat late in being acknowledged.

Rohmer's first real acclaim as a filmmaker came after his famous film series categorized as his "Contes moraux," six films that generally involve a male protagonist—often one engaged in unreliable narration—who must chose between two **women**. The most acclaimed of these is *Ma Nuit chez Maude* (1969). The five other tales in the 1962–1972 "Contes moraux" series are the shorts *La Boulangère de Monceau* (1962) and *La Carrière de Suzanne* (1963) and the features *La Collectionneuse* (1967), which won the **Prix Louis-Delluc**, *Le Genou de Claire* (1970), and *L'Amour l'après-midi* (1972). Rohmer subsequently won the Special Jury Prize at **Cannes** for *La Marquise d'O* (1976). His *Perceval le Gallois* (1979) was adapted from the romance by the twelfth-century poet Chrétien de Troyes.

Subsequent to the "Contes Moraux" Rohmer directed the series "Comédies et Proverbes," which focused on the points of view of women protagonists and include *La femme de l'aviateur* (1981), *Le beau mariage* (1982), *Pauline à la plage* (1983), *Les nuits de la pleine lune* (1984), *Le rayon vert* (1986), which won a Golden Lion at Venice, and *L'ami de mon amie* (1987). This was followed by the quartet, "Contes des quatre saisons," composed of *Conte de printemps* (1990), *Conte d'hiver* (1992), *Conte d'été* (1996), and *Conte d'automne* (1998). He also shot *Quatre aventures de Reinette et Mirabelle* (1987), *L'arbre, le maire et la médiathèque* (1993), *L'Anglaise et le duc* (2001), and *Triple Agent* (2004). He was awarded a Career Golden Lion at Venice in 2001.

Before he was recognized as one of France's most respected directors, Rohmer played a central role in the development of French film criticism. In well over two hundred reviews and essays, he helped to reaffirm the importance of cinema as an art form as he developed theories for interpreting formal and thematic elements of cinema. His films are also known for their philosophical content, often expressed as dialogues between characters who must make personal moral decisions.

ROMANCE, VIVIANE (1912–1991). Actress, producer, and screenwriter. One of the great femme fatales of French cinema, Viviane Romance was born Pauline Ortmans in Roubaix. She caught the attention of French cinema at the beginning of the sound era after being named Miss Paris. She made her screen debut in 1931 in **Jean Renoir**'s *La Chienne* and went on, during the early part of the decade, to appear in such films as **Louis Mercanton**'s *Il est charmant* (1932), **Claude Autant-Lara**'s *Ciboulette* (1933), **Marc Allegret**'s *Zouzou* (1934), Fritz Lang's *Liliom* (1934), **Julien Duvivier**'s *La Bandera* (1935), and Edmond T. Greville's *Princesse Tam Tam* (1935). Romance's breakthrough role came in 1936 when she appeared in Duvivier's *La Belle équipe*, and it was this performance that would define the roles she would play later in her career. Other films from the decade in which she appeared include **Jean Grémillon**'s *L'Étrange Monsieur Victor* (1937), **Pierre Chenal**'s *La Maison du Maltais* (1938), and **Roger Richebé**'s *Prisons de femmes* (1938) and *La Tradition de minuit* (1939).

During the 1940s, Romance starred in a number of films, including **Abel Gance**'s *Vénus aveugle* (1941), Gréville's *Une femme dans la nuit* (1943), **Christian-Jacque**'s *Carmen* (1945), Yves Allegret and Jean Choux's *La Boîte aux rêves* (1945), **Léon Mathot**'s *La Route du bagne* (1945), **Marcel L'Herbier**'s *L'Affaire du collier de la reine* (1946), and Duvivier's *Panique* (1947), among others. Romance continued to attract lead roles during the 1950s, but the caliber of the films in which she appeared declined somewhat. She had roles in Georges Lampin's *Passion* (1951), Pierre Cardinal's *Au cœur de la Casbah* (1952), Yves Allegret and Autant-Lara's *Les Sept péchés capitaux* (1952), Marcel Blistène's *Guele d'ange* (1955), and **Henri Decoin**'s *L'Affaire des poisons* (1955).

Romance appeared in only one major film during the 1960s, **Henri Verneuil**'s *Mélodie en sous-sol* (1963). She retired from the screen in 1974 after appearing in **Claude Chabrol**'s *Nada* (1974). In addition to acting, she contributed to the screenplay of *La Boîte aux rêves*

(1945), and she produced both *Passion* (1951) and Jean Josipovici's *Pitié pour les vamps* (1956), in which she also starred.

ROSAY, FRANÇOISE (1891–1974). Actress. Born Françoise Bandy de Nalèche, the daughter of an aristocrat and an actress, Françoise Rosay studied drama at the Paris Conservatoire d'art dramatique and began her career on the stage. She also became one of the great actresses of French cinema. Rosay began her film career during the silent era and went on to appear in well over one hundred films over a period of sixty years. She made her screen debut in 1913, appearing in **Henri Desfontaines**'s *film d'art* production of *Falstaff*. She had roles in a number of other silent films, mostly those by director **Jacques Feyder**, whom she later married. She appeared in Feyder's *Abrégeons les formalités* (1916), *La Trouvaille de Buchu* (1916), *Têtes de femmes, femmes de tête* (1916), *Frère de lait* (1917), *Le Billard cassé* (1917), *Crainquebille* (1922), and *Gribiche* (1926). She also worked with **René Clair** in *Les Deux timides* (1928) and Bethold Viertel in *The One Woman Idea* (1929).

Rosay's career flourished during the 1930s. She worked frequently with Feyder, acting in such films as *Si l'empereur savait ça* (1930), *Le Grand jeu* (1934), *La Kermesse héroïque* (1935), *Pension Mimosas* (1935), and *Les Gens du voyage* (1938). She also had roles in a significant number of films by other directors. These include Ludwig Berger's *Le Petit café* (1931), **René Guissart**'s *La Chance* (1931), **Jean-Paul Paulin**'s *L'Abbé Constantin* (1932), Alberto Cavalcanti's *Coralie et Cie* (1933), Marc Didier's *Le Billet de mille* (1934), **André Hugon**'s *Gangster malgré lui* (1935), **André Berthomieu**'s *Le Secret de Polichinelle* (1936), **Marcel Carné**'s *Jenny* (1936) and *Drôle de drame* (1937), **Julien Duvivier**'s *Un carnet de bal* (1937), and **Claude Autant-Lara** and Maurice Lehmann's *Le Ruisseau* (1938).

Rosay's career remained strong throughout the 1940s and 1950s, although she fled France, along with Feyder, during the Nazi Occupation. She spent some time in Great Britain, which introduced her to English-language film. She returned to France after the war and continued her career there, although the types of roles she played evolved as she aged. She appeared in such films as **Georges Lacombe**'s *Ils étaient douze femmes* (1940), Feyder's *Une femme disparaît* (1942),

Marcel Blistène's *Macadam* (1946), codirected with Feyder, **Marc Allegret**'s *Maria Chapdelaine* (1950), Autant-Lara's *L'Auberge rouge* (1951), Yves Allegret and Autant-Lara's *Les Sept péchés capitaux* (1952), Jean Dréville's *La Reine Margot* (1954), Léonide Moguy's *Le Long des trottoirs* (1956), and Denys de la Patellière's *Les Yeux de l'amour* (1959). Among the English-language films in which Rosay appeared are Terence Young's *That Lady* (1955), Douglas Sirk's *Interlude* (1957), and Martin Ritt's *The Sound and the Fury* (1959).

Rosay's film career slowed significantly during the 1960s and 1970s, although she continued to act. She had roles in such films as Gilles Grangier's *La Cave se rebiffe* (1961), Pierre Granier-Deferre's *La Métamorphose de cloportes* (1965), **Henri Verneuil**'s *La Vingt-cinquième heure* (1967), and Roger Pigaut's *Trois milliards sans ascenseur* (1972). A talented actress who did everything from comedy to romantic comedy to drama to crime films, Rosay also maintained her stage career throughout her life. Some critics have commented that Rosay owed her career to Feyder. It is true that he recognized her talent from the beginning and that their work together is some of her best and some of his best. However, she worked with many more directors than Feyder, and her career extended two decades beyond his death. Film history has perhaps not dealt fairly with Rosay, who was certainly one of the most prominent actresses of her day.

ROUCH, JEAN (1917–2004). Director. Jean Rouch was born in Paris, the son of a traveling naval officer who took his family to live in Algeria, France, Germany, and Morocco. Rouch studied civil engineering in Paris in the late 1930s, where he viewed films at the **Cinémathèque Française**. During that period, Parisians were fascinated with African art and artifacts. Africa was often the subject of exhibitions at the controversial Musée de L'Homme. Rouch also appreciated surrealist art, which had been inspired by African art. This interest in Africa would later characterize his filmmaking.

Rouch halted his studies temporarily as a result of Germany's pending invasion. In 1939, in an attempt to prevent German attacks, Rouch became part of a team that exploded bridges. In 1940, he returned to his studies and added courses in anthropology taught by Marcel Griaule. The following year Rouch left Paris to serve as an engineer in France's African colonies. In Niger he met Damouré

Zika, who would enable Rouch to examine Songhay traditions first-hand. After World War II, Rouch, Pierre Ponty, and Jean Sauvy traveled the Niger River and wrote articles under the name Jean Pierjean. During this exploration Rouch codirected his first film, *Au pays des mages noirs*, with a handheld 16 mm camera, a technique that would later influence the filmmakers of the *Nouvelle Vague* or New Wave.

Rouch directed several ethnographic films in Africa, especially in the regions colonized by France. He crafted what he termed "shared anthropology," or the practice of encouraging the participation of, rather than the objectification of, people being filmed. He also provided instruction in film technology to African students, among them the Senegalese filmmaker Safi Faye. In 1955, Rouch screened one of his most famous films, *Les Maîtres Fous*, at the Musée de l'Homme. The film was subsequently banned in Great Britain. He also made "ethno-fiction" films such as *Jaguar*, and in collaboration with Oumarou Ganda in 1958, *Moi, un noir*. Rouch's use of handheld cameras and Ganda's improvised narration in *Moi, un noir* further led scholars to view Rouch as a forerunner to the New Wave. *Moi, un noir* was awarded the **Prix Louis-Delluc** in 1959. Rouch later directed *La Pyramide humaine* (1960), a documentary about high school students' perceptions of racism in the Ivory Coast. In 1961, Rouch and the sociologist Edgar Morin directed *Chronique d'un été*, which received the Prix de la Critique at the **Cannes Film Festival**. It employed a pioneering *cinéma verité* style, the term a translation of Russian director Dziga Vertov's *kino pravda*, or "film truth." The cinéma verité style—Rouch is credited as being the first director to use the term—has also been linked, with variations, to French directors **Chris Marker** and **Raymond Depardon**.

In 1965, Rouch contributed a sketch, titled "Gare du Nord," to the film *Paris, Vu Par*, a series of shorts codirected with **Claude Chabrol**, **Jean-Luc Godard**, and **Eric Rohmer**, among others. He later directed the ethnographic film *La chasse au lion à l'Arc* (1965), and with Germaine Dieterlen and Gilbert Rouget, he directed *Batteries Dogon* (1966). In 1968, Rouch filmed *Petit à petit,* featuring Faye and Zika. Zika also appeared in Rouch's *Cocorico Monsieur Poulet* (1974). In 1969, Rouch, **Henri Langlois,** and Enrico Fulchignoni pioneered a doctoral program in cinema at Paris universities. He later directed a biographical short about Margaret Mead, *Ciné-portrait de*

Margaret Mead (1977). In addition to making films, Rouch was a professor and writer.

Rouch became the head of the Cinémathèque Française in 1985, a post he held until 1991. He continued directing; among his films were *Boulevards d'Afrique* (1989), codirected with Tam-Sir Doueb, *Madame L'Eau* (1993), *Faire-part: Musée Henri Langlois* (1997), and *Le Rêve plus fort que la mort* (2002), codirected with Bernard Surugue (2002). In the past few decades, depictions of Africans by French ethnographers have been examined with scrutiny, especially by African intellectuals. Manthia Diawara directed a playful and insightful reverse ethnography starring Rouch, titled *Rouch in Reverse* (1995). Other biographical films about Rouch include Julien Donada and Guillaume Casset's *L'inventaire de Jean Rouch* (1993), Jean-André Fieschi's *Mosso Mosso: Jean Rouch comme si* (1998), and Anne McIntosh's *Conversations with Jean Rouch* (2004). Rouch died in Niger in a car accident in 2004.

ROUDÈS, GASTON (1878–?). Director. Gaston Roudès was a director who made films during the silent era and at the early part of the sound era. He made his directing debut at Éclipse Studios working with **Joë Hamman** on the *Arizona Bill* series of **Camargue Westerns** made between 1911 and 1913. Episodes in the series include *Le Pouce* (1911), *La Piste argentée* (1911), and *La Consience de Cheval-Rouge* (1912). All of these have been lost. Roudès went on to make more than forty other silent films including *La Rose du radjah* (1913), *Le Scarabée d'or* (1913), *La Légende d'Œdipe* (1914), *Papillon et le roi nègre* (1914), *Les Gaz* (1918), *La Doute* (1920), *La Dette* (1920), *La Voix de l'océan* (1922), *Le Lac d'argent* (1922), *Le Petit moineau de Paris* (1923), *Le Crime des hommes* (1923), *L'Éveil* (1924), *La Douleur* (1925), *La Maternelle* (1925), *Le Prince Zilah* (1926), *Cousine de France* (1927), *La Maison au soleil* (1928), and *L'Âme de Pierre* (1928). He also directed a number of films with Marcel Dumont, including *Au-délà les lois humaines* (1920), *Les Élus de la mer* (1921), *Les Petits* (1925), and *La Dédale* (1927).

Roudès made several films during the sound era. These include *Un coup de mistral* (1931), *Le Carillon de la liberté* (1931), *Le Gamin de Paris* (1932), *Roger la honte* (1933), *L'Assomoir* (1933), *La Maison du mystère* (1933), *Flofloche* (1934), *Le Petit Jacques* (1934), *Le*

Chant de l'amour (1935), *Enfants de Paris* (1936), *La Joueuse d'orgue* (1936), *Un coup de rouge* (1937), *La Tour de Nesle* (1937), and *Une main à frappé* (1939). Most of Roudès's films, whether sound or silent, were melodramas, although he worked in other genres. His historical film *La Tour de Nelse* was one of his better films, as was his *Roger la honte*. Both films were later remade, the first by **Abel Gance** in 1955 and the second by André Cayatte in 1946. Many of Roudès's films feature the actress **France Dhélia**. Roudès stopped working in 1939 and may have died that year, although what precisely happened to him is not known. He has been largely overlooked by film historians, and many of his films are presumed lost, although several have been saved and archived by the Cinémathèque Suisse.

ROULEAU, RAYMOND (1904–1981). Actor and director. Raymond Rouleau made his film debut at the end of the sound era with a small part in **Marcel L'Herbier**'s silent classic, *L'Argent* (1928). He built his screen career throughout the 1930s with a steady series of supporting roles in films such as **Léo Joannen**'s *Suzanne* (1932), which Rouleau codirected, André Charlot and Alexander Esway's *Le Jugement de minuit* (1932), **Jean-Paul Paulin**'s *La Femme nue* (1932), Viktor Tourjansky's *Volga en flammes* (1934), **Marc Allegret**'s *Les Beaux jours* (1935), **Pierre Chenal**'s *L'Affaire Lafarge* (1938), Georg Wilhelm Pabst's *Le Drame de Shanghaï* (1938), **Pierre Fresnay**'s *Le Duel* (1939), and **Léonide Moguy**'s *Conflit* (1939).

Rouleau began the 1940s with roles in films such as **Christian-Jacque**'s *Premier bal* (1941) and *L'Assassinat du Père Noël* (1941), Maurice Tourneur's *Mam'zelle Bonaparte* (1942), and **Robert Vernay**'s *La Femme que j'ai la plus aimée* (1942). By the mid-1940s, Rouleau moved from supporting actor to lead actor status, attracting starring roles in a number of films, including L'Herbier and **Jacques de Baroncelli**'s *L'Honorable Catherine* (1943), Jacques Daniel-Norman's *L'Aventure est au coin de la rue* (1944), **Jacques Becker**'s *Falbalas* (1945), Richard Pottier's *Vertiges* (1947), and **André Hunébelle**'s *Mission à Tanger* (1949). Rouleau reprised the character of detective Georges Masse, played in Hunébelle's film, in later films including *Méfiez-vous des blondes* (1950) and *Massacre en dentelles* (1952). The type suited him well and he went on to play other hardboiled characters in Gilles Grangier's *Les Femmes sont* *folles* (1950), **Henri Verneuil**'s *Brelan d'as* (1952), **Henri Decoin**'s *Les Intrigantes* (1954), and Maurice Cloche's *Le Fric* (1959). Rouleau had small roles in a handful of films in the 1960s, including **Jean-Pierre Mocky**'s *La Grande frousse* (1964). He gave up screen acting after 1965.

In addition to acting, Rouleau directed a number of films, including *Une vie perdue* (1933), *Le Messager* (1937), and the musical dance film *Les Amants de Teruel* (1962). During the 1970s and early 1980s, he directed television productions and he also directed for the theater. Rouleau also wrote the screenplay for *Les Amants de Teruel* (1962) and for several of his television productions. He continued working in television until his death.

– S –

SADOUL, GEORGES (1904–1967). Film critic and film historian. Born in Nancy in 1904, Georges Sadoul, the son of a wealthy industrialist, became interested in cinema at an early age. He was a member of the surrealist movement and signed the second Surrealist Manifesto in 1930. Sadoul is best known for his work as a film historian and theorist and, in fact, some consider him the father of modern film scholarship. He published a number of works on the cinema, including *Histoire du cinéma* (1949), *Georges Méliès* (1961), *Louis Lumière* (1964), and *Histoire du cinéma français* (1965), as well as a number of film dictionaries. He also taught film and film history as professor at the **Institut des Hautes Études Cinématographiques** (IDHEC). In addition to his works on the cinema, he was also an important literary critic.

Sadoul's legacy in film history has been mixed. He was an early champion of independent directors and recognized the merits of such directors as **Robert Bresson**, Luis Buñuel, and **Jean-Luc Godard**. He was also one of the first scholars in the sound era to study silent film, although many of his assertions have been challenged by more recent scholars. He was completely dismissive of Hollywood cinema, with the exception of Frank Capra, because it clashed with his left-wing political views. In his defense, it may be said that Sadoul's evaluation of silent film was based on a very limited awareness of that period, as most silent films were unavailable at the time he was writing. Moreover, some of his judgments about Hollywood have been repeated and repeated in the years since he wrote. He remains, however, a problematic, if important, icon of French cinema, and although his view shaped the reception of French film decades, many of them were later challenged.

SAINT-CYR, RENÉE (1904–2004). Actress. Born Raymonde-Renée Vittoret in Beausoleil, Provence, Renée Saint-Cyr went on to become one of the most popular actresses of the 1930s and 1940s. She made her screen debut in 1933, appearing in Max de Vaucorbeil's *Une fois dans la vie* (1933), Jacques Tourneur's *Toto* (1933), Kurt Gerron's *Incognito* (1933), Félix Gandéra's *D'amour et d'eau fraîche* (1933), and Maurice Tourneur's *Les Deux orphélines* (1933). These early roles established Saint-Cyr as a talented comic actress, who was equally capable of drama and melodrama, and she went on to appear in films such as Pierre Colombier's *L'École des cocottes* (1934), **René Clair**'s *Le Dernier milliardaire* (1934), Marc Didier's *Le Billet de mille* (1934), **Jean Grémillon**'s *Valse royale* (1935), **Léon Mathot**'s *Les Loups entre eux* (1936), Richard Pottier's *27, rue de la Paix* (1937) and *L'Insaissable Frédéric* (1946), **Christian-Jacque** and **Sacha Guitry**'s *Les Perles de la couronne* (1937), **Roger Richebé**'s *Prisons de femmes* (1938), **Jean-Paul Paulin**'s *Le Chemin de l'honneur* (1939) and *La Voix du rêve* (1948), Christian-Jacque's *La Symphonie fantastique* (1942), **Henri Fescourt**'s *Retour de flame* (1943), and André Cayatte's *Pierre et Jean* (1943).

Saint-Cyr continued acting in the 1950s and 1960s, although the number of films in which she appeared dropped off during those decades. Among the films in which she had roles were André Zwaboda's *Capitaine Ardant* (1952), Robert Darène's *Le Chevalier de la nuit* (1954), which she also produced, Guitry's *Si Paris nous était conté* (1955), and **Jean Dréville**'s *La Fayette* (1961). She was the mother of director **Georges Lautner**, and she appeared frequently in his films, including *Le Monocle rit jaune* (1964), *Fleur d'oseille* (1968), *Quelques messieurs trop tranquilles* (1973), *Pas de problème!* (1975), *On aura tout vu* (1976), *Ils sont fous ces sorciers* (1978), *Est-ce bien raisonnable?* (1981), *Attention! Une femme peut en cacher une autre* (1983), *Le Cowboy* (1984), *L'Invité surprise*

(1989), and *Room Service* (1992). She also worked in television during the 1970s and 1980s. Despite the range of her performances, Saint-Cyr remains best remembered for her comic roles.

SAUTET, CLAUDE (1924–2000). Actor, director, and screenwriter. Claude Sautet studied at the **Institut des Hautes Études Cinématographiques** (IDHEC) before directing his first feature film, the comedy *Bonjour sourire* (1955), followed by *Classe tous riques* (1960) and *L'Arme à gauche* (1964). His first major film was *Les choses de la vie* (1969). It won the **Prix Louis-Delluc**, was nominated for a Golden Palm at **Cannes**, and was remade in Hollywood by Mark Rydell as *Intersection* (1994). Sautet's films have received critical attention because of their intimate portrayals of couples and their attention to detail. These include *César et Rosalie* (1972), *Une histoire simple* (1978), *Garçon!* (1983), *Un coeur en hiver* (1992), and *Nelly et Monsieur Arnaud* (1995).

Une histoire simple was nominated for an Oscar for Best Foreign Film and **César** awards for Best Director, Best Film, and Best Screenplay. Sautet won Césars for Best Director for *Un coeur en hiver* in 1993 and *Nelly et Monsieur Arnaud* in 1996. The former was awarded a Silver Lion at Venice in 1992 and the latter received the Prix Louis-Delluc in 1995. Sautet also directed *Max et les ferrailleurs* (1971), *Vincent, François, Paul, et les autres* (1974), *Mado* (1976), *Un mauvais fils* (1980), and *Quelques jours avec moi* (1988). He worked as a scriptwriter on his own films, in addition to **Jacques Deray**'s *Borsalino* (1970) and **Jean-Paul Rappeneau**'s *Les Maries de l'an II* (1970), among others. He often hired actors **Romy Schneider**, **Yves Montand**, **Michel Piccoli**, and **Emmanuelle Béart**.

SCHNEIDER, ROMY (1938–1982). Actress. Romy Schneider, or Rosemarie Albach-Retty, was born in Vienna, the daughter of actors Wolf Albach-Retty and Magda Schneider. She debuted in cinema in German director Hans Deppe's *Wenn der weisse Flieder wieder blüht* (1953). In 1954, she played a young Queen Victoria in the film *Mädchenjahre einer Königin* (1954), by Austrian director Ernst Marischka, followed by title roles in Marischka's *Sissi* trilogy, which follows the story of the Bavarian princess and later Austrian Empress Elizabeth. She costarred for the first time onscreen with her future partner **Alain Delon** in Pierre Gaspard'Huit's *Christine* (1958), a remake of **Max Ophüls**'s 1933 *Liebelei*. Her mother had played the same role in the Ophüls original.

In the late 1950s, Schneider and Delon became engaged, although they never married. She maintained a lively theater career and acted onstage with Delon in the play *Dommage qu'elle soit une putain*, directed by Louis Visconti in 1961. The following year, she acted in Visconti's cinematic sketch "Il Lavoro" in the film *Boccacio 70*.

Schneider settled in France but became a legendary international film star. In the 1960s, she played in Orson Welles's *The Trial* (1963), David Swift's 1964 *Good Neighbor Sam* (opposite Jack Lemmon), Clive Donner's 1965 film *What's New, Pussycat?*, with Peter O'Toole, Peter Sellers, and Woody Allen, and Terence Young's 1966 *Triple Cross* with Christopher Plummer. She continued to star in French films, such as **Alain Cavalier**'s *Le Combat dans l'île* (1962), **Henri-Georges Clouzot**'s unfinished *L'Enfer*, and Jean Chapot's *La Voleuse* (1966). She and Delon separated in 1963, but she still performed with him in films such as **Jacques Deray**'s *La Piscine* (1968). She acted for the first time for director **Claude Sautet** alongside **Michel Piccoli** in *Les choses de la vie* (1969). Schneider would become Sautet's preferred actress.

In the 1970s, Schneider acted opposite **Yves Montand** in *César et Rosalie* (1972), with Delon in Joseph Losey's *The Assassination of Trotsky* (1972), with **Jean-Louis Trintignant** in Pierre Granier-Deferre's *Le train* (1973), and again alongside Piccoli in Francis Girod's *Le Trio Infernale* (1974). She replayed the role of Empress Elisabeth in Visconti's *Ludwig* (1972). In the same decade, she received two **César** Awards for Best Actress in Andrzej Zulawski's *L'important c'est d'aimer* (1975) and Sautet's *Une histoire simple* (1978). She later costarred in **Constantin Costa-Gavras**'s *Clair de femme* (1979) with Montand. In the 1980s, she played starring roles in **Bertrand Tavernier**'s *La Mort en direct*, Girod's *La banquière* (1980), and **Claude Miller**'s *Garde à vue* (1981). Her last cinematic performance was in Jacques Ruffio's *La passante du Sans-souci* (1982). She was nominated for a César for Best Actress for her work.

SCHOENDOERFFER, PIERRE (1928–). Director and screenwriter. In the 1950s Pierre Schoendoerffer was a cameraman for the French army in Indochina. He was taken prisoner in 1954 at Dien Bien Phû in Vietnam and released in 1955. As a result of these experiences, the themes of war and colonization permeate his films. His first film was *La passe du diable* (1959), shot in Afghanistan with Jacques Dupont. His features *Ramuntcho* (1959) and *Pêcheur d'Islande* (1959) are both based on novels by Pierre Loti, a writer who often set his work in former French colonies. Schoendoerffer's experiences in Indochina were the basis of his 1963 novel, *La 317e section*, which he later adapted for the screen as *La 317e section* (1965). The film won Best Screenplay at **Cannes** in 1965. It was followed by the feature *Objectif 500 millions* (1966).

In 1968, Schoendoerffer won an Oscar for his documentary about American GIs in Vietnam, *La section Anderson* (1967). His most acclaimed feature films to date are *Le crabe-tambour* (1977) and *Dien Bien Phû* (1992), both of which center around questions of war. Derived from his novel of the same name, *Le Crabe-tambour* focuses on an officer who served in Algeria and Indochina. *Dien Bien Phû* depicts the pivotal battle in which French forces in Indochina were defeated. His next film, *L'honneur d'une capitaine* (1982), broached the sensitive topic of French war crimes in Algeria. Another film adapted from one of his novels, *Là haut, un roi au-dessus des nuages* (2003), is set in Thailand and features clips from his previous films that serve as flashbacks. In addition to directing and writing fiction, Schoendoerffer has worked as a journalist for *Paris-Match* and *Paris-Presse*.

SERRAULT, MICHEL (1928–). Actor. Michel Serrault was born in Brunoy. He performed in music halls with his colleague **Jean Poiret** in Robert Dhéry's theater troupe before acting beside Dhéry in director Jean Loubignac's *Ah! Les belles bacchantes* (1954). Shortly after, he played in **Henri-Georges Clouzot**'s classic, *Les Diaboliques* (1955). Serrault acted alongside Poiret in several films early in his career, such as Michel Boisrond's *Cette sacrée gamine* (1956), Roger Pierre and Jean-Marc Thibault's *La Vie est belle* (1956), Jean Boyer's *La Terreur des dames* (1956), Maurice Cloche's *Adorables démons* (1957), Philippe Agostini's *Le Naïf aux quarante enfants* (1958), Raoul André's *Clara et les méchants* (1958), Boyer's *Nina* (1959), Jean Berry's *Oh! Qué mambo* (1959), **Henri Diamant-Berger**'s

Messieurs les ronds de cuir (1959), and **Clément Duhour**'s *Vous n'avez rien à déclarer?* (1959). Serrault and Poiret costarred in Maurice Cloche's short film, *Ça aussi c'est Paris* (1957) and in **Sacha Guitry**'s *Assassins et voleurs* (1957). In 1958, Serrault acted in **Jacques Demy**'s short, *Musée Grévin*.

In the 1960s, Serrault appeared both onstage and in the cinema, especially in the genre of comedy. He acted in films such as Dhéry's *La Belle Américaine* (1961), Marcel Bluwal's *Carambolages* (1962), **René Clair** and Alessandro Blasetti's *Les quatre verités* (1962), Francis Rigaud's *Nous irons à Deauville* (1962), Boisrond's *Comment trouvez-vous ma soeur?* (1963), Michel Drach's *La Belle occase* (1964), **Georges Lautner**'s *Des pissenlits par la racine* (1964), **Edouard Molinaro**'s *Quand passent les faisans* (1965), Roland Quignon's *Bon Weekend* (1965), and **Jean-Pierre Mocky**'s *Les Compagnons de la Marguerite* (1966). He paired again with Poiret in several films, among them Raymond Bailly's *Ma femme est une panthère* (1960), Jacques Poitrenaud's *La Tête du client* (1965), Rigaud's *Les Baratineurs* (1965), and André's *Le Grande bidule* (1967), *Ces messieurs de la famille* (1967), and *Ces messieurs de la gâchette* (1969).

In the 1970s, Serrault would have more opportunities to demonstrate his versatility and talent. He played the principal role in Pierre Tchernia's *Le Viager* (1972), a leading role in Mocky's *L'Ibis rouge* (1975), and a supporting role in **Bertrand Blier**'s Oscar-winning *Préparez vos mouchoirs* (1978). He reached international stardom with his lead role, alongside Ugo Tognazzi, in **Edouard Molinaro**'s hugely successful film *La cage aux folles* (1978), based on the play by Poiret. Serrault won a **César** for Best Actor for his performance in 1979. That same year, he received a César nomination for Best Supporting Actor in Christian de Chalonge's *L'Argent des autres*. He would later receive two more Césars for Best Actor in **Claude Miller**'s *Garde à vue* in 1982 and **Claude Sautet**'s *Nelly et Monsieur Arnaud* in 1996. He also received four additional César nominations for Best Actor. In 1997, he received the Lumière Award for Best Actor in **Claude Chabrol**'s *Rien ne va plus*.

Serrault has been hailed as one of France's finest actors. He is admired for his intelligence, versatility, and intimate character studies (for example, in his title role for de Chalonge's *Doctor Pietot* in

1990). In addition to starring in the two sequels to *La cage aux folles*, Serrault has played several significant parts in French comedies, thrillers, and dramas. He played leading roles in Miller's *Mortelle randonée* (1983), **Jacques Deray**'s *On ne meurt que deux fois* (1985), Alain Jessua's *En toute innocence* (1988), Tchernia's *Bonjour l'angoisse* (1988), Italian director Luigi Comencini's *Buon Natale . . . Buon anno* (1989), Mocky's *Ville à vendre* (1992), *Bonsoir* (1994), *Le Furet* (2003), and *Grabuge!* (2005), Étienne Chatiliez's *Le Bonheur est dans le pré* (1995), **Mathieu Kassovitz**'s *Assassin(s)* (1997), de Chalonge's *Le Comédien* (1997), Christian Carion's *Une hirondelle a fait le printemps* (2001), Laurent Bouhnik's *24 heures de la vie d'une femme* (2002), and Philippe Muhl's *Le Papillon* (2002). Most recently he starred in Pierre Javaux's *Les Enfants du pays* (2006) and Mocky's *Le Bénévole* (2006).

SERREAU, COLINE (1947–). Actress, director, and screenwriter. Coline Serreau is one of France's most well-known **women** filmmakers. Before directing films, Serreau studied music and dance and later worked as an actress and writer in the theater. She wrote the script for Jean-Louis Bertucelli's film, *On s'est trompé d'histoire d'amour* (1974), in which she starred. Her first film, the short *Le rendez-vous*, was made for French television. Her debut fictional feature was *Pourquoi pas!* (1977), which was followed by *Qu'est-ce qu'on attend pour être heureux!* (1982).

Serreau's most popular film, and one of the most commercially successful in French cinematic history, is the comedy ***Trois hommes et un couffin*** (1985), which sold over 10 million tickets, won **César** Awards for Best Film and Best Original Screenplay, and was remade in Hollywood as *Three Men and a Baby* (1987). This film, like her other films, deals with controversial social issues in provocative ways. Although the film deals with gender roles, many feminists consider her earlier film *Qu'est-ce qu'elles veulent?* (1977) to be a stronger exploration of women's issues. The film is a documentary, based on interviews with women of diverse ages, economic backgrounds, and geographical regions.

In general, Serreau's work engages in several women's issues and invites reflection on gender roles and societal constructions of masculinity and femininity. Serreau also attempts to bridge the perceived gap between mainstream and **auteur** films. Her career is quite varied. She has directed films for the cinema, while also working in television and theater. Her fourth feature film, *Romauld et Juliette* (1989), a very loose adaptation of Shakespeare's drama, portrays an interracial, cross-class romance. Her next feature, *La crise* (1992), a film that also deals with women's roles, won Best Original Screenplay at the César Awards.

Serreau has also worked on the science-fiction feature, *Le belle verte* (1996), for which she composed the score and in which she stars, and *Chaos* (2001), a film that critiques patriarchal violence against an Algerian woman and the ensuing indifference of French men. Most recently, she directed a sequel to *Trois hommes et un couffin*, titled *18 ans après* (2003) and the film *Saint-Jacques . . . La Mècque* (2005).

SEYRIG, DELPHINE (1932–1990). Actress and director. Delphine Seyrig was born in Beirut, Lebanon. She acted on the stage in French theaters in the 1950s and in 1956 relocated to New York. In 1959, she appeared in Robert Frank and Alfred Leslie's *Pull My Daisy*, a short narrated by beat poet Jack Kerouac. Her career was launched with her starring role in **Alain Resnais**'s 1961 film *L'Année dernière à Marienbad*. In 1963, she won the Volpi Cup for best actress in Resnais's *Muriel* at the Venice Film festival. Fluent in English and French, she played in French and British films in the 1960s, notably Joseph Losey's *Accident* (1967) and *A Doll's House* (1973), **François Truffaut**'s *Baisers volés* (1968), and William Klein's *Mister Freedom* (1969). Her collaboration with **Luis Buñuel** was fruitful; after a small role in Buñuel's *The Milky Way* (1969), she landed a pivotal role in his classic *Le Charme discret de la bourgeoisie* (1972).

Seyrig worked for prominent **women** directors **Marguerite Duras** and Chantel Ackerman and starred in Duras's *India Song* (1975) and Ackerman's *Jeanne Dielman, 23 Quai de commerce, 1080 Bruxelles* (1975), *Golden Eighties* (1986), and *Letters Home* (1986). Seyrig was active in the women's rights movement and helped to establish the Simone de Beauvoir Center, a resource for documentary filmmakers with feminist concerns. Seyrig directed her own documentary about the careers of actresses, *Sois belle et tais-toi* (1977). It featured **Romy Schneider** and Jane Fonda, among others.

Seyrig was truly a pan-European actress, playing in French, British, German, Belgian, and Hungarian films. She acted in Belgian director Harry Kümel's *Les Lèvres rouges* (1971), British director Fred Zinneman's *The Day of the Jackal* (1973), British director Don Siegel's *The Black Windmill* (1974), French director Guy Gilles's *Le jardin qui bascule* (1975), French director Liliane de Kermadec's *Aloïse* (1975), Hungarian director Màrta Mészaros's *Utkozben* (1979), and German director Ulrike Ottinger's *Dorian Gray im Spiegel der Boulevardpresse* (1984) and *Johanna d'Arc of Mongolia* (1988).

SIGNORET, SIMONE (1921–1985). Actress. Born Simone Kaminker in Wiesbaden, Germany, Simone Signoret strove to become an actress from an early age; a member of the ***Groupe Octobre***, Signoret made her debut illegally during the Nazi Occupation of France. She was forced to change her name to disguise the fact that her father was Jewish and to work in secret in mostly uncredited roles during the war. Her first roles were in films such as Jean Boyer's *Boléro* (1942) and **Marcel Carné**'s *Les Visiteurs du soir* (1942), but it was her role in Yves Allegret's *Les Démons de l'aube* (1946) that changed her career. She married Allegret in 1944, but the two divorced in 1949. Signoret went on to appear in Marcel Blistène's *Macadam* (1946), Jean Sacha's remake of **Louis Feuillade**'s *Fantômas* (1947), and Maurice Tourneur's *Impasse des deux anges* (1948).

During the 1950s, Signoret became a leading lady, appearing in such films as Allegret's *Manèges* (1950), **Max Ophüls**'s *La Ronde* (1952), **Henri Calef**'s *Ombre et lumière* (1951), **Jacques Becker**'s *Casque d'or* (1952), Carné's *Thérèse Raquin* (1953), **Henri-Georges Clouzot**'s *Les Diaboliques* (1955), Luis Buñuel's *La Mort en ce jardin* (1956), and Raymond Rouleau's *Les Sorcières de Salem* (1957). She won an Oscar for her role in Jack Clayton's English-language film, *Room at the Top* (1959). The film made Signoret an international star.

In the 1960s and 1970s, Signoret had supporting roles in Michel Boisrond's *Amours célèbres* (1961), **Constantin Costa-Gavras**'s *Compartement tueurs* (1965), **René Clement**'s *Paris brûle-t-il?*

(1966), **Jean-Pierre Melville**'s *L'Armée des ombres* (1969), René Allio's *Rude journée pour la reine* (1973), and **Patrice Chéreau**'s *La Chair de l'orchidée* (1975). She also appeared in a number of English-language films. She had starring roles in Clément's *Le Jour et l'heure* (1963), Costa-Gavras's *L'Aveu* (1970), Pierre Granier-Deferre's *Le Chat* (1971) and *La Veuve Couderc* (1971), Moshe Mizrahi's *La Vie devant soi* (1977), Chéreau's *Judith Therpauve* (1978), and **Jeanne Moreau**'s *L'Adolescente* (1979).

During the 1980s, she appeared in only a handful of films including Mizrahi's *Chère inconnue* (1980), Granier-Deferre's *L'Étoile du nord* (1981), and Michel Drach's biopic *Guy de Maupassant* (1982). One of the most recognized and most talented actresses in French cinema, Signoret is almost universally remembered for her roles in Becker's *Casque d'or* (1952) and Ophüls's *La Ronde* (1952), films in which she played prostitutes. In fact perhaps these roles characterized her in the public mind, because she played a fair number of prostitutes on the screen. She is also widely known for her performance in Clouzot's *Les Diaboliques* (1955). Signoret was married to actor **Yves Montand** from 1951 until her death.

SIMON, MICHEL (1895–1975). Actor. Born François Michel Simon in Geneva, Michel Simon got his start as a stage actor in the renowned Pitoëff theater troupe in Geneva. He came to France in the 1920s to start a film career and appeared in a number of silent films, including **Jacque Catelain**'s *La Galerie des monstres* (1924), **Jean Choux**'s *La Vocation d'André Carel* (1925), Carl Theodor Dreyer's *La Passion de Jeanne d'Arc* (1928), and **Jean Renoir**'s *Tire-au-flanc* (1928). Simon was not really appreciated, however, until the sound era. He was one of the most popular and arguably most gifted actors to appear on the screen, and he appeared in more than one hundred films over the course of his career.

The 1930s and 1940s marked the peak of Simon's career. He reprised a part he had played on the stage in Choux's *Jean de la lune* (1931) and had a number of excellent roles early in the 1930s, including lead roles in Renoir's *La Chienne* (1931), *On purge bébé* (1931), and *Boudou sauvé des eaux* (1932), **Marc Allegret**'s *Lac aux dames* (1934), **Marcel L'Herbier**'s *Le Bonheur* (1934), and **Jean Vigo**'s *L'Atalante* (1934). These roles established him as a formidable actor with a broad range, able to perform comedy, drama, and everything in between. Simon also appeared in several less artistic, broadly popular films, including **Henri Diamant-Berger**'s *Miquette et sa mère* (1933), which demonstrated a willingness as well as an ability to perform in all sorts of films. Simon went on to appear in Allegret's *Sous les yeux d'occident* (1935), Raymond Bernard's *Amants et voleurs* (1935), Alexandre Ryder's *Mirages* (1937), **Marcel Carné**'s *Drôle de drame* (1937) and *Le Quai de brumes* (1938), **Sacha Guitry**'s *Faisons un rêve* (1937), Pierre Billon's *La Bataille silencieuse* (1937) and *Vautrin* (1944), Jean Boyer's *La Chaleur du sein* (1938) and *Circonstances attenuantes* (1939), **Christian-Jacque**'s *Les Disparus de Saint-Agil* (1938), **Georges Lacombe** and **Yves Mirande**'s *Derrière la façade* (1939), **Pierre Chenal**'s *Le Dernier tournant* (1939), Carl Koch and Renoir's *Tosca* (1941), L'Herbier's *La Comédie du bonheur* (1942), André Cayatte**'s** *Au bonheur des dames* (1943), and **Henri Decoin**'s *Les Amants du pont Saint-Jean* (1947), among other films.

Simon continued to be a draw in the 1950s and 1960s, and he continued the trend of acting in popular films as well as in more critically appreciated cinema. Among the films in which he appeared were **René Clair**'s *La Beauté du diable* (1951), Guitry's *La Poison* (1951) and *La Vie d'un hônnete homme* (1953), **Henri Verneui**'s *Brelan d'as* (1952), Billon's *La Marchand de Venise* (1953), Pierre Foucard and **André Hunébelle**'s *Mémoires d'un flic* (1956), René Jolivet's *Un certain Monsieur Jo* (1958), **Abel Gance**'s *Austerlitz* (1960) and *Cyrano et d'Artagnan* (1963), Norbert Carbonneaux's *Candide ou l'optimisme au XXe siècle* (1961), **Julien Duvivier**'s *Le Diable et les dix commandements* (1962), and **Claude Berri'**s *Le Vieil homme et l'enfant* (1967).

Simon appeared in only a handful of films in the 1970s, including Gérard Brach's *La Maison* (1970), Walerian Borowczyk's *Blanche* (1971), and **Jean-Pierre Mocky**'s *L'Ibis rouge* (1975), which was his last film. Simon remains an icon of the cinema, and it is for his work with Renoir, Vigo, and Carné that he is best remembered.

SOCIÉTÉ CINÉMATOGRAPHIQUE DES AUTEURS ET DES GENS DE LETTRES (SCAGL). SCAGL was the *film d'art* division launched by **Pathé** in about 1908. Pathé had been one of the financial backers of *Studio film d'art* but had launched its own rival, affiliate company, SCAGL, which was intended solely to produce films d'art in order to lure a more elite crowd to the cinema. Prior to that time, cinema had been regarded as a purely popular medium and Pathé, sensing market potential, sought to raise cinema's status. The company mostly went on to produce film adaptations of French literary classics, many of them directed by **Albert Capellani**. In 1910, as a result of the success of the SCAGL films, Pathé also directly launched an art series, released under the Pathé name. Films by theatrical director **Camille de Morhlon** as well as actor turned director **Henri Andréani** were featured in this series.

SOCIÉTÉ PATHÉ FRÈRES. Founded in 1898 by **Charles Pathé**, Société Pathé Frères was originally based in a studio at Vincennes that was built in 1902. Pathé later expanded to three studios, located at Vincennes, Joinville, and Belleville. Directed by **Ferdinand Zecca**, Pathé was, from 1902 until World War I, the most important studio and production company in France and perhaps the world. In addition to creating and producing films by directors such as **André Calmettes**, **Romeo Bosetti**, **Albert Capellani**, **Segundo de Chomon**, **Georges Denola**, **Louis Gasnier**, **André Heuzé**, **André Hugon**, **Charles-Lucien Lépine**, **René Leprince**, **Max Linder**, **Alfred Machin**, **Lucien Nonguet**, **Gaston Velle**, and of course Zecca himself, Pathé Studios was responsible for a number of technical and corporate innovations in the film industry.

Pathé Studios operated on a particular model of film creation, production, and distribution. That model was aggressive, formulaic, efficient, and highly successful. Under Zecca, an assembly-line approach to film creation was put in place that utilized teams of writers, directors, and actors. It was the job of directors and writers to quickly develop and film formulaic but effective films (often copied from **Gaumont** or British cinemas) designed to conform to audience demands. The studios produced many farces and chase films, for example, which were very easy to write and produce in a short period of time. Pathé therefore could produce films much more quickly than its competition.

In 1906, Pathé pushed film out of the fairground and into permanent sites of projection when it began to utilize permanent cinemas. In 1907, the studio began renting film prints to clients instead of selling them, melting down and reusing film stock, which made its films much less expensive that the films of other studios. In 1912, Pathé began to utilize mechanical colorization of films, a process that was perfected at the Pathé plants. This again gave the studio a great cost advantage over its competitors. Pathé also began expanding into the global market as early as 1907, establishing studios in Great Britain, the United States, and throughout Europe.

Pathé might have remained a dominant force in world cinema but World War I had a destructive impact on the French film industry and assured Hollywood's dominance. Moreover, Pathé was slow to adapt to sound cinema, and the process of converting production meant an enormous expense for the studio. Finally, it seems fairly clear that Pathé was guilty of mismanagement and potentially fraud. In order to save the company, various parts of it were sold off. Pathé sold his personal shares to film producer **Bernard Natan**, who took over control of the studios in 1929, at which point it was renamed **Pathé-Natan**.

STUDIO FILM D'ART. Founded in May 1908 by French businessman Paul Lafitte, Studio Film d'Art was created to fit Lafitte's conception of cinema, which was that film should reproduce, onscreen, great works of literature. To that end, Lafitte hired director **Charles Le Bargy** and playwright Henri Lavedan to make film versions of several "great works" of literature, and he built a glass-house studio (partly financed by Pathé), which was a type of early film studio constructed of steel and glass in order to allow for maximum exposure to natural light, in which these films were to be made. This type of filmmaking was later called *film d'art*, regardless of where the films were made. Film d'Art made a number of such literary films, among them *L'Assassinat du Duc de Guise* (1908), *Le Retour d'Ulysse* (1909), *Carmen* (1910), and *Camille Desmoulins* (1911). Film d'Art went out of business in 1911 due to financial problems. Nonetheless, the studio was central in promoting the idea that cinema could rival the theater and other "higher" arts and in pushing a more literary type of cinema.

– T –

TATI, JACQUES (1907–1982). Actor and director. Jacques Tati was born Jacques Tatischeff in Le Pecq. He studied the arts while also practicing boxing, rugby, and tennis. He worked in cabarets and music halls where he used his athletic talent to imitate famous sports players. He entered the cinema as a screenwriter and actor in Jacques Forrester's *Oscar, champion de tennis* (1932). He later scripted and acted in Charles Barrois's *On demande une brute* (1934), Jacques Berr's *Gai dimanche* (1935), and **René Clément**'s *Soigne ta gauche* (1936) and *Retour à la terre* (1938). After World War II, he acted in **Claude Autant-Lara**'s *Sylvie et Le fantôme* (1946) and *Le diable au corps* (1946).

Tati directed his first film, the short comedy *L'École des facteurs*, in 1947. It was also the inspiration for his first feature film, *Jour de fête* (1949), which was the top-selling French film in France in 1949. The film was nominated for best script at the Venice Film Festival. Tati's next films were **Les Vacances de Monsieur Hulot** (1953), which won the **Prix Louis-Delluc** and received an Oscar nomination, and *Mon oncle* (1958). Like *Jour de fête*, these comedies portray France's transformation into a modern industrial state. The character Monsieur Hulot, played by Tati himself, reemerged in his later films.

Tati's fourth film, *Playtime* (1967), was not as successful as the previous films but has been lauded by critics as a precursor to post-modern filmmaking and as a work of cinematic genius. Tati's last completed films were *Trafic* (1971) and *Parade* (1974). Tati is sometimes seen as an example of what **François Truffaut** dubbed *le cinéma de papa*, but he is best known for his meticulous directing, his revival of silent comedy, his creative use of sound, his brilliant comic acting, and his humorous portrayals of the social effects of modern mechanical gadgets. The intense preparation he spent on his films resulted in a career that was not prolific but much admired and widely successful.

TAUTOU, AUDREY (1978–). Actress. After acting in films made for television in the mid-1990s, Tautou entered the cinema with a breakthrough role in **Tonie Marshall**'s *Venus Beauté (Institut)* (1999). Her performance won her the **César** for Most Promising New Actress in 2000. She played the lead in *Triste à mourir* (1999), a short fiction film by Alexandre Billon. She subsequently landed leading roles in Serge Meynard's *Voyous Voyelles* (2000) and Laurent Firode's *Le Battement d'ailes du papillon* (2000). She also played supporting roles in Harriet Marin's *Épouse-moi* (2000) and Gabriel Aghion's *Le libertin* (2000).

In 2002, she received a Lumière Award and a César nomination for Best Actress in **Jean-Pierre Jeunet**'s *Le fabuleux destin d'Amélie Poulain* (2001), a film that launched her international stardom. She subsequently starred in Pascale Bailly's *Dieu est grand, je suis toute petite* (2001) and Laetitia Colombani's *À la folie, pas du tout* (2002), and she then played supporting roles in Cédric Klapisch's *L'Auberge espagnole* (2002) and Claire Devers's *Les marins perdus* (2002). She has acted in two Anglophone films to date: British filmmaker Steven Frears's *Dirty Pretty Things* and Amos Kollek's *Happy End*. She ventured into musical comedy with **Alain Resnais**'s *Pas sur la bouche* (2003) before pairing again with Jeunet to star in his feature *Un long dimanche de fiançailles* (2004). In 2006, she appeared alongside Jean Reno and Tom Hanks in Ron Howard's highly controversial film *The Da Vinci Code*.

TAVERNIER, BERTRAND (1941–). Actor, director, film critic, producer, and screenwriter. Bertrand Tavernier is one of France's most acclaimed directors. He began as a cinéphile and film critic for ***Positif*** and ***Cahiers du cinéma*** and as an assistant to **Jean-Pierre Melville**. His first feature film, *L'horloger de Saint Paul* (1974), won the **Prix Louis-Delluc** and a Silver Berlin Bear. The scenario for the film was written by Pierre Bost and Jean Aurenche, two writers who represented the *tradition de qualité* critiqued by **François Truffaut**. A crime or detective film, *L'horloger de Saint-Paul* stars **Philippe Noiret**, the actor with whom Tavernier would shoot several successful films.

Tavernier's next feature, *Que la fête commence . . .* (1975), won Césars for Best Director and Best Screenplay at the inauguration of the **César Awards** in 1976. Tavernier also won Best Screenplay at the César Awards for his third feature, *Le Juge et l'assassin* (1976). In the 1980s, Tavernier became one of the most prominent directors of the **heritage film**. Some critics argue that his films tend to be nostalgic, while others detect more subversive representations of French history. His 1981 film *Coup de Torchon* was inspired by Jim Thompson's *Pop.1280*. Tavernier transported Thompson's crime novel, which is set in the American South, to colonial French West Africa of the 1930s. Lynn Higgins has also established that the film reproduces scenes from the legendary American Western *The Virginian* (1923).

Another example of a Tavernier heritage film is his adaptation of Pierre Bost's novel, *Un dimanche à la campagne* (1984). The film won a César for Best Adaptation and the award for Best Director at Cannes. It was also nominated for a Golden Palm. Tavernier's interest in musical history is demonstrated in his documentary *Mississippi Blues* (1984), codirected with Robert Parrish in the United States, and *Round Midnight* (1986), a feature about an African American jazz musician (played by Dexter Gordon) in Paris in 1959. These films were followed by a historical feature set in medieval France, *La passion Béatrice* (1987). Tavernier's **heritage film** about World War I, *La vie et rien d'autre* (1989), won the British Film Academy Award for Best Foreign Film. Critics have argued that Tavernier's next film, *Daddy Nostalgie* (1990), consciously plays with the conventions of the nostalgia/heritage genre. In the 1990s Tavernier was engaged, along with other filmmakers and actors, in the *mouvement des sans-papiers,* a series of protests against attempts to deport African immigrants without legal papers. Several of his 1990s films engage in artistic social criticism. Tavernier's documentary, *La guerre sans nom* (1991), broaches the previously taboo and politically charged subject of the Algerian War. His feature *L.627* (1992), like **Mathieu Kassovitz**'s 1995 film *La Haine*, casts a critical lens on violent police tactics.

In 1994, Tavernier returned to heritage and cast Noiret in *La fille d'Artagnan* (1994). This was followed by *L'appât* (1995), which won a Golden Berlin Bear. His success continued with *Capitaine Conan* (1996), for which he received the César for Best director in 1997. It was followed by *Ça commence aujourd'hui* (1999), *Laissez-passer* (2002), which features Jean Aurenche in a leading role, and *Holy Lola* (2003). Tavernier was awarded a Lifetime Achievement Award at the Istanbul International Film Festival in 2001. In addition to winning numerous international film awards, he has been nominated for more than fifteen Césars.

TÉCHINÉ, ANDRÉ (1943–). Director, film critic, and screenwriter. Before directing films, André Téchiné worked as a critic at *Cahiers du cinéma* from 1964 to 1967 and later as an assistant to **Jacques**

Rivette and Marc'O. His first feature was *Paulina s'en va* (1975), which stars **Bulle Ogier**. It was followed by *Souvenirs d'en France* (1975), starring **Jeanne Moreau**.

Téchiné's films often pair several of France's most internationally recognized celebrities. *Barocco* (1976) pairs **Gérard Depardieu** and **Isabelle Adjani**, *Les soeurs Brontë* (1979) stars Adjani alongside **Isabelle Huppert**, *Hôtel des Amériques* (1981) features **Catherine Deneuve** and **Patrick Dewaere**, *Le lieu du crime* (1986) stars Deneuve and **Danielle Darrieux**, *J'embrasse pas* (1991) pairs **Philippe Noiret** and **Emmanuelle Béart**, *Ma saison préféré* (1993) stars Deneuve and **Daniel Auteuil** as does *Les voleurs* (1996). *Les temps qui changent* (2004) stars Deneuve and Depardieu. He chose the leading actress of *Rendez-vous* (1985), **Juliette Binoche**, to star again in *Alice et Martin* (1998), and Béart again in *Les Égarés* (2002). His most recent film is *LesTémoins* (2006), which stars Béart.

Téchiné's most acclaimed films to date are *Les roseaux sauvages* (1994), which received the **Prix Louis-Delluc**, and **César**s for Best Director, Best Film, and Best Screenplay in 1995, and *Rendez-vous*, which won him Best Director at **Cannes** a decade earlier. *Les roseaux sauvages* stars **Élodie Bouchez**, who received a Most Promising Actress award at the César Awards and Best Actress at Cannes for her role. Stéphane Rideau and Gaël Morel were both nominated for Césars for Most Promising Actor. Rideau also plays the lead in Téchiné's *Loin* (2001).

TRINTINGNANT, JEAN-LOUIS (1930–). Actor, director, and screenwriter. Jean-Louis Trintingnant began in the theater and has appeared in well over one hundred films. Trintignant first appeared on the screen in **Christian-Jacque**'s *Si tous les gars du monde* (1955). His breakthrough role was in **Roger Vadim**'s scandal-raising debut *Et Dieu créa la femme* (1956) alongside **Brigitte Bardot**. He landed a major role alongside **Romy Schneider** in **Alain Cavalier**'s *Le Combat dans l'île* (1962). His celebrity was solidified with **Claude Lelouch**'s *Un homme et une femme* (1966). He would star in several Lelouch films, among them *Le Voyou* (1970), *Partir, revenir* (1984), and *Un homme et une femme: vingt ans déjà* (1986). He won the Silver Berlin Bear for his performance in Alain Robbe-Grillet's *L'Homme qui ment* in 1968 and best actor at **Cannes** in 1969 for his role in **Constantin Costa-Gavras**'s political thriller, *Z*. He starred in key films by *Nouvelle Vague* or New Wave directors, appearing in **Eric Rohmer**'s *Ma nuit chez Maud* (1969), **Claude Chabrol**'s *Les biches* (1969), and **François Truffaut**'s *Vivement dimanche!* (1983), among other films.

Trintignant also played memorable roles in Krzysztof Kieslowski's *Trois couleurs: Rouge* (1993) and **Patrice Chéreau**'s *Ceux qui m'aiment prendront le train* (1997). He acted in several Italian films, among them Dino Risi's *The Easy Life* (1962), Bernardo Bertolucci's *The Conformist* (1970), and Ettore de Scola's *The Terrace* (1980). He directed two films: *Une journée bien remplie* (1973) and *Le maître nageur* (1979). He married **Stéphane Audran** and later Nadine Marquand (who became Nadine Trintignant), in whose films he would star. The actress Marie Trintignant is his daughter.

TROIS HOMMES ET UN COUFFIN **(1985).** Film. **Coline Serreau**'s comedy *Trois hommes et un couffin* narrates the story of three bachelors whose lives are changed when a baby girl is left at their apartment. The men, Pierre (Roland Giraud), Michel (Michel Boujenah), and Jacques (André Dussolier), have previously vowed not to allow women to inhabit their space for more than one night. Through their care for the infant, however, they find a space for women, or at least girls, in their lives and discover that they can be loving, capable fathers.

The film, which questions received gender roles, was an enormous success, despite Serreau's initial struggles to locate a producer. It was the best-selling film in France in 1985 and the fifth most commercially successful French film at the box office in the latter half of the twentieth century. It won **César Award**s for Best Film and Best Screenplay, and Boujenah, a little-known actor at the time, won the César for Best Supporting Actor. *Trois hommes et un couffin* was also nominated for an Oscar for Best Foreign Film. Serreau was expected to direct the Hollywood remake of the film, *Three Men and a Baby,* but dropped out of the project, leaving the remake to director Leonard Nimoy. Serreau has since made rather scathing remarks about what she sees as Hollywood's stifling influence on directors.

Serreau was one of several French women directors to emerge in the 1970s. Although there were prominent women directors before her, she came of age during a time when women were not expected to be directors, and thus her interest in challenging preassigned gender roles is not surprising. In *Trois hommes et un couffin*, men take on roles that have traditionally been assigned to women and eventually embrace their capacity as caregivers. Serreau's *Pourquoi pas!* (1977), made in the previous decade, also challenged conventional gender roles.

TRUFFAUT, FRANÇOIS (1932–1984). Director, film critic, producer, and screenwriter. While still a teenager in late 1947, François Truffaut initiated a *ciné-club* with his friend Robert Lachenay. Through his involvement with this club, *Cercle Cinémane*, and other ciné-clubs, Truffaut became acquainted with the critic **André Bazin**, who is often described as Truffaut's surrogate father. This relationship was pivotal in Truffaut's formation as a director. In 1953, Truffaut began writing for *Cahiers du cinéma* and *Arts*. As a critic, Truffaut boldly denounced the French cinematic *tradition de qualité*, most notably in his 1954 essay, "Une certaine tendence du cinéma français." The criticisms laid out in Truffaut's writing, and the underlying aesthetics implied in these criticisms, would be central in the formation of the *Nouvelle Vague* or New Wave.

Truffaut later established a small production company, Les Films du Carrosse, with the financial assistance of his father-in-law, the distributor Ignace Morgenstern. His first short was *Une visite* (1954), followed by *Les Mistons* (1957). In *Les Mistons* and in later films, Truffaut pays homage to the cinema through allusions to former films, such as **Louis Lumière**'s classic silent film *L'Arroseur arosé* (1895). This intertextual referencing would later also become a characteristic of the New Wave.

Truffaut went on to codirect a short about flooding around Paris, *Une histoire d'eau* (1958), with **Jean-Luc Godard**. His first feature film was the autobiographical *Les Quatre cent coups* (1959), which won the Grand Prix at the **Cannes Film Festival** and became a benchmark for the New Wave. In fact, some critics consider this film to be the first true New Wave film. The film's protagonist, Antoine Doinel, is played by one of Truffaut's regular actors, Jean-Pierre Léaud. Several critics have noted the similarities between the character Antoine's childhood and that of Truffaut. Truffaut himself did not comment on this, but referred to the film in only artistic terms, calling it an example of "cinema in the first person singular." Doinel would become a recurrent character in Truffaut's oeuvre. He subsequently made four other films featuring Doinel (all starring Léaud): the short *Antoine et Colette* (1962), *Baisers volés* (1968), which won the **Prix Louis-Delluc**, *Domicile conjugal* (1970), and *L'amour en fuite* (1979).

Following *Les Quatre cents coups*, Truffaut made his second feature, *Tirez sur le pianiste* (1960). This film was not as commercially successful as *Les Quatre cents coups,* but it later gained recognition for its divergence from an emphasis on plot and its innovative experimentation in film narrative, image, and cinematic style. It was also the first of Truffaut's films to employ the acclaimed cameraman Raoul Coutard. Truffaut's third feature, *Jules et Jim* (1962), was another success for the New Wave. It won the French Film Critics Award for best French film and has gained lasting international acclaim. It was followed by another acclaimed film, *La peau douce* (1964).

Truffaut directed one film in English, *Fahrenheit 451* (1966), which was derived from Ray Bradbury's famous science-fiction novel. In 1976, Truffaut authored his own book, a series of interviews with legendary director Alfred Hitchcock, *Le Cinéma selon Hitchcock*. Quite apart from this publication, it is quite evident from Truffaut's films that he had an interest in Hitchcock. Hitchcock's influence is apparent in *La marié était en noir* (1968) and *La sirène du Mississippi* (1969), both of which were based on novels by William Irish, who also wrote the story on which Hitchcock's *Rear Window* was based.

In 1970, Truffaut made *L'enfant sauvage* (1970), a film in which he also appears. This film was followed by *Les deux Anglaises et le continent* (1971) and *Une belle fille comme moi* (1972). Truffaut's tribute to filmmaking, *La Nuit américaine* (1973), was awarded an Oscar for Best Foreign Film and a British Film Academy Award for Best Film and Best Direction. His second book, *Les films de ma vie*, was published in 1975. Truffaut returned to literary adaptation in 1975 with his film *L'histoire de Adèle H*, which is adapted from the personal diaries of Victor Hugo's daughter, Adèle.

The recurring theme of youth, particularly troubled youth, returned in Truffaut's 1976 film, *L'argent de poche*, which sensitively narrates a series of stories about children in the town of Thiers. This film was followed by *L'homme qui aimait les femmes* (1977), which was made at the same time as Truffaut was working as an actor for Steven Spielberg on his film *Close Encounters of the Third Kind* (1977). In 1978, Truffaut directed and starred in *La chambre verte* (1978), another literary adaptation based on the writings of Henry James.

Truffaut's next film, *Le dernier métro* (1980), set during the German Occupation of France, is sometimes seen as the end of the **Mode Rétro** and/or as a problematic beginning to the **heritage film**. It won ten **César Award**s, including Best Director, Best Film, and Best Screenplay. It stars two icons of French cinéma, **Gérard Depardieu** and **Catherine Deneuve**, who received Best Actor and Best Actress at the César awards in 1981 for their performances. This film was followed by *La femme d'à côté* (1981) and *Vivement dimanche!* (1983), both of which star **Fanny Ardant**, who is the mother of Truffaut's youngest child.

Truffaut's influence on world cinema is vast and enduring. His films are invaluable to the New Wave, the heritage genre, and beyond. His writing inspired a reevaluation of cinema as it contributed to the serious study of film as an art form. Not only did Truffaut contribute to the theory of the **auteur**, in many ways he personifies the auteur.

– V –

VADIM, ROGER (1928–2000). Director and screenwriter. Roger Vadim was born Roger Vadim Plemiannikov in Paris. He studied drama under Charles Dullin and started as a stage actor. He acted in and contributed to the scripts of **Marc Allégret**'s *Maria Chapdelaine* (1950) and *Futures vedettes* (1955), and the latter starred Vadim's first wife, **Brigitte Bardot**. Vadim worked as Allegret's assistant for ten years and coscripted Michel Boisrond's *Cette sacrée gamine* (1956), also starring Bardot. He was also a journalist for *Paris-Match*.

Vadim made his directorial debut with the internationally successful *Et Dieu créa la femme*, with Bardot in the lead, which was released in 1956. *Et Dieu créa la femme* has been considered an important forerunner to the **Nouvelle Vague** or New Wave, because it opened the door for unknown film directors in its demonstration that newcomers could create commercially profitable films. In addition, **Jean-Luc Godard** and **François Truffaut** were impressed by Bardot's uncontained sexuality in the film. The film launched Bardot's international fame and has been acclaimed for its skillful use of Cinemascope and Eastmancolor.

Vadim's next films were *Sait-on jamais* (1957), a Berlin Bear–nominated film in which women protagonists continued to challenge traditional views of female sexuality, and *Les bijoutiers du clair de lune* (1958). His *Les liaisons dangereuses* , featuring **Jeanne Moreau** and **Gérard Philippe**, was among the top five French films at the box office in 1959. Vadim's vampiress film, *Et mourir de plaisir* (1960), starred his second wife, Annette Stroyberg Vadim. His next films were *La bride sur le cou* (1961) and *Le repos du guerrier* (1962), both starring Bardot. **Catherine Deneuve** played one of her early starring roles alongside **Annie Girardot** in Vadim's *Le vice et la vertu* (1963). He later directed *Château en Suède* (1963) and *La ronde* (1964), which marked his first collaboration with Jane Fonda, who became his third wife. She also starred in *La curée* (1966) and the Anglophone *Barbarella* (1968), a film adapted from a French science-fiction comic strip.

Some have argued that Vadim enjoyed flaunting the beauty of his wives and lovers in his films. He wrote a memoir titled *Bardot, Deneuve, Fonda: My Life With the Three Most Beautiful Women in the World* (1986), which seems to corroborate that theory. Vadim worked with other Hollywood stars besides Fonda. His *Pretty Maids All in a Row* (1971) featured Rock Hudson and Angie Dickenson. His next features were *Hellé* (1972) and *Don Juan ou si Don Juan était une femme* (1973), both with Bardot and another Vadim favorite, **Robert Hossein**. Also in the 1970s, Vadim directed *La jeune fille assassinée* (1974) and *Une femme fidèle* (1976), starring Sylvia Kristel, the actress who led in Just Jaeckin's 1974 erotic blockbuster, *Emmanuelle*. In the 1980s, Vadim directed *Night Games* (1980), *Hot Touch* (1982), and *Surprise-Party* (1983). His last film, before moving on to television, was the English-language *And God Created Woman* (1988), with Rebecca de Mornay.

VARDA, AGNÈS (1928–). Cinematographer, director, producer, and screenwriter. Agnès Varda is arguably France's most prominent

woman director. She was born in Belgium and went to France to study art history at the Ecole du Louvre and later changed her focus to photography at the Ecole de Vaugirard. She worked as the official photographer for the Théâtre National Populaire from 1951 to 1961 before shooting her first **auteur** film, the feature *La Pointe Courte* (1954). An independent film shot on location on a low budget, *La Pointe Courte* was a precursor to the *Nouvelle Vague* or New Wave, and it was edited by **Alain Resnais**.

Varda did not have much experience in cinema when she started her career, yet her first film received accolades from **André Bazin**. Her next feature, *Cléo de 5 à 7* (1961), has been associated with the New Wave, as has the feature *Le bonheur* (1964), which won the **Prix Louis-Delluc**. Varda's next feature, *Les Créatures* (1965), starring **Catherine Deneuve** and **Michel Piccoli**, was not generally as well received as her previous features. She shot *Lion's Love* (1968) while living in California with her husband **Jacques Demy**. It was followed by *L'Une chante, l'autre pas* (1976), which recounts the story of two women during different stages of the feminist movement. *Sans toit ni loi* (1985) is the story of a homeless girl and is one of her best-known feature films. The film won the Golden Lion at the Venice Film Festival and a César for its lead actress, **Sandrine Bonnaire**. Varda moved to California again and directed the feature *Documenteur* (1981), set in Los Angeles.

Varda's documentaries are known for their personal, subjective dimensions. One of the most acclaimed, Varda's short *Ulysse*, was awarded the **César** for Best Short Documentary. Varda also made a documentary about the actress Jane Birkin, *Jane B par Agnès V.* (1987). In the same year, she cowrote her feature *Kung-Fu Master* (1987) with Birkin, who is the leading actress. Another major documentary is *Jacquot de Nantes* (1991), which focuses on Demy, who died in 1990, as does *Les Demoiselles ont eu 25 ans* (1992) and *L'Univers de Jacques Demy* (1993). Among her other feature-length documentaries are *Daguerréotypes* (1975), *Murs Murs* (1980), *Les Glaneurs et la glaneuse* (2000), *Les Glaneurs et la glaneuse . . . deux ans après* (2002), and *Cinévardaphoto* (2004). Her film *Les Cent et une nuits de Simon Cinéma* (1995) was made for the centennial of cinema and features stars such as Michel Piccoli, **Jean-Paul Belmondo**, **Fanny Ardant**, Deneuve, and Bonnaire. In addition to directing feature-length films, she directed several shorts, including *O saisons, ô châteaux* (1957), *L'Opéra-Mouffe* (1958), *Du côté de la côté* (1958), *Salut les Cubains* (1963), *Elsa la Rose* (1965), *Oncle Yanco* (1967), *Black Panthers* (1968), *Réponse de femmes* (1975), *Plaisir d'amour en Iran* (1976), *Les Dites Caryatides* (1984), *7 P., cuis de b . . . à saisir* (1984), *T'as de beaux escaliers tu sais* (1986), *Le lion volatile* (2003), and *Ydessa, les ours et etc.* (2004).

Varda wrote a semi-autobiographical work that encompasses her life and her work, *Varda par Agnès* (1994). She coined the term *cinécriture*, a combination of the French words for cinema and writing, to describe a style in filmmaking. Her recent film *Les Glaneurs et la glaneuse* (2000) and its sequel *Les Glaneurs et la glaneuse . . . deux ans après* (2002) are both highly acclaimed documentaries dealing with issues ranging from the relationship between the past and the present, the urban and the rural. Both also foreground similarities between people regarded as normal by society and those whom society marginalizes. Her most recent films include *Le lion volatil* (2003) and *Ydessa, les ours et etc.* (2004).

VELLE, GASTON (1872–1948). Director. Like his contemporary and rival **Georges Méliès**, Gaston Velle began his career as a magician. He was hired on by **Pathé** in 1903 to make trick films or *trucs* to rival those of Méliès. Velle did not disappoint. He was able not only to make a good many well-received trick films, but also *féeries*, or fantasy films, the other genre for which Méliès was well known. During his initial period at Pathé from 1904 to 1907 he established a solid reputation in the two genres whether working alone or collaborating with the Spanish filmmaker **Segundo de Chomon**, also brought on to Pathé in an effort to rival Méliès.

In 1907, Velle went to Italy to become head of production for Cinca, the Italian film studio. He remained there until 1909 at which time Pathé lured him back by making him head of production for féeries. Velle remained at Pathé until 1911 or 1912, at which time no more films bearing his signature were made.

With respect to his films, Velle was considered a specialist in those two genres he helped pioneer, that is, the truc and the féerie. While his truc films were fairly popular and quite well done for the time, they lacked the sophistication of Méliès's films and were often centered on a single trick or effect. Among the best-known of these are *Le Chapeau magique* (1904), *Métamorphose du papillon* (1904), *La Valise de Barnum* (1904), *Les Cartes lumineuses* (1905), and *La Fée aux fleurs* (1905). *Les Invisibles* (1906), which is the first "invisible man" film and which helped establish this subgenre, is considered a classic.

Velle's féeries are probably the most enduring of the films he produced. He often collaborated with other Pathé filmmakers, such as **Ferdinand Zecca** or de Chomon in making féeries, and the films these collaborations produced are legendary. Films like *La Poule aux oeufs d'or* (1905), *Rêve à la lune* (1905), and *L'Écrin du Radjah* (1906) are silent-film classics and are still shown today. Little is known about Velle's life outside of his work.

VENTURA, LINO (1919–1987). Actor. Lino Ventura was born Angelo Borrini in Parma, Italy. His family immigrated to France in 1927. He was a professional wrestler before he debuted in **Jacques Becker**'s gangster film, *Touchez pas au grisbi* (1954). His second role was in Henri Decoin's crime drama, *Razzia sur la Chnouf* (1955). Both films star **Jean Gabin**, who is considered to be Ventura's acting mentor. In the 1950s, Ventura would work with Gabin in Georges Lampin's *Crime et châtiment* (1956), Gilles Grangier's *Le rouge est mis* (1957), and **Jean Delannoy**'s *Maigret tend un piège* (1957). Ventura also had a small role in **Louis Malle**'s *Ascenseur pour l'échafaud* (1957). At this point in his career, he mostly played hard-boiled characters in crime and detective films.

Ventura's status as a French film star was launched with his role in Bernard Borderie's *Le Gorille vous salue bien* (1958). He later led the casts in some of France's most popular films of the 1960s such as **Claude Sautet**'s *Classe tous risques* (1960), Denys de la Patellière's *Un taxi pour Tobrouk* (1961), **George Lautner**'s *Les Tontons flinguers* (1963), **Henri Verneuil**'s *Cent mille dollars au soleil* (1964), Robert Enrico's *Les Grandes gueules* (1965), and Verneuil's *Le Clan des Siciliens* (1969). Ventura played in a number of films by Italian directors, including Luciano Emmer's *La Ragazza in vetrina* (1961) and Vittorio De Sica's *Il Giudizio universale* (1961). He also acted in German director Wolfgang Staudte's *Die Dreigroschenoper* (1962) and Spanish director Carlos Saura's *Llanto por un bandido*

(1964). He starred in two 1960s films by **Jean-Pierre Melville**: *Le deuxième souffle* (1966) and *L'Armée des ombres* (1969).

In the 1970s, Ventura remained a frequent lead in box-office successes such as **Claude Lelouch**'s *L'aventure c'est l'aventure* (1972), **Edouard Molinaro**'s *L'Emmerdeur* (1973), and **Claude Pinoteau**'s *La Gifle* (1974). He often worked in films by the same directors, appearing in Enrico's *Boulevard du rhum* (1971), Pinoteau's *Les Silencieux* (1972), Lelouch's *La Bonne année* (1973), and Pierre Granier-Deferre's *La Cage* (1975) and *Adieu poulet* (1975). He acted in the Italian films *Uomini Duri* (1974), by Duccio Tessari, and *Cadaveri eccelenti* (1975), by Francesco Rosi. Ventura appeared in Anglophone films as well, most notably Terence Young's *The Valachi Papers* (1972) and Jack Gold's *The Medusa Touch* (1978).

In the 1960s and 1970s, Ventura ranked among France's most successful actors in top-selling features. In the 1980s, Ventura's image did not frequent the movie posters for France's most commercially profitable hits, yet arguably, he delivered two of his best performances. He received a **César** nomination for his role as Jean Valjean in **Robert Hossein**'s *Les Misérables* (1982) and has been lauded for his performance in Miller's *Garde à vue* (1981). In addition, he played leading roles in Yves Boisset's *Espion, lève-toi* (1982), José Giovanni's *Le Ruffian* (1983), and Pinoteau's *La 7ème cible* (1984). He also appeared in Michael Anderson's television film, *Sword of Gideon* (1986).

VERNAY, ROBERT (1907–1979). Director and screenwriter. Robert Vernay got his start in cinema as a director in the early 1930s. He made a handful of films, including *L'Éternelle chanson* (1932), *Le Béguin de la garnaison* (1932), and *Le Prince de six jours* (1934). He did not have much success on his own, however, and began working with some of France's best-known directors. He worked with **Julien Duvivier** as an assistant on such films as *La Bandera* (1935), *Pépé le Moko* (1937), *La Fin du jour* (1939), and *Untel père et fils* (1943), and with **Marc Allegret** on *Entrée des artistes* (1938). Vernay also assisted **Yves Mirande** on *Café de Paris* (1938) and **Georges Lacombe** on *Les Musiciens du ciel* (1940).

Vernay resumed directing on his own in the 1940s with more success, perhaps given a hand by the Nazi Occupation, which had sent many of the major directors into exile. His first independent film of the decade, *La Femme que j'ai la plus aimée* (1942), was directed from a screenplay written by Mirande and starred **Arletty** and **Mireille Balin**. His adaptation of *Le Comte de Monte Cristo* (1943) was a fairly successful adventure film that starred **Pierre Richard-Willm**. Vernay went on to make nearly thirty other films, including *Arlette et l'amour* (1943), *Le Père Goriot* (1945), *Le Capitan* (1946), *Emile l'Africain* (1948), *Fantômas contre Fantômas* (1949), another version of *Le Comte de Monte Cristo* (1955), *La Rue des bouches peintes* (1955), *Les Lumières du soir* (1956), and the spy film *Monsieur Suzuki* (1960). Vernay was a solid director but one who has not received much critical attention. In addition to directing, he also wrote the screenplays for a number of his films.

VERNEUIL, HENRI (1920–2002). Director and screenwriter. Henri Verneuil was born Achod Malakian in Rodesto, Turkey, of Armenian ancestry. He later immigrated to Marseilles with his parents. Verneuil studied engineering and later worked as a journalist and radio commentator. He started in cinema as an assistant to **Robert Vernay**. Verneuil made short documentary films in the 1940s then directed his first feature, *La table aux crevés* (1952), starring the famous comedian **Fernandel**. Fernandel then played a more serious starring role in Verneuil's very popular drama, *Fruit défendu* (1952). Fernandel was Verneuil's preferred actor in the 1950s. He played the lead in *Carnaval* (1953), *Le Boulanger de Valorgue* (1953), and *L'Ennemi public n.1* (1953), which also featured Zsa Zsa Gabor. *Le Mouton à cinq pattes* (1954), starring Fernandel alongside one of Verneuil's favorite actresses, **Françoise Arnoul**, was nominated for an American Academy Award for Best Screenplay. Verneuil's *La Vache et le prisonnier*, again starring Fernandel, was the top grossing French film of 1959.

Verneuil's collaboration with French stars such as Fernandel—and later **Jean Gabin**, **Alain Delon**, **Lino Ventura**, and **Jean-Paul Belmondo**—would bring him great commercial success. Verneuil's *Des gens sans importance* (1956) marked his first film with Gabin as the lead; Gabin would also star in *Le Président* (1960) and *Mélodie en sous-sol* (1963). *Mélodie en sous-sol* costarred Delon and was the second top French film of 1963. In 1962, Gabin paired with Belmondo in *Un singe en hiver*. Verneuil's *Le Clan des Siciliens,* with

Gabin, Delon, and Ventura, was the second most viewed French film in 1969. Verneuil directed several Belmondo films that scored among the top five French best sellers. These include *Cent mille dollars au soleil* (1964), *Le Casse* (1971), *Peur sur la ville* (1975), and *Les Morfalous* (1984). *Week-end à Zuydcoote* (1964) and *Le Corps de mon ennemi* (1976), both with Belmondo in the principal role, were also quite profitable at the box office.

Verneuil ventured into international cinema with his *La Vingt-Cinquième Heure* (1967), starring Anthony Quinn, and *La Bataille de San Sebastian* (1968), featuring Quinn and Charles Bronson. He also directed *The Serpent* (1973), starring Henry Fonda and Yul Brynner. He is best known for his French films, however, especially his dramatic thrillers. Verneuil received critical acclaim for the thriller *I . . . comme Icare* (1979), a film that recalled through fiction the assassination of John F. Kennedy as it simultaneously took its inspiration from psychologist Stanley Milgram's experiment on obedience to authority at Yale. Milgram viewed the shooting of the film, which stars actor **Yves Montand**. It received **César** nominations for Best Film and Best Screenplay.

In part because of his commercial savvy and fruitful use of French movie stars, Verneuil has been called "the most American of French cineastes." Yet not all of his films are clever, profit-producing vehicles. Verneuil directed a moving drama about an Armenian family's struggle in Turkey, *Mayrig* (1991). Based on his childhood and adapted from his own novel, *Mayrig* stars Claudia Cardinale and Omar Shariff. Verneuil directed a sequel, *588 Rue Paradis* (1992), inspired by his sometimes tumultuous experiences as an immigrant in France. He was assisted by his son, Patrick Malakian, who later directed *Pourquoi maman est dans mon lit?* (1994). In 1996, Verneuil received an honorary César.

VIGO, JEAN (1905–1934). Director. Born Jean Bonaventure de Vigo Almereyda in Paris, Jean Vigo was the son of Catalan revolutionary Miguel Almereyda. Vigo's father was convicted of espionage and found dead in his prison cell in 1917. He seemed never to recover from the loss. He spent his childhood in boarding schools, abandoned by his mother. The experience affected him profoundly and would influence his filmmaking. He was fascinated by the cinema at an early age, perhaps because of its offer of escape. He studied philosophy at the Sorbonne, then sought to work in the cinema, and was hired on at the independent Nice-based Studios de la Victorine, run by Serge Sandberg, in 1928.

Vigo made his first film, *A Propos de Nice*, in 1930. The film was a satiric documentary comment on the age and established the cinematographic interrogation of the political conditions of the age that would characterize Vigo's short career. His next film, *Taris ou la natation* (1931), was a documentary on swimming centered on champion swimmer Jean Taris. Vigo's third film was *Zéro de conduite* (1933), an exploration of oppression and rebellion in a boys' boarding school. Now recognized as one of the great classics of the cinema, the film was highly criticized and banned when it was released for its depiction of the overthrow of an oppressive order, which the government of the day deemed "anti-French." There was one last film, Vigo's only feature-length film, *L'Atalante* (1934). The film is a powerful exploration of the incompatibility of the desire for independence, self-determination, and harmony with the natural world and the materialism of modern society. *L'Atalante* was also panned when released but has since become considered one of the greatest films ever made. The studio cut and edited the film before its release to such an extent that it bore little resemblance to the director's original. It has been partially restored, but to date, no complete version has been released.

Tragically, Vigo died of tuberculosis before he could make any other films. However, it is fair to say that few other filmmakers, no matter how many films they made, have reached the stature he now holds in French film history. He is seen as an important contributor to *Le Réalisme poétique* or poetic realism and a master of film technique, who elevated film to the status of art, and who issued a challenge through his work that other filmmakers do likewise. He has been recognized as a significant influence on filmmakers as diverse as **Jean Renoir**, Luis Buñuel, and **Alain Resnais**.

– W –

WARGNIER, RÉGIS (1948–). Director and screenwriter. Régis Wargnier's first features were *La femme de ma vie* (1986) and *Je suis* *le seigneur du château* (1989). Two films about the relationships between Europeans and the people in their colonies have stirred critical interest: the epic *Indochine* (1992), which won an Oscar for Best Foreign Film and a **César** for its leading actress, **Catherine Deneuve**, takes place during France's colonization of former French Indochina. His English-language picture, *Man to Man* (2005), which opened the 2005 Berlin Film Festival, narrates the story of late nineteenth-century explorers who kidnap Africans and transport them to Europe for scientific observation. Wargnier's feature, *Est, Ouest* (1999), similarly emphasizes international politics through personal relationships. It tells the story of a French woman and a Russian exile who move to Stalinist Russia after World War II. He also directed *Une femme française* (1995).

WOMEN. Although women have been involved in French cinema from the beginning, they have, as in the case of other national film industries, had a great deal more difficulty than their male counterparts in establishing themselves, whether as directors, actors, screenwriters, or cinematographers or in any number of roles. The first director of a narrative film in France was **Alice Guy**. Her film *La Fée aux choux* (1896) was made for **Gaumont**, although for nearly a century, **Georges Méliès** was credited with having made the first narrative film. Guy went on to become head of production at Gaumont for a number of years, training all of the early directors at the studio and directing several hundred films. Yet she was virtually forgotten about. Her films were attributed to various other directors in many cases, and **Léon Gaumont** made no mention of Guy in his memoirs. In many ways, Guy is emblematic of the status of women in cinema. Their contributions have often been greater than the reputation afforded them.

Apart from Guy, there were a number of other women who made a significant contribution to cinema during the silent era. The great stage actress **Sarah Bernhardt** appeared in several early films, lending her tremendous artistic weight to a fledgling medium. Likewise, the stage performer **Mistinguett** appeared in film, bringing audiences to the cinema because of her enormous popular appeal. Early film stars such as **Stacia Napierkowska**, **Renée Carl,** and **Musidora** built audiences for the cinema by creating large followings interested in their work. Carl and Musidora also worked behind the camera, both directing films. Musidora also contributed as a screenwriter. **Germaine Dulac** was one of the first avant-garde directors, helping to cultivate impressionist cinema, and focusing her own films squarely on the lives of women. Her film *La Souriante Madame Beudet* (1922) interrogated gender roles at a remarkably early moment in film history. This is a theme later women directors would revisit. Dulac was also the first director to make a film based on a work by **Louis Delluc**. Her film *La Fête espagnole* (1920) preceded Delluc's entry into the cinema, and yet he has an award named for him and she does not.

In the early sound era, women's contribution in film was almost entirely in front of the camera. The so-called golden age of film was marked by the presence of numerous talented actresses, including **Arletty**, **Edwige Feuillière**, **Michèle Morgan**, **Danielle Darrieux**, and **Françoise Rosay**. Their presence onscreen was crucial to French cinema's success, both domestically and internationally, and yet not one of these actresses has come to hold the iconic status of someone like **Jean Gabin**, despite the fact that several of them had film careers longer than his.

Women did not often find themselves behind the camera during this period. One notable exception is **Marie Epstein**, the sister of impressionist director **Jean Epstein**. She codirected a number of films with **Jean-Benoît Lévy** starting in the 1920s and continuing into the 1930s. Another female director from the period is **Jacqueline Audry**, who got her start as a screenwriter working with directors such as **René Clément**. She made her first film, *Les Malheurs de Sophie*, in 1946 and went on to make nearly twenty other films.

The 1950s and 1960s were also periods during which women appeared with regularity on the screen. This period gave the world such starlets as **Brigitte Bardot** and **Martine Carol**, more known for their physical presence than their acting abilities. It also introduced audiences to actresses such **Catherine Deneuve** and **Jeanne Moreau**. Moreau is one of the iconic actresses of French stage and cinema, and Deneuve went on to become one of the most recognized and respected actresses in the world.

Agnès Varda began her career behind the camera in the 1950s. She is regarded as one of the most talented woman directors in the world. Varda made her first film, *La Pointe-courte*, in 1956 and she has directed nearly forty films since. Not simply a woman director, Varda puts women at the center of her films, and it is perhaps due to her influence that the 1970s produced a number of other women directors. Varda was not the only influential woman to make films during the period. **Marguerite Duras** began her film career working with the male directors of the *Nouvelle Vague* or New Wave. An accomplished novelist, Duras came to cinema by writing the screenplay for **Alain Resnais**'s *Hiroshima mon amour* (1959). She wrote numerous other screenplays as well, and in 1967, she began directing.

As noted, the 1970s marked a veritable revolution in women's filmmaking. Directors such as **Diane Kurys** and **Claire Denis** began their careers in that decade. They inspired yet another generation of woman filmmakers in the 1980s and 1990s, including **Anne Fontaine** and **Tonie Marshall**. In front of the camera, the actresses of the period were increasingly valued for dramatic ability and less for their physical appearances, a fact that also suggests something of a revolution in film. Deneuve continued to be a force, and the actress **Miou Miou** came into her own. Other talented actresses appearing onscreen included **Sandrine Bonnaire**, **Fanny Ardant**, **Juliette Binoche**, **Isabel Adjani**, and **Isabelle Huppert**. The present day is one in which increasing numbers of women have prominence in front of and behind the camera. They sit on film juries, teach at film schools, and encourage future generations of women to follow in their footsteps.

Beyond the direct contribution of women, French cinema is interesting for its representation of women onscreen. Very early on, it became evident that women constituted a significant share of the market for film. Filmmakers therefore tried to appeal to that audience, which perhaps explains the diversity of the representations of women that exist in French films. Even in the silent era, there are all sorts of women onscreen. Films such as **Pathé**'s *Dix Femmes pour un mari* (1905), featured women as aggressive husband hunters. *L'Honneur d'un père* (1905) featured women as cold, unfeeling, and cruel. **Louis Feuillade**'s *Les Vampires* (1915) presented women in the roles of victim and femme fatale. In contrast, films featuring Bernhardt depicted powerful women, and films featuring **Stacia Napierkowska** depicted exotic women.

Many of these types of roles held into the 1930s and 1940s. Certainly there were femme fatales such as Mireille Balin's Gaby in **Julien Duvivier**'s *Pépé le Moko* (1937) or **Arletty**'s Clara in **Marcel Carné**'s *Le Jour se lève* (1939). There were also femme fatales who turned out to be not so fatal, as in **Ginette Leclerc**'s Denise in **Henri-Georges Clouzot**'s classic film, *Le Corbeau* (1943). This period also offered melodramas and romantic comedies with women in roles ranging from matron to young lover. The most interesting variations to these types of roles began to appear in films by women. **Jacqueline Audry**'s *Gigi* (1948) in particular was a sort of deconstruction of women's roles in society, and several of Audry's other films would also offer diversity in the presentation of woman onscreen.

In the 1950s and 1960s, yet another incarnation of the screen woman appeared, the bombshell represented best by Bardot and Carol. In addition to foregrounding the woman's body, the cinema also began to explore women's sexuality (although it was still predominantly through male fantasy). Such films as **Max Ophüls**'s *Lola Montès* (1955) or **Roger Vadim**'s *Et Dieu . . . créa la femme* (1956) are obvious examples. In this period, Varda's filmmaking began to expand the possibilities for depicting women onscreen. *Cléo de 5 à 7* (1961) offered a more psychologically complex portrait of women (or at least one woman), and Varda would continue pushing boundaries in her exploration of other women, including herself. Even the seemingly macho directors of the *Nouvelle Vague* or New Wave offered fairly complex meditations on woman's existence. **Jean-Luc Godard**, in particular, created some very vivid and dynamic female characters in such films as *Vivre sa vie* (1962).

As more women have come into the film industry, particularly from the 1970s onward, the representation of women onscreen has been increasingly complex and interesting. **Diane Kurys** explored the ties that connect women in *Coup de foudre* (1983). **Claire Denis** and **Coline Serreau** have both examined various facets of womanhood in the contemporary world, questioning the construction of manhood in the same gesture. Brigitte Rouan has also focused on women in films such as *Outremer* (1990) and *Post coïtum* (1997). Her particular emphasis is on the psychology of women's everyday lives.

Even the women created by men have become more realistic and more diverse. Director **Claude Chabrol**, for example, has produced screen women as diverse as Emma Bovary in *Madame Bovary* (1991) and Catherine and Sophie of *La Cérémonie* (1995). While femme fatales and bombshells still do make their way to the silver screen, they find themselves increasingly in the company of much more complex female characters. This is true in films by both male and female directors. However, it is quite clear that if contemporary male directors do produce some complex portraits of women, it is without question the growing influence of women in the filmmaking industry that has encouraged these more serious explorations of woman onscreen.

– Y –

YANNE, JEAN (1933–2003). Actor, director, screenwriter, and producer. Born Jean Gouyé, Jean Yann started his career as a journalist and worked in radio and television. His debut acting role was in Alain Jessua's *La Vie à l'Envers* (1964). He landed significant roles in **Jean-Luc Godard**'s *Week-End* (1967) and in **Claude Chabrol**'s *Que la bête meure* (1969) and *Le Boucher* (1969). He later won best actor at **Cannes** for his performance in Maurice Pialat's *Nous ne vieillirons pas ensemble* (1971). He directed and starred in *Tout le monde il est beau, tout le monde il est gentil* (1972), a satire on radio journalism. He later directed and played the lead in several films, including *Moi y en a vouloir des sous* (1973), *Les Chinois à Paris* (1974), *Chobizenesse* (1975), and *Je te tiens, tu me tiens par la barbichette* (1979).

Yann was especially adept at satire and parody. His feature *Deux heures moins le quart avant Jésus-Christ* was one of the most popular films of 1982. Yanne plays a leading role in the film alongside **Coluche** and **Michel Serrault**, who is featured in many of his films. It was followed by the last film he directed, *Liberté, égalité, choucroute* (1985). He subsequently played memorable characters in **Régis Wargnier**'s *Indochine* (1992), Rémy Duchemin's *Fausto* (1993), Christophe Gans's *Le Pacte des loups* (2001), and Gilles Paquet-Brenner's *Gomez & Tavares* (2003).

– Z –

ZECCA, FERDINAND (1864–1947). Director and film pioneer. Ferdinand Zecca was born in Corsica in 1864 and later moved to Paris with his family. His father was a machinist at the Funambule and later a stage manager at the Théatre de l'Ambigu. Zecca originally followed in his father's footsteps, becoming at first a performer and stage manager himself, and later venturing into the new world of cinema. Zecca had a few brushes with the cinema early in his career. He did voice recordings of speeches for **Pathé** phono (his sister worked for Pathé as a projectionist) and acted in Pathé films for the Dufayel department stores (for whom **Méliès** also made films). He was also hired on at **Gaumont** (by **Alice Guy**) for a brief time in 1898, during which he made his first film, *Les Méfaits d'une tête de veau*, often credited to Guy (ironically, one of the few she is credited with but that she actually did not make).

Zecca's big "break" came in 1898 during the Paris Exposition, when he was hired by **Charles Pathé** to run the Pathé pavilion at the exposition. Pathé was so impressed by Zecca that he immediately hired him on as head of production at Pathé, and Zecca would ultimately become studio director at the enormous Vincennes studio when it opened in 1902.

In his early filmmaking career, Zecca made mostly very popular copies of films by other people. Two of his early successes, *Ce que l'on voit de mon sixième* (1901) and *Par la trou de la serrure* (1901) were copies of English comedies. Several of his *féeries*, including *Les Sept châteaux du diable* (1901), were clearly "inspired" by Méliès. And yet Zecca also demonstrated very early a talent for filmmaking in his own right and an ability to innovate and move film in completely new directions. His fantasy film *À la conquête de l'air* (1901), about a flying machine flying over Paris, is a silent film classic, for example.

Zecca is also credited with developing the sentimental social melodrama, one of the best known of which was the very successful ***Histoire d'un crime*** (1901), which recounts in several tableaux the fall of a gambler and his subsequent crime and punishment. The film is noteworthy both in its social and moralizing dimension and in its attempt to develop an extended narrative in film. However, even in this area, one might note the influence of others. Two of Zecca's other well-known social melodramas, *Au bagne* (1906) and *L'Honneur d'un père* (1906), are near exact copies of films by Guy, *Un cas de divorce* (1906) and *Le Fils du garde chasse* (1906).

The film widely considered to be Zecca's masterpiece is the four-part *La Vie et la passion de notre seigneur Jésus Christ* (1907). The film was codirected with **Lucien Nonguet** and featured the cinematography of **Segundo de Chomon**. Composed of thirty-eight scenes or tableaux, *La Vie et la passion* was made in the way that other long epics were made at Pathé, of reels of various lengths consisting of various combinations of scenes. This structure allowed theaters to decide how much of these long films they wanted to show and how much they would pay to do so.

Apart from its variable structure, *La Vie et la passion* is noteworthy in that it is one of the few life of Christ films made that was not inspired by the passion plays. Zecca and Nonguet created the story directly, inspired by paintings of the life of Jesus found in museums around Paris. In fact, many of the scenes in the film directly echo or represent such paintings. The same is true of Nonguet's epic biopic *Napoléon Bonaparte*. Another genre in which Zecca was a pioneer was that of the reconstructed *actualité* or newsreel. Such films represented events that were in the news. The most famous example is Zecca's *Catastrophe de la Martinique* (1902), which was not actually newsreel footage but instead re-created the eruption of Mont Pélé on the island of Martinique.

Over the course of his filmmaking career, Zecca made several hundred films and trained many, if not most, of the key directors at Pathé. He worked most closely with Lucien Nonguet in the beginning and with **René LePrince** near the end, but he collaborated at one time or another with many of the directors at Pathé. Among Zecca's other films are *L'Enfant prodigue* (1901), **Histoire d'un crime** (1901), *Quo Vadis* (1901), *Ali Baba et les quarante voleurs* (1902), *La Belle au bois dormant* (1902), *La Fée printemps* (1902), *Les Victimes de l'alcoolisme* (1902), *La Grève* (1904), *Brigandage moderne* (1905), *Le Pêcheur de perles* (1905), *Rêve à la lune/L'Amant de lune* (1905), *Excursion dans la lune* (1908), *Cléopatre* (1910), *La Fièvre de l'or* (1912), and *Coeur de femme* (1913).

As time went on Zecca became more and more involved in the business of the studio and less involved in filmmaking. By 1915, he had given up filmmaking altogether and was sent all over Europe and the United States attending to Pathé business. He returned to France in 1923, where he took over control of the Pathé Baby division, a manufacturing and marketing branch that sold home movie cameras.

ZEMMOURI, MAHMOUD (1946–). Actor, director, and screenwriter. Mahmoud Zemmouri was born in Algeria but came to France, where he became a director. His films, often placed under the rubrics *beur cinema* and *cinéma de banlieue*, explore the tensions between first-generation North African immigrants and their marginalized beur children. His *100% arabica* (1997), which features the raï music stars Khaled and Cheb Mami, critiques both Islamic fundamentalism and French treatment of the beur community. He also directed *Prends 10.000 balles et casse-toi* (1982), which explores the absurdity of the French "repatriation" incentive. His other films include *Les folles années du twist* (1986), *De Hollywood à Tamanrasset* (1990), *L'honneur de la tribu* (1993), and *Beur blanc rouge* (2005). He worked as an actor in **Claude Berri's** *Tchao Pantin* (1983), Gérard Jugnot's *Pinot simple flic* (1984), Jean-Loup Hubert's *La Smala* (1984), Bernard Nauer's *Nuit d'ivresse* (1986), *L'Oeil au beur(re) noir* (1987), Philipe Galland's *La Thune* (1991), Cheikh Doukouré's *Blanc d'ébène* (1992), Malik Chibane's *Hexagone* (1993), and his own *L'honneur de la tribu* and *100% arabica*.

ZIDI, CLAUDE (1934–). Director, producer, and screenwriter. Claude Zidi studied at the **Louis Lumière** School and later worked as a camera operator for **Claude Chabrol**. Although comedy is the most popular film genre in France, French comedies rarely receive the country's most prestigious awards. Zidi's police comedy *Les Ripoux* (1984), starring **Philippe Noiret** and **Thierry Lhermitte**, is one exception. It won Zidi **César** Awards for Best Film and Best Director. Although the sequel, *Les ripoux contre Ripoux* (1990), did not receive major awards, it, too, was a box-office success. To date, Zidi's *Astérix et Obélix contre César* (1999), derived from the famous French comic book series by Alberto Uderzo and Rene Goscinny, is the most expensive French film ever made. It features the French comedy star **Christian Clavier** and megastar **Gérard Depardieu**.

The majority of Zidi's films are comedies. His only drama to date is *Deux* (1989). His first films were *Les bidasses en folie* (1971), *Les fous du stade* (1972), *Le grand bazar* (1973), *Les bidasses s'en vont en guerre* (1974), *La Moutarde me monte au nez* (1974), and *La Course à l'échalote* (1975). His *L'Aile ou la cuisse* (1976) pairs two of France's most celebrated comedians of their time, **Louis de Funès** and **Coluche**. It was followed by *L'animal* (1977), *La Zizanie* (1978), and *Bête, mais discipliné* (1979). Coluche reappeared in *Inspecteur la Bavure* (1980) and *Banzaï* (1983). In addition to the *Les Ripoux* and *Les bidasses* sequels, Zidi made the popular *Les Sous-doués* (1980) and its sequel, *Les Sous-doués en vacances* (1982). Both feature **Daniel Auteuil**. Noiret and Lhermitte were paired again for *Ripoux 3*. Zidi has also directed *Les rois du gag* (1985), *Association de malfaiteurs* (1987), *La Totale!* (1991), *Profil bas* (1993), *Arlette* (1997), and *La Boîte* (2001).

Bibliography

As with every other aspect of the cinema in France, research and scholarship on the subject has been so extensive as to force us to make choices in the selection of bibliographic material. Film scholarship has been well developed in France, Great Britain, and the United States for several decades, and film theory and film criticism both extend back to the silent era. A complete bibliography on French cinema would be as long as this entire work, and we have not attempted it. In compiling this bibliography, we have privileged English-language works over French-language works, for the obvious reason that most readers will be English-speaking. We have included a sampling of French-language works, particularly when they are integral to the development of the cinema in France, when they are articles authored in French that appear in British or American journals, or when they are edited volumes that include studies in both languages. We have also privileged more recent scholarship over older scholarship, although, again, in those cases where it concerns a landmark work, age seems irrelevant.

The bibliography begins with general and reference works, then presents studies of periods, and then studies of the major topics that have shaped critical debate and film scholarship in recent years. It concludes with a list of major journals and useful Web sites. We have used, for studies of periods, the standard periodizations used in delineating the development of French film, recognizing that there are others. We have not included categories for major movements, such as *Le Réalisme poétique* or *La Nouvelle Vague*, because these studies tend to dominate the periods during which these films were produced, and were therefore somewhat redundant.

As concerns general studies of the cinema, there are a number that are of significance. *The Oxford History of World Cinema* (1996) contains a good deal of information about French cinema, although it is a work on cinema in general. There are also a number of fairly recent books that focus on French cinema. In French there is Jean-Pierre Jeancolas's *Histoire du cinéma français* (1995), along with the quite complete and more recent edited volume by Claude Beylie, titled *Une histoire du cinéma français* (2000), and in English Alan L. Williams's *Republic of Images: A History of French Filmmaking* (1992), Susan Hayward's *French National Cinema* (1993), as well as the more recent *French Cinema* (2002) by Rémi Fournier Lanzoni. Susan Hayward and Ginette Vincendeau's *French Cinema: Texts and Contexts* (2000) and *The Cinema of France* (2006), edited by Phil Powrie, are both also good general works. These last two books differ from the other studies in that they are volumes of studies on particular films, but the range of films included provides a fairly good overview of the trajectory of French cinema.

Reference works break down in the same way. There are general works that contain a good deal of information about French cinema, most notably the Larousse *Dictionnaire du cinéma* (2000), edited by Jean-Loup Passek, and in English *The International Dictionary of Films and Filmmakers* (2000), edited by Tom and Sara Prendergrast. A number of French "dictionaries" are quite good, particularly with respect to filmographies. These include Christian-Marc Bosseno and Yannick Dehee's *Dictionnaire du cinéma populaire français: des origines à nos jours* (2004) and Stéphane Roux's *Dictionnaire des réalisateurs français* (2002).

More in-depth studies are available for particular periods of French film. Richard Abel's books *Silent Film* (1996), *The Ciné Goes to Town: French Cinema 1896–1914* (1994), and *French Cinema: The First Wave, 1915–1929* (1984) are the definitive studies on silent film. David Bordwell's *French Impressionist Cinema: Film Culture, Film Theory, and Film Style* (1980) was also a groundbreaking work. It is not as recent as Abel's work, but is still important. A recent and very worthwhile volume on the early cinema, and on Pathé Studios in particular, is Michel Marie and Laurent Le Forestier's edited volume, *La Firme Pathé Frères: 1896–1914* (2004), which contains essays in both French and English and offers analyses of every aspect of Pathé, from industry practice to the comedies of Roméo Bosetti.

Studies of the 1930s, 1940s, and 1950s abound. Colin Crisp's *The Classic French Cinema: 1930–1960* (1993) is a fairly complete and worthwhile study, as is his later book, *Genre, Myth, and Convention in the French Cinema, 1929–1939*. Dudley Andrew's *Mists of Regret: Culture and Sensibility in Classic French Film* (1995) is also a valuable resource. In French, there is Pierre Billard's *L'Âge classique du cinéma français: du cinéma parlant à la Nouvelle Vague* (1995), and of course, numerous writings by the great André Bazin, including *Le cinéma français de la libération à la nouvelle vague (1945–1958)*, published in 1983. For those wishing to read some of what Bazin had to say in English, there is *French Cinema of the Occupation and Resistance: The Birth of a Critical Esthetic* (1981).

The period from 1960 to 1980 has also been a subject of great interest, most notably because of the *Nouvelle Vague* or New Wave. Books on this period include Jefferson T. Kline's *Screening the Text: Intertextuality in New Wave French Cinema* (1992), Jill Forbes's *The Cinema in France after the New Wave* (1992), Lynn Higgins's *New Novel, New Wave, New Politics: Fiction and the Representation of History in Postwar France* (1996), and Richard John Neupert's *A History of the French New Wave Cinema* (2002). In French, there are Antoine de Baecque and Charles Tesson's *La nouvelle vague: une légende en question* (1998), Jean Cleder and Gilles Mouellic's *Nouvelle vague, nouveaux rivages: permanences du récit au cinema, 1950–1970* (2001), and of course Jean-Michel Frodon's *L'âge moderne du cinéma français: de la Nouvelle Vague à nos jours* (1995), which also includes a study of much of the contemporary period.

There is probably as much on contemporary cinema as any cinema of any other period. However, studies of contemporary cinema are largely broken down along thematic lines, and there are relatively few overviews. Guy Austin's *Contemporary French Cinema* (1996) is a compact, concise overview of the period, and even includes a brief film history. Phil Powrie's *French Cinema in the 1980s: Nostalgia and the Crisis of Masculinity* (1997) is an interesting study of the 1980s, and his edited volume, *French Cinema in the 1990s: Continuity and Difference* (1999), contains a series of studies on key films from the decade. Lucy Mazdon's edited volume *France on Film: Reflections on Popular French Cinema* (2001) is likewise an interesting collection of essays on key films. In French, apart from Frodon's work, there is Claude Trémois's study of the 1990s, *Les enfants de la liberté: le jeune cinéma français des années 90* (1997).

For those interested in particular thematic studies of French cinema, there is Dina Sherzer's edited volume *Cinema, Colonialism, Postcolonialism: Perspectives from the French and Francophone World* (1996), and the more recent study, *Colonial Cinema and Imperial France, 1919–1939: White Blind Spots, Male Fantasies, Settler Myths* (2001), by David Henry Slavin. With respect to gender and French film, there are also numerous studies, including Sandy Flitterman-Lewis's *To Desire Differently: Feminism and the French Cinema* (1996) and Judith Mayne's *Framed: Lesbians, Feminists, and Media Culture* (2002). The journal *Camera Obscura* is also devoted to gender studies in film.

History in French film is another topic on which there is a wide variety of studies. They include Pierre Sorlin's *The Film in History: Restaging the Past* (1980), Maureen Turim's *Flashbacks in Film: Memory and History* (1989), and Marcia Landy's *Cinematic Uses of the Past* (1996). Specific to French cinema, there is Naomi Green's *Landscapes of Loss: The National Past in Postwar French Cinema* (1999). In French, there is Pierre Guibbert's *L'Histoire de France au cinéma* (1993). There are also studies on various aspects of history in film, including André Pierre Colombat's *The Holocaust in French Film* (1993), Philip D. Dine's *Images of the Algerian War: French Fiction and Film, 1954–1992* (1994), and Richard J. Golson's *Vichy's Afterlife: History and Counterhistory in Postwar France* (2000). On the relationship between literature and film, there is the volume edited by Andrew Horton and Joan Magretta, *Modern European Filmmakers and the Art of Adaptation* (1981). John J. Michalczyk's *The French Literary Filmmakers* (1981) is also a useful study.

There are too many studies of individual films, actors, and directors to cite, although we have given a good sampling. In general, the British dominate in this field. The British Film Institute has published several studies of films, but Manchester University Press is probably the most significant source in this area, with its evolving series on major French directors. The French publishing company Seghers has an equally impressive directors series in French. There are also so many interviews that summarizing them is impossible. Apart from book-length studies, there are several journals that provide excellent sources for research in the area of French cinema. The major film journals, such as *Screen* and *Sight and Sound*, regularly contain studies of French cinema. There are of course the legendary *Cahiers du cinéma*, and its rival *Positif,* both of which provide comprehensive opinions and analysis on French films, going back several decades. The French journal *La Révue du cinéma* is also quite good. In English, the only major journal devoted entirely to French cinema is the relatively recent *Studies in French Cinema*. Despite the fact that it is a newcomer, it has an editorial board consisting of most of the names cited in the bibliography, and publishes first-rate analyses of films from all periods.

The Web is fairly new territory with respect to French cinema studies, although there is a good deal out there. Noteworthy sites include *Cahiers du cinéma* (www.cahiersducinema.com/), the online film journal *Ecran noir* (www.ecrannoir.fr/index.php), *Il était une fois le cinéma* (www.iletaitunefoislecinema.com), *Le Film français* (www.lefilm francais.com/), and *Les Gens du cinéma* (www.lesgensducinema.com). There is also *Les Indépendents du premier siècle*, a site devoted to overlooked figures in French cinema (www.lips.org). The *Internet Movie Database* (www.imdb.com) has a good deal of information about French cinema, but it should be cross-checked. *DVDtoile* (www.dvdtoile.com) and *Allocine* (www.allocine.com) are very good companion sites, although they are less complete than the IMDB. The *Unifrance* site (www.unifrance.org/) has probably the most complete information on any films contained in its database, although it only contains fairly recent ones. In any format, there are a good many avenues for pursuing research in French cinema studies.

CONTENTS

FRENCH FILM: GENERAL

Alekan, Henri. *Des lumières et des ombres*. Paris: Le Sycamore/La Cinémathèque Française, 1984.

Andrew, Dudley. *Film in the Aura of Art*. Princeton, N.J.: Princeton University Press, 1984.

Armes, Roy. *French Cinema*. Oxford: Oxford University Press, 1985.

Bandy, Mary Lea, ed. *Rediscovering French Film*. New York: Museum of Modern Art, 1983.

Barrot, Olivier, and Raymond Chirat. *Les excentriques du cinéma français*. Paris: Veyrier, 1993.

Barsacq, Léon. *Le décor de film*. Paris: Seghers, 1970.

Beylie Claude, ed. *Une histoire du cinéma francais*. Paris: Larousse, 2000.

Bonitzer, Pascal. *Peinture et cinéma: décadrages*. Paris: Éditions de L'Étoile, 1985.

Braunberger, Pierre. *Cinémamémoire*. Paris: Centre Georges Pompidou, 1987.

Brunius, Jacques-Bernard. *En marge du cinéma français*. Paris: Arcanes, 1954.

Buss, Robin. *French Film Noir*. New York: Marion Boyars, 1994.

——. *The French through Their Films*. London: Batsford Press, 1988.

Butler, Margaret. *Film and Community in Britain and France: From La règle du jeu to Room at the Top*. New York: I. B. Tauris, 2004.

Chantal, Suzanne. *Le Ciné-monde*. Paris: Grasset, 1977.

Comes, Philippe de, and Michel Marmin, eds. *Le Cinéma français: 1630–1985*. Paris: Editions Atlas, 1985.

——. *Le Cinéma français: 1930–1960*. Paris: Editions Atlas, 1984.

Courtade, Francis. *Les malédictions du cinéma français: Une histoire du cinéma français parlant*. Paris: Moreau, 1978.

Danan, Martine. "From a 'Prenational' to a 'Postnational' French Cinema." In *The European Cinema Reader*, edited by Catherine Fowler, 232–45. London: Routledge, 2002.

Darré, Yann. *Histoire sociale du cinéma français*. Paris: La Découverte, 2000.

Dehee, Yannick. *Mythologies politiques du cinéma français 1960–2000*. Paris: PUF, 2000.

Delpierre, Madeleine. *French Elegance in the Cinema*. Paris: Société de l'histoire du costume, 1988.

Donahue, Walter, and John Boorman, eds. *Projections 9: French Film-Makers on Film-Making*. New York: Faber & Faber, 1999.

Durham, Carolyn A. *Double Takes: Culture and Gender in French Films and Their American Remakes*. Hanover, N.H.: University Press of New England, 1998.

Ellis, Jack. *A History of Film*. Englewood Cliffs, N.J.: Prentice Hall, 1979.

Ezra, Elizabeth, and Sue Harris, eds. *France in Focus: Film and National Identity*. Oxford: Berg Publishers, 2000.

Forbes, Jill. *The Cinema in France After the New Wave*. London: British Film Institute, 1992.

Fowler, Roy Alexander. *The Film in France*. London: Pendulum Publications, 1946.

Frodon, Jean-Michel. *L'âge moderne du cinéma francais: de la Nouvelle Vague à nos jours*. Paris: Flammarion, 1995.

Grossvogel, David I. *Didn't You Used to Be Depardieu?: Film as Cultural Marker in France and Hollywood*. New York: Peter Lang, 2002.

———. *Marianne and the Puritan: Transformations of the Couple in French and American Films*. Lanham, Md.: Lexington Books, 2005.

Guérif, François. *Le cinéma policier français*. Paris: Veyrier, 1981.

Hayward, Susan. *French National Cinema*. London: Routledge, 1993.

Hayward, Susan, and Ginette Vincendeau, eds. *French Film: Texts and Contexts*. London: Routledge, 2000.

Hill, John, and Pamela Church Gibson. *World Cinema: Critical Approaches*. Oxford: Oxford University Press, 2000.

Jeancolas, Jean-Pierre. *Histoire du cinéma français*. Paris: Natan, 1995.

La Breteque, Francois de. "Le cinéma populaire français: compromis et ambivalences." *CinémAction* 95, no. 2 (2000): 34–41.

Langlois, Henri. *Trois cents ans du cinéma*. Paris: Cahiers du Cinéma, 1986.

Lanzoni, Remi Fournier. *French Cinema: From Its Beginnings to the Present*. New York: Continuum Press, 2002.

Mazdon, Lucy. *Encore Hollywood: Remaking French Cinema*. London: British Film Institute, 2000.

Nowell-Smith, Geoffrey, ed. *The Oxford History of World Cinema*. Oxford: Oxford University Press, 1999.

Paris, James Reid. *The Great French Films*. Seacaucus, N.J.: Citadel, 1983.

Pauly, Rebecca M. *The Transparent Illusion: Image and Ideology in French Text and Film*. New York: Peter Lang, 1993.

Powrie, Phil, ed. *The Cinema of France: 24 Frames*. London: Wallflower, 2006.

Powrie, Phil, and Keather Reader. *French Cinema: A Student's Guide*. London: Arnold, 2002.

Prédal, René. *Cinquante ans de cinéma français*. Paris: Nathan, 1995.

Reader, Keith. *Cultures on Celluloid*. London & New York: Quartet Books, 1981.

Rohdie, Sam. *Promised Lands: Cinema, Geography, Modernism*. London: British Film Institute, 2001.

Sadoul, Georges. *Le cinéma français, 1890–1962*. Paris: Flammarion, 1962.

Siclier, Jacques. *Le cinéma français*. Paris: Ramsay, 1990.

Sorlin, Pierre. *European Cinemas, European Societies, 1939–1990*. London: Routledge, 1991.

Temple, Michael, and Michael Witt, eds. *The French Cinema Book*. London: British Film Institute, 2004.

Thiher, Allen. *The Cinematic Muse: Critical Studies in the History of French Cinema*. Columbia: University of Missouri Press, 1979.

Vincendeau, Ginette. *Stars and Stardom in French Cinema*. London: Continuum, 2000.

Williams, Alan L. *Republic of Images: A History of French Filmmaking*. Cambridge, Mass.: Harvard University Press, 1992.

Wilson, Emma. *French Cinema since 1950: Personal Histories*. Lanham, Md.: Rowman & Littlefield, 1999.

Zants, Emily. *Creative Encounters with French Films*. San Francisco: EmText, 1993.

REFERENCE

Bergan, Ronald, and Robyn Karney. *The Faber Companion to Foreign Films*. London: Faber & Faber, 1992.

Bessy, Maurice, Raymond Chirat, and André Bernard. *Histoire du cinéma français: Encyclopédie des films 1966–1970*. Paris: Pygmalion, 1992.

Biggs, Melissa E. *French Films, 1945–1993: A Critical Filmography of the 400 Most Important Releases*. London: McFarland, 1996.

Blandford, Steve, Barry Keith Grant, and Jim Hillier, eds. *The Film Studies Dictionary*. London: Arnold, 2001.

Bosseno, Christian-Marc, and Yannick Dehee. *Dictionnaire du cinéma populaire français: des origines à nos jours*. Paris: Nouveau Monde Editions, 2004.

Bousquet, Henri. *De Pathé Frères à Pathé Cinéma*. Paris: Henri Bousquet, 2001.

Garçon, François: *Gaumont: A Century of French Cinema*. New York: Harry Abrams, 1994.

Hayward, Susan. *Cinema Studies: The Key Concepts*. London: Routledge, 2000.

Katz, Ephraim. *The Film Encyclopedia*. 4th ed. New York: Harper Resource, 2001.

Mitry, Jean. *Filmographie universelle*. Bois d'Arcy: Service des Archives du Film, 1980–1982.

Nowell-Smith, Geoffrey. *The Oxford History of World Cinema*. Oxford: Oxford University Press, 1999.

Pallister, Janis, and Ruth Hottel. *Francophone Women Film Directors: A Guide*. Madison, N.J.: Fairleigh Dickinson University Press, 2005.

Paris, James. *The Great French Films*. Secaucus, N.J.: Citadel, 1983.

Passek, Jean-Loup. *Dictionnaire du cinéma*. Paris: Larousse, 2000.

Pearson, Roberta. *Critical Dictionary of Film and Television Theory*. London: Routledge, 2000.

Pendergast, Sarah, and Tom Pendergast. *International Dictionary of Films and Filmmakers*. Detroit: Saint James Press, 2000.

Pessis-Pasternak, Guitta. *Dictionnaire de l'audio-visuel, français-anglais et anglais-francais: cinéma, photographie, presse, radio, télévision, télédistribution*. Paris: Flammarion, 1976.

Rosenthal, Daniel. *Variety International Film Guide 2005: The Definitive Annual Review of World Cinema*. Los Angeles: Silman-James Press, 2005.

Roux, Stéphane. *Dictionnaire des réalisateurs français*. Paris: Dualpha, 2002.

Slide, Anthony. *Fifty Classic French Films, 1912–1982: A Pictorial Record*. New York: Dover, 1987.

Vincendeau, Ginette. *The Companion to French Cinema*. London: British Film Institute, 1996.

Vorontzoff, Alexis N. *Dictionnaire technique anglais-français du cinéma et de la télévision*. Paris: Technique et Documentation-Lavoisier, 1991.

Wakeman, John, ed. *World Film Directors*. New York: H. W. Wilson, 1987.

Waldman, Harry. *Paramount in Paris: 300 Films Produced at the Joinville Studios, 1930–1933*. Lanham, Md.: Scarecrow Press, 1998.

SILENT FILM: 1895–1929

Abel, Richard. *The Ciné Goes to Town: French Cinema 1896–1914*. Berkeley: University of California Press, 1998.

——. *Silent Film*. Rutgers, N.J.: Rutgers University Press, 1996.

——. *French Cinema: The First Wave, 1915–1929*. Princeton, N.J.: Princeton University Press, 1984.

Bordwell, David. *French Impressionist Cinema: Film Culture, Film Theory, and Film Style*. New York: Arno, 1980.

Bottomore, Stephen. "Dreyfus and Documentary." *Sight and Sound* 53 (Autumn 1984): 290–93.

Brownlow, Kevin. *Napoléon: Abel Gance's Classic Film.* New York: Knopf, 1983.

Crafton, Donald. *Émile Cohl, Caricature, and Film.* Princeton, N.J.: Princeton University Press, 1990.

———. *Before Mickey: The Animated Film: 1898–1928.* Cambridge: Massachusetts Institute of Technology Press, 1982.

Elsaesser, Thomas, ed. *Early Cinema: Space, Frame, Narrative.* London: British Film Institute, 1990.

Fell, John. *Film Before Griffith.* Berkeley: University of California Press, 1983.

Fescourt, Henri. *Le Cinéma, des origins à nos jours.* Paris: Cygne, 1932.

Frazer, John. *Artificially Arranged Scenes: The Films of Georges Méliès.* Boston: G. K. Hall, 1979.

Garçon, François. *Gaumont: A Century of French Cinema.* New York: Harry Abrams, 1994.

Gordon, Rae Beth. *Why the French Love Jerry Lewis: From Cabaret to Early Cinema.* Stanford, Calif.: Stanford University Press, 2001.

———. "Laughing Hysterically: Gesture, Movement and Spectatorship in Early French Cinema." In *Moving Forward, Holding Fast: The Dynamics of Nineteenth-Century French Culture,* edited by Barbara T. Cooper and Mary Donaldson-Evans, 217–37. Amsterdam: Rodopi, 1997.

Gunning, Tom. "The Cinema of Attraction: Early Film, Its Spectator and the Avant-Garde." *Wide Angle* 8, no. 3 (1986): 63–70.

Kaplan, Nelly. *Napoleon.* Edited by Bernard McGuirk. London: British Film Institute, 1994.

Marie, Michel, and Laurent Le Forestier. *La Firme Pathé Frères: 1896–1914.* Paris: AFRHC, 2004.

McMahan, Alison. "Eastern Westerns: Early French Constructions of American Identity." *Quarterly Review of Film and Video* 18, no. 3 (July 2001): 295–303.

Monaco, Paul. *Cinema and Society: France and Germany during the Twenties.* New York: Elsevier, 1976.

Pratt, George C. *Spellbound in Darkness: A History of the Silent Film.* Greenwich: New York Graphic Society, 1973.

Sorlin, Pierre. "France: The Silent Memory." In *The First World War and Popular Cinema: 1914 to the Present,* edited by Michael Paris, 115–37. New Brunswick, N.J.: Rutgers University Press, 2000.

FRENCH CINEMA: 1930–1960

Abecassis, Michaël. *The Representation of Parisian Speech in the Cinema of the 1930s.* Oxford: Peter Lang, 2005.

Andrew, Dudley. "French Cinema of the 1930s." In *European Cinema*, edited by Elizabeth Ezra, 97–114. Oxford: Oxford University Press, 2004.

——. *Mists of Regret: Culture and Sensibility in Classic French Film*. Princeton, N.J.: Princeton University Press, 1995.

Bazin, André. *Le cinéma français de la libération à la nouvelle vague (1945–1958)*, edited by Jean Narboni. Paris: Editions de l'Étoile, 1983.

——. *French Cinema of the Occupation and Resistance: The Birth of a Critical Esthetic*, translated by Stanley Hochman. New York: Ungar, 1981.

Billard, Pierre. *L'Âge classique du cinéma français: du cinéma parlant à la Nouvelle Vague*. Paris: Flammarion, 1995.

Buschsbaum, J. *Cinéma engagé: Film in the Popular Front*. Urbana: University of Illinois Press, 1988.

Buss, Robin. *French Film Noir*. New York: Marion Boyars, 1994.

Caille, Patricia. "From French Stars to Frenchmen in Postwar National Culture." *Quarterly Review of Film and Video* 19 (January 2002): 43–58.

Colombat, André Pierre. *Genre, Myth, and Convention in the French Cinema, 1929–1939*. Bloomington: Indiana University Press, 2002.

Comes, Philippe de, and Michel Marmin, eds. *Le cinema francais: 1930–1960*. Paris: Editions Atlas, 1984.

Conway, Kelley. *Chanteuse in the City: The Realist Singer in French Film*. Berkeley: University of California Press, 2004.

——. "Flower of the Asphalt: The Chanteuse Réaliste in 1930s French Cinema." In *Soundtrack Available: Essays on Film and Popular Music*, edited by Pamela Robertson Wojcik and Arthur Knight, 134–60. Durham, N.C.: Duke University Press, 2001.

Crisp, Colin. *Genre, Myth, and Convention in the French Cinema, 1929–1939*. Bloomington: Indiana University Press, 2002.

——. *The Classic French Cinema: 1930–1960*. Bloomington: Indiana University Press, 1993.

Ehrlich, Evelyn. *Cinema of Paradox: French Filmmaking under the German Occupation*. New York: Columbia University Press, 1985.

Faulkner, Christopher. *The Social Cinema of Jean Renoir*. Princeton, N.J.: Princeton University Press, 1986.

Fauré, Michel. *Le groupe Octobre*. Paris: Bourgeois Édition, 1979.

Ghali, Nourredine. *L'avant-Garde cinématographique des années vingt*. Paris: Expérimental, 1995.

Guillaume-Grimauld, Geneviève. *Le Cinéma du Front Populaire*. Paris: Lherminier, 1986.

Hillier, Jim, ed. *Cahiers du cinema, the 1950s: Neo-realism, Hollywood, New Wave*. Cambridge, Mass.: Harvard University Press, 1985.

Hubert-Lacombe, Patricia. *Le cinéma français dans la guerre froide: 1946–1956*. Paris: L'Harmattan, 1996.

Jeancolas, Jean-Pierre. *Quinze ans d'années 30; Le cinéma des Français, 1929–1944*. Paris: Stock, 1983.

Kaplan, Alice Yeager. *Reproductions of Banality*. Minneapolis: University of Minnesota Press, 1986.

Martin, John W. *The Golden Age of French Cinema, 1929–1939*. Boston: G. K. Hall, 1983.

O'Brien, Charles. *Cinema's Conversion to Sound: Technology and Film Style in France and the U.S.* Bloomington: Indiana University Press, 2005.

———. "Stylistic Description as Historical Method: French Films of the German Occupation." *Style* 32, no. 3 (Fall 1998): 427–29.

Reader, Keith. *Robert Bresson*. Manchester: Manchester University Press, 2000.

Sadoul, Georges. *French Film*. London: Falcon Press, 1953.

Sesonske, Alexander. *Jean Renoir, the French Films, 1924–1939*. Cambridge, Mass.: Harvard University Press, 1980.

Sorin, Cécile. "The Art of Borrowing: French Popular Cinema Before the New Wave." *Studies in French Cinema* 4, no. 1 (2004): 53–64.

Strebel, Elizabeth Grottle. *French Social Cinema of the Nineteen-Thirties: A Cinematic Expression of Popular Front Consciousness*. New York: Arno, 1980.

Vincendeau, Ginette, and Keith Reader, eds. *La Vie est a nous!: French Cinema of the Popular Front 1935–1938*. London: British Film Institute, 1986.

Weber, Alain. *Cinéma(s) français 1900–1939: Pour un monde différent*. Paris: Séguier, 2002.

Weiner, Susan. *Enfants terribles: Youth and Femininity in the Mass Media in France, 1945–1968*. Baltimore: Johns Hopkins University Press, 2001.

FRENCH CINEMA: 1960–1980

Baecque, Antoine de. *La nouvelle vague: portrait d'une jeunesse*. Paris: Flammarion, 1998.

Baecque, Antoine de, and Charles Tesson. *La nouvelle vague: une légende en question*. Paris: Cahiers du cinema, 1998.

Berliner, Todd. "The Genre Film as Booby Trap: 1970s Genre Bending and the French Connection." *Cinema Journal* 40, no. 3 (Spring 2001): 25–46.

Borde, Raymond, Freddy Buache, and Jean Curtelin. *Nouvelle Vague*. Lyon: Serdoc, 1962.

Buache, Freddy. *Le cinéma français des années 60*. Paris: Hatier, 1987.

Buache, Freddy. *Le cinéma français des années 70*. Paris: Hatier, 1990.

Chateau, Dominique. "La Nouvelle Vague entre l'autre et l'artiste." *Iris* 28 (Autumn 1999): 27–38.

Cleder, Jean, and Gilles Mouellic. *Nouvelle vague, nouveaux rivages: permanences du récit au cinéma, 1950–1970*. Rennes: Presses Universitaires de Rennes, 2001.

Clouzot, Claire. *Le cinéma français depuis la nouvelle vague*. Paris: Nathan, 1972.

Comes, Philippe de, and Michel Marmin. *Le Cinéma français, 1960–1985*. Paris: Editions Atlas, 1985.

Douchet, Jean. *Nouvelle vague*. Paris: Cinémathèque française: Hazan, 1998.

Douin, Jean-Luc, ed. *La Nouvelle Vague 25 ans après*. Paris: Cerf, 1983.

Frodon, Jean-Michel. *L'âge moderne du cinéma français: de la Nouvelle Vague à nos jours*. Paris: Flammarion, 1995.

Graham, Peter John. *The New Wave: Critical Landmarks*. Garden City, N.Y.: Doubleday, 1968.

Higgins, Lynn. *New Novel, New Wave, New Politics: Fiction and the Representation of History in Postwar France*. Lincoln: University of Nebraska Press, 1996.

Jeancolas, Jean-Pierre. *Le Cinéma des Français: la Ve République, 1958–1978*. Paris: Stock, 1979.

––––––. *Le Cinéma français 1969–1974*. Créteil: Maison des Arts et de la Culture de Créteil, 1974.

Kline, T. Jefferson. "The French New Wave." In *European Cinema*, edited by Elizabeth Ezra, 157–75. Oxford: Oxford University Press, 2004.

––––––. *Screening the Text: Intertextuality in New Wave French Cinema*. Baltimore: Johns Hopkins University Press, 1992.

Lipkin, Steve. "The New Wave and the Post-War Film Economy." *Current Research in Film* 2 (1986): 156–85.

Marie, Michel. *The French New Wave: An Artistic School*. London: Blackwell, 2003.

McCreary, Eugene. "Film and History: New Wave Cinema and '68." *Film & History* 19, no. 3 (1989): 61–68.

Monaco, James. *The New Wave: Truffaut, Godard, Chabrol, Rohmer, Rivette*. New York: Oxford University Press, 1976.

Neupert, Richard John. *A History of the French New Wave Cinema*. Madison: University of Wisconsin Press, 2002.

Sellier, Genevieve. "La Nouvelle Vague: un cinéma à la première personne du masculin singulier." *Iris* 24 (Autumn 1997): 77–89.

Siclier, Jacques. *Nouvelle vague?* Paris: Cerf, 1961.

Smith, Alison. *French Cinema in the 1970s: The Echoes of May*. Manchester: Manchester University Press, 2005.

Taylor, John Russell. *Cinema Eye, Cinema Ear: Some Key Filmmakers of the Sixties*. London: Methuen, 1964.

Turigliano, Roberto, ed. *Nouvelle Vague*. Turin: Festival Internazionale Cinema Giovani, 1985.

Wilson, David, ed. *Cahiers du Cinéma 1973–1978: History, Ideology, Cultural Struggle*. New York: Routledge, 2000.

CONTEMPORARY CINEMA

Austin, Guy. *Contemporary French Cinema: An Introduction*. Manchester: Manchester University Press, 1996.

Beugnet, Martine. *Marginalité, sexualité, contrôle dans le cinéma français contemporain*. Paris: Harmattan, 2000.

Bluher, Dominique. "Hip-Hop Cinema in France." *Camera Obscura: A Journal of Feminism, Culture, and Media Studies* 46 (2001): 77–96.

Bosséno, Christian. "Immigrant Cinema: National Cinema—the case of *beur* film." In *Popular European Cinema*, edited by Richard Dyer and Ginette Vincendeau, 47–57. London: Routledge, 1992.

Dhoukar, Hedi. "Les thémes du cinéma beur." *CinémAction* 56 (July 1990): 152–60.

Forbes, Jill. *The Cinema in France after the New Wave*. London: Palgrave Macmillan, 1992.

Harris, Sue. "New Directions in French Cinema." *French Cultural Studies* 15, no. 3 (October 2004): 219–324.

———. "The *Cinéma du Look*." In *European Cinema*, edited by Elizabeth Ezra, 219–32. Oxford: Oxford University Press, 2004.

Heathcote, Owen, Alex Hughes, and James S. Williams, eds. *Gay Signatures: Gay and Lesbian Theory, Fiction and Film in France, 1945–1995*. Oxford: Berg, 1998.

La Breteque, François de. "Films de banlieue, films de 'barrière.'" *Les Cahiers de la Cinématheque* 59/60 (February 1994): 128–32.

Mazdon, Lucy, ed. *France on Film: Reflections on Popular French Cinema*. London: Wallflower, 2001.

Orlando, Valerie. "From Rap to Rai in the Mixing Bowl: Beur Hip-Hop Culture and *Banlieue* Cinema in Urban France." *Journal of Popular Culture* 36, no. 3 (Winter 2003): 395–426.

Powrie, Phil, ed. *French Cinema in the 1990s: Continuity and Difference*. Oxford: Oxford University Press, 1999.

———. *French Cinema in the 1980s: Nostalgia and the Crisis of Masculinity*. Oxford: Oxford University Press, 1997.

Prédal, René. "Immigration et cinéma beur: vingt ans déjà." *Jeune Cinema* 204 (November/December 1990): 18–22.

——. *Le jeune cinéma français*. Paris: Nathan, 2002.

Tarr, Carrie. "Ethnicity and Identity in the *cinéma de banlieue*." In *French Cinema in the 1990s: Continuity and Difference*, edited by Phil Powrie, 172–84. Oxford: Oxford University Press, 1999.

——. "French Cinema and Post-Colonial Minorities." In *Post-Colonial Cultures in France*, edited by Alec G. Hargreaves and Mark McKinney, 59–83. London: Routledge, 1997.

——. "Gender, Ethnicity and Identity in Contemporary French Cinema: The Case of the Young Maghrebi-French Woman." *Iris* 24 (Autumn 1997): 125–35.

Trémois, Claude. *Les enfants de la liberté: le jeune cinéma français des années 90*. Paris: Seuil, 1997.

Wilson, Emma. *French Cinema Since 1950: Personal Histories*. Lanham, Md.: Rowman & Littlefield, 1999.

FILM THEORY AND CRITICISM: GENERAL

Abel, Richard. *French Film Theory and Criticism: A History/Anthology 1907–1929*. Berkeley: University of California Press, 1988.

Andrew, Dudley. *Concepts in Film Theory*. Oxford: Oxford University Press, 1984.

Astruc, Alexandre. *Du stylo à la caméra . . . et de la caméra au stylo: ecrits (1942–1984)*. Paris: L'Archipel, 1992.

Baudry, Jean-Louis. *L'Effet-cinéma*. Paris: Albatros, 1978.

Bazin, André. *Le cinéma français de la liberation à la nouvelle vague (1945–1958)*. Paris: Editions de l'Étoile, 1983.

Braudy, Leo, and Marshall Cohen, eds. *Film Theory and Criticism: Introductory Readings*. 6th ed. Oxford: Oxford University Press, 2004.

Deleuze, Gilles. Cinema 2: *The Time Image*. London, Athlone, 1992.

——. Cinema 1: *The Movement-Image*. London, Athlone, 1989.

Delluc, Louis. *Cinéma et cie*. Paris: Grasset, 1919.

Dulac, Germaine. *Écrits sur le cinéma, 1919–1937*. Paris: Expérimental, 1994.

Epstein, Jean. *Écrits sur le cinema*. Vol. 1. Paris: Seghers, 1974.

——. *Écrits sur le cinema*. Vol. 2. Paris: Seghers, 1975.

Fescourt, Henri. *La Foi et les montagnes*. Paris: Paul Montel, 1959.

Forrest, Jennifer. "The 'Personal' Touch: The Original, the Remake, and the Dupe in Early Cinema." In *Dead Ringers: The Remake in Theory and Practice*, edited by Jennifer Forrest and Leonard R. Koos, 89–126. New York: State University of New York Press, 2002.

Hammond, Paul, ed. *The Shadow and Its Shadow: Surrealist Writings on Cinema*. London: British Film Institute, 1978.

Hill, John, et al. *The Oxford Guide to Film Studies*. Oxford: Oxford University Press, 1998.

Hillier, Jim, ed. *Cahiers du cinéma, the 1950s: Neo-realism, Hollywood, New Wave*. Cambridge, Mass.: Harvard University Press, 1985.

Lowry, Edward. *The Filmology Movement and Film Study in France*. Ann Arbor: University of Michigan Research Press, 1985.

McCabe, Janet. *Feminist Film Studies: Writing the Woman into Cinema*. London: Wallflower, 2004.

McGregor, Andrew. "French Film Criticism and Cultural Hegemony: The Perpetual French 'Discovery' of Le Cinéma des Antipodes." *French Cultural Studies* 15, no. 2 (June 2004): 158–73.

Metz, Christian. *Psychoanalysis and Cinema: The Imaginary Signifier*. London: Macmillan, 1982.

Moussinac, Léon. *L'Âge ingrat du cinéma*. Paris: Sagittaire, 1946.

Powrie, Phil. "Out of This World (Cinema): French Cinema Studies Now." *Journal of Romance Studies* 1, no. 3 (Winter 2001): 143–52.

Rhodie, Sam. *Promised Lands: Cinema, Geography, Modernism*. London: British Film Institute, 2001.

Ricciardi, Alessia. *The Ends of Mourning: Psychoanalysis, Literature, Film*. Stanford, Calif.: Stanford University Press, 2003.

Rodowick, D. N. *Gilles Deleuze's Time Machine*. Durham, N.C.: Duke University Press, 1997.

Sadoul, Georges. *Lumière et Méliès*, edited by Bernard Eisenschitez. Paris: Lherminier, 1985.

Truffaut, François. "A Certain Tendency of the French Cinema." In *Movies and Methods: An Anthology*. Vol 1B, edited by B. Nichols. Berkeley: University of California Press, 1976.

COLONIAL AND POSTCOLONIAL CINEMA

Andrew, Dudley. "'Cinema Colonial' of 1930s France: Film Narration as Spatial Practice." In *Visions of the East: Orientalism in Film*, edited by Matthew Bernstein and Gaylyn Studlar, 207–31. New Brunswick, N.J.: Rutgers University Press, 1997.

Blum-Reid, Sylvie. *East-West Encounters: Franco-Asian Cinema and Literature*. London & New York: Wallflower Press, 2003.

Dine, Philip D. *Images of the Algerian War: French Fiction and Film, 1954–1992*. Oxford: Clarendon Press, 1994.

Jimenez, Floréal. "*L'Homme du Niger/The Man from Niger*: A Cinematographic Construction of Colonialist Ideology in the 1930s." *Studies in French Cinema* 5, no. 2 (2005): 111–22.

Langford, Rachael. "Colonial False Memory Syndrome? The Cinémémoire Archive of French Colonial Films and *Mémoire d'Outremer* (Claude Bossion, 1997)." *Studies in French Cinema* 5, no. 2 (2005): 99–109.

Lee, Sonia. "Mehdi Charef et le cinéma de l'intégration." *Contemporary French and Francophone Studies* 8, no.2 (Spring 2004): 185–91.

Norindr, Panivong. *Phantasmic Indochina: French Colonial Ideology in Architecture, Film, and Literature.* Durham, N.C.: Duke University Press, 1996.

———. "Filmic Memorial and Colonial Blues: Indochina in Contemporary French Cinema." In *Cinema, Colonialism, Postcolonialism: Perspectives from the French and Francophone World,* edited by Dina Sherzer, 120–46. Austin: University of Texas Press, 1996.

Sherzer, Dina. "Maghrebi-French Directors behind the Camera: The Cinema of the Second Generation." *Studies in Twentieth Century Literature* 26, no. 1 (Winter 2002): 144–71.

———, ed. *Cinema, Colonialism, Postcolonialism: Perspectives from the French and Francophone World.* Austin: University of Texas Press, 1996.

Slavin, David Henry. *Colonial Cinema and Imperial France, 1919–1939: White Blind Spots, Male Fantasies, Settler Myths.* Baltimore: Johns Hopkins University Press, 2001.

Spaas, Lieve. *The Francophone Film: A Struggle for Identity.* Manchester: Manchester University Press, 2000.

Tarr, Carrie. "Ethnicity and Identity in the *cinéma de banlieue.*" In *French Cinema in the 1990s: Continuity and Difference,* edited by Phil Powrie, 172–84. Oxford: Oxford University Press, 1999.

———. "French Cinema and Post-Colonial Minorities." In *Post-Colonial Cultures in France,* edited by Alec G. Hargreaves and Mark McKinney, 59–83. London: Routledge, 1997.

Ungar, Steve, and Tom Conley, eds. *Identity Papers: Contested Nationhood in Twentieth-Century France.* Minneapolis: University of Minnesota Press, 1996.

GENDER AND FRENCH CINEMA

Austin, Guy. "Vampirism, Gender Wars and the 'Final Girl': French Fantasy Film in the Early Seventies." *French Cultural Studies* 7, no 3 (October 1996): 321–42.

Balides, Constance. "Scenarios of Exposure in the Practice of Everyday Life: Women in the Cinema of Attractions." *Screen* 34 (Spring 1993): 19–37.

Bates, Robin. "Audiences on the Verge of a Fascist Breakdown: Male Anxieties and Late 1930s French Film." *Cinema Journal* 36, no. 3 (Spring 1997): 25–55.

Beugnet, Martine. *Marginalité, sexualité, contrôle dans le cinéma français contemporain*. Paris: Harmattan, 2000.

Burch, Noel, and Geneviève Sellier. "The 'Funny War' of the Sexes in French Cinema." In *Film and Nationalism*, edited by Alan Williams. New Brunswick, N.J.: Rutgers University Press, 2002.

Davies, Ann. "The Male Body and the Female Gaze in Carmen Films." In *The Trouble with Men: Masculinities in European and Hollywood Cinema*, edited by Phil Powrie, Ann Davies, and Bruce Babington, 187–95. London: Wallflower, 2004.

Fischer, Lucie. "The Lady Vanishes: Women, Magic, and the Movies." *Film Quarterly* 22 (Fall 1979): 30–40.

Flitterman-Lewis, Sandy. *To Desire Differently: Feminism and the French Cinema*. New York: Columbia University Press, 1996.

Freedman, Jane, and Carrie Tarr, eds. *Women, Immigration and Identities in France*. Oxford: Berg, 2000.

Gillain, Anne. "L'imaginaire féminin au cinéma." *The French Review* 70, no. 2 (December 1996): 259–71.

Hayward, Susan. "A History of French Cinema: 1895–1991: Pioneering Film-Makers (Guy, Dulac, Varda) and Their Heritage." *Paragraph: A Journal of Modern Critical Theory* 15, no. 1 (March 1992): 19–37.

———. "Varda's Cinematic Language, a New Mythology for Women? Some Considerations on *L'Une Chante, l'autre pas*." *Centerpoint: A Journal of Interdisciplinary Studies* 3, no. 3–4 (Fall–Spring 1980): 172–77.

Higgins, Lynn A. "Screen/Memory: Rape and Its Alibis in *Last Year at Marienbad*." In *Rape and Representation*, edited by Lynn A. Higgins and Brenda R. Silver, 303–21. New York: Columbia University Press, 1991.

Hottell, Ruth. "Including Ourselves: The Role of Female Spectators in Agnes Varda's *Le Bonheur* and *L'Une chante, l'autre pas*." *Cinema Journal* 38, no. 2 (1999): 52–71.

Hughes, Alex, and James S. Williams, eds. *Gender and French Cinema*. New York: Berg, 2001.

Karriker, Alexandra Heidi. *Film Studies: Women in Contemporary World Cinema*. New York: Peter Lang, 2002.

Mayne, Judith. "Inversion and Lesbian Plots in Henri-Georges Clouzot's *Les diaboliques*." In *Framed: Lesbians, Feminists, and Media Culture*, edited by Judith Mayne, 41–64. Minneapolis: University of Minnesota Press, 2000.

Nettelbeck, Colin. "Bazin's Rib? French Women Film-Makers and the Evolution of the Auteur Concept." *Nottingham French Studies* 41, no. 2 (Autumn 2002): 106–26.

Pallister, Janis. *French-speaking Women Film Directors*. Madison, N.J.: Fairleigh Dickinson University Press, 1998.

Powrie, Phil. "Transitional Woman: New Representations of Women in Contemporary French Cinema." *Esprit Créateur* 42, no. 3 (Fall 2002): 81–91.

Sellier, Genevieve. "Masculinity and Politics in New Wave Cinema." Translated by Dawn Cornelio. *Sites: The Journal of Twentieth Century Contemporary French Studies* 4, no. 2 (Fall 2002): 471–87.

Stehlin, Eve. "*Gueule d'amour* or the Eviction of the Femme Fatale: Towards the Homosexual Couple." *Studies in French Cinema* 5, no. 1 (2005): 37–47.

Tarr, Carrie, and Brigitte Rollet. *Cinema and the Second Sex: Women's Filmmaking in France in the 1980s and 1990s.* York: Continuum, 2001.

Weiner, Susan. *Enfants terribles: Youth and Femininity in the Mass Media in France, 1945–1968.* Baltimore: Johns Hopkins University Press, 2001.

Williams, James S., ed. *Revisioning Duras: Film, Race, Sex.* Liverpool: Liverpool University Press, 2000.

——. *The Erotics of Passage: Pleasure, Politics, and Form in the Later Work of Marguerite Duras.* New York: St. Martin's Press, 1997.

Worth, Fabienne. "Toward Alternative Film Histories: Lesbian Films, Spectators, Filmmakers and the French Cinematic/Cultural Apparatus." *Quarterly Review of Film and Video* 15, no. 1 (November 1993): 55–78.

FILM AND HISTORY

Atack, Margaret. *May 68 in French Fiction and Film: Rethinking Society, Rethinking Representation.* Oxford: Oxford University Press, 1999.

Baker, Geoff. "The Predication of Violence, the Violence of Predication: Reconstructing Hiroshima with Duras and Resnais." *Dialectical Anthropology* 24, no. 3–4 (December 1999): 387–406.

Benson, Ed. "The Screen of History in Clément's *Forbidden Games.*" *Literature Film Quarterly* 33, no. 3 (2005): 207–16.

Colombat, André Pierre. *The Holocaust in French Film.* Lanham, Md.: Scarecrow Press, 1993.

Dine, Philip D. *Images of the Algerian War: French Fiction and Film, 1954–1992.* Oxford: Clarendon Press, 1994.

Golsan, Richard J. *Vichy's Afterlife: History and Counterhistory in Postwar France.* Lincoln: University of Nebraska Press, 2000.

Greene, Naomi. *Landscapes of Loss: The National Past in Postwar French Cinema.* Berkeley: University of California Press, 1999.

——. "Dominer et Punir: The Historical Films of Bertrand Tavernier." *The French Review: Journal of the American Association of Teachers of French* 64, no. 6 (May 1991): 989–99.

Guibbert, Pierre. *L'Histoire de France au cinéma.* Conde-sur-Noireau: Association Les Amis de Notre Histoire, 1993.

Harvey, Sylvia. *May '68 and Film Culture*. London: BFI Publishers, 1978.

Higgins, Lynn. *New Novel, New Wave, New Politics: Fiction and the Representation of History in Postwar France*. Lincoln: University of Nebraska Press, 1996.

Hill, Leslie. "Filming Ghosts: French Cinema and the Algerian War." *Modern Fiction Studies* 38, no. 3 (Autumn 1992): 787–805.

King, Norman. "History and Actuality: Abel Gance's *Napoléon* vu par Abel Gance (1927)." In *French Film, Texts and Contexts*, edited by Susan Hayward and Ginette Vincendeau, 20–28. London: Routledge, 1990.

Landy, Marcia. *Cinematic Uses of the Past*. Minneapolis: University of Minnesota Press, 1996.

Murray, Alison. "Teaching Colonial History through Film." *French Historical Studies* 25, no.1 (Winter 2002): 41–53.

Norindr, Panivong. "Mourning, Memorials, and Filmic Traces: Reinscribing the Corps étrangers and Unknown Soldiers in Bertrand Tavernier's Films." *Studies in Twentieth Century Literature* 23, no. 1 (Winter 1999): 117–41.

O'Brien, Charles. "Stylistic Description as Historical Method: French Films of the German Occupation." *Style* 32, no. 3 (Fall 1998): 427–29.

Pauly, Rebecca M. "From Shoah to Holocaust: Image and Ideology in Alain Resnais's *Nuit et brouillard* and *Hiroshima Mon Amour*." *French Cultural Studies* 3, no. 3 (October 1992): 253–61.

Sellier, Geneviève. "*Saint-Cyr*, le film historique renouvelé par le cinéma d'auteur." *Sites: The Journal of Twentieth Century Contemporary French Studies* 6, no. 2 (Fall 2002): 395–401.

Short, K. R. M., ed. *Feature Films as History*. London: Croom Helm, 1981.

Sorlin, Pierre. "How to Look at an 'Historical' Film." In *The Historical Film: History and Memory in Media*, edited by Marcia Landy, 25–49. New Brunswick, N.J.: Rutgers University Press, 2001.

———. "France: The Silent Memory." In *The First World War and Popular Cinema: 1914 to the Present*, edited by Michael Paris, 115–37. New Brunswick, N.J.: Rutgers University Press, 2000.

———. "'Stop the Rural Exodus': Images of the Country in French Films of the 1950s." *Historical Journal of Film, Radio and Television* 18, no. 2 (June 1998): 183–98.

———. *The Film in History: Restaging the Past*. Totowa, N.J.: Barnes & Noble, 1980.

Turim, Maureen. *Flashbacks in Film: Memory and History*. New York: Routledge, 1989.

Vincendeau, Ginette. "Unsettling Memories." *Sight and Sound* 5, no. 7 (July 1995): 30–32.

Wild, Florianne. "Colliding with History in *La Bête humaine*: Reading Renoir's Cinécriture." *Literature-Film Quarterly* 31, no. 2 (2003): 111–17.

FILM AND LITERATURE

Anzalone, John. "Sound/Tracks: Zola, Renoir and *La Bête Humaine.*" *The French Review: Journal of the American Association of Teachers of French* 62, no. 4 (March 1989): 583–90.

Brami, Joseph. "Mme de Merteuil, Juliette, and the Men: Notes for a Reading of Vadim's *Liaisons Dangereuses* 1960." *Eighteenth-Century Life* 14, no. 2 (May 1990): 56–66.

Cousins, R. F. "Adapting Zola for the Silent Cinema: The Example of Marcel L'Herbier." *Literature Film Quarterly* 12, no. 1 (1984): 42–49.

Denby, David. "Gesture, Point of View and Proto-cinema in Victor Hugo's *Les Misérables.*" In *Reading Images and Seeing Words*, edited by Alan English, Rosalind Silvester, and David Scott, 137–55. Amsterdam: Rodopi, 2004.

Frohock, Richard. "Adaptation and Cultural Criticism: *Les Liaisons dangereuses* 1960 and *Dangerous Liaisons.*" In *Eighteenth-Century Fiction on Screen*, edited by Robert Mayer, 157–74. Cambridge: Cambridge University Press, 2002.

Golsan, Katherine. "From Theater to Cinema: Jean Renoir's Adaptation of *Nana* (1926)." *Excavatio: Emile Zola and Naturalism* 13 (2000): 225–28.

Griffiths, Katherine. "Scribbling Ghosts: The Textual Spectres and Spectral Texts of Emile Zola." In *Possessions: Essays in French Literature, Cinema and Theory*, edited by Julia Horn and Lynsey Russell-Watts, 51–65. Oxford: Peter Lang, 2003.

Herbst, Hildburg. "Coloring Word: Rohmer's Film Adaptation of Kleist's Novella *The Marquise of O . . .*" *Literature-Film Quarterly* 16, no. 3 (1988): 201–9.

Horton, Andrew, and Joan Magretta, eds. *Modern European Filmmakers and the Art of Adaptation.* New York: F. Unger, 1981.

Kline, T. Jefferson. "Truffaut's Adèle in the New World: Autobiography as Subversion of History." In *Identity Papers: Contested Nationhood in Twentieth-Century France*, edited by Steven Ungar and Tom Conley, 195–214. Minneapolis: University of Minnesota Press, 1996.

———. *Screening the Text: Intertextuality in New Wave French Cinema.* Baltimore: Johns Hopkins University Press, 1992.

Lynch, Joan D. "*Camile Claudel*: Biography Constructed as Melodrama." *Literature-Film Quarterly* 26, no. 2 (April 1998): 117–24.

Rider, Jeff, Richard Hull, and Christopher Smith, "The Arthurian Legend in French Cinema: *Lancelot du Lac* and *Perceval.*" In *Cinema Arthuriana: Essays on Arthurian Film*, edited by Kevin J. Harty, 41–56. New York: Garland, 1991.

Simpson, James R. "The Fox and the Lion's Share: Tyranny, Textuality and Jouissance in the *Roman de Renart* (Le Partage des proies)." In *Possessions:*

Essays in French Literature, Cinema and Theory, edited by Julia Horn and Lynsey Russell-Watts, 21–35. Oxford: Peter Lang, 2003.

Turk, Edward Baron. "The Film Adaptation of Cocteau's *Les Enfants Terribles*." *Cinema Journal* 19, no. 2 (Spring 1980): 25–40.

Woodhull, Winifred. "*Carmen* and Early Cinema: The Case of Jacques Feyder (1926)." In *Carmen: From Silent Film to MTV*, edited by Chris Perriam and Ann Davies, 37–59. Amsterdam: Rodopi, 2005.

Worth-Stylianou, Valerie. "Whose Life Is It Anyway? The Politics of the Representation of Motherhood in Two Female-Authored Memoirs of French Renaissance." In *Possessions: Essays in French Literature, Cinema and Theory*, edited by Julia Horn and Lynsey Russell-Watts, 37–49. Oxford: Peter Lang, 2003.

Zants, Emily. *Chaos Theory, Complexity, Cinema, and the Evolution of the French Novel*. Lewiston, Ill.: E. Mellen Press, 1996.

ACTORS, ROLES, AND FRENCH CINEMA

Austin, Guy. "The Life and Death of Star Bodies: Gérard Depardieu and Patrick Dewaere." *Modern & Contemporary France* 11, no. 2 (May 2003): 175–87.

——. *Stars in Modern French Film*. London: Arnold, 2003.

Callahan, Vicki. *Zones of Anxiety: Movement, Musidora, and the Crime Serials of Louis Feuillade*. Detroit, Mich.: Wayne State University Press, 2005.

——. "Screening Musidora: Inscribing Indeterminacy in Film History." *Camera Obscura: A Journal of Feminism, Culture, and Media Studies* 48 (2001): 59–81.

Cousins, Russell. "Revamping *Nana* as a Star Vehicle: The Christian Jaque/Martine Carol Screen Version." *Excavatio: Emile Zola and Naturalism* 9 (1997): 173–82.

French, Sean. *Bardot*. London: Pavilion, 1994.

Friel, Patrick. "Max Linder, the First Gentleman of Comedy." *Cinefocus* 1, no. 1 (January 1990): 8–12.

Gunning, Tom. "A Tale of Two Prologues: Actors and Roles, Detectives and Disguises in *Fantômas*, Film and Novel." *The Velvet Light Trap* 37 (Spring 1996): 30–36.

Hammond, Robert M. "Fernandel and Raimu as Informants." *Modern Language Journal* 43, no. 2 (February 1959): 85–86.

Handyside, Fiona. "Possessing Stars, Possessing Texts: Jeanne Moreau and the New Wave." In *Possessions: Essays in French Literature, Cinema and Theory*, edited by Julia Horn and Lynsey Russell-Watts, 151–64. Oxford: Peter Lang, 2003.

Hayes, Graeme. "Framing the Wolf: The Spectacular Masculinity of Alain Delon." In *The Trouble with Men: Masculinities in European and Hollywood Cinema*, edited by Phil Powrie, Ann Davies, and Bruce Babington, 42–53. London: Wallflower, 2004.

Hayward, Susan. "Signoret's Star Persona and Redressing the Costume Cinema: Jacques Becker's *Casque d'Or* (1952)." *Studies in French Cinema* 4, no. 1 (2004): 15–28.

Kuisel, Richard. "The Fernandel Factor: The Rivalry between the French and American Cinema in the 1950s." *Yale French Studies* 98 (2000): 119–34.

Leahy, Sarah. "'Neither Charm Nor Sex Appeal . . . ' Just What Is the Appeal of Simone Signoret?" *Studies in French Cinema* 4, no. 1 (2004): 29–40.

Le Gras, Gwénaëlle. "Soft and Hard: Catherine Deneuve in 1970." *Studies in French Cinema* 5, no. 1 (2005): 27–35.

O'Shaugnessy, Martin. "Le Surhomme à bout de souffle: Le Belmondo des années 1974–1985." In *Le Surhomme à l'écran*, edited by David Bigorgne, 107–15. Condé-sur-Noireau: Corlet, 2004.

Sellier, Geneviève. "Danielle Darrieux, Michèle Morgan and Micheline Presle in Hollywood: The Threat to French Identity." *Screen* 43, no. 2 (Summer 2002): 201–14.

Vanderschelden, Isabelle. "Jamel Debbouze: A New Popular French Star?" *Studies in French Cinema* 5, no. 1 (2005): 61–72.

Vincendeau, Ginette. "Anatomy of a Myth: Jean Gabin." *Nottingham French Studies* 32, no. 1 (Spring 1993): 19–31.

———. "The Beast's Beauty: Jean Gabin, Masculinity and the French Hero." In *Women and Film: A Sight and Sound Reader*, edited by Pam Cook and Philip Dodd, 115–22. Philadelphia: Temple University Press, 1993.

———. "Catherine Deneuve and French Womanhood." In *Women and Film: A Sight and Sound Reader*, edited by Pam Cook and Philip Dodd, 41–49. Philadelphia: Temple University Press, 1993.

———. "Gérard Depardieu: The Axiom of Contemporary French Cinema." *Screen* 34, no. 4 (Winter 1993): 343–61.

———. *Stars and Stardom in French Cinema*. London: Continuum, 2000.

———. "The Old and the New: Brigitte Bardot in 1950s France." *Paragraph: A Journal of Modern Critical Theory* 15, no. 1 (March 1992): 73–96.

STUDIES OF PARTICULAR DIRECTORS

Arnaud, Philippe. *Robert Bresson*. Paris: Cahiers du Cinema, 2003.

Austin, Guy. *Claude Chabrol*. Manchester: Manchester University Press, 1999.

Baecque, Antoine de. *Truffaut*. New York: Knopf, 1999.

Bazin, André. *Jean Renoir*. Paris: Editions champ libre, 1971.

Bergala, Alain. *Nul mieux que Godard*. Paris: Editions Cahiers du Cinéma, 1999.

Bertin, Celia. *Jean Renoir: A Life in Pictures*. Baltimore: Johns Hopkins University Press, 1991.

Beugnet, Martine. *Claire Denis*. Manchester: Manchester University Press, 2004.

Beylie, Claude. *Marcel Pagnol*. Paris: Seghers, 1974.

Billard, Pierre. *Louis Malle. Le Rebelle solitaire*. Paris: Plon, 2003.

Boiron, Pierre. *Pierre Kast*. Paris: Lherminier, 1985.

Bonitzer, Pascal. *Eric Rohmer*. Paris: Cahiers du Cinéma, 1991.

Brown, Royal. *Focus on Godard*. Englewood Cliffs, N.J.: Prentice Hall, 1972.

Callahan, Vicki. *Zones of Anxiety: Movement, Musidora, and the Crime Serials of Louis Feuillade*. Detroit, Mich.: Wayne State University Press, 2005.

Catelain, Jacques. *Marcel L'Herbier*. Paris: Jacques Vautrin, 1950.

Cerisuelo, Marc. *Jean-Luc Godard*. Paris: Editions des Quatre-Vents, 1989.

Crafton, Donald. *Émile Cohl, Caricature, and Film*. Princeton, N.J.: Princeton University Press, 1990.

Crisp, Colin. *Eric Rohmer: Realist and Moralist*. Bloomington: Indiana University Press, 1988.

Cunneen, Joseph E. *Robert Bresson: A Spiritual Style in Film*. New York: Continuum, 2003.

Dale, R. C. *The Films of Réné Clair*. Metuchen, N.J.: Scarecrow Press, 1986.

Daly, Fergus, and Garin Dowd. *Leos Carax*. Manchester: Manchester University Press, 2003.

Deschamps, Hélène. *Jacques Rivette: théâtre, amour, cinéma*. Paris: L'Harmattan, 2001.

Dixon, Wheeler W. *The Films of Jean-Luc Godard*. Albany: State University of New York Press, 1997.

Downing, Lisa. *Patrice Leconte*. Manchester: Manchester University Press, 2004.

Ezra, Elizabeth. *Georges Méliès*. Manchester: Manchester University Press, 2000.

Faulkner, Christopher. *The Social Cinema of Jean Renoir*. Princeton, N.J.: Princeton University Press, 1986.

Fischer, Lucy. *Jacques Tati*. Boston: G. K. Hall, 1983.

Frappat, Hélène. *Jacques Rivette, secret compris*. Paris: Cahiers du Cinéma, 2001.

Frey, Hugo. *Louis Malle*. Manchester: Manchester University Press, 2004.

Gauteur, Claude, and Ginette Vincendeau. *Jean Gabin: Anatomie d'un mythe*. Paris: Nathan, 1993.

Gillain, Anne. *François Truffaut*. Paris: Hatier, 1991.

Günther, Renate. *Marguerite Duras*. Manchester: Manchester University Press, 2002.

Hanlon, Lindley. *Fragments: Bresson's Film Style*. Rutherford, N.J.: Fairleigh Dickinson University Press, 1986.

Harris, Sue. *Bertrand Blier*. Manchester: Manchester University Press, 2001.

Hay, Stephen. *Bertrand Tavernier: The Film-Faker of Lyon*. London: I. B. Tauris, 2000.

Hayward, Susan. *Luc Besson*. London: Routledge, 1998.

Holmes, Diana, and Robert Ingram. *François Truffaut*. Manchester: Manchester University Press, 1998.

Ingram, Robert, and Paul Duncan, ed. *François Truffaut: Film Author 1932–1984*. London: Taschen, 2004.

King, Norman. *Abel Gance: A Politics of Spectacle*. London: British Film Institute, 1984.

Kramer, Steven, and James Welsh. *Abel Gance*. Boston: Twayne, 1978.

Lacassin, Francis. *Louis Feuillade*. Paris: Bordas, 1995.

Le Berre, Carole. *François Truffaut*. Paris: Cahiers du Cinéma, 1993.

Leger, Susan H. "Marguerite Duras's Cinematic Spaces." *Women & Literature*. 4 (1988): 231–57.

Leperchey, Sarah. *Alain Resnais: une lecture topologique*. Paris: L'Harmattan, 2000.

Lev, Peter. *Claude Lelouch, Film Director*. Rutherford, N.J.: Fairleigh Dickinson University Press, 1983.

Magny, Joel. *Claude Chabrol*. Paris: Cahiers du Cinéma, 1987.

———. *Eric Rohmer*. Paris: Rivages, 1986.

McGerr, Celia. *René Clair*. Boston, Twayne, 1980.

McMahon, Alison. *Alice Guy Blaché: Lost Visionary of the Cinema*. New York: Continuum, 2002.

Monaco, James. *Alain Resnais: The Role of Imagination*. New York: Oxford University Press, 1978.

O'Shaughnessy, Martin. *Jean Renoir*. Manchester: Manchester University Press, 2000.

Pérez, Michel. *Les films de Carné*. Paris: Ramsay, 1994.

Powrie, Phil. *Jean-Jacques Beineix*. Manchester: Manchester University Press. 2001.

Reader, Keith. *Robert Bresson*. Manchester: Manchester University Press, 2000.

Renoir, Jean. *My Life and My Films*. New York: Atheneum, 1974.

Rollet, Brigitte. *Coline Serreau*. Manchester: Manchester University Press, 1998.

Roud, Richard. *Jean-Luc Godard*. London: Secker & Warburg, 1967.

Serceau, Daniel. *Jean Renoir, l'insurgé*. Paris: Le Sycomore, 1981.

———. *Jean Renoir: La sagesse du plaisir*. Paris: Editions du Cerf, 1985.

Serceau, Michel. *Eric Rohmer: les jeux de l'amour du hasard et du discours*. Paris: Cerf, 2000.

Sesonske, Alexander. *Jean Renoir, the French Films, 1924–1939*. Cambridge, Mass.: Harvard University Press, 1980.

Simon, William G. *The Films of Jean Vigo*. Ann Arbor: University of Michigan Research Press, 1981.

Smith, Alison. *Agnès Varda*. Manchester: Manchester University Press, 1998.

Sterritt, David. *The Films of Jean-Luc Godard: Seeing the Invisible*. Cambridge: Cambridge University Press, 1999.

Tarr, Carrie. *Diane Kurys*. Manchester: Manchester University Press, 1999.

Turk, Edward Baron. *Child of Paradise: Marcel Carné and the Golden Age of French Cinema*. Cambridge, Mass.: Harvard University Press, 1989.

Walz, Eugene. *François Truffaut: A Guide to References and Resources*. Boston: G. K. Hall, 1982.

White, Susan M. *The Cinema of Max Ophuls: Magisterial Vision and the Figure of Woman*. New York: Columbia University Press, 1995.

Wilson, Emma. *Memory and Survival: The French Cinema of Kryzstof Kieslowski*. Oxford: Legenda, 2000.

Williams, Alan Larson. *Max Ophuls and the Cinema of Desire: Style and Spectacle in Four Films, 1948–1955*. Salem, N.H.: Ayer, 1980.

STUDIES OF PARTICULAR FILMS

Andrew, Dudley. "Revolution and the Ordinary: Renoir's *'La Marseillaise.'*" *Yale Journal of Criticism* 4, no. 1 (Fall 1990): 53–85.

——. "Desperation and Meditation: *Bresson's Diary of a Country Priest*." In *Modern European Filmmakers and the Art of Adaptation*, edited by Andrew Horton and Joan Magretta, 20–37. York: F. Ungar, 1981.

Brownlow, Kevin. *Napoléon: Abel Gance's Classic Film*. New York: Knopf, 1983.

Conley, Tom. "The Laws of the Game: Jean Renoir, *La Règle du jeu*." In *Legal Realism: Movies as Legal Texts*, edited by John Denvir, 95–117. Urbana: University of Illinois Press, 1996.

DeAngelis, Michael. "Inverting French Heritage Cinema: Melville, Carax, and *Pola X*." *Film Criticism* 27, no. 1 (Fall 2002): 20–35.

Ehrlich, Evelyn. "French Film During the German Occupation: The Case of *Le Corbeau*." *Wide Angle* 4, no. 4 (1981): 12–17.

Ennis, Tom. "Textual Interplay: The Case of Rohmer's *Ma nuit chez Maud* and *Conte d'hiver*." *French Cultural Studies* 7, no. 21 (October 1996): 309–19.

Forbes, Jill. *Les Enfants du paradis*. London: British Film Institute Film Classics, 1997.

Golsan, Katherine. "'Vous allez vous user les yeux': Renoir's Framing of *La Bête humaine*." *French-Review: Journal of the American Association of Teachers of French* 73, no. 1 (October 1999): 110–20.

Golsan, Richard J. "Collaboration and Context: *Lacombe Lucien*, the Mode Rétro, and the Vichy Syndrome." In *Identity Papers: Contested Nationhood in Twentieth-Century France*, edited by Steven Ungar and Tom Conley, 129–55. Minneapolis: University of Minnesota Press, 1996.

Hayward, Susan. "Beyond the Gaze and into Femme-Filmécriture: Agnes Varda's *Sans toit ni loi* (1985)." In *French Film: Texts and Contexts*, edited by Susan Hayward and Ginette Vincendeau. 2nd ed., 269–80. London: Routledge, 2000.

Higbee, Will. "The Return of the Political, or Designer Visions of Exclusion? The Case of Mathieu Kassovitz's Fracture Sociale Trilogy." *Studies in French Cinema* 5, no. 2 (2005): 123–35.

Homler, Scott. "Love Child: Mimesis and Paternity in Claire Denis' *Chocolat*." In *Cinema and Social Discourse in Cameroon*, edited by Alexie Tcheuyap, 305–24. Bayreuth, Germany: Thielmann & Breitinger, 2005.

Horne, John. "Film and Cultural Demobilization after the Great War: The Two Versions of *J'Accuse* by Abel Gance (1918 and 1938)." In *Vichy, Resistance, Liberation: New Perspectives on Wartime France*, edited by Hanna Diamond and Simon Kitson, 131–42. Oxford: Berg, 2005.

Kaplan, Nelly. *Napoleon*, edited by Bernard McGuirk. London: British Film Institute, 1994.

Kavanagh, Thomas M. "The Narrative of Chance in Melville's *Bob le flambeur*." *Michigan Romance Studies* 13 (1993): 139–58.

Kedward, H. R. "The Anti-Carnival of Collaboration: Louis Malle's *Lacombe Lucien* (1974)." In *French Film: Texts and Contexts*, edited by Susan Hayward and Ginette Vincendeau. 2nd ed., 227–39. London & New York: Routledge, 2000.

Lagny, Michele. "The Fleeing Gaze: Jean Renoir's *La Bête humaine* (1938)." In *French Film: Texts and Contexts*, edited by Susan Hayward and Ginette Vincendeau. 2nd ed., 42–62. London: Routledge, 2000.

Loshitzky, Yosefa. "The Post-Holocaust Jew in the Age of Postcolonialism: *La Haine* Revisited." *Studies in French Cinema* 5, no. 2 (2005): 137–47.

MacRory, Pauline. "Excusing the Violence of Hollywood Women: Music in *Nikita* and *Point of No Return*." *Screen* 40, no. 1 (Spring 1999): 51–65.

McArthur, Colin. "Mise-en-Scene Degree Zero: Jean-Pierre Melville's *Le Samourai* (1967)." In *French Film: Texts and Contexts*, edited by Susan Hayward and Ginette Vincendeau. 2nd ed., 189–201. London: Routledge, 2000.

Philippe, Antoine. "Celine et Julie vont à Marienbad." *The French Review* 78, no. 3 (February 2005): 458–70.

Powrie, Phil. "Configurations of Melodrama: Nostalgia and Hysteria in *Jean de Florette* and *Manon des sources*." *French Studies: A Quarterly Review* 46, no. 3 (July 1992): 296–305.

Reader, Keith. "'If I Were a Girl—and I am Not': Cross-Dressing in Alain Berliner's *Ma vie en rose* and Jean Renoir's *La Grande illusion*." *Esprit Createur* 42, no. 3 (Fall 2002): 50–59.

———. "The Circular Ruins? Frontiers, Exile and the Nation in Renoir's *Le Crime de Monsieur Lange*." *French Studies: A Quarterly Review* 54, no. 3 (July 2000): 287–97.

Sorlin, Pierre. "A Breath of Sea Air: Jacques Tati's *Les Vacances de M. Hulot* (1952)." In *French Film, Texts and Contexts*, edited by Susan Hayward and Ginette Vincendeau, 100–11. London: Routledge, 1990.

Ungar, Steven. "In the Thick of Things: Rouch and Morin's *Chronique d'un été* Reconsidered." *French Cultural Studies* 40, no. 1 (February 2003): 5–22.

Vincendeau, Ginette. "In the Name of the Father: Marcel Pagnol's 'Trilogy': *Marius* (1931), *Fanny* (1932), *César*." In *French Film, Texts and Contexts*, edited by Susan Hayward and Ginette Vincendeau, 9–26. London: Routledge, 1990.

Warehime, Marja. "Hospitality and Violence: Parasites and Hosts in Jean Renoir, Claude Chabrol and Karim Dridi." *Nottingham French Studies* 43, no. 2 (Summer 2004): 56–67.

Webster, Robert M. "Renoir's *Une Partie de campagne*: Film as the Art of Fishing." *The French Review: Journal of the American Association of Teachers of French* 64, no. 3 (February 1991): 487–96.

INTERVIEWS

Amiel, Vincent, and Alain Masson. "Entretien avec Marcel Ophüls." *Positif* 406 (December 1994): 15–21.

Anderson, Melissa. "The Modest Gesture of the Filmmaker: An Interview with Agnès Varda." *Cinéaste* 26, no. 4 (Fall 2001): 24–27.

Audé, Francoise, Michel Ciment, and Michel Sineux. "Entretien avec Jeanne Moreau." *Positif* 411 (May 1995): 6–14.

Bazin, Andre. Trans. Bert Cardullo. "An Interview with Jacques Tati by André Bazin, with the Participation of François Truffaut." *Quarterly Review of Film & Video* 19, no. 4 (October–December 2002): 285–98.

Berthomieu, Pierre, Jean-Pierre Jeancolas, and Claire Vasse. "Entretien avec Claude Chabrol." *Positif* 415 (September 1995): 8–14.

Bertin-Maghit, Jean-Pierre. "Entretien avec Christian-Jaque." *1895* 28 (October 1999): 47–52.

Bonnaud, Frederic. Trans. Kent Jones. "The Captive Lover: An Interview with Jacques Rivette." *Senses of Cinema: An Online Film Journal Devoted to the Serious & Eclectic Discussion of Cinema* 16 (September–October 2001).

Bourguignon, Thomas, and Yann Tobin. "Entretien avec Mathieu Kassovitz." *Positif* 412 (June 1995): 8–13.

Breitbart, Eric. "An Interview with Jean-Pierre Melville." *Film Culture* 35 (Winter 1964): 15–19.

Brunette, Peter, and Gerald Peary. "A child of the new wave: an interview with Benoît Jacquot." *Cinéaste* 25, no. 3 (2000): 23–27.

Caplis, Richard. "Why Not?: An Interview with French Director Coline Serreau." *Millimeter* (October 7, 1979): 178–83.

Coulombe, Michel. "Entretien avec Philippe de Broca." *Cine-Bulles* 17, no. 1 (1998): 4–9.

Cukier, Dan, and Jo Gryn. "Entretien avec François Truffaut." *Script* 5 (April 1962): 5–15.

Dieckmann, K. "Godard in his 'fifth period': an interview." *Film Quarterly* 39, no. 2 (1985): 2–6.

Duras, Marguerite, and Xaviere Gauthier. *Woman to Woman*. Lincoln: University of Nebraska Press, 1987.

Edelman, Rob. "Travelling a Different Route: An Interview with Agnès Varda." *Cinéaste* 15, no. 1 (1986): 20–21.

Ferenzi, Aurelien. "Entretien avec Eric Rohmer/Interview with Eric Rohmer." *Senses of Cinema: an Online Film Journal Devoted to the Serious & Eclectic Discussion of Cinema* 16 (September–October 2001).

French, Philip, ed. *Malle on Malle*. London: Faber & Faber, 1993.

Gillain, Anne. *Le Cinéma selon François Truffaut*. Paris: Flammarion, 1988.

Godard, Jean-Luc, and David Sterritt. *Jean-Luc Godard: Interviews*. Jackson: University Press of Mississippi, 1998.

Insdorf, Anette. "François Truffaut: Feminist Filmmaker?" *Take One* 6, no. 2 (January 1978): 6–17.

Johnson, William. "Recent Rivette: An Interreview." *Film Quarterly* 28, no. 2 (Winter 1974–75): 33–39.

Le guay, Philippe. "Jean-Paul Rappeneau." *Cinématographe* 97 (February 1984): 26–27.

Le Van Ra, Anne. "Entretien avec Yves Robert." *Les Cahiers de la Cinématheque* 63/64 (December 1995): 172–81.

Levitin, Jacqueline. "Mother of the New Wave: An Interview with Agnès Varda." *Women & Film* 1, no. 5–6 (1974): 62–66.

Mancini, Michele. "So Who Created . . . Vadim." *Film Comment* 24, no. 2 (March–April 1988): 18–23.

McGilligan, Patrick. "Journey into Light: French Film Maker and Critic Bertrand Tavernier." *Film Comment* 28, no. 2 (March–April 1992): 6–17.

Merigeau, P. "Entretien avec Claude Berri." *Revue du Cinéma* 419 (September 1986): 31–32.

Noel, Jacques. "La petite apocalypse: entretien avec Costa-Gavras." *Ciné-Fiches de Grand Angle* 160 (May 1993): 33–34.

Petrie, Graham. "Jacques Demy." *Film Comment* 8, no. 4 (Winter 1971–72): 46–53.

Porton, Richard, and Sandy Flitterman-Lewis. "The Spirit of Resistance: An Interview with Bertrand Tavernier." *Cinéaste* 28, no. 2 (Spring 2003): 4–10.

Prédal, Rene. "Entretien avec Jean Rouch." *CinémAction* 81, no. 4 (1996): 191–201.

———. "Rencontre avec Jean-Pierre Mocky." *Jeune Cinéma* 226 (February–March 1994): 13–16.

Renoir, Jean. Trans. Carol Volk. *Renoir on Renoir: Interviews, Essays, and Remarks*. Cambridge: Cambridge University Press, 1989.

Rosenbaum, Jonathan. "Godard in the Nineties: An Interview, Argument, and Scrapbook." *Film Comment* 34 (September–October 1998): 52–56.

———, ed. *Rivette: Texts and Interviews*. London: British Film Institute, 1977.

Roth-Bettoni, Didier. "Entretien avec Régis Wargnier." *Revue du Cinéma* 482 (May 1992): 36–37.

Sadr, Hamid-Reza. "An Interview with Alain Corneau: Film 'noir' and a French Director." *Film International: Iranian Film Quarterly* 11, no. 3 (Spring 2005): 34–39.

Toubiana, Serge. "Entretien avec Bertrand Blier." *Cahiers du Cinéma* 441 (March 1991): 22–27.

———. "Entretien avec Patrice Chéreau et Danièle Thompson." *Cahiers du Cinéma* 479/480 (May 1994): 12–15.

Quart, Leonard, and L. Rubenstein. "Blending the Personal with the Political: An Interview with Bertrand Tavernier." *Cinéaste* 8, no. 4 (Summer 1978): 25–27.

Walfisch, Dolores. "Interview with Chris Marker." *Vertigo* 1, no. 7 (1997): 38.

Ziolkowski, Fabrice. "Comedies and Proverbs: An Interview with Eric Rohmer." *Wide Angle—A Quarterly Journal of Film History Theory & Criticism* 5, no. 1 (1982): 63–67.

FRENCH FILM INDUSTRY

Abel, Richard. "Finding the French on American Screens, 1910–1914." In *Screen Culture: History and Textuality*, edited by John Fullerton, 137–57. London: Libbey, 2004.

———. *The Red–Rooster Scare: Making Cinema American, 1900–1910*. Berkeley: University of California Press, 1999.

——. *The Ciné Goes to Town: French Cinema 1896–1914*. Berkeley: University of California Press, 1998.

Bächlin, Peter. *Histoire économique du cinéma*. Paris: Nelle Édition, 1945.

Bellos, David. "Tati and America: Jour de fête and the Blum-Byrnes Agreement of 1946." *French Cultural Studies* 10, no. 2 (June 1999): 145–59.

Bousquet, Henri. *De Pathé Frères à Pathé Cinéma*. Paris: Henri Bousquet, 2001.

Danan, Martine. "French Cinema in the Era of Media Capitalism." *Media, Culture & Society* 22 no. 3 (May 2000): 355–65.

Delacroix, Jacques, and Julien Bornon. "Can Protectionism Ever Be Respectable? A Skeptic's Case for the Cultural Exception, with Special Reference to French Movies." *Independent Review* 9 no. 3 (Winter 2005): 353–75.

Federico, Salvatore. "La Guerre culturelle entre le David français et le Goliath américain: Les Accords du GATT et le cinéma." *RLA: Romance Languages Annual* 7 (1995): 51–55.

Garçon, François. *Gaumont: A Century of French Cinema*. New York: Harry Abrams, 1994.

Gomery, Douglas. "Economic Struggle and Hollywood Imperialism: Europe Converts to Sound." *Yale French Studies* 60 (1980): 80–93.

Gubach, T. *The International Film Industry: Western Europe and America since 1945*. Bloomington: University of Indiana Press, 1969.

Jäckel, Anne. "Broadcasters' Involvement in Cinematographic Co-Productions." In *Television Broadcasting in Contemporary France and Britain*, edited by Michael Scriven and Monia Lecomte, 175–97. New York: Berghahn, 1999.

Loutfi, Martine Astier. "Imperial Frame: Film Industry and Colonial Representation." In *Cinema, Colonialism, Postcolonialism: Perspectives from the French and Francophone World*, edited by Dina Sherzer, 20–29. Austin: University of Texas Press, 1996.

Menand, Louis. "Paris, Texas: How Hollywood Brought the Cinema Back from France." *New Yorker* 79 (February 17, 2003): 169–77.

Nesselson, Lisa. "Cinematic History Seen Through Gaumont's Lens." *Variety* 398 (May 9, 2005): A13–A15.

O'Brien, Charles. *Cinema's Conversion to Sound: Technology and Film Style in France and the U.S.* Bloomington: Indiana University Press, 2005.

Pitts, Brent A. "Using Industry Profiles in Business French: A Survey of the Seventh Art." *MIFLC Review* 2 (October 1992): 84–93.

Scott, Allen J. "French Cinema: Economy, Policy and Place in the Making of a Cultural-Products Industry." *Theory, Culture & Society* 17, no. 1 (February 2000): 1–38.

Ulff-Moller, Jens. *Hollywood's Film Wars with France: Film-Trade Diplomacy and the Emergence of the French Film Quota Policy*. Rochester, N.Y.: University of Rochester Press, 2001.

Williams, Alan. "Industrial Organization and Cinematic Art: An American Perspective on the Economic History of French Cinema." *Cinefocus*, 4 (1996): 10–17.

PERIODICALS

L'Avant-Scene du Cinéma. Paris. 1961– .
Bref: Le Magazine du Court Métrage. Paris. 1983– .
Bright Lights Film Journal. Portland, Ore. 1974– .
Cahiers du cinema. Paris. 1951– .
Camera Obscura: A Journal of Feminism, Culture, and Media Studies. Durham, N.C., and Bloomington, Ind. 1976– .
Caméra-Stylo. Paris. 1981– .
Cinéaste. New York. 1967– .
Ciné-Bulles. Montreal. 1982– .
Cinéma. Paris. 1954– .
CinémAction. Conde-sur-Noireau. 1978– .
Cinema Journal. Austin, Tex. 1961– .
Cinémas. Montreal. 1990– .
Cinématographe. Paris. 1971–1987
Ciné-télé-revue. Brussels. 1921– .
Écran. Paris. 1972–1979.
L'Écran français. 1943–1953.
Études cinématographiques. Paris. 1960– .
Film and History. Newark, N.J. 1971– .
Film Comment. New York. 1962– .
Film Criticism. Meadville, Pa. 1976– .
Le Film Français. Paris. 1944– .
Film History. Bloomington, Ind. 1987– .
Film Quarterly. Berkeley, Calif. 1958– .
Film Review. London. 1944– .
Iris. Iowa City, Iowa. 1983– .
Jeune Cinéma. Paris. 1964– .
Literature/Film Quarterly. Salisbury, Md. 1973– .
Positif. Paris. 1952–
Première. Paris. 1976– .
Présence du cinéma. Paris. 1959–1967.
Quarterly Review of Film Studies. New York. 1976–1989.
Quarterly Review of Film and Video. Lincoln, Neb. 1976– .
Le Revue du cinéma. Paris. 1946–1994.
Screen. Oxford. 1959– .

Sight and Sound. London. 1932– .
Studies in French Cinema. Exeter. 2001– .
TéléCiné. Paris. 1946–1978.
Télérama. Paris. 1950– .
Trafic. Paris. 1991– .

WEB SITES

AFEMIC: www.afemic.com
AFRHC: www.dsi.cnrs.fr/AFRHC/AFRHC.html
Allocine: www.allocine.fr
Cahiers du cinéma: www.cahiersducinema.com
Césars: www.lescesarducinema.com/cesar/home.html
Chez.com French Film Guide: www.chez.com/guides/cine
Ciné-fiches: www.cine-fiches.com
Discover France: www.discoverfrance.net/France/Movies/mov_index.shtml
DVD toile: www.dvdtoile.com
Ecran noir: www.ecrannoir.fr
FEMIS: www.lafemis.fr
French Institute of London: www.institut-francais.org.uk/cinema/ci_about.php
Il était une fois le cinéma: www.iletaitunefoislecinema.com
In Black and White: www.inblackandwhite.com/FrenchFilmsv2.0/index.html
Institut Lumière: www.institut-lumiere.org
Institut National de l'Audiovisuel: www.ina.fr
Internet Movie Database: www.imdb.com
Le Film français: www.lefilmfrancais.com
Les Gens du cinéma: www.lesgensducinema.com
Les Indépendants du premier siècle: www.lips.org
Les Rails du cinéma: www.cinema-francais.net
Lumière Films: www.atelierpix.com/lumiere/challenge/index.html
Magic Machines: www.acmi.net.au/AIC/MAGIC_MACHINES.html
Modern Times: www.moderntimes.com/palace/contents.htm
On Set with French Cinema: www.onsetwithfrenchcinema.com/osintro.htm
Plume noire: www.plume-noire.com/movies/reviews/french.html
Screening the Past: www.latrobe.edu.au/screeningthepast
Senses of Cinema: www.sensesofcinema.com/index.html
Silent Movies: www.csse.monash.edu.au/~pringle/silent
The Golden Years: www.thegoldenyears.org
They Shoot Pictures Don't They: www.theyshootpictures.com/index.htm
Unifrance: www.unifrance.org

About the Authors

Dayna Oscherwitz, Ph.D., is an assistant professor of French and Francophone Studies at Southern Methodist University in Dallas, Texas. Her areas of interest include French cinema, African cinema, contemporary French culture, and the French Caribbean. She has published in *Mots Pluriels* and *Contemporary French and Francophone Studies* and in the volumes *The Cinema of France: 24 Frames*, edited by Phil Powrie, and *Memory, Empire, and Postcolonialism: Legacies of French Colonialism*, edited by Alec G. Hargreaves. She is currently completing a book on the relationship between popular culture, particularly film and music, and identity politics in France.

MaryEllen "Ellie" Higgins, Ph.D., is an assistant professor of Comparative Literature and English at the Greater Allegheny Campus of the Pennsylvania State University. Her areas of research are African cinema and literature, Caribbean cinema and literature, and French cinema. Recently, she has published in *Research in African Literatures*, *The Journal of Commonwealth Literature*, *Tulsa Studies in Women's Literature*, and the volume *Writing Gender, Race, and Diaspora*. She is presently writing a book on Senegalese cinema.